Fundamentals of Health Psychology

Thomas Hadjistavropoulos & Heather D. Hadjistavropoulos

OXFORD

UNIVERSITY PRESS

OXFORD
UNIVERSITY PRESS

Oxford University Press is a department of the University of Oxford.
It furthers the University's objective of excellence in research, scholarship,
and education by publishing worldwide. Oxford is a registered trade mark of
Oxford University Press in the UK and in certain other countries.

Published in Canada by
Oxford University Press
8 Sampson Mews, Suite 204,
Don Mills, Ontario M3C 0H5 Canada

www.oupcanada.com

Library and Archives Canada Cataloguing in Publication
Fundamentals of health psychology / edited by Thomas Hadjistavropoulos
and Heather Hadjistavropoulos.

Includes bibliographical references and index.
ISBN 978-0-19-900275-7 (bound)

1. Clinical health psychology. I. Hadjistavropoulos, Thomas, 1963-, editor
II. Hadjistavropoulos, Heather D., 1967-, editor

R726.7.F86 2014   616.001'9   C2014-902169-0

Cover image: Jordan Siemens/Digital Vision/Getty

Part 1 opener image: Vetta/Getty Images
Part 2 opener image: Hero Images/Getty Images
Part 3 opener image: © Directphoto.org/Alamy

This book is printed on permanent (acid-free) paper ∞.

Printed and bound in the United States of America.

1 2 3 4 — 18 17 16 15

Brief Contents

Contents

Preface

It was a pleasure for us to work with the authors and with Oxford University Press on the creation of this important volume. This text, most suitable for health psychology courses offered in the United States, Canada, and elsewhere, is unique in many ways. Unlike many university textbooks in the Canadian market, this volume is not a Canadian edition (i.e., an edition with added Canadian content) of a pre-existing US text. We felt that such an approach would not be optimal. Instead, this book was developed from the ground up with the intent of providing both American and Canadian content (e.g., prevalence information for each country, descriptions of the health systems in Canada and the US, emphasis on cultural minority populations of both countries) in order to be optimally suited for both countries. Given its breadth, the book would also be appropriate for adoption by universities outside North America.

A second strength of this volume is its collection of contributors. Most university texts are written by one to four authors who are not experts in each and every major topic covered. Unlike such texts, chapters in this volume are authored by individuals who are leading experts on the topics covered.

A third strength of the book is its range of topics. While we cover the broad areas often found in health psychology textbooks (e.g., stress and coping, general overview of health psychology, prevention, cardiovascular disease), we have also included briefer chapters focusing on a variety of specific health conditions (e.g., asthma, gastrointestinal problems) that are managed and researched by health psychologists.

A fourth strength of the book is that chapters are dedicated to special populations/issues (i.e., children, older adults, cross-cultural issues). Most health psychology texts do not include specialized chapters covering these most important areas. Study of the issues affecting these populations is of critical importance within our pluralistic society.

This book was written with advanced (i.e., third- and fourth-year) undergraduate students in mind but would also be appropriate as an introductory health psychology text for more advanced students. It is organized conceptually as follows. Chapters 1–4 cover very general and broad issues (e.g., introduction to health psychology, body systems, psychological determinants of health and immunity, the health-care system and the role of psychologists within that system, and prevention/health promotion). Chapters 5–7 examine common problems that can affect large numbers of people, both healthy individuals and those with a wide variety of chronic illnesses (e.g., stress and ability to cope with it, anxiety about one's health and pain). Chapters 8–11 explore some of the most common serious health problems (i.e., cancer, cardiovascular disease, diabetes, and HIV). Chapters 12–16 look at a variety of significant health conditions that are studied and managed by health psychologists yet are not commonly covered in detail in undergraduate health psychology texts (e.g., multiple sclerosis, renal conditions). Finally, Chapters 17–19 consider special populations (children and older adults) and cross-cultural issues.

We hope that you will enjoy this book and that it will kindle your interest to learn more about health psychology.

Thomas Hadjistavropoulos
Heather D. Hadjistavropoulos

From the Publisher

Oxford University Press is pleased to present *Fundamentals of Health Psychology*, a comprehensive introduction to the key topics and approaches in the fast-growing field of health psychology. This expansive new text, the work of an impressive team of internationally respected experts, offers students the foundation they need to engage critically with the most pressing issues in health psychology and to pursue future study in this fascinating field.

Important Features of This Book

Fundamentals of Health Psychology incorporates a number of high-interest features that enhance its value as a reliable, useful, and up-to-date teaching and learning tool:

- **Distinguished contributors**—hailing from Canada, the United States, and beyond—offer authoritative and up-to-date insight into the current state of research and collaboration in health psychology.
- **Balanced coverage** of general issues as well as specific conditions and illnesses provides students with a well-rounded understanding of the field.
- **In-depth discussions of special populations** in Part III explore pediatric psychology, geropsychology, and cross-cultural concerns, allowing students to learn about issues and challenges that extend beyond their personal frames of reference.
- **Two types of themed boxes** highlight significant issues, theories, and practice-based solutions.
  - **"In Focus" boxes** offer a closer look at topics of health promotion, illness prevention, research, and treatment.
  - **"In Practice" boxes** present students with case studies and show how researchers and other professionals apply theories to explain and solve health issues.
- **Visually engaging photos, figures, and tables** help students envision and interpret complex concepts and data, bringing the discussion to life.
- **"Future Directions" discussions** explore where current research and treatments may lead, providing highly relevant insight to students considering a career in the field.
- **End-of-chapter summaries, questions for critical thought, and reading lists** improve student comprehension and encourage active engagement with key concepts.

Online Supplements

Fundamentals of Health Psychology is supported by an outstanding array of ancillary materials, including a **test bank** and **PowerPoint slides** for instructors as well as a **study guide** and a **companion website** for students. These resources are available online at **www.oupcanada.com/HealthPsychology**.

Acknowledgements

We are sincerely grateful to all of our distinguished chapter contributors for their work, and to Eleni Gardikiotis for her assistance with the formatting and organization of the manuscript. We also are grateful to Suzanne Clark, Tamara Cupar, Elizabeth Mazur, and Tanuja Weerasooiya of Oxford University Press, Canada for encouraging and facilitating this work. The contribution of Richard Tallman, who completed the copyediting of this text, is also acknowledged.

The editors, along with Oxford University Press, would like to acknowledge the reviewers whose thoughtful comments and suggestions have helped to shape this text:

Theresa Bianco, Concordia University

Anita DeLongis, University of British Columbia

Kelly Haskard Zolnierek, Texas State University, San Marcos

Diane LaChapelle, University of New Brunswick

Tara-Leigh McHugh, University of Alberta

Susana Phillips, Kwantlen Polytechnic University

Julia Roncoroni, University of Florida

Stacey Wareham-Fowler, Memorial University of Newfoundland

The editors would like to note that the case studies (In Practice boxes) presented in the text, with the exception of that in Chapter 1, are fictitious. Any similarity to actual persons is purely coincidental.

Thomas Hadjistavropoulos
Heather D. Hadjistavropoulos

About the Editors

Thomas Hadjistavropoulos, Ph.D., ABPP, FCAHS, is Professor of Clinical Psychology, Research Chair in Aging and Health, and Director of the Centre on Aging and Health, University of Regina. He served in 2007–8 as the President of the Canadian Psychological Association (CPA). His research focuses on psychological issues in pain. An area of recent focus has been pain assessment and management among seniors, with a special emphasis on seniors who have severe limitations in ability to communicate because of dementia. He has received numerous awards, including a Canadian Institutes of Health Research Investigator Award, the Year 2000 Canadian Pain Society Early Career Award for Excellence in Pain Research, the Canadian Association on Gerontology Distinguished Member Award, the Saskatchewan Health Research Foundation Career Achievement Award, and a Saskatchewan Health Care Excellence Award. He is a Fellow of both the Canadian Psychological Association and the American Psychological Association in recognition of his distinguished contributions to the science and profession of psychology. More recently, he was inducted as Fellow in the Canadian Academy of Health Sciences, one of the highest honours available to Canadian health scientists. Thomas has served as editor of *Canadian Psychology/Psychologie canadienne*, psychology section editor of the *Canadian Journal on Aging*, and on other editorial boards. He has published over 130 peer-reviewed papers and book chapters as well as four books. (Photo: Courtesy of Debra Marshall for SHRF.)

Heather D. Hadjistavropoulos (Ph.D., University of British Columbia, 1995) is a Professor of Psychology and Director of Clinical Training at the University of Regina (U of R), Canada. She founded the Psychology Training Clinic at the U of R in 2002, and trains graduate students in the assessment and treatment of anxiety and mood disorders, most commonly among individuals with co-morbid medical conditions. Heather's research is focused on: (a) assessing and treating psychological problems that impact health; and (b) understanding and improving the quality of health care in an attempt to reduce the burden of illness. Heather received a Canada Innovation Foundation grant to develop a state-of-the-art Clinical Health Psychology research area. She has published and presented her research widely, and is the recipient of many awards for her research as well as her contributions to training and the profession of psychology. In 2010, Dr Hadjistavropoulos was funded to develop and evaluate an Online Therapy Unit for Service Education and Research (onlinetherapyuser.ca). The Online Therapy USER is having a substantive impact on delivery of psychological care in Saskatchewan. (Photo: Courtesy of University of Regina Department of Photography.)

Contributors

Jenna Albiani, M.A.
Ryerson University

Rebecca S. Allen, Ph.D.
University of Alabama

Casey B. Azuero, M.A., M.P.H.
University of Alabama

Sarah K. Ballou, M.A.
Northwestern University Feinberg School of Medicine

Danielle Blackmore, M.A.
Ryerson University

Alexa Bonacquisti, M.A.
Drexel University

Christine T. Chambers, Ph.D.
Dalhousie University

Nicholas J. S. Christenfeld, Ph.D.
University of California, San Diego

Blaine Ditto, Ph.D.
McGill University

Pamela A. Geller, Ph.D.
Drexel University

Sherry L. Grace, Ph.D.
University Health Network, Toronto & York University

Konstadina Griva, Ph.D.
National University of Singapore

Heather D. Hadjistavropoulos, Ph.D.
University of Regina

Thomas Hadjistavropoulos, Ph.D., ABPP
University of Regina

Tae Hart, Ph.D.
Ryerson University

Trevor A. Hart, Ph.D.
Ryerson University & University of Toronto

Stanley Ing, B.A.Sc.
University of Toronto

Thomas Janssens, Ph.D.
University of Leuven, Belgium

Laurie Keefer, Ph.D.
Northwestern University Feinberg School of Medicine

Amanda C. Kentner, Ph.D.
Massachusetts College of Pharmacy and Health Sciences

Gerald P. Koocher, Ph.D., ABPP
Simmons College

Adrienne H. Kovacs, Ph.D.
University Health Network, Toronto

Britta A. Larsen, Ph.D.
University of California, San Diego

Rachel C. Lawton, M.Sc.
Northwestern University Feinberg School of Medicine

Gregory Marchildon, Ph.D.
University of Regina

Laura L. Mayhew, M.A.
University of South Florida

Anne Moyer, Ph.D.
State University of New York at Stony Brook

Bojana Petrovic, M.P.H.
University of Toronto

James O. Prochaska, Ph.D.
University of Rhode Island

Janice M. Prochaska, Ph.D.
Pro-Change Behavior Systems, Inc.

Chantelle Richmond, Ph.D.
University of Western Ontario

Thomas Ritz, Ph.D.
Southern Methodist University

William P. Sacco, Ph.D.
University of South Florida

Elizabeth A. Sarma, B.A.
State University of New York at Stony Brook

Natalie Stratton, B.A.
Ryerson University

Tyler G. Tulloch, M.A.
Ryerson University

Kristi E. White, Ph.D.
University of Minnesota

Jaime Williams, Ph.D.
University of Regina

Part I

Fundamentals of Health Psychology

1

Introduction to Health Psychology

THOMAS HADJISTAVROPOULOS | HEATHER D. HADJISTAVROPOULOS

Learning Objectives

In this chapter you will:

- Learn what health psychology and behavioural medicine are.

- Read a brief history of health psychology from its roots in ancient Greece to the tremendous growth the field has experienced in recent years.

- Find out about careers in health psychology (e.g., research vs clinical positions).

- Be introduced to key theories and models in health psychology (e.g., the biopsychosocial model, social cognitive theory, theory of planned behaviour, health belief model).

What Is Health Psychology?

Health psychology can be thought of as a subspecialty of psychology, but also as a discipline-specific descriptor within the broad interdisciplinary field of **behavioural medicine**. The 1977 Yale Conference on Behavioural Medicine was organized to support the early stages of behavioural medicine, which at that time was a young, growing interdisciplinary field (Belar, Mendonca McIntyre, & Matarazzo, 2003). The conference led to the following definition of "behavioural medicine":

> "Behavioral medicine" is the field concerned with the development of behavioral-science knowledge and techniques relevant to the understanding of physical health and illness and the application of this knowledge and these techniques to diagnosis, prevention, treatment and rehabilitation. Psychosis, neurosis and substance abuse are included only insofar as they contribute to physical disorders as an end point. (Schwartz & Weiss, 1977)

Three years after the Yale conference, a formal definition of health psychology was developed by American psychologist J.D. Matarazzo (1980; 1982; Gatchel, Baum, & Krantz, 1989), who was the first president of the Health Psychology Division (Division 38) of the American Psychological Association (APA). This definition remains widely accepted to this day:

> Health psychology is the aggregate of the specific educational, professional and scientific contributions to the discipline of psychology to the promotion and maintenance of health, the prevention and treatment of illness, and the identification of etiologic and diagnostic correlates of health, illness and related dysfunction.

Over the years, several applied subspecialties of health psychology have developed. **Clinical health psychology** is one of the most influential (American Psychological Association, 2011). Clinical health psychologists help people diagnosed with health conditions manage the symptoms of their health condition and address the psychological consequences of these symptoms. **Occupational health psychology** is another subspecialty that focuses on the prevention and management of occupational stress, the prevention of injury, and the maintenance of health of workers (Centers for Disease Control and Prevention, 2012). Another subspecialty, **community health psychology**, concerns itself with community-wide health needs and health-care systems. More specifically, community health psychologists aim to effect change and to promote access and cultural

PHOTO 1.1 | Joseph D. Matarazzo developed the formal definition of health psychology.

competence within health-care systems so that these systems can more effectively serve diversity within communities (De La Cancela, Lau Chin, & Jenkins, 1998).

Psychologists have made tremendous contributions to the prevention of illness, the maintenance of good health, and the management of a variety of conditions including but not limited to asthma (e.g., Grover, Kumaraiah, Prasadrao, & D'souza, 2002), diabetes (e.g., Grey, Boland, Davidson, Li, & Tamborlane, 2002), cardiovascular disease (e.g., Smith & Ruiz, 2002), and chronic pain (e.g., McCracken & Turk, 2002). They have also helped thousands of people cope with the psychological consequences of serious illnesses such as cancer (e.g., McGregor et al., 2002) and AIDS (Smith Fawzi et al., 2012). Moreover, psychological interventions for patients with chronic illnesses can result in substantial medical cost savings (e.g., Hunsley, 2003). For example, Schlesinger and colleagues (1983) studied approximately 2,000 patients diagnosed with hypertension, ischemic heart disease (characterized by reduced blood supply of the heart muscle), diabetes, or airflow limitation disease (a lung-related condition). Approximately 700 of these patients received psychological services whereas 1,300 did not. Compared to those who did not receive such services, the patients who received psychological therapy evidenced a 40 per cent reduction in annual medical costs. Once the cost of the psychological treatment was taken into account, the net saving for those who received psychological treatment was 5 per cent. Although 5 per cent may seem like a small amount, it could translate into many millions of dollars if these psychological treatments were to be applied on a larger scale. Similar results were obtained in a Canadian study involving cancer patients (Simpson, Carlson, & Trew, 2001). Specifically, women who completed medical treatment for breast cancer were randomly assigned to receive either standard psychosocial care available to patients or a structured group therapy intervention. The results showed that patients in the structured group intervention fared better with respect to adjustment and quality of life and that there were significant per patient cost savings even after accounting for the cost of the psychological intervention.

A Brief History of Health Psychology

The roots of health psychology can be traced back to early thinkers such as Hippocrates (460–377 BC), who is considered by many to be the father of modern medicine, and Galen (AD 129–99). These early Greek physicians held a holistic view of health and considered the mind and the body to be part of the same system (Belar et al., 2003). They also believed that a balance between physical and emotional states was necessary to sustain overall health (Belar et al., 2003). Over the years, the popularity of these ideas varied. During the Renaissance, Descartes (1596–1650) argued in favour of what is now referred to as **Cartesian dualism** or the idea that mind and body are separate entities and that explanations for illness can be found in the body alone. This idea formed the basis for much of physical medicine in Western societies (Belar et al., 2003). Following Descartes, the role of psychological factors in illness was revived again in the nineteenth century. This eventually gave rise to the development of psychosomatic medicine, with the word "psychosomatic" having been coined by Johann Christian August Heinroth (1773–1843), a German psychiatrist (Belar et al., 2003; Lipsitt, 1999). Psychosomatic medicine initially focused on illness behaviour that could be attributed to psychological causes. Consistent with this, Benjamin Rush (1746–1813) argued that "actions of the mind could cause many illnesses." Rush is considered to be

the father of modern psychiatry for publishing the book *Medical Inquiries and Observations upon the Diseases of the Mind* (1812) and is credited with founding the American Medico-Psychological Association, which later became the American Psychiatric Association (Belar et al., 2003).

Development of the ideas that lead to the emergence of health psychology are also linked to more recent thinkers, including Freud and other psychoanalysts who believed that certain symptoms such as paralysis and blindness represented manifestations of unconscious conflicts. In the 1940s, Franz Alexander helped establish psychosomatic medicine, which focused on the idea that physical disease can be the result of "fundamental, nuclear, or psychological conflict." Although these views did not adequately capture the multifactorial causation of disease (Straub, 2007), they led to explorations that contributed to today's accumulated knowledge of health. These explorations, concerning the multifactorial causation of disease, have been more directly stimulated by the behavioural sciences (Schwartz & Weiss, 1977).

In contrast to behavioural medicine, which has been more directly concerned with behavioural approaches (e.g., biofeedback, health-promoting behaviours) to the treatment and prevention of physical disease

PHOTO 1.2 | Benjamin Rush (1746–1813).

© Classic Image/Alamy

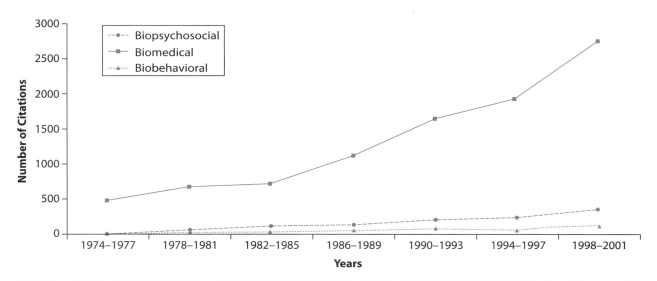

FIGURE 1.1 | Frequency of citations of "biopsychosocial," "biobehavioral," and "biomedical" in Medline.
Source: Suls & Rothman (2004).

(Schwartz & Weiss, 1977), psychosomatic medicine has traditionally emphasized etiology and pathogenesis of physical disease. Gradually, psychosomatic medicine developed as a field through the work of clinicians such as Helen Flanders Dunbar, who became the founding editor of the *Journal of Psychosomatic Medicine*, which published its first issue in 1939 (Belar et al., 2003). The American Psychosomatic Society was founded in 1942 by an interdisciplinary group that included psychiatrists, psychoanalysts, psychologists, physiologists, and internists, with neurologist Tracy Putnam as its first president (Belar et al., 2003). Over time, psychodynamic theory and psychoanalysis gradually became less popular in North America because of criticisms about insufficient scientific rigour. Nonetheless, a variety of scholars and clinicians continued to explore the interdependence of psychological factors, such as stress and disease, and Guze, Matarazzo, and Saslow (1953) published an account of the **biopsychosocial model** as a foundation of comprehensive medicine, although later work by George Engel (1977) on the biopsychosocial model became more widely cited (Belar et al., 2003).

In terms of the organized discipline of psychology, in 1973 the American Psychological Association appointed a task force to explore psychology's role within behavioural medicine and in 1978 created a health psychology division (Division 38) (Straub, 2007). The Health Psychology Division of APA is one of the five largest divisions within the organization (France, 2011). The Health Psychology Section of the

PHOTO 1.3 | The journal *Health Psychology* is published by the American Psychological Association and is "devoted to understanding the scientific relations among psychological factors, behaviour, and physical health and illness."

Canadian Psychological Association (CPA) was founded in the early 1980s (John Conway, personal communication, 10 November 2011). According to a 2011 count, the Health Psychology Section of the CPA was the seventh largest section (out of a total of 32 sections). Developments similar to those pertaining to the formation of formal health psychology groups in North America also took place in Europe and Asia, with a variety of special interest groups and organizations developing over the 1980s and 1990s (Belar et al., 2003). Health psychology is also recognized as a specialty by the American Board of Professional Psychology, the oldest credentialling group in psychology (Belar, 1997).

The growth of the field is demonstrated not only by an explosion in the number of articles in the field of health psychology but also by dramatic growth in government research support for health-related behavioural and psychological research, especially in the United States (Suls & Rothman, 2004). As an example of the growth, during the years 1974–7 the term "biopsychosocial" was mentioned in six articles, but in the 1999–2001 period it appeared in 350 articles (Suls & Rothman, 2004). Another way of illustrating the rapid growth of the field is to point out that the word "biomedical" increased in frequency by a factor of 5 during the same period whereas the word "biopsychosocial" increased by a factor of 60 (Suls & Rothman, 2004).

 ## IN FOCUS

Competencies in Research for Health Psychologists

The following lists describe the suggested competencies that are taught in many programs in health psychology without reference to clinical training. Of course, not all health psychology programs require all of the same competencies from all of their graduates. It is the unique feature of research oriented Ph.D. programs to provide sufficient flexibility to allow the developing scientist to acquire a unique set of skills. Similarly, different health psychology programs have different research emphases ranging from epidemiological studies, to exploring mechanisms of disease, to developing individual or population based interventions. Nevertheless, it is appropriate at this time for our academic colleagues to ask about the competencies that help to define health psychology researchers and for health psychology programs to emphasize such competencies in their curriculum. The list of competencies described are intended to cover in a general way the broad field of health psychology research as it exists today.

A. Knowledge base: The entry-level health psychologist researcher should have knowledge of:

1. The historical relationship of health psychology to the basic sciences, public health, and clinical investigation.
2. Scientific foundations and methods of psychology and exposure to allied health disciplines (e.g., epidemiology, physiology, genomics, bioinformatics)
3. Biobehavioural, social-environmental, and psychological factors associated with health behaviours, illness, and disease.

4. Mechanistic and mediational pathways between contextual, psychosocial, and biological phenomena as they relate to disease progression, health promotion, and illness prevention.
5. Biological, psychological, behavioral, and sociocultural tools (e.g., psychophysiological assessment, interview techniques, assessment development, observational coding, focus groups, web-based informatics tools) relevant to individuals and systems.
6. Dynamic interactions between populations and contextual variations (age, gender, ethnicity, culture, religion, etc.) on health behaviour and health outcomes.
7. Pathophysiology of disease and the implications for development of biopsychosocial treatments.
8. Appropriate methods and procedures to develop a program of research.
9. Strengths and potential pitfalls of role relationships that characterize interdisciplinary collaborative research.
10. Regulatory and ethics competence in relation to interdisciplinary research.

B. Applications: The entry-level health psychologist should be able to:

1. Evaluate biopsychosocial findings related to physical health or illness/injury/disability.
2. Assess biopsychosocial and behavioural risk factors for the development of physical illness, injury, or disability.

Careers in Health Psychology

Health psychologists are often trained to conduct both applied (e.g., clinical) work and research. However, health psychologists interested in academic or related research careers are sometimes trained exclusively as researchers. Generally speaking, health psychologists in North America tend to seek doctoral and/or post-doctoral training, although some acquire terminal master's degrees. A program leading to a doctoral degree typically requires 5–7 years of graduate study. Clinical health psychologists are often trained within clinical psychology doctoral programs with faculty members qualified and interested in health psychology. This allows these graduate students to conduct health psychological research, take courses relevant to health psychology, and complete internships and practica with a focus on health psychology. Post-doctoral training opportunities are also available. The accompanying In Focus box lists the core competencies, according to the Health Psychology Division of the APA, that health psychologists should have.

Many CPA-accredited graduate programs in Clinical Psychology have faculty members with strong interests and expertise in health psychology.[1] For example, within

---

1 The material and examples concerning training and research opportunities in health psychology are based on information gathered at the

---

3. Assist in assessment of new and emerging health technologies.
4. Develop health psychology research protocols and evaluate their effectiveness and quality.
5. Evaluate biopsychosocial and cognitive assessment tools appropriate to understanding physical illness, injury, or disability.
6. Design and evaluate empirically supported health promotion, prevention, and other interventions appropriate to target populations in the context of an interdisciplinary team.
7. Apply diverse methodologies to address contextual, psychosocial, and biological processes as they relate to disease progression, health promotion, and illness prevention.
8. Select, apply, and interpret data analytic strategies that are best suited to the diverse research questions and levels of analysis characteristic of health psychology.
9. Work toward translation of research findings to applied settings.
10. Translate issues presented by professionals from other disciplines into research questions and appropriate methods for investigation.
11. Integrate the talents and skills of professionals from different disciplines and different levels of training (e.g., masters, doctoral) to optimize research.
12. Integrate within and lead in the formulation of interdisciplinary research teams.
13. Accurately and efficiently communicate research findings in a manner that is consistent with the highest standards within the profession in ways that can be understood by fellow psychologists, professionals from other disciplines, and lay audiences alike.
14. Write a research proposal of a quality sufficient to be submitted to a granting agency.
15. Publish in peer-reviewed journals in the area of health psychology.
16. Understand the bounds/limits of one's research competence.
17. Obtain proficiency in a traditional area of psychology such as psychophysiology, psychometrics, statistics, affect and cognition, or social psychology.
18. Obtain knowledge, exposure, and competency outside of an area of traditional psychology (e.g., epidemiology, genetics, neural imaging, body imaging, assaying biomarkers, nutrition, exercise, sleep).
19. Demonstrate adequate training and evidence of skill as a teacher, and have the requisite knowledge to develop and implement an undergraduate health psychology course.
20. Understand the role and responsibilities of an effective mentor, and have the ability to promote the development of research and teaching competencies in graduate and undergraduate students.

Source: American Psychological Association Division 38 (2014).

University of Regina Photography Dept. Used with permission.

PHOTO 1.4 | The health psychology laboratory at the University of Regina has studied the effects of anxiety on balance performance and fall risk in older persons. In this photograph a volunteer is walking on a computerized sensor mat (the GaitRite® System) that is used in the evaluation of gait and balance while psychophysiological indicators of anxiety (heart rate and skin conductance) are being monitored.

the University of Regina Clinical Psychology graduate program, there are strong interests in the areas of pain and health anxiety. A wide range of health psychology interests are represented in Canadian psychology departments (e.g., McGill University, Université de Montréal,

time of writing of this chapter. Some of the information concerning program offerings and research interests in various universities may have changed since then. Interested students are encouraged to examine university websites and contact departments of psychology directly for more up-to-date information.

University of Manitoba, and many others). Research interests in health psychology can be found in numerous departments in the US (e.g., University of Washington, George Washington University). Training in experimental health psychology with a primarily research focus is also offered at some universities (e.g., the University of British Columbia and the University of Pittsburgh).

At present, specialized occupational health psychology training is being offered by several universities, including but not limited to the University of Nottingham (UK), Leiden University (The Netherlands), and several US schools such as the University of Connecticut, Central Michigan University, Portland State University, Colorado State University, and others.

Health psychologists are employed by general and specialized (e.g., cancer, physical rehabilitation) hospitals and private clinics treating patients with complex problems (e.g., chronic pain clinics), as well as in private practice. As private practitioners, health psychologists often serve as consultants to the legal and insurance systems and provide expert opinion about a variety of case scenarios (e.g., psychological consequences of accidents, extent of disability). They also provide psychological treatment services to patients diagnosed with various health conditions. Many practising health psychologists often combine their professional work with some university teaching (e.g., teaching an evening course or supervising practica and internships of graduate students in psychology). Health psychologists often are employed as instructors and researchers in psychology, psychiatry, and a wide variety of other university (e.g., health studies, gerontology, anesthesiology, general medicine) and teaching hospital departments. Funding sources for health psychology research include such agencies and organizations as the National Institutes of Health (US), the Canadian Institutes of Health Research, and the Heart and Stroke Foundation.

At the time of this writing, valuable information about careers and training in health psychology was available on the website of the Health Psychology Division of APA (www.health-psych.org/). Additional information about health psychology was available on the website of the Health Psychology Section of CPA (www.cpa.ca/aboutcpa/cpasections/healthpsychology/).

Theories and Models in Health Psychology

Throughout this text we present a variety of theories and models that have been used and validated within the context of health psychology and behavioural

⊞ IN PRACTICE

From the Life of a Health Psychologist: Dr Christine Chambers

A Typical Day

Dr Christine Chambers is a Pediatric Health Psychologist at the IWK Health Centre and a Professor of Pediatrics and Psychology at Dalhousie University. Clinically, she has expertise in providing behavioural and cognitive behavioural interventions for children with acute and chronic medical illnesses and their families, with a focus on management of chronic pain and preparation for painful medical procedures. Her research examines the role of a variety of developmental, psychological, and social factors that influence children's pain, with a focus on family factors in pediatric pain and pain measurement in children.

8:30 a.m. to 10:00 a.m.: Undergraduate health psychology class

Dr Chambers delivers a lecture at the university on the topic of managing chronic illnesses to a classroom of undergraduate students, most of whom are interested in various careers as health professionals, such as medicine, nursing, physiotherapy, and psychology. The students have a few last-minute questions, before the paper is due next week, about their personal health projects, for which they have chosen a health-related behaviour to modify, measure, and assess the effectiveness of their intervention.

10:00 a.m. to 11:00 a.m.: In the office

Dr Chambers heads over to the IWK Health Centre to her office and research lab in the Centre for Pediatric Pain Research, where she catches up on the latest issue of the *Journal of Pediatric Psychology* and gives feedback to a graduate student on the results section of the student's dissertation on the role of children's memories for pain. She also speaks briefly with a reporter from *Today's Parent* magazine who has contacted her for input on an article about how parents can help their children better cope with immunization pain.

11:00 a.m. to 12:00 p.m.: Teleconference

Just before lunch, Dr Chambers has a teleconference with colleagues on the development of a multi-site Internet-based intervention to address children's sleep problems. This work is a team grant funded by the Canadian Institutes of Health Research and is led by a colleague of Dr Chambers at the university, but

Photo by Nick Pearce. Used by permission of Christine Chambers.

PHOTO 1.5 | Dalhousie University health psychologist Christine Chambers.

includes team members at various other universities and children's hospitals across Canada.

12:00 p.m. to 1:00 p.m.: Lunch and clinical rounds

Dr Chambers enjoys her lunch during an interesting clinical rounds presentation by a colleague on the Pediatric Health Psychology Service. The colleague describes a challenging case of an adolescent with celiac disease who has had difficulties adhering to a gluten-free diet—if the youth cannot maintain the diet, this could have a significant negative impact on long-term health. The psychologists on the service, including Dr Chambers, offer various ideas and suggestions.

1:00 p.m. to 2:30 p.m.: Lab meeting

After lunch Dr Chambers attends her weekly lab meeting with her research team. An undergraduate honours student working with Dr Chambers presents preliminary results from a study examining the relationship between general parenting style and how parents report responding to the pain children experience during daily minor injuries.

(Continued)

2:30 p.m. to 3:30 p.m.: In the clinic

Dr Chambers follows up with one of her patients, a 10-year-old boy, who was referred for treatment of a severe needle phobia. It is their second session together and today they are gradually working their way through various exposure exercises related to the fear hierarchy they generated in the first session. For example, today Dr Chambers has brought pictures of children getting needles and a toy needle for the child to view and manipulate.

3:30 p.m. to 5:00 p.m.: Treatment group for children with recurrent abdominal pain

Dr Chambers provides supervision for a group of practicum students who are leading a six-week cognitive behavioural therapy group for children with recurrent abdominal pain and their parents. The group focuses on teaching children coping strategies to deal with their pain by targeting the thoughts, feelings, and behaviours associated with their pain and symptoms by employing evidence-based strategies, like deep belly breathing, guided imagery, and positive self-talk. In this session, the children practise progressive muscle relaxation while the parents learn about the importance of their own responses to their child's pain.

5:00 p.m. to 10:00 p.m.: Evening at home

Dr Chambers heads home and enjoys some play time with her young children before preparing dinner and helping her husband put the children to bed. She replies to a few e-mails from her students and colleagues and does some last-minute editing on the final draft of the chapter she has been writing on families and pain before heading to bed to get a good night's sleep.

medicine. These theories and models include, but are not limited to, the biopsychosocial model of health (Chapters 7 and 19), the gate control theory of pain (Chapter 7), cognitive behavioural theory (Chapters 6, 7, and elsewhere), and the stages of change model (i.e., transtheoretical model, Chapter 4). Some of these broad perspectives are presented in this chapter. The biopsychosocial model is discussed because of its breadth and impact on the entire discipline, while other formulations (e.g., the health belief model, social cognitive theory) are presented as specific introductory examples of the wide range of theoretical foundations that influence the work of health psychologists.

The Biopsychosocial Model

Health psychology operates within the biopsychosocial model of health that considers the interplay and integration of biological, psychological, and social factors on health (see Figure 1.2).

The biopsychosocial model forms the conceptual basis of health psychology (Suls & Rothman, 2004). This approach contrasts with the medical model of disease that separates the physical and psychosocial. An assumption of the medical model of disease is that illness is entirely physical and questions about illness are answerable objectively and deterministically (Child, 2000). However, such conceptualizations fail to fit the data because the role of psychological, social, and behavioural factors in the causation and maintenance of disease are well established (Rozanski, Blumenthal, & Kaplan, 1999; Schneiderman, Antoni, Saab, & Ironson, 2001). For example, social support has been shown to have a

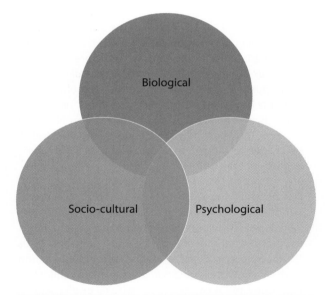

FIGURE 1.2 | The biopsychosocial model of health recognizes the importance of biological, psychological, and socio-cultural influences.

Source: Figure I Biopsychosociocultural Framework July 10, 2010 © A.E. Núñez available at http://culturegenderhealth.blogspot.com/2010/07/which-is-correct-term-sex-gender-both.html

positive effect on health-related self-care behaviours of cardiac patients (Salyer, Schubert, & Chiaranai, 2012), and inadequate social support and reduced use of problem-solving coping strategies by patients are associated with increased pain and lower functional outcomes in post-surgical samples (Lopez-Olivo et al., 2011). It is also well documented that psychological stress can have negative consequences for human immune responses (Segerstrom & Miller, 2004).

Many health problems can be conceptualized through the biopsychosocial model (e.g., obesity, drug addiction). In the case of obesity, for instance, biological factors (e.g., some people may inherit a tendency to gain more weight or a slower metabolic rate), psychological factors (e.g., depression and low self-esteem may lead a person to eat more calorie-dense foods such as desserts and/or to become physically inactive), and social factors (e.g., socio-economic factors such as ability to afford healthier foods that may be more expensive than "junk food"; absence of social support) can contribute to the problem as well as play an important role in one's ability to lose weight and maintain the weight loss.

The biopsychosocial model is detailed elsewhere in this volume. Chapter 7, for example, presents a detailed illustration of the model in relation to pain; Chapter 19 discusses the important role of culture in biopsychosocial conceptualizations of health and illness. The breadth of the biopsychosocial perspective has encouraged the development of other theories and models that provide more detailed description and hypotheses related to specific components of the biopsychosocial model (e.g., the specific role of beliefs and cognitions and the role of reinforcement in health and illness). Some of these models/theories (i.e., the health belief model, social cognitive theory, and the theory of planned behaviour) are described below while other theories (e.g., the stages of change theory [Chapter 4] and cognitive behavioural theory [e.g., Chapters 6, 7]) are detailed elsewhere in this book.

Health Belief Model

The **health belief model** (Janz & Becker, 1984; Rosenstock, 1974) has been very influential in health psychology (Glanz & Bishop, 2010). The model postulates that readiness to take action in relation to health problems is a function of people's beliefs (e.g., perceived severity of one's health condition, perceived risk of getting the condition, perceived barriers to adopting a health-promoting behaviour) and of their perception of the benefits of taking action to prevent health problems (Champion & Skinner, 2008; Rosenstock, 1974). The model, therefore, facilitates an understanding of possible reasons for non-compliance with health-care recommendations (Turner, Hunt, Dibrezzo, & Jones, 2009). Factors that may affect these types of beliefs (e.g., demographic variables) are also considered in the model (see Figure 1.3). Empirical support for the model is available in that attitudes and beliefs have been shown repeatedly to affect health-related behaviour (Janz &

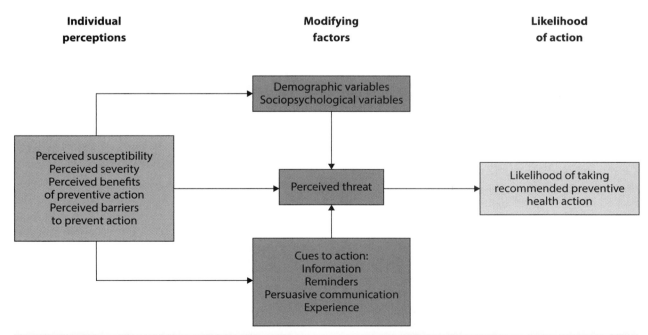

Individual perceptions **Modifying factors** **Likelihood of action**

Demographic variables
Sociopsychological variables

Perceived susceptibility
Perceived severity
Perceived benefits of preventive action
Perceived barriers to prevent action

Perceived threat

Likelihood of taking recommended preventive health action

Cues to action:
Information
Reminders
Persuasive communication
Experience

FIGURE 1.3 | The health belief model.

Used with the permission of Albert Bandura.

PHOTO 1.6 | Originally from Alberta, Canada, Stanford University psychologist Albert Bandura has served as Honorary President of the Canadian Psychological Association.

Becker, 1984). For example, beliefs regarding susceptibility to disease (i.e., the flu) and beliefs regarding disease severity and potential benefits of influenza vaccines predict whether individuals will obtain an influenza vaccine (Larson, Olsen, Cole, & Shortell, 1979). On the other hand, the model does not fully explain the full range of reasons (e.g., economic factors) that affect decisions to engage in health behaviours (Janz & Becker, 1984; see also Chapters 10 and 19).

Social Cognitive Theory

Social cognitive theory is based on the work of Albert Bandura (1986; 1991a; 1991b) and considers human behaviour as being reflected in a three-way model in which personal factors, environmental influences, and behaviour commonly interact (McAlister, Perry, & Parcel, 2008).

Reinforcement, observational learning, self-control, and self-efficacy (i.e., people's beliefs about their ability

to effectively address a situation and to yield desirable results) are central constructs in this theory. According to Bandura, self-efficacy develops through social experiences, observing others, and personal experiences, including any internal experiences that provide the person with information about his or her personal strengths and weaknesses. Social cognitive theory helps explain the socio-cultural and personal determinants of health (Bandura, 1998) and is largely consistent with the biopsychosocial model of health, with a greatest emphasis, however, placed on describing social variables involved in health.

Many aspects of the theory have been well supported. For example, self-efficacy beliefs concerning one's ability to control one's health play an important role in our understanding of health-related functioning, including recovery from coronary artery surgery (Allen, Becker, & Swank, 1990; Bastone & Kerns, 1995), coping with cancer (Beckham, Burker, Lytle, Feldman, & Costakis, 1997), renal disease (Devins et al., 1982), adherence to medication (Brus, van de Laar, Taal, Rasker, & Wiegman, 1999; De Geest et al., 1995), decreasing risk of osteoporosis through calcium intake and physical activity (Haran, Kim, Gendler, Froman, & Patel, 1998), and other conditions. This influence occurs largely as a result of the behaviours (e.g., health-promoting behaviours) that self-efficacy beliefs influence and regulate. Specifically, beliefs about self-efficacy influence our health behaviours, which then affect health outcomes. Similarly, social support helps alleviate depression and physical dysfunction, and leads to health-promoting behaviours largely because it raises perceived coping self-efficacy (Bandura, 1998; Cutrona & Troutman, 1986; Duncan & McAuley, 1993; Major, Mueller, & Hildebrandt, 1985). Moreover, effective coping with stressors has been shown to improve immune function (Antoni et al., 1990; Gruber, Hall, Hersh, & Dubois, 1988; Kiecolt-Glaser et al., 1986).

Theory of Planned Behaviour

The **theory of planned behaviour** (e.g., Ajzen, 1991) is an expansion of a pre-existing formulation known as the theory of reasoned action (e.g., Ajzen & Fishbein, 1980). According to Ajzen (1991; n.d.), our behaviour is determined by three types of beliefs: (1) *behavioural beliefs* (i.e., beliefs about the likely consequences of behaviour); (2) *normative beliefs* (i.e., beliefs about others' expectations); and (3) *control beliefs* (i.e., beliefs about factors that facilitate or prevent performance of behaviour). As Figure 1.4 illustrates, behavioural beliefs lead to favourable or unfavourable *attitudes* about the behaviour; normative beliefs lead to perceived social pressure related to the *subjective*

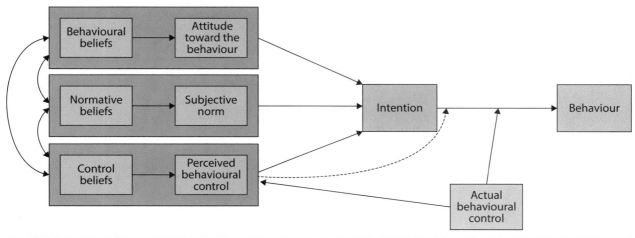

FIGURE 1.4 | Theory of planned behaviour.
Source: © 2006 Icek Ajzen.

norm; and control beliefs lead to a *perception of behavioural control*. In turn, the attitudes, subjective norms, and perceived behavioural control affect the strength of the *intention* to perform the behaviour and, ultimately, the actual performance (or lack thereof) of the behaviour. The theory also gives consideration to the extent to which the individual has *actual* (as opposed to just *perceived*) *control* over the behaviour, as shown in the figure.

A considerable body of research has supported the use of the theory of planned behaviour in the prediction of intention and behaviour, although the prediction of self-reported behaviour appears to be stronger than the prediction of actual behaviour (Armitage & Conner, 2001). Similarly, evidence has shown a distinction between desire and intention, as well as between self-efficacy and perceived control over behaviour (Armitage & Conner, 2001). Nonetheless, the theory has been criticized for neglecting the important role of emotion, as well as cultural factors, in the determination of behaviour (e.g., Munro, Lewin, Swart, & Volmink, 2007). Within health psychology, the theory of planned behaviour has been used to study a wide range of health-related behaviours, such as adherence to diet and physical activity, in diverse clinical populations (e.g., Vallance, Lavalee, Culos-Reed, & Trudeau, 2012; Welsh et al., 2013). This theory is discussed further in Chapter 11.

Future Directions

In a review of the state of the discipline of health psychology, Miller, Chen, and Cole (2009) concluded that although health psychology has shown considerable growth in documenting the relationship between psychological factors and disease, the most significant challenge that remains for future research involves the need for a better understanding of the biological processes mediating this relationship. Miller and colleagues also identified a series of advanced methodologies that are becoming increasingly influential and have the potential to help resolve the puzzle of how psychological variables impact health. These methodologies include, but are not limited to, sophisticated statistical approaches for testing complex relationships among variables, use of non-invasive imaging systems (e.g., magnetic resonance imaging [MRI]), use of biomarkers such as C-reactive protein (CRP; an inflammatory biomarker that appears to increase in response to stress), and use of laboratory analyses that permit the capture of a wide range of basic scientific information, including patterns of gene activity. With respect to applied areas, future research is expected to emphasize questions about the cost-effectiveness of health psychology, how to translate knowledge in health psychology into practice, and how to improve delivery of health psychology services through the use of technology, such as the Internet. Health psychologists must also not lose sight of the changing demographics, and ensure that interventions are appropriate for a population that is becoming increasingly ethnically diverse and older (Smith, Orleans, & Jenkins, 2004). Health psychology must also pay greater attention to non-industrialized parts of the world, where it is estimated that 90 per cent of the global burden of disease exists, but where only 10 per cent of the world's health-care resources are found (Lyons & Chamberlain, 2006).

SUMMARY

Health psychology is a subspecialty within the field of psychology, but also a discipline-specific descriptor within the interdisciplinary field of behavioural medicine. The field is concerned with education, research, and practice related to the promotion and maintenance of health and the prevention and treatment of illness. The discipline has grown tremendously since it was defined by Matarazzo (1980), and now has several subspecialties, including clinical health psychology, occupational health psychology, and community health psychology.

The roots of health psychology can be traced back to early Greek physicians who believed that the mind and body are part of the same system and intricately related. These holistic ideas of health re-emerged in the nineteenth century, after a predominant conceptualization in Western society of the mind and body as separate entities (Cartesian dualism) over the previous two centuries. This re-emergence began with the field of psychosomatic medicine, which acknowledged that psychological factors could explain physical symptoms. Gradually, scholars and clinicians began to explore the interdependence of psychological factors and physical health, and the field of behavioural medicine emerged, with an emphasis on behavioural approaches to treating physical disease.

The field has attracted many psychologists, and today health psychologists are often trained to conduct both applied (e.g., clinical) work and research. Health psychologists in North America tend to seek doctoral and/or post-doctoral training. In terms of employment settings, health psychologists are often employed in academic institutions or in clinical settings, such as general and specialized (e.g., cancer, physical rehabilitation) hospitals, private clinics treating patients with complex problems (e.g., chronic pain clinics), or private practice.

Health psychologists typically conceptualize health and illness using a biopsychosocial model of health that regards both health and illness as stemming from interactions among biological (e.g., genetic), psychological (beliefs, emotions, behaviours), and social (relational) variables. Other models/theories that health psychologists commonly draw on in both research and clinical work are the health belief model, social cognitive theory, and the theory of planned behaviour. These models are consistent with the assumptions of the biopsychosocial model, but focus on identifying variables that predict health behaviour. The health belief model identifies beliefs (e.g., perceptions of health, benefits of taking action) as central to understanding readiness to adopt health behaviours. The social cognitive theory also puts emphasis on beliefs, but emphasizes the importance of self-efficacy beliefs (developed through personal experiences, observing others, and social experiences) in determining health behaviour. Similarly, the theory of planned behaviour identifies beliefs as important, but proposes that behaviour is determined by three types of beliefs: (1) behavioural beliefs (i.e., beliefs about the likely consequences of behaviour); (2) normative beliefs (i.e., beliefs about others' expectations); and (3) control beliefs (i.e., beliefs about factors that facilitate or prevent performance of behaviour).

Critical Thought Questions

1. Have you considered a career in health psychology? If you were to consider such a career would you be most interested in the applied or research aspects of the discipline? Which areas of focus within health psychology (represented in the various chapters of this book) would interest you the most and why?

2. To what extent do you believe that in 25 years professional psychologists will be engaged in clinical work with people who present primarily with physical conditions (e.g., chronic pain, cancer, cardiovascular disease) as opposed to working largely with people whose primary problems are related to mental health issues? Justify your response.

Recommended Reading

Hunsley, J. (2003). Cost effectiveness and medical cost-offset considerations in psychological service provision. *Canadian Psychology, 44,* 61–73.

Miller, G., Chen, E., & Cole, S.W. (2009). Health psychology: Developing biologically plausible models linking the social world and physical health. *Annual Review of Psychology, 60,* 501–524.

Suls, J., & Rothman, A. (2004). Evolution of the biopsychosocial model: Prospects and challenges for health psychology. *Health Psychology, 23,* 119–125.

2

An Introduction to Body Systems and Psychological Influences on Health

BLAINE DITTO

Learning Objectives

In this chapter you will:

- Learn the basic functions of key body systems.

- Discover how these body systems work together to support behaviour and health.

- Explore some of the ways these systems malfunction and produce disease.

- Be introduced to how the brain, behaviour, and psychological processes influence risk for disease.

Body Systems

Introduction

Imagine you're a single-celled organism floating in a primeval sea. Life is good! The warm sun stimulates cellular activity and food is plentiful. On the other hand, things aren't perfect. Without a means of locomotion, you rely on currents and waves to make contact with food. Your ability to avoid becoming someone else's food is also limited.

There are problems with this fanciful scenario, including the fact that without a central nervous system you have no organ with which to consider these issues. However, the example raises several issues, including the origin of the field of health psychology. Biological structures and processes evolved because they allowed animals to *do* things that increased their chances of survival and reproduction, such as obtain food and avoid predators. This went beyond the development of simple structures such as legs to complex nervous systems that could support perception, evaluation of the environment, decision-making, and emotion. In a sense, Charles Darwin (1872) became the first health psychologist when he suggested that emotional reactions such as fear and anger are the product of evolution and have widespread effects on behaviour and the body. Unfortunately, close integration of thought, emotion, and physiology cuts both ways. In the context of early evolution (or participation in the "Hunger Games"), emotions such as fear and anger increased one's chances of survival by motivating behaviour (e.g., to flee or fight), preparing the body for an emergency, and communicating your situation to others by facial and bodily expression. On the other hand, in the modern world where vigorous physical reactions are usually unnecessary and most people die of chronic, degenerative illness, the wear and tear of these ancient responses has become a major source of illness (Sapolsky, 2004).

This chapter is an introduction to body systems and psychological influences on health. We begin with a brief overview of some of the body's major systems before introducing mechanisms of psychological influences on body function, such as the autonomic nervous system. The concept of stress is introduced (though discussed in more detail in Chapter 5), followed by some examples of stress-related illness. Throughout the chapter, the integration of psychological processes, physiological activity, and risk for illness is emphasized.

© pictore/iStockphoto

PHOTO 2.1 | Charles Darwin (1809–82).

The Cardiovascular System

Complex multicellular organisms require some means of distributing nutrients internally since not all cells can be in contact with the environment. This was a crucial step in evolution, though different species developed different circulatory systems. For example, a number of species have more than one heart, e.g., octopi have three and hagfish have five (Choy & Ellis, 1998).

In comparison, the human circulatory system (Figure 2.1) seems relatively simple and similar to closed-loop arrangements, such as a heating system, that circulate water. A strong central pump—the heart—maintains blood flow through a system of outgoing and incoming "pipes" (arteries, capillaries, and veins). Pressure in the system is higher after the heart beats and ejects blood (the systolic phase of the heart) compared to the resting phase (the diastolic phase), but in general flow is uninterrupted. The obvious importance of continual flow is indicated by what happens when the heart becomes an inefficient pump during a heart attack. Although there are some interesting exceptions (e.g., when someone falls in ice-cold water, slowing metabolism dramatically), death usually occurs within a few minutes in the absence of treatment. See Chapter 9 for a more detailed discussion of cardiovascular disease.

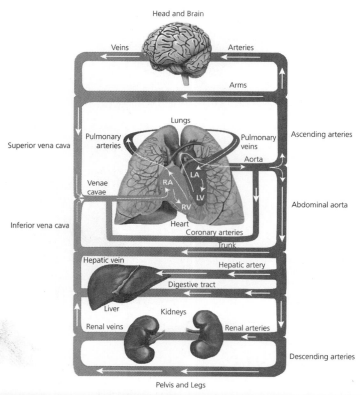

FIGURE 2.1 | Schematic view of the cardiovascular system.

Source: © medical-artist.com

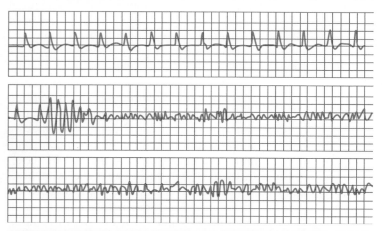

FIGURE 2.2 | A normal electrocardiogram (heart rhythm), top, and two cases of ventricular fibrillation.

Source: Ventricular fibrillation is not provoked by chest compression during post-shock organized rhythms in out-of-hospital cardiac arrest, by Erik P. Hess and Roger D. White, *Resuscitation*, Volume 66, No. 1.

human heart is actually two pumps side-by-side. Blood from the venous circulation collects in the right atrium and is ejected into the right ventricle. At the same time, blood that has just passed through the lungs collects in the left atrium and is ejected into the left ventricle. Afterward, simultaneous contraction of the right and left ventricles sends the blood out to the lungs and rest of the body via the aorta. These actions are co-ordinated by a repeated, reliable pattern of electrical activity that spreads from the atria to the ventricles. The activity associated with the contraction of the two atria is reflected as the P-wave in the electrical signature of the heart, the electrocardiogram (a normal rhythm is displayed in the top panel of Figure 2.2). Contraction of the more powerful ventricles is reflected by the R-wave (the large spikes in the top panel of Figure 2.2). Death of heart muscle cells as the result of a myocardial infarction can produce, depending on the area of cell death, various forms of fibrillation—an interruption of the smooth flow of electrical activity across the heart. This may cause the remaining cells to contract in an unco-ordinated fashion, decreasing the efficiency of the pump (bottom panels of Figure 2.2). Typically, defibrillation involves the use of a large shock in the hope of resetting the electrical profile of the heart.

In general, myocardial infarctions are the result of the process of atherosclerosis. That is, a number of stimuli such as cigarette smoke and high blood pressure can damage the interior lining of the arteries, the endothelium. This may lead to an excessive repair process involving **inflammation**, clotting, cholesterol buildup, and eventually plaques that extend into the artery, and reduce blood flow (Figure 2.3). Atherosclerosis can occur in any artery, but those that supply the heart muscle are especially important, given the body's dependence on the heart to distribute oxygen and nutrients.

As can be seen by the effects of wrapping a rubber band around your finger, pain is often experienced in areas of the body that have a reduction in blood flow. In the case of reduced blood flow to the heart, pain is often experienced in the form of angina, a pain or tightness in the chest or shoulder. Angina is

While the basic features are simple, the details of the cardiovascular system are complex and interesting. The an important though not universal warning sign of risk for myocardial infarction and fibrillation.

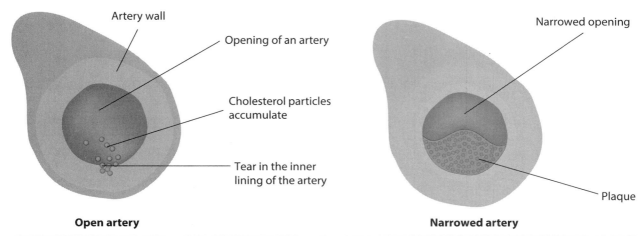

Open artery

- Artery wall
- Opening of an artery
- Cholesterol particles accumulate
- Tear in the inner lining of the artery

Narrowed artery

- Narrowed opening
- Plaque

FIGURE 2.3 | The build-up of atherosclerosis in an artery.

Source: Adapted from an image courtesy of www.myvmc.com.

The Gastrointestinal System

The human body is often described humorously as a doughnut—its exterior surface includes an interior passage (Figure 2.4). That said, the movement of food through the gastrointestinal system is not a leisurely journey. Digestion transforms food using both mechanical and chemical processes to a form where nutrients can be easily absorbed. The breakdown begins in the mouth where it is chewed and mixed with saliva. Patterned muscle contractions move the mixture through the esophagus to the stomach. Smooth muscle in the stomach contracts, further mixing food with corrosive substances such as hydrochloric acid. Additional materials from the liver and pancreas are added in the small intestine. Eventually, the component parts such as sugars and amino acids are small enough for absorption into capillary blood. Waste materials proceed through the large intestine.

This active process is monitored locally (e.g., more fat in the mixture will trigger release of the digestive fluid bile, originally produced by the liver, from the gallbladder into the small intestine) as well as by the brain. While most people acknowledge the influence of the brain on cardiovascular activity, the idea of central control of digestive activity is less appreciated. However, the involvement of muscle activity throughout the process suggests possible means of disruption and a mechanism for functional gastrointestinal disorders that

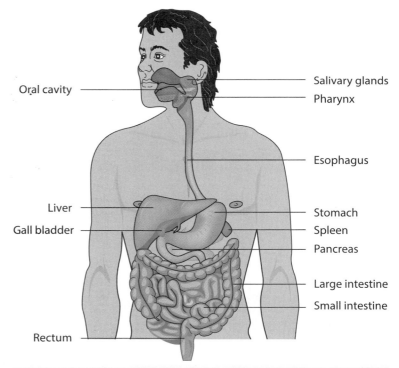

- Oral cavity
- Salivary glands
- Pharynx
- Esophagus
- Liver
- Stomach
- Gall bladder
- Spleen
- Pancreas
- Large intestine
- Small intestine
- Rectum

FIGURE 2.4 | The gastrointestinal system.

Source: Adapted from an image courtesy of www.myvmc.com.

some experience during stress. A more positive example is the increase in saliva often experienced in anticipation of a tasty meal. Some of the mechanisms of such control and their adaptive and maladaptive effects will be discussed below. Chapter 15 includes a detailed discussion of gastrointestinal problems encountered by health psychologists.

The Respiratory System

The respiratory system is also involved in bringing materials from the environment to cells deep within the body (Figure 2.5). Most animals require oxygen to utilize nutrients absorbed from the gastrointestinal system. Oxygen is required to convert glucose to the important molecule adenosine triphosphate, which, in turn, powers the body's chemical reactions. Carbon dioxide is a waste product of this process. Since both oxygen and carbon dioxide are gases, a different system for their intake and excretion was necessary. The primary organs in the respiratory system are the lungs. Other organs include the nose, mouth, trachea, and diaphragm. Similar to the cardiovascular system, air passes through progressively narrower passages in the lungs to allow efficient extraction of oxygen and uptake of carbon dioxide. At the end of the trachea, the pathway divides into two bronchi (the primary bronchi), one for each lung. After entering the lungs, the bronchi subdivide into secondary bronchi, bronchioles, and alveoli. Alveoli are small cavities surrounded by a mesh of capillaries. Carbon dioxide–rich blood from the venous circulation is pumped through the lungs by the heart's right ventricle. Carbon dioxide diffuses out into the alveoli, and oxygen from inspired air is absorbed and proceeds to the left atrium for circulation to the rest of the body. Air is moved in and out of the lungs primarily by contraction of the diaphragm located below the lungs.

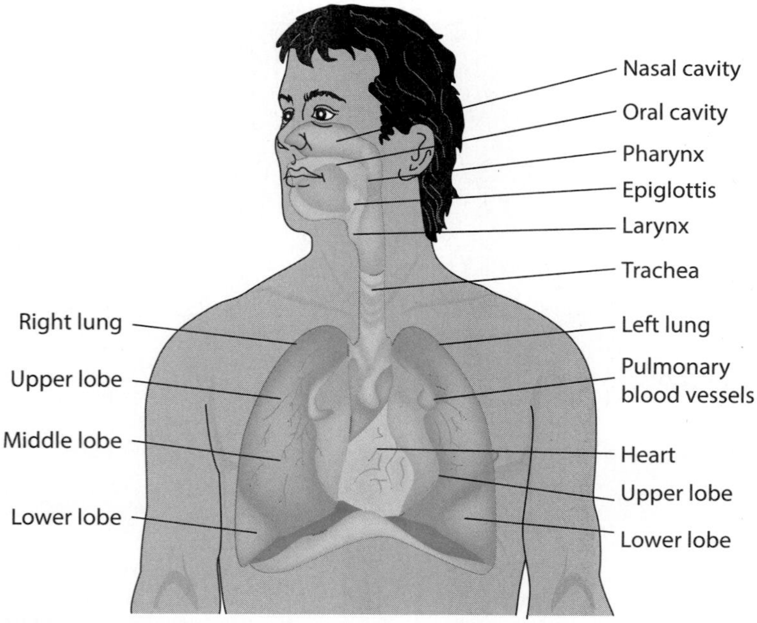

Although they require the activity of nearby muscles to move air in and out, the lungs are not simply passive bags of air. As in the gastrointestinal system, the brain monitors the chemical composition of the blood and can speed or slow respiration via stimulation of the diaphragm. Smooth muscle cells surrounding bronchioles also control airflow. Degree of bronchodilation or constriction can be influenced by both the central nervous system and local processes if inspired air seems problematic, or in response to other environmental challenges. See Chapter 14 for a discussion of respiratory conditions.

The Renal System/Urinary System

The gastrointestinal and respiratory systems are involved in both the intake of substances into the body and the removal of waste products, e.g., carbon dioxide. The renal system also participates in waste removal as well as other processes such as blood pressure regulation. At any point in time, a considerable amount of the body's blood is being filtered in the two kidneys, the main component of the system. They remove waste products from the blood, concentrate urine that is subsequently passed through the urinary system, control the retention and excretion of electrolytes such as sodium and potassium, and are important in blood pressure control. As a result, kidney disease can have widespread effects on the body. See Chapter 16 for a discussion of relevant conditions.

The Immune System

As suggested by the previous discussion, a great deal of human physiology is involved in the intake and distribution of nutrients to cells in the interior of the body (this is not to imply that other systems, such as the reproductive system [see Chapter 13], are unimportant, but these will not be discussed here due to space limitations). Yet not everything that is eaten, inhaled, or otherwise enters the body is useful. Some substances, e.g., certain microorganisms, can be especially harmful. The **immune system** protects the body from infection.

The immune system is more diverse and much less compartmentalized than previously discussed systems. A widespread

FIGURE 2.5 | The respiratory system.

Source: Adapted from an image courtesy of www.myvmc.com.

Nasal cavity
Oral cavity
Pharynx
Epiglottis
Larynx
Trachea
Left lung
Pulmonary blood vessels
Heart
Upper lobe
Lower lobe

Right lung
Upper lobe
Middle lobe
Lower lobe

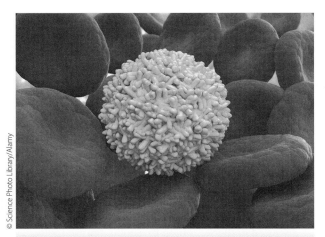

PHOTO 2.2 | A white blood cell, or leukocyte.

© Science Photo Library/Alamy

system is necessary given the diversity of ways that substances can enter the body. As a result, the primary components of the immune system are individual cells that circulate in the bloodstream, though there are also fixed components such as lymph vessels and nodes, the thymus and spleen.

Circulating leukocytes (i.e., white blood cells) develop from stem cells located in bone marrow. They have the potential to develop into many different kinds of blood cells and are initially distinguished into myeloid and lymphoid types. A number of different cells develop from the myeloid line, including some that are not part of the immune system such as oxygen-carrying erythrocytes (red blood cells) but also immune system components neutrophils, eosinophils, and macrophages (Figure 2.6). Most of these attack and digest suspect

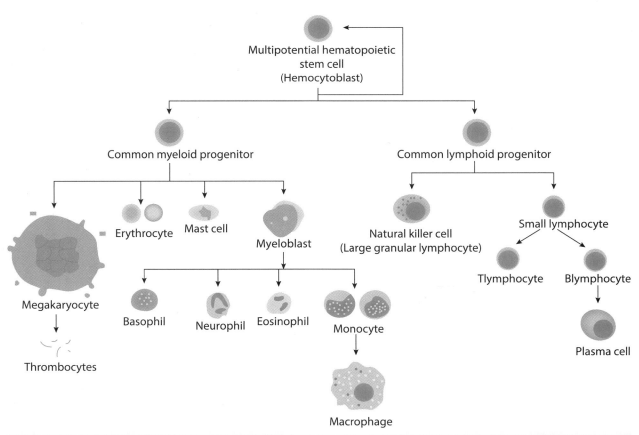

FIGURE 2.6 | Circulating immune system cells.

Source: Copyright © A. Rad

substances. Some also release substances to aid destruction and organize the immune response. For example, macrophages release molecules called cytokines, which activate other immune cells and promote inflammation.

Inflammation is a classic sign of infection. Cytokines and other inflammatory mediators such as histamine dilate and increase the permeability of blood vessels in the area, facilitating the influx of other immune cells attracted to the mediators. An increase in fluid in the area also causes it to balloon out, tightening connections between cells to create a physical barrier to isolate the infection. Red, puffy areas are a sign that the immune system is working.

Cells derived from the myeloid line as well as some from the lymphoid line (natural killer cells) provide what is described variously as natural, innate, or "non-specific" immunity. They are pre-programmed to attack many types of invaders by the presence of receptors that lock on to common proteins used by these bacteria, etc. However, this leaves open the possibility of attack by novel threats that may have developed recently, such as a new strain of the flu virus. "Specific" immune cells derived from the lymphoid line are more flexible in that they can be programmed to respond to protein patterns on new threats. Although this two-pronged system usually works well, it also means that specific immunity is ineffective during one's first encounter with the threat. For example, most people become quite sick when infected by the chickenpox virus the first time, though non-specific immune activity usually prevents death. However, lymphocytes are programmed to attack and remember the virus, thus providing more or less lifelong immunity after the initial infection.

Different types of lymphocytes have complementary functions and are classified as T or B cells (depending on where the cells mature) and subdivided into groups with the prefix CD (cluster of differentiation refers to molecules on cell surface). Cytotoxic T cells (CD8+ cells) are similar to neutrophils and macrophages in the sense that they directly attack dangerous cells, especially those infected with a virus. Other T cells support the immune response in various ways. For example, Helper T cells (CD4+ cells) stimulate cytotoxic T cells and macrophages by releasing cytokines. Although they do not attack cells directly, their importance is indicated by the devastating effects of the human immunodeficiency virus (HIV), which targets CD4+ cells. B-lymphocytes play a key "humoral" support role, releasing antibodies that bind to invaders and attract immune cells.

The immune system developed to respond to a variety of threats. However, the process of detection is not perfect. At times, the system reacts to innocuous external and internal stimuli. Allergies are caused by unnecessary responses to innocuous external stimuli. Reactions are usually mild but can be life-threatening, as in the case of peanut allergy. The immune system can also attack healthy internal cells. Autoimmune disorders such as rheumatoid arthritis, Type 1 diabetes, and lupus are caused by inappropriate targeting of healthy cells in the joints, pancreas, etc. To some degree, immune system cells are like a gang of hired gunslingers who generally follow orders but occasionally shoot the wrong person. Thus, there are mechanisms to dampen as well as stimulate immune activity, some of which involve central nervous system control mediated by actions of the **peripheral nervous system** and hormones. Central nervous system control of immune function will be discussed in the section on psychoneuroimmunology.

Psychological Influences on Body Systems

Complex organisms that could adapt to their surroundings were more likely to survive and produce offspring. The development of systems for the internal delivery of nutrients was a key step as this allowed other systems to execute behaviour. Nervous systems process information about the environment and internal condition of the body, adjusting physiology and behaviour accordingly. The human central nervous system can exert incredible control over physiology and behaviour via the peripheral nervous system and the **endocrine system**. Imagine the rapid-fire adjustments of muscle activity necessary to play a Mozart concerto (or at least to play it well)! At the same time, the brain has to adjust blood flow, respiratory activity, perspiration, etc. to support the behaviour.

Physiological activity is also adjusted according to internal as well as external sensory information. In addition to "efferent" fibres that transmit orders from the brain to muscles, the peripheral nervous system includes "afferent" fibres that transmit information from receptors sensitive to pressure, temperature, chemicals, and pain to the brain. A simple example is the baroreflex. To maintain adequate blood flow to the brain and reduce the chances of fainting as we move through daily activities, receptors sensitive to stretch are attached to the carotid arteries in the neck and elsewhere. If blood flow in this area goes down, e.g., if you stand up quickly, information is transmitted to the brain by afferent fibres in the glossopharyngeal nerve. This is combined with other information about the state of the cardiovascular system and organism, usually leading to compensatory cardiovascular responses organized by efferent fibres of the autonomic nervous system (discussed below), such as an increase in heart rate. The reverse—a decrease in heart rate—occurs when the arteries are stretched by an increase in blood pressure. Interestingly, external pressure to this area, such as wearing a tight collar or tie, can also produce a decrease in heart rate and, at times, fainting (for *Star Trek* fans, this is the origin of the Vulcan death grip). The baroreflex is a simple example of the continuous back-and-forth of information about the external and internal environment to the brain and adjustment of body function.

The Peripheral Nervous System

The peripheral nervous system (Figure 2.7) allows the brain to make quick adjustments of body function. The central nervous system (CNS) is comprised of the brain and spinal cord. Neurons (i.e., nerve cells) of the peripheral nervous system are located outside the CNS. Fibres of the peripheral nervous system exit in bundles (nerves) from the brain stem or from the spinal cord

between spinal vertebrae. Some fibres proceed directly to their "target organ" whereas others synapse with other neurons along the way in clusters called ganglia.

The peripheral nervous system has two subsystems—the **somatic nervous system** and the **autonomic nervous system**. The somatic nervous system consists of neurons that exit the spinal cord and proceed without synapse to striated muscle cells that control body movement, often referred to as voluntary muscle cells. As exemplified by the impact of severe spinal cord injury, proper function of the somatic nervous system is important. If the spinal cord is severed due to an event such as car accident, the brain is unable to control somatic nervous system neurons that exit the spinal cord below the injury, resulting in paralysis of muscles innervated by those fibres. That said, since somatic nervous system neurons do not innervate organs such as the heart and the lungs, they are less important in terms of the major causes of illness. As a result, the autonomic nervous system will be described in greater detail.

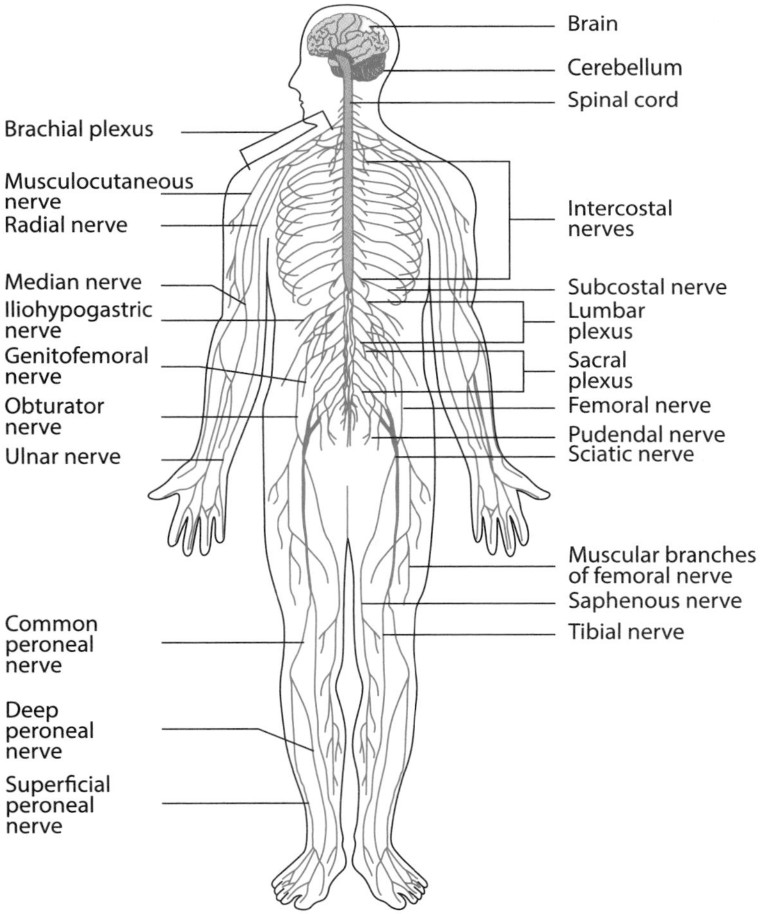

Brain
Cerebellum
Spinal cord

Brachial plexus

Musculocutaneous nerve
Radial nerve

Intercostal nerves

Median nerve
Iliohypogastric nerve
Genitofemoral nerve
Obturator nerve
Ulnar nerve

Subcostal nerve
Lumbar plexus
Sacral plexus
Femoral nerve
Pudendal nerve
Sciatic nerve

Muscular branches of femoral nerve
Saphenous nerve
Tibial nerve

Common peroneal nerve

Deep peroneal nerve
Superficial peroneal nerve

FIGURE 2.7 | The peripheral nervous system.

The Autonomic Nervous System

The autonomic nervous system (ANS) consists of neurons that exit the brain stem or spinal cord, synapse with other ANS neurons, and proceed to cardiac muscle or smooth muscle cells that influence activity in different organs. Muscle activity influenced by the ANS is often referred to as "involuntary" since it occurs continuously without conscious thought, e.g., you do not have to remember to tell your heart to contract. On the other hand, the word "involuntary" is somewhat inaccurate since the results of biofeedback experiments indicate that it is possible to develop some control over processes such as heart rate (Levenson & Ditto, 1981). Regardless, the ongoing nature of muscle tension means that ANS effects are revealed by increases and decreases in activity, e.g., increased or decreased heart rate, rather than the presence or absence of activity. It also means that ANS activity affects muscle tension somewhat more slowly than somatic nervous system activity but has longer-lasting effects (imagine pushing a moving automobile as opposed to a stationary one).

Another similarity to automobiles is the fact that the ANS is subdivided into two relatively independent parts, similar to acceleration and braking systems (Figure 2.8). In

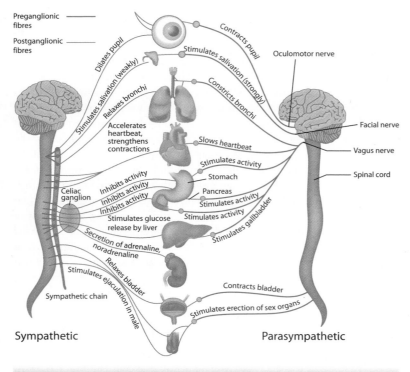

FIGURE 2.8 | The autonomic nervous system.

general, the **sympathetic nervous system** (SNS) stimulates smooth muscle activity whereas the **parasympathetic nervous system** (PNS) usually inhibits activity.

The PNS is sometimes called the craniosacral system since these ANS fibres exit the central nervous system in the upper (cranial) and lower (sacral) regions. Typically, "pre-ganglionic" neurons proceed most of the way to their target organs before they synapse with "post-ganglionic" neurons. The post-ganglionic neurons are relatively short. Acetylcholine is used as the neurotransmitter at the junctions of the pre- and post-ganglionic PNS neurons and at the junctions between post-ganglionic PNS neurons and the target organ.

The SNS is sometimes called the thoracolumbar system since these fibres exit the spinal cord in the central thoracic and lumbar regions. In contrast to the PNS, these pre-ganglionic neurons do not travel far before synapsing in large clumps called sympathetic ganglia, which are located close to the spinal cord. As a result, the post-ganglionic neurons of the SNS are much longer. As in the PNS, acetylcholine is used as the neurotransmitter at the junctions of the pre- and post-ganglionic SNS neurons whereas norepinephrine is used as the neurotransmitter at the junctions between post-ganglionic SNS neurons and the target organ.

These differences in anatomy influence function. Though slower and less precisely targeted than somatic nervous system activity, PNS activity is generally quicker and more specific than SNS activity. There is much greater opportunity for sympathetic activity to spread and linger compared to parasympathetic activity. Imagine walking down a deserted street late at night. Unexpectedly, a cat knocks over a trash can. Sympathetic activity will probably lead to a number of different responses—increased sweating, heart rate, constriction of blood vessels, etc.—that may leave you feeling "wired" for some time. Another interesting example has to do with nicotine. Nicotine from cigarette smoke stimulates a subtype of receptor for acetylcholine that is found in the brain and peripheral nervous system. This might suggest that nicotine produces physiological relaxation, consistent with the subjective experience of many smokers. However, since acetylcholine is also used as a transmitter in sympathetic ganglia, nicotine is mostly a stimulant in terms of its effects on peripheral physiology. Exceptions to this "all or nothing" description of SNS activity will be discussed later.

The Endocrine System

In addition to the peripheral nervous system, the brain can influence body function by stimulating the release of hormones. Hormones are similar and in some cases identical to neurotransmitters released by neurons of the peripheral nervous system and influence different aspects of target organ function. However, since they are released into the bloodstream they can influence physiological activity longer. The effects of hormones complement and extend peripheral nervous system activity. This is especially the case for hormones released from the central portion of the **adrenal glands**, the adrenal medulla (Figure 2.8). The adrenal medulla is somewhat unusual in that release of its hormones, primarily epinephrine and norepinephrine, is controlled by sympathetic nervous system fibres. SNS activity stimulates the adrenal medulla to release epinephrine and norepinephrine into the bloodstream, reinforcing and maintaining SNS activity.

Most other hormones are controlled by the hypothalamus and the pituitary gland, often referred to as the "master gland" (Figure 2.9). Descending activity from the brain stimulates different patterns of hypothalamic

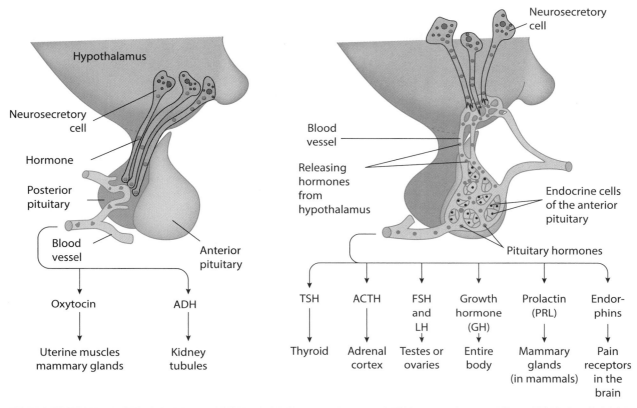

FIGURE 2.9 | Pituitary hormones.

output to the pituitary. Neurons connecting the hypothalamus to the posterior portion of the pituitary gland control release of hormones such as antidiuretic hormone, which influences water retention by the kidneys and blood pressure, and oxytocin. Traditionally, oxytocin was viewed primarily in terms of its effects on reproductive activities, though more recently it has also been found to have stress-buffering properties. In fact, Taylor (Taylor et al., 2006) has suggested that oxytocin is a key component of a motivational system ("tend and befriend") promoting social engagement to address collective needs, including safety and protection.

The anterior pituitary releases a wider array of hormones than the posterior pituitary and functions somewhat differently. The primary function of hormones released from the anterior pituitary is to stimulate the release of hormones from more distant glands. For example, thyrotropic hormone is released to control the thyroid gland. As well, the hypothalamus controls anterior pituitary function by secreting its own set of "releasing factors," that is, hormones that travel the short distance to the anterior pituitary to influence function. For example,

hypothalamic gonadotropin-releasing factor controls the release of pituitary hormones regulating the gonads (testes and ovaries). Similarly, corticotrophin-releasing factor (CRF) controls the release of adrenocorticotrophic hormone (ACTH) from the anterior pituitary, which in turn regulates the adrenal cortex.

The hypothalamic-pituitary-adrenal (HPA) axis is especially important vis-à-vis psychological influences on body systems and the development of illness. The adrenal cortex releases a number of hormones, including glucocorticoids, mineralocorticoids, androgens, and estrogens. As the name suggests, mineralocorticoids (e.g., aldosterone) affect mineral balance (e.g., sodium) and often reinforce the effects of stress on variables such as blood pressure. Glucocorticoids (e.g., cortisol) free up glucose and other energy resources during times of stress. While this may be useful in some circumstances it can pose problems in others. Glucocorticoids also influence inflammation and other aspects of immune system activity that may have beneficial effects in some circumstances and adverse effects in others. This will be discussed in the section on psychoneuroimmunology.

The Development of the Stress Concept

The brain strives to maximize the efficiency of body function and adjust to the environment. Typically, adjustments are small and involve specific aspects of ANS or hormonal activity. For example, standing up may produce a brief decrease in baroreceptor stimulation that triggers an increase in cardiac-related SNS activity and a decrease in cardiac-related PNS activity (causing an increase in heart rate), but not much else occurs in terms of ANS or hormonal activity.

However, the brain also responds to stimuli that challenge the entire human organism. Stimuli such as extreme cold or heat, exercise, and blood loss elicit complex, widespread patterns of ANS and hormonal activity to prepare the body for different challenges. In the early 1900s, the physiologist Walter Cannon noted many common features of responses to strong, challenging stimuli, including stimuli primarily psychological in nature. In his classic book, *Bodily Changes in Pain, Hunger, Fear, and Rage* (1929), he argued that we possess a broad pattern of response to threat that he called the "fight-or-flight response pattern." Cannon believed that the extensive connections of the sympathetic nervous system allow the brain to prepare the body for a potentially life-threatening situation. SNS activity during a fight-or-flight response increases heart rate to facilitate delivery of nutrients to the muscles. It also constricts blood vessels in the skin and gastrointestinal system, though SNS activity *dilates* vessels supplying large muscles in the arms and legs. The fact that SNS activity stimulates smooth muscle in some blood vessels and relaxes it in others shows that the view of the SNS as producing uniform "arousal" is oversimplified. The SNS produces a pattern of peripheral physiological activity that prepares the body for vigorous physical action. Some processes are stimulated, others are inhibited. SNS activity also inhibits smooth muscle contraction in the gastrointestinal system (though this may disrupt digestion) and the bronchioles of the lungs (to allow greater intake of oxygen). The impact of the fight-or-flight response—more commonly described today as the stress response—on a wide variety of body functions has become increasingly recognized and now extends to aspects of physiology once believed unaffected, such as immune function.

Cannon was not an epidemiologist and thus did not extensively study associations between the fight-or-flight response and illness (an interesting exception was

"It was the classic fight or flight response. Next time, try flight."

PHOTO 2.3 | "Next time, try flight."

his study of the extreme example of voodoo death; see In Focus box, below). World events in the 1930s and 1940s also slowed appreciation of his work (Cannon had an interesting life that included rescuing scientists in the turmoil of the Spanish Civil War and World War II). However, interest in the topic of stress skyrocketed after World War II. To a large degree, this was due to the physician and researcher Hans Selye. Similar to Cannon, Selye believed that a wide range of stimuli can elicit a pattern of physiological activity—the stress response—that is problematic in modern life. His focus on the effects of stress on hormonal activity, particularly the adrenal hormone **cortisol**, complemented Cannon's interest in the ANS. As a physician, he was also more focused on how stress contributed to disease and was noted for his work linking stress, cortisol, and ulcer formation in rats. Selye's greatest contribution, though, may have been to popularize the idea of stress in the scientific community and the general public. His classic book, *The Stress of Life* (1956), was read widely largely because it argued that stress is a daily occurrence. This idea struck a chord in the years of the Cold War and, more generally, during an era of growing concern about the effects of industrialization, the growth of suburbs, and the "rat race" of modern, Western human life. Selye's message fit the times and provided a boost to stress research and the development of health psychology.

⊚ IN FOCUS

Cannon and "Voodoo Death"

Walter Cannon was a well-travelled man with diverse interests. Although not an epidemiologist (someone who studies disease trends in human societies) or an anthropologist, Cannon became fascinated by examples of death that seemed to be linked to extreme stress in several non-Western societies. In particular, he was interested in a phenomenon he called "voodoo death" where someone died after being "cursed" by a religious leader. He collected records from adventurers, anthropologists, missionaries, and physicians in South America, Africa, Australia, the Caribbean, and elsewhere. Given the unusual nature of the events, these were case reports rather than controlled experiments, but they were often quite detailed and allowed him to discount alternative explanations such as murder by poison or intentional suicide. Occasionally, Cannon was able to correspond with the observer to extend his detective work.

Cannon viewed voodoo death as essentially the flip side of the placebo effect—a powerful effect of expectation on health. However, in this case, the expectation was death, leading to intense fear and a self-fulfilling prophecy of "death from fear" (Cannon, 1942). In addition to cultural beliefs, this was usually accentuated by withdrawal of all social support and acceptance of the victim's fate by others. Although he could not examine the victims directly, Cannon suggested that strong sympathetically mediated blood vessel constriction was the key feature of the process. Reports of looking extremely pale and "white as a sheet" were common. He believed that this led eventually to a state of physiological shock not unlike a wartime injury. It is likely that other processes were involved, such as cardiac arrhythmias (Sternberg, 2002), but this was an early, creative attempt to link life stress, emotion, physiological activity, and health.

Theories of stress and coping will be discussed in Chapter 5. For the moment, the only issue to note before turning to a few examples of stress-related illness is the association between stress and emotion.

Emotion

Although Cannon and Selye emphasized the idea of a broad, generic stress response, subsequent research revealed interesting differences as well as similarities in reactions to many strong stimuli, including emotional stimuli. These findings complement rather than undercut the notion of a stress response since the differences usually seem to match the nature of adaptive behaviour most likely to occur in the situation. However, the precise pattern of the stress response is more tailored to the situation than once believed. One of the most important differences concerns reactions to situations that elicit anger as opposed to fear. Both being in an angry confrontation and walking on a deserted street late at night, for example, can elicit large increases in heart rate mediated by an increase in SNS activity and decrease in PNS activity directed at the heart. However, anger-inducing situations are more likely to elicit sympathetically mediated blood vessel constriction than are fear-inducing

situations, which may even elicit vasodilation (Ax, 1953; Sinha, Lovallo, & Parsons, 1992). This may be due to the fact that the odds of an angry confrontation leading to physical aggression, injury, and blood loss are much greater (at least in an evolutionary context) than a fearful situation that encourages you to run. Blood vessel constriction might reduce blood loss due to injury.

Differences in stress responses may set the stage for different stress-related disorders and be part of the reason that not everyone suffers from a stress-related illness. For example, the development of stress-related hypertension appears to be associated with a certain type of stressful life environment and emotional predisposition that, along with genetic susceptibility, increases risk for high blood pressure. This idea of environmental and emotional patterning will be elaborated in the discussion of specific illnesses.

The fact that emotions are the immediate stimulus for many stress reactions raises one other important issue. Stress responses do not require actual exposure to challenging life situations. Strong reactions can be produced by the anticipation of an event that may never occur or the memory of an event that has already occurred. This may have been a useful conservative error at one time in evolutionary history (better safe than sorry that one hasn't anticipated and prepared for an attack), but it leads to even more unnecessary stress responses involving, for example, irritation of arteries by increased blood pressure.

Psychological Factors in the Development of Medical Illnesses

Without question, environmental challenges or "stressors" can influence body function. However, can the stress response actually make you sick? Since human beings are not assigned randomly to stressful and non-stressful circumstances at birth, this question has always been controversial. A number of different approaches have been employed, often blending human and animal research. These are illustrated in the following discussion of several stress-related disorders.

Gastrointestinal Ulcers: Executive Monkeys and Helpless Rats

Historically, gastrointestinal ulcers were viewed as the prototypic stress-related illness. In the middle of the twentieth century many believed that the pressures of modern life and business contributed to the development of ulcers, especially among people with executive responsibility. This was common in scientific circles (based largely on Selye's research) as well as the popular media (e.g., the high-pressure newspaper editor in the Spider-Man comics, J. Jonah Jameson, had an ulcer).

In addition to stereotypes of the time, the idea was boosted by an influential experiment that seemed to confirm the importance of executive stress. The "executive monkey" experiment (Brady, Porter, Conrad, & Mason, 1958) was one of the most widely cited studies in psychology and a staple of introductory psychology textbooks for decades (see also Chapter 5). In this study, monkeys trained to avoid the delivery of electric shocks by pressing a bar were much more likely to develop ulcers compared to control monkeys who were placed in the same environment and received the same number of shocks but were not given this "responsibility." Unfortunately, the experiment had a crucial flaw that was not appreciated for some time. To save time during initial training, monkeys who learned the desired behaviour quickly were non-randomly assigned to be executives! The other monkeys were assigned to be the controls. As a result, ulcer formation in the executives may have been due to pre-existing differences in activity, fearfulness, or sensitivity to pain.

The executive monkey study is a useful cautionary tale of the dangers of uncritical adoption of stereotypes

and over-enthusiasm for the idea that stress causes illness. However, it does not imply that stress cannot cause illness, including gastrointestinal ulcers. In fact, subsequent animal research showed that certain stressful situations reliably increase risk for ulcers. Weiss (Weiss, Pohorecky, Salman, & Gruenthal, 1976) conducted a well-known series of more tightly conducted studies with rats and found that animals placed in the more helpless situation of receiving electric shocks that they were unable to control were more susceptible to ulcers. Unpredictability also increases risk. The similarity between these animal experiments and the learned helplessness paradigm of psychological depression is obvious, and a number of unpleasant, uncontrollable situations have been found to induce ulcers in animals. For example, simply restraining rats for long periods of time significantly increases risk for ulcers. Underscoring the association with depression, recent research indicates that the likelihood of restraint-induced ulcers in rats is reduced by the anti-depressive medication fluoxetine (Prozac) (Abdel-Sater, Abdel-Daiem, & Sayyed Bakheet, 2012). Another interesting finding from Weiss's experiments (Weiss et al., 1976) was that rats exhibiting signs of aggression towards another rat when shocked were significantly *less* likely to develop lesions, even if this did nothing to terminate the shocks. This is an interesting contrast to research that will be discussed below indicating the importance of anger and aggression in the development of cardiovascular disease. In sum, there is good evidence that uncontrollable stress can contribute to gastrointestinal ulcers in animals.

However, the field took another unexpected turn in the 1980s in the context of human research on ulcers. Two Australian researchers, Barry Marshall and Robin Warren, discovered that a bacterium, Helicobacter pylori (H. pylori), was present in many ulcer patients and that antibiotic treatment often produced remarkably beneficent effects. This led some to argue that the problem was essentially "solved" and that even if stress could produce ulcers in animals it was irrelevant for human ulcers. On the other hand, while the importance of H. pylori continues to be acknowledged, views have become more nuanced in recent years. For example, about 30 per cent of people with ulcers do not have H. pylori and ulcers sometimes reoccur in people treated for H. pylori despite elimination of the bacterium. Most important, most people with H. pylori do not develop ulcers (Fink, 2011). Thus, it is more accurate to view it as a strong risk factor for ulcers that can be exacerbated by other factors, including stress. An interesting study found that stomach ulcers increased significantly following the Hanshin-Awaji earthquake of January 1995 in Japan, especially among those most personally affected and less able to rebuild (Aoyama et al., 1998). Another large population-based study found an association between personality disorders and stomach ulcer (Schuster, Limosin, Levenstein, & Le Strat, 2010). Levenstein (2000) developed a model that integrates influences of infection, stress, and lifestyle factors such as smoking and alcohol use on ulcer formation. The idea that stress may contribute to ulcer formation by reducing immune activity is consistent with the growing area of psychoneuroimmunology. It is also consistent with the role of depression, which is known to have a particularly strong effect on cortisol release. In sum, after some interesting twists and turns, there has been a revival of interest in the role of stress in gastrointestinal ulcers that reflects the growing sophistication of stress research.

Vasovagal Reactions: A Brief but Dramatic Response

Most people are familiar with the symptoms of a vasovagal reaction (VVR), often through personal experience, even if they are unfamiliar with the term. Many people experience dizziness, weakness, and even fainting at some point in their lives that is not due to an external insult such as concussion or drug use or internal disease such as epilepsy. Vasovagal reactions are caused by a decrease in blood flow to the brain in the absence of other illness. Historically, this was believed to be due to the combined effects of a large decrease in heart rate (mediated by parasympathetic *vagal* activity) and changes in blood vessel constriction. This description is not incorrect, though more recent research suggests that blood vessel constriction in the brain may be especially important (Folino, 2006). If blood flow to the brain is reduced sufficiently, fainting or "vasovagal syncope" occurs.

Fortunately, the majority of faints are brief and do not require treatment, though injury from falling is not unusual and longer faints can lead to seizures and on rare occasions death. Fainting and milder symptoms are also associated with avoidance of health-care behaviour such as injections and dental exams as well as clinical phobias. As a result, vasovagal reactions are more serious than the comic depictions of a Victorian matron who swoons at the receipt of bad news or a cartoon character who faints when startled. In fact, a vasovagal reaction is probably the clearest, most dramatic example of stress-related illness. In the span of a few moments, an individual with no pre-existing illness can be rendered *unconscious* by a psychological stressor.

Similar to some early views on the development of stress-related ulcers, vasovagal syncope was first thought to be the result of a stress-related parasympathetic rebound—essentially a side effect of "relief." In a classic article, Graham (Graham, Kabler, & Lunsford, 1961) noted that vasovagal symptoms during injections and blood draws generally follow a period of strong sympathetic nervous system activity and often occur towards the end of the procedure, sometimes after removal of the needle. On the other hand, though a full discussion of the psychology and physiology of the vasovagal response is beyond the present scope, the idea of relief is inadequate. For example, students rarely faint at the end of exams! This does not seem to be a general response to the termination of a stressful event. Nor is there a general association with anxiety or fear. For example, among people with strong fears, a number of studies have showed that people with blood, injury, and injection phobias are especially susceptible to vasovagal reactions whereas people who might have extreme fears of animals or social situations are no more likely to faint than people in the general population. Ost (1992) found that 70 per cent of people with blood phobias had fainted at least once during their lives. Vasovagal reactions seem to be related to the anticipation of physical harm.

In some respects, this sounds similar to the situation that sets the stage for stress-related ulcers, though there are differences as well. In particular, people do not faint or get dizzy in the context of every unpleasant, uncontrollable situation. As suggested above, there seems to be a special association with having to endure "puncture" in the context of injections, blood draws, and dental work. Another clue may be the fact that postural stress such as standing contributes significantly to risk for vasovagal symptoms. This has been observed even in people who are otherwise extremely healthy, such as young soldiers required to stand at attention for a long time (Fitch & Rippert, 1992). Finally, the vasovagal reaction is virtually identical to the physiological response to severe actual blood loss. In fact, hemorrhage-related fainting is observed reliably across species when blood loss approaches 30 per cent of total volume.

Recently, Diehl (2005) proposed that hemorrhage-related fainting developed as an active, adaptive response to severe injury. Some aspects of sympathetic activity are stimulated to increase perspiration and blood vessel constriction near the surface of the body. However, other aspects of sympathetic activity are decreased and some aspects of parasympathetic activity are increased in an attempt to lower blood pressure and thus blood loss. Lower blood pressure leads to less blood loss from a wound and greater opportunity for clotting. Metabolic activity is also reduced if this leads to loss of consciousness. This may also be a convincing way to "play dead" in the presence of a predator or overwhelming opponent (Bracha, 2004). Regardless, stress-related vasovagal reactions may have developed as a response to the *anticipation* of major blood loss. This would explain why people who are afraid of blood and blood loss are especially at risk of VVR (Ditto, Gilchrist, & Holly, 2012) and why standing, which causes blood to pool in the lower part of body and creates a sensation of blood loss, contributes to this process. While the details remain to be determined, this is an interesting example of how psychological and physical risk factors interact with specific characteristics of a stressful situation to elicit a patterned stress response, including both sympathetic and parasympathetic activity that may lead to a specific illness.

High Blood Pressure

In many respects, hypertension is the flip side of a vasovagal reaction. The most obvious difference is that hypertension is defined by high rather than low blood pressure. It is also sustained across the day rather than acute. The sustained nature of hypertension is exemplified by the fact that pressure does not drop or "dip" to the same extent when hypertensives sleep. In recent years, the degree of nocturnal blood pressure dipping has been used as a predictor of negative outcomes associated with hypertension such as stroke and coronary heart disease. In other words, the less blood pressure goes down at night, the greater the likelihood of stroke/heart disease.

The psychological profile of hypertension is also quite different from vasovagal reactions and ulcers. Vasovagal reactions and ulcers are typically related to uncontrollable stress, though there are some differences between them. Vasovagal reactions are most likely to occur in situations involving short-term uncontrollable stress that may lead to acute physical injury or blood loss whereas ulcers are more likely to occur in situations involving long-term uncontrollable stress, hopelessness, and depression. In contrast, theories of high blood pressure typically focus on situations and emotions related to struggle and aggression. A simple manipulation found to raise blood pressure in rats is crowding. The number of rats housed in a cage is positively associated with blood pressure, though the effect is stronger among males and those at greater genetic risk for hypertension (Bernatova, Puzserova, & Dubovicky, 2010). This is an interesting contrast to Weiss's (Weiss et al., 1976) finding that rats

who engaged in shock-related aggressive behaviour were significantly *less* likely to develop stomach lesions.

Considerable research in humans also suggests that conditions involving irritation, struggle, conflict, and crowding are linked to risk for hypertension and may begin to influence blood pressure early in life. Regecova and Kellerova (Regecova & Kellerova, 1995) found that kindergarten children whose schools were located in neighbourhoods with higher levels of traffic noise had higher blood pressure than children who went to school in quieter neighbourhoods. The young age of participants eliminates alternative explanations involving smoking and alcohol use. As well, they observed an interesting *negative* association between noise and heart rate—children who attended kindergarten in noisier neighbourhoods displayed lower heart rates. The authors attributed this to a normal baroreflex response of healthy children. Over time, the baroreflex becomes

PHOTO 2.4 | Chronic exposure to noise has been found to be related to blood pressure elevation and hypertension.

© chrisgon/iStockphoto

desensitized in hypertension, contributing to the upward progression of blood pressure. Associations between environmental noise and blood pressure have also been observed in adults. A recent review showed that chronic exposure to noise is significantly related to blood pressure elevation and risk for hypertension (van Kempen & Babisch, 2012) though the effect is seen mainly in men and those who are more annoyed by noise.

Other research has focused more explicitly on the idea of anger, extending from the original psychoanalytic hypothesis that the chronic experience of anger is often important in the development of high blood pressure (Alexander, 1939). An interesting subset of this research concerns the effects of racial discrimination on emotions and blood pressure in African Americans. African Americans are at greater risk for hypertension due to a combination of genetic and environmental factors. In a creative study, Sweet et al. (Sweet, McDade, Kiefe, & Liu, 2007) controlled for genetic background by examining the relationship between blood pressure and socio-economic position (income) in African Americans as a function of skin colour. Among lighter-skinned African Americans, they observed the expected negative association between income and blood pressure. However, among participants with darker skin, they found that those with higher incomes actually had higher blood pressure. These individuals may have been special targets of discrimination once successful, or their success may have required greater struggle. A recent study of the effects of stress on blood pressure dipping found that African-Americans who experience more racial discrimination on an everyday basis had smaller decreases in blood pressure at night, possibly as a result of rumination about injustice (Tomfohr, Cooper, Mills, Nelesen, & Dimsdale, 2010). Relatedly, several studies of stress management strategies that may reduce anger (e.g., transcendental meditation) have observed significantly greater effects in African Americans (Schneider et al., 2005).

The mechanisms of stress-induced hypertension are still under study, but one reason for the involvement of anger may be the fact that it often produces strong increases in both cardiac output and blood vessel constriction (Ax, 1953; Sinha et al., 1992), placing extra stress on the endothelium. In principle, increased cardiac output combined with blood vessel constriction and decreased flow to the skin would be useful in situations that might lead to violent conflict. However, repeated exposure may impair the ability of blood vessels to relax and self-regulate (a condition referred to as endothelial dysfunction; it is interesting that one complication of hypertension is erectile dysfunction)

as well as thwart other compensatory responses such as the baroreflex. Diet, abdominal obesity, and, more generally, the "metabolic syndrome" (a common cluster of symptoms including abdominal obesity, high blood sugar, high cholesterol, and high blood pressure) are also probably involved in this process via the effect of insulin on endothelial function.

Other Diseases

Coronary heart disease will be discussed in Chapter 9. Many similarities have been identified between psychological aspects of hypertension and coronary heart disease, including the focus on anger. Evidence also links stress to many other diseases. Cortisol is often implicated as the culprit. For example, high cortisol reactivity has been associated with poor blood sugar control in diabetes (Dutour et al., 1996). This is perhaps unsurprising given that its primary function is to increase the availability of glucose during emergencies. Relatedly, stress appears to be a risk factor for obesity, over and above the well-known phenomenon of emotional eating. In addition to its effects on glucose, cortisol facilitates the storage of abdominal fat, perhaps preparing the body for the "long haul" of a stressful situation (Epel et al., 2000).

Cortisol also has intriguing effects on central nervous system function, particularly memory. Animal studies indicate that cortisol may even have toxic effects on brain cells in certain areas (Sapolsky, 2000). Some have speculated that this originated as an adaptive means of coping with trauma, preventing excess fear that may inhibit subsequent behaviour (some mothers joke that if they remembered all the details of their pregnancy and childbirth, they would never do it again). Regardless, the belief that stress may contribute to dementia and age-related cognitive decline is a hot though controversial topic (Fink, 2011). Another hot topic with implications for many stress-related disorders is the effect of stress on immune system function.

Psychoneuroimmunology

Development of the Field

The growth of psychoneuroimmunology is probably the most important development in health psychology in the last 20 years. Cannon's description of the autonomic nervous system set the stage for early theories of stress-related problems such as high blood pressure, asthma, and ulcers. Observable connections between the brain and the heart, blood vessels, etc. provided a framework for speculation. Clinicians and theorists wondered for years about associations between psychological variables and a number of other disorders, but they were stymied by the lack of a plausible mechanism. For example, inspired by Cannon's work, Ishigami (1919) studied people with tuberculosis and observed connections between life stress, personality, and progress of the disease. Unfortunately, this work was largely ignored even though the author noted an additional tantalizing cue—the adverse effects of stress were associated with increased blood glucose.

The tide changed with the arrival of Hans Selye. As discussed earlier, he emphasized the role of cortisol release in the stress response (which may have explained Ishigami's blood glucose finding). He was also aware of its anti-inflammatory properties. In fact, he suggested that stress-related ulcers were due to the effect of cortisol on inflammation, reducing the ability of the stomach to protect itself from acid-related damage. In support of this idea, he found that surgical removal of the adrenal glands prevented stress-induced ulcers in rats (Selye, 1956). While connections among stress, cortisol, immune function, and ulcers are more likely to involve control of Helicobacter pylori, the idea that stress and cortisol can impair one aspect of immune function was influential and encouraged further research in the area.

Years later, Ader coined the term "psychoneuroimmunology" and propelled the field by demonstrating that aspects of immune system function can be influenced by classical conditioning (Ader & Cohen, 1975). In general, stress appears to reduce immune system function, perhaps explaining its impact on risk for a number of diseases.

Stress, Immune Function, and Illness

One of the most popular ways to study the impact of stress on immune function has been to look at the effects of examination stress (Glaser, 2005). For example, Kiecolt-Glaser et al. (1984) found lower natural killer cell activity and T-lymphocytes in blood samples obtained from students during exam periods, especially in more lonely students.

However, are such effects strong enough to lead to illness? Cohen conducted a creative set of studies on the clinical implications of stress-related immune suppression (Cohen, 2005). Participants who differed in life stress, social support, etc. were exposed to a virus that produces a common cold. Those with more life stress were more likely to develop symptoms independent of other risk factors such as cigarette smoking and sleep quality.

In some studies, participants were hospitalized to further control possible confounds. While the investigators studied a minor health problem, the controlled exposure to a virus in these studies provides strong evidence of the importance of stress in susceptibility to illness. The accompanying In Practice box discusses a possible case example of psychological influences on health.

What about more serious illness? The results are less clear but emerging evidence suggests that stress can influence the progression of more serious diseases such as AIDS and cancer. An effect of stress on the progression and consequences of the human immunodeficiency virus (HIV) that leads to AIDS is especially plausible given that the disease is defined by the influence of HIV on immune function. Life stress has been associated with accelerated progression to AIDS in HIV+ men (Leserman et al., 2002) and possibly faster progression of cervical cancer in HIV+ women (Pereira et al., 2003).

The possible role of stress in the onset and course of cancer in people without HIV is more controversial. In part, this is due to the difficulty of studying the question given the diversity, complexity, and long time frame of most types of cancer. Some of the most persuasive studies in the area concern the effects of stress reduction interventions on the progression of cancer, that is, what happens when stress is *reduced*. Andersen et al. (2008) found that women with breast cancer who participated in stress reduction groups after surgery were significantly less likely to experience a recurrence and lived longer than women with only medical treatment. While concerns about the reliability and ethics (e.g., raising false hopes) of particular studies have been expressed, examining effects of stress reduction strategies on cancer provides a more experimental approach where potential confounding variables (e.g., smoking, diet, and exercise) and mediators (e.g., different aspects of immune function) can be measured carefully. The possible benefit of treatments that reduce depression also fits the large body of research showing increased cortisol release in people with clinical depression (Giese-Davis et al., 2011).

Unfortunately, there are some important additional qualifications to this relatively tidy picture. Most important, the impact of stress on immune function is not uniformly inhibitory (Segerstrom & Miller, 2004). In addition to evidence of decreased immune function, investigators have observed *higher* cytokine levels, inflammation, and greater risk for autoimmune disease in some stressed groups. Another puzzle is why stress reduces immune function. At first glance, from an evolutionary perspective, it would make more sense for

🔲 IN PRACTICE

Ron vs the Warts

Ron always had problems with warts on his hands. Nothing dramatic—months would pass with nothing, but then one or two would pop up on or between his fingers. Sometimes they went away on their own, though he also became very familiar with his local dermatologist. While they are caused by a virus (the human papillomavirus), his dermatologist joked that the best way to remove them was simply "nuke" the buggers, that is, freeze or cut (after local anesthesia, of course) them off. This was usually effective in the short term. They seldom returned in exactly the same spot, but they never completely went away, occasionally popping up in a different location. Unfortunately, during a stressful first semester in university, they became much worse. Tired of the nuisance and embarrassment, Ron decided to look into alternative, hopefully more permanent approaches. Being a bright college student, he knew that they definitely did *not* spring from contact with toads (not common in downtown

Toronto). He also discounted "distant healing," the idea that illness can be treated by spiritual or mental energy from a healer, after reading about an interesting but unsuccessful test of this popular alternative treatment applied to warts (Harkness, Abbot, & Ernst, 2000). On the other hand, after reading a study that found that hypnotic relaxation and suggestion worked as well as if not better than salicylic acid (Spanos, Williams, & Gwynn, 1990), he decided to give it a try. This approach is based on the idea that viral activity leading to warts is influenced by the immune system, which, in turn, is influenced by emotional state. Following a training session with a psychologist, he practised a tailored 20-minute relaxation and imagery procedure daily for a month. The warts may have gotten a bit smaller (it was hard to tell) but he eventually became impatient and had them frozen. On the other hand, his mood and general physical health were better and he signed up for a yoga class in the winter semester.

stress to strengthen rather than weaken immune function. For example, a fight-or-flight situation involving possible injury could lead easily to introduction of bacteria from a cut or bite of a predator.

Recent research on the effects of the sympathetic nervous system on immune function clarifies the picture somewhat (Kin & Sanders, 2006). Historically, SNS activity was viewed as irrelevant to immune function. How could fixed nerves affect the activity of cells moving freely in the bloodstream? However, it has been established that (1) most immune cells have receptors for norepinephrine; (2) SNS fibres innervate organs like the lymph nodes and thymus where many immune cells congregate; and (3) SNS activity can stimulate certain aspects of immune function. A clever study by Benschop et al. (1996) examined SNS, hormonal and immune system activity in novice parachutists. Not surprisingly, people who were just about to jump out of an airplane for the first time experienced large increases in sympathetic activity as evidenced by high heart rate and norepinephrine levels. More important, a number of immune changes were observed, such as increases in the number and activity of natural killer cells. The authors demonstrated that these were the result of sympathetic activity by administering the

drug propranolol. Propranolol blocks receptors for norepinephrine and eliminated the changes in natural killer cells.

In sum, life stress can both increase and decrease immune function, depending in part on the length of the stressful situation. Brief stressors appear to produce an adaptive, sympathetically mediated increase in immune function that, if repeated, might contribute to problems such as asthma or rheumatoid arthritis. On the other hand, stressors of longer duration can lead to a cortisol-related reduction in immune activity. This may have developed as a way of modulating the immune response to reduce inflammation that may hinder ongoing escape behaviour and perhaps reduce the risk of autoimmune disorders.

That said, even more recent results suggest that the pendulum may swing back to immune enhancement with *very* prolonged stress. Cohen et al. (2012) suggest that long-term release of cortisol may desensitize glucocorticoid receptors, decreasing the body's ability to control immune function. As a result, inflammation and other aspects of immune function may go up. For example, caregivers of children with cancer have been found to have dysregulated cytokine activity (Miller, Cohen, & Ritchey, 2002).

⦿ IN FOCUS

Illness as Metaphor and the Ethics of Stress

Ironically, one problem with the idea that psychological factors can influence health for better or ill is widespread acceptance by the general public. The idea has been around for a long time and is reflected in everyday language—we speak of dying of embarrassment or a broken heart. In 1728, the Scottish physician, John Hunter, is reported to have said, "My life is in the hands of any rascal who chooses to annoy me." Dr Hunter died during an argument at a hospital board meeting.

Illness is portrayed as an invader we need to battle. This is especially the case for cancer, which is often described in terms of the mythological Hydra that springs two more heads after each is cut off. And if you look at newspaper obituaries or media reports generally, invariably you encounter descriptions of cancer victims who succumbed following a brave or courageous "battle" or "fight" with the disease. However, the feminist author Susan Sontag, herself a victim of cancer, warned against the dangers of "illness as metaphor" (Sontag, 1978).

Why? Unfortunately, psychological and behavioural influences on health can convey the notion of blame. There is a long, sad history of illness being viewed as the "wages of sin." In fact, much of modern medicine was built on the idea of removing blame for illness by emphasizing biological causes, leading to more charitable attitudes about the sick.

Even if a person's psychological state may have contributed to an illness, should he or she be blamed for "pushing too hard" or for "not coping with problems"? The goal of reducing depression and maintaining a positive outlook may be useful for many with cancer, but should those whose health deteriorates feel as if this was due to a lack of "fighting spirit"?

© ZU_09/iStockphoto

PHOTO 2.5 | Hercules battling the Hydra.

Collectively, these findings fit a reasonable pattern; at the same time, it is clear that further research is required. For example, the duration of stress does not explain all contradictory findings (Segerstrom & Miller, 2004). Just as different stressors elicit qualitatively different patterns of autonomic nervous system activity, there seems to be patterning of immune responses to stress (Kin & Sanders, 2006).

Future Directions

Future research will undoubtedly reveal more connections between psychological variables and illness, with implications for treatment. Many of these effects likely will be complex and multi-directional. For example, while long-term depression may contribute to inflammation, recent research suggests that inflammatory cytokines can enter the central nervous system and exacerbate depression. The future will also see greater clarification of genetic and other risk factors for stress-related illness. Even more interesting are recent findings showing that genetic activity is influenced by the environment. Traditionally, a person's genes have been viewed as the blueprint for their physical (including neural) structure that influences how they respond to the environment. However, we now know that environmental experiences can regulate gene expression. Genes promoting inflammation have been found to be particularly active in lonely people (Cole et al., 2007) and those with low socio-economic status (Chen et al., 2009). On many levels, you are in a dynamic relationship with the environment.

SUMMARY

The field of health psychology stems from the integration of biological, behavioural, psychological, and social processes in the evolution of complex multicellular organisms. Complex organisms did not evolve to lie quietly on a beach, at least not all the time. Searching for food, defending from predators, and developing collaborative networks to aid in these and other tasks required the development of complex nervous systems and organs to support the intake and distribution of nutrients. This chapter has discussed the key systems involved in the intake and distribution of nutrients and protecting the body from unhelpful substances. To some degree, these systems are capable of self-regulation, though activity is also influenced by the brain in accordance with information about the internal and external environment.

Major life challenges can elicit a strong pattern of physiological response called the stress response.

This is not a recent development. Given its importance in the survival of primitive animals, the stress response developed early in evolution. Snakes, frogs, and fish have well-developed stress responses (Bonga, 1997). Stress–immune system interactions even have been observed in insects (Davies et al., 2012). Thus, it appears that humans are "stuck" with these reactions. Unfortunately, modern life challenges do not usually require the kinds of vigorous physical responses that were once necessary, setting the stage for stress-related illness (Sapolsky, 2004). On the other hand, human beings also have the potential for creative problem-solving and stress management so we are not necessarily prisoners of the "stress of life."

Critical Thought Questions

1. What are some similarities and differences between the respiratory and gastrointestinal systems?
2. What are some similarities and differences in control of physiology by the somatic nervous system, the sympathetic nervous system, the parasympathetic nervous system, and the endocrine system?
3. Why did animals develop a stress response and what kind of considerations influence how the stress response is "tailored" to the situation?
4. What are the differences in the effects of stress on immune system function as a function of time?

Recommended Reading

Kiecolt-Glaser, J.K., McGuire, L., Robles, T.F., & Glaser, R. (2002). Emotions, morbidity, and mortality: New perspectives from psychoneuroimmunology. *Annual Review of Psychology, 53*, 83–107.

Krantz, D.S., & McCeney, M.K. (2002). Effects of psychological and social factors on organic disease: A critical assessment of research on coronary heart disease. *Annual Review of Psychology, 53*, 341–369.

McEwen, B.S. (1998). Protective and damaging effects of stress mediators. *New England Journal of Medicine, 338*, 171–179.

3

Health Psychology within the Health-Care System

GREGORY P. MARCHILDON | HEATHER D. HADJISTAVROPOULOS | GERALD P. KOOCHER

Learning Objectives

In this chapter you will:

- Discover that health systems in various countries are financed and organized differently and how these differences affect health psychology services.

- Learn how health services are typically classified by time, duration, and complexity of treatment.

- Understand problems with misuse of medical services and how health psychologists can address overuse or delayed medical care.

- Become familiar with the role of health psychologists within health systems.

- Learn how adherence to medical treatment is defined and measured and how health psychologists can improve patients' adherence to treatment.

- Learn about patient satisfaction and dissatisfaction with health systems and services.

- Understand the impacts of interventions by health psychologists, including potential cost savings to health systems.

Introduction

The approach health professionals, including health psychologists, take in caring for patients is largely shaped by the **health system**. The unique public and private funding arrangements, administrative structures, government regulation, and delivery modes all influence the interaction between providers and their patients. This chapter describes the health systems in the United States, Canada, and other areas of the world, and then focuses on the role of health psychologists in North America. In general, all health systems include different levels of care, sources of funding, and administrative and delivery arrangements. Research shows that health-care use varies with patient differences, such as age, gender, and cultural group. The second half of this chapter focuses on several topics of interest to health psychologists in relation to health systems, such as medical service misuse, adherence to medical care, patient satisfaction with health care, and **medical cost offset** of psychological interventions.

Health Systems in the United States, Canada, and Elsewhere

The term "health system" has many different definitions. According to the World Health Organization (WHO), a health system consists "of all the people and actions whose primary purpose is to improve health" whether or not these people or actions are "integrated and centrally directed" (WHO, 2000, p. 2). In a published background document prepared for a summit of European ministers of health, the European Observatory on Health Systems and Policies provided a more specific operational definition that identifies the following three functions of a health system: (1) to deliver both personal and population-based health services; (2) to enable the delivery of health services, including finance, resource generation, and *stewardship*; and (3) to influence what other sectors do when it is relevant to health (Figueras, McKee, Lessof, Duran, & Menabde, 2008).

By using the word "stewardship," which means the responsible oversight and protection of something worth caring for and preserving, this definition gives priority to the role of governments in financing, directing, coordinating, and regulating health systems. This can occur at the national level or, as is sometimes the case in federations such as the United States and Canada, at both the national and state/provincial levels of government.

PHOTO 3.1 | Otto von Bismarck (1815–98).

PHOTO 3.2 | Sir William Beveridge (1879–1963).

While the private sector, including relatively autonomous professions (e.g., physicians), can have a significant position in a health system, they can be influenced in performing their roles by government funding and regulation (Saltman & Ferroussier-Davis, 2000). In fact, there has been a long-term trend since 1945 towards greater government involvement in health care in almost all advanced industrial countries, including the United States and Canada (Marchildon & Lockhart, 2012).

Health systems in advanced industrial countries generally follow one of three models based on their financing and organizational mechanisms (Burau & Blank, 2006; Freeman & Frisina, 2010): social health insurance, national health systems, and private health insurance. **Social health insurance systems** originated with employment-based social insurance pools regulated by the state. The version developed in late nineteenth-century Germany was introduced by then German Chancellor Otto von Bismarck (Saltman & Dubois, 2004). National health systems are often called **Beveridge systems**, after William Beveridge, the British public servant who first introduced the idea of a tax-funded health service that later became the National Health Service (NHS) in the United Kingdom. **Private health insurance systems** rely on private insurance carriers setting premiums based on risk and establishing the basic terms of coverage, even if this is done in response to government regulation. Table 3.1 briefly

TABLE 3.1 | Types of Health Systems

Type of Health System	Definition	Country Examples
Social Health Insurance (Bismarck)	A government-regulated health insurance scheme where the people must buy insurance, but may do so through an employer. In Bismarck's Germany, for example, the government obliged employers to pay and employees to join these social insurance funds. In other countries, trade unions and political parties have played a similar role. The government provides health coverage for those people without jobs and without the means to purchase insurance.	Austria, Belgium, France, Germany
National Health System (Beveridge)	A general tax-funded system directed by government for its entire population. Established in 1948, the National Health Service (NHS) in the United Kingdom provided a reasonably comprehensive set of health services without user fees to all citizens.	Australia, Canada, Italy, Norway, Spain, Sweden, United Kingdom
Private Health Insurance	Funded by private individuals, employees, and employers, private health insurance carriers determine the terms of coverage, payment, and risk assessment, although there may be some government regulation and some targeted programs to address scope of coverage and affordability by the poor or unemployed.	Singapore, Switzerland, United States*

*The US represents a mixed system drawing from a variety of models, but remains primarily a private health insurance system.

describes these three types of health systems and how various high-income countries can be classified.

While the United States represents a mixed health system drawing on all three models, it remains a predominantly private health insurance system. When Medicare and Medicaid were introduced in 1965, they sought to address gaps rather than replace employment-based private health insurance (Hacker, 2002). Similarly, the reforms introduced through the Affordable Care Act of 2010 (sometimes referred to as Obamacare), although now sharing some features in common with social health insurance, focused on regulating private health insurance and mandating its purchase by individual Americans (Starr, 2011). Unlike European-style universal systems, the United States did not historically provide coverage for everyone. When the Affordable Care Act was passed, the Congressional Budget Office estimated that the law would expand coverage to 94 per cent of the population (Starr, 2011). Unfortunately, politically and ideologically driven differences in states' implementation policies will result in differences in coverage and affordability based on where people live. At least some Americans will continue to face financial obstacles in obtaining needed medical care for years to come.

In Canada, the predominant form of financing for the majority of health care is through general government taxation, hence the country's classification as a Beveridge or NHS-style system. Approximately two-thirds of publicly financed health care flows on a universal basis covering 100 per cent of the population, based on a set of five criteria set out in the Canada Health Act.

Paid entirely through general taxation at the provincial and federal levels of government and offered free at the medical office or hospital, these universally available services include only medically "necessary" hospital and medical care. As a result, people needing psychological services generally pay through private health insurance or out of pocket unless these services are provided through government-operated clinics/hospitals or school boards by psychologists on salary. The provinces are responsible for administering their own coverage systems while private insurance for medically necessary hospital and medical care services is either prohibited or discouraged (Flood & Archibald, 2001).

With the rapid escalation in the growth of health expenditures since the 1980s in the United States and Canada, concerted efforts have been made to contain costs and increase efficiency. This has resulted in changes to permit more effective management of health organizations and health providers. As a consequence, a significant percentage of Americans receive services through health maintenance organizations (HMOs). HMOs provide a range of health services in a single package and typically direct patients to a particular group of medical professionals and facilities. HMOs provide a less expensive alternative to traditional insurance plans that allow consumers to freely choose providers and facilities within limits, based on the nature of the particular plan. In an effort to contain the rapidly growing demand for high-tech medical care, HMOs emphasize prevention and more cost-effective treatments (Tovian, 2004). However, HMOs faced a backlash by the mid-1990s led by patients

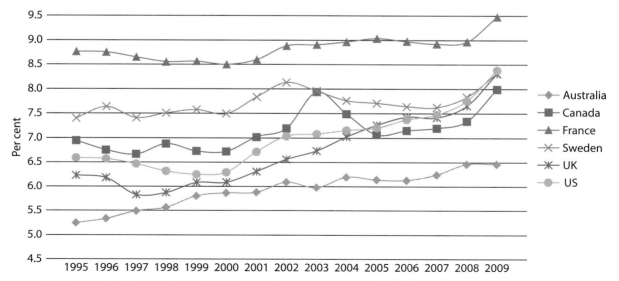

FIGURE 3.1 | Trends in public health expenditure as a share of gross domestic product (GDP), selected countries, 1995–2009.

Source: Based on Gregory P. Marchildon. *Canada: Health System Review, Health Systems in Transition*, 2012, 14(7): 1–179.

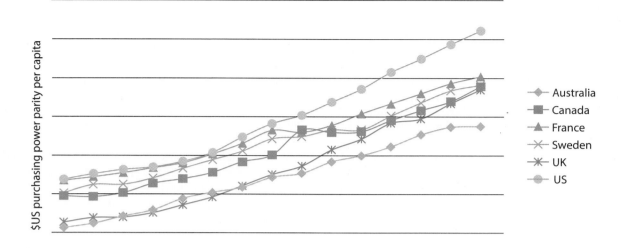

FIGURE 3.2 | Trends in public health expenditure per capita ($US), selected countries, 1995–2009.

Source: Based on Gregory P. Marchildon. *Canada: Health System Review, Health Systems in Transition,* 2012, 14(7): 1–179.

and providers who concluded that quality of care was often sacrificed to achieve cost efficiencies (Gray, 2006). In response to this growing level of dissatisfaction with HMOs, a majority of states began to regulate HMOs in an effort to protect the quality of care (Gray, Lowery, & Godwin, 2007).

In the United States, consumers face a diverse patchwork of coverage at the most basic levels, because states have differing coverage mandates under both private insurance and Medicaid. Medicare provides more uniform coverage for those over 65, but many people continue to work or purchase supplemental coverage beyond that age. As a result, making clear generalizations about coverage of psychological services across individuals on a national basis presents a significant challenge. In addition, according to a recent CNN report, up to 16 per cent of US residents do not have any health insurance coverage (Smith & Stark, 2012).

The Canadian system also emphasizes illness prevention and more cost-effective treatment, but led by provincial governments and their regional health authorities (RHAs) instead of private HMOs.

As part of a sweeping effort to contain costs, better integrate and co-ordinate care, and shift resources to illness prevention and health promotion, all provincial governments except Ontario (which has restricted the RHA function to a funding role) have arm's-length RHAs manage most services. The two main exceptions to this delegated administration include prescription drug plans and physician payment, both of which are

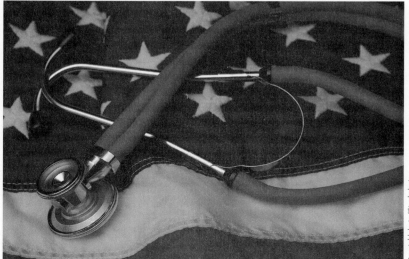

PHOTO 3.3 | The United States has a mixed health system that is highly reliant for its financing on private health insurance.

PHOTO 3.4 | The bulk of funding for the Canadian health system comes from general taxation.

centrally administered by provincial ministries of health (Marchildon, 2013).

Impact of Health Systems on Health Psychology

The biopsychosocial model (see Chapter 1) posits that biological, psychological, and social processes are "integrally and interactively involved in physical health and illness" (Suls & Rothman, 2004, p. 119). As such, many believe that health psychologists should play an important role in assisting patients with medical concerns. Nevertheless, patient access to health psychologists in the US and Canada remains limited.

We can summarize the problems addressed by health psychologists in current health systems as follows (Belar, 1997):

- Treating psychological conditions secondary to illness (e.g., post-myocardial infarction depression, and disorders associated with traumatic injuries).
- Addressing physical conditions responsive to behavioural interventions (e.g., anticipatory nausea, improved pain control).
- Reducing the physical and psychological discomforts and consequences accompanying stressful medical procedures (e.g., surgery, cardiac catheterization, magnetic resonance imaging, lumbar punctures, bone marrow biopsies, chemotherapy).

- Altering behaviours in terms of risk factors for disease or disability (e.g., promoting smoking cessation, weight reduction, improving exercise levels, and reducing substance abuse).
- Diagnosing and referring people with psychological presentations of organic problems (e.g., steroid-induced psychosis, hypothyroidism presenting as depression).
- Identifying and treating psychological dysfunctions that first appear as physical problems (e.g., tension and migraine headaches, spastic colitis, chest pains as part of panic attacks, conversion reactions).
- Facilitating the recovery or adaptation of individuals with chronic physical or mental conditions (e.g., cancer, cystic fibrosis, diabetes, muscular sclerosis, depression, schizophrenia).
- Helping health-care providers and patients deal with health system stresses (e.g., improving physician–patient relationships, reducing staff burnout).

Although the United States and Canada have very different health systems, especially when it comes to hospital and physician care, health psychologists have faced strikingly similar obstacles in terms of providing the types of services described above. In particular, both countries lack a comprehensive public payment mechanism to reimburse psychological services, and this has limited their integration into these health systems (Romanow & Marchildon, 2003; Tovian, 2004).

In the US, under federal Medicare and state Medicaid rules, recent development of "health and behaviour" CPT codes (see Table 3.2) now permit licensed psychologists to access reimbursement for services provided to patients with non-psychiatric conditions without needing to fit their services under existing mental health codes or seeking physician approval. In Canada, publicly funded fee-for-service remuneration is limited to physicians. While RHAs can decide whether to hire health psychologists, this remains a relatively rare practice (Romanow & Marchildon, 2003; Tovian, 2004). While citizens of both countries can pay for health psychological services completely out of pocket or use private (largely employment-based) insurance, many people are not aware of these services, cannot afford the services, or do not have access to private practitioners trained to provide services.

TABLE 3.2 | Selected Current Procedural Terminology Codes, United States

Selected Current Procedural Terminology (CPT Codes) Used in Billing in Mental Health Care in the US (Developed by the American Medical Association)	Selected Health and Behaviour Assessment and Intervention CPT Codes Used in the US When a Physical Diagnosis Is Present (Developed by the American Medical Association)
90834: Psychotherapy, 45 minutes **90839:** Psychotherapy for crisis, first 60 minutes **90840:** Add-on each additional 30 minutes of psychotherapy for crisis	**96150:** The initial assessment of the patient to determine the biological, psychological, and social factors affecting the patient's physical health and any treatment problems. **96151:** A reassessment of the patient to evaluate the patient's condition and determine the need for further treatment. **96152:** The intervention service provided to an individual to modify the psychological, behavioural, cognitive, and social factors affecting the patient's physical health and well-being. Examples: increasing the patients' awareness about their disease, or using cognitive/behavioural approaches to initiate physician-prescribed diet and exercise regimens. **96153:** Group intervention—service provided in group context. Example: smoking cessation program that includes educational information, cognitive-behavioural treatment, and social support. Group sessions typically last for 90 minutes and involve 8 to 10 patients.

Note: You can view all of the 2013 codes at: www.apapracticecentral.org/reimbursement/billing/psychotherapy-codes.pdf
Source: Based on http://www.apapracticecentral.org/reimbursement/billing/psychotherapy-codes.pdf.

Types of Health Services

There are many ways to classify care within health-care systems. A distinction is sometimes made between primary, secondary, and tertiary levels of care. **Primary care** refers to the main health care aimed at prevention (e.g., immunizations) and a broad spectrum of problems. Typically, we get such care from a family physician, but nurses, physicians' assistants, or other health-care clinic staff may also fall in this category. The primary care provider is usually the first contact, responsible for comprehensive care and, at least initially, co-ordination if referral to specialists is needed. In other words, the primary provider often acts as a de facto gatekeeper to the health system. Psychologists are typically not primary care providers, but may serve on teams in primary health clinics (Frank, McDaniel, Bray, & Heldring, 2004).

Secondary care refers to a broad range of specialized services, such as care provided by medical specialists or health psychologists. While physicians' services can be delivered on an in- or outpatient basis, most health psychology services at the secondary level are delivered on

an outpatient basis. These are generally not first-contact services and typically follow a referral from a first-contact health provider. Nonetheless, there are some exceptions. For example, a psychologist on staff at a hospital serving in the emergency department alongside other providers (e.g., evaluating and providing urgent care to sexual assault victims and suicide attempters) would represent one such exception. Referral to a psychologist for help with a specific health problem, such as coping with a diagnosis of cancer, would be another form of secondary care.

Tertiary care refers to even more specialized care, often delivered in a teaching hospital or academic health centre, that has a supporting infrastructure of specialized equipment and facilities as well as a range of available specialists. Some psychological interventions are delivered within tertiary care settings (e.g., psychological interventions delivered to chronic pain and organ transplant inpatients).

In addition to classifying care in terms of whether it is primary, secondary, or tertiary, health care can be described in terms of duration. Acute care refers to care that is for an injury or illness. Chronic care refers to care for a pre-existing or long-term illness, such as diabetes, asthma, or congestive heart failure. As can be seen

IN PRACTICE

Surviving Myocardial Infarction: A Team Approach

Margaret, a 48-year-old divorcee, did not worry very much about her health. Yes, she did smoke a handful of cigarettes each day. Yes, she was about 15 kg overweight for a woman of her height and age. She'd tell herself that she'd get to work on losing some weight right after the holidays, and could really quit smoking anytime she wanted to—and would someday soon. With that mindset, she did not become concerned when she started to feel some "mild indigestion" at work. One day at work she became a bit more concerned when she started having some trouble catching her breath and felt some pain shooting down her left arm. Margaret mentioned these symptoms to her co-worker, who recognized symptoms of a myocardial infarct (MI, or heart attack). Her colleague had some aspirin in her desk and gave it to Margaret, telling her to chew it up while she called 911.

In some ways, Margaret was very fortunate. Her MI occurred in the presence of someone who recognized what was happening and who assisted her well. Following emergency implantation of two stents to restore cardiac circulation and a few tense days in the cardiac intensive care unit, Margaret was ready for discharge. Her medical condition was stable, but her anxiety shot through the roof. Thoughts of, "How will I manage all the things I have to remember now? What if this happens again?" ran through her mind constantly. On discharge, a nurse gave Margaret a set of prescriptions, heart-healthy diet instructions, and a warning about her weight and smoking. That night Margaret could barely sleep, feeling intensely aware of her own mortality, and uncertain about how she could possibly manage the lifestyle changes necessary to maintain her health.

Fortunately, she had access to an outpatient cardiac rehabilitation program that used a team approach. The team included a cardiologist, nurse practitioner, dietician, and psychologist. Working together, the team was able to present an integrated plan of care relying on psychological principles to optimize adherence. In addition, the psychologist was able to forewarn Margaret about the hazards of depression during recovery from MI and work with her using cognitive behavioural and medical crisis counselling techniques. She was able to take control of her care, beginning with an improved diet, a moderate exercise program, and a nicotine patch to help end her smoking habit. It wasn't easy, but with the support of the team, Margaret was soon on the road to restored health. She wondered how she'd ever have managed without them. Health statistics show that without such services, Margaret might well have faced a need for expensive and risky re-hospitalizations in the following months.

from the list of problems addressed by psychologists, chronic illnesses form an important part of the work conducted by health psychologists. Table 3.2 provides examples of typical procedural codes used for billing by psychologists in the United States. The CPT billing codes described earlier are used uniformly to classify all health insurance billing procedures for both private and government-sponsored programs. Note that some codes apply only to mental health services, while other "health and behaviour" codes focus on services related to patients with physical illness.

Health care is also sometimes classified in terms of the setting in which it is delivered, such as a hospital, the home, the community, a rehabilitation setting, or a long-term care facility. Health psychologists work in all of these settings. For example, in a hospital a health psychologist may assist patients with coping with medical procedures, while in the home, community, or rehabilitation setting health psychologists may assist patients with development of strategies for coping with and adherence to treatment of a chronic condition. In long-term care, health psychologists may assist with development of strategies for working with patients with dementia (e.g., identifying pleasant activities or managing behavioural problems such as aggression).

Patterns of Health-Care Use

Despite sharp differences in health systems, the health-care cultures of the US and Canada are remarkably similar. In particular, the health professions, including the medical, nursing, and health psychology professions, are similarly organized. All are self-regulating professions with similar scopes of practices and specializations. Contrary to the European practice of separating social care from health care, long-term care in the US and Canada, including home and community care, is treated as part of the health-care system—at least from a conceptual perspective.

The people these providers serve are also very similar in terms of their respective demands on the health system. While overall health status is somewhat better in Canada than the United States, both countries have similar rates of acute and chronic disease incidence and suffer from similar high-risk factors for disease (Marchildon, 2013). Table 3.3 compares the two countries to four other mature and high-quality health systems.

Citizens in both countries also have high expectations, at least relative to the citizens in some Western European countries, in terms of timely, effective, and high-quality medical interventions. This has led to substantial public and private investments in medical care. At the same time, high expectations may contribute to low patient satisfaction ratings in the US and Canada relative to other high-income countries in Western Europe and Australasia (Schoen, 2011).

Even with these similarities, some important differences exist between Canada and the US in their patterns of health-care use. On a per capita basis, Americans spend more on health care than the citizens of any other country. However, in regard to public

TABLE 3.3 | Male and Female Causes of Death (Disease Burden), Selected Countries, Age-Standardized Rates per 100,000 People

Cause of Death per 100,000 people	United States	Canada	Australia	France	Sweden	United Kingdom
Year of Data	2007	2004	2006	2008	2008	2009
Ischemic heart disease, males	129	123	99	50	118	110
Ischemic heart disease, females	68	61	52	19	58	50
Stroke, males	32	34	36	31	45	42
Stroke, females	29	29	34	22	36	39
All cancers, males	185	205	184	221	165	199
All cancers, females	130	143	115	111	125	141
Lung cancer, males	57	60	40	57	29	48
Lung cancer, females	36	36	20	14	22	30
Breast cancer	19.8	22.4	18.5	22.3	19.1	23.2
Prostate cancer	17.5	21.2	24.3	20.0	32.7	23.3
Road accidents, male	21.1	12.8	10.9	10.8	6.3	6.2
Road accidents, female	8.3	4.9	3.4	2.9	2.0	1.7
Suicide, males	17.1	15.7	11.9	21.6	16.1	9.8
Suicide, females	4.3	4.9	3.3	6.8	6.0	2.6

Source: Adapted from Marchildon (2013, p. 15, Table 1.11).

financing, per capita government health expenditures are almost identical in both countries, in part due to the historical growth and high expense of Medicare and Medicaid in the US relative to medicare in Canada (Marchildon, 2013).

There are also significant differences in the use of new technologies, particularly advanced diagnostic imaging technologies. The number of CT (computerized tomography), MRI (magnetic resonance imaging), and PET (positron emission tomography) machines per capita in the United States significantly exceeds that in Canada, and evidence suggests that American physicians use health information technology more intensively than their Canadian counterparts (OECD, 2011; Schoen et al., 2009).

In both the United States and Canada, health-care use varies with certain demographic variables. For instance, older adults tend to seek and use more care as their health fails and they develop chronic health conditions (Alemayehu & Warner, 2004). Another characteristic involves men making less use of health-care services than women (Alemayehu & Warner, 2004). Pregnancy, female birth control, childbirth, and symptoms associated with menopause account for some of the sex differences in health-care use. Other factors that may contribute to this difference involve somatic perception and symptom labelling, as well as socialization that leads men to be less prone to disclose and more prone to ignore symptoms (Barsky, Peekna, & Borus, 2001). Socio-economic status (SES) also plays a role in health-care use. Recent research suggests that in both the US and Canada, SES is not related to hospital use. In the US but not Canada, physician use is lower among those with lower income and those without health insurance (Blackwell, Martinez, Gentleman, Sanmartin, & Berthelot, 2009). There is also a significant gap in the extent to which those of lower SES seek preventative health care, such as immunizations against disease (Abramson, Oshea, Ratledge, Lawless, & Givner, 1995). Ethnicity also plays a role, with lower use of health-care services among ethnic minorities (e.g., Quan et al., 2006; Scheppers, van Dongen, Dekker, Geertzen, & Dekker, 2006). This topic is given in-depth consideration in Chapter 19. One implication of these differences is that health psychologists are more likely to provide treatment to patients who are high users of health services. Nevertheless, psychologists must be competent to work with diverse groups and to find ways to ensure that all patients who need their services have access to and are aware of these services.

Medical Service Misuse

Prevention of medical service misuse is of vital importance to a sustainable health-care system. Such misuse refers not only to the overuse of medical services but also to delays in obtaining medical services. Both situations can harm people and result in increased costs.

Overuse

Overuse of medical services is discussed briefly in Chapter 6 in reference to excessively elevated health anxiety associated with high levels of seeking medical care (Noyes, Happel, & Yagla, 1999; Tomenson et al., 2012). People with health anxiety may seek out unnecessary medical services in an attempt to alleviate this anxiety. This results in higher health-care costs, but also in an increased likelihood of patients undergoing unnecessary medical tests or procedures that can cause complications and trigger additional usage.

Other psychological conditions associated with significantly greater use of medical care include depression and general anxiety (Deacon, Lickel, & Abramowitz, 2008; Kimerling, Ouimette, Cronkite, & Moos, 1999). For example, people with panic disorder often become frequent users of medical services, especially if not effectively treated for their psychological condition (Deacon et al., 2008). Panic disorder occurs when people experience recurrent, unexpected panic attacks followed by anxiety about having another attack, worry about the implications of the attack or its consequences, or a change in behaviour (e.g., avoidance) because of the attack (American Psychiatric Association, 2013). Compared to people with other anxiety disorders, those with panic disorder have the greatest number of medical visits overall, as well as the most frequent visits to cardiology, family medicine, and emergency medicine units (Deacon et al., 2008).

Similarly, people with depression also show high levels of medical use (Kimerling et al., 1999). Depression is diagnosed when people have prolonged depressed moods or loss of interest, and experience other symptoms, such as a change in weight or appetite, insomnia or hypersomnia, psychomotor agitation or retardation, fatigue, feelings of low self-worth, difficulties concentrating, or recurrent thoughts of death or suicidal ideation (American Psychiatric Association, 2013). Higher levels of depressive symptoms correlate with increased medical usage over a 10-year period, even when controlling for age, sex, marital status, and medical co-morbidity (Kimerling et al., 1999).

It is important for health-care professionals to recognize and treat patients with psychological disorders to prevent the overuse of medical care (Kraft, Puschner, Lambert, & Kordy, 2006). Despite widespread knowledge about these principles, psychological disorders remain consistently undertreated (Collins, Westra, Dozois, & Burns, 2004). Undertreatment sometimes occurs because the conditions are not identified and instead the focus remains on the unexplained medical symptoms. At other times, undertreatment occurs because of inadequate access to appropriately trained mental health providers, or because patients have limited time available to seek care, mobility difficulties, or concerns about stigma (Collins et al., 2004).

Delayed Health Care

While overuse of medical services is a significant concern, people who significantly delay seeking health care (including psychological services) when they are needed also raise concerns. Delayed use of medical services can lead to increased morbidity and mortality and result in increased health-care spending. Some health system features may encourage or create delays. High user fees, including deductibles and co-payments, are common in private health insurance systems in the US, as contrasted to the more modest user fees or free services more typical of social health insurance and national health systems. Significant user fees may encourage people with limited financial means to delay seeking necessary medical care. By the same token, national health systems often have long waiting times for services deemed necessary but not urgent. In addition, they may not cover costs of psychological or other non-medical services.

As an example of the importance of timely care, consider those who delay seeking care after experiencing an acute myocardial infarction or a stroke. Many deaths and significant disability could be prevented if these patients obtained prompt care for such conditions (Kainth et al., 2004; Rawles, 1996). Survival rates after acute myocardial infarction improve by up to 50 per cent if patients receive treatment within one hour of symptom onset. A shorter interval between onset of symptoms and medical treatment is associated with better cardiac function (Moser et al., 2007). Similarly, shorter time of administration of stroke medications is associated with substantially improved outcomes (Hacke et al., 2004).

Why do patients delay seeking or fail to seek health care? As discussed in Chapter 6, often people delay treatment because they fail to recognize early symptoms as requiring intervention, or fail to grasp the benefits of more rapid treatment. If people do not feel vulnerable, or do not believe that care will be helpful, they will likely not seek it (Hagger & Orbell, 2003). At the system level, patients may delay or avoid seeking treatment if they face onerous user charges or potentially long waits for needed treatment.

In the case of acute myocardial infarction, demographic, clinical, social, psychological, and health-care variables are associated with delays in seeking treatment. In the US, demographic variables associated with delays in seeking care for myocardial infarction include older age, being female, lower education, lower SES, and being Black. In terms of clinical variables, surprisingly, those with more chronic health conditions as well as those who have a history of angina (see Chapter 9) also delay medical care for symptoms of acute MI. It seems these patients may attribute symptoms to other conditions and not to MI and thus delay treatment seeking. Social factors associated with delayed treatment include being at home alone, resting, or sleeping. Psychologically, anxiety is associated with seeking care quickly, while feelings of embarrassment or indecision increase the delay. It also appears that living further from care is associated with delays in seeking care, and, interestingly, calling a physician for advice is associated with delays in receiving care as compared to calling emergency medical services (Moser et al., 2007).

Although multiple variables are associated with delays in seeking care or underutilization of health care, one variable that seems to be quite consistent across health-care conditions is that individuals from visible minority groups in the United States have lower levels of health-care use than those who identify themselves as White (Burgess, Ding, Hargreaves, van Ryn, & Phelan, 2008). Of note, recent research suggests that perceived discrimination is greater among minority groups and that anticipated discrimination results in decreased utilization of health care among minority groups (Burgess et al., 2008). Chapter 19 discusses cross-cultural considerations in more detail.

Another recent study points to the role of medical mistrust in delaying care, with medical mistrust found to be associated with failure to take medical advice, failure to keep follow-up appointments, postponing receiving care, and failing to fill prescriptions (LaVeist, Isaac, & Williams, 2009). Medical mistrust in the United States and Canada is correlated with individuals of lower education or who belong to an ethnic minority.

What can be done to reduce delays in seeking appropriate medical care? In the case of ischemic stroke and myocardial infarction, it appears that community-based public education has largely been ineffective in reducing patient delays in seeking medical care (Luepker et al., 2000; Moser et al., 2007), even when enormous resources are put into improving education (Hand, Brown, Horan, & Simons-Morton, 1998). More sophisticated approaches are needed to target high-risk populations and address the diverse factors associated with delays in seeking medical care.

Unfortunately, psychologists do not typically encounter patients who delay seeking medical treatment until the patient's condition has deteriorated to the point where they must seek treatment. When psychologists do work with people who have a history of delaying treatment, in an effort to avoid future delays in seeking care, a component of treatment is likely to involve the review and discussion of factors that may have contributed to this delay. One common strategy that psychologists use with patients who are at risk of treatment delay is to encourage use of a symptom diary so that patients have a better awareness of symptoms. Psychologists are also likely to encourage patients to discuss symptoms with significant others so that they have support and assistance in interpreting and responding to symptoms. Psychologists will also review the patient's knowledge and awareness of symptoms that may signal a need to seek care.

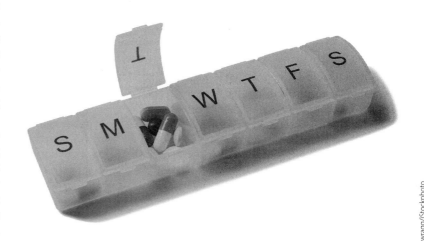

© wragg/iStockphoto

PHOTO 3.5 | Pill boxes are often used to help ensure that patients remember to take their medication and to improve adherence with medical regimens.

Adherence to Medical Care

Adherence to medical care is another issue given considerable attention by health psychologists. Patient adherence to medical recommendations is vital to good health outcomes, including reduced morbidity and mortality. Non-adherence is generally associated with poorer health and increased health-care costs. Patients who follow medical advice are almost three times more likely to have a positive treatment outcome compared to those who are non-adherent (DiMatteo, Giordani, Lepper, & Croghan, 2002).

Definition and Measurement

Adherence refers to patients following treatment recommendations made by their health-care professionals (DiMatteo, et al., 2002). The words "adherence" and "compliance" are sometimes used interchangeably, but "adherence" is a better term as it recognizes that patients are actively involved in sticking to their care. There are many forms of adherence for psychologists to consider, such as whether patients are taking medications as recommended, keeping appointments, or following recommended health behaviours such as exercise or diet plans (DiMatteo et al., 2002). Psychologists can measure adherence in different ways. They can ask patients to keep diaries, count pills, or share results of physical tests related to adherence (e.g., urine or blood assays). Alternatively, they can ask patients to self-report or electronically monitor health behaviours. Self-reporting is often used because it is simple and inexpensive, but this has the disadvantage that memory for the adherence behaviour can be distorted. Many smart-phone apps can assist in promoting adherence. Sometimes, collateral information is collected from a family member by a health-care professional, but this assumes the informant has accurate information. Sometimes psychologists think of patients as adhering or not, but, in fact, adherence falls on a continuum ranging from 100 per cent to zero. It can be difficult at times for psychologists to decide whether patients require treatment to improve adherence.

Rates and Predictors of Adherence

Adherence links to a number of different variables. Adherence to medical recommendations, for example, is highest in patients with HIV disease (88.3 per cent), arthritis (81.2 per cent), gastrointestinal disorders (86.2 per cent), and cancer (79.1 per cent), and lowest in patients with pulmonary disease (68.8 per cent), diabetes (67.5 per cent) and sleep conditions (65.5 per cent) (DiMatteo et al., 2002). What accounts for these differences? It appears that patients are more likely to adhere if the condition is severe, the treatment is believed to be effective, and the treatment recommendations are straightforward and less complex to follow.

Adherence is also related to other variables, such as education, income, and SES, with individuals of higher education, income, and SES more likely to adhere to medical recommendations (DiMatteo, 2004). Adherence decreases with less understanding of what is required, but also decreases as the complexity of the patient's life increases.

Sometimes patients are non-adherent because they do not perceive their condition as severe, because they do not understand the importance of treatment, or because they feel unable to implement the changes required. Emotional problems can also increase non-adherence. Problematic alcohol and drug use and history of mental health problems predict non-adherence (DiMatteo, Haskard-Zolnierek, & Martin, 2012). Social factors are also related to adherence, with adherence found to be greater among those who have good social supports (DiMatteo, 2004). Finally, health-care relationships also factor into adherence, such that the greater trust an individual has in a provider the greater the adherence (DiMatteo et al., 2002).

Improving Adherence

Health-care professionals, including health psychologists, have worked on improving patient adherence. However, many interventions designed to improve adherence fail. Simplistic interventions that do not target the patients' key motivations are particularly ineffective (McDonald, Garg, & Haynes, 2002). Multifaceted approaches that combine strategies, regularly review or examine adherence over time, and account for individual patient needs have the greatest chance of success.

Recently, a three-pronged approach, referred to as the Information-Motivation-Strategy Model, was proposed as a method for professionals to assist patients

"What fits your busy schedule better, exercising one hour a day or being dead 24 hours a day?"

PHOTO 3.6 | "What fits your busy schedule better ...?"

with adherence (DiMatteo et al., 2012). The first step encourages health-care professionals to focus on providing patients with information, and emphasizes the importance of effective patient–provider communication. Adherence cannot take place if patients do not understand the information they are given. For patients to understand, providers must give clear information, check for understanding, allow patients opportunities to clarify misunderstandings, and express empathy towards patients. The second important component of patient adherence, according to this model, is addressing patient motivation. This step recognizes that patient beliefs about disease severity, vulnerability, treatment efficacy, self-efficacy, and barriers to treatment have a significant impact on motivation. As a final step in improving patient adherence, health-care professionals need to clearly and systematically examine the strategies patients use to adhere to treatment recommendations as well as the barriers that may interfere with success. Practical barriers may need to be overcome to help patients with adherence, such as difficulties in coping with the dose frequency and regimen complexity

⊞ IN PRACTICE

Improving Adherence: The Case of Lucas

Lucas, a 16-year-old male, lives with his biological parents. At age 13, Lucas developed Type I diabetes, an autoimmune disease in which the pancreas gradually ceases to produce insulin, making it impossible for the body to process glucose normally. At the time of the assessment, Lucas's prescribed regimen involved injecting two types of insulin (i.e., one long-acting and additional injections of instant-acting insulin with meals) to control his blood sugar levels. Because of erratic blood sugar results, Lucas was referred to a psychologist working with adolescents who have diabetes.

The psychologist treating Lucas first evaluated how well he and his parents understood the prescribed regimen and blood sugar control. The assessment revealed that Lucas thought involving his parents in the psychological management of his diabetes was desirable. Assessment proceeded by having Lucas and his parents keep a detailed record of Lucas's self-management, including food intake, exercise levels, insulin doses, and peripheral blood glucose levels. The record helped clarify variables affecting good control. Specifically, the psychologist wanted to understand the antecedents of poor self-management (e.g., inadequate diabetes education, dietary issues, lack of exercise, incorrect medication, failure to check blood glucose levels). Lucas had primary responsibility for keeping the journal. The psychologist learned that Lucas's parents both worked full-time and had become less involved in his diabetes care since his initial diagnosis. They expected Lucas to manage his condition by himself. Lucas would often skip meals or snack irregularly. He did not consistently check his blood glucose. The journal revealed that Lucas paid less attention to insulin dosing and monitoring when he was with his friends or busy playing computer games. In fact, he spent considerable time playing sedentary games and got little physical exercise.

Following the assessment period, intervention first began with diabetes management education: the psychologist talked to Lucas and his family about basic diabetes care and effective behavioural strategies for improving adherence. The psychologist also engaged Lucas in developing a list of reasons why he wanted better control of his diabetes. Intervention then focused on developing strategies to assist Lucas in remembering how to balance food intake, exercise, and medication co-ordinated with blood glucose monitoring. One important strategy involved downloading an app on his smart phone allowing him to better track blood glucose levels and adherence to medications. This app also sent him reminders to check his blood glucose. Importantly, his parents could also monitor the results. Lucas's parents also agreed to a reward system contingent on improved blood glucose levels. Rewards were negotiated each week (e.g., use of car, time with friends) and were linked to a progressively higher level of adherence (80 per cent adherence increased to 100 per cent adherence over treatment). Another key to success involved problem-solving and regular meal times (e.g., helping Lucas choose foods when his parents were working), as well as organization of his diabetic supplies (e.g., blood glucose meter, insulin).

Following treatment, Lucas was able to improve his monitoring of his peripheral blood glucose from 1–2 times day to four times a day (before each meal and at bedtime). He also became more consistent in taking his medications as prescribed. Furthermore, his sleep and meal schedule became much more regular than it had been in the past. His glycosylated hemoglobin (HgA1c) dropped from 11 per cent to a much healthier 7 per cent.

(Ingersoll & Cohen, 2008). Other practical issues that may require consideration include exploring whether patients have the necessary money, skills, resources, or time to adhere to treatment recommendations.

Health-care professionals need to recognize that many treatment recommendations require patients to exert considerable self-control and to give up short-term rewards for long-term outcomes (Hagger, Wood, Stiff, & Chatzisarantis, 2009). Non-adherence results when self-regulation fails or the individual has difficulties overcoming bad habits. Difficulties with self-regulation thus need attention from health-care professionals. Some strategies that assist with self-regulation include limiting the number of activities that require self-control and recommending that patients obtain sufficient rest and relaxation to replenish their ability to exercise self-control (Hagger et al., 2009). Health psychologists have an important role to play in helping patients with self-control or similar problems. The accompanying In Practice box discusses how a psychologist worked with an adolescent to improve treatment adherence to diabetes treatment recommendations.

Patient Satisfaction

Patient satisfaction with health care is another topic of interest to health psychologists. When patients feel dissatisfied with care, it is not uncommon to spend time during sessions with a psychologist discussing concerns about individual providers or the health system in general. Hardly surprising, patients are less likely to follow advice from providers they do not like, understand, or agree with (Rodin & Janis, 1979).

Since the 1980s there has been a steady increase in research on patient satisfaction (Sitzia & Wood, 1997), with extensive study among different patient groups, different treatments, different settings, and different organizational structures (Xiao & Barber, 2008). The interest in assessing patient satisfaction suggests that health-care providers and organizations value the patient's point of view and collect this information in order to improve services (Worthington, 2005).

When global ratings of care are used, patients report very high levels of satisfaction with care, with as many as 85 per cent reporting they are satisfied with health-care services (Worthington, 2005). When patients are asked about specific aspects of care, however, there is more variability and lower ratings of satisfaction are reported (Worthington, 2005).

Given the centrality of physicians within health systems, considerable research has examined patient satisfaction with physicians. This research is highly relevant to health psychologists, as past experience with physicians can become a central topic of discussion when patients seek psychological services. Certain key physician behaviours are related to higher levels of satisfaction with one's physician. Specifically, patients report greater satisfaction with care when their physicians have strong verbal and non-verbal communication skills, question patients effectively, readily share information, express empathy, and collaborate with their patients to make decisions (Zolnierek & DiMatteo, 2009). One of the single best predictors of patient satisfaction is feeling the provider is listening (Xiao & Barber, 2008).

Female physicians are generally preferred over male physicians. This may be because female physicians have greater patient-centred communication and more reciprocal interactions with their patients. Female physicians spend, on average, two minutes longer with patients than male physicians, which translates to 10 per cent more time with patients (Roter, Hall, & Aoki, 2002). Female physicians also engage in more positive talk, psychosocial counselling, and emotion-focused talk with patients compared to male physicians

Perhaps not surprisingly, the healthier one is, the more satisfied one is with one's provider (Xiao & Barber, 2008). It is not entirely clear, however, if greater satisfaction leads to better health outcomes or if better health outcomes result in greater satisfaction with care.

A significant consequence of dissatisfaction with the physician–patient relationship is that patients subsequently seek more health-care services, commonly seeking second opinions (LaVeist et al., 2009), and show lower adherence to medical recommendations and treatment protocols (Zolnierek & DiMatteo, 2009). In other words, if you feel your physician has poor communication skills, you are less likely to follow his or her advice and will be more likely to seek care elsewhere (Zolnierek & DiMatteo, 2009). Clearly, training physicians in communication is extremely important and results in higher adherence among patients than when physicians receive no such training (Zolnierek & DiMatteo, 2009).

Since the 1990s there has been a sustained movement towards more patient-centred care and choice in health systems, in part because of poor patient satisfaction. The Institute of Healthcare Improvement (IHI), based in Cambridge, Massachusetts, has been prominent in putting patient-centred care on the agenda of health system decision-makers in the United States and Canada. The first dimension in IHI's influential Triple Aim is improving the patient experience of care, now a key element in the reform agendas of individual health-care organizations, regional health authorities, and governments in both countries.

Medical Cost Offset of Psychological Interventions

As described in other chapters in this book, a growing body of evidence shows that effective psychological treatments can assist individuals with recovery and adaptation to medical conditions, such as diabetes, headaches, arthritis, chronic pain, and medically unexplained physical symptoms (Hunsley, 2003). Suls and Rothman (2004) described three areas in which behavioural interventions by health psychologists have been particularly effective: (1) smoking cessation; (2) reducing stress and mitigating the consequences of medical procedures; and (3) facilitating the recovery or adaptation of persons with chronic illness. One question you may have—and one shared by all governments that fund or subsidize health psychology services—is whether providing psychological services to medical patients ultimately reduces health-care costs. That is, by receiving psychological services, do patients improve their health in a significant way and thus reduce their use of health-care services? From a health system perspective, government decision-makers want to know not only whether costs will be reduced through such interventions, but also their precise impact over successive annual budgets.

In fact, it appears that providing psychological services to patients reduces their subsequent use of other health-care services by approximately 20–30 per cent (Chiles, Lambert, & Hatch, 1999). It is very rare for the costs of psychological treatment to exceed cost savings from the psychological intervention. The cost offset is greatest for behavioural interventions delivered to medical inpatients (e.g., surgery, oncology, cardiac rehabilitation) compared to outpatients. The cost offset is also significantly greater when structured psychological interventions (e.g., psycho-education for medical patients) are offered compared to non-specific psychotherapy.

Research on psychological treatment for hostility among coronary disease patients provides a recent specific example of cost offset research (Davidson, Gidron, Mostofsky, & Trudeau, 2007). This research involved randomizing male patients with myocardial infarction or unstable angina to either two months of cognitive behavioural group therapy or an information session. Those in the cognitive behavioural treatment condition had a significantly shorter length of hospital stay over six months following therapy and lower hospitalization costs compared to those in the information session. More specifically, for every dollar spent on therapy, there was an approximate savings of two dollars in hospitalization costs over a six-month period. Demonstrating the cost-effectiveness of health psychological interventions is critical for the advancement of health psychology. Nevertheless, as noted above, financial constraints limit the expansion of the profession and delivery of these services to the population, even when cost-effectiveness data are available and favourable.

Future Directions

In addition to helping patients maintain or improve their health, health psychologists have the potential to work with patients on issues that significantly impact the functioning and sustainability of the health system, such as overuse or delayed use of medical services, adherence to medical care, and patient satisfaction. By working with patients on issues that impact health-care use, health psychologists also can help reduce health-care spending and thereby make health systems more fiscally sustainable. Despite the cost-effectiveness of health psychological services, however, the current structure of the health system limits the availability of these services. As we have seen, physicians have a central position in both United States and Canadian health systems—though for slightly different reasons—in providing referrals for the services of health psychologists, especially for secondary and tertiary care. As a consequence, there may be an opportunity for health psychologists to play a larger role in the future if more health psychologists are involved in the primary care of patients.

This chapter raises some important directions for future research in the field of health psychology with specific reference to the health system. A question that deserves greater attention is how we can best educate health psychologists to work with diverse health-care disciplines and make their competencies known and valued. Despite being cost-effective and effective in treating individual patients' health and well-being, health psychology interventions are not integrated in routine clinical practice (Nicassio, Meyerowitz, & Kerns, 2004). We need to ensure that knowledge gained through health psychological research is appropriately disseminated and effectively translated into practice. Health psychologists also need to continue to conduct research that demonstrates the cost-effectiveness of health psychology, and this research should be more effectively disseminated to policy decision-makers. Thus far, research in this area (Chiles et al., 1999) has not had a significant impact on our health system (e.g., increased public access to health psychologists). As a result, considerably more attention should be turned to addressing health system barriers to incorporating health psychology into routine care (e.g., insurance coverage, both public or private), and this may require greater attention to how best to communicate how health psychology can improve our health systems.

In terms of improving patient access to health psychologists, it is possible that further research on how health psychologists can use technology to improve access to health services would be beneficial. Although this field is growing, we have much to learn about the use of computerized assessment and treatment programs to deliver health psychology services. Further research is also needed on how health psychologists can best work with ethnically diverse populations and older adults. Most research in health psychology tends to be on middle-aged, middle-class, and ethnically homogeneous adults in industrialized countries. This is problematic because our population is rapidly becoming ethnically diverse populations and older (Smith, Orleans, & Jenkins, 2004), and we need to ensure that health psychologists are competent to meet the needs of all patients who come in contact with our health system.

SUMMARY

Due to different public and private funding arrangements, regulatory structures, and delivery modes, health systems vary from country to country and shape the way health psychologists provide services to their patients. The US has a predominantly private health insurance system supplemented by public programs, the most notable of which are federal Medicare and state-administered Medicaid. Canada has a predominantly public coverage system in which provincial governments provide medically necessary hospital, diagnostic, and physician services.

Due to restrictive public coverage, patient access to the services of health psychologists is limited in both countries, despite the fact that health psychologists can provide an array of services directly connected to medical care. These include: treating psychological conditions secondary to illness; treating physical symptoms that are responsive to behavioural interventions; addressing the physical and psychological consequences of stressful medical procedures; altering behaviours that lower the risk factors for disease and disability; diagnosing and referring individuals with psychological presentations of organic problems; and identifying and treating psychological dysfunctions that first appear as physical problems. Despite these health system barriers, health psychologists are involved in every stage of care, from primary (first-contact) and secondary (specialized outpatient) to tertiary (specialized inpatient) care.

When working with patients, health psychologists often need to consider whether patients are misusing medical services. There are two common types of misuse: overuse and delayed use. Overuse is particularly common among individuals who have health anxiety, depression, and panic disorder. Delayed use is particularly problematic among individuals who delay seeking care for myocardial infarctions, strokes, or cancer and is related to demographic, clinical, social, psychological, and health-care variables.

Health psychologists also often assist patients with adherence to medical care. Adherence refers to patients following treatment recommendations made by their health-care professionals. Psychosocial variables predict adherence, and thus psychologists have an important role to play in assisting patients with adherence to medical recommendations. The Information-Motivation-Strategy Model has been proposed as a method to assist professionals in assisting patients with adherence.

While it is estimated that 85 per cent of patients are satisfied with the health care they receive, when patients are dissatisfied with health care, they may spend considerable time elaborating on their concerns when talking to psychologists. There is growing evidence that there are effective psychological treatments to assist individuals with recovery and adaptation to medical conditions as well to problems they encounter within the health-care system. These psychological services can reduce health-care spending.

Critical Thought Questions

1. What type of health system, if any, do you think is most conducive to ensuring that patients obtain access to health psychology services when they are most needed?

2. What do you perceive to be a greater problem— overuse of medical services, delayed use of medical services, or patient non-adherence to medical recommendations?

3. Could you imagine physicians using the Information-Motivation-Strategy Model to improve patient adherence to use of prescribed medications? What would the strengths and challenges of this be?

Recommended Reading

DiMatteo, M.R., Haskard-Zolnierek, K.B., & Martin, L.R. (2012). Improving patient adherence: a three-factor model to guide practice. *Health Psychology Review, 6*, 74–91.

Hunsley, J. (2003). Cost-effectiveness and medical cost-offset considerations in psychological service provision. *Canadian Psychology-Psychologie Canadienne, 44*, 61–73.

Romanow, R.J., & Marchildon, G.P. (2003). Psychological services and the future of health care in Canada. *Canadian Psychology/Psychologie Canadienne, 44*, 283–295.

Tovian, S.M. (2004). Health services and health care economics: the health psychology marketplace. *Health Psychology, 23*, 138–141.

4

Prevention of Illness and Health Promotion Intervention

JAMES O. PROCHASKA* | JANICE M. PROCHASKA*

Learning Objectives

In this chapter you will:

- Learn about the importance of a healthy lifestyle.

- Learn the core constructs of the Transtheoretical Model of Behaviour Change (TTM).

- Identify which TTM principles and processes to use at each stage of change.

- Learn about multiple behaviour change.

- Read about the challenges to TTM.

- See how TTM interventions have been applied to exercise, nutrition, and smoking.

- Compare patient health to population health.

*Conflict of interest disclosure: The authors of this chapter are affiliated with the Pro-Change Behavior Systems company that is mentioned in this chapter.

Importance of a Healthy Lifestyle

Health risk behaviours like smoking, inactivity, unhealthy diets, alcohol abuse, and ineffectively managed stress significantly contribute to a population's morbidity, disability, mortality, reduced functioning and productivity, and escalating health-care costs. In contrast, a healthy lifestyle including abstinence from smoking, eating five servings of fruits and vegetables each day, adequate physical activity (e.g., walking **10,000 steps a day** or doing 150 minutes of **moderate exercise** a week), and striving to maintain a body mass index (BMI) of less than 25 is being shown to increase life expectancy up to 14 years (Khaw et al., 2008; van den Brandt, 2011; Pronk et al., 2010). However, having a healthy lifestyle of 0 (smoking), 5 (fruits and vegetables), 10 (10,000 steps), and 25 (<25 BMI) has been an elusive goal for 97 per cent of the population (Reeves & Rafferty, 2005).

To have a significant and sustainable impact on attaining these healthy behaviours, a model of behaviour change is needed to address the needs of entire populations, not just the minority who are motivated to take immediate action for better health. The Transtheoretical Model of Behaviour Change (TTM) is founded on stages of change, which categorize segments of populations based on where they are in the process of change. Principles and processes are applied to initiate movement through the stages of change. Interventions based on TTM principles can produce interactive and broadly applicable programs for treatment of entire populations. The programs include computer-tailored interventions (CTIs) delivered through various modalities, such as counsellor guidance, telephonic coaching, and the Internet. The programs can have a high impact on disease prevention and management behaviours. These interventions involve new approaches that complement existing ones, such as proactive stage-matched interventions for multiple behaviours delivered to homes via computers with interventions that have the potential to provide the foundation for a well-care system, which will complement the existing sick-care system.

PHOTO 4.1 | A healthy lifestyle consisting of healthy diet and regular exercise has been an elusive goal for much of the population.

PHOTO 4.2 | Physical activity, such as walking, has been shown to lead to increases in life expectancy.

Core Constructs of the Transtheoretical Model of Behaviour Change

TTM uses stages to integrate principles and processes of change across major theories of intervention, hence the name "Transtheoretical." This model emerged from a comparative analysis of leading theories grounded in psychotherapy and behaviour change. Because more than 300 psychotherapy theories were found, the authors determined there was a need for systematic integration (Prochaska, 1979). Ten processes of change emerged, including consciousness-raising from the Freudian tradition, contingency management from the Skinnerian tradition (emphasizing reinforcement for modifying behaviours), and helping relationships from the Rogerian tradition (relating with caring, empathy, and unconditional positive regard to support change).

In an empirical analysis of self-changers compared to smokers in professional treatments, researchers assessed how frequently each group used each of the 10 processes (DiClemente & Prochaska, 1982). Research participants indicated that they used different processes at different times in their struggles with smoking. These self-changers were teaching us about a phenomenon that was not included in any of the multitude of therapy theories. They were revealing that behaviour change unfolds through a series of stages (Prochaska & DiClemente, 1983).

From the initial studies of smoking, the stage model rapidly expanded in scope to include applications to a broad range of health and mental health behaviours. Examples include alcohol and substance abuse, stress, bullying, delinquency, depression, eating disorders and **obesity**, high fat diets, HIV/AIDS prevention, mammography screening, medication compliance, unplanned pregnancy prevention, pregnancy and smoking, radon testing, sedentary lifestyles, and sun exposure. Over time, behaviour studies have expanded, validated, applied, and challenged the core ideas of the Transtheoretical Model (Hall & Rossi, 2008; Noar, Benac, & Harris, 2007; Prochaska, Wright, & Velicer, 2009).

The Transtheoretical Model has concentrated on five stages of change, 10 processes of change, decisional balance (the pros and cons of changing), self-efficacy, and temptation. Stage of change serves as the key integrating construct. Studies of change have shown that people move through a series of stages when modifying behaviour. While the time a person can stay in each stage is variable, the tasks required to move to the next stage are not. Certain principles and processes work best at each stage to reduce resistance, facilitate progress, and prevent relapse. Only a minority (usually less than 20 per cent) of a population at risk is prepared to take action at any given time. Thus, action-oriented strategies are not helpful for those in the early stages of the change. Strategies based on each of the TTM stages result in increased participation in the change process because they are tailored to each individual in the whole population rather than the minority ready to take action.

Stages of Change

The stage construct implies progress occurring over time. Surprisingly, none of the leading theories of therapy contained a core construct representing time. Traditionally, behaviour change was often construed as an event, such as quitting smoking, drinking, or overeating, but the TTM recognizes change as a process that unfolds over time involving progress through a series of stages (see Figure 4.1).

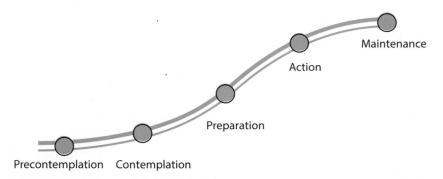

FIGURE 4.1 | The stages of change.
Source: © Pro-Change Behavior Systems, Inc. Reprinted with permission.

Precontemplation

People in the precontemplation stage are not intending to take action in the foreseeable future, usually measured as the next six months. Being uninformed or under-informed about the consequences of one's behaviour may cause a person to be in precontemplation. Multiple, unsuccessful attempts at change can lead to demoralization about ability to change. Both the uninformed and under-informed tend to avoid reading, talking, or thinking about their high-risk behaviours. They are often characterized in other theories as resistant, unmotivated, or not ready for health promotion programs. In fact, traditional population health promotion programs were not ready for such individuals and were not motivated to meet their needs.

Contemplation

Contemplation is the stage in which people are intending to change in the next six months. They are more aware of the pros of changing but are also acutely aware of the cons. In a meta-analysis across 48 health risk behaviours (Hall & Rossi, 2008), the pros and cons of changing were equal. This weighting between the costs and benefits of changing can produce profound ambivalence that can cause people to remain in this stage for long periods of time. This phenomenon is often characterized as chronic contemplation or behavioural procrastination. Individuals in contemplation are not ready for traditional action-oriented programs that expect participants to act immediately.

Preparation

Preparation is the stage in which people are intending to take action in the immediate future, usually measured as the next month. Typically, they have already taken some significant steps towards changing the behaviour in the past year. These individuals have a plan of action, such as joining an exercise class, consulting a counsellor, talking to their physician, buying a self-help book, or relying on a self-change approach. These are the people who should be recruited for action-oriented programs such as traditional smoking cessation or weight-loss clinics.

Action

Action is the stage in which people have made specific overt modifications in their lifestyles within the past six months. Since action is observable, the overall

© James Brey/iStockphoto

PHOTO 4.3 | Preparation is the stage in which people are intending to take action in the immediate future, usually measured as the next month.

process of behaviour change often has been equated with action. But in the TTM, action is only one of five stages. Typically, not all modifications of behaviour count as action in this model. In most applications, people have to attain a criterion that scientists and professionals agree is sufficient to reduce risk of disease. For example, reduction in the number of cigarettes or switching to low tar and nicotine cigarettes were formerly considered acceptable actions towards smoking cessation. Now the consensus is clear—only total abstinence counts, as those other changes do not necessarily lead to quitting and do not lower the risks associated with smoking to zero.

Maintenance

Maintenance is the stage in which people have made specific, overt modifications in their lifestyles and are working to prevent relapse; however, they do not apply change processes as frequently as do people in action. They are less tempted to relapse and grow increasingly more confident (have greater self-efficacy) that they can continue their changes. Based on temptation and self-efficacy data, researchers have estimated that maintenance lasts from six months to about five years. While this estimate may seem somewhat pessimistic, longitudinal data in the 1990 Surgeon General's report support this temporal estimate (USDHHS, 1990). After 12 months of continuous abstinence, 43 per cent relapsed to regular smoking. It was not until five years of continuous abstinence that the risk for relapse dropped to 7 per cent (USDHHS, 1990).

Termination

Termination is, in a sense, a sixth stage, when people are not tempted; they have 100 per cent self-efficacy. Whether depressed, anxious, bored, lonely, angry, or stressed, individuals in this stage are sure they will not return to unhealthy habits as a way of coping. It is as if the habit was never acquired in the first place or their new behaviour has become an automatic habit. Examples include people who have developed automatic seatbelt use or who automatically take their medications at the same time and place each day. In a study of former smokers and alcoholics, researchers found that less than 20 per cent of each group had reached the criteria of zero temptation and total self-efficacy (Snow, Prochaska, & Rossi, 1992). The criterion of 100 per cent self-efficacy may be too strict or it may be that this stage is an ideal goal for population health efforts. In other areas, like exercise, consistent condom use, and weight control, the realistic goal may be a lifetime of maintenance. Termination has not been given as much emphasis in TTM research since it may not be a practical reality for populations and it occurs long after interventions have ended.

Processes of Change

Processes of change are the experiential and behavioural activities that people use to progress through the stages. They provide important guides for intervention programs, serving as independent variables that are applied to move from stage to stage. Ten processes have received the most empirical support in our research to date.

Consciousness-Raising

Consciousness-raising involves increased awareness about the causes, consequences, and cures for a particular problem behaviour. Interventions that can increase awareness include feedback, interpretations, bibliotherapy (i.e., using self-help books or manuals), and media campaigns. Sedentary people, for example, may not be aware that their inactivity can have the same risk as smoking a pack of cigarettes a day.

Dramatic Relief

Dramatic relief initially produces increased emotional experiences followed by reduced affect or anticipated relief, if appropriate action is taken. Role-playing, grieving, personal testimonies, and health risk feedback are examples of techniques that can move people emotionally.

Self–Re-evaluation

Self–re-evaluation combines both cognitive and affective assessments of one's self-image with and without a particular unhealthy habit, such as one's image as a couch potato versus an active person. Values clarification, identifying healthy role models, and imagery are techniques that can help people apply self–re-evaluation. One might ask, "Imagine if you were free from smoking, how would you feel about yourself?"

Environmental Re-evaluation

Environmental re-evaluation combines both affective and cognitive assessments of how the presence or absence of a personal habit affects one's social environment, such as the effect of smoking on others. It can also include the awareness that one can serve as a

 **IN FOCUS**

Mastering Your Own Change

1. Think about what behaviour health risks you may have—smoking, unhealthy diet, sedentary behaviour, overweight.
2. Choose a risk to focus on.
3. Assess what stage you are in for reducing that health risk, e.g., how ready you are to exercise 150 minutes per week: not intending to do so in the next six months (precontemplation); intending to do so in the next six months (contemplation); intending to do so in the next month (preparation).
4. Now go to Table 4.1 and the chapter section on processes of change and work on the processes of change that match your stage of change.
5. One month later, reassess your stage of change for the risk behaviour you are focusing on and see if there is movement, and if so, use the processes of change that match your new stage. If you are still at the same stage, increase you usage of the processes.

positive or negative role model for others. Empathy training, documentaries, and family interventions can lead to such assessments.

Self-Liberation

Self-liberation is the belief that one can change and the commitment, as well as re-commitment, to act on that belief. New Year's resolutions, public testimonies, or a contract are ways of enhancing what the public calls willpower. One might say, "Telling others about my commitment to take action can strengthen my willpower. Who am I going to tell?"

Social Liberation

Social liberation requires an increase in social opportunities or alternatives, especially for people who are relatively deprived or oppressed. Advocacy, empowerment procedures, and appropriate policies can produce increased opportunities for minority health promotion, gay health promotion, and health promotion for impoverished segments of the population. These same procedures can also be used to help populations change; examples include smoke-free zones, salad bars in college dining halls, and easy access to condoms and other contraceptives.

Counterconditioning

Counterconditioning requires learning healthy behaviours as substitutes for problem behaviours. Examples of counterconditioning include nicotine replacement as a safe substitution for smoking or walking as a healthier alternative than "comfort" foods as a way to cope with stress.

Stimulus Control

Stimulus control removes cues for unhealthy habits and adds prompts for healthier alternatives. Examples are removing all the ashtrays from the house and car or removing high-fat foods that are tempting cues for unhealthy eating.

⚏ IN PRACTICE
Motivation for Healthy Change

Sometimes it takes a health scare to motivate us to change—and sometimes witnessing someone else's scare is enough.

Jennifer used the dramatic relief process of change to move herself to action when someone she loved had an unexpected emergency. Her experience may inspire you to get ready to make healthy changes.

"When I first got to school, I had a hard time getting everything done—I felt like I was drowning all the time. So I wasn't sleeping or eating well and there was no way I had time to exercise. But that all changed after my dad had a heart attack."

"He's fine now, but it was really scary. My mom called me to tell me to come home because he had to be rushed to the emergency room. The whole way there I kept thinking, he is so young, how could this have happened? I was terrified that he would die like my grandfather did after his heart attack."

"The doctors put a stent in one of his arteries, so the problem was fixed. But he had to go to a program for three months to start exercising, eating healthier foods, and learning how to manage stress. The doctors also told me that because so many people in my family have had heart attacks, I need to start living a healthier life too. She said if I changed things now, I could avoid this when I was my dad's age."

"Now I see how important it is to make time to take care of my health. I made a choice to exercise each day. Sometimes I just go for a 30-minute walk between classes, and other times I get **aerobic exercise** by playing tennis with a friend. I'm eating healthier too. Don't get me wrong, I still eat cookies occasionally and don't even try to resist popcorn when we go to the movies, but overall, I'm making better choices. And my dad gave me some good ideas about managing stress—like managing my time better—that he got from his classes. I was surprised at how much of a difference creating a schedule could make."

"I know I am doing a lot to be as healthy as I can. And the best part is that I'm also more relaxed—instead of feeling like I'm just getting by, I feel like I'm doing well. Somewhere along the way, making these changes helped me fit everything in."

Reinforcement Management

Reinforcement management provides positive consequences for taking steps in a positive direction. While reinforcement management can include the use of punishment, we found that self-changers rely on reward much more than punishment. Reinforcements are emphasized since a philosophy of the stage model is to work in harmony with how people change naturally. People expect to be reinforced by others more frequently than what actually occurs, so they should be encouraged to reinforce themselves through self-statements like "Nice going—you handled that temptation." They also can treat themselves at milestones as a reinforcement to increase the probability that healthy responses will be repeated.

PHOTO 4.4 | Temptation reflects the intensity of urges to engage in an unhealthy habit while in the midst of difficult situations.

Helping Relationships

Helping relationships combine caring, trust, openness, and acceptance, as well as support for healthy behaviour change. Rapport-building, a therapeutic alliance, supportive calls, social media, and buddy systems can be sources of social support.

Decisional Balance

The process of reflection and weighing the pros and cons of changing is decisional balance. Originally, TTM relied on Janis and Mann's (1977) model of decision-making that included four categories of pros: instrumental gains for self; instrumental gains for others; approval from self; and approval from others. The four categories of cons were instrumental costs to self; instrumental cost to others; disapproval from self; and disapproval from others. In a long series of studies attempting to produce this structure of eight factors, a much simpler structure was almost always found: the pros and cons of changing. Sound decision-making requires the consideration of the potential gains (pros) and losses (cons) associated with the consequences of a behaviour. For example, there are more than 65 scientific benefits of **regular physical activity**. One could be encouraged to make a list to see how many can be identified. One can also list the cons. The more the list of pros outweighs the cons, the better prepared one will be to take effective action.

Self-Efficacy

Self-efficacy is the situation-specific confidence that people have while coping with high-risk situations without relapsing to their unhealthy habit. This construct was integrated from Bandura's (1982) social cognitive theory (see Chapter 1).

Temptation

Temptation reflects the intensity of urges to engage in an unhealthy habit while in the midst of difficult situations. Typically, three factors reflect the most common types of tempting situations: negative affect or emotional distress, positive social situations, and craving. People could ask themselves how they will cope with emotional distress (without relying on a cigarette or comfort foods) to help them cope more effectively and thereby build their confidence or self-esteem.

Critical Assumptions of TTM

The Transtheoretical Model is also based on critical assumptions about the nature of behaviour change and population health interventions that can best facilitate such change. The following are a set of assumptions that drive transtheoretical theory, research, and practice:

1. Behaviour change is a process that unfolds over time through a sequence of stages, and health promotion programs will need to assist individuals as they progress over time.
2. Stages are both stable and open to change, just as chronic behavioural risk factors are both stable and open to change. Population health initiatives can motivate change by enhancing the understanding of the pros and diminishing the value of the cons.
3. Most at-risk populations are not prepared for action and will not be served by traditional action-oriented prevention programs. Helping individuals set realistic goals, like progressing to the next stage, will facilitate the change process.
4. Specific principles and processes of change need to be emphasized at specific stages for progress through the stages to occur. Table 4.1 outlines which principles and processes to emphasize at each stage.

These critical assumptions need to be taken into consideration when developing health promotion interventions for behaviour change and to facilitate progress through the stages.

Empirical Support

Each of the core TTM constructs (a theoretical dimension represented by two or more variables) has been studied across a broad range of behaviours and populations. Applying TTM to new behaviours involves research and measurement (Redding, Maddock, & Rossi, 2006), followed by intervention development, and refinement, eventually leading to studies of intervention success. We have selected a sample of these studies for discussion.

Stage Distribution

If interventions are to match the needs of entire populations, it is important to know the stage distributions of specific high-risk behaviours. A series of studies on smoking in the US clearly demonstrated that less than 20 per cent of smokers are in the preparation stage in most populations (e.g., Velicer et al., 1995; Wewers, Stillman, Hartman, & Shopland, 2003). Approximately 40 per cent of smokers are in the contemplation stage and another 40 per cent are in precontemplation. In countries that have not had a long history of tobacco

control campaigns, the stage distributions are even more challenging. In Germany, about 70 per cent of smokers are in precontemplation and about 10 per cent of smokers are in the preparation stage (Etter, Perneger, & Ronchi, 1997), while in China, more than 70 per cent are in precontemplation and about 5 per cent are in preparation (Yang et al., 2001). With a sample of 20,000 members of an HMO across 15 health risk behaviours, only a small portion were ready for the action stage of behavioural change (Rossi, 1992a).

Pros and Cons across 12 Behaviours

In studies of 12 different behaviours (smoking cessation, quitting cocaine, weight control, dietary fat reduction, safer sex, condom use, exercise acquisition, sunscreen use, radon testing, delinquency reduction, mammography screening, and physicians practising preventive medicine), it was confirmed that helping people to make better decisions involves focus on the pros and cons of changing.

Systematic relationships were found between stages and the pros and cons of changing for these 12 behaviours. In all 12 studies the cons of changing were higher than the pros for people in the precontemplation stage (Prochaska et al., 1994). Likewise, in all 12 studies the pros increased between the precontemplation and contemplation stages, and the cons of changing were lower in the action stage than in the contemplation stage. In 11 of the 12 studies, the pros of changing were higher than the cons for people in action. These relationships suggest that to progress from precontemplation, the pros of changing need to increase; to progress from contemplation, the cons need to decrease; to progress to action, the pros need to be higher than the cons. These same patterns of relationships have been replicated in a meta-analysis of the pros and cons of changing across the stages of change for 48 different health behaviours (Hall & Rossi, 2008).

Processes of Change across Behaviours

One of the assumptions of the Transtheoretical Model is that people can apply a common set of change processes across a broad range of behaviours. The higher-order structure of the processes (experiential and behavioural) has received more research support across problem behaviours than have the specific processes (Rossi, 1992b). Typically, support has been found for the standard set of 10 processes across behaviours such as smoking, diet, cocaine use, exercise, condom use, and sun exposure. However, the structure of the processes across studies has not been as consistent as the structure of the stages and the pros and cons of changing. The processes used to initiate change vary by behaviour. An infrequent behaviour such as conforming to an annual screening test (e.g., mammogram) may require fewer processes to progress to long-term maintenance (Rakowski et al., 1998).

Relationship between Stages and Processes of Change

One of the earliest empirical integrations was the discovery of systematic relationships between the stages people were in and the processes they were applying (Prochaska & DiClemente, 1983). This discovery allowed an integration of processes from theories typically seen as incompatible and in conflict. For example, Freudian theory relied almost entirely on consciousness-raising for producing change. This theory was viewed as incompatible with Skinnerian theory, which relied entirely on reinforcement management for modifying behaviour. But self-changers did not know that these processes were theoretically incompatible and their behaviour revealed that processes from very different theories needed to be emphasized at different stages of change. This integration suggests that in early stages of health promotion interventions, efforts should support the application of cognitive, affective, and evaluative processes to progress through the stages. In later stages these programs should rely more on commitments, conditioning, rewards, environmental controls, and support to progress toward maintenance or termination.

Table 4.1 has important practical implications for health promotion interventions. To help people progress from precontemplation to contemplation, processes such as consciousness-raising and dramatic relief need to be applied. Applying reinforcement management, counter-conditioning, and stimulus control processes in precontemplation would represent a theoretical, empirical, and practical mistake. Conversely, such strategies would be optimally matched for people at the action stage. Integration of the processes and stages has not been as consistent as the integration of the stages with the pros and cons of changing. Part of the problem may be the greater complexity of integrating 10 processes across five stages. The processes of change require more basic research.

Applied Studies

A large, diverse body of evidence on the application of TTM has revealed several trends. The most common application involves TTM computerized tailored interventions, which match intervention messages to individuals' particular needs (e.g., Kreuter, Strecher, & Glassman, 1999; Skinner, Campbell, Rimer, Curry, & Prochaska, 1999). Tailored interventions are population-based. They combine the best of population health with clinical health to provide individualized help. For example, individuals in precontemplation could receive feedback designed to increase their pros of changing to help them progress to the contemplation stage. These interventions, such as suggested readings, testimonials from others successful in changing, and encouragement to

TABLE 4.1 | Principles and Processes of Change That Mediate Progression between the Stages of Change

Precontemplation	Contemplation	Preparation	Action	Maintenance
Consciousness Raising				
Dramatic Relief				
Environmental Reevaluation				
	Social Liberation			
	Self-Reevaluation			
		Self-Liberation		
			Counter Conditioning	
			Helping Relationships	
Pros of Changing Increasing			Reinforcement Management	
	Cons of Changing Decreasing		Stimulus Control	
		Self-Efficacy Increasing		

reduce defences, originally were printed and given to participants at work or mailed to participants at home (Velicer et al., 1993); however, a growing range of applications are developing, including multimedia, computerized, tailored interventions (Mauriello, Sherman, Driskill, & Prochaska, 2007) that can be delivered in clinic settings, worksites, colleges, online at home, or on smart phones on the go. To view a demo of a college health Internet intervention, go to www.prochange .com/livewell-video.

The growing range of settings where TTM is being applied also includes primary care offices (Goldstein et al., 1999; Hoffman et al., 2006; Hollis et al., 2005), churches (Voorhees et al., 1996), campuses (Prochaska, J.M., et al., 2004), and communities (CDC, 1999). Increasingly, employers and health plans are making such TTM-tailored programs available to entire employee or subscriber populations. A recent meta-analysis of tailored print communications found that TTM was the most commonly used theoretical model across a broad range of behaviours (Noar, Benac, & Harris, 2007). TTM or Stage of Change Model was used in 35 of the 53 studies. In terms of effectiveness, the best results were produced when tailored communications included each of the following TTM constructs: stages of change, pros and cons of changing, self-efficacy, and processes of change (Noar et al., 2007). In contrast, interventions that included the non-TTM construct of perceived susceptibility had significantly worse outcomes. Tailoring non-TTM constructs like social norms and behavioural intentions did not produce significant differences (Noar et al., 2007). These unprecedented impacts require scientific and practice shifts in our approach to health promotion interventions:

1. from an action paradigm to a stage paradigm;
2. from reactive to proactive recruitment of participants;
3. from expecting participants to match the needs of our programs to having our programs match their needs;
4. from clinic-based to community-based behavioural health programs that apply the field's most powerful individualized and interactive intervention strategies; and
5. from assuming some groups do not have the ability to change to making sure that all groups have easy accessibility to evidence-based programs that provide stage-matched tailored interventions. Without such access, behaviour change programs cannot serve entire populations.

© kzenon/iStockphoto

PHOTO 4.5 | The liveWell college health program encourages students to engage in more physical activity.

Motoyuki Kobayashi/Getty Images

PHOTO 4.6 | Regular physical activity helps people to maintain health and become energized.

Challenging Studies

As with any model, not all of the research is supportive. Here are samples of some of the more challenging studies. Farkas et al. (1996) and then Abrams, Herzog, Emmons, and Linnan (2000) compared addiction variables to TTM variables as predictors of cessation over 12 to 24 months. Addiction variables, like number of cigarettes smoked and duration of prior quits (e.g., more than 100 days) out-predicted TTM variables, suggesting that addiction models were preferable to TTM. Responses to these comparative studies included concerns that Farkas et al. (1996) compared 14 addiction-type variables to just the single stage variable from TTM (Prochaska & Velicer, 1996; Prochaska, J.J., Velicer, Prochaska, Delucchi, and Hall, 2006). The Abrams et al. (2000) study included self-efficacy and the contemplation ladder—an alternative measure of readiness or stage—as part of its addiction model, but these are part of TTM. Also, for those intervening, how much you can predict is less important than how much you can change. Although duration of previous quits (e.g., 100 days) may predict better than stage, little can be done to change history, while stage can be changed.

In one study, Herzog, Abrams, Emmons, Linnan, and Shadel (1999) found that six processes of change did not predict stage progress over 12 months. In a second study, processes predicted stage progress but only when the contemplation ladder measure was used (Herzog et al., 2000). In a third report, TTM measures predicted 12-month outcomes, but self-efficacy and the stage measure were not counted as TTM variables (Abrams et al., 2000). Other researchers have found that change processes and other TTM variables predict stage progress (e.g., Prochaska et al., 1985, 1991, 2004, 2008; DiClemente et al., 1991; Dijkstra, Conijm, & De Vries, 2006; Johnson et al., 2000; Sun, Prochaska, Velicer, & Laforge, 2007). Johnson et al. (2000) explained some inconsistencies in previous research by demonstrating better predictions over 6 vs 12 months, and better predictions using all 10 processes of change instead of just a few.

One productive response to studies critical of TTM is to conduct further research. In response to the criticism that addiction severity is a better predictor of outcomes than stage of change, a series of studies to determine predictors of outcomes across multiple behaviours was done. To date, four such predictors have been found (Blissmer et al., 2010). The first is the severity effect, in which individuals with less severe behaviour risks at baseline are more likely to progress to action or maintenance at 24-month follow-up for smoking, diet, and sun exposure. This effect includes the level of addiction that Farkas et al. (1996) and Abrams et al. (2000) preferred. The second is stage effect, in which participants in preparation stage at baseline have better 24-month outcomes for smoking, diet, and sun exposure than those in contemplation, who do better than those in precontemplation. This effect is what Farkas et al. (1996) and Abrams et al. (2000) criticized. The third is treatment effect, in which participants in treatment do better at 24 months than those in control groups for smoking, diet, and sun exposure. The fourth is effort effects, in which participants in both treatment and control groups who progressed to action and maintenance at 24 months were making better efforts with TTM variables like pros and cons, self-efficacy, and processes at baseline. Moreover, no single demographic group did better across these multiple behaviours. What these results indicate is that either–or thinking (such as *either* severity *or* stage) is not as helpful as a more inclusive approach that seeks to identify the most important predictors of change, whether they are based on TTM or on an addiction or severity model.

Increasing Impacts with Multiple Behaviour Change Programs

A challenge for any theory is to keep raising the bar, that is, to be able to increase the theory's impact on enhancing health. One challenge for TTM is to treat multiple behaviours, since populations with multiple behaviour risks are at greatest risk for both chronic disease and premature death. These multiple-problem populations also account for a high percentage of health-care costs. The best estimates are that about 60 per cent of health-care costs are generated by about 15 per cent of populations, who have multiple behaviour risks (Edington, 2001).

The studies to date on multiple behaviour changes have been limited by the frequent use of poor research designs, and by not applying the most promising interventions, such as interactive and individualized TTM-tailored communications (Prochaska et al., 2001). From a TTM perspective, applying an action paradigm to multiple behaviours risks overwhelming populations, since action is the most demanding stage and taking action on two or more behaviours at once could be overwhelming. Furthermore, in individuals with four health behaviour risks, like smoking, diet, sun exposure, and sedentary lifestyles, less than 10 per cent were ready to take action on two or more behaviours (Prochaska & Velicer, 1997). The same was true with diabetes patients who needed to change four behaviours (Ruggiero et al., 1997).

Applying our best practices of a stage-based multiple behaviour manual and computerized tailored feedback reports over 12 months, we reached out to a population of parents of teens who were participating in parallel projects at school (Prochaska et al., 2004). We were able to engage 83.6 per cent of the eligible parents. The treatment group received up to three expert system reports at 0, 6, and 12 months. At 24 months, the treatment group was outperforming the controls on all three cancer prevention behaviours: smoking cessation, healthier diets, and safer sun exposure practices.

With a population of 5,545 patients from primary care practices, we were able to recruit 65 per cent for a second multiple behaviour change project (Prochaska et al., 2005). In this project, mammography screening (i.e., screening aimed at the early detection of breast cancer) was targeted in addition to the three aforementioned cancer prevention behaviours. Significant treatment effects were found for all four target behaviours at 24 months.

Comparisons across three multiple-risk behaviour studies demonstrated that the efficacy rates for smoking cessation were in the same 22 to 25 per cent abstinence range that we consistently find when targeting only smoking (Prochaska, J.J., et al., 2006). Further, it was found that smokers with a single risk were no more successful in quitting than smokers who were treated for two or three risk behaviours. The same was found for participants with a single risk of diet or sun exposure compared with those with two or three risk behaviours. Overall, these results indicate that TTM-tailored interventions may be producing unprecedented impacts on multiple behaviours for disease prevention and health promotion.

Applying TTM Interventions to Exercise, Nutrition, and Smoking

With a population of 1,277 overweight and obese patients in a workplace who were invited to participate in the study through mailings at work, we applied our original strategy for multiple behaviour change. We call this the modular approach, where participants receive a separate TTM computerized tailored intervention (CTI) module for each of their risk behaviours. The treatment groups had significant changes at 24 months on healthy eating, exercise, and emotional eating. This study was the first to report significant coaction in the treatment group

and significant changes in fruit and vegetable intake, specific behaviours that were not targeted. Coaction is the increased probability that individuals who take effective action on one behaviour (like exercise) are more likely to take action on a secondary behaviour (like diet). Also, the intervention resulted in a mean of about 0.8 behaviours changed per participant in the TTM group, which was 60 per cent greater than the 0.5 behaviours in the control group (Johnson et al., 2008).

One of our exciting developments in simultaneously changing multiple behaviours is the phenomenon of coaction. We have found that significant coaction typically occurs only in our TTM treatment groups (e.g., Paiva et al., 2012; Johnson, Paiva, Mauriello, Prochaska, Redding, & Velicer, 2013; Mauriello et al., 2010) and not in control groups, suggesting it is likely to be treatment-induced.

With a population of 1,400 employees in a major medical setting, the study of Prochaska et al. (2008) made available online modular TTM computerized tailored interventions or three motivational interviewing (a psychotherapeutic approach designed to enhance motivation for positive change) telephonic or in-person sessions for each of four behaviours (smoking, inactivity, BMI >25, and stress). Patients chose which behaviours to target and how much time and effort to spend on any behaviour. At six months, both treatments outperformed the Health Risk Intervention (HRI), which included feedback on the person's stage for each risk and guidance on how they could progress to the next stage.

With a population of 1,800 students recruited from eight high schools in four states, Mauriello et al. (2010) applied a second-generation strategy with exercise as the primary behaviour. Students received three online sessions of fully tailored CTIs. The secondary behaviours of fruit and vegetable intake and limited television watching alternated between moderate and minimal (stage-only) tailoring. Over the course of the six-month treatment, there were significant treatment effects in each of the three behaviours, but only changes in fruit and vegetable intake were sustained at 12 months. Significant coaction was found for each pair of behaviours in the treatment group but none in the control group. The amount of coaction decreased after treatment, suggesting that longer treatment may be needed for this age population where health risk behaviours tend to increase.

Prochaska et al. (2012) recruited 3,391 adults from 39 states who were at risk for lack of exercise and ineffective **stress management**. This study involved a strategy for multiple tailored behaviour change. One treatment group received a fully tailored TTM online for the primary behaviour of stress management and minimal tailoring for exercise. A second group received three sessions of optimally tailored telephonic coaching for exercise and minimal tailoring for stress. In this study, the TTM exercise coaching outperformed the TTM online stress management, which outperformed the controls. Also, the exercise coaching produced significant effects on healthy eating and depression management, which were not treated. Finally, the same order of effective treatment was found for enhancing five domains of well-being: emotional health, physical health, life evaluation, thriving, and overall well-being. This study represents the greatest impact to date on decreasing health risk behaviours and increasing health and well-being. It also underscores the importance of tailoring change interventions.

Limitations of the Model

Although TTM has been applied across at least 48 behaviours and populations from many countries, the model still has limitations. The problem area that has produced the most disappointment has been primary prevention of substance abuse in children. To date, population studies based on TTM have not produced significant prevention effects (e.g., Aveyard et al., 1999; Hollis et al., 2005). Unfortunately, little can be concluded from non-significant results. For example, Peterson et al. (2000) also reported that 16 out of 17 such studies failed, and suggested that the field should move beyond social influence models. Prevention trials have proved challenging across theories.

Part of the challenge from a TTM perspective is that almost all young people who have not yet used substances like tobacco, alcohol, or other drugs are in precontemplation stage for acquisition of such use. One promising approach was to identify subgroups based on pros, cons, and temptation to try using. Those with a profile of low pros for using, high cons, and low temptations were clearly the most protected. This profile showed the best effort effects at baseline and the least acquisition at 12, 24, and 36 months (Velicer, Redding, Sun, & Prochaska, 2007). The first studies applying such profiles did not produce the expected positive outcomes, but new investigation can involve application of more creative and effective interventions. It remains to be seen whether effective TTM-tailored prevention

programs that build on both theoretical and empirical insights can be developed.

A promising new finding (Velicer et al., 2013) related to the use of an energy balance program (Health in Motion) with middle school students. Specifically, a smoking and alcohol prevention intervention lacked effectiveness to prevent substance use, but the energy balance program in the comparison group did prevent it. A focus on having a healthy lifestyle through exercise, healthy eating, and less than two hours of screen time each day may be a more engaging and helpful intervention than a target of just avoiding substances.

It might be assumed that TTM does not apply very well to children and adolescents. There is a basic question as to the age at which intentional behaviour change begins. Applied studies in bullying prevention in elementary, middle, and high schools, however, have all produced impressive results (Evers, Prochaska, Van Marter, Johnson, & Prochaska, 2007). Similarly, early intervention with adolescent smokers using TTM-tailored treatments produced significant abstinence rates at 24 months that were almost identical to rates found with treated adult smokers (Hollis et al., 2005). This was also true of TTM-tailored interventions targeting sun protective behaviours in adolescents (Norman et al., 2007). One problem is that there has been much more research applying TTM to reducing risks than to preventing risks.

Given the global application of TTM, it will be important to determine in which cultures TTM can be applied effectively and in which cultures it may require major adaptations. In basic meta-analysis research on the relationships between stages and pros and cons of changing in 10 countries, there was no significant effect by country (Hall & Rossi, 2008).

Future Directions

While research results to date are encouraging, much still needs to be done to advance practical behaviour change through evidence-based efforts such as the Transtheoretical Model. Basic research needs to be done with other theoretical variables, such as processes of resistance, framing, and problem severity, to determine if such variables relate systematically to the stages and if they predict progress across particular stages. More research is needed on the structure or integration of the processes and stages of change across a broad range of behaviours, including acquisition behaviours such as exercise, and extinction behaviours like what has been accomplished for smoking cessation (Rosen, 2000). What modifications are needed to better address specific types of behaviours?

Since tailored communications represent the most promising interventions for applying TTM to entire populations, more research is needed comparing the effectiveness, efficiency, and impacts of alternative technologies. The Internet is excellent for individualized interactions at low cost but has not produced the high participation rates generated by person-to-person outreach via telephone or visits to primary care providers. Increasingly, employers are encouraging and offering incentives to employee populations to participate in more integrated Internet, telephone, and provider programs. Interventions once seen as applicable only on an individual basis are being applied as high-impact programs for population health.

How do diverse populations respond to stage-matched interventions and to high-tech systems? How might programs best be tailored to meet the needs of diverse populations? Might menus of alternative intervention modalities (e.g., telephone, Internet, neighbourhood or church leaders, person-to-person or college programs) empower diverse populations to best match health-enhancing programs to their particular needs?

Changing multiple behaviours presents special challenges, such as the number of demands placed on participants and providers. Alternative strategies need to be tried beyond the sequential (one at a time) and simultaneous (all treated intensely at the same time). Integrative approaches are promising. For example, with bullying prevention, there are multiple behaviours (e.g., hitting, stealing, ostracizing, mean gossiping and labelling, damaging personal belongings) and multiple roles (bully, victim, and passive bystander) that need to be treated. An integrated approach is needed to address these needs in the given time constraints. If

behaviour change is construct-driven (e.g., by stage or self-efficacy), what higher-order construct could integrate all of these more concrete behaviours and roles? In a study where relating with mutual respect was used as a higher-order construct, significant and important improvements across roles and behaviours were found for elementary, middle, and high school students (Evers et al., 2007). We are presently testing the concept of living well with college students as they work on the multiple behaviours of stress management, exercise, and healthy eating. As with any theory, effective applications may be limited more by our creativity than by the ability of the theory to drive significant research and effective interventions.

Applying TTM on a population basis to change multiple health risks has required the use of innovative paradigms that complement established paradigms. Table 4.2 illustrates how a population paradigm, using proactive outreach to students, complements the individual patient paradigm that passively reacts when students seek clinical services. The use of the stage paradigm complements the action paradigm, which assumes that because students are seeking services they are prepared to take action. The use of computerized tailored interventions complements the traditional reliance on clinicians, and the treatment of multiple behaviours complements the established clinical wisdom of treating one behaviour at a time. The population theme paradigm based on impacts (reach × efficacy × number

TABLE 4.2 | Inclusive Care from Two Clusters of Paradigms for Individual Patients and Entire Populations

Patient Health	Complemented by	Population Health
1. Individual patients		1. Entire populations
2. Passive reactance		2. Proactive
3. Acute conditions		3. Chronic conditions
4. Efficacy trials		4. Effectiveness trials
5. Action-oriented		5. Stage-based
6. Clinic-based		6. Home-based
7. Clinician-delivered		7. Technology-delivered
8. Standardized		8. Tailored
9. Single target behaviour		9. Multiple target behaviours
10. Fragmented		10. Integrated

of behaviours changed) complements individualized clinical trials with select samples that rely on efficacy. Integrating these new paradigms can produce the foundation for a well-care system to complement the established sick-care system. Combining the two systems would enhance the health and well-being of many more people by healing the sick, while maximizing wellness for all.

SUMMARY

In this chapter, we described the 15 core constructs of TTM and how these constructs can be integrated across the stages of change. Empirical support for the basic constructs of TTM and for applied research was presented, along with conceptual and empirical challenges from critics of TTM. Applications of TTM-tailored interventions with entire populations were explored with examples for single behaviours and for multiple health-risk behaviours. A major theme is that programmatically building and applying the core constructs of TTM at the individual level can ultimately lead to high-impact programs for enhancing health at the population level.

The Transtheoretical Model is a dynamic model of change and must remain open to modifications and enhancements as more students, scientists, and practitioners apply the stage paradigm to a growing number of diverse theoretical issues, public health problems, and at-risk populations.

Critical Thought Questions

1. What are the advantages of a stage paradigm vs an action-oriented paradigm?
2. Historically, it was thought a person could only change one behaviour at a time. Evidence is now showing that multiple behaviour change can happen. What are some new ideas that make this possible?
3. What stage of change are you in for a health risk behaviour that you have? What TTM processes of change would you use to get to the next stage of change?

Recommended Reading

Prochaska, J.O., Norcross, J.C., & DiClemente, C.C. (1994). *Changing for good: A revolutionary six-stage program for overcoming bad habits and moving your life positively forward*. New York: William Morrow.
Cancer Prevention Research Center: www.uri.edu/research/cprc
Coaches Guide for Using TTM with Clients: contact info@prochange.com

Pro-Change Behavior Systems, Inc.: www.prochange.com
Basic Transtheoretical Model training: contact elearning@prochange.com
MyHealth behaviour change programs: www.prochange.com/myhealth

5

Stress, Coping, and Health

NICHOLAS J.S. CHRISTENFELD | BRITTA A. LARSEN

Learning Objectives

In this chapter you will:

- Learn about different sorts of stress—good stress versus bad stress, chronic versus acute stress—and how these distinctions can matter for health.

- Discover what sorts of situations are likely to produce stress, and how it matters how one thinks about, or appraises, the challenges one faces.

- Find out about groups that are most subject to stress and most at risk of long-term health consequences from that stress.

- Explore coping techniques that can mitigate the impact of stress.

- Learn beneficial effects of social support, how this may differ by gender, and how formal support groups can help.

Introduction

We all know the feeling. You're sitting in class waiting for a lecture to begin, and suddenly you realize that people around you have their notes put away and their #2 pencils out: it's exam time. You completely forgot and are totally unprepared. Your heart starts pounding, you start sweating a little, your mouth gets dry, and you feel ready to jump from your seat and sprint out of the classroom. While you may not have experienced this exact scenario, chances are you've experienced something close enough to imagine the feelings involved, one in particular: stress.

Most people identify stress as a negative experience. However, a life without stress, while conceptually appealing, may be no more medically advisable than extending the life of one's car by never driving it. Nonetheless, stress is linked in various ways to impaired health and reduced well-being, and some understanding of its nature, variety, mechanisms, and impact is worthwhile. As with the car, while stress is unavoidable, where you go and how you navigate your world can impact the wear and tear on the system.

Most generally, stress involves some perturbation of the system, or movement away from homeostasis or resting state, usually in response to some perceived threat or demand. The study of the body's response to stress (also see Chapter 2) was largely launched by Cannon's (1929) work on the fight-or-flight response and by Selye's idea of a **General Adaptation Syndrome** (Selye, 1976). Various situations require rapid preparation for action, and the hypothalamic-adrenal-pituitary axis (HPA) co-ordinates the body's neuroendocrine response. (See Chapter 2 for a detailed discussion of these physiological responses.) While preparation for action is often adaptive, repeated or chronic activation can produce long-term harm. It may also be that the bodily response—a primitive one in evolutionary terms—is well suited to dealing with immediate physical threats that are acute and worth some long-term risk, but is less functional in dealing with the vaguer psychological threats of modern life, which cannot often be resolved by either fighting or fleeing (Sapolsky, 2004). Because of the breadth of the bodily stress response, with cardiovascular, immune,

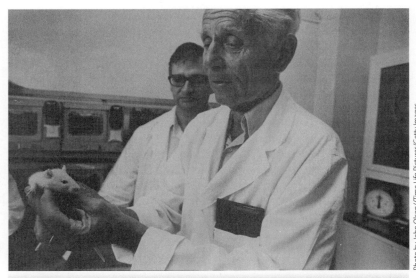

PHOTO 5.1 | Hans Selye (1907–82) of the Université de Montréal.

digestive, reproductive, and other systems involved, the health effects of stress are widespread, and are apparent in many health outcomes (see Chapter 2). Heart disease (see Chapter 9) has perhaps received the most attention, with much research based on the "reactivity hypothesis" that repeated blood pressure spikes lead to hypertension and heart disease.

Of course, not all threats or demands are equal; some are frightening, some are exciting. Similarly, some last only a few moments, and others linger for years. When discussing stress and its effect on physical and mental health, important distinctions need to be made in the vast array of deviations from homeostasis we experience.

Good vs Bad Stress

One issue raised by the literature on coping is the distinction between responses likely to be beneficial versus those likely to be harmful. This is an intrinsically difficult issue, as harm and benefit occur along multiple dimensions. Sometimes active coping with a threat, even if it produces some long-term damage to the cardiovascular system, may well be worthwhile if, for example, it prevents one from being fired, or, in more primitive times, eaten by a lion (Sapolsky, 2004). While stress is generally regarded as a negative experience, the stress response, including physiological and cognitive changes, is actually meant to give us the resources to deal with threats, rather than add to the negative experience of the situation.

While Selye (1976) described a General Adaptation Syndrome when demands are placed on the system, he also distinguished between **distress**, which has negative health consequences, and **eustress**, which is positive. This good stress generally comes from confronting challenges that one can adequately deal with, and thus can provide a sense of meaning and well-being (O'Sullivan, 2010). On the other hand, distress comes from feeling that one's resources are insufficient to meet the demands of a situation. There has not been much research on the health benefits of eustress, though it is connected to the notion of optimal arousal, and there is considerable evidence that people can perform better, if not live longer, when they reach an optimal level of arousal (i.e., with some pressure on them) (Le Fevre, Matheny, & Kilt, 2003).

Acute vs Chronic Stress

One factor underlying the difference between positive and negative stress is its duration. While the notions of acute and chronic stress are much used, there is little conceptual clarity about their meaning (Gerin et al., 2012). Most models of how stress leads to disease suggest that the impact will persist even after the stress has passed, with, for example, brief elevations in blood pressure that can gradually cumulate into damage to the arterial wall, and so produce hypertension (Folkow, 1978). As such, the difference between an acute stressor and a chronic one could be simply how many times it recurs and how long it lasts.

Stress researcher Robert Sapolsky (2004) has theorized that the physiological stress response was designed (in evolutionary terms) to address acute threats, such as being chased by a predator. It is when these short-term changes, such as increases in blood pressure, become long-term that stress can lead to disease. There is some evidence that short-term stress can actually be beneficial (Edwards et al., 2006); ample evidence, however, shows that chronic stress is harmful. In one famous example, Cohen and colleagues (1997) exposed willing volunteers to a cold virus, quarantined them, and waited to see who got sick and who remained healthy. While experiencing acute stress over the previous year was not associated with infection rates, people who had experienced chronic stressors, in this case those lasting at least one month, were more likely to become sick than those who had not experienced chronic stressors.

Chronic stress is not always a product of the actual stressor being extended or recurring; rather, dwelling on events that are themselves very brief ("You're fired!" "I'm leaving you!") can turn these acute stressors into chronic ones. This process is known as **rumination**. Research shows that ruminating on a stressor can extend elevated blood pressure response, or later recreate it (Glynn, Christenfeld, & Gerin, 2002). People who tend to ruminate also have a higher incidence of cardiovascular disease (Larsen & Christenfeld, 2009), suggesting that this tendency to extend acute stressors into chronic ones can be damaging to one's health.

Rumination, then, has the potential to turn acute stressors into chronic ones, and also to explain, in part, the difference between positive and negative stressors. It also, as discussed later in this chapter, may be part of the link between stress and various co-morbid disorders.

Whether stress is good, bad, acute, or chronic naturally depends on many factors. Of course, there are the aspects of the events themselves, such as what is at stake (one's grade, one's health, etc.) and how. Also important in determining the nature of a stressful event, however, is the nature of the person experiencing it; the same event (e.g., a failing grade) could happen to two people and evoke very different reactions. In the sections below, we discuss common sources of stress and how some people might find them more stressful than others.

Stressful Situations

Job and Primary Role Stress

Among the most studied sources of situational stress have been various occupations, although attention has also been paid to the stress caused by traumatic life events, and more recently there has been growing interest in stress caused by having chronic caregiver responsibilities. Given the strong indication that stress matters, that people spend a good fraction of their lives at work, and that many people find work stressful, research on this topic is abundant and important.

At the extremes, there is good evidence that occupation matters. Timio et al. (1988) followed for two decades a group with particularly low **job stress**: nuns living in a secluded order in Umbria. They lived isolated from urban life, rarely spoke, spent time praying and meditating, suffered no economic stress, had no family responsibilities, and, to the extent possible, no earthly anxieties. If such things matter, the comparison of these nuns with a control group living in the same area should reveal it. And it does. Over the span of the study, blood

PHOTO 5.2 | Stress is associated with certain occupations and life roles.

pressure rose significantly—roughly 40 mmHg SBP—for people in the control group, while for the nuns it did not rise at all. This difference emerged despite no difference in body mass index (BMI) increases for the two groups, and withstood control for activities such as bearing children.

There are also health studies of cloistered life roles rather different from life in the convent. D'Atri, Fitzgerald, Kasl, and Ostfeld (1981) studied prisoners, also looking longitudinally at changes in resting blood pressure, and found that those assigned to live in solitary cells showed a significant decrease in blood pressure compared to those living in crowded dorms, despite the fact that daily activities, diet, and other lifestyle factors were rigidly controlled and standardized for all prisoners.

While both of these studies show compelling evidence that specific occupations and life circumstances influence blood pressure, neither prisoners nor nuns are representative of the general population. The most simple, intuitive notion of job strain is that some professions intrinsically come with high levels of stress, while others are naturally more relaxing. However, it is not immediately clear what the most stressful jobs would be. Are jobs more stressful if they involve menial tasks, manual tasks, or low wages and endless drudgery? Or instead, are the most stressful jobs ones that involve supervisory positions, with the responsibility not just for oneself but for many or even many thousands of subordinates? Or perhaps stress is not related to status, but instead to the particular details of the job—traders on the floors of the New York or Toronto stock exchanges with relentless time pressure, or Transportation Security Administration screeners who are expected to maintain constant vigilance?

One key question about job stress (and stress in general) is the issue of control; namely, is it more stressful to have control in a demanding situation or to have no control? This has been explored in animal studies, with conflicting results. Brady (1958) and Brady and colleagues (Brady, Porter, Conrad, & Mason, 1958) compared rhesus monkeys that could exert control over receiving electric shocks with yoked monkeys that could not. The former died of perforated ulcers, while the latter survived, suggesting that high control in stressful situations may be more damaging. However, there are several reasons not to apply this too literally to human job stress. In addition to methodological objections (see Chapter 2), the finding runs counter to Seligman's animal work (Seligman & Maier, 1967), which suggests that not having control leads to a negative state of learned helplessness and depression. Moreover, the effect does not replicate in another species, namely rats (Weiss, 1968). Thus, it is questionable how useful these studies are in speaking to control and occupational stress in humans; in addition to finding contradictory results, the stressors used in animal studies do not have clear correlates in human jobs.

Studies with humans show that the effect of job stress on health seems to rely on multiple factors, though there is not complete agreement on what those factors are. For example, the model of occupational stress developed by Karasek et al. (1988) suggests that job stress is a function of job demands and "decision latitude," or amount of autonomy. The argument is that jobs with high demands but little autonomy would be highly stressful and, consequently, damaging to health. This clearly moves away from a simple hierarchical view, since upper executives may have high demand, but this can be offset by high control, and those nearer the bottom of the pyramid may have fewer demands, but also less control. People holding high-demand/low-autonomy jobs, such as waiters and firemen, are roughly four times as likely to suffer heart attacks as those with the greatest balance of autonomy and strain (Karasek et al., 1988). Moreover, it appears that while neither demands (e.g., jobs reported as "hectic") nor control (e.g., jobs affording control over pace) had any predictive value separately with respect to daily blood pressure, the ratio of demands to control predicted both sleeping and waking diastolic blood pressure (Theorell et al., 1991).

Those who put in high effort and receive few rewards are also at risk for high job strain. In other words, the imbalance of effort and reward can predict, in large samples of blue-collar workers, negative health events such as coronary heart disease (CHD, or, colloquially, hardening of the heart's arteries), myocardial infarction (MI, or, colloquially, a heart attack), and death (colloquially, kicking the bucket) (Matschinger, Siegrist, Siegrist, & Dittmann, 1986; Siegrist, 1996). Kivimaki et al. (2002), in tracking workers over 25 years, found that CHD (see Chapter 9) was roughly doubled in those with a high effort–reward imbalance. Another model suggests that damage results from a misfit or incongruence between the person and the environment, or the demands of the job and capabilities of the employee

(French, Caplan, & Harrison, 1982). For example, a worker who values creativity would suffer working on an assembly line.

In general, these job strain models rely on some interactive aspect of the effort involved in the job and whether that job includes factors that make its successful completion viable. The models discussed so far deal with such success at the level of structural occupational factors, but this can also be seen as depending on the resources or coping ability of the individual employee. That approach suggests a different sort of model, which is discussed in the section on the interaction of person and situation below.

Life Events

In keeping with the notion that stressful jobs are health-damaging, various views have suggested that life stresses in general, whether at work, at home, in relationships, or elsewhere, should be seen as risk factors for morbidity and mortality. There have been efforts to quantify the general level of stress in a person's life, with one classic tool being the Social Readjustment Rating Scale (SRRS), more commonly known as the Holmes and Rahe Stress Scale (Holmes & Rahe, 1967). This scale includes numerous possible life events, and people obtain a score for each event they have experienced in some given interval, with more points assigned for the more major events (Table 5.1). For example, serious trouble with the law warrants 63 points, and trouble with the in-laws gets 29. One notable feature of this scale is that it does not distinguish between positive and negative events; both contribute to the total stress score. Marriage, thus, gets 50 points, while being fired earns 47. The scores for each event were obtained from subjective magnitude estimates of a group of research participants, and were in fact calibrated off marriage, which was set at 50.

This approach to assessing life stress has received its share of criticism. One argument points out the somewhat arbitrary weighting of the various factors (Rabkin & Struening, 1976). A nuanced response had a panel assign weights to an individual's life stressors based on contextual information, so that the end of a happy marriage, for example, would be rated as more stressful than the end of one that was less idyllic and whose end might even be welcome (Brown & Harris, 1978). Another issue has been the question of whether positive items produce the same sort of stress as negative ones. Few would deny the stress of planning a big wedding but pleasant events such as a vacation also add points in the original formulation.

TABLE 5.1 | Events, and Corresponding Points, for Life Stress, from Holmes and Rahe's Social Readjustment Rating Scale

	Life Event	Value		Life Event	Value
1	Death of spouse	100	22	Change in responsibilities at work	29
2	Divorce	73	23	Son or daughter leaving home	29
3	Marital separation	65	24	Trouble with in-laws	29
4	Jail term	63	25	Outstanding personal achievement	28
5	Death of close family member	63	26	Spouse begins or stops work	26
6	Personal injury or illness	53	27	Begin or end school/college	26
7	Marriage	50	28	Change in living conditions	25
8	Fired at work	47	29	Revision of personal habits	24
9	Marital reconciliation	45	30	Trouble with boss	23
10	Retirement	45	31	Change in work hours or conditions	20
11	Change in health of family member	44	32	Change in residence	20
			33	Change in school/college	20
12	Pregnancy	40	34	Change in recreation	19
13	Sex difficulties	39	35	Change in church activities	19
14	Gain of new family member	39	36	Change in social activities	18
15	Business readjustment	39	37	A moderate loan or mortgage	17
16	Change in financial state	38	38	Change in sleeping habits	16
17	Death of close friend	37	39	Change in number of family get-togethers	15
18	Change to a different line of work	36	40	Change in eating habits	15
19	Change in number of arguments with spouse	35	41	Vacation	13
20	A large mortgage or loan	31	42	Christmas	12
21	Foreclosure of mortgage or loan	30	43	Minor violations of the law	11

Source: Holmes and Rahe (1967).

Another debate about the measurement of life stress is whether stress problems depend on rare major events, or whether they have a greater relationship to frequent and minor ones. The death of a spouse (100 points in the Holmes and Rahe Stress Scale) is unquestionably stressful, but it could be that, given how rare such events are, the damage to the system is more profound from trying to get one's kids to finish their homework every night for a dozen years. To assess such questions, Kanner and colleagues (1981) developed a scale with questions about more than 100 life hassles. People indicate which events they have experienced in the past month and also rate the severity of the events. The events listed include major changes such as being laid off, but also more minor events like auto maintenance, gossip, and attending too many meetings. Following 100 people for nine months, Kanner and colleagues (1981) found a large and significant correlation between reports of these daily hassles and psychological symptoms. In fact, these daily hassles were more associated with scores on a self-reported symptom checklist (including such symptoms as headaches and feeling lonely) than were the more major events.

It does seem clear that people's health and well-being can be impacted by many events of their lives, though questions about the necessary magnitude and valence of those events are not yet fully settled. Questions of causality also complicate the issue, as those with poor coping resources, or those who are simply poor, are likely to encounter more stresses to begin with.

Caregiver Stress

The person tasked with caring for an older or a sick relative experiences significant stress. An aging population, the treatment of infectious diseases, neonatal care, and battlefield first aid have all likely contributed to the number of people needing chronic care, and, accordingly, the number of people providing it. This sort of responsibility perhaps exemplifies the daily hassles approach to stress. The caretaker's role, while interspersed with crises, is mostly known for its relentless responsibility, vigilance, and hassles. This sort of stress has been shown actually to reduce telomere length, which is a marker of cellular aging (Epel et al., 2004). Chronically caring for others, it seems, even makes one's cells feel old.

Some approaches to caregiver stress are conceptually very similar to job stress models. For example, Nolan, Grant, and Ellis (1990) suggested that caregiver stress is produced by the perceived nature of the demand exceeding the perceived capabilities of the person. Other views of caregiver stress are more specific to this stressor and suggest that caregiving is stressful because it interferes with the caregiver taking care of himself or—more commonly—herself. In addition to such objective burdens (Jones, 1996; Maurin & Boyd, 1990), there is also the subjective burden, which includes the feelings experienced when providing care (Nijboer et al., 1999).

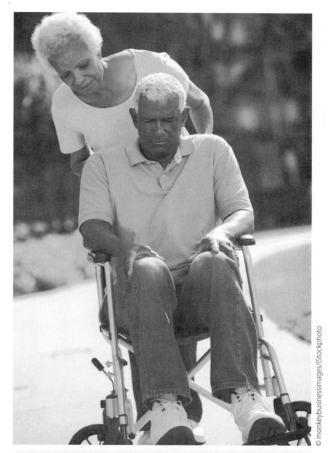

PHOTO 5.3 | The role of caregiver is stressful, and increasingly common and long-lasting.

The stress of caregiving does not seem to impact all caregivers equally. With traumatic brain injury, partners seem particularly affected (Verhaeghe, Defloor, & Grypdonck, 2005), perhaps because it represents a more profound or unexpected change to the prior relationship. Women seem to report more caregiver-associated stress and depression than men (Kreutzer, Serio, & Bergquist, 1994). The consequences of caregiver stress include self-reported symptoms (Teel & Press, 1999), increased use of medical services despite having less time to seek care (Son et al., 2007), and also an elevation in mortality risk (Schulz & Beach, 1999). Importantly, and it is a point we will return to, subjective assessments of stress are important in understanding the impact of stressors on health (Son et al., 2007). Despite the burden, people value caring for family members (Lawton, Moss, Kleban, Glicksman, & Rovine, 1991).

Sociological Stress: SES, Gender, and Race

Some forms of stress are thought to result not from the particulars of one's employment, family responsibilities, or specific life events, but more generally from one's status in society. The positions thought to be associated with poor health outcomes are those subjected to discrimination, harassment, and limited opportunities. Again consistent with some job strain models and caregiver stress, people in positions of less power often experience demands that overwhelm their personal resources.

Blood pressure and other health outcomes relate to socio-economic status (SES) (Luepker et al., 1993; Garrison, Gold, Wilson, & Kannel, 1993). Some of these relationships seem to be due to the relatively poorer health behaviours of those in lower SES groups as compared to those of higher SES (Stringhini et al., 2011). People of lower SES and those who are marginalized, for

example, are likely to have poorer nutrition and are more likely to smoke. Evidence, however, indicates that education interventions improve health (Lleras-Muney, 2005). Stress due to societal status is different from the other sorts of stress we have discussed in that it is due to relative position, rather than to any absolute level of daily events, task demands, and the like (Eibner & Evans, 2005).

As more women entered the workforce and were unable to correspondingly reduce their burdens at home, researchers addressed the corresponding stress of dual roles. Role conflict for women, for example, has been associated with increased psychosocial symptoms (Coverman, 1989). In contrast to findings showing working women endure greater stress, women have a considerably longer lifespan than men—5.3 more years in Canada, and 5.0 in the United States (CIA World Factbook, 2012)—and, at least through menopause, women have significantly lower blood pressure levels (Oparil, 1995).

◎ IN FOCUS

Stress and New York City

Causes of death vary by occupation, race, and nationality, but also, more locally, by region. In the southeastern US—a region known as the "stroke buckle"—there is an excess of stroke mortality (Lanska & Kuller, 1995). Even more locally, New York City is a hot spot for heart attack mortality (McNutt, Strogatz, Coles, & Fehrs, 1994). While there are numerous possible explanations for this pattern, one is that the level of stress associated with a city is a trigger for MI. If this is the case, then one ought to be able to detect not just an effect of chronic exposure to New York City (NYC) among its residents, but also an acute effect among people who are visiting the city. Similarly, it might be possible to detect a reduction in heart attack risk among residents when they are outside the city.

To test such notions, Christenfeld and colleagues (1999) used federal death records to examine the fraction of deaths in various groups attributed to ischemic heart disease (IHD). Examining all deaths over the period of a decade, they found a dramatically higher proportion were due to IHD among NYC residents. They also found a significant elevation, about half that observed for residents, among people who did not live in NYC but who died while visiting there. Likewise, NYC residents, out of the city, show a proportion of deaths due to IHD that, while

PHOTO 5.4 | New York City.

still elevated, is about halfway down to the population level. All of these effects persist when controls are put in place for age, race, gender, and ethnicity differences and for being in or out of county of residence. The findings taken together suggest that something about being in NYC disposes people to this cause of death, and that about half the effect is from chronic exposure—living there—and about half from acute exposure—being there. The findings do not reveal exactly what it is about the city that matters, but stress, crowding, vigilance, and even excitement could all be involved.

Racial minority populations are often studied with respect to health disparities (see Chapter 19). Evidence shows that differences are due not simply to socio-economic factors, but more directly to being the victim of racist interactions. Williams, Neighbors, and Jackson (2003), for example, found that incidents of racial bias were associated with poor physical health, as well as psychological distress. Reports of racial discrimination were associated with red blood cell oxidative stress (Szanton et al., 2011). Oxidative stress involves free radicals (which are molecules that, having a single unpaired electron in their outer shell, are highly chemically reactive since they seek to steal an electron from neighbouring molecules) damaging DNA and other cellular components. While African Americans clearly suffer worse health outcomes than Caucasians, the same appears not to be true of persons of Hispanic heritage, an effect at least partly attributable to health behaviour differences such as alcohol consumption and cigarette smoking (Pérez-Stable, Marín, & Marín, 1994).

Contributors to Stress: The Person

Jobs, life events, caregiving, and socio-economic status are all examples of situations or circumstances causing stress. Another approach is to identify the people who, across a wide range of circumstances, are more prone, or vulnerable, to stress. The notion of stressful people has a long history, going back at least to Alexander (1939), who, appropriately in the first issue of *Psychosomatic Medicine*, suggested that people who channel their hostile anger inward activate the autonomic nervous system, and are therefore more likely to develop hypertension. The stress-prone personality reached its apotheosis, in popular fame, if not research support, in Friedman and Rosenman's (1959) notion of a Type A personality (see also Chapter 9). Irvine, Garner, Craig, and Logan (1991) found a significantly higher prevalence of Type A in persons with hypertension than in matched controls, but, going back to Alexander's notion, also found that hostility seemed to be the key factor, rather than the more general Type A pattern, and more recently attention has moved to that dimension (Barefoot, Dodge, Peterson, Dahlstrom, & Williams, 1989; Williams & Barefoot, 1988). There is some debate about just what aspect of the general bundle of anger, hostility, and aggression is critical (Cook & Medley, 1954; Buss & Perry, 1992; Brummett, Maynard, Haney, Siegler, & Barefoot, 2000), with further distinctions such as anger-in versus anger-out used (Spielberger et al., 1985).

Another personality dimension that has received some attention is negative affectivity (NA), a trait that characterizes people prone to negative emotions such as anger, fear, disgust, contempt, and the like. This is related to other constructs such as neuroticism, having to do with anxiety, worry, envy, and such. There seems little doubt that this is associated with reports of poor health, but whether its action is on the reporting or on the health itself is harder to assess. There is some evidence for each, with Eysenck (1991) finding higher death rates (an outcome not so biased by self-report) in those high in NA, and others suggesting that NA can confound reporting (McCrae, 1990).

Contributors to Stress: The Interaction of Person and Situation

In addition to the investigations of the types of situations likely to be stressful and the sorts of people likely to experience stress, there have been studies of the interaction between person and situation to identify the sorts of situations that produce health-damaging stress in particular sorts of people. For example, an Effort-Distress Model (Frankenhauser, 1983) suggests that distress depends not only on effortful situations, but also on the individual seeing events as excessive or feeling out of control. Another model (Dressier, 1990; 1991) has suggested that it is not being poor that is stressful, but rather living beyond one's means—that is, the stressfulness of SES is a combination of available resources and the ways individuals use them.

Another interaction showing that stress depends on the particulars of the person and the situation emerges in work with New York City traffic enforcement agents (TEAs) (Brondolo et al., 2009). In general, most people are in favour of the existence and even enforcement of parking regulations, but nobody is pleased to be ticketed, and the TEA's days are filled with aggressive and hostile encounters. TEAs wore ambulatory blood pressure monitors, and their activities were tracked, so that it was possible to determine whether certain sorts of people in those positions had elevated blood pressure, whether the job in general produced elevations, or whether there was an interaction between person and situation factors. The findings showed that people with the personality trait of high hostility indeed showed high levels of ambulatory blood pressure during the periods of hostile interactions with members of the public. In summary, consistent with the general trend in psychology of moving away from rigid divisions between personality and situational factors, and towards an understanding of the person-by-situation interaction, stress research has embraced the way that people's traits interact with, and create, the situations that can impact health.

Appraisal

The interactionist's view suggests that some stressors are too much for some individuals and overwhelm their resources. Another way of expressing this view is that how people view life's events, rather than just what those events are, is likely to be critical. As Shakespeare suggested in *Hamlet* (Act II, scene ii, 250–251), "there is nothing either good or bad, but thinking makes it so." Going back to the example at the beginning of the chapter, if you don't care about your grade in the class, then you probably won't find a surprise exam very stressful. This process of determining the stressfulness of a situation is known as appraisal.

One of the early, and still most influential, theorists on the role of appraisal is Richard Lazarus. In his early writings on the issue (1966), he illustrated the role of appraisal with the example of his family staying in Japan, in a wooden house in a district known for its high risk of fires, and listening at night to the wail, he thought, of nearby fire trucks. The simple discovery, after a few stressful days, that in fact he was near a hospital and was hearing the arriving ambulances transformed the meaning of same stimuli into something no longer considered a threat.

Lazarus's discovery of the nature of the sirens illustrates the concept of **primary appraisal**, which involves a determination of the magnitude and nature of the threat that the situation presents (Lazarus & Folkman, 1984). Primary appraisal is then followed by **secondary appraisal**, a determination of the resources available to deal with that threat. In his case, that appraisal suggested there was no threat, and so a secondary appraisal was not necessary. When resources are judged to be adequate, the situation can be seen as a challenge, and when inadequate, as a threat. These judgements have been shown to have changed the physiological response (Tomaka, Blascovich, Kelsey, & Leitten, 1993). Reappraising electric shocks as interesting new sensations, for example, leads to reductions in physiological response (Holmes & Houston, 1974).

PHOTO 5.5 | Richard Lazarus (1922–2002) of the University of California, Berkeley.

With the permission of Joseph Campos.

Coping

Problem- vs Emotion-Focused Coping

Just as everyone experiences stress, everyone employs different strategies to cope with that stress. While stress itself tends to spring from primary appraisal, the coping process is focused around secondary appraisal, or an assessment of one's resources available for meeting stressful demands. These resources and the coping strategies that utilize them generally fall into two categories: **problem-focused coping** and **emotion-focused coping**. In problem-focused coping, one copes with stress by directly addressing the demands of the situation, such as borrowing money to pay an unexpected bill. In emotion-focused coping, one copes with stress by addressing the emotions that come with stressful situations, such as turning to friends for encouragement and support (Obrist, 1981).

Some evidence suggests that problem-focused coping for health problems is associated with better health outcomes. There is, of course, a problem with assuming this is causal rather than reflecting a correlation without causality; it could be that people who use problem-focused coping are those who can take specific actions for their health, while those turning to emotion-focused coping may be people who have fewer medical options, and can only learn to deal with the emotions that come from being ill. Really, one type of coping is not necessarily better than the other; when facing a serious illness, for example, it is likely that an individual will have to engage in both problem-focused coping, such as seeking treatment options, and emotion-focused coping, such as learning to deal with uncertainty. The most appropriate coping response will depend on the situation, and most situations will call for some combination. In fact, Folkman and Lazarus (1980) have suggested that the most effective coping strategy is a flexible one—that is, being able to switch coping strategies based on the demands of the situation. One type of coping, however, sometimes classified as a type of emotional coping, appears to be less effective than the others: **avoidant coping**. Rather than dealing with the situation or emotions about the stressor, the goal of avoidant coping is to ignore the problem and its resulting emotions. This type of coping is quite robustly shown to lead to worse physical and mental health outcomes (Holahan & Moos, 1986), and is often associated with substance abuse disorders. This emphasizes that, while there is not necessarily one right way to deal with a stressor, avoidance is often a maladaptive strategy.

Coping strategies can be further differentiated. Coping can be assessed in various ways. Much research on coping has involved the Ways of Coping Scale, a 66-item measure developed by Folkman and colleagues (1986). The scale identifies distinct coping strategies within the categories mentioned above (problem-focused, emotion-focused, and avoidant). Data from couples who completed the Ways of Coping measure to describe their response to a particular recent stressor were used to identify eight distinct coping strategies:

1. confrontative coping (e.g., "I tried to get the person responsible to change his or her mind");
2. distancing (e.g., "I went on as if nothing had happened");
3. self-controlling (e.g., "I tried not to act too hastily or follow my first hunch");
4. seeking social support (e.g., "I talked to someone about how I was feeling");
5. accepting responsibility (e.g., "I realized I brought the problem on myself");
6. escape-avoidance (e.g., "I slept more than usual");
7. planful problem-solving (e.g., "I made a plan of action and followed it");
8. positive reappraisal (e.g., "I changed something about myself").

Other measures of coping have included more specific categories, such as turning to religion or substance abuse (Carver, Scheier, & Weintraub, 1989). Measures such as the Ways of Coping Scale can be used to examine how coping changes over time, within or across stressful events (Stone & Neale, 1984). Clearly, coping is a complex, dynamic process. In the pages that follow, we will explore just a few of these specific coping strategies and their interactions with mental and physical health.

TABLE 5.2 | Types of Social Support

Type of Support	Description	Examples
Emotional	Providing empathy, sympathy, and reassurance	Assuring a friend that you love and care about him or her; sharing a time you went through something similar
Instrumental	Providing tangible goods and services	Loaning someone money to pay a bill; giving someone a ride to the physician's office
Informational	Providing useful information pertinent to the stressful situation	Telling someone about a newly approved drug for her/his health problem; directing someone to government services she/he qualifies for
Appraisal	Providing feedback about someone's response to a stressor	Reassuring someone that she/he performed well while being evaluated at work; telling a friend that his or her response to an angry co-worker was appropriate

Social Support

One of the most common ways of coping with stress—whether everyday hassles like school or work deadlines, or significant stressors like loss of a job or a death of a loved one—is to turn to friends and family for support. **Social support** has many forms, but it can generally be described as a social network in which others care about one's well-being and provide help and assistance. This help is generally divided into four categories (Table 5.2): **emotional support**, such as providing encouragement and empathy; **instrumental support**, which refers to providing tangible goods and services, like loaning someone money or offering them a ride; **informational support**, in which one provides valuable information relevant to addressing the situation; and **appraisal support**, or helping someone identify a stressor and potential coping options (Wills, 1990). It turns out that our inclination to seek social support during stress is a good one, as support is one of the most effective ways of dealing with stress—not just emotionally, but also physiologically. However, determining who will seek social support and the type of benefits they will receive from it is complicated. There are several theories about when and how social support can help us deal with stress. Some of these theories are summarized below.

Main Effects vs Buffering

Is social support only important during severe stress? Certainly not—we enjoy having supportive friends and family whether or not we are facing a stressor. But is social support *more* important during stress? It might be. These two perspectives (i.e., main effects vs buffering) represent two different prevailing theories about social support and health: that social support has a main effect on health, and that social support buffers—or protects us from—the negative effects that stress has on our health (Cohen & Wills, 1985). It is important to remember that these are not duelling or mutually exclusive perspectives. Rather, both can be true, and there is scientific data supporting both models.

The **main effects model** suggests that social support is generally beneficial to health and well-being, whether we are carefree or stress-ridden. This has been shown for myriad measures of health; people with more social support tend to have lower blood pressure, are less likely to suffer from heart disease, have stronger immune systems, and live longer (Uchino, Cacioppo, & Kiecolt-Glaser, 1996). In viral challenge studies, Cohen and colleagues (1997) found that when people were exposed to a rhinovirus (the cause of the common cold), they were less likely to get sick if they had good social support back home.

More compelling evidence for the main effects model is shown in studies on marriage and health. Marriage, it turns out, is robustly health-protective: married people live longer and generally get sick less than single people do, one reason being that they have a constant source of social support (Kiecolt-Glaser & Newton, 2001). Of course, it is important to remember that these studies are not randomized trials, so we cannot assume that having better social support actually *causes* better health. It could be that people who are healthy are more easily able to make friends and interact with people, and that people who are chronically ill are kept from participating in social activities. While it may not be possible to randomly assign people to strong or weak social circles, some of these complications can be addressed by conducting prospective studies in which people who are healthy at baseline are followed for many years to see if they develop health problems. Such prospective studies show that among initially healthy people, those with better social support at baseline are less likely to develop health problems (e.g., heart disease) and tend to live longer (Hemingway & Marmot, 1999). While this is not definitive proof of a causal effect, it does suggest that social support may play a protective role.

The buffering model suggests that one of the main ways that social support leads to better health is by reducing stress and, therefore, reducing the negative effects of stress on one's health (Cohen & Wills, 1985). This model has received growing support in recent years. While marriage protects against getting sick in the first place, it also appears to be particularly important when facing a health crisis: married people are more likely to survive a heart attack, more likely to recover from cancer, and less likely to relapse after remission (Chandra, Szklo, Goldberg, & Tonascia, 1983; Goodwin, Hunt, Key, & Samet, 1987). Similar results have been found in prospective studies. In a large prospective study of men in Sweden, Rosengren, Orth-Gomer, Wedel, and Wilhelmsen (1993) found that those who experienced significant stressful events during the seven-year study were more than three times more likely to die (10.9 per cent) than those who had not (3.3 per cent). However, when the authors divided participants into those with low and high emotional support, they found that this increased risk of mortality associated with stress was only found in those with low emotional support. This suggests that those with high social support were somehow protected from the physiological consequences of stress. Again, this study did not involve random assignments so we cannot make causal claims about support being protective.

Some studies on the **buffering hypothesis** have employed an experimental approach because support only needs to be observed during a stressor in order to test the model (rather than throughout daily life, as is the case with tests of the main effects model). Using laboratory studies, researchers evaluated physiological responses to stress, such as changes in blood pressure, when people do and do not have supportive others present. Participants in one study (Glynn, Christenfeld, & Gerin, 1999) were asked to do something many people find particularly stressful: give a speech in front of an evaluative audience. For a random sample of these participants, one of the audience members was a confederate (working for the experimenter) who provided supportive feedback by using body language that might suggest the participant was doing a good job, such as nodding and smiling. The researchers found that those who received this feedback during the speech had lower blood pressure than those who did not receive supportive feedback, suggesting that support during the stressor made the experience not quite as stressful. Short-term increases in blood pressure are not likely to have important effects on health, but over time they can add up and increase risk of heart disease and other health problems (McEwen, 1998). The notion of "allostatic load" captures the idea that not just the magnitude of the elevation but also the duration and frequency of the blood pressure response will contribute to disease outcomes. Having support throughout a chronic stressor, then, could be important for health.

Important health outcomes have been observed with social support during stressors outside the laboratory. Kulik and Mahler (1987) examined the effects of social support in an especially stressful situation: awaiting major surgery. These researchers found that coronary bypass patients whose pre-operative roommate was a patient who had already had surgery had better recovery and returned home from the hospital sooner than those whose roommates had not yet had surgery. In this case, social support was not only a source of encouragement, but also a source of valuable information on what to expect. This study represents a particularly useful real-world example because roommates in hospitals are essentially assigned at random. Thus, while the authors did not plan to conduct a randomized controlled trial, they were able to observe the effects of random assignment in the real world.

Social support, then, appears to be an especially important resource during stressful times. This is one of the most robust findings (across laboratory studies and real-world evidence) in health psychology research.

The Great Gender Divide

People do not use social support equally when they experience stress. Although not all sex and gender stereotypes are true, this one generally is: during stressful times, women are much more likely than men to turn to friends and family for support. In fact, it may be that this is the main difference in the way men and women face stress (Taylor, Klein, Gruenewald, Gurung, & Taylor, 2003). This disparity is seen for different types of support and different types of stress. Given the same physiological symptoms, men are less likely than women to see a physician (Green & Pope, 1999), and men facing personal life stressors are less likely than women to turn to support networks for help (Padesky & Hammen, 1981). This does not mean that men do not benefit from social support—quite the opposite. As mentioned earlier, marriage appears to have great benefits for health, yet these benefits are not distributed equally; men experience more health benefits from marriage than women do (Kiecolt-Glaser & Newton, 2001). This could be for a variety of reasons. The important point is that although men do seem to benefit from support, they do not seek it out the way that women do.

This gender difference is so pronounced that some researchers believe that women's physiological stress response should be classified differently from that of men. Taylor and colleagues (2000) have argued that the typical fight-or-flight response may actually be a more appropriate description of men's response to stress, and that women's much more social response could more accurately be classified as **tend-and-befriend**. This captures the two social responses that women exhibit when experiencing stress: social bonding and caring for children. According to Taylor and colleagues, this social response to stress is not simply socially learned but has an evolutionary basis. In species where females are physically smaller and weaker, relying on a group for protection may be a better survival strategy than fighting or running away. Fight-or-flight may also be less feasible for females who are pregnant or have young children. Reproductive roles for males and females are such that males can have almost unlimited offspring, whereas reproduction for females is much more finite, making protection of offspring a greater priority for females. Tending and befriending, then, may be the best ways for females to survive and pass on their genes.

The tend-and-befriend hypothesis does not suggest that women do not have a sympathetic fight-or-flight response to stress—of course a woman's heart, like a man's, pounds when she is scared. Central to the tend-and-befriend hypothesis is the idea that women may have a modified stress response due to the hormone oxytocin. Research with oxytocin is still limited, but it appears to encourage affiliation and caregiving. While both men and women secrete oxytocin during stress, oxytocin may affect women more because its effects are modulated by estrogen and suppressed by androgens.

Women have especially elevated levels of oxytocin when pregnant and nursing; thus, if oxytocin suppresses the fight-or-flight response, this urge would be especially blunted when women have young offspring.

The tend-and-befriend viewpoint is not universally accepted (Geary & Flinn, 2000). While it is difficult to prove any evolutionary hypothesis, there is some evidence for the tend-and-befriend effect. As part of a study, researchers interviewed children about their parents' behaviours after work and found that the days that children reported the most nurturing from their mothers were the days that women reported the most stress at work. Fathers' stressful days, however, aligned with days children reported their fathers being distant and isolating themselves (Repetti & Wood, 1997). In rodents, group housing acts as a stressor for males but is calming for females. This affiliative response may be stronger for lactating mothers with high oxytocin levels. However, nursing mothers can also become especially aggressive and territorial. There is still a good deal of research to be done on oxytocin and the stress response in women.

A large study of Canadians explored gender differences in the use of social support and the severity and duration of depression (Wareham, Fowler, & Pike, 2007). Positive social interactions were found to be beneficial for both sexes, but men who used more emotional/informational support actually did worse. It may be that men, with less of this sort of support available in reserve, were harmed by using up so much of it.

Some social interactions are stressful for some people and calming for others, which emphasizes an important aspect of social support: the right type of support must be offered in order to be effective in reducing stress. Sometimes, as discussed below, social interactions can actually create more stress than they eliminate.

Social Stress

Are social interactions always good for our health? Certainly everyone can think of some social interactions that have increased their blood pressure rather than decreased it. Being part of social networks is generally good for health, but it can also be stressful when social interactions become negative. Looking at measures of life events, one can see that many major ones are social, such as divorce. Not surprisingly, people who go through major social stressors like divorce report more health problems than people with stable, happy social structures.

Social networks can actually become a liability to health when they do not provide the support that is needed or expected. Kulik and Mahler (1989), in their study of male coronary bypass patients, examined recovery time in relation to how often the patients' wives visited them in the hospital. They found that those who recovered fastest and went home earliest, not surprisingly, were the ones whose wives visited most often. The surprising finding, however, was that the group slowest to recover was not single men, but married men whose wives visited rarely or never. In this case it appeared that having an unsupportive spouse was actually worse for health than having no spouse at all. This effect of spousal support is so strong that one study showed that marital quality predicted the progression of heart disease in heart failure patients just as accurately as objectively measured physiological risk factors (Coyne et al., 2001).

Just like with social support, not everyone responds to social conflict equally, and in this case the division is again drawn along gender lines. Women generally report more distress over social conflict than men, which is not surprising because women appear to rely more on social networks than men do. However, there is one large exception to this trend: while men receive more health benefits from marriage, they appear to suffer just as many health consequences from divorce as women (Umberson, 1987). One suggested explanation for this disparity is that women tend to have wide, complex social networks, and are often able to list multiple people as close friends and confidants. Men, on the other hand, often list many friends and acquaintances but only one close friend with whom they can discuss their problems: their wives. Thus, when men get married they receive a major boost to their social resources, but when they get divorced they may lose it all at once (Gerstel, Riessman, & Rosenfield, 1985).

People going through significant stressors may also report negative effects of support if they get the *wrong type* of support. People going through treatment for cancer, for example, generally benefit from social support, but report that receiving informational support and treatment suggestions from friends and family can actually be more distressing than helpful, and that they would rather receive such information only from their physicians (Arora, Rutten, Gustafson, Moser, & Hawkins, 2007).

Other Coping Strategies

Emotional Disclosure

While many benefits are gained from discussing stressful events with others, it appears that there may be some benefits in simply "discussing" a problem with *oneself*. For several decades, James Pennebaker and colleagues have researched the effects of emotional self-disclosure by having participants write about stressful experiences

IN FOCUS

Support Groups

Turning to support groups to deal with stressful experiences is an increasingly popular coping option, and it seems these days there is a support group for nearly every type of major stressor: serious physical illness, mental disorders, substance abuse, divorce, single parenting, and so on. By gathering and talking with others who face the same challenges, people can empathize with others who know the stressful experience first-hand and can also glean useful information on overcoming challenges. Whether support groups are actually beneficial for physical and mental health, however, is a matter of some debate. Like with many things, the answer is "it depends." In one study of stage 1 breast cancer, women were assigned to an education group or peer discussion group for eight weeks. The researchers found that those in the education group experienced sustained improvements in physiological and psychological functioning while those in the peer discussion group showed no benefits and experienced more negative affect than those in the control group (Helgeson, Cohen, Schulz, & Yasko, 2000). Conversely, another study showed that women with metastatic breast cancer benefited greatly from a support group (Spiegel, Bloom, & Yalom, 1981), and similar results were obtained in a

PHOTO 5.6 | Many people who suffer from stress attend support groups.

study of HIV+ men with depression (Kelly et al., 1993). Overall, research suggests that for those with less serious conditions and/or who already have sufficient support at home, support groups may not be useful and may lead them to focus on the problem rather than coping with it. For others who do not have sufficient support at home and/or who have more serious, potentially terminal conditions, support groups may be a valuable resource.

---

in a journal. In a seminal study with college freshmen, Pennebaker, Colder, and Sharp (1990) assigned students to write in a journal three times per week about either stressful experiences and feelings (such as the stress of leaving home and starting college) or trivial topics (such as the weather). Over the course of the study, those who wrote about stressors reported fewer visits to the student health centre than those who wrote about trivial topics, and they showed a slight trend in improvements in their grades from first semester to second semester. Whether this showed actual health improvements due to writing about stress is debatable, as fewer visits to the health centre do not necessarily imply that these people became ill less often. In addition, while the number of visits in the stress writing group differed from the visits taken by those in the trivial topics writing group, it did not actually differ from the number of visits taken by students who were not in the study. An effective intervention ought to be

not only better than the placebo, but also better than no treatment at all.

Other studies have since explored further the effects of emotional writing, and have led to mixed results. Pennebaker and colleagues have found that emotional writing may lead to enhanced immune function (Petrie, Booth, Pennebaker, Davison, & Thomas, 1995), fewer absences from work (Francis & Pennebaker, 1992), and enhanced liver functioning (Francis & Pennebaker, 1992), but not all studies have been consistently positive. However, people with chronic diseases benefit more consistently from emotional writing. Smyth and colleagues (1999) showed that patients with asthma and patients with arthritis demonstrated improvements in objective measures of functioning after regularly writing about traumatic experiences.

The question that arises from the writing and stress studies is *why* would emotional writing lead to psychological and physiological benefits? There is no clear answer, but according to Pennebaker and Seagal (1999), writing about traumatic events can help place these events in a meaningful narrative. Writing about an event could help someone find purpose in relation to the event, or to place it in the context of his or her life in a meaningful way. This is supported by an analysis of the content of these journal entries. Pennebaker and Seagal found that those who benefited most from the writing exercise were those who used the most cause-and-effect words—e.g., "because," "therefore"—which could indicate that these people were recognizing the causes and consequences of the stressors.

Exercise

One common approach to coping with stress is to head to the gym. Given the vast literature on the benefits of exercise and the popularity of this coping strategy, there is surprisingly little research on the effectiveness of exercise as a coping strategy. People who report frequent exercise also tend to report lower levels of stress (Penedo & Dahn,

2005), yet this again is only a correlation, and does not necessarily speak to the effects of exercise on stress.

Limited experimental studies suggest that exercise may be an effective way to cope with and reduce stress. One laboratory study showed that participants who were physically active following an emotional stressor (giving a speech in front of an audience) had greater blood pressure reactivity while exercising than controls who sat quietly (Figure 5.1). When they stopped exercising, however, they returned to baseline blood pressure levels more quickly than controls—that is, the exercise seemed to help them get over the stress faster (Chafin, Christenfeld, & Gerin, 2008). It is not clear whether this is purely a physiological effect, or whether stress actually is lowered by exercise. Randomized controlled trials have also generally shown that those assigned to exercise conditions report less stress by the end of the study than those in control conditions (Penedo & Dahn, 2005).

It is unclear what type of exercise is most beneficial. Norris, Carroll, and Cochrane (1992) found that only high-intensity aerobic exercise was effective in reducing

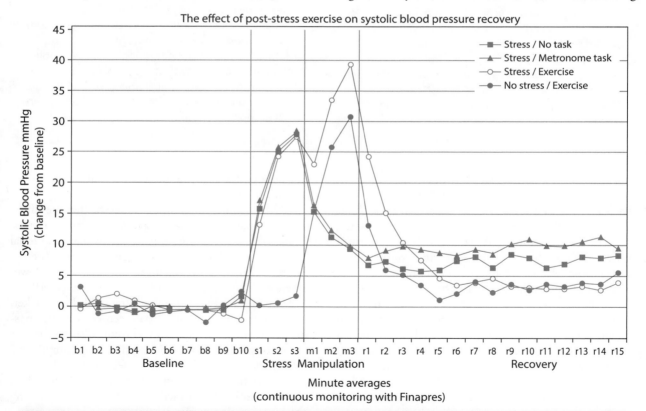

FIGURE 5.1 | Average systolic blood pressure (SBP) change from baseline score (per minute) across the experimental session.

Source: Chafin, Christenfeld, & Gerin (2008).

stress in adolescents. Others, however, have found that more mindful forms of exercise, such as yoga and Tai Chi, are effective in reducing depression and anxiety and increasing positive affect (Schell, Allolio, & Schonecke, 1994; Sandlund & Norlander, 2000). Women undergoing radiation therapy for breast cancer and who were randomly assigned to an integrated yoga therapy not only reported reduced stress, anxiety, and depression, but also showed slightly less damage to their DNA than controls following radiation (Banerjee et al., 2007). In summary, evidence supports exercise as an effective coping strategy but it remains unclear how much or what type is needed to prevent or reduce stress, or how and why exercise reduces stress. It could be that planned, purposeful activity in which one accomplishes goals is generally beneficial for mental health. The effects may also be physiological. As stress engages the sympathetic nervous system, using the resulting increased energy could help initiate recovery to baseline. This could also be achieved by actively engaging the parasympathetic nervous system through yoga, Tai Chi, or other mindful, breathing-focused exercises.

Stress and Mental Health

As excessive stress is generally a negative psychological experience, it is not surprising that it is also a significant factor in many psychological disorders. Extreme stress is a major risk factor for depression and, not surprisingly, anxiety disorders (Tennant, 2001; Cutrona et al., 2005). Post-traumatic stress disorder (PTSD) represents an extreme example of the connection between stress and mental health (American Psychiatric Association, 2013, pp. 271–280). Furthermore, this disorder is characterized by intrusive thoughts, often even when sleeping, of the traumatic event, and this rumination, whether of war, assault, abuse, or other such acute trauma, extends the duration of the stressor and multiplies its impact.

Of course, feeling anxiety after losing a job or being depressed following the death of a loved one is not unusual and not necessarily a sign of psychopathology or dysfunction. As with stress in general, whether people experience anxiety or depression is only partly influenced by the situations in which they find themselves, and largely by the way they cope with stressful events. In fact, a key component of mood and anxiety disorders is fixating and dwelling on events that might be considered minor—in other words, ruminating. Nolen-Hoeksema (2000) found that trait rumination, or one's usual tendency to ruminate, was predictive of future anxiety and depression, even in people who had not been depressed before. In depressed individuals, ruminating seems to make depression even worse, and learning not to ruminate can actually ameliorate depression (Larsen & Christenfeld, 2009).

This overlap between rumination and anxiety is significant even down to the molecular level: it turns out that neurotransmitters that influence mood, such as serotonin, are also important for shifting and altering thinking patterns (Clarke, Dalley, Crofts, Robbins, & Roberts, 2004). This chronic ruminating and resulting activation of the stress response could partially explain why people with anxiety and mood disorders are at two to three times greater risk for stress-related diseases like cardiovascular disease (Larsen & Christenfeld, 2009). This again emphasizes the interplay of situations and personal characteristics in determining how stress will affect individuals. While stressors are of course significant, the appraisal and coping processes are just as significant, if not more so.

Stress Management

As stress is a ubiquitous feature of modern life, researchers have explored effective strategies for stress management. Such strategies vary in effectiveness and range from behavioural approaches to medication management. One popular behavioural approach is **cognitive behavioural therapy (CBT)**, a form of therapy focused on changing cognitions and beliefs in order to change behaviour and emotions (Ellis, 1962). As discussed elsewhere in this book (see Chapter 6), CBT is one of the most popular forms of therapy for stress, depression, and other mood and anxiety disorders, and research shows that this intervention, in which people learn to reinterpret stressful situations and inoculate themselves to stress, is generally an effective approach to stress management (Bryant, Harvey, Dang, Sackville, & Basten, 1998; Butler, Chapman, Forman, & Beck, 2006; Saunders, Driskell, Johnston, & Salas, 1996).

Biofeedback, relaxation, and mindfulness are part of a set of strategies, largely inspired by Eastern practices and Buddhism, for dealing with stress. Such strategies involve taking some control over one's own stress responses, both physical and mental. These therapeutic approaches are based on the notion, discussed earlier, that stress responses, while perhaps useful in the face of acute physical threats, may quickly become maladaptive. Biofeedback techniques allow people to monitor, often with the use of devices, their physiological responses, such as heart rate, and so come to have more control over those bodily systems. Relaxation interventions can involve a variety of other techniques to promote calmness, including music, meditation, massage, and the like. While not studied to the degree of CBT, relaxation techniques have been found to be effective in reducing stress (Jacobs, 2001). Mindfulness aims to reduce anxiety about future events and rumination about past ones by having people more focused on their experiences in the moment, and this has also been shown to be effective in reducing anxiety and stress (Kabat-Zinn et al., 1992; Jain et al., 2007).

Pharmacological treatments for stress are widely— and some would say sometimes inappropriately—used. A class of drug called benzodiazapines is often prescribed for people experiencing extreme stress and anxiety. Even among people who have never taken these drugs, their common names are quite familiar, the most popular being Xanax and Valium. These drugs are typically taken only on a short-term basis to increase functioning and improve sleep. Common antidepressants, usually selective serotonin reuptake inhibitors (SSRIs) such as Prozac and Paxil, might be prescribed for longer-term stress and anxiety. Much less common in the treatment of short-term stress is the use of beta-blockers, a class of drugs typically used to treat hypertension. Because these drugs reduce heart rate, they have been used experimentally to treat performance anxiety in actors and musicians. The effectiveness of beta-blockers in treating performance anxiety is debatable; they appear effective in addressing physiological manifestations of anxiety, such as shaking, but are less effective in treating cognitive and emotional aspects of stress (Kenny, 2006). While pharmacological treatments are widely prescribed in treating stress and anxiety, people taking these medications are often encouraged to complement them with behavioural approaches.

Future Directions

While most are convinced that stress impacts health, and that techniques that reduce stress—its frequency, intensity, and duration—are thereby likely to promote health, central questions about the connection remain unanswered and are the focus of much investigation. One critical question relates to the mechanism by which acute responses are translated into chronic disease. Also, while heart disease has been a main focus of stress researchers, stress has a broad impact, suggesting that the focus on the stress–disease link is broadening. For example, the immune system is involved, with

⊞ IN PRACTICE

The Support Group: Stress Welcomes Company

Mary's life, like most, had a mix of challenges and worries. She had just been made regional manager at work, a promotion she had long sought. But with cutbacks by headquarters, the staff she inherited was smaller than what she felt was needed. The vice-president had pointed out that her predecessor had had the same staff, and Mary had thought, but managed not to say out loud, that the reason she now had the job was that her predecessor had predeceased her. There was an early performance evaluation coming up, and Mary had not yet figured out if that would be a chance for her to demonstrate her mastery of the job or instead a moment to let her doubters gloat. She did not feel that her aging father-in-law, to whom she tended almost every day, quite understood the burdens she was operating under, and taking care of him had not been balanced by any reduction in other duties. Mary had talked to her husband about the stress she felt with her new responsibilities, and he had offered a lot of appropriate advice, and even some

ideas she had implemented, but she still sometimes felt overwhelmed.

Mary thought she could keep it up, but then she started to get sick. Every virus going around seemed to find a home in her, and it was taking her longer and longer to evict them. One of her college roommates, listening to Mary talk, suggested that she might try a support group. She did—not with much enthusiasm as first, but she quickly found she treasured the weekly sessions. Other people were going through similar things—taking care of ailing or needy relatives while still working full-time—and just having them listen and understand without even offering advice was very soothing for her. She was as busy as before. In fact, the support group added another commitment each week. But she believed again that she could master the various challenges, and even new tasks at work now were opportunities rather than oppressions. And, she noted to herself in the supermarket checkout line, she had not needed to buy Kleenex.

inflammatory responses being connected to a wide range of outcomes. A better understanding of this link would likely shed light on what responses are most likely to be damaging, and whether interventions should focus, for example, on limiting exposure to stressors or on enhancing the speed of recovery from stress.

Various societal trends also make some types of stress research especially important. Among these research areas is work on caretaker stress. Moreover, worth additional investigation is the role of modern social networking in stress reduction, with relationships increasingly electronically mediated.

SUMMARY

Human stress can be broadly understood as resulting from some event that upsets the equilibrium of the system. Moreover, such perturbations are thought to produce long-term damage and adverse health outcomes. This stress can come from aspects of the situation, from aspects of the person, and from the interaction of the two. Job stress has been studied extensively, and most models suggest that it results from the interplay of factors such as a high workload and low autonomy or low reward. Other situational sources of stress include caregiving roles, as well as situations produced by one's position in society (e.g., as a woman, a member of a minority group, having low SES). Looking at aspects of the person, it seems that the sorts of people who are predisposed to stress are those who are prone to hostility and negative affectivity. Such people will find themselves in more stress-provoking situations and respond to them more negatively. The interactionist view is that certain people, those high in hostility, will be prone to stress under certain situations, such as negative interpersonal encounters.

While some efforts to define stress have relied on objective factors, most views recognize that the subjective appraisal of the situation is critical. That is, one must determine whether the situation represents a threat, and then whether one has sufficient resources to cope with that threat. Various external resources can contribute to people's ability to cope, and social support is among the most studied of these. People with more extensive networks enjoy better health, and interventions that provide social support have been shown to reduce blood pressure and promote well-being. Some findings regarding gender differences in the seeking of social support are consistent with women using a different evolutionary strategy when dealing with stress that includes more affiliative responses. Other strategies that may enhance coping include emotional disclosure, with some evidence that expressing one's thoughts on past events can promote health. Similarly, in enhancing recovery after the event has passed, vigorous physical exercise has been shown to be beneficial.

Critical Thought Questions

1. In what way are positive events likely to be as stressful as negative ones, and in what ways might they be expected to cause less damage to long-term health?
2. When should friends help out, and when might it be better to be alone?

3. How readily can stress be dealt with simply by changing the way one thinks about the situation?

Recommended Reading

Sapolsky, R.M. (2004). *Why zebras don't get ulcers: The acclaimed guide to stress, stress related diseases, and coping* (3rd rev. ed.). New York: W.H. Freeman.

Lazarus, R.S., & Folkman, S. (1984). *Stress, appraisal and coping*. New York: Springer.

Health Anxiety and Other Psychological Responses to Bodily Symptoms

HEATHER D. HADJISTAVROPOULOS

Learning Objectives

In this chapter you will:

- Discover how thinking about and appraising physical signs and symptoms influences the way we feel and behave when we experience physical signs and symptoms.

- Learn about the common-sense model of illness representations and how this model can be used to understand how we appraise bodily signs and symptoms as either normal or threatening.

- Examine various influences (e.g., culture, personality, social relationships) on the way we appraise bodily symptoms as being either normal sensations or signs of illness.

- Gain knowledge of the prevalence and nature of health anxiety, which can result when people catastrophically appraise physical signs and symptoms as threatening to their health.

- Develop an understanding of the cognitive behavioural conceptualization of health anxiety and how this conceptualization is used to understand the development and maintenance of health anxiety.

- Learn how health psychologists commonly assess and treat health anxiety.

Introduction

In January 2012, Nick Cannon, actor, comedian, host of *America's Got Talent*, and husband of singer Mariah Carey, was hospitalized for kidney failure at the age of 31. In a YouTube documentary, Cannon shared that one day he was out enjoying time with his family, when he suddenly experienced his body swelling up, shortness of breath, and severe right-sided pain. He was subsequently diagnosed with a disease called lupus nephritis, which is an autoimmune inflammation of the kidney and a serious complication caused by systemic lupus erythematosus (also known as lupus). In patients diagnosed with lupus, the immune system cannot differentiate between harmful and healthy substances and therefore attacks healthy cells and tissues (de Zubiria Salgado & Herrera-Diaz, 2012). Lupus has an unpredictable course, with a wide variety of symptoms such as arthritis, fever, photosensitivity, cold fingers or toes, and mouth sores (Jimenez, Cervera, Font, & Ingelmo, 2003).

Cannon has documented his extensive medical treatment in a YouTube series called *NCredible Health Hustle*. The documentary includes his victories and the obstacles he faced while coping with his condition (Cannon, 2012a). While viewing the documentary, you observe Cannon responding to a life-threatening illness by constantly striving to return to his former state of health. He not only relies on his health-care providers, but takes an active role in his own care by exercising and changing his diet, and ultimately reducing some of his work commitments. Cannon's thoughts about his health condition evolve over time. At first, Cannon shared that he was "working on the condition" and feeling very "optimistic" (Cannon, 2012b). Over time, however, he described viewing his condition as "life-threatening" and "unexpected," and noted that he was having increasing thoughts about how "life is important and tomorrow definitely isn't promised." He later described doing all he can to "stay positive" (Cannon, 2012c).

Not all people respond to having a serious medical condition in the same way. Thoughts and behaviours vary widely. Some individuals may rely solely on formal medical care, while others may avoid such care at all costs. Some people are consumed with thoughts about the worst-case scenario, while others attempt to remain positive despite conflicting evidence. This chapter will help you understand diverse responses to bodily sensations, beginning with common reactions and then turning to less common, more anxious responses such as **health anxiety**.

© Allstar Picture Library/Alamy

PHOTO 6.1 | Nick Cannon, actor, comedian, host of *America's Got Talent*, and husband of singer Mariah Carey, was hospitalized for kidney failure at the age of 31.

Common-Sense Model of Illness Representation

The common-sense model of illness representation (CSM) (Leventhal, Meyer, & Nerenz, 1980) is a useful information-processing model for understanding how we respond to physical signs and symptoms with a cognitive appraisal, evaluating how threatening our physical signs and symptoms are. A *physical sign* refers to observable evidence of a physical change in our bodies. The edema experienced by Cannon is an example of a physical sign. In contrast to a physical sign, a *physical symptom* is something that is only experienced by us and cannot be directly observed by others. Pain is an example of a physical symptom. It cannot be observed directly; others must rely on our non-verbal or verbal reports (see Chapter 7). Surveys that examine the prevalence of physical signs and symptoms suggest that the vast majority of people experience at least one physical sign or symptom a day (e.g., Pennebaker, 1982). Ultimately, this means that there is considerable opportunity for us to appraise and respond to physical signs and symptoms we experience.

According to the CSM (Figure 6.1), after we notice physical sensations (stimuli), we form a "common-sense" or "lay" representation of these sensations in an attempt to determine the meaning of the physical sensations. We are, in essence, processing information and considering whether a health threat is (or is not) present. This mental representation is sometimes called a schema, belief, cognition, or perception. According to the CSM, this mental representation then influences how we cope with the physical sensations we experience. If we ultimately view the physical sensations as threatening, we will employ coping strategies in an attempt to manage the health threat. If we do not regard the physical sensations as threatening, however, no coping behaviours will be required. If implemented, coping behaviour is subsequently followed by a further appraisal process, in which we consider our success in coping with the physical sensations. This appraisal,

in turn, influences our representation of the physical sensations. In parallel to processing the meaning of physical sensations, we also simultaneously process our emotional response to the physical sensations. Central to the model is the interaction between our perceptions of physical sensations and our emotional response to the physical sensations. That is, how we view our physical sensations influences our emotions and our emotions influence our views of the physical sensations. How do you think this model applies to Cannon's experience? Can you see how his appraisals of illness influenced his emotions and behaviours and vice versa?

Dimensions of Illness Representations

Research on the CSM has revealed that we do not develop a single schema or representation of our health/illness, but instead that we conceptualize our health/illness along multiple dimensions. These dimensions include forming a representation of the identity, cause, consequences, timeline, and controllability of the physical signs and symptoms (Hagger & Orbell, 2003). **Identity** refers to how we label the signs and symptoms we experience (e.g., lupus, cancer, heart disease). Identity is often measured by asking individuals about their physical signs and symptoms (e.g., pain, breathlessness, fatigue). **Cause** refers to our beliefs about what brought on the signs and symptoms; we might consider

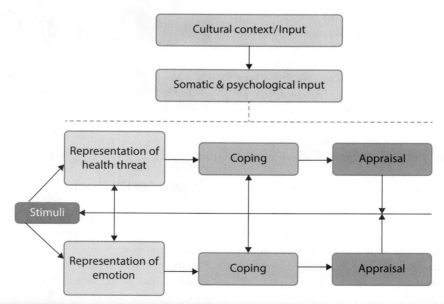

FIGURE 6.1 | The common-sense model of illness representation.

Source: Diefenbach & Leventhal (1996).

biological, emotional, environmental, or psychological causes. In terms of **consequences**, we also tend to think about the impact of the signs and symptoms on our everyday lives (e.g., self-care, household responsibilities, family, work, emotional well-being). **Timeline** refers to our beliefs about how long the signs and symptoms will last (e.g., acute versus chronic) and whether they will fluctuate or persist over time. Finally, **controllability** refers to our beliefs about whether we have control over our signs and symptoms and whether we believe treatment will be efficacious. These representations of our signs and symptoms are not static but change over time, especially in response to treatment (Fischer et al., 2010).

The Illness Perception Questionnaire was developed to measure these specific illness representations (Weinman, Petrie, Moss Morris, & Horne, 1996). A revised version of this measure, the Illness Perceptions Questionnaire-Revised (IPQ-R) (Moss-Morris et al., 2002) also assesses these constructs, but includes several other subscales. For instance, control is divided into two subscales, including *personal control* (belief that one can manage signs and symptoms) and *treatment control* (belief that treatment will be efficacious). The timeline construct is also divided into subscales measuring an *acute/chronic timeline* (a short-term or long-term problem) and a *cyclical timeline* (unpredictable and cyclical nature of illness). A further modification is that the questionnaire measures the emotional response to illness with two subscales, *emotional representations of illness* (feelings of depression, anger, worry, and anxiety in response to the illness) and *illness coherence* (how much the individual understands or comprehends the illness).

Relationship between Illness Representations and Coping Behaviour

In terms of coping, the CSM predicts that how we view our signs and symptoms determines how we cope (see Chapter 5 for a broader discussion of coping strategies). The model recognizes wide variability in the types of coping strategies we use, and how we view our signs and symptoms determines how we select a coping strategy. For example, with the advancement of the Internet, many people cope by seeking information about symptoms online (Baker, Wagner, Singer, & Bundorf, 2003). Alternatively, they may attempt to divert their attention and ignore their signs and symptoms. In other cases, people may try to change their beliefs about their signs and symptoms, viewing them as benign and non-threatening (Cameron & Jago, 2008). In contrast to those who attempt to cope with physical symptoms

on their own and avoid seeking medical care, some people seek health-care services for very minor medical symptoms (Shapiro, Ware, & Sherbourne, 1986). As many as 40 per cent of individuals seek care for minor medical symptoms that could have been managed without medical intervention (Shapiro et al., 1986).

There are multiple examples of how thoughts about our body influence how we cope with illness. Consider patients with diabetes. Those who hold negative beliefs about their ability to control their illness and negative perceptions about its course and consequences are less likely to attend medical appointments regularly (Lawson, Bundy, Lyne, & Harvey, 2004). Our views regarding illness not only predict whether we seek medical care, but they also predict whether we follow medical advice provided. For example, individuals with asthma who believe that asthma can be cured and/or controlled are more likely to adhere to medical recommendations, while those who believe that asthma has been caused by external factors are less likely to adhere to care recommendations (Jessop & Rutter, 2003). As another example, cardiac patients who perceive their health condition as having few consequences and who believe they have great personal control over their illness and that the treatment is ineffective are more likely to drop out of cardiac rehab programs compared to those who hold the opposite beliefs (Yohannes, Yalfani, Doherty, & Bundy, 2007).

Overall, there is considerable support for the association between how we view our signs and symptoms and our coping behaviour (Hagger & Orbell, 2003). In a meta-analysis of this research, it was found that those who perceive themselves as having many symptoms and view their symptoms as chronic and disabling are more likely to cope with symptoms by using avoidance (e.g., they deny that they have problems and avoid medical care) and emotional expression (Hagger & Orbell, 2003). On the other hand, those who view their signs and symptoms as controllable are more likely to cope by using problem-focused coping strategies (e.g., they use strategies to try and solve their medical problems, such as asking for medical help).

Illness Representations and Health Outcomes

How could our views of illness and how we cope with illness impact our emotional and physical health? Research evidence, in fact, suggests that certain illness representations are associated with improved emotional and physical well-being, while other illness representations are associated with emotional distress and poorer physical health. In terms of emotional well-being, viewing an illness as within our control is associated with greater psychological well-being and social functioning; in contrast, perceiving one's illness as having multiple symptoms and being chronic is associated with negative psychological well-being (Hagger & Orbell, 2003). These findings are evident across multiple medical conditions such as diabetes, epilepsy, and cardiac disease (Hagger & Orbell, 2003).

In terms of physical well-being, a similar pattern is found. The CSM suggests that our views of an illness determine our behaviours, which in turn impact our physical health. Supporting this idea, McSharry and colleagues (2011) conducted a meta-analytic study of patients with diabetes. They found that higher scores on identity, negative consequences, cyclical timeline, concern, and emotional representations and lower scores on personal control were positively associated with higher HbA1c in individuals with Type 2 diabetes. HbA1c is a measure of blood glucose or glycemic control, with higher scores suggesting that the individual is not following treatment recommendations and is at greater risk of diabetic complications (McSharry, Moss-Morris, & Kendrick, 2011).

Also supporting a relationship between illness representations and illness outcomes, Petrie et al. (2002) found that if patients altered their illness perceptions, they experienced improved health outcomes. More specifically, patients who suffered their first myocardial infarction (MI; heart attack) were assigned to usual care or to an intervention (led by nurses) designed to alter their perceptions about their MI (Petrie, Cameron, Ellis, Buick, & Weinman, 2002). The intervention resulted in patients being more likely to believe their heart condition could be controlled and less likely to believe that their heart condition would be chronic and cause serious consequences. In the intervention group, but not the control group, patients reported fewer angina symptoms and more often reported that they were better prepared for discharge. At three-month follow-up, they returned to work at a significantly faster rate than the usual care group. Overall, this is consistent with the view that thoughts influence behaviour, which ultimately influences health.

Determinants of Illness Representations

How do we develop our beliefs or views about our physical sensations? According to the CSM, we actively seek information to understand our physical sensations and base our mental representations on the physical sensations we are experiencing. These illness appraisals, however, are also influenced by other factors, such as our past experiences, cognitive heuristics (e.g., simple mental rules that help us form judgements and make decisions), social factors, and culture, as well as personality and mood.

Physical Stimuli

How we view our signs and symptoms is to some degree influenced by what we feel physically. Take, for example, a study of patients faced with end-stage renal disease. In this study, those who were undergoing dialysis (and thus experiencing many physical symptoms) and those who had a kidney transplant (and thus no longer experiencing significant symptoms) differed in how they perceived illness. Specifically, those who had dialysis (see Chapter 16) had stronger timeline beliefs, lower control beliefs, and stronger beliefs about disruptiveness of illness compared to those who had a kidney transplant (Griva, Jayasena, Davenport, Harrison, & Newman, 2009). In other words, beliefs about illness were shaped by the physical input the individuals experienced. This relationship between physical symptoms and beliefs is also evident in a recent study of patients with osteoarthritis (Bijsterbosch et al., 2009). In this study, investigators examined if illness perceptions changed over a six-year period in individuals diagnosed with osteoarthritis. Indeed, over time, as osteoarthritis worsened, people with osteoarthritis perceived their condition as more chronic and less controllable.

While physical sensations are important in shaping our beliefs, the CSM recognizes that appraisal of physical sensations is highly individualized and does not always correspond with physical input. As an example, women who have the most invasive breast cancer have been found to have a strong sense of control over their cure (Henselmans et al., 2010). What, then, are the other factors that influence how we interpret and respond to troubling physical sensations?

Personal Experiences

The CSM suggests that our beliefs about our physical signs and symptoms are influenced by our history with illness (Leventhal et al., 1980). Based on past experience with illness, we develop memories of illness that influence how we interpret and respond to our current physical signs and symptoms. To illustrate, children with a history of previous negative medical experiences demonstrated more distress during a throat culture examination than did children with previous positive or neutral medical experiences (Dahlquist et al., 1986). Knowledge of family history of illness can also be part of our illness history. Our illness history provides a context that colours how we interpret current somatic changes.

Heuristics

Diefenbach and Leventhal (1996) have suggested that in addition to our personal history, most of us have decision rules or heuristics that influence how we appraise signs and symptoms. One such rule is the *symmetry rule*, which refers to the fact that we tend to believe we are ill if we experience symptoms, and believe we are healthy if we do not experience symptoms. A further rule that influences how we appraise symptoms is the *stress–illness rule*. This holds that symptoms that develop in the context of stressful events are assumed to be part of stress rather than illness. In contrast, the *prevalence rule* refers to the fact that rare conditions are perceived as threatening, whereas common conditions are perceived as less serious. The *age–illness rule* refers to our tendency to believe that mild symptoms that develop gradually are a normal part of aging. In general, these rules are helpful, but they can also lead to errors. Consider, for example, the case of a man in his early sixties who gradually began to experience fatigue. Applying the age–illness rule, he ignored his fatigue and assumed it was associated with the natural aging process, when the fatigue was in fact a sign of coronary artery disease.

Social Influences

How we interpret and view physical sensations is also a function of our social environment. As one would expect, information that medical professionals communicate to us has a powerful influence on how we interpret and respond to physical signs and symptoms (Zolnierek & DiMatteo, 2009). That is, if we are told by a medical professional to be concerned about a sign or symptom, most of us will be concerned. Beyond medical professionals, family, friends, and others we interact with also influence how we interpret and respond to our signs and symptoms and how we cope with illness. A classic study demonstrates how others in our environment impact how we interpret our physical sensations (Craig & Weiss, 1971). In this study, all participants were exposed to experimentally induced

pain. Some participants, however, observed a confederate modelling low pain tolerance, while other participants observed a confederate modelling high pain tolerance. Exposure to the confederate displaying low pain tolerance led participants to report greater pain than when they observed confederates displaying high pain tolerance. This experimental study provides a great example of how social factors influence our views of physical sensations and also our behaviour.

Another example of how social variables influence how we respond to symptoms comes from a study conducted by Block, Kremer, and Gaylor (1980). These researchers examined pain levels reported by patients with chronic pain when they were in the presence of their spouse compared to when they were in the presence of a ward clerk. Chronic pain patients who described their spouse as highly supportive and always eager to help reported more pain when they were in the presence of their spouse than when they were in the presence of a ward clerk. Chronic pain patients who described their spouse as not always eager to help, however, reported lower pain when their spouse was present compared to the ward clerk.

At least three divergent approaches to how family and friends respond to patient illness have been described (Vilchinsky et al., 2011). One such approach is referred to as *active engagement*. This approach involves family and friends discussing illness with the patient, asking how he is or she is feeling, and attempting to assist the patient with

© Juanmonino/iStockphoto

PHOTO 6.2 | Spouses of chronic pain patients respond to their loved one's pain condition in varying ways.

constructive problem-solving activities. Another way in which family and friends influence illness perceptions is through *protective buffering*, which consists of withholding their concerns about the patient and denying being worried about the patient's health condition. A third approach is referred to as *overprotection*, which involves family and friends underestimating the patient's ability to cope and providing unnecessary and excessive assistance. These varying reactions to patients significantly influence how patients view and respond to illness. More specifically, when support involves active engagement compared to the other approaches, patients respond to illness with the less distress and greater self-efficacy (Vilchinsky et al., 2011).

Culture

Related to social influences, one's cultural background also influences how we interpret and respond to illness. The health beliefs of Caucasians, for instance, are quite different from those of other ethnic groups (Landrine & Klonoff, 1992). A study of critically ill patients who were in an intensive care unit for more than three days illustrates this difference (Ford, Zapka, Gebregziabher, Yang, & Sterba, 2010). In this study, African-American patients tended to perceive illness as less enduring than Caucasians did, and reported more confidence in treatment efficacy as well in their own personal control (Ford et al., 2010). They also tended to view illness as less serious, having less emotional impact, while simultaneously perceiving illness as less coherent. Another example of research showing cultural differences in illness beliefs comes from a study of inpatients with coronary artery disease; in this study, patients who identified themselves as South Asian reported having lower personal control over their illness compared to those who identified themselves as Caucasian (Grewal, Stewart, & Grace, 2010). They were also more likely to attribute their illness to worry and poor medical care in the past, and, compared to Caucasian patients, less likely to attribute illness to aging. Chapter 19 reviews further research on cross-cultural factors in health psychology.

Personality and Mood

Personality, in particular **neuroticism**, influences how we view physical symptoms. Neuroticism, also referred to as negative affectivity, is the tendency to experience negative emotions and emotional instability. Neuroticism is associated with a tendency to report somatic complaints (Charles, Gatz, Kato, & Pedersen, 2008). It appears that negative affectivity influences our attention to and interpretation of symptoms (Charles et al.,

2008). For example, women who scored higher on neuroticism were more likely to view their newly diagnosed and surgically treated breast cancer as not being under their control (Henselmans et al., 2010).

Depression, anxiety, and stress, which tend to be correlated with neuroticism, also have a significant impact on how we view and respond to signs and symptoms. For example, when daily mood is negative and stress is high, people tend to report increased pain, miss work more often, and seek out health care more frequently (Gil et al., 2004). Positive mood, on the other hand, has the opposite effect. Those who have a positive mood report lower pain and lower health-care use (Gil et al., 2004). Norman Cousins (1976) is widely known for providing a personal account or anecdotal evidence on how viewing comedy films assisted him in coping with pain and illness. Experimental studies also support the relationship between mood and appraisals of health. In a classic laboratory study, it was found that inducing a positive mood as compared to a negative mood by watching pre-selected movie clips resulted in more favourable perceptions of health (Croyle & Uretsky, 1987). These results serve to highlight that personality and mood influence how we perceive our health. It should also be acknowledged, however, that relationships are bi-directional and our physical health has a direct impact on our mood (Pollard & Schwartz, 2003).

Health Anxiety

Some people, when faced with physical signs and symptoms, become extremely overwhelmed and consequently report experiencing severe levels of health anxiety. Here, our focus on health anxiety emphasizes cognitive behavioural therapy for the treatment of health anxiety. Before proceeding, consider the case of Linda presented in the In Practice box.

Clinical Considerations

The case of Linda, described in the accompanying box, illustrates health anxiety. Health anxiety specifically refers to the experience of excessive anxiety about one's present or future health and is often based on a misinterpretation of signs and symptoms (Rachman, 2012). Health anxiety is recognized as a dimensional construct characterized by a lack of concern about one's health at one end of the continuum and excessive anxiety about health on the other (Ferguson, 2009). Transitory or fleeting health anxiety is a common experience in the

⊞ IN PRACTICE
The Fear of Illness

Linda is a self-employed 55-year-old single woman who works as a freelance journalist. She reported being extremely anxious about her health and concerned that she would develop lung cancer. Linda shared that the fear developed in 2005 after she heard that Peter Jennings, a TV reporter and anchorman, died from lung cancer. She noted that as a teenager and young adult she often smoked socially when out with friends. She also described growing up in a home where both her parents smoked. Linda indicated that after hearing about the death of Peter Jennings, she began to notice that she was short of breath when walking up stairs. She also began to notice an unexplained pain in her shoulder. Linda indicated that she subsequently spent several days on the Internet searching the potential meaning of her symptoms. After becoming alarmed by what she was reading, she spoke to her physician. He ordered a chest x-ray, which did not reveal any suspicious areas in her lungs. Linda initially found this reassuring, but later requested that her physician order a CT scan. Her physician complied with her request. Consistent with the x-ray, the CT scan showed no suspicious areas in Linda's lungs. She once again felt reassured, but only for a brief period of time. She later returned to her physician and requested an MRI. Although reluctant, the physician complied with Linda's request and ordered an MRI, which, similar to the other tests, did not reveal any suspicious areas in Linda's lungs.

Despite this reassurance, Linda found that she continued to be preoccupied with the idea that she had lung cancer or would develop lung cancer in the future. Linda reported that she began to keep a daily diary of her symptoms. She also reported spending about a half an hour on the Internet each day reading about lung cancer. Linda described feeling "immobilized" and "fatigued" by her worry, and as a result neglected her regular household chores as well as her work responsibilities. She further reported limiting her recreational activities and isolating herself from her family and friends.

general population. In this case, the fleeting health anxiety is suspected to be adaptive by motivating individuals to take necessary action to prevent the development of a medical condition or deterioration of health (Asmundson, Taylor, & Cox, 2001). Health anxiety is regarded as excessive when it is continuous, results in distress, and causes extreme behaviours designed to alleviate anxiety but that ultimately heighten anxiety and interfere with daily functioning. When health anxiety is extreme, it can be the subject of clinical attention. In the past, extreme health anxiety was referred to as **hypochondriasis**. This label is no longer used in the current edition of the *Diagnostic and Statistical Manual of Mental Disorders*, as it was considered unclear (American Psychiatric Association, 2013). Instead, those with extreme health anxiety are now diagnosed with either somatic symptom disorder or illness anxiety disorder. A diagnosis of somatic symptom disorder is given to those with one or more distressing somatic symptoms who also experience persistently high levels of anxiety about health. A diagnosis of illness anxiety disorder is given to those who are preoccupied with having or acquiring

a serious illness and who have a high level of health anxiety but do not have significant somatic symptoms. It is important to note that excessive health anxiety also exists among individuals who have a medical condition (Hadjistavropoulos et al., 2012). That is, even people diagnosed with a medical condition can become overly health anxious. In this case, health anxiety presents as a preoccupation with the medical condition that is substantially greater than typically experienced by other people with the same medical condition and is associated with increased distress and disability.

In terms of prevalence among medical patients, approximately 20 per cent have extreme health anxiety (Tyrer et al., 2011), with patients with neurological problems having greater health anxiety than other patient groups. In comparison, extreme health anxiety is found in about 7.7 per cent of the population (Noyes, Happel, & Yagla, 1999). Some argue that as you age and experience an increased number of medical conditions, you will become more health anxious. While this is a common assumption, no solid research evidence supports this (Barsky, Frank, Cleary, Wyshak,

© Cartoonstock/Mike Baldwin

© Mike Baldwin / Cornered

"No, you haven't missed much. Pretty well everyone called in sick."

PHOTO 6.3 | Hypochondriac convention: "everyone called in sick."

& Klerman, 1991). In fact, older adults who are healthy may be at decreased risk of health anxiety compared to older adults with medical problems or younger adults (Bourgault-Fagnou & Hadjistavropoulos, 2009).

Extreme health anxiety is associated with considerable emotional distress and increased disability (Looper & Kirmayer, 2001; Noyes et al., 1999), including higher rates of unemployment (Barsky, Wyshak, Klerman, & Latham, 1990). Extreme health anxiety also results in a substantial increase in medical care (Tomenson et al., 2012), which then increases the risk of unnecessary, invasive, potentially dangerous, and expensive medical procedures (Abramowitz & Braddock, 2008; Noyes et al., 1999). Adding to the severity of the condition, elevated health anxiety is associated with lifetime history of diagnoses of anxiety and depressive disorders (Faravelli et al., 1997; Noyes et al., 1999), and it is estimated that 50–70 per cent of patients diagnosed with extreme health anxiety do not recover.

Genetics

Limited research to date has examined the heritability of health anxiety, and what has been done in this area is largely inconclusive (Torgerson, 1986). On the other hand, a number of predisposing traits are suspected of increasing vulnerability to health anxiety, and these traits seem to have a genetic component. One such trait is anxiety sensitivity or the tendency to be fearful of anxiety-related sensations such as increased heart rate; this trait has been linked to health anxiety and also appears to be inherited to some degree (Stein, Jang, & Livesley, 1999). Similarly, somatization or the occurrence of reoccurring multiple somatic complaints also appears to have a genetic component and increases risk for health anxiety (Gillespie, Zhu, Heath, Hickie, & Martin, 2000). Finally, neuroticism or a tendency to experience negative affectivity and mood instability is also thought to increase vulnerability to health anxiety (Costa & Mccrae, 1985) and again seems to involve genetic predispositions (Birley et al., 2006).

Cognitive Behavioural Model of Health Anxiety

Beyond genetics, it is suspected that health anxiety results through a learning experience whereby people either directly or indirectly (e.g., someone the person knows or hears about) experience a distressing event (e.g., illness) that leads them to believe that their health is in danger (Salkovskis & Warwick, 1986). These experiences are thought to be responsible for the development of core cognitions and behaviours that consequently produce health anxiety. This is referred to as the cognitive behavioural model (see Figure 6.2). This model is commonly used to understand health anxiety. Similar to the common-sense model of illness representation, the cognitive behavioural model recognizes that thoughts significantly impact how people feel about and respond to physical sensations. The approach emphasizes, however, that the individual with health anxiety has developed dysfunctional thoughts based on past experience and that health anxiety arises when these dysfunctional thoughts are triggered. The thoughts about health can be triggered by internal physical sensations but also by external events, such as hearing about another person's illness. These thoughts in essence result in people being preoccupied with their health and misinterpreting innocuous or benign bodily sensations as more threatening than they actually are.

Several thoughts are believed to be central in the development of health anxiety, including holding beliefs that: (1) the feared disease is serious and catastrophic; (2) one is vulnerable to disease; (3) one is not capable of coping with the feared illness; and (4) inadequate medical resources are available to treat the illness. Indeed, the presence of these thoughts in individuals who are

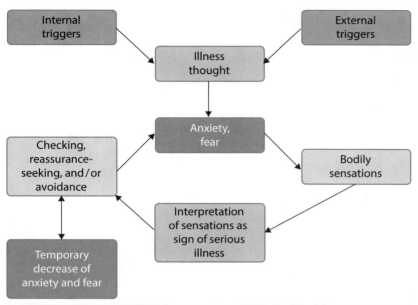

FIGURE 6.2 | Cognitive behavioural model of health anxiety.

Source: Adapted from Page 42 of Furer, Walker, & Stein (2007).

are health anxious engage in **safety behaviours** that, although designed to reduce threat and anxiety, in the longer term have the opposite effect. Safety behaviours can be quite variable. The classic behaviour associated with extreme health anxiety is repeated *information-seeking* or *reassurance-seeking* from medical professionals or family and friends. *Body monitoring*, which refers to monitoring one's physical sensations and appearance, is another form of safety behaviour. Other behaviours relevant to health anxiety include avoidance behaviours, such as avoiding situations that may provoke health anxiety (e.g., television shows, hospitals, people with illness).

The cognitive behavioural model posits that when health anxiety is triggered, the person who is anxious becomes vigilant and engages in these behaviours to reduce threat. A study by Abramowitz and Moore (2007) supports this notion. These researchers had participants expose themselves to personally significant health-related stimuli and found this provoked anxiety and resulted in individuals reporting urges to perform safety behaviours. The problem with safety behaviours is that, contrary to expectations among health-anxious individuals, they increase rather than decrease anxiety (Radomsky, Shafran, Coughtrey, & Rachman, 2010). For example, engaging in hygienic safety behaviours (e.g., using sanitized wipes) increases rather than decreases health anxiety scores (Olatunji, Etzel, Tomarken, Ciesielski, & Deacon, 2011). It seems that engaging in the behaviour reinforces the belief that there is danger and the individual should be fearful.

Cognitive Behavioural Therapy

Cognitive behavioural therapy has emerged in the past 20 years as the treatment of choice for health anxiety. CBT has the greatest empirical support and also has other attractive features, such as being patient-centred and collaborative in nature. CBT for health anxiety focuses on addressing thoughts and behaviours as described previously. A number of books describe this approach in considerable detail (Abramowitz & Braddock, 2008; Furer, Walker, & Stein, 2007; Owens & Antony, 2011; Taylor & Asmundson, 2004).

health anxious has been confirmed (Hadjistavropoulos et al., 2012). In addition to these thoughts, people with extreme health anxiety hold other general dysfunctional beliefs, such as the belief that *there must be an explanation for all aches, pains, and unusual sensations and that there is far more illness in the world than people realize* (Fulton, Marcus, & Merkey, 2011).

In addition to thoughts or beliefs, people with extreme health anxiety have several cognitive biases that make them vulnerable to anxiety. One such bias is a **confirmatory bias** whereby individuals with health anxiety tend to focus on information that confirms their fears and ignore information that disconfirms their fears (Warwick & Salkovskis, 1990). A second bias of relevance to health anxiety is referred to as *thought–action–fusion bias*, which is the tendency of anxious people to believe that when they think a negative thought the thought will come true (e.g., "If I think about cancer, I will develop cancer") (Shafran & Rachman, 2004). Also identified as relevant to health anxiety is *ex-consequentia reasoning*, which refers to the tendency of anxious individuals to believe that if they feel anxious, there must be danger present (Arntz, Rauner, & Vandenhout, 1995).

The cognitive behavioural approach to health anxiety also identifies behaviour as playing a role in its development and maintenance. Specifically, this approach emphasizes that, when exposed to physical sensations or information about health, people who

© nullplus/iStockphoto

PHOTO 6.4 | Cognitive behavioural therapy (CBT) has emerged in recent years as the treatment of choice for health anxiety.

Core Features

Most clients who receive CBT for health anxiety visit their therapist for approximately 12 sessions of 50–60 minutes, but the exact number of sessions depends on the client. More sessions are provided to clients who experience greater health anxiety and a greater number of health fears. Also notable about CBT is that clients typically are responsible for the completion of assignments and homework between sessions. The accompanying In Focus box contains some homework sheets completed by Linda as part of her therapy. The assumption is that the more a client works on the homework, the greater the efficacy of treatment and the shorter the treatment duration.

Some factors are known to complicate treatment of health anxiety. Review of the research, for instance, suggests that treatment is more difficult if clients:

1. have had extreme health anxiety for a longer period of time;
2. suffer from severe symptoms;

3. have strongly held beliefs;
4. present with a personality disorder;
5. experience co-morbid general medical conditions;
6. report the presence of stressful life events;
7. appear to benefit in some way (e.g., financially) from having health anxiety (Taylor, Asmundson, & Coons, 2005).

The relationship between treatment outcome and age is ambiguous, in that some studies show better outcomes with younger clients, while other studies suggest outcomes are not related to age (Taylor et al., 2005).

Typically, CBT begins by providing psycho-education to clients, covering similar details to those described above. The key to this component of therapy is for clients to understand how health anxiety develops, with specific attention to how thoughts lead to health anxiety, which leads to selective attention to bodily sensations or changes and behaviours (e.g., avoidance, seeking reassurance, checking) that serve to further increase health anxiety. Clients are also often

⊘ IN FOCUS

Linda's Homework

THOUGHT RECORD: As part of therapy, Linda was required to keep a thought record whereby she identified her anxious thought and then identified evidence for and against the thought. Following this, she was asked to generate a new balanced thought.

Trigger	Anxious Thought	Anxiety (0–100)	Evidence for the Thought	Evidence against the Thought	New Balanced Thought
Noticed that I had a heavy feeling in my chest	This must be a sign that I have lung cancer	85	I used to smoke and so it is highly likely that this is a sign of lung cancer. Peter Jennings had a heavy feeling in his chest and this ended up being lung cancer.	I have been examined extensively and been reassured that I do not have lung cancer. There are many other reasons to cough other than having lung cancer. Focusing on my cough makes it more likely I will cough.	It is not likely that this is a sign that I have lung cancer. I have a habit of thinking the worst. Just because I think the worst does not make it likely.

EXPOSURE HIERARCHY: As part of her therapy, Linda created an exposure hierarchy and then worked on exposing herself to these activities, situations, persons, places, and sensations in order to reduce her anxiety.

Easy (provokes least anxiety: 0–35)	Anxiety rating (0–100)
1. Watch a movie where the main character has an illness	30
2. Imagine walking past someone who is smoking	35
3. Read obituaries	40
Medium (provokes moderate anxiety: 35–70)	
1. Go for coffee with a friend who had cancer	60
2. Walk up three flights of stairs	65
3. Sit near someone who is smoking	70
Hard (provokes the most anxiety: 70–100)	
1. Imagine I will be diagnosed with lung cancer	90
2. Visit the oncology ward at the hospital	95
3. Imagine that I will die of lung cancer	100

SAFETEY BEHAVIOUR RECORD: As part of her therapy, Linda identified safety behaviours that she performs to alleviate her health anxiety and was asked to identify both the benefits and drawbacks of the behaviour.

Safety Behaviour	Benefits	Downside
Checking Internet for at least ½ hour a day	Makes me feel that I am keeping up to date on knowledge. Makes me feel like I am doing something to avoid getting lung cancer.	Actually increases my health anxiety because it reinforces the idea that I am in danger. There is always something that is frightening that increases my anxiety rather than decreases it.
Keeping diary of symptoms	Makes me feel like if my symptoms get worse, I will notice this and be able to go to my doctor immediately.	Keeps my attention focused on my symptoms and increases the likelihood that I will identify a symptom that will lead me to go to my doctor.

encouraged to keep a diary. In the diary, they record the date, the level of health anxiety experienced, triggers for health anxiety, thoughts, behaviours, and physical symptoms they may be experiencing. One challenge during psycho-education is that sometimes clients are focused on proving they have a medical condition, and therefore may not be open to exploring alternative explanations for their physical sensations. Following the initial psycho-education, sessions turn to helping clients identify the specific thoughts they are having about their health that may be triggering health anxiety. It is common at this stage to have clients examine the evidence for and against their thoughts and explore whether they are able to formulate and accept an alternative, more balanced thought. One thought that is likely contributing to Linda's health anxiety is her belief that feelings of discomfort in her chest must be a sign of lung cancer. A further important thought in Linda's case is that she felt she would not be able to cope with a diagnosis of lung cancer and would die if she developed the condition. The following box presents a sample thought record Linda might complete as part of treatment.

After this initial attention to thoughts, the cognitive behaviour therapist normally focuses on exposure with response prevention, a therapeutic technique that involves having clients first formulate a hierarchy of the stimuli and thoughts that they tend to avoid. Clients order the hierarchy so that they work on exposing themselves to items that are lower (i.e., less anxiety provoking) on the hierarchy first before graduating to items that are higher on the hierarchy. Key when completing exposure exercises is the concept of response prevention, which involves ensuring that clients do not employ strategies that they typically use to manage their anxiety (e.g., repeatedly checking the body for signs of change, seeking reassurance), but instead fully expose themselves to stimuli or events that produce anxiety. Exposure sometimes begins by presenting images rather than actual stimuli to clients. This can then be followed by direct exposure to a feared object, situation, or stimulus. During exposure exercises, clients rate their fear on the subjective units of discomfort scale (SUDS), which ranges from 0 or no fear to 100 or maximal fear. Ultimately, the therapist helps clients build hierarchies that range from a low level to a high level of fear. The accompanying box shows a sample exposure hierarchy.

A further component to CBT is helping clients examine their safety behaviours, such as body-checking or reassurance-seeking. It is not realistic to ask clients to never perform a checking behaviour or to see a physician. Instead, it is important for the therapist to discuss realistic levels of safety behaviours. In terms of medical visits, some authors have suggested that clients be encouraged to take a "wait-for-two-weeks" approach to certain types of symptoms (Furer et al., 2007). This approach assumes that most symptoms resolve on their own in two weeks and do not require further medical attention. If the symptoms persist beyond this period, then it is reasonable to see a physician. In working in this area we have found that, rather than imposing limits on how often clients seek medical services, it is important for clients to decide what is reasonable after discussing it with their physician and/or friends and family members.

Adjunctive Strategies

Additional strategies can be incorporated into treatment, depending on the client. Stress management, for instance, has been advocated by some and involves helping clients identify stressors and applying various strategies to the stressor, such as relaxation, time management, and problem-solving (Taylor & Asmundson, 2004). It is also not uncommon to find clients who are anxious about their health to be fearful of death; when this occurs, this fear must also be addressed in therapy (Furer et al., 2007). Other authors advocate the importance of focusing on improving general life satisfaction and enjoyment since individuals with health anxiety are commonly overly focused and preoccupied with their health at the expense of other activities (Furer et al., 2007). In addition, mindfulness has recently been incorporated into the treatment of health anxiety (Wattar et al., 2005). In this case, therapists assist clients with bringing their complete attention to the present moment to aid clients in learning how to be present-focused rather than focused on future health problems. Beyond working with the individual with health anxiety, it is often necessary in CBT to work with the family during the course of treatment. In this case, the therapist may attend to sick-role behaviours (Barsky & Ahern, 2004). This involves helping clients consider how others respond to their behaviour and how this may be impacting their anxiety (e.g., do others only pay attention to the individual when the individual expresses worry about his or her health?). Furthermore, it can be helpful for therapists to work with health-care providers to ensure they recognize that providing excessive reassurance may exacerbate rather than improve client health anxiety.

Empirical Evidence

Considerable evidence supports the efficacy of CBT (e.g., Barsky & Ahern, 2004; Greeven et al., 2007; Seivewright et al., 2008; Warwick, Clark, Cobb, & Salkovskis, 1996).

For instance, when randomly assigned to a CBT or a control condition, clients significantly improve in response to CBT in comparison to the control. Of note, treatment improves not only health anxiety, but also associated problems such as generalized anxiety, depression, social function, and use of medical services (e.g., Seivewright et al., 2008). Particularly noteworthy, CBT has also been found to be efficacious for treating health anxiety when delivered in cost-efficient manners. When treatment is presented online in weekly modules and paired with therapist support, for instance, clients improve in comparison to individuals who receive no treatment (Hedman et al., 2011). It is also found that when CBT is provided in a group format, clients improve in comparison to a waiting list control condition (Avia et al., 1996).

The above review is not meant to suggest that other approaches to health anxiety are ineffective. In fact, studies suggest that medication (e.g., paroxetine) (Greeven et al., 2007), behavioural stress management (Clark et al., 1998), group psycho-education based on a problem-solving approach (Buwalda, Bouman, & van Duijn, 2007), and short-term psychodynamic psychotherapy (Sorensen, Birket-Smith, Wattar, Buemann, & Salkovskis, 2011) are all effective in treating health anxiety. The main limitation of the other approaches is that results have generally not been replicated across multiple studies.

Future Directions

Future research is needed to enhance our understanding of the continuum of responses to physical sensations. We do not fully understand why some individuals become health anxious while others do not. More sophisticated studies that concurrently examine biological and psychosocial determinants of health anxiety are needed. In the area of treatment, evidence clearly shows that CBT is efficacious for health anxiety, and emerging evidence supports other treatment approaches for health anxiety as well. There is a trend in the recent literature to add techniques to CBT; the question remains whether more is better. If all treatments are effective, then it is important that we give further consideration to determining which treatment approaches are the most cost-effective. Preliminary research has been conducted in this area and suggests that when individuals participate in CBT, medical and non-medical costs are substantially lowered (Hedman et al., 2010). Other important areas for research include examining the efficacy of CBT with diverse populations. Based on our review of the literature, we do not yet know whether CBT is efficacious among ethnic minorities or if it is equally effective across the lifespan.

SUMMARY

According to the common-sense model of illness representations, after perceiving physical sensations we form a common-sense representation of these sensations in an attempt to determine their meaning. The representations are multi-dimensional in nature in that we form beliefs about the identity, cause, consequences, timeline (acute/chronic and cyclical), controllability (personal and treatment control), and emotional impact of the physical sensations. The representations we form of our physical sensations are determined not only by our physical sensations, but also by our past experiences with our health, cognitive heuristics, social factors, and culture. Personality and mood are other determining factors.

The mental representations we form are important because they influence how we cope with the physical sensations. In parallel to processing the meaning of physical sensations, we also simultaneously process how we will emotionally respond to these sensations. The way we view our physical sensations influences our emotions and health outcomes, and our emotions and health outcomes influence our representations of the physical sensations.

When physical sensations are perceived to be extremely threatening, people may experience health anxiety. Health anxiety specifically refers to excessive anxiety about one's present or future health and is often based on a misinterpretation of signs and symptoms. Health anxiety is regarded as excessive when it is persistent and results in distress, and extreme behaviours ultimately heighten anxiety and interfere with functioning.

The cognitive behavioural model of health anxiety was introduced in this chapter. This model suggests that health anxiety results when individuals develop dysfunctional cognitions based on past experience. These cognitions result in the individual being preoccupied with his/her health and misinterpreting innocuous or benign bodily sensations to be more threatening than they actually are. The cognitive behavioural model suggests that individuals who are anxious about their health also engage in safety behaviours, such as seeking information and reassurance, and these behaviours can contribute to the anxiety. While safety behaviours are designed to reduce threat and anxiety, they have the opposite effect and usually exacerbate an individual's health concerns.

CBT has emerged as the treatment of choice for health anxiety. Key strategies include identifying and challenging dysfunctional thoughts and exposing individuals to feared stimuli while simultaneously modifying or eliminating safety behaviours. Randomized controlled trials comparing CBT to usual care suggest CBT reduces not only health anxiety but also associated problems such as generalized anxiety, depression, social function, and use of medical services. CBT is also found to be efficacious for treating health anxiety when delivered online or in groups.

Critical Thought Questions

1. Think of your most recent experience with a health concern. Apply the common-sense model of illness representations to your experience.
2. In the research literature and clinical practice, attention has been given primarily to severe health anxiety. Do you think individuals who significantly underestimate the probability/seriousness of illness and have an unrealistic optimism about their health should also be treated? How could CBT be used with these clients?

Recommended Reading

Hagger, M.S., & Orbell, S. (2003). A meta-analytic review of the common-sense model of illness representations. *Psychology & Health, 18*, 141–184.

Rachman, S. (2012). Health anxiety disorders: A cognitive construal. *Behaviour Research and Therapy, 50*, 502–512.

Seivewright, H., Green, J., Salkovskis, P., Barrett, B., Nur, U., & Tyrer, P. (2008). Cognitive-behavioural therapy for health anxiety in a genitourinary medicine clinic: Randomised controlled trial. *British Journal of Psychiatry, 193*, 332–337.

7

The Psychology of Pain

THOMAS HADJISTAVROPOULOS

Learning Objectives

In this chapter you will:

- Learn the difference between acute and chronic pain.

- Understand how pain is both a psychological and a physical experience.

- Examine important pain theories (e.g., the gate control theory) and models of pain (e.g., the biopsychosocial model).

- Learn about the psychological assessment and management of pain.

Acute and Chronic Pain, Prevalence, and Medical Management

Pain is a universal source of distress and, due to its high prevalence, represents a serious public health concern. Pain is often classified as acute or chronic. Acute pain is usually associated with recent ongoing tissue damage (e.g., an injury) while chronic pain has persisted beyond the normal expected healing period or is otherwise persistent over time (Merskey & Bogduk, 1994). Often chronic pain is defined as pain that has lasted for at least three to six months (Merskey & Bogduk, 1994). Chronic pain, the primary focus of this chapter, affects people's lives in diverse ways. Its prevalence is estimated to be as high as 30 per cent of the adult population in the Western world (Tsang et al., 2008), but this estimate varies from country to country (e.g., Breivik, Collet, Ventafridda, Cohen, & Gallacher, 2006) and as a result of different research methodologies used. In Canada, close to 20 per cent of the adults are estimated to suffer from chronic pain (Schopflocher, Taenzer, & Jovey, 2011). In the United States, approximately 116 million Americans suffer from chronic pain (Skinner, Wilson, & Turk, 2012; Institute of Medicine, 2011). According to the National Center for Health Statistics (2006) up to 10 per cent of adults reported that they had pain that lasted a year or more, and 40 per cent indicated that their pain had a moderate or severe negative impact on their lives (Skinner et al., 2012).

A World Health Organization (WHO) survey of primary care patients in 15 countries showed that 22 per cent of patients reported pain lasting for six months or longer requiring medical attention or medication, or causing significant interference with activity (Gureje, Von Korff, Simon, & Gater, 1998; Skinner et al., 2012). Persistent pain is also a prevalent problem in children and adolescents, with estimates ranging from 15 to 30 per cent (Stanford, Chambers, Biesanz, & Chen, 2008). According to an Institute of Medicine (2011) report, cumulative costs in the US, including treatment, disability payments, lost work days and tax revenue, and legal fees, attributed to chronic pain may exceed $600 billion per year. In Canada, where the population is roughly 10 per cent of that of the US, the costs are also very high. Specifically, the Canadian costs are estimated to be over $37 billion per year, including an estimated $6 billion in direct health-care costs (Phillips & Schopflocher, 2008). Moreover, the typical annual cost of care per pain patient waiting for treatment at Canadian pain clinics is $17,544 (most often this is privately funded by patients) (Canadian Pain Society, 2011; Guerriere et al., 2010).

From a biomedical standpoint, depending on its nature, pain can be managed with medications, surgical interventions, physical therapy, and other related modalities. A recent review of non-cancer-related chronic pain treatments led to the conclusion that such treatments tend to provide only modest improvements in pain and minimal improvements in physical and emotional functioning (Turk, Wilson, & Cahana, 2011). This finding was not surprising, given the complexity of chronic pain, and points towards the need for multi-disciplinary approaches that incorporate psychological modalities.

Understanding the Nature of Pain

Pain is primarily a psychological experience (Hadjistavropoulos & Craig, 2004). The International Association for the Study of Pain (IASP), which is the most highly influential group of pain researchers and clinicians, defines pain as "an unpleasant sensory and emotional experience associated with actual or potential damage, or described in terms of such damage" (Merskey & Bogduk, 1994). This definition stresses the psychological nature of the experience by clarifying that pain is not merely a sensation but a perception that incorporates emotional components.

Although pain is often thought of as a sensation, this is incorrect. A sensation is defined as the process by which stimulation of a sensory receptor gives rise to neural impulses that result from an experience outside the body (Gerrig, Zimbardo, Desmarais, & Ivanco, 2010). A potentially painful sensation, however, will not be perceived as pain until it is interpreted as such by the brain. Related to this, it is important to clarify the distinction between the terms "nociception" and "pain." **Nociception** refers to the processing of stimuli associated with the stimulation of nociceptors (i.e., specific receptors) and has the potential of being experienced as pain (Turk & Melzack, 2011). In other words, nociception frequently (but not always) leads to the experience of pain. In contrast to nociception, pain represents a perceptual process associated with selective abstraction, conscious awareness, ascribed meaning, learning, and appraisal (Hadjistavropoulos & Craig, 2004; Melzack & Casey, 1968). In fact, motivational and psychological states are of primary importance in the conceptualization of pain (Price, 2000). For example, the experience of pain has been shown to be closely tied to emotions such as anger, sadness,

"Does it hurt when I do this. . .?"

PHOTO 7.1 | "Does it hurt when I do this ...?"

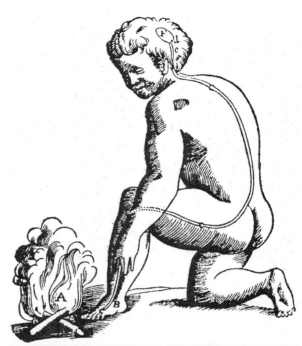

FIGURE 7.1 | Descartes's conception of the pain pathway. From R. Descartes, *Traite de l'Homme* (1648). Source: The Granger Collection, NYC — All rights reserved.

and disgust (Hale & Hadjistavropoulos, 1997). In addition to pain being a psychological experience in and of itself, it also leads to direct behavioural (e.g., facial expressions of pain) and psychological consequences (e.g., mood deflation). For example, a very large portion of chronic pain sufferers also present with depression. According to a comprehensive literature review, and depending on the study, 31–100 per cent of people with chronic pain suffer from depression; the percentage varies depending on the nature of the patient population studied and the criteria and measures used (Romano & Turner, 1985). Regardless of these discrepancies in the prevalence of depression within chronic pain populations, most investigators seem to agree that patients with chronic pain are at risk of suffering from depression (Miller & Cano, 2009). Similar conclusions were drawn in a more recent comprehensive review of studies that showed that depression is present in 5–85 per cent of pain patients (Bair, Robinson, Katon, & Kroenke, 2003).

Chronic pain can also be associated with other psychological conditions such as anxiety and substance abuse (Morasco, Corson, Turk, & Dobscha, 2011; Cimmino, Ferrone, & Cutolo, 2011) with patients often using alcohol and non-prescribed drugs in an effort to palliate pain.

At the social level, chronic pain can lead to disruption of social relationships, social isolation, and reduced quality of life (e.g., Sessle, 2011; Breivik, Collett, Ventafridda, Cohen, & Gallacher, 2006). Given the strong psychological elements of the pain experience as well as the psychosocial consequences of pain, psychologists have played a central role in research designed to better conceptualize the pain experience (Melzack & Wall, 2004), to better understand the manner in which pain is expressed verbally and non-verbally (T. Hadjistavropoulos et al., 2011), and to treat chronic pain patients whose quality of life suffers as a consequence of pain.

Theories of Pain

Early theories of pain had a biophysical focus. Figure 7.1 depicts the concept of the pain pathway conceptualized by Descartes (1596–1650). This conceptualization has been viewed as being analogous to a string with a bell attached to it. According to this early view, tissue damage results in pain being experienced in the same way as a pull on the string causes the bell to ring. Descartes implied a direct one-on-one correspondence between pain and tissue damage, which is known as **specificity**

PHOTO 7.2 | Ronald Melzack, McGill University psychologist.

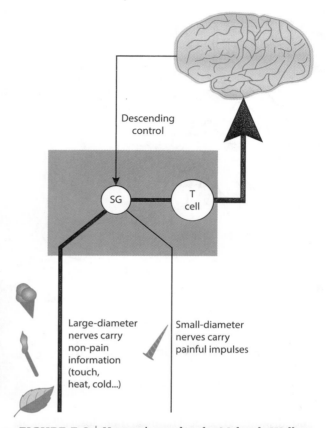

FIGURE 7.2 | How pain works: the Melzack–Wall pain gate.

Source: Starkey, C. (1991). *Therapeutic Modalities for Athletic Trainers* (p 28). Philadelphia: FA Davis.

theory. That is, the greater the tissue damage, the greater the pain. Although specificity theory was influential for many years, it failed to help patients with severe chronic pain (Melzack & Katz, 2004).

Several attempts were made to find a new theory, but these led to accounts of pain mechanisms that were vague and inadequate, and none of these theories considered the brain as anything more than a receiver of pain messages (Melzack & Katz, 2004). This changed as a result of the pioneering work of Melzack and Wall (1965), who developed the most dominant theory of pain today (i.e., the gate control theory). Subsequent work by these and other pain researchers has moved our focus from pain as a physical experience to pain as a complex psychological phenomenon.

Key elements of the theory are summarized in Figure 7.2. Melzack and Katz (2004) outlined the **gate control theory** as follows: nerve impulses are transmitted from afferent fibres to spinal cord transmission cells modulated by a gating mechanism in the dorsal horn of the spinal cord. This gating mechanism is affected by the amount of activity in small pain pathway fibres and large-diameter

sensory neural pathways. Specifically, the large-diameter fibres tend to "close the gate" by inhibiting transmission while small fibres "open the gate" by facilitating transmission. As a concrete example, rubbing a painful area often helps reduce pain because the act of rubbing activates the large-diameter fibres that tend to inhibit nociceptive transmission. These small and large-diameter fibres synapse on projection cells, which go to the brain through the spinothalamic tract (i.e., a sensory pathway originating in the spinal cord and transmitting signals to the thalamus). When the output of spinal transmission cells reaches a critical level, it activates the neural areas that underlie the complex, sequential patterns of experience and behaviour that characterize pain. Cortical descending signals (i.e., messages from the brain) also have the potential to inhibit nociceptive message transmission to the brain and close the "gate." The description of the process whereby descending cortical input (that can represent beliefs, attitudes, attentional processes, and other psychological responses) can close the gating mechanism provides a physiological basis for the role of psychological factors and strengthens justification for use of psychological treatments for pain. Moreover, recognition of the role of cortical function in pain modulation serves to explain a variety of phenomena and establishes the important role of psychological influences in the pain experience (e.g., the ability of many people to endure increased pain under hypnosis) (Facco et al., 2011).

Melzack (2001) has complemented the gate control theory of pain with the **neuromatrix model**, which emphasizes the role of the brain in pain perception. The neuromatrix model is capable of explaining phenomena such as phantom limb pain (i.e., pain felt as if it is coming from an amputated limb that is no longer there). More specifically, Melzack (2001; 2005) argued that the body is perceived as a unit and is identified as the "self" distinct from its surroundings. The perception of unity of the body with all of the qualities felt from the body, including pain, is produced by a central neural process. The anatomical process of the body-self, the neuromatrix, is described as a widespread network of neurons that form loops between the cortex and the limbic system (comprising complex sets of brain structures) as well as the thalamus and the cortex. The neuronal loops separate to allow for parallel processing in different components of the neuromatrix and come together repeatedly to permit interactions between the processing outputs. Melzack conceptualized the neuromatrix as initially being genetically determined, but subsequently sculpted by sensory inputs. Characteristic inputs from the body undergo cyclical synthesis so that patterns are impressed on them in the neuromatrix. The repeated cyclical processing and synthesis of nerve impulses through the neuromatrix reveal a characteristic pattern, the neurosignature, which is produced by the arrangement of synaptic connections in the entire neuromatrix. The neurosignature can be conceptualized as output from the neuromatrix. In other words, pain perception can be generated by the output of the neuromatrix as a function of sensory inputs as well as of information from regions of the brain involved in affective and cognitive functions. Moreover, pain behaviours can be generated or perpetuated by previously conditioned cues in the environment or by the expectation of pain and suffering (Loeser & Melzack, 1999). Phantom limb pain is therefore believed to be related to activity of the neuromatrix. Various treatments can affect the output of the neuromatrix to the extent that they change the inputs and the influences on the neuromatrix (Loeser & Melzack, 1999).

A variety of **biopsychosocial models of pain** are consistent with and build on the gate control theory of pain by elaborating on social and psychological influences that affect the pain experience. Such models focus on the interplay of biological, psychological, and social parameters in pain. Like the gate control theory, biopsychosocial models contrast with strict biomedical models, which are losing popularity. Specifically, biomedical models do not take into account social and psychological factors on the pain experience and focus only on biological processes. Biomedical models fail to explain a wide variety of phenomena, including but not limited to the effect of hypnosis on the pain experience, the role of coping styles in functioning with pain and rehabilitation outcomes, and the success of psychological interventions in chronic pain management (T. Hadjistavropoulos et al., 2011).

Various influential biopsychosocial models/conceptualizations have been developed to describe and clarify different aspects of the pain experience. These models recognize the importance of biological factors in pain but emphasize the interaction of biology with psychological (including cognition, affect, and behaviour) and social factors (e.g., social support, culture) (e.g., T. Hadjistavropoulos et al., 2011; Waddell, 1987; 1991; 1992; Waddell, Newton, Henderson, Somerville, & Main, 1993). Such models/conceptualizations include, for example, the *operant model, fear avoidance model, communications model*, and *cognitive behavioural* conceptualizations of chronic pain. We review each of these below.

The Operant Model

This model stresses the importance of reinforcement in the development and maintenance of pain behaviour. For example, if excessive pain behaviour (e.g., excessive complaining) is reinforced by attention, it tends to persist and be maintained by the attention (e.g., Fordyce, 1976; Fordyce, Shelton, & Dundore, 1982). Moreover, behaviours (e.g., inactivity) that are reinforced because they temporarily reduce pain may also persist and become maladaptive, especially when they are associated with additional rewards such as reduced aversive work-related responsibilities. Empirical support for many aspects of this model exists. Experimental laboratory studies have demonstrated that pain reports in relation to induced pain can increase as a function of verbal reinforcement (Jolliffe & Nicholas, 2004; Flor, Knost, & Birbaumer, 2002). Moreover, therapy based on operant principles has been found to be effective, relative to being on a waiting list, at least in the short term (Henschke et al., 2010). In actual clinical practice, however, therapy components based on the operant model are often incorporated within broader cognitive behavioural therapy approaches (i.e., approaches that incorporate a variety of additional psychological methods). The operant model has been criticized for failing to take into account interpretations and appraisals of pain (Sharp, 2001).

The Fear Avoidance Model of Pain

The fear avoidance model (Vlaeyen & Linton, 2000) is based on the idea that certain movements and behaviours become associated with pain or exacerbations of pain (Meulders, Vansteenwegen, & Vlaeyen, 2011). Such associations, especially when coupled with catastrophic thoughts about pain and concern about the possibility of reinjury, can lead to excessive avoidance. According to the model, excessive avoidance can then lead to stiffness and deconditioning, thus increasing the probability of future

pain. Important aspects of the model have been supported with empirical research. For example, fear avoidance beliefs (e.g., "I must avoid most activities because I am afraid of reinjury") are predictors of future disability and chronicity (Fritz, George, & Delitto, 2001). Nonetheless, clinical studies generally find small effects and it has been argued that fear of pain leading to avoidance may be better construed as one of many variables that influence the experience of pain and disability (Moseley, 2011).

The Communications Model of Pain

The communications model of pain (e.g., Prkachin & Craig, 1994; T. Hadjistavropoulos et al., 2011) is summarized in Figure 7.3. Based on an earlier formulation by Rosenthal (1982), the chain of pain communication is seen as a three-step A–B–C process whereby the internal

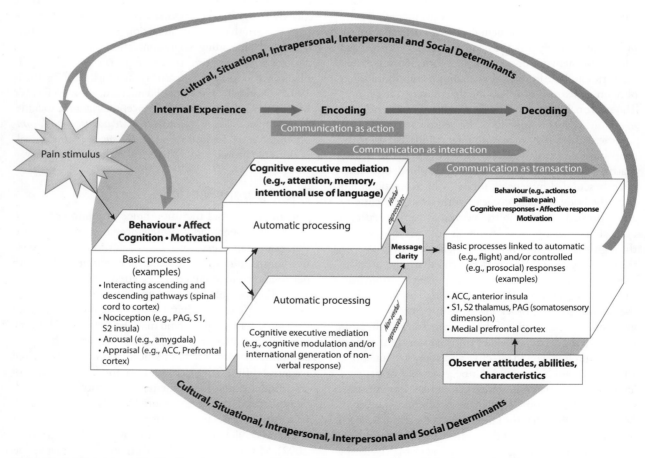

ACC = anterior cingulate cortex; S1 = Somatosensory area; S2 = Second somatosensory area; PAG = Periaqueductal gray.

FIGURE 7.3 | The communications model of pain.

Source: Hadjistavropoulos et al. (2011).

experience of pain (A), which is determined by biological, social/cultural, and psychological factors, is encoded into verbal and non-verbal expressive behaviour (B) that can be potentially decoded (C) by observers. External influences, including cultural, interpersonal, and intrapersonal determinants, can affect this process at any stage. The first step of the model describes a variety of processes that take place during the experience of pain. These include affective (e.g., negative emotion), cognitive (e.g., thoughts about the pain), and brain correlates (reflecting a complex system that conveys nociceptive information from the spinal cord to the cerebral cortex) (Dube et al., 2009; T. Hadjistavropoulos et al., 2011; Price, 2000; Rainville, 2002; Staud, Craggs, Robinson, Perlstein, & Price, 2007).

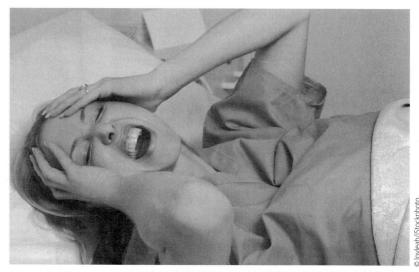

PHOTO 7.3 | Non-verbal pain expressions are believed to be more automatic and less under voluntary control than self-reported pain.

In terms of the encoding of pain in expressive behaviour (i.e., verbal and non-verbal), the model specifies that expressive behaviours vary with respect to the extent to which they are characterized by automaticity (e.g., reflexive withdrawal) or cognitive executive mediation (e.g., as is the case with self-reported pain) (Hadjistavropoulos & Craig, 2002). Non-verbal pain behaviours are seen as, generally, being more automatic and less under voluntary control than self-report. On the other hand, self-report is considered to be under more voluntary control but easier to decode by an observer. Characteristics of the observer (e.g., sex, gender, health professional or not) (Hadjistavropoulos et al., 1998) and of the person expressing pain have also been shown to affect the decoding process (Hadjistavropoulos, LaChapelle, Hale, & MacLeod, 2000; Hadjistavropoulos, McMurtry, & Craig, 1996; MacLeod, LaChapelle, Hadjistavropoulos, & Pfeifer, 2001). In turn, observer actions (often based on decoding of the pain experience) have the potential to palliate or worsen the pain experience.

Examples of contextual influences on the pain process are derived from studies demonstrating that people are less likely to express pain in the presence of a tolerant model (i.e., an individual who demonstrates that he or she can tolerate well relatively high pain intensities) (Craig & Weiss, 1972; Craig, 1986), that children whose mothers were taught to interact in a pain-promoting manner reported more pain than children in a control group (Chambers, Craig, & Bennett, 2002), and

that pain can be expressed with varying levels of intensity as a function of cultural background (Nayak, Shiflett, Eshun, & Levine, 2000). Moreover, social stereotypes such as those based on physical attractiveness seem to affect the decoding of pain, with more physically attractive people being perceived as healthier and as experiencing less pain (Hadjistavropoulos, McMurtry, & Craig, 1996). Although aspects of the model require more testing, particularly in naturalistic contexts (i.e., healthcare settings), a strength of the communications model is that it provides a high level of detail with respect to the various variables that influence the pain experience.

Cognitive Behavioural Conceptualization of Pain

Cognitive behavioural conceptualizations focus on the role of cognitive factors and beliefs in the pain experience and recognize the interconnections among thoughts, feelings, and behaviours (Turk, Meichenbaum, & Genest, 1987; Sharp, 2001). The assumption is that a fundamental difference between those who adjust well to pain and those who do not lies in their appraisals and interpretations of the situation (e.g., holding maladaptive beliefs such as "I can never enjoy anything with this pain problem" as opposed to "I can still enjoy many things in my life, despite the pain"). Such beliefs also affect emotions and behaviour (e.g., exaggerated concern about reinjury may lead to reduced activity) and, in turn, negative emotions and associated physiological changes can affect the thinking process (Skinner et al., 2012). As such, this conceptualization also postulates that patients' beliefs have an impact on the manner in which they present themselves to others, such as health-care providers, which in turn would affect how others react to the patient in pain (e.g., by encouraging or discouraging pain complaints) (Skinner et al., 2012). Cognitive behavioural theorists have argued that pain-related beliefs and cognitions develop as a result of the patients' early histories, cultural backgrounds, and other social experiences. Indeed, research has supported many predictions of this model. For example, catastrophic thinking about pain is a risk factor in the development of chronic pain and is an indicator of poor prognosis (Haythornthwaite, Clark, Pappagallo, & Raja, 2003; Linton, 2005; Picavet, Vlaeyen, & Schouten, 2002; Sullivan, Feuerstein, Gatchel, Linton, & Pransky, 2005). Psychological interventions based on this model are reviewed below and incorporate a variety of techniques and procedures designed to influence affective, behavioural, cognitive, and sensory aspects of the pain experience (Skinner et al., 2012).

Psychological Assessment of Pain

Health psychologists are frequently involved in the assessment of patients experiencing pain, especially those who suffer from chronic pain. It is important to recognize that such psychological assessments tend to incorporate complete evaluations of patients' psychological functioning (e.g., psychological co-morbidities, coping efforts) and involve both detailed clinical interviews covering personal and psychological history and psychological tests.

The psychological assessment of pain is typically based on biopsychosocial formulations of the pain experience. It focuses on a variety of domains capturing information about the person, psychological and problem history, co-morbidities, coping styles, dimensions of the pain experience itself, functional analysis of pain behaviour (i.e., examination of antecedents and consequences of pain behaviour) and impact of pain on quality of life.

Full History, Co-morbidities, Coping Styles, and Overall Psychological Functioning

The psychological assessment of the pain patient involves obtaining a full personal and psychological history and assessment of co-morbidities and coping styles. Coping styles are important because some strategies for coping with pain (e.g., strategies that focus on problem-solving) are associated with better outcomes than more passive strategies (e.g., heavy reliance on hope that pain will be alleviated as a result of the actions of others) (e.g., Covic, Adamson, & Hough, 2000). Historical information includes information on past treatments, substance use, and vocational and social history, as well as the client's goals and expectations related to current treatment.

Dimensions of the Pain Experience

Pain is a multi-dimensional experience. In the first instance, a psychologist may assist with the standardized measurement of self-reported pain intensity using scales that vary in complexity. A simple tool would be a 0–10 numeric rating scale anchored by the polar opposites "no pain" and "pain as bad as it can be" or verbal rating scales where the patient selects a word out of a list that depicts different levels of pain intensity (e.g., "no pain," "mild pain," "moderate pain," "severe pain"). However, pain also has affective (i.e., it is accompanied by negative emotions), sensory, and evaluative components (e.g., perceptions of the nature of pain such as throbbing or sharp).

One of the most widely used psychometric tools is the McGill Pain Questionnaire (MPQ) (Melzack, 1975), which consists of groups of words designed to capture various dimensions of the pain experience (see Figure 7.4). The tool consists of pain descriptors that the patient can select from (e.g., throbbing, stabbing, burning, dull). In addition, the questionnaire includes line drawings of the human body so that the patient can mark the spatial distribution of the pain. Moreover, there is an overall rating of pain intensity based on a 1–5 scale (with each number associated with an intensity word ranging from "mild" to "excruciating". Descriptors of the temporal properties of the pain (e.g., brief, momentary, transient) are also included. The MPQ provides assessment of the following pain dimensions: (1) sensory: linked to words describing the sensory quality of the experience in terms of properties such as thermal and pressure; (2) affective: linked to words relating to affective elements such as fear; and (3) evaluative: e.g., whether pain is evaluated as unbearable, annoying etc.

The MPQ has shown remarkable accuracy in classifying people correctly with a variety of pain syndromes. For example, Melzack, Terrence, Fromm, and Amsel (1986) showed that the tool was 91 per cent accurate in classifying patients who suffered from trigeminal neuralgia, a nerve disorder that causes intense pain in

McGill Pain Questionnaire

Patient's Name ______ Date ______ Time ______ am/pm

PRI: S ______ (1 –10) A ______ (11 –15) E ______ (16) M ______ (17 –20) PRI(T) ______ (1 –20) PPI ______

1 FLICKERING ___
QUIVERING ___
PUSING ___
THROBBING ___
BEATING ___
POUNDING ___

2 JUMPING ___
FLASHING ___
SHOOTING ___

3 PRICKING ___
BORING ___
DRILLING ___
STABBING ___
LANCINATING ___

4 SHARP ___
CUTTING ___
LACERATING ___

5 PINCHING ___
PRESSING ___
GNAWING ___
CRAMPING ___
CRUSHING ___

6 TUGGING ___
PULLING ___
WRENCHING ___

7 HOT ___
BURNING ___
SCALDING ___
SEARING ___

8 TINGLING ___
ITCHY ___
SMARTING ___
STINGING ___

9 DULL ___
SORE ___
HURTING ___
ACHING ___
HEAVY ___

10 TENDER ___
TAUT ___
RASPING ___
SPLITTING ___

11 TIRING ___
EXHAUSTING ___

12 SICKENING ___
SUFFOCATING ___

13 FEARFUL ___
FRIGHTFUL ___
TERRIFYING ___

14 PUNISHING ___
GRUELLING ___
CRUEL ___
VICIOUS ___
KILLING ___

15 WRETCHED ___
BLINDING ___

16 ANNOYING ___
TROUBLESOME ___
MISERABLE ___
INTENSE ___
UNBEARABLE ___

17 SPREADING ___
RADIATING ___
PENETRATING ___
PIERCING ___

18 TIGHT ___
NUMB ___
DRAWING ___
SQUEEZING ___
TEARING ___

19 COOL ___
COLD ___
FREEZING ___

20 NAGGING ___
NAUSEATING ___
AGONIZING ___
DREADFUL ___
TORTURING ___

PPI
0 NO PAIN ___
1 MILD ___
2 DISCOMFORTING ___
3 DISTRESSING ___
4 HORRIBLE ___
5 EXCRUCIATING ___

BRIEF ___	RHYTHMIC ___	CONTINUOUS ___
MOMENTARY ___	PERIODIC ___	STEADY ___
TRANSIENT ___	INTERMITTENT ___	CONSTANT ___

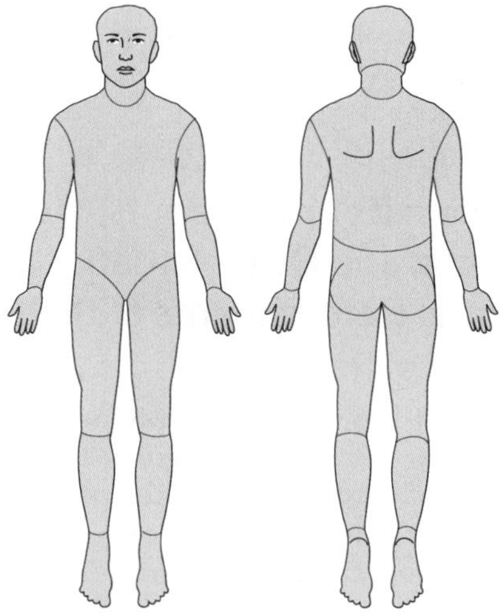

E = EXTERNAL
I = INTERNAL

COMMENTS:

FIGURE 7.4 | The McGill Pain Questionnaire.

Source: Copyright R. Melzack 1970, 1975; reprinted with permission.

the face, or atypical pain. Moreover, Dubuisson and Melzack (1976) showed that the MPQ was accurate in correctly classifying 77 per cent of patients who presented with eight different types of pain syndromes.

Other aspects of the pain experience commonly evaluated by health psychologists include cognitions. For example, the Pain Catastrophizing Scale (Sullivan, Bishop, & Pivik, 1995) is often used to evaluate the extent to which patients engage in catastrophic thinking. Catastrophic thinking involves a cognitive appraisal in which situations are viewed as being threatening and beyond an individual's ability to cope. Similarly, psychologists often measure whether patients show certain behavioural tendencies, such as the tendency to avoid activity due to fear of pain or fear of reinjury. Dimensions such as pain catastrophizing and fear of pain predict poor rehabilitation outcomes (e.g., Piva, Fitzgerald, Wisniewski, & Delitto, 2009) and are, thus, important to assess.

Pain Behaviour: Its Antecedents, Consequences, and Other Situational/Environmental Determinants of the Pain Experience

Health psychologists assess pain behaviours observed during the interview (e.g., a patient grimacing due to pain) and through discussion of what the patient does when he or she is in pain (e.g., does he or she ask for assistance from significant others?). Standardized observational approaches are also often used with special populations, including persons with limited ability to communicate, such as infants (Ruskin, Amaria, Warnock, & McGrath, 2001) and older adults with severe dementia (Lints-Martindale, Hadjistavropoulos, Lix, & Thorpe, 2012; also see Chapter 18).

Antecedents (i.e., what precedes the pain behaviour) are examined. For example, some patients report that their pain feels worse when they find themselves in stressful situations. Similarly, the consequences of pain behaviour are discussed (e.g., how does a spouse react to pain complaints?). Consistent with the operant model, the environment can sometimes serve to encourage or discourage pain behaviour. For example, an individual may receive more help and attention because he or she is in pain (although the opposite can also occur with potentially detrimental consequences for social relationships). Other environmental/social elements relating to the pain experience are also evaluated. Social support is a good example. An optimal amount of social support has been linked to more positive physical rehabilitation outcomes among

pain patients (Burckhardt, 1985; Faucett & Levine, 1991; Murphy, Creed, & Jayson, 1988; Turner & Noh, 1988). On the other hand, excessive social support (i.e., social support that becomes solicitous) can be counterproductive (Boothby, Thorn, Overduin, & Ward, 2004; McCracken, 2005; Paulsen & Altmaier, 1995). Other examples of environmental/social influences on the pain experience are the work environment the patient is in (or is planning to return to) and whether or not the patient is operating within an adversarial compensation system. Adversarial compensation systems, where the patient's veracity is being questioned, have been linked to poorer rehabilitation outcomes (Hadjistavropoulos, 1999).

Effects of Pain on Quality of Life

Chronic pain often affects a variety of spheres of human functioning. These spheres include the following:

- a person's mood and psychological functioning with pain possibly leading to clinical depression or anxiety;
- social relationships (pain, can result in social isolation due to physical limitations preventing the individual from participating in various social activities);
- intimate relationships (pain leading to irritability or physical discomfort interfering with sexual activity);
- vocational functioning, that is, workplace productivity and security;
- economic circumstances, resulting, for example, from a person being less able to engage in his or her regular occupation;
- use of substances, with the individual abusing alcohol and other drugs in order to cope with the pain experience.

As such, using interview techniques and other psychological assessment tools, such as psychological inventories, the psychologist evaluates the extent to which each of these areas is affected and makes treatment recommendations to address these concerns.

Acceptance of the biopsychosocial formulations of pain has supported the development of and increased emphasis on psychological treatments for chronic pain. Cognitive behaviour therapy (CBT) is gaining popularity as a modality designed for the treatment of chronic pain. CBT perspectives recognize the reciprocal relationships among cognition (including beliefs, schemata, automatic thoughts, and appraisals), behaviour, and interpersonal variables.

ⓩ IN FOCUS

Pain in Persons with Limited Ability to Communicate

The case of Tracy Latimer attracted tremendous Canadian media attention in the 1990s (McGrath, 1998). Tracy was a 12-year-old girl who suffered from cerebral palsy and had serious limitations in her ability to communicate pain due to the severe motor and cognitive impairments associated with her condition. There was little question, though, that she suffered severe pain, which was caused by the neuromuscular pathologies of cerebral palsy and probably by surgery performed to relieve contractures. Nonetheless, systematic assessment of pain represented a real challenge (Hadjistavropoulos, von Baeyer, & Craig, 2001). Tracy's father, Robert, decided to end her life because of what he described as her continuous suffering and pain. His legal representatives argued that he was left with limited choice as he had been told that nothing could be done to relieve his daughter's suffering. Following considerable public debate and legal battles, the Supreme Court of Canada eventually heard the case and ruled that Mr Latimer must spend at least 10 years in jail for killing his severely disabled daughter. Mr Latimer's decision concerning Tracy was supported by many people, who argued that her extreme pain justified euthanasia. Others, however, expressed concern about vulnerable persons who cannot effectively express themselves. Canadian psychologist Patrick McGrath (1998), in an article titled "We all failed the Latimers," argued that although much of the media attention had focused on the right to live or die, the most important issue (i.e., the right of people with severe communication impairments to adequate pain assessment and management) was not discussed sufficiently.

Tracy Latimer's case sparked considerable attention within the pain research community and contributed to considerable efforts to improve pain assessment and management for people with severe cognitive impairments. As an example, the Non-Communicating Children's Pain Checklist (Breau, Finley, McGrath, & Camfield, 2002) was developed and subsequently validated as an effective behavioural observation tool to improve pain assessment in children with severe to profound intellectual disabilities (see Hadjistavropoulos, Breau, & Craig, 2011, for a review of this work). Similar efforts have been undertaken to improve the pain assessment of older adults with severe dementia (see Chapter 18).

PHOTO 7.4 | Tracy and Robert Latimer.

Psychological Treatments for Chronic Pain

CBT is used widely. It is not typically considered to be an alternative to medical and physical treatment modalities but complementary to these. Generally, the best approach to address chronic pain is interdisciplinary, and CBT is often offered as a component of such interdisciplinary approaches (Turk, Wilson, & Cahana, 2011). In addition to psychologists, interdisciplinary pain management teams tend to include physicians, physiotherapists, occupational therapists, pharmacists, and/or other health professionals. Rather than simply

PHOTO 7.5 | Relaxation procedures are often used for pain management.

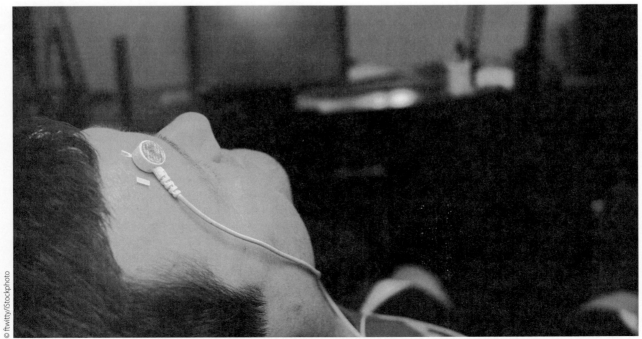

PHOTO 7.6 | Patient undergoing electromyographic biofeedback therapy for headache pain.

targeting the pain itself, CBT for chronic pain patients also targets a variety of psychological consequences of pain, such as depression and anxiety.

CBT not only incorporates cognitive techniques, such as challenging dysfunctional automatic thoughts (e.g., "I am useless because I have pain"), but also a wide variety of behavioural procedures, including, but not limited to, pacing of activity, building coping skills, problem-solving, relaxation training, and biofeedback. Skinner et al. (2012) organized the methods that tend to be incorporated into CBT for pain:

1. Cognitive techniques such as cognitive restructuring (e.g., challenging negative thoughts and maladaptive beliefs through Socratic dialogue) and problem-solving (e.g., defining problems and working on solutions);
2. behavioural techniques such as relaxation training and pacing (e.g., breaking up tasks into smaller components and performing them throughout the day) and behavioural activation (e.g., pleasant activity scheduling, pacing activity);
3. supportive educational techniques (e.g., offering support and providing information about the nature of pain);
4. other techniques including biofeedback (a procedure that helps clients become more aware of specific physiological functions using psychophysiological measuring instruments), hypnosis, and relapse prevention strategies (e.g., developing coping skills to deal with possible relapses, identifying triggering events as a means of preventing relapse).

With respect to biofeedback, a variety of different types are used (e.g., thermal biofeedback or electromyography), depending on the type of pain experienced. For example, electromyography biofeedback has been used with tension headache patients who learn to reduce tension in muscles of the head (e.g., the frontalis muscle).

Given that thoughts, emotions, and behaviours can affect one another, targeting maladaptive beliefs can have a positive impact on behaviour. For example, overcoming a belief such as "socialization can never be pleasant when one has a chronic pain condition" could lead the person to participate in social activities more frequently, and rewarding social experiences can lead to improved mood. Cognitive behavioural therapists often aim to modify maladaptive beliefs and behaviours that patients with chronic pain may hold or engage in (e.g., "unless my pain problem can be treated, I cannot experience any joy"). More specifically, such thoughts

are challenged through Socratic examination and dialogue. Often, "behavioural experiments" are set up within the context of therapy. Consider, for example, a client who believes that "I can't enjoy going out because I am in pain" and agrees to go to a social event in order to test the belief that "there is no way I can have fun if in pain." Testing such beliefs directly and finding evidence against such beliefs is often a far more powerful tool in changing maladaptive thoughts than convincing a client through dialogue that the belief may not be accurate.

Generally, CBT has been found to be effective in the management of chronic pain, leading to reductions in self-reported pain intensity and negative affect, although the effect sizes are only moderate (Eccleston, Williams, & Morley, 2009; Morley, Eccleston, & Williams, 1999). To put this in perspective, however, it is important to note that many pain problems are highly resistant to treatment, and physical/medical treatment modalities often also lead, at best, to only modest benefits. As is the case with most other treatments for chronic pain, some patients do not benefit from CBT. As such, it has been argued that rather than conducting more studies simply examining the effectiveness of CBT in the treatment of chronic pain, it is important to identify subgroups of patients who are most likely to benefit from this therapy, as well as the circumstances under which CBT is likely to be beneficial (Skinner et al., 2012; Day, Thorn, & Burns, 2012).

More recently, CBT-based programs have begun to be delivered via the Internet and tend to focus on pain education, coping skills acquisition, and other cognitive behavioural procedures. Macea, Gajos, Daglia Calil, and Fregni (2010) conducted a systematic review and meta-analysis of these studies and concluded that such interventions offer a small but statistically significant benefit in terms of pain reduction.

In recent years, in addition to CBT, acceptance and commitment therapy has also gained in popularity. According to this approach, acceptance of pain rather than changing one's thoughts about pain is the focus of treatment. The approach (Hayes & Wilson, 1994) emphasizes the manner in which the client relates to distressing thoughts and incorporates mindfulness, that is, a mental state of awareness that has commonalities with meditation and involves being intentionally present in the moment and without judgement (Kabat-Zinn, 1990). The assumption is that suffering is an unavoidable part of human experience and trying to control distressing thoughts about pain (or other forms of suffering) can ultimately increase distress. Patients

IN PRACTICE

Learning to Adapt to Pain through CBT

Jim is a 49-year-old mechanic who is married with one adult son. He presented with neck and back pain as a result of a work injury, which persisted despite repeated medical and physical treatments. Not only was he unable to work but he was no longer able to play golf, which was his favourite pastime and provided him with social opportunities. Since he went off work and stopped playing golf, Jim began spending more time at home and minimal time with his friends, since most of the socialization took place at the golf club. As a result of boredom and frustration, he became depressed and irritable. In turn, his irritability created considerable strain in his marriage. He believed that he "could not have his life back" as long as he had his pain.

He was referred for psychological therapy by his disability insurance provider. Jim was skeptical when he came for therapy and quickly questioned the purpose of the referral. As he told the therapist, "The problem that I have is with my back and I know that you can't fix that. When my back gets better, I will feel better. So I don't know what you are going to do for me."

The psychologist asked Jim a number of questions about the quality of his life. Jim confided that he was feeling depressed and had many catastrophic and other negative thoughts about pain (e.g., "I can never have a nice time unless my pain goes away"; "there is nothing that I can do to cope with my pain"; and "I can't stop thinking about the pain"). He talked about his marriage and how his irritability had strained his relationship with his wife. Through discussion, Jim also came to recognize that the more he thought and focused on his pain, the more upset he became. He saw a vicious cycle of how increased distress made him focus even more on the pain, which only increased his distress. The psychologist asked Jim whether he would be willing to see if cognitive behaviour therapy could improve the quality of his life, despite the pain.

Over the weeks that followed, Jim tried a number of "therapy experiments." That is, the psychologist encouraged him to test out some of the beliefs that he held about his pain. For example, Jim created a list of activities that were once pleasurable. These included getting in touch with friends he had not seen for several months as well as high school friends he had not seen for longer. In fact, he was able to attend a high school reunion and had a good time. As he visited with old friends, he realized that he often did not think about his pain. As a result of this, he had tested the beliefs "*I can never have a nice time until my pain problem goes away*" and "*I cannot stop thinking about the pain*." Through discussions in therapy, he began to adopt more adaptive beliefs, such as "I can distract myself from my pain problem by engaging in activities that interest me" and "When I participate in certain pleasant and interesting activities, I derive a sense of pleasure and a sense of mastery."

Gradually, he started to become more active. He and his wife began to go to the movies together and he even visited the golf club, where he was able to socialize with his friends at the clubhouse. As his mood improved, he explored vocational options and was able to find a job at the service desk of an automobile repair shop. He also learned to use relaxation strategies that reduced muscle tension in his back, which contributed to his pain experience, and he began to pace himself with home projects, breaking each project into small jobs and taking breaks before experiencing pain exacerbation. By doing this, he was able to break the mental association of pain with physical activity. Jim had managed to change his thinking and behaviour and to improve the quality of his life despite the pain.

are encouraged to be mindful and to notice, observe, and accept private events, rather than fight them. This, in turn, is expected to help them experience life more fully, because they will no longer be consumed and preoccupied with fighting distressing thoughts.

A meta-analysis of the effectiveness of mindfulness-based interventions and of acceptance and commitment therapy showed that, although these approaches were not superior to CBT, they were good alternatives in that the outcomes were comparable (Veehof, Okam, Schreurs, & Bohlmeijer, 2011). Nonetheless, the authors of the meta-analysis acknowledged that the CBT approach remains the standard, given the larger number of quality studies evaluating CBT.

Psychological Management of Acute Pain

Although psychologists are more likely to become involved in chronic pain management, there are many opportunities for clinical health psychologists to engage in the management of acute pain. For example, psychological interventions for post-surgical pain have been associated with reduced length of hospital stay and improved outcomes (Kiecolt-Glaser, Page, Marucha, & MacCallum, 1998). Psychologists have also been involved in the management of burn pain, dental pain, and pain due to non-surgical medical procedures. The types of psychological interventions typically used for acute pain management include a variety of different relaxation procedures (e.g., progressive muscle relaxation, imagery-based relaxation), hypnosis (i.e., a state of consciousness that involves attention being diverted away from the pain and onto a narrowly focused area or the hypnotist), cognitive procedures (e.g., distraction, use of coping self-statements), and psycho-education (e.g., providing information about the steps involved in the procedure to reduce unrealistic anxiety-provoking expectations that could have a negative impact on pain levels) (Bruehl & Chung, 2004). More recently, technological advances have also been incorporated into these treatments. For example, immersion in virtual reality environments has been used as a distraction strategy with good results (Li, Montaño, Chen, & Gold, 2011). Psychological interventions for acute pain management have been studied as adjuncts to standard pharmacological approaches and have shown considerable promise, although the extent to which they can be effective in the absence of pharmacological pain management has been studied less (Bruehl & Chung, 2004) and there is a need for more systematic controlled clinical trials.

Future Directions

Plenty of evidence supports the social-contextual elements of the pain experience and expression, but much of this research has been conducted in laboratory settings with healthy research participants (T. Hadjistavropoulos et al., 2011). Thus, more research is needed in real-world settings. Similarly, much of the research on pain assessment (Turk & Melzack, 2011) and management has focused on populations treated in multi-disciplinary settings, yet only a select subsample of patients with chronic pain are treated in such settings. More research with pain patients who receive pain services in more typical community facilities is needed.

An exciting area in which health psychologists are engaged involves the use of imaging such as functional magnetic resonance imaging (fMRI). For example, psychologist Philip Jackson and his colleagues have investigated specific brain activity in response to the observation of pain in others (Jackson, Meltzoff, & Decety, 2005; Jackson, Rainville, & Decety, 2006). More research, however, is needed to better understand the psychosocial variables affecting brain mechanisms involved in the direct experience of pain but also when observing pain in others (T. Hadjistavropoulos et al., 2011). Increased study of these phenomena with pain patients (as opposed to healthy volunteers) would be especially welcome. Moreover, we anticipate increased research and clinical application of protocols designed to address pain over the Internet, with the potential of reaching thousands of patients who now have limited access to psychological services for chronic pain (H. Hadjistavropoulos et al., 2011).

SUMMARY

Pain is both a physical and a psychological experience. The gate control theory of pain describes the mechanisms involved in the perception of pain, while biopsychosocial formulations, consistent with the gate control theory, emphasize the role of social, cultural, psychological, and cognitive influences on pain and its communication. Given the well-documented influence of psychological factors in pain, psychologists have been involved in research and clinical applications with pain patients. Cognitive behavioural and other related procedures are of demonstrated effectiveness in helping people cope with pain problems.

Critical Thought Questions

1. Can you think of psychological strategies (e.g., distraction through engagement in pleasant activities, repeating coping self-statements) that you have used to cope with pain? Did these strategies make it easier for you to manage your pain? Besides what you may have already tried on your own, what are some other psychological strategies that a person could use to manage pain and its consequences?

2. Even today, many health professionals underplay the extent to which psychological intervention can help with serious chronic pain problems. If you were discussing this issue with a health professional who argued that a physical problem can only be managed by physical/medical methods, what position would you take and what arguments and evidence would you use to support your position?

Recommended Reading

Flor, H., & Turk, D.C. (2011). *Chronic pain: An integrated biobehavioural approach*. Seattle: IASP Press.

Hadjistavropoulos, T., et al. (2011). A biopsychosocial formulation of pain communication. *Psychological Bulletin, 137*, 910–939.

Part II

Health Conditions

8

Cancer

ANNE MOYER   ELIZABETH A. SARMA

Learning Objectives
In this chapter you will:

- Learn to explain the basic biological processes underlying cancer.

- Familiarize yourself with the most common types of cancer.

- Learn to describe cancer risk factors and cancer prevention strategies.

- Learn to explain how psychosocial factors may contribute to cancer initiation and progression.

- Compare and contrast the features and purpose of different psychological treatments for cancer patients.

Understanding Cancer

Cancer is not a single disease, but rather a term to refer to a group of more than 100 illnesses (Benson & Liau, 2010). The basic process underlying different types of cancer, however, is the same. Cell proliferation normally is stringently regulated so that new cells are created to replace damaged or dying cells. Mechanisms are in place during cell division to repair damaged deoxyribonucleic acid (DNA, the basic genetic material that controls cell growth, division, and death) or to activate programmed cell death if the DNA damage is too extensive to repair. DNA damage can occur due to genetic processes or damage from **carcinogens** or viruses. Importantly, cancer is typically a result of multiple gene mutations, and these mutations are usually acquired during the lifespan. When genes that regulate cell division have mutations (i.e., DNA damage), the result is a breakdown in the regulation of cell division, leading to uncontrolled cell proliferation (see Photo 8.1). The new tissue that develops from unregulated cell growth is called a tumour or neoplasm.

The resulting tumour may or may not be harmful. Malignant tumours are cancerous. Cells in malignant tumours can invade surrounding tissue and spread to a distant site in the body through the blood or lymph systems in a process called **metastasis**. Benign tumours are not cancerous and typically are not life-threatening.

Often, they can be removed and do not invade nearby tissue or metastasize (Benson & Liau, 2010). The main categories of cancer are broadly classified according to the tissue in which the cancer originates. These categories include the following (NCI, 2012a):

1. Carcinoma: malignant neoplasms (i.e., new, abnormal tissue growth) that develop in the cells of the skin or tissues that line or cover organs (e.g., respiratory tract, reproductive tract). Most human cancers are carcinomas.
2. Sarcoma: malignant neoplasms that develop in connective tissue, muscle, or bone.
3. Leukemia: cancer that develops in blood-forming tissue (e.g., bone marrow), causing a rapid proliferation of white blood cells.
4. Lymphoma: cancers of the lymphatic system.
5. Central nervous system cancer: cancers that develop in brain tissue or the spinal cord.

Cancer type is typically named for the organ or type of cell in which the cancer initially develops (e.g., breast cancer for cancer that begins in breast tissue).

Types and Prevalence of Cancer

Cancer is a leading cause of death worldwide: approximately 7.6 million (13 per cent) of all deaths are cancer-related (WHO, 2012). In Canada, cancer is the leading cause of death, accounting for 30 per cent of all deaths each year (Statistics Canada, 2011). Every day, approximately 500 people are diagnosed with cancer and 200 die of cancer-related causes (CCS, ·2012a). In 2012, it was estimated that approximately 186,400 Canadians would be diagnosed with cancer and 75,700 Canadians would die of cancer.

Over the past 30 years the number of new cases diagnosed and cancer-related deaths have increased, mainly due to the growth of the aging population (CCS, 2011). However, incidence rates are becoming stable or increasing only modestly, and mortality rates are decreasing, suggesting that survival rates are improving for some

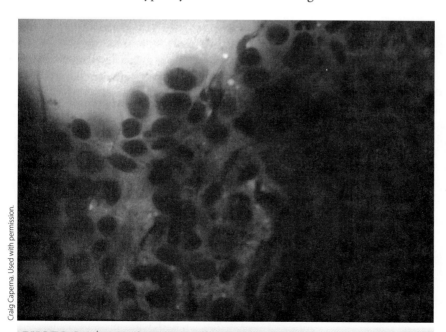

Craig Caperna. Used with permission.

PHOTO 8.1 | Hepatic cancer cells.

cancers (see Figure 8.1). The five-year survival rate (i.e., the probability that a person diagnosed will be living five years from the diagnosis) for all cancer types is between 60 per cent and 70 per cent in North America (ACS, 2012; CCS, 2012a). Table 8.1 shows the annual incidence and mortality rates for select cancers, adjusted

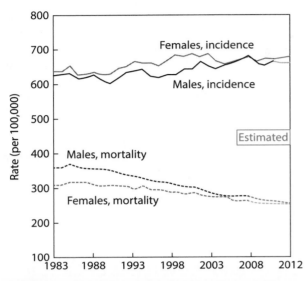

FIGURE 8.1 | Age-standardized incidence and mortality rates for all cancers, ages 50–59, Canada, 1983–2012.

Source: Canadian Cancer Society's Steering Committee on Cancer Statistics. Canadian Cancer Statistics 2012. Toronto, ON: Canadian Cancer Society. May 2012, ISSN 0835-2976.

for age of the patient, in Canada and the US. Testicular cancer has been highly publicized in recent years and accounts for approximately 13 per cent of cancers diagnosed in Canadians aged 15 to 29 years (CCS, 2013). Although testicular cancer is a relatively common cancer among young men, it usually responds to treatment when detected early.

Lung Cancer

Lung cancer is the second most commonly diagnosed cancer among North Americans, accounting for approximately 14 per cent of new cancer diagnoses (ACS, 2012; CCS, 2012a). Over 25,500 people in Canada and 226,160 people in the US were expected to be diagnosed with lung cancer in 2012. In addition, lung cancer is the most common cause of cancer death in the world (Swerdlow, Peto, & Doll, 2010). Indeed, 27 per cent of all cancer deaths in Canada are attributed to lung cancer. In both Canada and the US, the five-year survival rate for lung cancer for all stages is just 16 per cent. The survival rate is 52 per cent when the cancer is localized, but unfortunately only 15 per cent of lung cancer diagnoses are made at this early stage.

Lung cancer incidence and mortality rates began to decrease in the mid-1980s for men but did not do so until the mid-2000s for women (ACS, 2012; CCS, 2012a). This lag is attributed to gender differences in smoking behaviour. Specifically, tobacco consumption decreased among men in the mid-1960s, while among women it did not decrease until the mid-1980s. It should be noted, however, that men still have numerically higher incidence and mortality rates of lung cancer than women.

Prostate Cancer

Other than non-melanoma skin cancer, prostate cancer is the most commonly diagnosed cancer among North American men (CCS, 2012a; NCHS, 2012). Prostate cancer accounts for approximately 30 per cent of new cancer diagnoses in men, and an estimated 26,500 men in Canada and 241,740 men in the US were expected to be diagnosed with prostate cancer in 2012 (ACS, 2012; CCS, 2012a). In Canada, prostate cancer is

TABLE 8.1 | Annual Incidence and Mortality Rates of Select Cancer Types per 100,000 Males and Females, Canada and the US

	General		Lung		Prostate	Breast
	M	F	M	F	(M only)	(F only)
Canada						
Incidence	448.8	364.2	65.1	47.4	114.6	97.6
Death rate	200.1	141.2	57.0	36.1	20.4	21.8
Unites States						
Incidence	541.8	412.3	76.4	52.7	154.8	124.9
Death rate	219.4	151.1	65.7	39.6	23.6	23.0

Sources: CCS (2012a) for Canada; SEER (2012) for the United States.

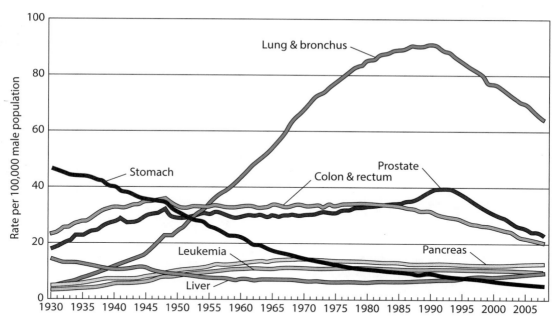

*Per 100,000, age adjusted to the 2000 US standard population.
Note: Due to changes in ICD coding, numerator information has changed over time. Rates for cancer of the liver, lung and bronchus, and colon and rectum, are affected by these coding changes.

FIGURE 8.2 | Age-adjusted cancer death rates,* males by site, US, 1930–2008.

Source: © 2014, American Cancer Society, Inc, Surveillance Research.

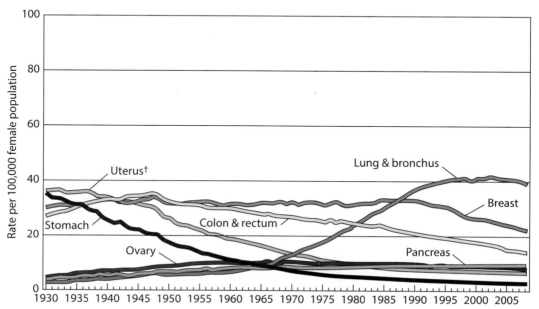

*Per 100,000, age adjusted to the 2000 US standard population. †Uterus cancer death rates are for uterine cervix and uterine corpus combined.
Note: Due to changes in ICD coding, numerator information has changed over time. Rates for cancer of the lung and bronchus, colon and rectum, and ovary are affected by these coding changes.

FIGURE 8.3 | Age-adjusted cancer death rates,* females by site, US, 1930–2008.

Source: © 2014, American Cancer Society, Inc, Surveillance Research.

Moredun Animal Health Ltd/Science Photo Library

PHOTO 8.2 | A scanning electron micrograph provides a colour depiction of a small cancerous tumour within a human lung. The tumour is covered in microscopic hair-like structures called microvilli, which enable absorption and secretion. Smoking and other tobacco use are responsible for nearly all cases of lung cancer.

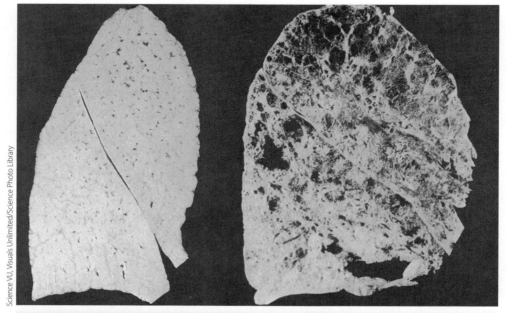

Science VU, Visuals Unlimited/Science Photo Library

PHOTO 8.3 | A healthy human lung compared to a tobacco smoker's lung.

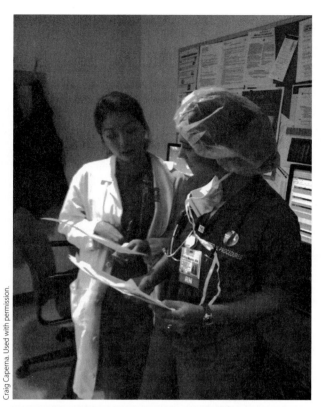

Craig Caperna. Used with permission.

PHOTO 8.4 | Screening is designed to detect cancer at an early stage, before symptoms have developed.

the third leading cause of cancer death, while in the US it is the second leading cause. The five-year survival rate for all stages of prostate cancer combined is 99 per cent (ACS, 2012; CCS, 2011), which is quite high compared to, for example, lung cancer. This rate becomes 100 per cent when the cancer is localized, an encouraging fact, given that 90 per cent of prostate cancers are discovered in the local or regional stages. Incidence rates have fluctuated due to increased rates of cancer screening but have generally decreased since the early 2000s in both Canada and the US. Mortality rates have also decreased since the mid-1990s because of the improved effectiveness of treatment.

Breast Cancer

Around the world, breast cancer is the most diagnosed cancer, with approximately 1 million cases diagnosed each year (Swerdlow et al., 2010). Breast cancer is the most commonly diagnosed cancer among North American women, aside from non-melanoma skin cancer, with an estimated 22,700 and 226,870 new cases in Canada and the US, respectively, in 2012 (ACS, 2012; CCS, 2012a). Breast cancer accounts for approximately 26–29 per cent of all cancer diagnoses in women and is the second most common cause of cancer death in North America (NCHS, 2012; CCS, 2012a). Across all stages of the disease, 89 per cent of women survive at least five years after diagnosis (ACS, 2012; CCS, 2011). This rate is as high as 99 per cent when the cancer is localized and 84 per cent when the cancer has spread just to surrounding regions. Fortunately, approximately 60 per cent of breast cancer diagnoses are at the local stage (SEER, 2012). Incidence rates have generally decreased since the early 2000s due to screening and the decreased use of hormone replacement therapy for menopausal symptoms (ACS, 2012; CCS, 2012a). Mortality from breast cancer has generally decreased since the mid-1980s thanks to early detection and more effective adjuvant therapy after surgery.

Medical Management Approaches

Treatment for cancer involves procedures that address cancerous cells locally, such as surgery and radiation, and treatments, such as chemotherapy, that eradicate cancerous cells that may have metastasized to other areas of the body where they may develop into secondary tumours. Surgical removal of tumours allows them to be examined further by a pathologist to determine how aggressive they may be and whether they are likely to respond to particular types of adjuvant treatment. Radiation therapy may be given daily over an extended period of time, often necessitating time off from work or even temporary relocation to be near a treatment centre. Radiation may be delivered by external beams or by the insertion of radioactive seeds or needles to a target area of the body (Rosenbaum et al., 2005). While a person receiving external beam radiation is not radioactive, radioactive seeds are, and necessitate caution, for example, by avoiding close proximity to other people. Chemotherapy may be given as intravenous infusions or taken orally as pills. Hormonal therapy, such as tamoxifen, is given to combat tumours whose growth is promoted by hormones. Bone marrow transplant is performed following very high-dose chemotherapy treatment that is so radical that it depletes one's bone marrow (Rosenbaum et al., 2005). Sometimes chemotherapy is administered to shrink a tumour before

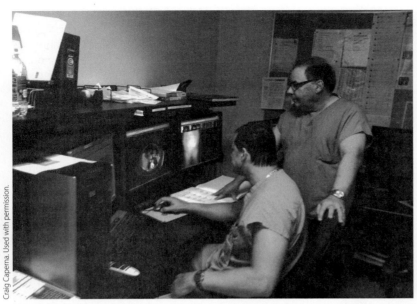

Craig Caperna. Used with permission.

PHOTO 8.5 | Surgical removal of tumours allows them to be examined further by a pathologist to determine how aggressive they may be and whether they are likely to respond to particular types of adjuvant treatment.

surgery, or even palliatively, to alleviate symptoms associated with a tumour's growth.

Cancer Risk Factors

The long delay between exposure to risk factors, such as carcinogens, and the onset of cancer makes the determination of the cause of cancer a challenge (Swerdlow et al., 2010). Although different cancers share similar clinical characteristics, the causes and risk factors associated with cancers at different sites varies. In addition, cancer is often the result of the interaction of various risk factors, which can be biological, environmental, behavioural, or demographic. Epidemiological research provides much of the information regarding risk factors for cancer.

Biological risk factors for cancer include genetic susceptibility, age, and sex. People who carry cancer susceptibility genes are at a heightened risk of developing cancer. For example, mutations in the *BRCA1* and *BRCA2* genes confer an increased risk of breast and ovarian cancers (Swerdlow et al., 2010). Approximately 5–10 per cent of cancers are due to inherited gene mutations; however, most cancers are due to sporadic mutations that are acquired during the lifespan, such

as from carcinogen damage or irregularities during cell division (ACS, 2012; CCS, 2012b). In addition, a family history of cancer, specifically in first-degree relatives, can indicate increased risk; however, families share not only genetics, but may also share lifestyle behaviours that increase risk (e.g., diet) or exposure to the same environmental risk factors. Genetic testing for gene mutations that suggest increased risk for cancer has become increasingly popular, as tests have become more accessible (see In Focus box). Those who test positive for carrying a mutation can opt for increased surveillance, prophylactic surgical removal of potentially affected organs (e.g., breasts or ovaries), or preventive medications (NCI, 2009). They may also share this information with family members, particularly first-degree relatives, who have a 50 per cent chance of carrying the mutation themselves, and who may also opt for testing. Those who test negative for a mutation should continue to engage in screening at recommended rates.

The incidence of cancer generally increases with age. Indeed, 70 per cent of new cancer cases and 62 per cent of cancer deaths in Canada are among adults 50 to 79 years of age (CCS, 2012b). The increased risk with age may be due to a combination of risk factors, including an accumulation of genetic mutations, a weaker immune system, and more carcinogen exposure (Parkin & Bray, 2006). When age is taken into account, men generally have higher cancer incidence and mortality rates than women (CCS, 2012a; Swerdlow et al., 2010). For instance, the lifetime probability of developing cancer is approximately 45 per cent in men and 40 per cent in women living in North America (ACS, 2012; CCS, 2012b).

In addition to and in interaction with biological risk factors, environmental and behavioural factors may also increase one's risk for cancer. Environmental factors include exposure to carcinogens, such as asbestos, radon, and formaldehyde (Swerdlow et al., 2010). Exposure to ionizing radiation, such as ultraviolet radiation (the principal cause of skin cancer), can increase cancer risk through damaging DNA. Approximately 10 per cent of cancers in developed countries are attributable to infections, and 5 per cent of all cancer deaths are a result of viral infections (CCS, 2012b; Swerdlow

Patenting and Commercializing Breast Cancer Susceptibility Genes

Since the discovery in the early 1990s that mutations in the BRCA1 and BRCA2 genes confer increased susceptibility to breast, ovarian, and other cancers in both men and women, battles have raged about whether it should be to obtain US patents on genetic material and on methods to use that genetic material for diagnostic tests. Proponents suggest that patenting is necessary to protect the significant investments of companies that have conducted essential scientific research. Such protection, it is argued, allows companies to develop further products and services, advancing innovations in the field of personalized medicine. Detractors, including some scientists and professional medical organizations, counter that patenting stifles the open sharing of information and data essential to scientific discovery. For companies that seek to hold the patents on tests for hereditary cancer, such testing represents significant revenues. The commercialization of such testing has been criticized, based on concerns about conflicts of interest and the lack of appropriate counselling and delivery of such information outside of clinical settings (Matloff & Caplan, 2008).

et al., 2010). The human papillomavirus (HPV), particularly the strains that are sexually contracted, causes about 70 per cent of cervical cancers, although having HPV does not always lead to cervical cancer (CCS, 2012b). In addition, longer exposure to sex hormones can increase the risk of some reproductive cancers (CCS, 2012b).

It is estimated that 35 per cent of cancers are related to lifestyle choices. Tobacco is a major cause of cancer, especially lung and bronchial cancers, in developed countries (Swerdlow et al., 2010; see Figure 8.4). It is estimated that tobacco use is linked to 20–30 per cent of cancer deaths worldwide. Tobacco smoke contains over 70 carcinogens and greatly increases the risk of lung cancer. In fact, smokers are 20 times more likely to develop lung cancer than non-smokers, and the risk increases with the amount smoked (CCS, 2012b). Other behavioural factors linked to increased risk of cancer include high alcohol consumption, a diet high in fat, lack of exercise, and obesity.

Finally, some demographic factors are associated with risk for cancer. For example, socio-economic status (SES) is linked to increased risk for certain types of cancer. Low SES is associated with increased risk for lung, stomach, and cervical cancers (Kawachi & Kroenke, 2006). In addition, low SES is a risk factor for cancer mortality in general (Booth, Li, Zhang-Salomons, & Mackillop, 2010). The reasons for the association between SES and cancer risk and survival are unclear. It has been suggested that later stage of diagnosis, a more aggressive biology of cancer, lower quality of care, and differences in behavioural risk factors (e.g., higher smoking rates, higher rates of obesity) may help to explain the SES difference in cancer risk and mortality (Clegg et al., 2009; Kawachi & Kroenke, 2006; Woods, Rachet, & Coleman, 2006).

Differences in cancer incidence and mortality have also been observed based on nationality. For example, breast cancer is most common in Western countries, such as the US and Europe, whereas breast cancer incidence is relatively low in Africa and Asia (Parkin & Bray, 2006; Swerdlow et al., 2010). Asian-American women born in the US have been found to have a breast cancer risk 60 per cent higher than Asian-American women who were born in the East (Ziegler et al., 1993). Furthermore, those who had lived in the US longer had an increased risk of breast cancer, with incidence rates closer to those of White women than rates of women in their home country. National differences in cancer incidence and mortality are believed to be due to environmental and behavioural differences, rather than genetic differences (Parkin & Bray, 2006). For instance, the differences observed in breast cancer incidence are likely related to lifestyle factors in the host country that are adopted after immigration, such as dietary fat intake, that may increase body mass index and the influence of reproductive hormones (Keegan, Gomez, Clarke, Chan, & Glaser, 2007; Kolonel & Wilkens, 2006; Parkin & Bray, 2006).

There are also racial and ethnic differences in the incidence and mortality of various cancers. For example, non-Hispanic White women in the US are more likely to develop breast cancer than any other race/ethnicity group, but African-American women are more likely to die from the disease (ACS, 2011; see Figure 8.5). This discrepancy is attributed to later stages at detection and poorer stage-specific survival among African-American women (Curtis, Quale, Haggstrom, & Smith-Bindman, 2008).

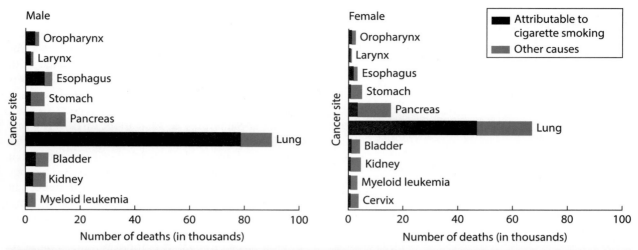

FIGURE 8.4 | Annual number of cancer deaths attributed to smoking, by sex and site, US, 2000–4.

Source: © 2014, American Cancer Society, Inc, Surveillance Research.

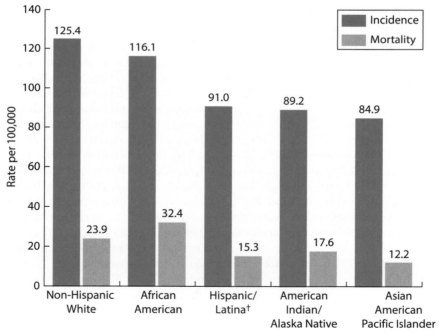

* Rates are age adjusted to the 2000 US standard population.
† Persons of Hispanic origin may be any race.

FIGURE 8.5 | Female breast cancer incidence (2004–8) and mortality (2003–7) rates (adjusted to the 2000 US standard population) by race and ethnicity.

Source: © 2014, American Cancer Society, Inc, Surveillance Research.

Biopsychosocial Factors in Cancer Incidence and Progression

We have thus far considered the biological, environmental, behavioural, and demographic risk factors for cancer. The biopsychosocial model posits that, besides biological factors, social and psychological factors must be taken into account in explaining and treating patients' dysfunction (Engel, 1977). In this section, we consider the role of psychosocial factors, particularly stress, in concert with biological mechanisms that may play a role in the initiation and progression of cancer.

In general, the evidence linking psychosocial factors to cancer initiation has been ambiguous (Antoni et al., 2006; Lutgendorf & Sood, 2011). The most consistent evidence has linked cancer incidence with severe life events (e.g., bereavement), extreme distress, and chronic depression (Chida, Hamer, Wardle, & Steptoe, 2008; Lutgendorf & Sood, 2011). For example, major life events, such as the death of a loved one, have been linked to an increased risk of developing cancer (Levav et al., 2000). Lillberg and colleagues (2003) examined whether major life events were related to increased cancer incidence in a prospective study with approximately 11,000 Finnish women. At baseline, women in the study were asked to report stressful life events that had occurred in the past five years. Cancer registry information was checked 14 years later to determine which women developed breast cancer. Women who had experienced a major life event, including divorce or separation, death of a spouse, or death of a friend or relative, were at an elevated risk for breast cancer. Depression has also been linked to an increased risk of developing cancer (Chida et al., 2008; Penninx, Guralnik, & Havlik, 1998).

It is difficult to establish a causal link between psychosocial factors and cancer onset for several reasons. The use of retrospective designs can greatly limit our ability to make causal conclusions (Chida et al., 2008; Reiche, Nunes, & Morimoto, 2004; Sklar & Anisman, 1981). Cancer patients who are asked to recall past life events may remember these events differently based on having knowledge of their diagnosis. In addition, it is possible that the disease was present before and during the stressful life events. Importantly, there is typically a long delay between the development of and the detection of cancer, further obscuring causal links between psychosocial factors and cancer onset (Bleiker, Hendriks, Otten, Verbeek, & van der Ploeg, 2008; Reiche et al., 2004).

In general, the evidence linking psychosocial factors to cancer progression and mortality has been stronger than the evidence for cancer onset (Antoni et al., 2006; Lutgendorf & Sood, 2011). In particular, depression, stressful life events, and social isolation have been associated with more rapid cancer progression and poorer survival in individuals with cancer (Lutgendorf & Sood, 2011). Depression in cancer has been associated with mortality rates up to 39 per cent higher (Chida et al., 2008; Satin, Linden, & Phillips, 2009). Stressful life events, such as loss of a spouse, have also been associated with higher mortality rates in cancer patients (Chida et al., 2008). In a study investigating the experience of traumatic and stressful life events in women with metastatic or recurrent breast cancer, women who had experienced at least one traumatic or stressful life event had a significantly shorter disease-free interval, relative to women who had not had such an experience (Palesh et al., 2007).

Cancer progression and mortality are associated with social isolation and a lack of social support (Pinquart & Duberstein, 2010; Reynolds & Kaplan, 1990), although not all studies support this relationship (e.g., Chida et al., 2008). For example, in a study of women with breast cancer, women who reported they were socially isolated before their diagnosis were twice as likely to die of breast cancer. Furthermore, women without close relatives, friends, or living children had a higher risk of breast cancer mortality than women with more social ties (Kroenke, Kubzansky, Schernhammer, Holmes, & Kawachi, 2006). However, a decrease in cancer mortality is associated with high levels of perceived social support, a larger network size, and being married (Pinquart & Duberstein, 2010). Among the unmarried, cancer mortality appears to be differentially associated with marital history. In a study of marital status and cancer survival, patients who were separated from their spouse at the time of their diagnosis had the lowest five- and 10-year survival rates, followed by those patients who were widowed, divorced, and never married (Sprehn, Chambers, Saykin, Konski, & Johnstone, 2009).

How might psychosocial factors influence the initiation and progression of cancer? Both indirect behavioural and direct physiological pathways have been proposed. First, behavioural changes that accompany psychosocial factors may play a role in cancer onset and development. For instance, psychosocial factors can lead to behavioural changes that increase one's risk of cancer, including increased smoking, less exercise, and poor diet (Reiche et al., 2004; Sprehn et al., 2009). Furthermore, psychosocial factors, such as stress and depression, can lead to a decrease in compliance with medical regimens, which may increase the progression of cancer (Spiegel & Giese-Davis, 2003; Sprehn et al., 2009). Social support may be linked to lower mortality because one's social network encourages healthy behaviours and allows for greater access to the health-care system (e.g., getting to medical appointments).

Psychosocial factors have also been postulated to influence cancer initiation and progression through physiological pathways. Psychoneuroimmunology research (see Chapter 2 for a general discussion of psychoneuroimmunology) has helped to clarify possible biological mechanisms. Stress and the immune system are linked through the sympathetic nervous system (SNS), which releases catecholamines (e.g., norepinephrine and epinephrine), and the hypothalamic-pituitary-adrenal (HPA) axis (a pathway that connects the brain with the endocrine system), which releases cortisol (Antoni et al., 2006; Segerstrom & Miller, 2004). Chronic stressors (e.g., bereavement, depression, isolation) and the resulting constant exposure to stress hormones generally impair immune function (Antoni et al., 2006; Glaser & Kiecolt-Glaser, 2005). When the immune system detects transformed cells, it attempts to destroy these cancerous cells, a process referred to as **immunosurveillance** (Dunn, Koebel, & Schreiber, 2006). If the immune system is inhibited and all tumour cells are not destroyed, the tumour will grow, leading to cancer.

How do stress hormones and immunosuppression influence cancer? Stress hormones can cause DNA damage, impair mechanisms involved in DNA repair, and inhibit programmed cell death in cancer cells, all of which may promote the onset and progression of cancer (Antoni et al., 2006; Lutgendorf & Sood, 2011; Reiche et al., 2004). Stress, through the release of catecholamines, may also promote tumour growth by facilitating angiogenesis (the development of a blood supply for the tumour, allowing growth, invasion, and metastasis) (Antoni et al., 2006; Lutgendorf & Sood, 2011). High levels of social support have been associated with lower levels of these growth factors in women with ovarian cancer, suggesting a potential physiological pathway through which a lack of social support influences cancer progression (Costanzo et al., 2005; Lutgendorf et al., 2002). Cortisol, which is a significant steroid hormone (a glucocorticoid, produced by the adrenal cortex), has also been shown to stimulate growth and proliferation of cancer cells (Lutgendorf & Sood, 2011). Negative psychosocial states, through their effects on stress hormones, have been associated with inhibition of the cellular immune response, thus decreasing immunosurveillance (Antoni et al., 2006; Lutgendorf & Sood, 2011). For example, women who were diagnosed and treated surgically for breast cancer and who reported high levels of psychological distress (intrusive and avoidant thoughts and behaviours about

cancer) had reduced natural killer (NK)-cell response relative to women who reported low levels of psychological distress (Andersen et al., 1998). Breast cancer patients with higher levels of perceived social support, especially high-quality emotional support from a spouse or intimate other, had greater NK-cell activity and increased NK-cell cytotoxicity (Levy et al., 1990).

Cancer Prevention

Behavioural changes can be made to help reduce one's risk of developing cancer. For example, wearing sunscreen to protect against harmful ultraviolet radiation can help reduce risk of skin cancer. Avoiding smoking can help reduce risk of lung cancer. Exercising regularly can help reduce the risk of colon and breast cancer. However, as we have seen in previous sections, cancer is typically caused by multiple factors, so primary prevention measures can reduce but not entirely eliminate the risk of developing cancer.

Cancer screening is a secondary prevention measure. Screening is designed to detect cancer at an early stage, before symptoms have developed. Screening reduces cancer morbidity and mortality through early detection because early-stage cancer is typically easier to treat, and treatment interventions tend to be less aggressive and invasive (NCI, 2012b). Examples of efficacious cancer screening tests are mammography for breast cancer, Pap tests for cervical cancer, and fecal occult blood tests and colonoscopy for colorectal cancer.

Although screening tests have benefits for morbidity and mortality, there are also associated harms. Some screening tests can be directly harmful to the patient, for example, perforation of the colon from a colonoscopy (Levin & Prorok, 2006). Also, screening tests may incorrectly detect absent cancer or may miss present cancer. False positives (i.e., a positive screening result when cancer is not present) cause stress and anxiety. In addition, unnecessary follow-up diagnostic tests, such as biopsies, can be painful and invasive. False negatives (i.e., a negative screening result when cancer is present) usually result in a delay in diagnosis and treatment. The issue of **overdiagnosis**, which has been alleged for mammography and breast cancer, has also been identified as a problem of cancer screening in that it can lead to unnecessary treatment (Levin & Prorok, 2006).

Screening mammography is a low-dose x-ray procedure used to look at breast tissue and detect early-stage breast cancer (ACS, 2011). Mammography screening decreases breast cancer mortality by 15 per cent to 30 per cent (Jorgensen, Keen, & Gøtzsche, 2011; Nelson et al., 2009).

Although mammography involves radiation, the radiation risk from mammography is small, and the mortality benefit of screening outweighs the risks of radiation exposure (Yaffe & Mainprize, 2011). In general, mammography correctly identifies those with breast cancer approximately 80 per cent of the time and those without breast cancer approximately 90 per cent of the time (Nelson et al., 2009). In Canada, it is recommended that women between the ages of 50 and 69 years of age be screened every two to three years (CTF, 2011). Similarly, women in the US are advised to receive screening every two years between the ages of 50 and 74 (USPSTF, 2009), although screening guidelines are not universally agreed upon (e.g., ACS, 2011). Approximately 70 per cent of women aged 50 and older have had a screening mammogram in the past two years (NCHS, 2011; Shields & Wilkins, 2009).

Although screening mammography can help to reduce breast cancer morbidity and mortality, some women do not receive mammograms. Barriers to engaging in mammography screening exist at the health-care system level, the social level, and the individual level (Sarma, 2013). Reasons for non-adherence include a fear of radiation (Champion & Skinner, 2003), fear of pain (Rawl, Champion, Menon, & Foster, 2000), anxiety about a positive screening result (Miller, O'Hea, Block Lerner, Moon, & Foran-Tuller, 2011), and a lack of accessibility to a screening centre (Ogedegbe et al., 2005). Despite this, health psychology researchers have used mainly individual-level theories such as the health belief model (Rosenstock, Strecher, & Becker, 1988) to examine such barriers to obtaining mammograms. For instance, the health belief model (see Chapter 1), in predicting the likelihood of getting a mammogram, considers one's beliefs about barriers to engaging in a behaviour (e.g., mammography is painful) in combination with one's beliefs about one's susceptibility to a condition (e.g., breast cancer), the severity of the consequences of that condition (e.g., surgery, death), the perceived benefits of the behaviour (e.g., a clear mammogram would provide peace of mind), and one's perceived sense of self-efficacy in performing the behaviour.

Like other screening tests, mammography can sometimes be inaccurate. Indeed, the chance of a false positive at the first screening is 7.4 per cent (CTF, 2011). What are the psychological consequences of false positive results? In the short term, women may be anxious when they receive the results (Brett, Bankhead, Henderson, Watson, & Austoker, 2005). In the long term, women with false positives have an increase in thoughts, anxiety, and worry about breast cancer (Brewer, Salz, & Lillie, 2007), although it is not known how long this anxiety lasts.

Psychosocial Adjustment to Cancer

As treatments have improved and cancer mortality has decreased in some cancer types, cancer is increasingly becoming a chronic illness. For cancer patients and their families, cancer diagnosis and treatment mean multiple adjustment challenges due to the disease, including changes in interpersonal relationships and social roles, the physical effects of treatment, and coping with the uncertainty and stress of the diagnosis and treatment (Franks & Roesche, 2006; Helgeson & Cohen, 1996). In this section, we consider how patients adapt to and cope with living with cancer.

A diagnosis of cancer can create a period of crisis. Common initial reactions to a cancer diagnosis include disbelief and denial of the veracity of the diagnosis. This initial phase typically lasts less than a week. Patients then move to the dysphoria phase, during which the diagnosis is acknowledged. This dysphoria phase is characterized by anxiety, depression, insomnia, poor concentration, lack of appetite, and trouble maintaining daily activities, and usually lasts one to two weeks, although this varies. Finally, patients typically adjust to the diagnosis and treatment for cancer and attempt to resume regular routines. The quality of this long-term adaptation phase depends on many factors and varies greatly among individuals (Holland & Gooen-Piels, 2003).

Psychosocial adaptation to cancer is an ongoing process that changes with the disease stage, symptoms, prognosis, and treatment (Holland & Gooen-Piels, 2003). Patients need to attend treatment sessions, manage emotional distress, and adjust to changing social roles. In addition, patients are faced with the consequences of cancer and its treatment, including pain, fatigue, lack of appetite, and sexual dysfunction, all of which can cause impairment and influence the patient's daily life (Nicholas & Veach, 2000).

Coping with cancer involves the use of different coping strategies according to the nature of the stressor. For instance, patients receiving palliative care for cancer reported using problem-focused coping less frequently for existential issues and emotion-focused coping less frequently for physical stressors (De Faye, Wilson, Chater, Viola, & Hall, 2006). The appraisal of cancer-related stressors is also an important factor that determines which coping strategies a patient will use. For example, if cancer is appraised as a threat or a challenge, problem-focused coping is more likely to be used to deal with the stressor (e.g., medical compliance, problem-solving). On the other hand, if cancer is appraised as a harm or loss, then avoidance coping is more likely to be used (e.g., denial, minimizing the threat of cancer, wishful thinking, substance use). Again, cancer patients use multiple types of coping to deal with the stress of cancer (Franks & Roesch, 2006). Helplessness and hopelessness are associated with poor adjustment (van't Spijker, Trijsburg, & Duivenvoorden, 1997) and increased risk of cancer relapse or death (Watson, Haviland, Greer, Davidson, & Bliss, 1999); however, that evidence linking helplessness and hopelessness to cancer survival has not been consistent (Petticrew, Bell, & Hunter, 2002). Optimism has been linked to greater psychological well-being in cancer patients (van't Spijker et al., 1997). In a study of newly diagnosed cancer patients, psychological well-being was associated with higher optimism and lower pessimism before the start of chemotherapy, and pessimism predicted a negative change in psychological well-being nine months after chemotherapy (Pinquart, Fröhlich, & Silbereisen, 2007).

Social support is thought to have positive effects on psychological and physical health both directly, by enhancing health behaviours, and indirectly, by acting as a buffer against cancer-related stressors (Costanzo, Sood, & Lutgendorf, 2011; Nicholas & Veach, 2000). Emotional support and, more specifically, emotional expression (i.e., having someone to talk with about cancer-related concerns) may be especially important for successful adjustment to cancer (Helgeson & Cohen, 1996). For instance, in a sample of breast cancer patients, women who reported high emotional expression about cancer had fewer medical morbidities, better physical health, and less distress eight months after medical treatment than women who reported low emotional expression (Stanton et al., 2000). Emotional expression is also associated with better survival (Reynolds et al., 2000). Cancer is a strain on interpersonal relationships and is also stressful for the patient's friends and family (Helgeson & Cohen, 1996). The patient may have to limit social activities due to treatment schedules and side effects. Friends and family may act in unintentionally harmful ways towards the patient, such as avoiding physical contact or open communication about cancer, because they are unsure of how to behave (Wortman & Dunkel-Schetter, 1979).

Cancer is a major source of stress, and more severe psychological problems, such as depression, can develop in patients. The likelihood that a patient will develop psychological problems depends on medical (e.g., site, stage, hospitalization) and personal factors (e.g., quality of social support) (Manne et al., 2008). Although general distress affects 5 per cent to 50 per cent of patients (van't Spijker et al., 1997), inpatients are more likely to be distressed because of the greater disability and pain associated with their conditions (Holland & Gooen-Piels, 2003). Depression affects between 9 per cent and 46 per cent of patients (van't Spijker et al., 1997), and is more common among cancer patients than in the general population (Massie, 2004; van't Spijker et al., 1997). However, depression can be difficult to diagnose in cancer patients because the symptoms of depression (e.g., weight loss, insomnia, fatigue) may be mistaken for symptoms of the disease (Spiegel & Giese-Davis, 2003). Patients who are socially isolated and have greater physical impairment due to cancer are more at risk for poor adjustment (Holland & Gooen-Piels, 2003; Manne et al., 2008). Knowledge of risk factors that predict poor adjustment can help health-care providers to identify patients who may be at risk.

Psychological Assessment of the Cancer Patient

Treatment for cancer has changed from being focused solely on medically managing the disease to also preserving quality of life. This has become especially important as medical advances have allowed cancer patients to live long after their treatment is complete. Thus, more attention has been paid to the psychological needs of patients. Psychosocial health needs can be identified when patients bring this up themselves, when providers ask about them directly, or when clinicians administer screening assessments (Adler & Page, 2008). Screening is useful in that it may identify patients who do not perceive themselves to be in need of psychosocial services. Specific instruments include the Distress Thermometer, a single-item scale that depicts a thermometer and asks respondents to indicate the level of distress that they have experienced over the past week from 0 (no distress) to 10 (extreme distress). The Patient Care Monitor 2.0 uses 86 items to identify difficulties commonly encountered by cancer patients, including psychological distress, problems with performing their roles in life, physical problems, and lowered overall quality of life. The instrument is administered via computer, taking about 11 minutes, and the results can be forwarded automatically to clinicians in advance of meeting with a patient (Adler & Page, 2008).

Current practice guidelines recommend that psychological assessment be part of an ideal plan to identify cancer patients whose psychosocial needs are likely to affect their health. However, such screening is not yet routine in cancer care (Adler & Page, 2008). Such screening, however, is useful only in environments where resources are available to link patients who screen positive for distress and difficulty coping with psychosocial health services to assistance. Thus, such screening is recommended only in settings where effective follow-up treatment and monitoring is possible.

A predominant belief underpinning the development of psychosocial interventions for cancer patients was that the challenges that cancer presents are so disruptive that most patients could benefit from some type of psychological intervention. Recent research, however, has shown that those who are more distressed appear to benefit the most from such interventions (Hart et al., 2012; Schneider et al., 2010), suggesting that screening and then targeting treatment to those who are actually experiencing difficulties may be a more appropriate approach. Nonetheless, it has also been suggested that psychological interventions may be instrumental in preventing distress, even in patients who are not currently troubled, as they go through the stages of cancer treatment and beyond.

Psychological Interventions for Cancer Patients

As has been outlined above, the challenges that cancer patients face are many. As Karen's example (see In Practice box) demonstrates, upon diagnosis, in addition to the shock of a potentially life-threatening diagnosis, there is often much new information to take in and understand, and decisions regarding the course of treatment often need to be made. Like Karen, many women with breast cancer will be in the position of deciding between being treated with **mastectomy** versus **breast-conserving surgery** plus radiation. Being offered this type of choice is helpful in allowing patients to maximize the aspects of quality of life that are particularly important to them, such as body image concerns versus worry about being exposed to radiation. However, this latitude also brings with it the burden of making a decision during an already stressful time.

🔲 IN PRACTICE
Adjusting to a Cancer Diagnosis

Karen, a 61-year-old mother of two grown daughters, was looking forward to spending more time in her garden and travelling during her upcoming retirement. She was relatively active, took vitamins and calcium supplements, and, at the recommendation of her physician, received a mammogram semi-annually. One morning in the shower she felt a pea-sized bump under her left arm. Although somewhat alarmed, she wondered whether it really could be an indicator of something serious. Her most recent mammogram had been clear, so she decided to just keep an eye on it for a while and not let herself get too worked up thinking about the "C word." She felt healthy and the lump wasn't painful. About a month later, when the lump hadn't changed, she scheduled an appointment with her physician who, upon physical examination, ordered a mammogram. When the diagnostic mammogram indicated suspicious findings in the form of visible calcifications, Karen was scheduled to have a needle biopsy. This would allow the cells themselves to be examined, to definitively determine if the tumour was cancerous. She was anxious about the procedure, which would occur under a local anaesthetic, but, although it was somewhat uncomfortable, it was over quickly.

Although Karen had been fairly composed when she had identified the lump, waiting for the results of the biopsy sent her into a bit of a tailspin. She began to worry about worst-case scenarios, wondering if she would lose her breast, her femininity, the admiration of her husband, her robust lifestyle and social life, and, most importantly, she wondered if she would live to see grandchildren. She sat up late into the night searching the Internet for information, and at times it was overwhelming to process so many new terms and concepts: tumour staging, lumpectomy, mastectomy,

(Continued)

breast prostheses, reconstructive surgery, the dangers of silicone breast implants. When the news came that she indeed had breast cancer, Karen felt shocked and numb, despite having prepared herself as best she could. It was difficult to concentrate on all that was said during her consultation and she was relieved when she learned that a **patient navigator** would help her negotiate the process of understanding her options and getting information from the various specialists that formed her medical team.

Fortunately, like a large proportion of women diagnosed with breast cancer, Karen's cancer was detected at an early stage and she could be effectively treated by either mastectomy, having her entire breast removed, or lumpectomy, having just the tumour removed. The breast-conserving treatment, however, would involve several weeks of daily radiation therapy to eradicate any remaining malignant cells. Removing the entire breast might make her feel as if she'd had a more "complete" procedure, but what would it be like to be without a breast? Although she did not consider herself vain and felt confident in her husband's love and support, she was somewhat invested in her image of herself as healthy, "whole," and attractive. She found testimonies on the Internet from women satisfied with each of the procedures, and even from women who had had breast reconstruction following a mastectomy and a breast augmentation on the other side that resulted in an overall enlarged bust. She didn't think that an enhanced body image was worth that amount of follow-up surgery, so she opted for lumpectomy plus radiation. The surgery went smoothly, and during the procedure the surgeon also biopsied one of the lymph nodes under her arm. The pathology report revealed that, because cancer had not appeared to have metastasized beyond the breast, chemotherapy would not be necessary.

Karen's radiation therapy was five days a week over six weeks. Each session was brief and wasn't painful, but the sight of unfamiliar medical equipment was somewhat alarming at first. Although she kept working through her treatment, she experienced some additional fatigue, and the skin of the treated breast often felt sunburned and dry.

Karen's family and friends were as supportive and caring as she could have wished and her husband took on additional household tasks to allow her extra time to rest. However, intimacy between them dropped off for a while, arousing insecurities for Karen that she was no longer a vibrant, sexually attractive woman. After some frank and tearful discussion, Karen realized that her husband's withdrawal was based in a concern for her comfort and well-being. With that, the pressure to resume sexual activity felt lessened and they settled into more affectionate forms of intimacy, a time that intensified their bond and led to the eventual resumption of their regular patterns of lovemaking. As the completion of her treatment approached, Karen was looking forward to having these trips to the hospital behind her, but, somewhat unexpectedly, without the schedule of appointments and the care, attention, and concern of the medical staff, she felt somewhat unmoored. Although she would have regular follow-up visits to monitor her condition, she felt strange when no longer taking an active role in fighting her cancer.

Karen was an avid reader and noticed how many self-help books related to cancer there were in the bookstores and her local library. Some were authoritative, written by doctors, and some were written by women who had cancer themselves. Some of the books were irreverent and upbeat in tone, and focused on how to maintain a positive body image and family and sexual relationships; some were more clinical in tone and packed with medical terminology and information. She read one focused on life beyond cancer and found it useful and encouraging. However, Karen craved some kind of personal connection with others who had been through what she had experienced. But she was busy, and admittedly somewhat hesitant to discuss her concerns in a group of people. She noted that several mainstream cancer support organizations such as the Wellness Community, Cancer Care, and American Cancer Society had online support communities, where one could post one's own concerns and read the posts of others. This worked well for her, as she often found herself brooding later at night after the concerns of the day had faded. When she had trouble sleeping, spending some time online gave her some peace of mind. Soon she found that not only was it uplifting to connect with others in her situation but that sharing her own insights and encouraging others was empowering. This forum was a place where more personal issues, such as how to communicate with her husband about intimacy post-cancer and worries about her own daughters' health, could be explored with people who knew what she was going through.

Part of what had spurred her concern about her daughters' risk for also developing breast cancer was seeing an advertisement about genetic tests to determine if one carried a breast cancer mutation that could be passed on. Karen began thinking about other cases of cancer in her family—an aunt on her mother's side who also had breast cancer, a sister who had had skin cancer, and a great-aunt on her father's side who she seemed to remember may have had some kind of ovarian or gynecological cancer—and she worried there might be something genetic going on.

When she asked her physician about this at her next follow-up visit, she was referred to a **genetic counsellor** specializing in cancer. Karen found the genetic counsellor supportive and especially good at communicating the complexities of genes, mutations, and what types of information genetic testing could and could not provide. The counsellor took a detailed family history and created a diagram, called a pedigree. It depicted all of the relatives on both sides of her family and documented whether they were alive, and, if dead, what they had died of, and at what age. There were some details of distant relatives' health histories that were hard for her to remember, but telephone calls to her older sister and a still-living aunt filled in some of the details. The counsellor explained that, despite the multiple cases of cancer in Karen's family, cancer is a common disease and her family history did not appear to be indicative of a hereditary pattern. Because genetic testing is uninformative in cases like this, it was not recommended for her. This assessment was reassuring for Karen to hear, along with the fact that hereditary cancers represent a very small proportion of all cases of breast cancer. The counsellor explained further, however, that Karen's daughters, because they have a family history of breast cancer in a first-degree relative, had a risk twice that of women without a family history of cancer (Rosenbaum & Rosenbaum, 2005). Thus, they should continue to obtain screening mammography at recommended intervals and to have regular clinical breast exams by their physicians.

Patients often vary in the extent to which they desire to share their treatment-related decision-making with their physicians. Some make their decisions on their own while others rely on their physician's best clinical recommendation, so this process must be negotiated skilfully by clinicians (Adler & Page, 2008). Several American states mandate that women diagnosed with breast cancer who are medically eligible for them be informed of breast-conserving options in addition to mastectomy. These mandates arose in reaction to a history of surgical treatment for breast cancer that was extensive in its degree of breast tissue removal. This radical surgical approach was in keeping with a now-outdated notion of cancer's spread and a treatment focus that was primarily on survival per se rather than on the quality of that survival. Breast cancer activists and individuals within the medical community equally were important in bringing about these changes, both in the revised standards of medical care and in legal actions (Lerner, 2001).

Men diagnosed with prostate cancer may be offered a similar type of decision between having their tumour surgically removed or treated with radiation and "active surveillance" or watchful waiting to detect signs that a cancer is aggressive or has started to progress. This is because most prostate cancers are not life-threatening and evidence suggests that survival time is similar for men who are treated with either radical prostatectomy or active surveillance (Wilt et al., 2012). Deciding between treatment or watchful waiting is made more arduous by the fact that the side effects of prostate cancer treatment, including impotence and urinary incontinence, are threatening to quality of life, and some men may consider these quite problematic. However, taking no action against a tumour may also be anxiety-promoting and risky.

As described earlier, the array of treatments for cancer, including surgery, radiation therapy, chemotherapy, hormone therapy, and bone-marrow transplant, bring side effects that often are debilitating. These include loss of function, disfiguration, **lymphedema**, fatigue, nausea, vomiting, hair loss, skin burns or irritation, mouth sores, neuropathy, and even "chemo brain," the awareness that one's thinking is no longer sharp. These side effects result in diminished body image and self-esteem; depression and anxiety; disruptions in family, marital, and social relationships; and occupational and financial consequences. The side effects or ramifications of cancer treatment may last months or even years so that ongoing support is essential. Even the end of treatment may present a difficult adjustment for patients, as it brings about a change in routines, the withdrawal of frequent contact with medical personnel, and a halt to a sense of actively engaging with the disease.

eireann/123RF

PHOTO 8.6 | Hair loss can be a consequence of chemotherapy.

Fortunately, now more than ever, a wealth of psychosocial resources are available for cancer patients through various social service and charitable organizations. These resources assist in meeting the informational, emotional, social, and practical needs that arise during the various stages of cancer diagnosis, treatment, and recovery. They include information on cancer-related treatments, peer support, counselling/psychotherapy, pharmacological management of mental symptoms, medical supplies, transportation, family and caregiver support, assistance with activities of daily living, legal services, cognitive and educational services, financial and insurance advice, benefits counselling, and financial assistance (Adler & Page, 2008).

Among the types of treatments that have been subjected to empirical evaluation, a major theoretical orientation has been the cognitive behavioural approach (Moyer, Sohl, Knapp-Oliver, & Schneider, 2009), which focuses on recognizing and altering problematic thoughts and behaviours and on reducing negative emotions related to cancer. An example of this type of treatment involved developing effective problem-solving skills and identifying and challenging maladaptive thoughts; learning relaxation techniques; and using resources such as family and friends and pleasurable activities to cope (Edelman & Kidman, 1999). Supportive-expressive group therapy focuses on expressing emotions, generating social support among group members, and exploring existential concerns like the fear of dying (Classen et al., 2008). Another type

of well-researched treatment is education, which focuses on increasing knowledge and reducing uncertainty by providing information on topics such as treatment options, side effects, and psychosocial challenges.

One popular type of coping assistance is provided in the form of support groups. These may be offered through organizations such as Cancer Care, The Wellness Community, or through the hospitals where medical treatment occurs. These may be offered in person, or online, and may be led by professionals such as nurses, social workers, or clinical psychologists, or by cancer survivors or "peers." These groups may be comprised of members with various types or stages of cancers, or may be restricted to those with a particular cancer, gender, age, or stage of disease or treatment. Opinion varies regarding the extent to which insisting on commonalities among support group members is important or not. One reason why this may be important is that group members often engage in social comparison, a process whereby they contrast their own condition, abilities, qualities, etc. to those of similar others. Often, cancer patients selectively use downward social comparison (comparing oneself to those who are doing less well) and upward social comparison (comparing oneself to those who are doing better). Women being treated for breast cancer were observed to use downward social comparison spontaneously and frequently (Wood, Taylor, & Lichtman, 1985). This strategy is presumed to be a means of coping and self-enhancement when under threat. This suggestion was borne out by the fact that downward social comparison was used more frequently by women who were closer in time to their surgery and presumably experiencing more threat. However, in some instances, downward social comparisons to similar others who were physically much worse proved to be frightening and sobering. In a review of the ways in which individuals in threatening situations satisfy their need to be with others and gain information, cancer patients were found to seek contact with individuals they perceive as more fortunate (Taylor & Lobel, 1989). Thus, peer discussion groups may be problematic when they expose cancer patients to others doing poorly psychologically or physically.

Another type of intervention useful for many cancer patients is physical activity, including aerobic exercise and resistance training. Such training can actually reduce fatigue and improve mood (Brown et al., 2011; Puetz & Herring, 2012). In previous years, cancer patients experiencing fatigue were encouraged to rest, take things easy, and refrain from exerting themselves. However, this strategy is thought to lead to a vicious cycle that promotes deconditioning and further fatigue. Research indicates that even patients currently undergoing chemotherapy can benefit physically and psychologically from exercise training. Similarly, breast cancer patients were once discouraged from using the arm on their treated side to lift heavy objects like groceries or grandchildren. This advice was intended to prevent lymphedema, irreversible damage to the lymphatic system that may have already been weakened by surgery and radiation. However, research now indicates that weight training is safe for women with breast cancer who have or are at risk for lymphedema and decreases the symptoms or incidence of lymphedema (Ahmed, Thomas, Yee, & Schmitz, 2006). Interventions for terminally ill cancer patients aim not only to manage psychological distress, but also to promote coping with the end of life and fostering a good death by focusing on spiritual well-being and finding meaning in one's life. One such activity used to do this is a short-term life review (Ando, Morita, Akechi, & Okamoto, 2010). This involves bringing to mind and sharing the important events and memories from one's life during an interview with a therapist. Patients respond to questions such as "what was the proudest moment in your life?" and then review their recorded statements with a therapist who has compiled them, along with relevant images, into an album, to develop a sense of continuity and coherence in these memories.

For students interested in specializing in working psychotherapeutically with cancer patients it is important, in addition to appropriate psychotherapy training, to become knowledgeable about the medical aspects of cancer (Watson & Kissane, 2011). Such professionals must often communicate with medical personnel to be aware of the disease, prognostic, and treatment context affecting their patients. Most importantly, such professionals must manage their own emotional responses to this potentially demanding work. The supportive care of cancer patients involves dealing with highly charged psychological, physical, relationship, and existential issues.

Future Directions

Both medical and psychosocial treatment for cancer is likely to become more individualized with the emergence of personalized medicine and more emphasis on screening and targeting of appropriate psychological services. Future research investigating psychosocial interventions for cancer patients will likely focus on understanding the role of particular patient characteristics (e.g., personality traits, mental and physical quality of life, social environment, and self-efficacy) that moderate their effects (Tamagawa, Garland, Vaska, & Carlson, 2012) and the mechanisms of action as well as the active ingredients of treatment that are most effective in improving quality of life (Moyer et al., 2012; Stanton, Luecken, Mackinnon, & Thompson, 2012).

SUMMARY

Cancer is the term used for a number of diseases. Cancerous tumours result when genes that regulate cell division have damaged DNA, leading to uncontrolled cell proliferation. Mortality rates for some cancers are decreasing. Treatment for cancer includes surgery, radiation therapy, chemotherapy, hormonal therapy, and bone marrow transplant.

Risk for cancer involves the interaction of biological, environmental, behavioural, and demographic factors. Specific factors include genetic susceptibility, age, sex, exposure to carcinogens, infections, tobacco use, high alcohol consumption, a diet high in fat, lack of exercise, and obesity. The evidence linking psychosocial factors to cancer initiation has been ambiguous. The evidence linking psychosocial factors such as depression, stressful life events, and social isolation to cancer progression and mortality is somewhat stronger. Potential mechanisms include behavioural factors, such as adherence to treatment, and physiological factors, such as elevated stress hormones and immunosuppression. Primary prevention measures, like avoiding smoking, can reduce but not entirely eliminate the risk of developing cancer. Cancer screening, including mammography, is a secondary prevention measure designed to detect cancer at an early stage, before symptoms have developed. Screening has both benefits and harms.

Cancer diagnosis and treatment bring changes in interpersonal relationships and social roles, physical effects, and uncertainty and stress. Targeting coping strategies appropriately, appraising threats as challenges, maintaining optimism, and benefiting from interpersonal support are related to psychological adjustment and well-being. Screening for distress is not yet routine in oncology care and needs to be linked to follow-up psychosocial care services. Treatment decision-making, side effects, and survivorship pose burdens that often require assistance. Resources such as information, peer support, counselling/psychotherapy, pharmacological agents, medical supplies, transportation, family and caregiver support, and practical, legal, educational, and financial assistance are readily available to cancer patients through social service and charitable organizations.

Critical Thought Questions

1. As screening has both benefits and harms, how do we decide whether the general population should use a screening test, such as mammography?
2. For an individual with a family history indicating a high likelihood of a hereditary cancer, what are the potential advantages and disadvantages of pursuing a genetic test to determine if he or she carries a cancer-related mutation?
3. Is it appropriate to patent a gene?

Recommended Reading

Lerner, B.H. (2001). *The breast cancer wars*. New York: Oxford University Press.

Love, S. (2010). *Dr. Susan Love's breast book* (5th ed.). South Boston, Mass.: Da Capo Press.

Miller, S.M., Bowen, D.J., Croyle, R.T., & Rowland, J.H. (2009). *Handbook of cancer control and behavioral science: A resource for researchers, practitioners, and policymakers*. Washington: American Psychological Association.

Rosenbaum, E.H., & Rosenbaum, I. (2005). *Everyone's guide to cancer supportive care: A comprehensive handbook for patients and their families*. Kansas City: Andrews McMeel.

Watson, M., & Kissane, D. (Eds.). (2011). *Handbook of psychotherapy in cancer care*. Hoboken, NJ: John Wiley & Sons.

9

Cardiovascular Disease

| AMANDA C. KENTNER | ADRIENNE H. KOVACS | SHERRY L. GRACE

Learning Objectives

In this chapter you will:

- Learn how psychological distress is linked to the behavioural and biological risk factors that underlie heart disease (the biopsychosocial model).

- Learn to distinguish between types of cardiovascular diseases and their medical management through secondary prevention measures.

- Learn to identify and describe several psychosocial factors that contribute to cardiovascular disease onset and reoccurrence.

- Gain an understanding of how these psychosocial factors are assessed in heart patients.

- Be able to compare and contrast common pharmacological, psychotherapeutic, psycho-educational, and behavioural interventions offered to those living with heart disease.

Cardiovascular Disease Description, Prevalence, and Medical Management

Diseases of the cardiovascular system include those that occur within the heart and the blood transport or circulatory system (i.e., veins and arteries). Together, these diseases are among the leading causes of death for North American men and women (Table 9.1). Fortunately, due to advances in treatment, mortality rates from cardiovascular disease (CVD) have significantly declined in developed nations such as Canada and the United States (Figure 9.1). Since mortality rates have declined, and onset of disease has not, this means that many people are living with chronic CVD.

Psychological factors are associated with the onset of CVD and its progression, as well as the quality and

© Goodluz/iStockphoto

PHOTO 9.1 | Due to advances in treatment, mortality rates due to cardiovascular disease (CVD) have significantly declined in developed nations such as Canada and the US. This means many more people are living with chronic CVD today than ever before.

TABLE 9.1 | Male and Female Mortality (%) due to Cardiovascular Disease, Canada and the US

Country	All Deaths	Male Deaths	Female Deaths
Canada	29%	28%	29.7%
United States	26%	26%	26%

Source: Adapted from Statistics Canada (2011); Heron et al. (2009).

quantity of life of those with CVD. For example, people suffering from depression are more likely to develop heart disease, and once they do they are more likely to die from it. Further, it is known that optimal management of heart disease requires multiple behavioural changes, such as smoking cessation, regular physical activity, and adhering to a heart-healthy diet low in sodium and saturated fat. Coping with a heart condition and its treatment can cause stress in interpersonal relationships and role functioning (e.g., paid and unpaid work), directly impacting **quality of life**.

This chapter explores each of these issues in terms of the psychological risk factors that underlie CVD development and its prognosis, in addition to the different assessment tools for evaluating the psychological functioning of people with CVD. Finally, the evidence base for common psychological interventions offered to patients living with heart disease is discussed. Information about the physiology of the cardiovascular system is presented in Chapter 2. We recommend that you review it before continuing with this chapter.

The Disease Process

The biopsychosocial model provides a framework describing how behavioural and social factors contribute to the onset of CVD (Buselli & Stuart, 1999; Ferris, Kline, & Bourdage, 2012). Specifically, injury to the endothelium (see Chapter 2) is often caused by hypertension (high blood pressure), diabetes (problems regulating blood sugar), and hyperlipidemia (too much cholesterol). These injuries are associated with behavioural and social risk factors such as smoking, abdominal obesity, physical inactivity, unhealthy diet, and psychosocial distress. All these factors are modifiable through behavioural changes.

The result is atherosclerosis, where endothelial cells become inflamed and lipids start to form plaque in the endothelium, causing calcification (i.e., hardening). This, in turn, means the heart has to work harder to pump blood, and the diameter of the heart vessel often gets smaller. This interrupts blood flow, and hence the distribution of oxygen and nutrients to the heart. A temporary restriction of blood flow is known as *ischemia* (tissue cells remain alive but their functioning is disrupted), in which the heart tissue by the vessel is deprived of oxygen. Damaged arterial walls are also vulnerable to plaque rupture and blood clots, which can completely block the vessel (see Stone & Mancini, 2009). In the instance of complete blockage, there is no distribution

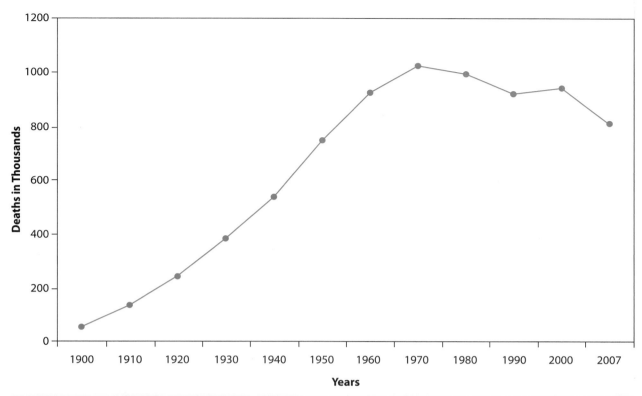

FIGURE 9.1 | Deaths due to cardiovascular disease, United States, 1900–2007.

Data Source: National Center for Health Statistics.

▦ IN PRACTICE

CVD and Depression

James was a 62-year-old man, married to his homemaker wife, with three adult children and two young grandchildren. He worked long hours in real estate, and was planning to work for five more years in order to retire more comfortably at the age of 67. While showing a house to clients, he experienced the sudden onset of chest pain and collapsed to the ground. His clients called 911 and James was taken by ambulance to the hospital where an angiogram revealed three-vessel blockage. He subsequently underwent emergency coronary artery bypass grafting (CABG). He remained in the hospital for seven days. When he was discharged from the hospital, he was referred to **cardiovascular rehabilitation (CR)** and informed that he could plan to return to work, on a part-time basis, in approximately six months.

After James returned home, he spent much of his time sleeping in his bedroom and ignored telephone calls from the CR team to arrange an intake session. James had never behaved like this before and his wife and children were unsure how to handle the situation. As a result of his wife's encouragement, James discussed his situation with his cardiologist, who easily recognized the symptoms of a major depressive episode. The cardiologist told James about the elevated rate of depression among cardiac patients and co-ordinated a referral to a psychologist. The psychologist provided emotional support as well as cognitive behavioural therapy. The psychological benefits of physical activity were strongly emphasized. By the end of a 12-session course of psychotherapy, James had initiated CR, re-engaged with his family and professional colleagues, and reported significantly improved mood.

⊘ IN FOCUS

Know the Warning Signs of a Heart Attack

- Chest discomfort—most heart attacks involve discomfort in the centre of the chest that lasts more than a few minutes, or that goes away and comes back. It can feel like uncomfortable pressure, squeezing, fullness, or pain.
- Discomfort of other areas of the upper body—symptoms can include pain or discomfort in one or both arms, the back, neck, jaw, or stomach.
- Shortness of breath—with or without chest discomfort.
- Other signs—may include breaking out in a cold sweat, nausea, or light-headedness.

If these signs are present dial 911!

Source: Reprinted with permission. © 2014 American Heart Association, Inc.

of oxygen and other nutrients to the myocardial (i.e., heart muscle) tissues supplied by that artery, known widely as a "heart attack," or **myocardial infarction (MI)**.

Prevalence of CVD

In Canada, over 70,000 individuals experience a myocardial infarction (MI) each year (Public Health Agency of Canada, 2009), and 16,000 of these result in death (Heart & Stroke Foundation of Canada, 2012). In the United States, recent annual estimates anticipate that 785,000 adults will have an MI and 500,000 will have **angina** (Roger et al., 2011). **Heart failure** primarily affects older adults (Figure 9.2), and the increasing prevalence has been related to an aging population demographic (Hunt et al., 2005). An estimated 5.7 million American adults have chronic heart failure (Roger et al., 2011). The average lifespan of heart failure patients is approximately five years following hospital discharge (Alter et al., 2012). Every year, CVD costs the Canadian and American economies more than $20.9 billion and $444 billion, respectively (Figure 9.3), in physician services, hospital costs, lost wages, and decreased productivity (Heart & Stroke Foundation of Canada, 2012; CDC, 2011).

There are health disparities in CVD in terms of sex, race, and socio-economic status.

For example, CVD occurs in men and women of African ancestry at an earlier age than in Caucasians (Feinstein et al., 2012); subsequently, death rates are higher in persons of African ancestry in all age categories (Mensah, Mokdad, Ford, Greenlund, & Croft, 2005). Moreover, in North America, CVD is most common among people in lower income brackets, such that socio-economic status is a major factor associated with later chronic disease risk and mortality (Johnson-Lawrence, Kaplan, & Galea, 2013).

Medical Management of CVD

Once a patient is diagnosed with heart disease, it is important to restore blood flow to the heart in the short term. But patients need to work towards improving the health of their vasculature in the long term, so they can prevent another blockage from occurring as well as preserve the pumping ability of the heart. Secondary prevention focuses on the initiation of treatments to stop the progression of diseases and disabilities once they have already occurred. Secondary prevention of **ischemic**

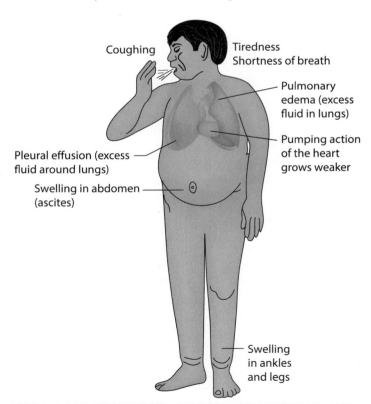

Coughing

Tiredness
Shortness of breath

Pulmonary edema (excess fluid in lungs)

Pumping action of the heart grows weaker

Pleural effusion (excess fluid around lungs)

Swelling in abdomen (ascites)

Swelling in ankles and legs

FIGURE 9.2 | The major signs and symptoms of heart failure.

Source: National Heart, Lung, and Blood Institute; National Institutes of Health; US Department of Health and Human Services

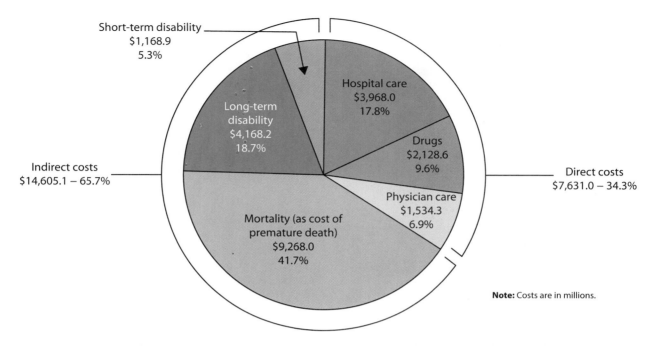

Short-term disability
$1,168.9
5.3%

Long-term
disability
$4,168.2
18.7%

Hospital care
$3,968.0
17.8%

Drugs
$2,128.6
9.6%

Indirect costs
$14,605.1 – 65.7%

Direct costs
$7,631.0 – 34.3%

Physician care
$1,534.3
6.9%

Mortality (as cost of
premature death)
$9,268.0
41.7%

Note: Costs are in millions.

FIGURE 9.3 | Percentage of costs due to cardiovascular disease in Canada.

heart disease specifically includes reducing risk factors through behavioural approaches (e.g., exercise, smoking cessation) and pharmacotherapy (e.g., aspirin, cholesterol-lowering drugs). Often, **revascularization** interventions are performed in hospital to restore sufficient blood flow. Revascularization procedures include angioplasty, also known as percutaneous coronary intervention (PCI), and coronary artery bypass grafting (CABG). Angioplasty is a procedure in which a catheter is used to place a balloon or wire mesh tube to dilate coronary vessels that have narrowed. This mesh tube ("stent") is inserted into the narrowed portion of the artery to prevent further occlusion (Figure 9.5). CABG uses arteries or veins from another area of the body to graft onto the coronary arteries (Figure 9.4), restoring the delivery of the blood supply to heart tissues (Ryan et al., 1996).

Angioplasty generally requires a single overnight hospital stay for patients, whereas CABG requires approximately a week-long hospitalization. For patients who have had their "chests opened" for CABG surgery, there may be a stronger psychological impact of the treatment.

Patients may perceive their disease as more severe and life-threatening. They have an extended recovery period during which time their usual activities are limited.

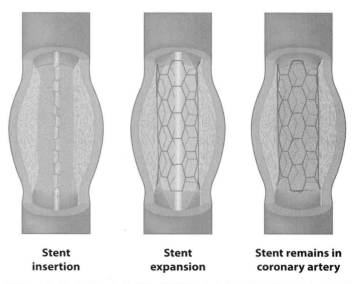

Stent insertion · **Stent expansion** · **Stent remains in coronary artery**

FIGURE 9.4 | Percutaneous coronary interventions (PCI).

Source: Adapted from http://www.adamimages.com/Coronary-artery-balloon-angioplasty—series—Procedure,-part-4-Illustration/PI9967/F4

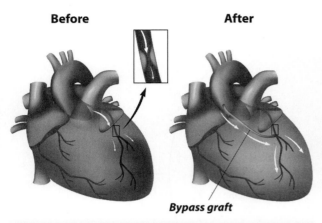

Before   **After**

Bypass graft

FIGURE 9.5 | Coronary artery bypass grafting (CABG).

Source: Alila07 / Dreamstime.com

PHOTO 9.2 | Cardiovascular rehabilitation (CR) is a comprehensive secondary prevention program, providing risk factor modification through education, behavioural counselling, and individualized exercise training. Participation in CR significantly reduces mortality and repeat hospitalization rates (Davies et al., 2010; Heran et al., 2011).

There has also been evidence of negative cognitive effects following bypass surgery (Goulding, Furze, & Birks, 2012; van Harten, Scheeren, & Absalom, 2012).

Cardiovascular rehabilitation is a comprehensive secondary prevention program, providing risk factor modification through education, behavioural counselling (e.g., pharmacological therapy adherence, nutrition and weight management, smoking cessation), and individualized exercise training. In addition, CR provides social support to patients with CVD, often offers stress management classes, and may screen for psychological distress. CR can be provided on an outpatient basis, in a hospital setting, in a community gym, or even through telephone support at home. Participation in this rehabilitation significantly reduces mortality and repeat hospitalization rates, irrespective of the form in which the program is offered (Davies et al., 2010; Heran et al., 2011).

The diagnosis of CVD and the acute experience of having a CVD event often lead to psychological distress in patients and their loved ones. Recovery requires adaptive and supportive patient–provider interactions, patient education, long term patient follow-up, and chronic disease management, in addition to communication among health-care providers and the patient to ensure optimal self-management. Patients require support to cope with their chronic condition and to successfully change their health behaviours over the long term. Behavioural change models such as motivational interviewing (i.e., a psychological approach designed to increase motivation for change) assist health-care professionals in addressing risk factors such as smoking, lack of exercise, and poor nutrition and medication adherence with their patients. Such behavioural change models focus on cognitively restructuring patient ambivalence and motivation towards risk factor modification. They also encourage self-efficacy and self-regulation (core features) in the adoption of sustainable health-promoting behaviours and the elimination of health-damaging ones. Finally, successful interventions have been developed to support physicians in their communication to patients, resulting in greater heart-healthy behaviour changes than following usual care.

Psychological Factors in Cardiovascular Disease and Prevention

Traditional risk factors (e.g., diabetes, hypertension, smoking, dyslipidemia) only explain about two-thirds of new CVD cases. Psychosocial factors may also be related to the development of CVD and its prognosis. For example, in an international study called INTERHEART, over 24,000 people from 52 countries who had heart attacks were age- and sex-matched to people who had not had infarctions. Patients who had MIs were more likely to recall periods of perceived work and home stress, financial stress, and major life events (i.e., business failure, intra-family conflict), in addition to depression and lower control, during the 12 months *prior* to their cardiac events. These factors accounted for a large proportion of their risk for CVD. Moreover, the results were generally consistent across regions of the world, ethnic groups, and between men and women (Rosengren et al., 2004). These psychosocial risk factors in the development and prognosis of CVD, including perceived job and home stress, social isolation, depression, anxiety, and personality traits, are discussed below.

Stress

Stress-related vulnerability to disease may stem from a discrepancy between a real or perceived appraisal of environmental demands (stressful life events) and the biopsychosocial coping mechanisms of an individual. For example, students may experience stress if they perceive they do not have enough time to study for an exam to achieve their desired grade. The external demands of stress on the individual may be acute or chronic in nature, and each can affect the cardiovascular system. Acute stressors are those of shorter duration but strong intensity (e.g., losing a job, the death of a loved one, undergoing CABG). Chronic stressors are those of a longer duration and may be intermittent or continuous (e.g., ongoing financial challenges or marital conflict).

Acute Stress

The effects of acute stressors on CVD are supported by studies of life stressors such as bereavement and disasters. For example, one study reported the highest relative mortality risk following the death of a spouse was over the first week after the loss (Kaprio, Koskenvuo, & Rita, 1987). Other studies have confirmed that the risk for death is increased during the first six months following bereavement; both men and women appear to be at increased risk of chronic ischemic heart disease (Martikainen & Valkonen, 1996).

Environmental disasters, such as earthquakes, have also been associated with CVD. Indeed, during the first month following the 1995 Hanshin-Awaji earthquake in Japan, there was a significant increase in MI and stroke among those living near the epicentre. Of note, compared to the two-week period prior to the disaster, in well-controlled hypertensive patients, one clinic reported prolonged elevations in blood pressure 2–4 weeks after the disaster (Kario, McEwen, & Pickering, 2003). However, it appeared that the risk of a fatal outcome following this acute stressor was associated with having underlying CVD prior to the earthquake.

Acute mental stress has also been reported to bring on cardiac ischemia (i.e., insufficient supply of blood to the heart), particularly "silent" ischemia (i.e., no overt chest pain). Rozanski et al. (1988) assessed cardiac functioning in patients with CVD while they completed either a series of mental tasks that included arithmetic, reading, and public speaking, or exercise. In a majority of the patients, mental stress, particularly public speaking, was accompanied by "silent" myocardial ischemia similar to what was observed during exercise.

Chronic Stress

Like acute stressors, chronic stressors are characterized as external pressures that may directly impact daily functioning and cardiovascular health. Although chronically stressful situations are those that persist for longer durations, the specific stressors themselves are varied and often arise unexpectedly (such as an argument in an overall situation of marital strife). These types of stressors are often unpredictable in their frequency and duration, but occur numerous times over long periods. The core feature of chronic stress is that the person perceives himself or herself as having limited control over the situation in which the chronic stressor(s) occur. Stressors that have been shown to impact CVD onset and prognosis include job strain, family conflict, and social isolation.

Job Strain

Components of chronic job strain have been linked to the development of CVD. Primarily, low decision-making control (i.e., the demand-control model) (Karasek & Theorell, 1990) and an imbalance between employees' efforts at work and the rewards they gain in return (i.e., the effort-reward imbalance model) (Siegrist, 2010) underlie psychological distress and cardiovascular disease (Aboa-Éboulé et al., 2011; Aboa-Éboulé, Brisson, & Maunsell, 2011; Kuper, Singh-Manoux, Siegrist, & Marmot, 2002; Siegrist et al., 2004; Siegrist, 2010).

A Canadian study established that chronic job strain, as characterized by "high psychological demands" and "low decision control," is a predictor of *recurrent* CVD events following an initial CVD event (Aboa-Éboulé et al., 2007). In this study, middle-aged male and female participants who returned to work after an MI were followed until (a) their first recurrent CVD event, (b) death, or (c) until six years after their initial heart attack (whichever occurred first). Patients were assessed on their psychological work demands, which included quantity of work, time constraints, and intellectual requirements, in addition to their freedom to use and develop new skills, make independent decisions, and be creative. After adjusting for other work characteristics,

Photo courtesy of Amanda C. Kentner

PHOTO 9.3 | A discrepancy between the effort that employees put into their work and the payoffs received has been linked to the development of cardiovascular disease (Siegrist, 2010; Kuper et al., 2002). Low decision-making control is also a factor in the psychological distress and cardiovascular risk associated with work strain.

often have more CVD risk factors, such as smoking and reduced physical activity. The negative CVD outcomes associated with these behavioural risk factors occur in people at a younger age than would be expected in the general population (Haupt et al., 2008). For example, in the landmark Nurses' Health Study, female nurses who worked rotating night shifts had a higher rate of MI and death from CVD, even after considering other CVD risk factors. Overall, the risk for CVD among women who worked more than six years on shifts was 1.5 times greater than it was among the women who were not on shifts (Kawachi et al., 1995).

Family Strain

The INTERHEART study highlighted the negative effects of chronic family stress on cardiovascular health (Rosengren et al., 2004). Marital strain in particular may be related to the development of CVD. In the Framingham Offspring Study, men and women were assessed on measures of marital status, marital strain, and risk factors for CVD and followed for 10 years on CVD outcomes (i.e., MI, coronary death) and death from all causes. In this work, the *development* of a CVD event was primarily related to the reaction to conflict with one's spouse (Eaker, Sullivan, Kelley-Hayes, D'Agostino, & Benjamin, 2007). Importantly, men and women who perceive low marital support or have marital conflict tend to have higher blood pressure (a risk factor for CVD) compared to individuals who perceive high support or who engage in collaborative problem-solving (Broadwell & Light, 1999; Smith et al., 2009). Moreover, *prognosis* following a CVD event is related to the frequency of marital disagreements, individual marital happiness, and comparison of their marital satisfaction to other couples (Orth-Gomer et al., 2000; Eaker et al., 2007). The impact of marital strain on CVD prognosis appears to affect both men and women.

demographics, lifestyle (i.e., alcohol consumption, physical activity), and clinical characteristics, survival rates for patients with greater chronic job strain were lower. These patients had a higher risk for fatal CVD, MI, or angina in the 2–6 years after their initial MI (Aboa-Éboulé et al., 2007).

The effort-reward model suggests that a lack of reciprocity between work effort and rewards can lead to emotional distress (Siegrist, 2010). Rewards include money, potential for promotion, as well as job security. There is an increased risk of CVD in employees who perceive an imbalance between the work they put in for their employer and the rewards they receive in return (Siegrist, 2010). Overall, high effort-to-reward imbalances are predictive of CVD and poor physical and mental health functioning (Kuper et al., 2002). The effect of effort–reward imbalances are particularly evident in employees with limited occupational social support networks (Kuper et al., 2002).

Shift work patterns that go beyond the typical eight-hour workday and disrupt normal biological rhythms are associated with a higher prevalence of atherosclerosis (i.e., narrowing of the arteries) and MI. Shift workers

Approximately 12 per cent of Americans over the age of 45 have family caregiving responsibilities for someone with a chronic illness or disability (Roth, Perkins, Wadley, Temple, & Haley, 2009). Providing support to a spouse or other family member who requires assistance increases the risk of CVD onset in the caregiver. This is often due to chronic stress and the specific strains associated with physically and psychologically demanding tasks, financial difficulty, filling multiple roles, social isolation, and watching the deterioration and suffering of another person. Caregivers are often older persons and their own health and emotional adjustment to the situation may decline during the process of taking care of another (Haley, Roth, Howard, & Safford, 2010; Low, Thurston, & Matthews, 2010).

Social Isolation

Social isolation refers to low rates of contact with other people. A social network, on the other hand, includes family, friends, co-workers, pets (Friedmann & Thomas, 1995), and even the patient-centred care network (Cossette, Frasure-Smith, & Lespérance, 2001). Stronger social networks are related to a lower incidence of CVD (Orth-Gomer, Rosengren, & Wilhelmsen, 1993, O'Shea

et al., 2002), and higher-quality relationships are particularly protective (Dickens et al., 2004).

On the other hand, social isolation has been related to decreased heart functioning and poor health behaviours. For example, those who know fewer than three people well enough to visit their home are at an increased risk for CVD compared to those who are not socially isolated (Rodriguez et al., 2011). Moreover, social isolation and loneliness are associated with a greater risk of being inactive, smoking, and engaging in multiple health-risk behaviours, in addition to having high blood pressure (Shankar, McMunn, Banks, & Steptoe, 2011). People who feel that they have limited social support (Burg et al., 2005; Leifheit-Limson et al., 2010) or who live alone are more likely to die, to have a recurrent cardiovascular event (Schmaltz et al., 2007), or to experience decreased quality of life and/or depression (Leifheit-Limson et al., 2010). It could also be possible that people who are depressed are likely to experience decreased quality of life, to have a recurrent cardiovascular event, to live alone, and to have limited social support.

Psychological Disorders

Two psychological conditions—depression and anxiety—have been related to CVD onset and prognosis. Depression is characterized by low mood and/or a diminished feeling of pleasure or interest in normal everyday activities. Other prominent features include significant changes in appetite, weight, sleep disturbance, fatigue/decreased energy, psychomotor retardation or agitation, sense of worthlessness or guilt, difficulty concentrating and making decisions, and/or recurrent thoughts of death or suicide. The difference between clinical depression and psychological distress ("the blues") is the severity and duration of the symptoms. An elevated risk of depression occurs among individuals with CVD (Ormel et al., 2007). The 12-month prevalence of depressive disorder in the general American population is 6.7 per cent (Kessler, Chiu, Demler, & Walters, 2005); this rate increases to approximately 15–20 per cent for those who have an underlying CVD condition (NIH, 2004; Thombs et al., 2006).

A history of depression is recognized to be a psychological predictor for developing CVD (Hemingway & Marmot, 1999; Rugulies, 2002; Wulsin & Singal, 2003; Van der Kooy et al., 2007). Reviews of studies have shown depression is a moderate risk factor for MI (i.e., smoking is a greater risk factor). Of particular note, patients diagnosed with depression are at the greatest risk for developing CVD, and this risk level is

Photo courtesy Insert of Amanda C. Kentner

PHOTO 9.4 | Those who believe they have a poor social network are more likely to suffer from depression and are at an increased risk of a recurrent cardiovascular event (Leifheit-Limson et al., 2010; Schmaltz et al., 2007).

comparable to that of traditional risk factors such as smoking. The risk for CVD onset is still elevated but lower in those who present with depressive symptoms only (not clinically diagnosable) (Van der Kooy et al., 2007).

Patients with angina or MI who have depressive symptoms in the hospital tend to still have these symptoms 6 and 12 months later (Grace et al., 2005). There is also an association between depression and death in patients who already have CVD (Hemingway & Marmot, 1999; Frasure-Smith & Lespérance, 2003; Lespérance, Frasure-Smith, Talajic, & Bourassa, 2002; Smith & Ruiz, 2002). Importantly, depression in the first two years after MI predicts poor prognosis in terms of quality of life, greater symptoms, disability, and death (de Jonge et al., 2006; Frasure-Smith, Lespérance, & Talajic, 1995a). These poor outcomes are particularly evident in women (Frasure-Smith, Lespérance, & Talajic, 1995b). Specifically, depression in CVD patients is related to twice greater mortality in the two years after CVD diagnosis when compared to non-depressed CVD patients (Barth, Schumacher, & Herrmann-Lingen, 2004; van Melle et al., 2004).

Anxiety and Trauma/Stressor-Related Disorders

An anxiety disorder is a negative emotional state underscored by worry, apprehension, and a sense of threat. Other symptoms include restlessness, fatigue, irritability, sleep difficulties, and hyper-arousal. To be classified as a disorder, anxiety symptoms must be persistent and arise during inappropriate situations, i.e., where no real threat exists. Moreover, these symptoms must be disruptive to social and/or occupational functioning. Anxiety disorders include, but are not limited to, generalized anxiety disorder (GAD), phobias, and panic disorder. The most notable trauma-related disorder is post-traumatic stress disorder (PTSD). The overall 12-month prevalence of all anxiety disorder subtypes (including trauma-related disorders) in the general American population is about 18 per cent (Kessler et al., 2005). The documented prevalence of cardiac patients meeting the criteria for at least one anxiety disorder is approximately 36 per cent (Todaro et al., 2007). CVD populations have a higher risk of anxiety disorders irrespective of socio-economic background, geographic location, and culture (Ormel et al., 2007). However, the impact of anxiety on CVD appears to be stronger for men than for women (Fiedorowicz, He, & Merikangas, 2011).

The role of anxiety in the development of CVD is less clear than that of depression (Fleet, Lavoie, & Beitman, 2000) and may be dependent on the specific anxiety disorder subtype (Hemingway & Marmot, 1999). For example, the presence of phobic anxiety increases the risk of sudden cardiac death, but not of non-fatal MI (Kawachi et al., 1994; Albert, Chae, Rexrode, Manson, & Kawachi, 2005). It has been proposed that phobic anxiety may elevate this risk of cardiac death through increased ventricular arrhythmia (abnormal rapid heart rhythms) (Albert et al., 2005; Watkins et al., 2006).

Not surprisingly, anxiety levels tend to be high following a CVD event and have been shown to persist for longer than six months following angina or MI. Post-MI anxiety has been associated with a range of CVD events, including ischemia, MI, and sudden death (Denollet & Brutsaert, 1998; Frasure-Smith et al., 1995b; Moser & Dracup, 1996). High levels of anxiety are also related to longer hospital stays and reduced quality of life (Lane, Caroll, Ring, Beevers, & Lip, 2000).

Some evidence suggests a differential impact of anxiety dependent on disorder subtype (Herrmann, Brand-Driehorst, Buss, & Ruger, 2000). For example, MI patients with a lifetime history of agoraphobia (a specific phobia indicated by an irrational fear of open and/or public spaces) had poorer cardiac outcomes than patients with GAD (Parker, Owen, Brotchie, & Hyett, 2010). It was suggested that the worrying tendencies among individuals with GAD might actually promote help-seeking behaviour and better CVD self-management (Herrmann et al., 2000; Parker et al., 2010).

In addition, PTSD has also emerged as a potential contributor to CVD onset. PTSD is characterized by intrusive memories of a traumatic event, avoidance, and hyper-arousal. It has been linked to poor health behaviours (e.g., less physical activity, higher rates of medication non-adherence, and smoking) (Zen, Whooley, Zhao, & Cohen, 2012), and may be associated with increased risk of atherosclerosis and mortality (Ahmadi et al., 2011). Furthermore, PTSD may occur in response to a traumatic cardiovascular event, thus further increasing CVD recurrence and death.

It must be noted that mood and anxiety disorders are highly co-morbid (i.e., they often occur together) (Kessler et al., 2005), and thus their unique contribution to CVD development and prognosis can be difficult to determine. In one study, CVD patients with co-morbid depression *and* GAD were not at a greater risk for poorer outcomes (cardiac death, cardiac arrest, or revascularization procedures) than those patients who had either major depression *or* GAD alone (Frasure-Smith & Lespérance, 2008). In another study, anxiety alone was an independent risk factor for hospitalization and outpatient clinic visits (Strik, Denollet,

Lousberg, & Honig, 2003). This suggests that although depression and anxiety are highly co-morbid, they may relate to CVD in different ways.

Personality

In general, "personality" refers to an individual's characteristic way of acting and thinking, although there is little consensus for a specific definition (Griggs, 2012). Personality is likely a malleable construct influenced by the interaction between our genes and our environment. In particular, aspects of personality appear to contribute to CVD onset and other clinical cardiovascular markers of recurrent disease (Hemingway & Marmot, 1999).

Type A and B behavioural patterns, also known as *Type A and B personality*, respectively, were the first aspects of personality hypothesized to have an independent role in the onset of heart disease (Friedman and Rosenman, 1959). *Type A* individuals are competitive high achievers who display anger and hostility, and tend to be engaged in multiple tasks; individuals with a *Type B behavioural pattern* are described as lacking drive and a competitive nature (Friedman and Rosenman, 1959). Aspects of personality consistently related to both CVD onset and prognosis are anger and hostility (Chida et al., 2009), which are specific dimensions of the Type A personality subtype. For example, anger and hostility levels in those with and without CVD are associated with a significantly higher risk for mortality and non-fatal CVD outcomes, particularly in healthy men compared to women (Chida & Steptoe, 2009).

Subsequently, the focus of personality subtypes centred on the *Type D* personality, referring to people who display both a high level of negative affect and social inhibition (Denollet, 2005). Negative affectivity is the predisposition for worry and irritability, while social inhibition is the tendency to be insecure and uncomfortable in social situations (Denollet, 2005). However, researchers have not consistently shown a connection between this personality type and CVD (Grande et al., 2011; de Voogd, Sanderman, & Coyne, 2012).

Positive Psychology: Resilience and Coping

So far we have explored the role of negative psychosocial factors (anxiety, depression) on CVD onset and prognosis. Now we shift focus to another arm of cardiac psychology that explores more positive perspectives. Specifically, a focus on "resilience" or "psychological thriving" in the face of a cardiac or other health diagnosis, as positive ways of coping that lead to health-protective behaviours (e.g., participating in physical activity, smoking cessation, choosing heart-healthy foods), or engaging one's support networks. Indeed, struggling with life-threatening adversity can be a catalyst for personal growth and transformation (Johnson, 1991; Tedeschi, Park, & Calhoun, 1998). Patients may change their view of themselves, their priorities, and their interactions with others (e.g., "having a heart attack has made me stop and appreciate my life and the people around me") in response to a health-related trauma such as CVD (Aldwin, 1994; Tedeschi et al., 1998).

Vitality is a positive emotional state associated with a renewable sense of enthusiasm and energy (Rozanski & Kubzansky, 2005). People who have "vitality" have effective coping skills and can regulate their emotions in response to stress. Whereas negative emotions may deplete energy and contribute to poor health, positive emotions such as optimism may reduce the progression of atherosclerosis and result in better recovery following MI and heart surgery (Agarwal, Dalal, Agarwal, & Agarwal, 1995; Leedham, Meyerowitz, Muirhead, & Frist, 1995, Scheier et al., 1999; Matthews, Räikkönen, Sutton-Tyrrell, & Kuller, 2004).

When people who have survived a CVD trauma such as an MI begin to recognize benefits and take steps towards positive changes in their lives, they may undergo "post-traumatic growth," defined as the experience of positive consequences arising from the struggle with a traumatic experience. The resulting transformation is thought to lead not only to a return to previous levels of well-being, but to a higher level of functioning in some aspects of life (Aldwin, 1994; Tedeschi et al., 1998; Chan, Lai, & Wong, 2006). In particular, angioplasty patients who experienced such positive psychology in the weeks after their cardiac event had better health outcomes (i.e., lower cholesterol and better performance on a six-minute walk test) following an exercise rehabilitation program than patients with lower personal resilience (Chan et al., 2006).

How? The Biopsychosocial Model

Together, behavioural and pathophysiological mechanisms explain the relationship between psychological factors and heart disease. Behavioural factors include smoking, physical inactivity, non-adherence to medications, and poor diet as a response to psychological distress (Rozanski, Blumenthal, & Kaplan, 1999). Psychological factors, including depression, anxiety, and other stressors, are also associated with biological mechanisms that promote atherosclerosis. For example, individuals who are chronically stressed may present with hyper-arousal and continual activation of the hypothalamic-pituitary-adrenal axis and the sympathetic nervous system. In response to this, multiple adverse cardiovascular effects ensue, such as an elevated resting heart rate. A more specific example, family distress (reflecting aspects of the social environment), has been linked to the cardiovascular reactivity (e.g., blood pressure changes in response to stress) of adults, and more recently of adolescents as well (Low et al., 2010). Together, these fluctuations may be followed by endothelial inflammation and a process whereby lipid plaques accumulate and calcification occurs. These plaques narrow the vascular walls, obstructing blood flow and oxygen delivery, which may eventually progress to an MI (see Rozanski et al., 1999).

Summary of Psychological Factors in Cardiovascular Disease and Prevention

Overall, it appears that psychosocial factors, both negative and positive, are related to CVD onset and prognosis. However, evidence is mixed regarding the contribution of each of the psychological factors discussed, with some studies showing no association between the factors and CVD. Moreover, most research in this field is observational in design, so we cannot rule out that some unmeasured factor other than the psychological factor under study explains the relationship with CVD. For example, it is possible that depression could be secondary to compromised health (i.e., shortness of breath leads to fatigue, the inability to sleep, and feeling down), as opposed to leading to compromised health (i.e., depression leads to CVD) (Bunker et al., 2003). Nevertheless, recall that the traditional risk factors such as smoking, hypertension, and diabetes do not account for all cases of CVD, and psychological factors are thought to play a role. Next we examine the issue of reliably identifying these psychological constructs in CVD patients through measurement.

Psychological Assessment of Patients with Cardiovascular Disease

Psychological risk factors are best assessed via clinical interview by a trained professional (e.g., psychiatrist or psychologist) or self-administered standardized questionnaires or surveys. Structured clinical interviews can be used to "diagnose" a psychological disorder. Results of the assessment and relevance to quality of life and medical outcomes should then be discussed with the patient. Notably, most medical care for cardiac patients focuses on their physical health, despite the large burden of psychological distress in those with heart disease. Some experts recommend screening for psychological distress (i.e., brief surveys) within the context of routine cardiac care for patients, although this recommendation is not without its critics (see Gilbody, House, & Sheldon, 2005; Gilbody, Sheldon, & House, 2008; Ziegelstein, Thombs, Coyne, & de Jonge, 2009). Finally, psychological researchers often assess cardiac patients as well through the use of questionnaires.

Depression/Anxiety

Diagnosis of a cardiac patient with a mood or anxiety disorder can be complicated by the fact that many symptoms of depression or anxiety, such as fatigue, sleep disturbance, and appetite-related weight change, are also symptoms associated with CVD (Simon & Von Korff, 2006). For these reasons, structured diagnostic interviews are often recommended (Berkman et al., 2003; Freedland et al., 2002). Self-report assessments of depression/anxiety symptoms are used often because they allow for a quick and cost-effective evaluation of patient populations. Examples include the Patient Health Questionnaire (PHQ) (Kroenke, Spitzer, & Williams, 2003) and the Hospital Anxiety Depression Scale (HADS) (Hunt-Shanks, Blanchard, Reid, Fortier, & Cappelli, 2010).

Personality Factors

Hostility, arguably the most hazardous trait of the Type A personality, can be measured via the Cook-Medley Hostility (Ho) Scale (Barefoot et al., 1989). The Ho Scale assesses hostility according to six subscales: cynicism, hostile attributions, hostile affect, aggressive responding, social avoidance, and "other." High scores on cynicism, hostile affect, and aggressive responding are most predictive of mortality (Barefoot et al., 1989).

Social Support

Many scales are available to assess social support. One recommended measure in the CVD literature is the ENRICHD (Enhancing Recovery in Coronary Heart Disease) Social Support Inventory (ESSI) (Vaglio et al., 2004). The ESSI was developed for use in a major randomized control trial called ENRICHD (Berkman et al., 2003) to identify patients who had low social support following an MI. The ESSI can be administered as either a five- or a seven-item test that allows for validated quick and reliable scoring in CVD populations (Berkman et al., 2003; Mitchell et al., 2003; Vaglio et al., 2004). The items on the ESSI evaluate factors such as love and affection, help with daily chores, and whether someone is available to help sort through problems and/or offer advice (Vaglio et al., 2004).

Interventions for Patients with Cardiovascular Disease

Given the burden of psychological distress in patients with CVD and the negative effects on health, therapies demonstrated to reduce distress in non-medically ill populations have also been applied and tested in CVD patients. The main therapies for psychological disorders are pharmacological, psychotherapeutic, and behavioural interventions.

Pharmacotherapy (Medications)

Anti-depressant and anxiolytic medications are used to treat depression and/or anxiety. The Sertraline Antidepressant and Heart Attack Randomized Trial (SADHART) (Glassman et al., 2002) was conducted across seven countries, including the United States and Canada. Eligible male and female patients had had an MI or had been hospitalized for unstable angina and also had been diagnosed with a current episode of depression. Half of the patients were given a selective serotonergic reuptake inhibitor (SSRI) drug by the name of sertraline. SSRIs increase the availability of a neurotransmitter (i.e., chemical messenger) in the brain called serotonin, which is thought to relieve depression. In this study, sertraline was not associated with negative changes in any cardiovascular indicators, suggesting that it is safe for use in CVD populations (Glassman et al., 2002). In addition, sertraline was more effective than a placebo in reducing depressive symptoms; interestingly, scores of lower depression were more commonly observed among patients who had a previous history of depression.

In the MI and Depression Intervention Trial (MIND-IT) (Honig et al., 2007), MI patients with depression were randomized to receive either mirtazapine or a placebo for a 24-week period. Mirtazapine is part of a newer class of antidepressants, activating serotonin and other receptors in the brain involved in mood. In MIND-IT, MI patients who received mirtazapine had lower depressive symptoms at follow-up. Similar to SADHART, those who responded best to the antidepressant treatment tended to be those with a history of depressive episodes. Overall, a review of the studies in this field concluded that SSRIs offer a small, but clinically meaningful, effect on depression symptoms in CVD patients and that hospitalization rates may also be reduced (Baumeister, Hutter, & Bengel, 2011).

Psychotherapy or Talk Therapy

Psychological therapies are effective in treating psychological distress in both mental health-care settings and medically ill populations. Well-established therapies include cognitive behavioural therapy (CBT) (see Prior, Francis, Reitav, & Stone, 2009) and interpersonal therapy (IPT) (see Prior et al., 2009). These structured interventions of short duration involve the interaction between a client and a trained therapist for the purpose of addressing the underlying factors that contribute to anxiety or mood disorders. As indicated in previous chapters, the goal of CBT is to identify cognitive patterns and behaviours that generate these psychological manifestations, while IPT is focused more on the patient's relationships and social environment.

Given the evidence suggesting depression and low social support are related to poor CVD prognosis following MI, the ENRICHD trial (Berkman et al., 2003) was designed to address whether treating depression and increasing social support would reduce recurrent CVD events and death. In this US study, consenting MI patients who were depressed and/or had low social support were assigned at random to either a usual care or a CBT intervention. Part of the CBT intervention was for patients to complete homework assignments that addressed maladaptive cognitive patterns and behaviours that contributed to their psychosocial distress, including low social support. Usual care consisted of the standard care provided by physicians, in addition to written materials about CVD risk factors.

Results showed that treatment allocation had no effect on clinical event outcomes such as recurrent MI or death during the four-year follow-up period. Depression symptoms were reduced and social support was significantly increased in the intervention group versus patients in usual care; however, benefits were not sustained over a long term (Berkman et al., 2003). A closer look at the findings showed that improvements

© Mark Bowden/iStockphoto

PHOTO 9.5 | Cognitive behavioural therapy is used to identify patterns of thoughts and behaviours that contribute to anxiety and mood disorders. Evidence suggests that this form of therapy assists to elevate mood but does not provide a significant role in cardiovascular outcome (Thombs et al., 2008).

in mood and social support were found to be related to the adherence of the patient to the CBT-related homework assignments (Cowan et al., 2008). Moreover, depressed patients who did not benefit from the CBT were at higher risk for mortality (Carney et al., 2004).

Another trial tested an SSRI antidepressant, citalopram, alongside IPT. The Canadian Cardiac Randomized Evaluation of Antidepressant and Psychotherapy Efficacy (CREATE) study (Lespérance et al., 2007) was a 12-week trial that included patients with both clinical depression and CVD (i.e., MI, angioplasty). Patients were randomized to one of four groups: (1) IPT + clinical management + citalopram, (2) IPT + clinical management + placebo, (3) clinical management + citalopram, or (4) clinical management + placebo. Clinical management was a standardized protocol of patient depression treatment offered by a clinician. Results showed that citalopram was significantly better than the placebo in the reduction of depression scores 12 weeks after initiation of the antidepressant treatment. There was no

effect of IPT. Therefore, the investigators recommended that citalopram be considered as a first-line treatment for co-morbid depression in CVD patients (Lespérance et al., 2007).

Overall, despite the lack of efficacy evidence for IPT in the management of depression in CVD patients, CBT is recognized as having a modest role in the improvement of mood, but not CVD outcomes (Thombs et al., 2008). While more recent studies suggest that depression treatment may improve CVD outcomes (Gulliksson et al., 2011), the role of evidence-based psychosocial interventions in improving quality of life should not be overlooked.

Psycho-educational and Behavioural Interventions

Behavioural interventions aim to address the physical and psychosocial aspects underlying the CVD process, such as smoking cessation, increasing physical activity, medication adherence, improvements in diet, and stress management. Education is also necessary for patients to understand their disease, its causes, and treatments.

Physical activity, a core component of CR, is excellent for the primary and secondary prevention of CVD. The success of CR is likely because of its ability to effect physiological changes as well as enhance mood. Indeed, physical activity is associated with significantly reduced psychological distress in the form of depression, anxiety, and hostility. These reductions in those who participate in CR are associated with a reduced risk for death during the first two years or more following CVD diagnosis (Milani & Lavie, 2009).

In one CR intervention study, patients were followed for one year and their quality of life, as well as their anxiety and depression, was measured by the HADS. Participation in CR significantly lowered both depression and anxiety severity across the follow-up period. Interestingly, a reduction in depression severity independently accounted for improvements in quality of life (Yohannes, Doherty, Bundy, & Yalfani, 2010). Combined, the ability of physical activity to directly target both physiological and psychological risk factors makes it an important biopsychosocial intervention for the improvement in long-term prognosis of CVD patients.

Another psycho-educational intervention is stress management, which typically includes relaxation training, cognitive restructuring (see Chapter 7), and communication and problem-solving skill development to provide patients with the skills to manage acute episodes of stress and chronically reduce depression, anxiety, and hostility (Blumenthal et al., 2010; Blumenthal et al., 2005). In one randomized trial (a gold standard method of study in which patients are randomly allocated to receive an intervention or a comparison treatment ensuring that any unmeasured alternative explanations for the findings would be balanced in both groups), patients who received either exercise or stress management training had reductions in depressive symptoms, regardless of the intervention, suggesting both are beneficial (Blumenthal et al., 2010). However, another study has since demonstrated no additional benefit on biochemical markers of CVD in patients attending an expanded CR program that included both physical activity and stress management versus CR with physical activity alone (Plüss, Karlsson, Wallen, Billing, & Held, 2008).

In the Secondary Prevention in Uppsala Primary Health Care Project (SUPRIM) trial (Gulliksson et al., 2011), patients who had been discharged from hospital with CVD in the last year were randomized to CBT with a focus on either stress management or traditional care. CVD patients who were randomized into the CBT/stress

management intervention demonstrated a significant decrease in recurrent cardiovascular endpoints compared to controls. Moreover, higher attendance rates across the 20 CBT stress management sessions was associated with the lowest recurrent CVD risk (Gulliksson et al., 2011).

Overall, there is limited evidence that psychosocial interventions reduce the morbidity and mortality of individuals with established CVD (Linden, Phillips, & Leclerc, 2007). More randomized clinical trials are necessary to properly evaluate elements of these interventions (i.e., timing of treatments and effectiveness) on both physical and psychosocial health outcomes. Further, there are currently no clinically accepted treatment programs to specifically address social support, job stress, or hazardous personality factors in CVD. Notwithstanding the effect of psychological illness on future morbidity, CVD patients with co-morbid psychological illness are under-treated. In one sample, less than 20 per cent of eligible patients attended CR despite evidence of its benefit; the rate of attendance is even lower for depressed patients, who attend the fewest sessions (Grace et al., 2005).

Future Directions

There is now substantial evidence that anxiety, and predominantly depression, are associated with CVD development and worse prognoses. However, no psychological factor has been accepted as a "cause" in either the development or recurrence of CVD. Although the level of severity of depressive symptoms is associated with CVD and plausible mechanisms for the relationship have been established, three main gaps/inconsistencies in the findings need to be addressed by future research. First, some researchers have postulated that the relationship can be explained by alternative factors such as the experience of being hospitalized or fatigue induced by CVD itself. Second, depression treatment has not been definitively shown to improve cardiac outcomes. Third, there have been methodological differences between studies in terms of timing of study initiation, methods of psychosocial assessment, duration of interventions, and differences in treatment types. Combined, these methodological differences have resulted in inconsistencies between studies with respect to various psychosocial factors and their effects on CVD onset/outcomes (Prior et al., 2009). Because traditional risk factors do not account for all cases of CVD, future research is needed to definitively establish or negate the role of psychosocial risk factors in the onset and recurrence of CVD disease. This research might best consider the combination of these factors and how they interact with basic cardiovascular physiology.

SUMMARY

CVDs are among the leading killers of North American men and women. Advances in treatments have reduced the risk of mortality, such that an increasing number of individuals live with CVD. The chronicity of CVD requires long-term medical follow-up and often re-hospitalizations, and may reduce patients' capacity to maintain gainful employment, which can have a negative effect on security and quality of life as well as on both the Canadian and American economies.

Psychosocial factors are associated with CVD onset and reoccurrence, in addition to quality and quantity of life. Major psychosocial factors implicated in the development and prognosis of CVD include depression and anxiety, job and marital/family stress, social isolation, and personality factors such as hostility. These factors may directly influence the disease process through pathophysiological changes, such as inflammation and endothelial damage, resulting in atherosclerosis.

Psychosocial distress also indirectly affects disease progression by promoting poor health behaviours (i.e., smoking, low physical activity, poor treatment adherence) that can lead to the development of traditional risk factors such as diabetes, hypertension, and high cholesterol. Although the role of these biopsychosocial factors in both the direct and indirect progression of CVD is highly plausible, these factors have never been proven to be causal.

In summary, the role of psychology in the management of heart patients is based on many interrelationships. This chapter has established that psychological distress (a) is linked to behavioural and cardiovascular risk factors, and may itself be a risk factor for CVD; (b) may trigger acute cardiac events; (c) can form a barrier to the receipt of evidence-based therapies; (d) is highly prevalent in cardiac patients; and (e) can masquerade as cardiac symptoms (Rozanski, Blumenthal, & Davidson, 2005).

Critical Thought Questions

1. How might mood or anxiety disorders impact CVD patients throughout their medical management process and in their interactions with health-care providers?
2. How can researchers assess the effectiveness of a psychosocial intervention for heart patients?
3. How might a psychologist approach a patient whose social support circle includes people thought to negatively influence health behaviours?
4. What psychological factors might be at play for a CVD patient undergoing an angioplasty?

Recommended Reading

Allan, R., & Scheidt, S. (1996). *Heart and mind: The practice of cardiac psychology*. Washington: American Psychological Association.

Jordan, J., Bardé, B, & Zeiher, A.M. (Eds.). (2006). *Contributions towards evidence-based psychocardiology: A systematic review of the literature*. Washington: American Psychological Association.

Molinari, E., Compare, A., & Parati, G. (Eds.). (2006). *Clinical psychology and heart disease*. Italia: Springer-Verlag.

Skala, J.A., Freedland, K.E., & Carney, R.M. (2005). *Heart disease (advances in psychotherapy, evidence-based practice)*. Cambridge, Mass.: Hogrefe & Huber.

10

Diabetes

KRISTI E. WHITE | LAURA L. MAYHEW | WILLIAM P. SACCO

Learning Objectives

After reading this chapter you will:

- Learn the differences among prediabetes, type 1, type 2, and gestational diabetes.

- Understand how diabetes is diagnosed.

- Identify and define the different medical complications of diabetes.

- Understand how the different types of diabetes are medically managed.

- Know how psychological and behavioural factors play a role in diabetes management.

- Understand the different types of psychological interventions commonly used with people with diabetes.

Diabetes Overview

Diabetes is characterized by a deficiency in the body's ability to metabolize (break down and use) glucose (sugar). Unsuccessfully treated diabetes can result in serious medical complications. The prevalence of diabetes has been increasing at an alarming rate. Over the past three decades, for example, the prevalence of diagnosed diabetes in the United States has increased by 176 per cent (CDC, 2012). This chapter provides an overview of diabetes: the types of diabetes, prevalence rates, risk factors, common complications, and medical management. Psychosocial factors involved in diabetes are then presented, including how they are assessed in clinical settings. The chapter concludes with a description of psychological interventions used to enhance diabetes self-management.

Endocrine Disorders

The endocrine system (see Chapter 2) contains glands that make and control hormones, chemical messengers that regulate many bodily processes. Endocrine disorders occur when hormone levels are too high or too low, or when the body does not properly respond to hormones (MedlinePlus, 2012). **Insulin**, a hormone produced by the pancreas, is necessary for cells to metabolize glucose. Insulin works like a key that opens locked glucose gates on cells of the body. It binds with cells and opens glucose channels, allowing glucose to move from the blood into body cells (see Figure 10.1). Insulin also enables glucose to be stored in the liver and other body tissues (ADA, 2009).

Diabetes mellitus is the most common endocrine disorder. It is characterized by chronic dysregulation of the use and/or production of insulin. The hallmark feature of diabetes (ADA, 2012) is **hyperglycemia**, or elevated levels of glucose in the blood (**blood glucose**). The classic symptoms of hyperglycemia include frequent hunger, frequent urination, frequent thirst, blurred vision, and fatigue. Chronic hyperglycemia has serious long-term health consequences. Another problem for diabetes patients can be **hypoglycemia**, which refers to blood

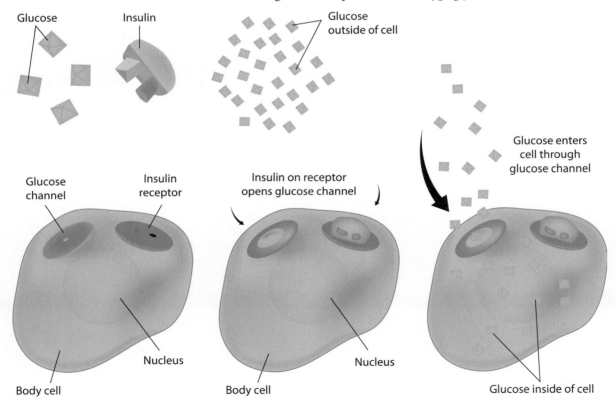

FIGURE 10.1 | Insulin works like a key that opens locked glucose gates on cells of the body. Insulin binds with cells and opens glucose channels that allow glucose to move from the blood into body cells.

Source: From *Human Diseases and Conditions, 2E*. © 2010 Gale, a part of Cengage Learning, Inc. Reproduced by permission. www.cengage.com/permissions

glucose levels that drop too low. Common symptoms of hypoglycemia include shakiness, dizziness, sweating, hunger, and confusion or altered consciousness (ADA, 2012).

Diabetes Classification

There are three different types of diabetes: type 1, type 2, and gestational. Type 1 and type 2 diabetes account for nearly all diabetes cases. Type 1 accounts for about 5 to 10 per cent of diabetes cases, and type 2 accounts for about 90 to 95 per cent. Gestational diabetes is the least common form of diabetes. According to the **Centers for Disease Control and Prevention (CDC)**, it affects between 2 and 10 per cent of pregnant women in the US (CDC, 2011). Prevalence of gestational diabetes among pregnant women in Canada ranges from 3.7 per cent in non-Aboriginal populations to 8–18 per cent in Aboriginal populations (CDA, 2008).

Type 1 Diabetes

Formerly known as juvenile or insulin-dependent diabetes, type 1 diabetes usually occurs in childhood and adolescence. Type 1 diabetes is an autoimmune disease that destroys the insulin-producing beta cells of the pancreas. This results in insulin deficiency. People with type 1 diabetes must rely entirely on self-administered insulin supplementation to survive.

Type 2 Diabetes

Type 2 diabetes was formerly known as non-insulin dependent or adult-onset diabetes. It is characterized by insulin resistance, relative insulin deficiency, or both. Insulin resistance is a condition where the body does not respond as well as it should to the action of insulin. This hampers the body's ability to properly metabolize carbohydrates, fats, and proteins (ADA, 2012). Relative insulin deficiency means that the pancreas produces some insulin, but not enough to meet the body's needs (ADA, 2012). Both insulin resistance and relative insulin deficiency can contribute to chronic hyperglycemia in type 2 diabetes.

Gestational Diabetes

Gestational diabetes sometimes develops during pregnancy because of hormonal changes and increased metabolic demands. These changes can reduce insulin production and/or effectiveness. Gestational diabetes occurs more frequently among obese women and those with a family history of diabetes. While only about 5 to 10 per cent of women who develop

PHOTO 10.1 | Actor Jerry Lewis was diagnosed with type 1 diabetes.

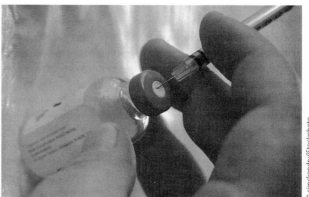

PHOTO 10.2 | People with type 1 diabetes must rely entirely on self-administered insulin supplementation to survive.

gestational diabetes remain diabetic after pregnancy, their risk of developing type 2 diabetes is higher later in life (CDC, 2011).

Prediabetes

Chronic hyperglycemia develops gradually and may go undetected for many years. Consequently, health-care systems are now attempting to identify people with a condition called **prediabetes**, a likely precursor to diabetes. Prediabetes is defined as having blood glucose levels higher than normal but not high enough to meet criteria for a diabetes diagnosis. Nearly 25 per cent of the populations in the US and Canada are estimated to have prediabetes (CDA, 2011; CDC, 2011). People with untreated prediabetes are 20 times more likely to develop type 2 diabetes over a five-year period than those with normal blood glucose levels (ADA, 2012). About 50 per cent of Canadians with prediabetes are estimated to develop type 2 diabetes (CDA, 2011).

Diagnosis

Diagnosis of diabetes is determined primarily by several different blood tests that measure glucose levels. It is possible to diagnose someone based on one test alone. However, it is common for physicians to repeat a test or give more than one test before making a final diagnosis. The diagnosis is easier to make if the person is already showing classic symptoms of hyperglycemia. The tests typically used for diabetes diagnosis are: (1) a fasting plasma glucose test, which measures blood glucose levels after fasting for at least eight hours; (2) an oral glucose tolerance test, which measures blood glucose levels two hours after ingesting a sweet liquid following an eight-hour fast; and (3) the **hemoglobin A1c** (A1c) test, which shows the average blood glucose levels over the prior two to three months (ADA, 2012). The A1c test is a bit more complicated than the other tests. Here is how it works: Glucose in the cells attaches to hemoglobin, a protein in red blood cells that carries oxygen. The A1c test measures the percentage of hemoglobin that has been coated with glucose. Red blood cells form and die constantly and have a typical lifespan of three months. Therefore, A1c represents the average blood glucose over the past few months. (US Department of Health and Human Services, 2011).

Diabetes Statistics

Diabetes, primarily type 2 diabetes, has become one of the most prevalent chronic diseases in the world. In 2010, an estimated 285 million adults worldwide had diabetes. Within the US, approximately 25.8 million people (8.3 per cent of the population) had diabetes (CDC, 2011). Of those, approximately 3 million had type 1 and about 23 million had type 2 (CDC, 2011; JDRF, 2011). Within Canada, it is estimated that 6.4 per cent of people age 12 or older have diabetes (Statistics Canada, 2010). In both Canada and the US, men are about 1–2 per cent more likely than women to have diabetes (CDC, 2011; Statistics Canada, 2010).

There are sizable racial and ethnic differences in risk for diabetes. In the US, type 2 diabetes risk is significantly higher for all other racial and ethnic groups compared to non-Hispanic White adults (CDC, 2011). Specifically, risk is 77 per cent higher for non-Hispanic Black persons, 66 per cent higher for Hispanics, and 18 per cent higher for Asian Americans. Data from 2007–9 indicate that among adults, 7.1 per cent of non-Hispanic Whites, 12.6 per cent of non-Hispanic Blacks, 11.8 per cent of Hispanics, and 8.4 per cent of Asian Americans were diagnosed with diabetes. In contrast, type 1 diabetes is more prevalent in non-Hispanic Whites than in other racial and ethnic groups (SEARCH for Diabetes in Youth Study Group, 2006). In Canada, members of the Aboriginal population tend to be diagnosed with diabetes at a younger age (PHAC, 2009). They also have a higher rates of gestational diabetes and of type 2 diabetes in children and adolescents, and experience diabetes complications more often than their non-Aboriginal counterparts (PHAC, 2011).

The prevalence of diabetes has been increasing. Figure 10.2 shows a dramatic increase in US diabetes cases, mainly within the past 20 years. The prevalence of diabetes among Canadians increased by 70 per cent between 1999 and 2009 (PHAC, 2011). By 2030 world diabetes rates are expected to increase by 54 per cent, with 7.7 per cent of the adult population suffering from the disease (Shaw, Sicree, & Zimmet, 2010; see Figure 10.3). Higher rates of diabetes are most likely due to large increases in the number of people who are overweight and obese in North America and worldwide (ADA, 2012; PHAC, 2011). The increasing prevalence of diabetes over the past two decades is especially notable

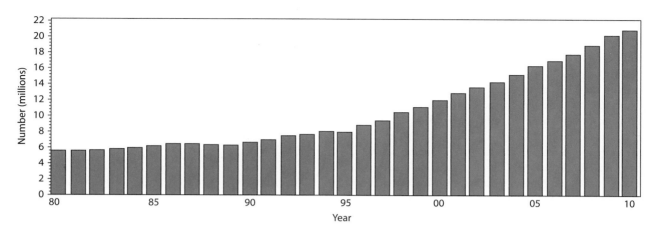

FIGURE 10.2 | Number (in millions) of civilian, non-institutionalized persons with diagnosed diabetes, United States, 1980–2010. Diabetes is becoming more common in the US. From 1980 through 2010, the number of Americans with diagnosed diabetes has more than tripled (from 5.6 million to 20.9 million).

Source: http://www.cdc.gov/diabetes/statistics/prev/national/figpersons.htm

FIGURE 10.3 | Projected percentage rates of diabetes worldwide in 2030 for people 20–79 years of age.

Source: IDF Diabetes Atlas, 5th edition, p. 29, Map 2.2 at http://www.idf.org/sites/default/files/da5/5eDiabetesAtlas_2011.pdf

in children and adolescents. Nearly 25 per cent of children and adolescents in the US now meet criteria for diabetes or prediabetes. Between 2000 and 2008 the prevalence of diabetes and prediabetes in US adolescents increased from 9 per cent to 23 per cent (May, Kuklina, & Yoon, 2012). The increase in diabetes and prediabetes among young people is especially concerning because early onset of the disease increases the risk of later diabetes-related complications (CDA, 2008; PHAC, 2011).

Etiology and Risk Factors

The etiology—the cause or origin—of diabetes is not fully understood. More is known about risk factors—factors associated with developing a disease but not proven to be a cause. A family history of diabetes, obesity, and a sedentary lifestyle are the most significant risk factors for developing type 2 diabetes (ADA, n.d.; Van Dam et al., 2005). First-degree relatives (e.g., children, siblings) of a person with diabetes are more likely to develop type 2 diabetes than someone in the general population without that sort of genetic link. Twin studies indicate that shared genes are partly—but not entirely—the reason why diabetes tends to run in families (Florez, Hirschhorn, & Altshuler, 2003). When considering the role of genes versus the environment, it is important to recognize that the prevalence of type 2 diabetes has risen markedly over the past 20 years, but the genetic makeup of the population cannot change in such a short period of time. What has changed is the number of people who are overweight or obese (defined as a body mass index (BMI) ≥25 kg/m²). Obesity rates have increased over the same period that diabetes rates have risen (Mokdad et al., 2001). It is likely that a combination of genetic vulnerability and obesity-related lifestyle behaviours (poor diet and sedentary lifestyle) increase the risk of developing type 2 diabetes (Li, Qi, Workalemahu, Hu, & Qi, 2012).

Although obesity is a risk factor for type 2 diabetes, not all obese people develop type 2 diabetes, and not all people with type 2 diabetes are obese. Other risk factors for type 2 diabetes include prediabetes, hypertension (high blood pressure), delivering a baby heavier than nine pounds, prior diagnosis of gestational diabetes, low HDL cholesterol and/or high triglyceride levels, and being a member of certain racial and ethnic groups, including African Americans, Latinos, Native Americans/Canadians of Aboriginal ancestry, Asian Americans, and Pacific Islanders (ADA, 2012). Low socio-economic status (SES) is another known risk factor for diabetes. Low SES is related to increases in diabetes prevalence, risk of diabetes-related complications, and risk of diabetes-related death (Rabi et al., 2006; Saydah & Lochner, 2010). Obesity rates are higher among those with low SES, which may partly explain the relationship between low SES and increased diabetes risk. Increased diabetes risk among those with lower SES may also be related to community factors that make healthy lifestyles harder to maintain (e.g.,

"The red circles are your red blood cells. The white circles are your white blood cells. The brown circles are donuts. We need to talk."

PHOTO 10.3 | "We need to talk."

unsafe neighbourhoods, lack of parks, low income, and, consequently, poorer nutrition). Genetic vulnerability also appears to play a role in the development of type 1 diabetes, but again, genes are not entirely responsible. Environmental factors likely interact with genetic vulnerability to produce type 1 diabetes. The specific environmental factors that are critical, however, remain unclear. Environmental factors that may increase risk include exposure to certain toxins and viruses, certain foods, early feeding practices (e.g., exposure to cow's milk, vitamin D deficiency), and stressful life events. However, these findings should be viewed as speculative, as more research is needed (Åkerblom, Vaarala, Hyöty, Ilonen, & Knip, 2002; Peng & Hagopian, 2006).

Common Medical Complications

Chronic high glucose levels cause serious medical complications. These complications are usually categorized as either macrovascular or microvascular. **Macrovascular complications** are diseases involving

 **IN FOCUS**

Risk Assessment for Diabetes

The American Diabetes Association (ADA) offers a free risk assessment for type 2 diabetes on its website. Fill out a short quiz and determine your risk for developing this chronic illness. You can also learn what to do to lower your risk at: <www.diabetes.org/diabetes-basics/prevention/diabetes-risk-test/?loc=DropDownDB-RiskTest>.

the large blood vessels. These include cardiovascular diseases (CVD) such as coronary artery disease, peripheral arterial disease, and stroke. Individuals with type 2 diabetes have a 150–400 per cent increased risk of stroke (Beckman, Creager, & Libby, 2002). CVD contributes the most to the medical costs of diabetes (ADA, 2012).

Microvascular complications are diseases of the small blood vessels. These include retinopathy, nephropathy, and neuropathy. *Retinopathy* involves damage to the blood vessels of the eye and is a leading cause of blindness in adults (Nathan, 1993). Retinopathy is so common among people with diabetes that most will experience some degree of retinopathy during their lifetime. Other eye disorders (e.g., glaucoma, cataracts) occur earlier and more often in people with diabetes (ADA, 2012). Diabetic *nephropathy* is a condition in which both chronic hyperglycemia and hypertension cause damage to the kidneys. Patients with nephropathy often require dialysis (having a machine perform kidney functions) or kidney transplantation. Nephropathy affects 20–40 per cent of people with diabetes. It is the leading cause of long-term kidney failure and end-stage kidney disease and is a major cause of illness and death in people with diabetes (ADA, 2012). Diabetic *neuropathy* involves damage to nerves throughout the body. It causes symptoms such as tingling, numbness or pain in the extremities (i.e., toes, feet, legs, hands, and arms), stomach and intestinal problems, sexual dysfunction, weakness, and dizziness. Deterioration of muscles in the foot and hand can also occur (ADA, 2012). Peripheral neuropathy (i.e., neuropathy in the extremities) combined with peripheral vascular disease (a macrovascular diabetic complication) increases the risk for lower limb amputations. This occurs because peripheral neuropathy deadens the sensation in the feet, making it less likely that a person will notice a foot wound. At the

same time, peripheral vascular disease reduces blood circulation to the extremities, which interferes with wound healing. The combination of deadened sensation in the feet and slower wound healing often leads to amputation. In Canada, people with diabetes are nearly 20 times more likely to have non-traumatic lower limb amputations than are people without diabetes (ADA, 2012; PHAC, 2011).

Medical Management of Diabetes

The ADA, the Canadian Diabetes Association (CDA), and the European Association for the Study of Diabetes (EASD) are among the largest worldwide diabetes associations. These associations regularly publish guidelines for diabetes medical management and offer very similar recommendations. The ADA and the EASD have collaborated to create common guidelines for diabetes management (Inzucchi et al., 2012). An attractive feature of both the ADA and CDA guidelines is an evidence-based grading system, which ranks the strength of scientific support for each recommendation (ADA, 2012; CDA, 2008). Recommendations based on studies using the best scientific methods are ranked the highest. Recommendations that have not been tested using empirical scientific methods are given the weakest ranking (ADA, 2012). Greater confidence is placed in recommendations that are scientifically supported. These ranking systems help health practitioners make well-informed decisions.

The primary goal of diabetes medical management is to maintain healthy blood glucose levels. Most patients are advised to keep their A1c level at or below 7 per cent, because doing so substantially reduces the risk of medical complications from diabetes (ADA, 2012). However, recent guidelines offer the option of tailoring A1c goals to each patient based on his or her own needs or medical history. For example, a lower A1c goal (less than 6.5 per cent) might be established for patients who experience no side effects from lower blood glucose levels. A higher A1c goal (up to 8 per cent) might be made for patients who have severe reactions to low blood glucose levels, who have limited life expectancy, or who have serious medical problems (ADA, 2012).

Specific medical practice guidelines have been established to help patients maintain healthy blood glucose levels. Somewhat different recommendations are made based on the stage, severity, duration, and type of diabetes. These recommendations are briefly described next.

Prediabetes, Type 2, and Gestational Diabetes

Healthy Lifestyle Behaviours

A major goal of diabetes medical management is to promote healthy lifestyle behaviours. Recommendations for those with prediabetes and newly diagnosed type 2 diabetes include healthy eating, calorie reduction, regular exercise, and a 5–10 per cent reduction in body weight. ADA diet guidelines for people with prediabetes are relatively flexible. It states that "for weight loss, either low-carbohydrate, low-fat calorie-restricted, or Mediterranean diets may be effective in the short-term (up to 2 years)" (ADA, 2012, p. S21). People with prediabetes should also reduce fat intake, eat the recommended amounts of fibre and whole grains, and limit sugar-sweetened beverage intake (ADA, 2012). For those with type 2 diabetes, the ADA and EASD advise tailoring dietary recommendations while maintaining a healthy diet that includes high-fibre foods, low-fat dairy products, and fresh fish. Foods high in carbohydrates (e.g., sweet desserts) and saturated fats should be limited (Inzucchi et al., 2012). Exercise recommendations for those with prediabetes and type 2 diabetes include at least 150 minutes of moderate-intensity exercise per week. The lifestyle recommendations that government health agencies make for preventing and controlling diabetes reflect a healthy lifestyle for all people. The CDA makes similar healthy lifestyle recommendations.

As noted earlier, medical management recommendations should be based on strong scientific evidence. Large-scale studies of lifestyle interventions for people with prediabetes have been conducted in the US, Finland, China, Japan, and India. All of these studies reached the conclusion that lifestyle changes including regular exercise and weight loss reduce the risk of developing diabetes (Ahmad & Crandall, 2010). For example, the Diabetes Prevention Program Research Group (DPRG) intensive lifestyle intervention reduced the probability of developing diabetes by 58 per cent (DPRG, 2002). The DPRG also found that intensive healthy lifestyle modifications were superior to a medication intervention. Moreover, the DPRG results applied to various ethnic groups, not just Caucasians (DPRG, 2009). Figure 10.4 shows that approximately 11 per cent of the placebo group developed diabetes each year. By contrast, only about 5 per cent of the lifestyle intervention group developed diabetes annually. In

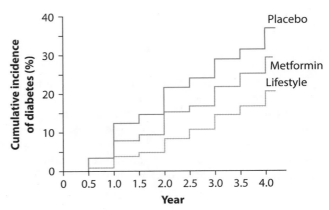

FIGURE 10.4 | Cumulative incidence of diabetes according to study group. The diagnosis of diabetes was based on the criteria of the American Diabetes Association. The incidence of diabetes differed significantly among the three groups (P<0.001 for each comparison).

Source: Diabetes Prevention Program Research Group (2002).

summary, healthy lifestyle behaviours are keys to preventing and managing diabetes.

Oral Medication

Some people with prediabetes and type 2 diabetes do not achieve adequate **glucose control** (keeping blood sugar levels in the prescribed range) with lifestyle change alone. In such cases, health-care providers often prescribe oral medication. Metformin is one oral medication that is widely used, is inexpensive, has few-side effects, and is very effective in controlling high blood glucose. Metformin is used to manage existing diabetes and to prevent future diabetes in those with prediabetes. For example, the DPRG (2002) found that metformin alone reduced the risk of developing type 2 diabetes by 31 per cent (see Figure 10.4). Metformin is also recommended for type 2 diabetes (Inzucchi et al., 2012) and for those with prior gestational diabetes (ADA, 2012). When metformin alone does not achieve target A1c levels for type 2 patients, health-care providers usually prescribe a second drug from a different class of diabetes medications. Adding a second class of oral diabetes medications has been shown to lower A1c approximately 1 per cent more (Bennett et al., 2011), which is impressive. However, all oral diabetes medications can have adverse side effects that must be considered before deciding on a two-drug combination.

Insulin

Approximately 53 per cent of people with type 2 diabetes use oral diabetes medications (Koro, Bowlin, Bourgeois, & Fedder, 2004). However, sometimes even a combination of two or three oral medications from different classes does not successfully reduce A1c levels. In these cases, insulin replacement therapy is usually prescribed (ADA, 2012). Recall that insulin is a hormone that is necessary to metabolize glucose. Recall also that people with type 2 diabetes produce some insulin, but it is either too little or does not work effectively. Because people with type 2 diabetes produce some working insulin, they are usually prescribed a low dose of long-lasting insulin to support their body's supply. Approximately 11 per cent of people with type 2 diabetes take insulin along with one or more oral medications (Koro et al., 2004).

A major risk of using insulin is severe hypoglycemia. Symptoms of hypoglycemia range from relatively mild (e.g., shakiness, sweating, confusion) to severe (e.g., seizures, confusion, loss of consciousness). Whenever a person experiences hypoglycemia, he or she should immediately ingest food with high glucose content (e.g., orange juice, glucose tabs, non-diet soft drink) to bring the glucose levels back to a normal level. With mild hypoglycemia, a person can correct glucose levels him- or herself (self-treat). *Severe hypoglycemia* is defined as any episode that requires external assistance (unable to self-treat). Severe hypoglycemia is potentially dangerous and could be fatal in some situations, such as when driving a car. People with type 1 diabetes are more likely to experience severe hypoglycemia than are those with type 2 diabetes. About 30–40 per cent of people with type 1 diabetes experience at least one severe hypoglycemic episode every year (Frier, 2009). In contrast, about 11 per cent of people with type 2 diabetes report at least one severe episode of hypoglycemia each year (Lipska et al., 2013).

Youth with Type 2 Diabetes

Less is known about how best to treat type 2 diabetes in youth. A large randomized clinical trial was conducted by the Treatment Options for Type 2 Diabetes in Adolescents and Youth (TODAY) Study Group (2012). The researchers concluded that metformin plus rosiglitazone (another class of diabetes oral medications) was more effective than metformin alone. Adding a lifestyle intervention to metformin did not significantly improve outcomes beyond the effect of metformin alone. While the TODAY study provides useful information, additional research is needed to establish clear standards for treating type 2 diabetes in children and in adolescents.

Self-Monitoring of Blood Glucose (SMBG)

People with diabetes are usually given a portable blood glucose monitoring device (called a glucometer) to test blood glucose levels throughout the day. The test requires drawing a small drop of blood using a finger-pricking device. The blood is then placed on a monitoring strip that has been inserted into the glucometer. Within seconds, the blood glucose level is shown. In people with diabetes, blood glucose levels fluctuate throughout the day depending on food intake, exercise, medication use, and even stress. Regular self-monitoring helps determine if blood glucose levels are in an unhealthy range. Regular SMBG can also help patients identify factors related to changes in their blood glucose levels. It can also prompt immediate action to bring their blood glucose level to a healthy range and may help prevent future incidents of unhealthy blood glucose levels.

Recently, SMBG has been de-emphasized for people with type 2 diabetes who do not use insulin or use insulin only once per day. For this group of patients, SMBG appears to have an insufficient benefit with regard to reducing A1c and improving quality of life (Farmer et al.,

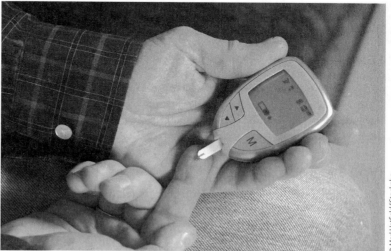

PHOTO 10.4 | Testing blood glucose. Within seconds after the test strip touches the drop of blood, the glucometer will show the blood glucose level.

2012). On the other hand, SMBG is highly recommended for type 2 patients using insulin several times a day. These patients should measure their blood glucose level three or more times daily, because doing so is likely to improve their A1c level and reduce risk for hypoglycemia (ADA, 2012). Most people with type 2 diabetes do not regularly monitor their blood glucose levels. Only about 15 per cent of people with type 2 diabetes monitor their blood glucose more than once per day. More than 50 per cent never monitor at all or do so less than once per month (Harris, 2001).

Bariatric Surgery

Bariatric surgery for obese type 2 patients has become more frequent in recent years. The most common types of bariatric surgery are gastric banding and gastric bypass. Both of these surgeries are designed to reduce the size of the stomach. Bariatric surgery results in substantial weight loss and significant improvement in glucose levels (Buchwald et al., 2009). Diabetes is either fully resolved or improved in 80 per cent of those receiving gastric banding and in 90 per cent of those receiving gastric bypass surgery. Other medical problems associated with obesity and diabetes are also improved (e.g., reduced cholesterol, blood pressure, and sleep apnea). Bariatric surgery is not without risks, including death. Death rates range from as few as 0.1 per cent for gastric banding procedures to as high as 1.1 per cent from procedures that involve removing portions of the stomach (Buchwald et al., 2009). Nevertheless, these procedures are considered reasonable treatment options for some obese type 2 diabetes patients. Those with medical complications who are unable to achieve adequate glucose control are the likely candidates.

Type 1 Diabetes

The treatment regimen for type 1 diabetes is relatively complex and demanding. SMBG should occur at least three times per day. Based on blood glucose readings along with carbohydrate intake and level of physical activity, the proper dose of insulin must be administered three to four times per day. Most people with type 1 diabetes use a needle to inject insulin. However, some use a continuous insulin infusion system that is placed below the skin, also called insulin pump therapy. The

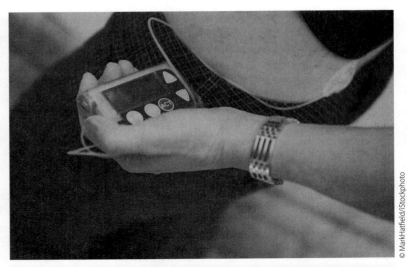

© MarkHatfield/iStockphoto

PHOTO 10.5 | Insulin pump therapy allows easy injection of short-acting doses of insulin throughout the day.

insulin pump allows easy injection of short-acting doses of insulin throughout the day, rather than relying on fewer injections of long-lasting insulin. This technique allows for more flexibility in their lives. By and large, the same recommendations for exercise and a healthy diet described earlier are also made for people with type 1 diabetes.

People with type 1 and type 2 diabetes are vulnerable to the long-term health consequences of poor glucose control. However, those with type 1 diabetes are much more likely to experience short-term fluctuations in blood glucose levels that can lead to serious medical consequences. A common problem for people with type 1 diabetes is hypoglycemia. Hypoglycemic episodes occur about twice per week in people with type 1 diabetes.

Hypoglycemia usually results from taking too much insulin relative to the amount of glucose in the blood. For example, hypoglycemia could happen if something interferes with plans to eat food to balance out previously injected insulin. It could also occur after too much exercise without enough food (glucose) to offset previously injected insulin.

People with type 1 diabetes also face risks if they take too little insulin relative to the amount of glucose in their blood. Insufficient levels of insulin prevent glucose from being used properly, which forces the body to break down fat for energy. This process produces **ketones** (poisonous acids). High levels of ketones can cause a condition called **ketoacidosis**, which can lead to a diabetic coma or even death. In summary, for people with type 1 diabetes, failing to control blood glucose levels throughout the day can lead to both short- and long-term adverse health consequences.

Other Medical Management Issues

The risk for medical complications from diabetes must be addressed routinely by health-care providers (ADA, 2012). Health-care providers should carefully monitor and treat known risk factors for CVD, especially blood pressure and cholesterol. To reduce CVD risk, diabetes patients may be prescribed a daily dose of acetylsalicylic acid (e.g., Aspirin) and are always advised not to smoke. Regular screenings for retinopathy (e.g., annual eye exams), nephropathy, and neuropathy are also essential. Diabetes also creates a higher risk for foot wounds with potentially dangerous consequences, including amputation. Therefore, a comprehensive annual foot examination by a physician is considered vital. Diabetes patients must also continually guard against foot wounds (e.g., wear proper footwear, use care when clipping toenails) and visually inspect their feet every day. Diabetes patients are also more prone to complications from influenza and pneumonia. Therefore, all recommended influenza and pneumonia vaccines should be received. Due to higher risk for severe periodontal disease (a disease that affects tissues surrounding the teeth), diabetes patients should receive a dental examination twice a year. People with diabetes—possibly only those with type 2—may also be at increased risk for some forms of cancer, including colon, breast, liver, and pancreatic cancer (Suh & Kim, 2011). Therefore, they should be screened regularly and encouraged to alter behaviours that place them at risk for cancer (e.g., stop smoking, lose weight, increase physical activity).

Diabetes Self-Management Education (DSME)

Diabetes patients must continuously follow a complex medical regimen to have the best chance for physical and psychological well-being. However, many patients fall short of the self-management goals they have been prescribed (Delamater, 2006). A large multinational study showed that only 46 per cent of type 1 patients and just 39 per cent of type 2 patients achieved complete success in at least two-thirds of their self-care domains (Peyrot et al., 2005). Ultimately, the responsibility for successful outcomes rests primarily with the patients themselves. Therefore, formal diabetes education and support programs are considered essential to improve patient success (ADA, 2012).

Most DSME programs are multidisciplinary, meaning that they include physicians, nurses, dieticians, and diabetes educators. Sometimes social workers and psychologists are included. The goals of DSME are to encourage proper self-care behaviours while enhancing patient decision-making and problem-solving. Family members of child and adolescent patients usually attend DSME sessions because poor family support is related to poor adherence (Anderson et al., 2002; Wysocki, 2006). Patients of all ages are encouraged to maintain contact with their health-care team for ongoing education and support (ADA, 2012). DSME has been found to have a significant positive effect on a variety of diabetes-related outcomes (Cochran & Conn, 2008; Deakin, McShane, Cade, & Williams, 2005; Norris, Lau, Smith, Schmid, & Engelgau, 2002). However, even with DSME, many people with diabetes continue to have problems adhering to their self-care regimen. As a result, there has been increased interest in the role that psychosocial factors play in diabetes self-management. See Chapter 3 for a more detailed discussion of adherence.

Psychosocial Factors in Diabetes

Psychosocial factors play such an important role in diabetes that both the ADA and CDA have dedicated large sections of their treatment recommendations to psychological issues (ADA, 2012; CDA, 2008). A wide variety of psychosocial factors can influence diabetes self-management. The most studied factors include stress and coping, beliefs and expectations, depression, anxiety, eating disorders, and social support.

Stress and Coping

Stress

Stress can be physical (e.g., surgery, illness), psychological (e.g., dreading deadlines, fear of giving a presentation), or environmental (e.g., living in an unstable relationship or household). Stress can be positive (e.g., planning a wedding, accepting a promotion) or negative (e.g., attending a funeral, losing one's job). For the purposes of this section, "stress" is defined as any set of experiences that cause psychological unrest (see Chapter 5 for a detailed discussion of stress). Physical stress (e.g., surgery, infection, chronic illness) can directly influence glucose regulation through physiological processes (see McCowen, Malhorta, & Bistrian, 2001, and Wellen & Hotamisligil, 2005, for more information). This section focuses on psychological reactions to stress that can affect diabetes.

Psychological stress influences diabetes in two primary ways: through physiological stress responses and through behavioural stress responses. Psychological stress triggers a complex series of physiological processes that involve the brain, nervous system, and endocrine system. The primary systems involved in the stress response include the hypothalamic-pituitary-adrenal (HPA) axis and the sympathetic-adrenal-medullary (SAM) system. When faced with stress, the body moves into action, releasing stress hormones and glucose so the muscles and brain have easy access to energy (Black, 2003; Padgett & Glaser, 2003). This response can be very helpful when stress requires a large increase in metabolic demand (e.g., chasing a perpetrator or fighting off an intruder). However, when stress requires a minimal increase in metabolic demand (e.g., giving a speech or remembering an argument), excess hormones and glucose are not "used up." When that happens, substances produced by psychological stress remain in the bloodstream and disrupt blood glucose regulation (Charmandari, Tsigos, & Chrousos, 2005).

PHOTO 10.6 | Unhealthy coping responses such as eating comfort food, increasing alcohol consumption, decreasing physical activity, and smoking can adversely influence diabetes.

Behavioural reactions to stress can also affect diabetes by interfering with adherence. For example, during periods of stress, a person may use unhealthy coping responses such as eating comfort food, increasing alcohol consumption, decreasing physical activity, and smoking. Stressful events can also be distracting and time-consuming, which may lead to skipped meals, less sleep, forgetting to take medication, and failing to test blood glucose. For more information on the relationship between stress and diabetes, visit the ADA website at: <www.diabetes.org/living-with-diabetes/complications/stress.html>.

Coping

Stress is unavoidable and a normal part of life. For people with diabetes, the goal is not to eliminate stress, but rather to reduce and manage it. The different ways of coping can be grouped into two broad categories: approach and avoidant (see Chapter 5 for a detailed discussion of coping). Approach coping involves active or problem-solving strategies (e.g., active planning). These approaches are associated with positive diabetes outcomes and well-being (Duangdao & Roesch, 2008; Fisher, Thorpe, DeVellis, & DeVellis, 2007; Gherman et al., 2011). Avoidant coping involves passive, emotion-focused coping such as wishful thinking, denial, and substance abuse. These approaches tend to be less effective (Graue, Wentzel-Larsen, Bru, Hanestad, & Søvik, 2004). For example, emotional coping (e.g., avoiding worries about high blood glucose) is associated with higher A1c levels (Gherman et al., 2011). In summary, stress is related to poorer glucose control in people who use less effective coping strategies (Peyrot & McMurry, 1992). Healthy coping appears to protect people from the negative effect of stress on glucose control and improves quality of life. Learning to use healthy coping strategies is considered an important part of diabetes self-management (Fisher et al., 2007).

Beliefs and Expectations

A person's beliefs about diabetes are also considered important in diabetes management. The health beliefs model (Rosenstock, Strecher, & Becker, 1988), which was briefly introduced in Chapter 1, suggests that diabetes self-care will be better in patients who believe: (a) they are at risk of experiencing the negative consequences of diabetes; (b) that the consequences of diabetes are serious, and (c) that they will benefit from using self-care behaviours. Further, those who believe the costs of self-care are too great (e.g., time, effort, money) are expected to be less motivated. Many of these beliefs and expectations are related to engaging in diabetes self-care (Gherman et al., 2011; Harvey & Lawson, 2009). Beliefs about the personal consequences of adherence, in particular, have been found to be strongly related to diabetes adherence (Gherman et al., 2011).

Diabetes self-efficacy refers to confidence in one's ability to manage the demands of diabetes self-care. Basically, self-efficacy taps into a person's perceived control over diabetes. Self-efficacy expectations are strongly related to positive diabetes outcomes, including diabetes self-care and A1c levels (Gherman et al., 2011). The relationship between self-efficacy and positive diabetes outcomes is bi-directional. That is, higher self-efficacy should foster better adherence. In turn, better adherence should foster higher self-efficacy (Sacco et al., 2007).

Depression

In recent years, the relationship between depression and diabetes has received increased attention, and for good reasons. Figure 10.5, shows that depression prevalence rates are nearly twice as high among those with diabetes (both type 1 and type 2) compared to those without diabetes (Anderson, Freedland, Clouse, & Lustman, 2001). Moreover, when people with diabetes are depressed, they adhere less, have higher blood glucose levels, have more medical complications, and even die

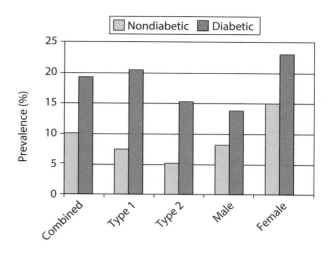

FIGURE 10.5 | Depression prevalence rates are approximately twice as high in adults diagnosed with diabetes as in those without diabetes.

Source: Adapted from Anderson, Freedland, Clouse, & Lustman (2001).

at an earlier age (Figure 10.6) (Ciechanowski, Katon, & Russo, 2000; de Groot, Anderson, Freedland, Clouse, & Lustman, 2001; Egede, Nietert, & Zheng, 2005).

Researchers have attempted to understand the complex relationships among depression, diabetes, and adverse health outcomes. First, depression may pave the way for increased risk of developing

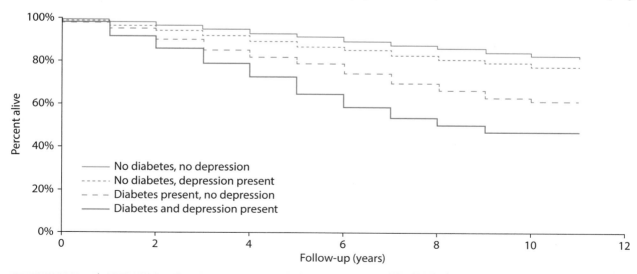

FIGURE 10.6 | Estimated probability of survival (all-cause mortality) according to diabetes and depression diagnosis in 1982. People with depression and diabetes have a 2.5-fold increased risk of death compared with people without either diabetes or depression (Egede et al., 2005).

Source: Egede, Nietert, & Zheng (2005).

type 2 diabetes (Knol et al., 2006; Mezuk, Eaton, Albrecht, & Golden, 2008). Depressed people tend to engage in unhealthy behaviours that may put them at risk for type 2 diabetes. For example, when a person is depressed, he or she may be more likely to eat unhealthy foods (e.g., a high calorie diet) and avoid exercise (Golden et al., 2008). Also, chronic stress associated with depression can lead to prolonged activation of the HPA axis and ANS dysregulation (described above). This dysregulation could increase the risk of developing diabetes by disrupting the body's ability to regulate insulin (Rosmond, 2005; Stetler & Miller, 2011). Second, in the same ways that it could lead to future diabetes, depression could worsen diabetes after it has been developed. Higher levels of stress in depressed people with diabetes could hamper the ability to metabolize glucose. Also, symptoms of depression (e.g., fatigue, hopelessness) could interfere with diabetes self-care (Katon et al., 2010).

A third possibility is that depression could be a *consequence* of developing diabetes. Being diagnosed with diabetes, being unable to control blood glucose levels, or having diabetes-related health problems could cause depression. For example, researchers measured depression in two groups of people. One group had received a diagnosis of type 2 diabetes from a health-care provider. The other group had blood glucose levels high enough to warrant a diagnosis but had never been told they had diabetes. Depression was higher in the group that had received the diabetes diagnosis (Knol et al., 2007). These results suggest that simply knowing that one has diabetes could increase depression. In addition, diabetes patients who are less successful in adhering to their self-care program are more depressed. Those less successful at adhering are also more likely to report feeling lower diabetes-related self-efficacy (Sacco & Bykowski, 2010; Sacco et al., 2007). Finally, diabetes patients with more diabetes-related medical problems tend to be more depressed (Sacco et al., 2007). Thus, depression could be a consequence of the burden of diabetes, particularly when diabetes is poorly controlled (Sacco & Bykowski, 2010; Sacco et al., 2007).

These findings suggest that the relationship between depression and diabetes is probably bi-directional. That is, depression may increase the risk of developing and worsening diabetes, and having diabetes may also increase the risk for depression (Pan et al., 2010; Renn, Feliciano, & Segal, 2011). Consequently, assessment and treatment of depression has become an increasingly important aspect of diabetes care (Renn et al., 2011; ADA, 2012; CDA, 2008).

Anxiety and Eating Disorders

Anxiety and eating disorders are two other types of psychological disorders that the ADA and CDA have identified as potentially problematic for those with diabetes (ADA, 2012; CDA, 2008). Although less is known about the role of these disorders in diabetes, anxiety and eating disorders are more common among people with diabetes. Both disorders are related to worse diabetes adherence and health outcomes (Collins, Corcoran, & Perry, 2009; Kenardy et al., 2001; Li et al., 2008; Young-Hyman & Davis, 2010). The relationship between glycemic control and disordered eating appears relatively straightforward. For example, imagine that a person with diabetes is over-eating (e.g., binge eating disorder), under-eating (e.g., anorexia), or bingeing and purging (e.g., bulimia). The variability in this person's caloric intake can make it hard for his or her body to regulate blood glucose levels.

The relationship between anxiety and diabetes is less clear. It is possible that the autonomic dysregulation described earlier in this section may explain the link between anxiety and poor glycemic control (Tsigos & Chrousos, 2002). Also, symptoms of anxiety (such as avoidance behaviours) may interfere with successful adherence (Wysocki, 2006). In considering the possible role of anxiety, it must be noted that anxiety and depression are often co-morbid, meaning they often occur together in the same person. Thus, perhaps anxiety plays a role in poor diabetes management because it can co-occur with depression. Anxiety and eating disorders have received enough attention that the ADA and CDA recommend screening for both of these psychological disorders in diabetes patients (ADA, 2012; CDA, 2008).

Social Support

Social support from family, peers, and health-care professionals can play an important role in diabetes management. Social support may be helpful in several different ways. For example, social support can provide direct assistance and useful information, protection against the negative effects of stress, and ideas about alternative coping strategies to deal with stress (van Dam et al., 2005). In people with diabetes, greater social support has been linked to a variety of positive clinical outcomes. These outcomes include: lower A1c, lower blood pressure and cholesterol, better self-management behaviours (e.g., diet, exercise, blood testing), and lower levels of depression and stress-related symptoms (Strom & Egede, 2012). In addition, and even more importantly, interventions designed to increase social support can improve various diabetes outcomes (Strom & Egede, 2012; van Dam et al., 2005).

Theories and Models Related to Diabetes

Biopsychosocial Model

We have discussed biological, psychological, and social factors that influence diabetes. Although these factors are often discussed separately, most experts agree that they are interrelated. The biopsychosocial model, which was introduced in Chapter 1, is often used when discussing diabetes. Recall that the biopsychosocial model stresses the importance of addressing all of these factors when thinking about health and well-being. This model is easily applied to diabetes, and there is support for using it to predict patients' success with glucose control (e.g., Peyrot, McMurry, & Kruger, 1999). The case example presented later in this chapter shows how the biopsychosocial model can be applied to a person with diabetes.

Theory of Reasoned Action/Planned Behaviour

Another model introduced in Chapter 1 is the theory of reasoned action/planned behaviour. Recall that this model proposes three psychological factors that influence a person's intentions to engage in a given behaviour (e.g., exercising). The stronger a person's intentions, the more likely the person is to actually perform the behaviour. The three factors are (1) attitudes towards the behaviour; (2) beliefs about how other people who are important to the person view the behaviour; and (3) perceived control over the behaviour. For example, let's say that a person with diabetes is told by his physician that he should begin exercising three times per week. If this person has a supportive attitude towards exercise (e.g., thinks exercise is a good thing), his friends exercise regularly, and he believes he has control over how often he exercises, he is likely to intend to exercise. However, if this person's attitudes are not positive (e.g., believes exercise won't improve his health), his friends never exercise, and he believes he has little control over how much he exercises, he is much less likely to follow his physician's recommendation. This model has been shown to be useful in predicting diabetes health behaviours (e.g., Harvey & Lawson, 2009).

Psychosocial Assessment of Patients with Diabetes

Psychosocial factors play an important role in diabetes. Therefore, the health-care team must be able to assess these factors, especially when diabetes self-management is poor (ADA, 2012; CDA, 2008).

Formal psychological tests and structured clinical interviews are the best method for assessing psychosocial factors. However, less formal questioning during meetings with patients is most common because of time and resource constraints (Martin, 2012). For example, the CDA makes the following recommendation: "Healthcare professionals should actively explore psychological factors by asking empathetic but frank open-ended questions." The CDA recommends the following topics for discussion: "stress, social support, unhealthy self-care behaviours, health beliefs about risk of complications, treatment efficacy and the degree of interference with normal functioning" (CDA, 2008, p. S83). Informal interviewing can be quite informative. Two simple questions can effectively screen for depression (Whooley, Avins, Miranda, & Browner, 1997). Therefore, the CDA recommends asking patients: (1) Have you been bothered during the past month by feeling down, depressed, or hopeless? and (2) Have you been experiencing little interest or pleasure in doing things? If a patient experiences either symptom on a regular basis, further inquiry about depressive symptoms would be warranted. To assess self-efficacy and social support, health-care professionals could also use simple questions such as these: "How confident do you feel in your ability to manage your diabetes using a scale from 1 (little confidence) to 10 (highly confident)?" Or, "How satisfied are you with the support you receive from your family using a scale from 1 (very unsatisfied) to 10 (very satisfied)?"

Helping the patient achieve diabetes self-management goals is of utmost importance. Accomplishing a goal is more likely if a person has established implementation intentions (Gollwitzer & Sheeran, 2006). Implementation intentions are specific plans for when, where, and how a desired behaviour will be achieved as part of an individual's current routine. Implementation intentions require patients to change broad goals (e.g., exercise more) to goals tied to specific behaviours and situations. For example, a good implementation intention would be: "When I get home from work on Mondays, Wednesdays, and Fridays, I will take a 15-minute walk around the block." Health-care providers should assess a patient's intentions about any aspect of diabetes self-care. If the patient's intentions are too broad, providers should help the patient make them more specific.

Formal psychological testing is usually limited to patients who show signs of more serious psychological problems (e.g., depression, eating disorders). Many reliable and valid psychological tests are used in diabetes research (Peyrot & Rubin, 2007). With recent advances in computer-assisted assessment, these tests may be administered more routinely in clinical settings (e.g., Snoek et al., 2011). One instrument widely used in research and sometimes administered in clinical settings is the Patient Health Questionnaire (PHQ) (Spitzer, Kroenke, & Williams, 1999). The PHQ is a brief self-report measure designed for use in primary-care medical settings. The PHQ screens for eight different mental disorders, including depression, panic disorder, other anxiety disorders, bulimia, binge eating, and alcohol abuse. Another widely used research measure is the Problem Areas in Diabetes Questionnaire (PAID). The PAID is designed to tap into diabetes-related stress (Welch, Jacobson, & Polonsky, 1997). These are just a few examples of tests that have been developed and could be used to formally assess psychosocial factors related to diabetes. Most health-care providers recognize the importance of psychosocial factors in diabetes, but many do not feel confident in their ability to assess these factors or intervene (Peyrot et al., 2005). Therefore, diabetes health-care teams often rely on clinical psychologists, who are trained to assess and treat psychological problems.

Psychological Interventions for People with Diabetes

As you now know, many people with diabetes struggle with their self-care regimen, and many experience psychological problems. In some cases, psychological interventions are recommended. A trained mental health clinician usually provides these interventions. Psychological interventions for diabetes can be delivered to individuals one-on-one or in groups. Interventions might focus on diabetes adherence problems, psychological problems (e.g., depression, anxiety, stress, binge eating), or both. The length of psychological interventions for diabetes varies. In most cases, the sessions last for one hour and extend over a 6–16 week period (Ismail, Winkley, & Rabe-Hesketh, 2004). Psychological interventions for people with diabetes are helpful (Fisher et al., 2007; Ismail et al., 2004; Winkley, Landau, Eisler, & Ismail, 2006). Some of the most commonly used interventions are described next.

Cognitive Behavioural Therapy (CBT)

CBT is the most frequently administered psychological intervention for people with diabetes. It is based on theory and research showing that cognition (thoughts, expectations, beliefs, imagery) directly influences emotion and behaviour (Ismail et al., 2004).

From a diabetes perspective, CBT often includes setting goals and scheduling activities. The therapist and patient collaboratively plan self-management activities such as blood glucose testing and exercise. They might also schedule pleasant events to improve depressed mood (Sacco, Malone, Morrison, Friedman, & Wells, 2009). The CBT therapist works with the patient to anticipate obstacles that might interfere with successful completion of the plan. These obstacles are usually in the form of unhelpful thoughts (e.g., "It will take too long"; "I can't do it"; "Other people will get mad at me"; "None of this will help my diabetes"). Patients are taught to carefully examine each specific thought. After helping the patient become aware of these negative thoughts, the therapist helps the patient objectively examine them. For example, he or she would be asked to evaluate the evidence that supports each negative thought, and might also be asked to consider alternative, less negative interpretations of events the person has experienced. The goal of this therapeutic process is for the patient to learn to think about life with diabetes in a more realistic and functional way.

Behavioural experiments and data-gathering are other key components of CBT (Sacco & Beck, 1995). For example, an "experiment" might be planned to test the patient's negative expectations about eating a healthy substitute for a high-fat food. Or the therapist might design an "experiment" to test how much satisfaction the patient will get from taking a walk around the neighbourhood. The patient would be asked to predict how much satisfaction he or she expects from engaging in those behaviours (e.g., using a scale from 0 to 10). After engaging in the behaviour, the patient writes down the actual amount of satisfaction experienced. Patients often find that the event was more satisfying than expected. Hopefully, the patient learns to recognize that negative expectations are often inaccurate and interfere with healthy behaviour change. If therapy is successful, the patient will continue to evaluate negative cognitions in a more objective manner.

Problem-Solving Therapy (PST)

PST provides a systematic framework for solving problems that interfere with goal attainment and psychological well-being. The therapist helps patients solve problems using the following four steps: (1) problem definition and formulation; (2) generation of alternative solutions (brainstorming); (3) decision-making (choosing one solution to try); and (4) solution implementation followed by evaluation of its effectiveness. If successful in solving the problem, the patient would continue with the same strategy. If not, another solution would be developed and attempted (D'Zurilla & Nezu, 2010). PST is well suited to helping patients overcome barriers to diabetes self-care, as well as other problems that may be causing psychological distress (Weinger et al, 2011).

Relaxation Training

Relaxation training is designed to give diabetes patients a coping skill to deal with stress and anxiety (Henry, Wilson, Bruce, Chisholm, & Rawling, 1997; Ismail et al., 2004). Various relaxation techniques are available. Three common techniques are diaphragmatic breathing, guided imagery, and progressive muscle relaxation (PMR). Diaphragmatic breathing involves breathing deeply and slowly into the abdomen. This type of breathing reduces anxiety and stress due to better blood oxygenation. It has the added benefit of helping patients focus on something non-stressful (the breath) instead of upsetting thoughts. Diaphragmatic breathing is often combined with other types of relaxation exercises, such as guided imagery. In guided imagery the patient is encouraged to use all five senses to visualize a relaxing, stress-free image. For example, one might imagine a scene such as "lying on the beach, hearing the waves, smelling the water, feeling the sand and the sun's warmth, seeing the blue sky and clouds." PMR involves learning to systematically tense and then relax different groups of muscles throughout the body, one at a time (e.g., forearms, shoulders, thighs). Patients are asked to practise these techniques at home in a comfortable setting to acquire the ability to relax. They are encouraged, then, to practise condensed versions of these relaxation techniques before, during, or after stressful events. Learning to effectively relax has a variety of positive outcomes for diabetes patients. Some of these positive outcomes include reduced physiological arousal, improved mood, and increased adaptive behaviour (Manzoni, Pagnini, Castelnuovo, & Molinari, 2008).

CBT, PST, and relaxation therapy are effective in improving glucose control in adults with type 2 diabetes, and in children and adolescents with type 1 diabetes. These interventions are also effective at reducing psychological problems frequently found in people

with diabetes, including depression, anxiety, and eating disorders (Ismail et al., 2004; Winkley et al., 2006).

Motivational Interviewing (MI)

The diabetes regimen can be demanding. Even though people may know how to effectively manage their diabetes, they may lack sufficient motivation. MI was designed specifically to increase a person's motivation. It does so by exploring and resolving ambivalence (Miller & Rose, 2009; Resnicow et al., 2002). Ambivalence refers to feeling strongly about both the advantages and disadvantages of a behaviour. For example, a person with diabetes might feel ambivalent about exercising. He or she knows that exercise will help control blood glucose levels, and it is good for overall health. But on the other hand, he or she also thinks it takes too much time and effort. Whenever the perceived disadvantages of behaviour change outweigh the advantages, motivation to change is low.

In MI, the therapist helps patients notice the discrepancy between where they are and where they want to be, and how feeling "torn" (ambivalence) is affecting them. For example, the therapist might gently point out that the patient says she wants to feel better, but at the same time she is not doing what is necessary to feel better. In MI, the therapist avoids any attempt to coerce or argue with the patient. Doing so would decrease motivation for changing. Rather, the MI therapist remains non-judgmental. The therapist gently asks questions and listens carefully to help the patient freely explore and resolve the ambivalence. The goal is to get patients to make their own arguments for changing their behaviour (i.e., "change talk"). This fosters motivation from within. Once the patient expresses motivation to change, the therapist assists behaviour change efforts by offering a "menu" of options. The patient then makes his or her own plan of change using this menu. Throughout this phase, the MI therapist also works to enhance the patient's self-efficacy.

MI can be a useful intervention for diabetes. A recent review found MI alone or in combination with other psychological interventions led to improvement in a variety of diabetes-related outcomes. Specifically, MI had positive effects on glucose control, diet and exercise, weight loss, diabetes self-efficacy, and perceived control over diabetes (Hettema, Steele, & Miller, 2005; Martins & McNeil, 2009).

⊞ IN PRACTICE

Gaining Control

Mary is a 57-year-old Latina woman who recently was diagnosed with type 2 diabetes. She is not surprised by this news because she has a family history of type 2 diabetes. Mary is 5′4″ and weighs 230 pounds. She and her husband recently moved across the country because of his job relocation. Mary's new job is extremely stressful and exhausting, but it pays well, so she doesn't look for a new one. Mary now lives very far away from her three adult children and has no friends in her current city. Her husband works the night shift, so they have opposite schedules. Lately, Mary has noticed that she feels tired and sad all the time, and she doesn't really like doing the things she used to enjoy. Mary usually gets fast food on her way home from work because she is too tired to make anything at home (her favourite meal is a cheeseburger, fries, and a 20-oz. cola). When she arrives home in the evening, she has some chips and a soda around nine, and sits in her recliner watching TV until she goes to bed around 10. On nights when she feels really low, she treats herself to a bowl of ice cream to make herself feel better. On her next medical visit, Mary learns that her A1c level is 10.5. Her physician warns her about the health complications she could experience if she doesn't get her diabetes under control.

Mary decides to join a gym and starts going to an exercise class three times per week. She becomes friends with other members who inspire her to continue going to classes. She also decides to see a psychologist for her symptoms of depression. After six months of CBT for depression, and at the same time maintaining her exercise program, Mary feels much better and is relying less on food to improve her mood. At her next checkup, she discovers that her A1c level is 8.3. She feels even more confident about her ability to manage her diabetes regimen. Her physician praises her for the results and tells her to keep up the good work. After one year, Mary has lost 70 pounds and her A1c is down to 7.0. She has completed her full course of CBT for depression. She no longer feels sad or tired and enjoys a variety of activities with her new-found exercise buddies. Her husband, children, and friends are all very proud of her. But most of all, she is very proud of herself and feels extremely confident about her ability to manage her diabetes self-care regimen. She hopes that someday she will be able to stop her diabetes medications.

Future Directions

Diabetes has become one of the most serious health problems facing the world today. There has been an alarming increase in the prevalence of type 2 diabetes over the past several decades. Type 1 and type 2 diabetes can be controlled with proper self-care. Type 2 diabetes is preventable (Hopper, Billah, Skiba, & Krum, 2011). Unfortunately, the personal demands of diabetes self-care and prevention are challenging. People are often unsuccessful even when they know what to do. Psychosocial factors play a role in diabetes. However, more research is needed. The following topics seem especially important for future research:

1. *Prevention.* A better understanding is needed of psychosocial factors that influence lifestyle behaviours (diet and exercise) in at-risk children, adolescents, and adults. This research will help develop effective prevention programs for type 2 diabetes.

2. *Psychological distress.* It has become apparent that psychological distress, especially depression, is involved in the development and worsening of diabetes. Nevertheless, there is still much to be learned. For example, will treatment for depression prevent the onset of diabetes or reduce A1c in those already diagnosed (Bykowski, Sacco, & Mayhew, 2009)?

3. *Cost-effective interventions.* Effective psychological interventions to improve diabetes self-management are available. However, most health-care providers do not have sufficient resources or expertise to deliver them (Cardona-Morrell, Rychetnik, Morrell, Espinel, & Bauman, 2010). Given the large number of people with or at risk for diabetes, cost-effective interventions are needed that will have widespread and long-lasting positive effects (Glasgow, McKay, Piette, & Reynolds, 2001; Ruzic, Sporis, & Matkovic, 2008).

Along these lines, different ways of providing interventions must be investigated, including the use of computers, the Internet, telephones, smart phones, video-conferencing, and written self-help material.

SUMMARY

Diabetes is the most common endocrine disorder. It is characterized by chronic dysregulation of the use and/or production of the hormone insulin, which is required to metabolize glucose. The three major categories of diabetes are: type 1, type 2, and gestational. Prediabetes, a relatively new diagnosis, is a significant risk factor for developing type 2 diabetes. Millions of people worldwide have diabetes, and its prevalence is increasing dramatically. Uncontrolled diabetes can lead to a host of severe medical problems. Methods to prevent and treat diabetes employ a comprehensive approach that addresses biological, psychological, and social factors. However, the treatment regimen is complex and multi-faceted. Consequently, adherence to diabetes prevention and self-management regimens remains less than optimal. Psychological distress, especially depression, is more common among people with diabetes and appears to be involved in its development and course. Other psychological factors also appear to play an important role. Additional psychosocial research is needed to increase our understanding of diabetes and to enhance prevention and treatment.

Critical Thought Questions

1. Consider the major diabetes categories, including prediabetes. In what ways are they the same and how do they differ?
2. What are the main medical complications that people with diabetes should be concerned about?
3. What beliefs are more likely to increase the likelihood that a person will be motivated to manage his or her diabetes?
4. Based on the information provided in this chapter, what would you do to decrease your risk of developing diabetes in the future?

Recommended Reading

American Diabetes Association website: www.diabetes.org/?loc=logo
Canadian Diabetes Association website: www.diabetes.ca/
Centers for Disease Control and Prevention (CDC) website for diabetes: www.cdc.gov/diabetes/#

Polonsky, K.S. (2012). The past 200 years in diabetes. *New England Journal of Medicine, 367*, 1332–1340.
World Health Organization (WHO) website for diabetes: www.who.int/diabetes/en/

11

HIV and Sexually Transmitted Infections

TYLER G. TULLOCH | NATALIE L. STRATTON | STANLEY ING | BOJANA PETROVIC | TREVOR A. HART

Learning Objectives

In this chapter you will:

- Identify common sexually transmitted infections (STIs) and how their transmission is facilitated by behaviour.

- Learn about the human immunodeficiency virus (HIV) and how its transmission is facilitated by behaviour.

- Learn how thoughts and behaviours are associated with the transmission of HIV and STIs.

- Learn about the psychological effects of living with HIV and STIs.

- Identify different types of psychological interventions to prevent HIV and STIs.

- Identify different types of psychological and community-level health promotion interventions for people living with HIV.

Sexually Transmitted Infections in the National and Global Context

According to the World Health Organization, 499 million new cases of curable **sexually transmitted infections (STIs)** occur annually throughout the world (WHO, 2013a). This statistic does not include cases of **human immunodeficiency virus (HIV)/acquired immunodeficiency syndrome (AIDS)** and other non-curable STIs, which continue to adversely affect the lives of individuals worldwide. The World Health Organization estimated that at any point in 2008, 100.4 million people were infected with *Chlamydia trachomatis*, 36.4 million with *Neisseria gonorrhoeae*, 36.4 million with syphilis, and 187 million with *Trichomonis vaginalis*. In 2011, approximately 34 million people were living with HIV/AIDS, and the area most affected was sub-Saharan Africa where 23.5 million, or 69 per cent, of all people living with HIV/AIDS reside (UNAIDS, 2012). Across the world, social, economic, political, and environmental factors, such as poverty, discrimination, and gender inequalities, influence the susceptibility of HIV/AIDS and STI transmission among a variety of communities and populations (GIFHT, 2013; WHO, 2013b). A comprehensive and sustained response to these social and structural factors may adequately address HIV/AIDS globally (Seeley et al., 2012).

STIs are mainly transmitted through unprotected sexual contact, but can also be transmitted through non-sexual means, such as blood transfusions, contaminated needles (used by infected individuals), and from mother to child during birth or while breastfeeding. If left untreated, HIV and STIs can pose serious health risks, so it is important for individuals who are sexually active to be tested for HIV and STIs to prevent further spread of infection and to seek appropriate treatment.

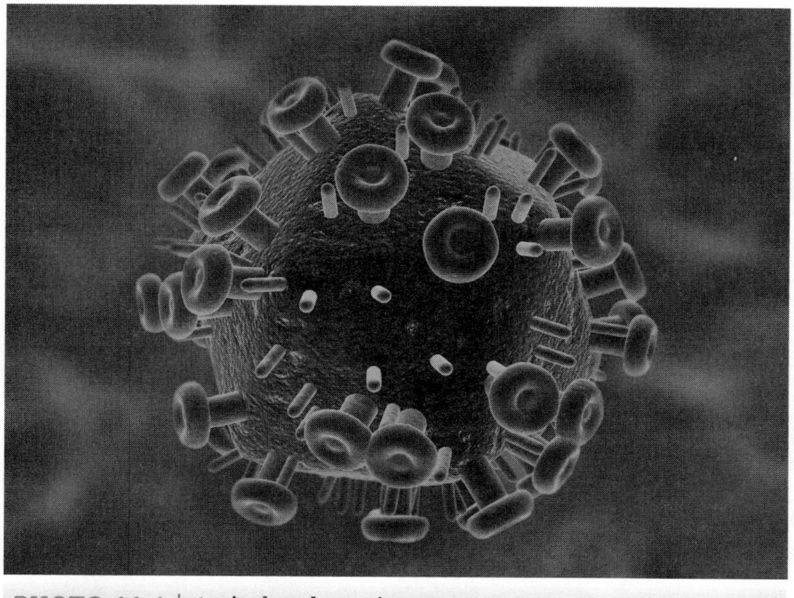

Overview of STIs in the US and Canada

STIs, especially incurable viral infections such as herpes and HIV, are a public health concern in the US and Canada. Many people with STIs do not experience symptoms and, therefore, may not get tested. As a result, asymptomatic individuals may unknowingly transmit STIs. The pathogenic agents that cause STIs can be **viruses**, **bacteria**, or parasites.

Adolescents and young adults (15–24 years old) in the US and Canada comprise the group with the highest STI rates (PHAC, 2007; CDC, 2012a). National survey studies report low rates of condom use during sexual intercourse as well as low rates of STI testing among adolescents and young adults (Rotermann, 2012; Eaton et al., 2012). In light of this situation, there have been many sexual health support and education programs developed for adolescents. In addition to the high prevalence of STIs in adolescents and young adults, other factors such as socio-economic status and poverty, gender, and ethnicity/race can influence whether people are at greater risk of getting an STI (CDC, 2011a; CDC, 2012b; Springer, Samuel, & Bolan, 2010). Females are more likely to suffer long-term consequences of STIs due to differences in anatomy—bacteria and viruses can penetrate the lining of the vagina more easily than a penis—and symptoms of STIs may not be seen as quickly and easily for females when compared to men (CDC, 2011a). In the US, African Americans bear a disproportionate burden of STIs due to factors that relate to: (1) less access to STI testing and health care resulting from an overall lower socio-economic status; (2) higher rates of incarceration; and (3) social discrimination (CDC, 2012b). It has been recommended that STI prevention efforts be targeted to these communities to reduce the spread of STIs (Springer et al., 2010).

Sebastian Kaulitzki

PHOTO 11.1 | An isolated HIV virus.

Unless otherwise specified, all STI and HIV/AIDS descriptions and epidemiological data in this overview are provided by the Centers for Disease Control in the US and the Public Health Agency of Canada (CDC, 2012c; PHAC, 2007). Table 11.1 outlines common types of STIs, their pathogens, and how they are transmitted and treated medically.

HIV is a viral infection that weakens the immune system and causes AIDS. AIDS is diagnosed when an individual has HIV and an **opportunistic infection**, defined as an infection that occurs when the immune system is no longer working (WHO, 2012). In the US, a person must also have less than 200 CD4$^+$ T-cells per cubic millimetre of blood to receive an AIDS diagnosis (CDC, 2008). CD4$^+$ T-cells are responsible for orchestrating the immune response, so a low number of these cells leads to the poor immune system found in people with HIV/AIDS. In Canada, a total number of 2,358 HIV cases were

reported in 2010 (PHAC, 2012b). A greater proportion of these cases are among men who have sex with men and among injection drug users. Since 2000, the rate of HIV infection among adults has been relatively stable. In the US, an estimated 48,100 new HIV infections were reported in 2009, a number that has remained relatively stable. A disproportionate number of new US HIV infections are among men who have sex with men, among African Americans, and among Hispanics/Latinos (CDC, 2012d). In Canada the most vulnerable populations are men who have sex with men, injection drug users, street youth, and First Nations individuals.

As HIV is a virus, it needs a host to replicate itself. The routes by which HIV enters the body are unprotected sexual contact, sharing of contaminated needles, from mother to child, and, less commonly, through tattooing, body piercing, or transfusion of HIV-infected blood. Also less commonly, HIV can enter the body via

TABLE 11.1 | Summary of Sexually Transmitted Infections

Disease and Pathogen	Transmission	Medical Treatment
Viral Infections		
HIV/AIDS Human immunodeficiency virus	Unprotected sexual intercourse; injection drug use; mother to child	*Not Curable* Treatment available: combined active antiretroviral therapy reduces the rate at which the virus will replicate.
HPV Genital human papillomavirus	Unprotected sexual contact	*Not Curable* No specific treatment available. Treatment for the health problems that HPV can cause is available.
Genital Herpes Herpes simplex virus 2	Unprotected sexual contact	*Not Curable* Treatment available for symptom management. Antiviral medications can shorten and prevent outbreaks during period of time person takes medication.
Hepatitis A Hepatitis A virus	Fecal–oral route	*Curable* No specific treatment available. Recommend bed rest and adequate intake of fluids.

TABLE 11.1 | (*Continued*)

Disease and Pathogen	Transmission	Medical Treatment
Hepatitis B Hepatitis B virus	Direct blood-to-blood contact; unprotected sexual intercourse; contaminated needles; mother to child	*Curable* No specific treatment available. Recommend bed rest, adequate nutrition and intake of fluids. Some people may need to be hospitalized.
Hepatitis C Hepatitis C virus	Direct blood-to-blood contact; unprotected sexual intercourse; contaminated needles	*Potentially Curable* Treatment available. Antiviral medications are taken for several months, but may not be effective.
Bacterial Infections		
Chlamydia *Chlamydia trachomatis*	Unprotected sexual contact	*Curable* Treatment: single dose of azithromycin or a week of doxycycline twice a day.
Gonorrhea *Neisseria gonorrhoeae*	Unprotected sexual contact	*Curable* Treatment: single dose of ceftriaxone or azithromycin
Syphilis *Treponemapallidum*	Direct sexual contact with sore from infected individual	*Curable* Treatment: a single intramuscular injection of penicillin, an antibiotic, will cure a person who has had syphilis for less than a year. Additional doses are needed to treat someone who has had syphilis for longer than a year.
Parasitic Infections		
Trichomoniasis *Trichomonasvaginalis*	Direct sexual contact	*Curable* Treatment: a single dose of metronidazole or tinidazole.
Pediculosis (pubic lice) *Phthirus pubis*	Sexual contact May also spread by close personal contact or contact with articles used by an infected person	*Curable* Treatment: a lice-killing lotion can be used to treat pubic ("crab") lice.
Scabies *Sarcoptesscabiei*	Direct, prolonged, skin-to-skin contact with person infected with scabies; indirectly by sharing articles such as clothing, towels, or bedding used by an infected person	*Curable* Treatment: products used to treat scabies are called *scabicides* because they kill scabies mites; some also kill eggs.

Source: Based on BC Centre for Disease Control (2012); CDC (2012b); PHAC (2007).

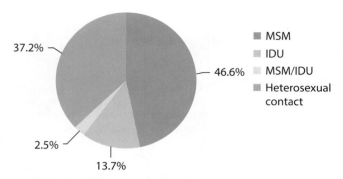

FIGURE 11.1 | Proportion of new HIV infections by exposure category, Canada, 2011. N = 3,175. MSM = male-to-male sexual contact. IDU = injection drug use.

Source: PHAC (2012c).

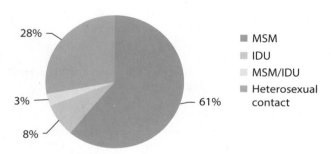

FIGURE 11.2 | Proportion of new HIV infections by exposure category, United States, 2010. N = 48,076. MSM = male-to-male sexual contact. IDU = injection drug use. Data from 46 states and five US dependent areas.

Source: Adapted from CDC (2012g).

accidental needle stick injuries that occur when a needle pierces the skin, which can be a workplace hazard for medical health providers and for medical laboratory workers. Once the virus enters the body, it invades the CD4+ T-cells (NIAID, 2012). The virus enters the CD4+ T-cell by first fusing with the outside surface of the cell (AVERT, 2012). CD4+ T-cells therefore become host cells for HIV and help the virus to self-replicate. Once new copies of the virus are produced by the host cell, they leave to enter other CD4+ T-cells. Antiretroviral medications, which are used to treat viruses such as HIV, do not cure HIV but instead reduce the ability of HIV to enter cells or replicate itself. Highly active antiretroviral therapy is the use of a combination of antiretroviral medications to treat HIV, which is now often called **combination antiretroviral therapy**. HIV/AIDS

symptoms occur in four primary stages (WHO, 2007), illustrated in Table 11.2.

Genital human papillomavirus (HPV) (CDC, 2013) is the most common STI transmitted in the US and is mainly transmitted through genital contact and oral sex; it can be transmitted even when an infected person is asymptomatic. A number of serious health problems can arise from HPV, including genital warts and various types of cancers (i.e., cancers of the head, neck, vagina, cervix, anus, and penis). However, HPV usually goes away (in 90 per cent of cases) before it can cause any serious complications. To prevent HPV infection, vaccines are recommended for males and females between 11 and 12 years old, which could potentially protect people from the most common types of HPV. Although there are no treatment options for HPV infection, there are treatments to alleviate the symptoms of HPV.

Genital herpes is transmitted through sexual contact with infected individuals. Most individuals with herpes will never have sores or will experience only very mild symptoms. Symptoms usually occur two weeks after transmission and resolve within two to four weeks. Symptoms during the initial episode may include secondary sores and flu-like symptoms (i.e., fever, swollen glands). Although genital herpes cannot be cured, treatment such as antiviral medication is available for symptom management. Treatment can shorten and/or prevent future outbreaks.

Hepatitis A (CDC, 2009a; PHAC, 2009a) is caused by the hepatitis A virus and is transmitted through anal–oral contact or contaminated food and water from infected food handlers with poor hygiene. Individuals generally experience fever, fatigue, loss of appetite, nausea, vomiting, abdominal pain, dark urine, clay-coloured bowel movements, joint pain, and jaundice. Symptoms usually last less than two months, although 10–15 per cent of individuals have prolonged or relapsing disease for up to six months. There is no specific treatment for hepatitis A, but adequate bed rest and fluid intake aid in the healing process. The hepatitis A vaccine prevents acquiring hepatitis A.

Hepatitis B (CDC, 2009b; PHAC, 2010; see also BCCDC, 2011) is an infection caused by the hepatitis B virus (HBV). Differing from hepatitis A transmission, hepatitis B is transmitted mainly through sexual contact, contaminated needles, and from mother to child during childbirth. Some people are asymptomatic yet can still spread the virus. Symptoms during the acute phase of HBV are similar to those of hepatitis A. Symptoms

TABLE 11.2 | Stages of HIV Infection

Acute HIV Infection	Symptoms include rash, fever, swollen or enlarged lymph nodes, pharyngitis, muscle pain, malaise, diarrhea, and vomiting. A large majority remain asymptomatic.
Asymptomatic HIV Infection	This stage often lasts up to 10 years. As HIV takes over the immune system, more specifically CD4+ T-cells, CD4+ T-cell count is used to indicate disease progression. At this stage, CD4+ T-cell count is usually above 500 cells/mL.
Early Symptomatic HIV Disease	Symptoms include fever, weight loss, recurrent diarrhea, fatigue, and headache. Skin infections such as herpes simplex or inflammation of the skin may occur. CD4+ T-cell count continues to decline.
Late Symptomatic HIV Disease	Occurs when CD4+ T-cell count has fallen below 200 cells/mL, and the risk of developing AIDS-related opportunistic infections or malignancy is very high. Examples of opportunistic infections are Kaposi sarcoma, a tumour caused by human herpes virus 8 (HHV8), and thrush, a yeast infection in the mouth or throat.

Source: Based on World Health Organization (2007).

may last from a few weeks to as long as six months. Chronic HBV occurs when the disease is left untreated and people may either experience ongoing symptoms or remain symptom-free for as long as 20–30 years. Approximately 15–25 per cent of persons with chronic HBV develop serious liver conditions such as cirrhosis (scarring of the liver) or liver cancer, and some individuals may require hospitalization. Like hepatitis A, no specific treatment is available for HBV, but adequate bed rest and fluid intake aid in the healing process. The hepatitis B vaccine prevents acquiring HBV.

Hepatitis C (CDC, 2012e; PHAC, 2009b) is an infection caused by the hepatitis C virus. Also unlike hepatitis A, hepatitis C is transmitted mainly through contaminated needles, other forms of contact with blood such as an open sore or wound, through penetrative sexual contact, and, more rarely, from mother to child during childbirth. Some people are asymptomatic yet can spread the virus. Symptoms during the acute phase of hepatitis C are similar to those of hepatitis A and B. Symptoms can last indefinitely. Unlike hepatitis B, treatments may cure the infection. Treatment is administered for several months to a year, but is not always successful at curing the infection. This treatment involves antiviral medication that can cause or exacerbate depression. No vaccine exists.

Chlamydia is transmitted through vaginal, oral, or anal intercourse with an infected person. Although most infected individuals are asymptomatic, some may experience symptoms such as painful or difficult urination, inflammation of the rectum, genital discharge, or rectal pain and bleeding. For men, testicular pain and swelling are other common symptoms. For women,

additional symptoms include abnormal vaginal bleeding and lower abdominal pain. In rare cases, infected women may experience pelvic inflammatory disease, in which infection of the uterus, fallopian tubes, and other reproductive organs causes lower abdominal pain. Chlamydia is curable with antibiotics. Chlamydia is prevalent among youth and young adults and is the most commonly reported notifiable disease in the US and Canada (PHAC, 2012a; CDC, 2012f). In 2011, the rate of chlamydia among African Americans in the US was 7.5 times higher as compared to White Americans and three times higher as compared to Hispanics (CDC, 2012h). Since 1990, the incidence rates of chlamydia have increased in both countries. The increase in chlamydia cases in the last 20 years may be due to increases in actual incidence, but also may reflect improved screening, testing, and reporting of the disease in medical and public health settings. This increase in chlamydia is illustrated in Figures 11.3 and 11.4.

Gonorrhea can lead to severe complications and spread to other parts of the body, such as the eyes, if left untreated. It is transmitted mainly via sexual contact and common symptoms include anal itching, soreness, bleeding, or painful bowel movements. Some men and most women never experience any symptoms. Some symptomatic men experience a burning sensation when urinating, a yellow, white, or green discharge from the penis, and painful or swollen testicles. For women, symptoms may include increased vaginal discharge, burning sensation while urinating, and vaginal bleeding between periods. Furthermore, women with gonorrhea are at risk of developing serious complications, even if symptoms are mild or absent. Gonorrhea is curable

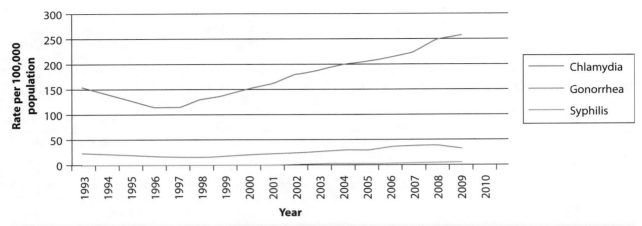

FIGURE 11.3 | Reported rates for chlamydia, gonorrhea, and syphilis, Canada, 1993–2009.

Data Source: PHAC (2011a, 2011b, 2011c).

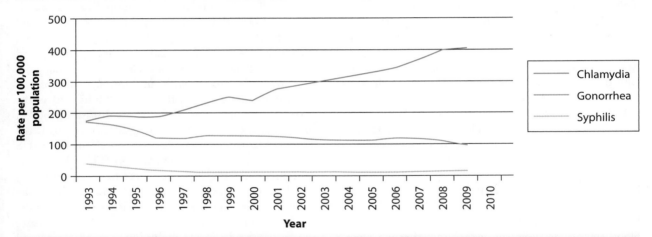

FIGURE 11.4 | Reported rates for chlamydia, gonorrhea, and syphilis, United States, 1993–2009.

Data Source: CDC (2011b).

with antibiotics. In 2011, the rate of gonorrhea among African Americans in the US was 17 times higher as compared to Caucasian Americans and eight times higher as compared to Hispanics (CDC, 2012h).

Syphilis is contracted through sexual contact. Most people who contract syphilis are asymptomatic for years, but remain at risk for later complications if it is left untreated. Syphilis occurs in three stages: the primary, secondary, and late stages, with a latent stage between the secondary and late stages when the virus remains hidden. In the primary stage, sores appear approximately 21 days after infection and usually last from three to six weeks, healing without treatment. If treatment is not administered, infection can progress to the secondary stage.

During the secondary stage, a non-itchy rash appears, as well as other symptoms like fever, swollen lymph glands, headaches, weight loss, muscle aches, and fatigue. Secondary stage symptoms heal without treatment; however, infection will progress to the latent and late stages of disease. The final latent and late stage begins when symptoms of the primary and secondary stages of syphilis disappear. Without treatment, individuals remain infected yet symptom-free for years. In the late stage of syphilis, internal organs and tissues such as the brain, nerves, eyes, heart, and liver may be damaged. Symptoms of late-stage syphilis include paralysis, numbness, gradual blindness, and dementia. Fortunately, syphilis is often curable in the primary and secondary stages with injections of penicillin. In Canada and the US there has been an increase in the rate of syphilis among men who have sex with men and in African-American communities (CDC, 2012b; PHAC, 2012a).

Trichomoniasis is a parasitic infection. Most individuals have no symptoms, but when symptoms occur they range from mild irritation to severe inflammation of the genital area. Without treatment, infection can last for years. Itching or irritation may occur during urination, and for men, during ejaculation. A thin discharge with an unusual smell may accompany symptoms. Trichomoniasis is curable with antibiotics.

Pediculosis, or *pubic lice* (CDC, 2010a), is caused by a tiny insect called *Phthirus pubis* and is usually transmitted through sexual contact with someone infected with pubic lice but can occasionally be spread via close personal contact or contact with articles of clothing used by an infected individual. The most common symptom of pediculosis is itching in the genital area. Pediculosis is curable with a lice-killing lotion.

Scabies (CDC, 2010b) is caused by *Sarcoptesscabiei*, a type of mite, and is usually transmitted by direct, prolonged, skin-to-skin contact with an infected individual. Just like pediculosis, scabies can sometimes be spread indirectly by sharing articles of clothing, towels, or bedding used by an infected person. The spread of scabies may be increased if the person has crusted scabies. The illness is characterized by intense itching and a rash that may include tiny blisters and scales. Sometimes sores become infected with bacteria due to scratching the rash. Topical treatments, also called scabicides, kill scabies mites and some also kill scabies eggs.

Psychosocial Risk and Protective Factors in HIV/STI Acquisition

Knowledge, Motivation, and Skills

Knowing how STIs are transmitted and the level of risk of contracting an STI from a given behaviour allows people to make informed choices about which sexual activities they feel comfortable performing. The level of risk associated with certain sexual behaviours varies depending on the STI's mode of transmission. Table 11.3 illustrates the level of risk of STI transmission for given behaviours.

TABLE 11.3 | Level of Risk of STI Transmission Associated with Sexual Behaviours

	Skin on Skin; Rubbing of Genitals	Mutual Masturbation	Oral Sex without a Condom	Vaginal/Anal Intercourse without a Condom
Viral Infections				
Genital herpes	High risk if sores are present or just before an outbreak	Low risk if hands are clean before touching genitals	Receiving: High risk if sores are present on the mouth Giving: High risk if sores are present on the genitals	High risk
Hepatitis A	Low risk if fecal matter is not present	Low risk if hands are clean and fecal matter is not present on hands	Receiving: No real risk Giving: Low risk	High risk
Hepatitis B	No real risk	No real risk	Receiving: No real risk Giving: Low risk	High risk

(Continued)

TABLE 11.3 | *(Continued)*

	Skin on Skin; Rubbing of Genitals	Mutual Masturbation	Oral Sex without a Condom	Vaginal/Anal Intercourse without a Condom
Hepatitis C	No real risk	No real risk	Receiving: No real risk Giving: Low risk	High risk
HIV/AIDS	No real risk	No real risk	Receiving: No real risk Giving: Low risk	High risk
HPV (genital warts)	High risk if sores are present or just before an outbreak	Low risk if hands are clean before touching genitals	Receiving: No real risk Giving: High risk	High risk
Bacterial Infections				
Gonorrhea (the clap)	No real risk	No real risk	Receiving: No real risk Giving: High risk	High risk
Chlamydia	No real risk	No real risk	Receiving: No real risk Giving: High risk	High risk
Syphilis	High risk if chancre or rash is present	Low risk	Receiving: High risk Giving: High risk	High risk
Parasitic Infections				
Trichomoniasis	High risk	Low risk if hands are clean before touching genitals	Receiving: No real risk Giving: Low risk	High risk
Pubic lice (crabs)	High risk	Low risk if hands are clean before touching genitals	Receiving: No real risk Giving: High risk	High risk
Scabies	High risk	Low risk: If hands are clean before touching genitals	Receiving: No real risk Giving: High risk	High risk

Note: Activities listed as no real risk either never lead to infection or never pose a potential risk of transmission, or the possibility is extremely unlikely. Low-risk activities include behaviours where a few reports of transmission have been documented. A significant number of scientific studies link high-risk activities with transmission.

Source: CDC (2012b); Rathus, Nevid, Fichner-Rathus, Herold, & McKenzie (2007).

Condoms

Despite having accurate knowledge about STIs and the risks associated with certain sexual behaviours, many people continue to engage in unprotected sex. Although condoms remain the most effective method of protection against the transmission of STIs and unintended pregnancies (e.g., CDC, 2011c; Kulig, 2003), rates of consistent condom use among adolescents and young adults are low (e.g., Shiely, Horgan, & Hayes, 2009). One explanation for these low rates may be that adolescents and young adults tend to engage in unplanned sexual activity, especially when using alcohol or illicit substances (e.g., Poulin & Graham, 2001). Another explanation is that adolescents may be uncomfortable obtaining condoms. In a US national survey, more than one-third of adolescents reported that purchasing condoms was embarrassing and found discussing condom use challenging (Kulig, 2003). Cost may be another barrier to consistent condom use (Cohen, Scribner, Bedimo, & Farley, 1999).

In order to protect against the transmission of STIs and unintended pregnancies, condoms must be used consistently and correctly. Common improper techniques include using a condom after first putting it on inside out, not holding the base of the condom during withdrawal, and not leaving enough air at the tip of the condom, thus increasing its chance of breaking (Grimley, Annang, Houser, & Chen, 2005). People who feel confident that they are capable of and likely to use condoms correctly during sexual activity are more likely to use condoms consistently and to refuse to have sex when condoms are not available (DiIorio et al., 2001; Farmer & Meston, 2006). Individuals who intend to use condoms during their next sexual encounter are also less likely ever to have contracted an STI, which suggests that they may use condoms consistently (Small, Weinman, Buzi, & Smith, 2009). These individuals report more positive attitudes towards taking responsibility for their health and are less concerned with whether their partner endorsed condom use (Small et al., 2009).

© LuckyBusiness/iStockphoto

PHOTO 11.2 | Safe sex practices can help prevent the spread of sexually transmitted diseases.

Number of Sexual Partners

People who have a higher number of sexual partners are at greater risk for acquiring STIs (e.g., Shiely, Horgan, & Hayes, 2009; Tapert, Aarons, Sedlar, & Brown, 2001). Participating in sexual activity with numerous casual partners ("one-night stands") increases an individual's chance of acquiring an STI, as the sexual history of each partner then becomes linked to the individual. Each partner who has previously engaged in unprotected sex with others exponentially increases the number of partners an individual has indirectly come into contact with. Furthermore, condom use declines throughout the duration of a relationship with a primary partner (Kulig, 2003). To minimize the chance of acquiring STIs, it is important for individuals (1) to discuss whether the relationship is monogamous and (2) to be tested for STIs before making the decision to stop using condoms.

Communication

Similar to gaining accurate information about the transmission of STIs, it is important to find out about a potential partner's sexual and drug history. That knowledge allows people to make informed decisions about which activities they are comfortable performing. In fact, partners who discuss each other's sexual history are more likely to use condoms during future sexual encounters (e.g., Rickman et al., 1994). However, partners who do not communicate with one another about condom use or STI and pregnancy prevention strategies are less likely to use condoms (Crosby et al., 2002).

Substance Use

Illicit drug and alcohol use before or during sexual situations may facilitate sexual activity by lowering inhibitions, calming anxieties, and improving confidence (Drumright, Patterson, & Strathdee, 2006). At the same time, individuals who consume alcohol before or during a sexual encounter are less likely to use a condom (e.g., Logan, Cole, & Leukefeld, 2002), specifically with a casual sexual partner (Brown & Vanable, 2007). In fact, alcohol and substance abusers

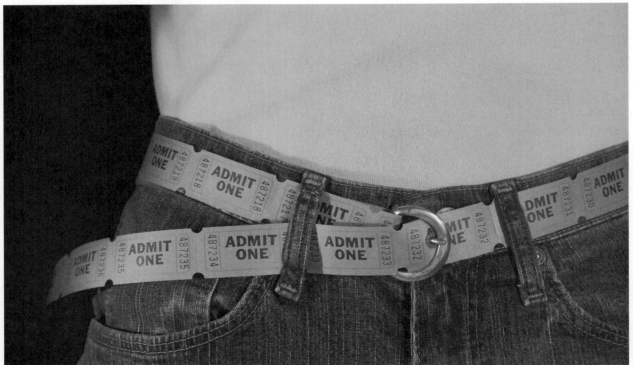

© Christine Glade/iStockphoto

PHOTO 11.3 | Individuals with a high number of sex partners are at greater risk for acquiring sexually transmitted infections.

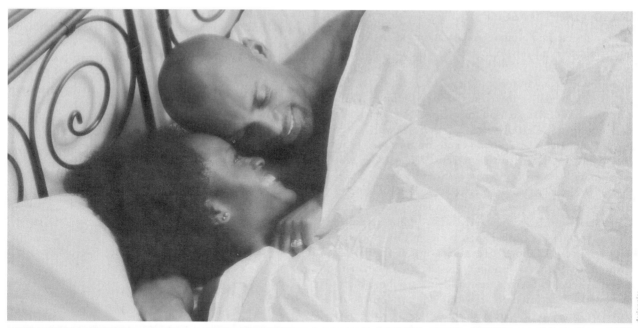

designpics

PHOTO 11.4 | Partners who discuss each other's sexual history are able to make informed choices and are more likely to practice safe sex.

are more likely to have a higher number of casual sexual partners and a history of STIs (Tapert, Aarons, Sedlar, & Brown, 2001).

Internalized Homophobia

Gay, lesbian, and bisexual persons may internalize society's negative beliefs and assumptions regarding same-sex attraction, which is also known as internalized homophobia (e.g., Newcomb & Mustanski, 2011). People with high internalized homophobia may feel more shame and, therefore, not protect themselves during sexual situations (Kashubeck-West & Szymanski, 2008). Gay and bisexual men who report high internalized homophobia are more likely to engage in unprotected anal intercourse (Dew & Chaney, 2005). Gay and bisexual men who experience high internalized homophobia and loneliness also have a greater number of sexual partners (DeLonga et al., 2011).

Personality Factors

Sensation-seeking and impulsivity are examples of personality factors related to unsafe sexual behaviour (e.g., McCoul & Haslam, 2001; Teva, Bermudez, & Buela-Casal, 2010). Sensation-seeking describes people who search for new, exciting, and intense experiences and are willing to take various risks (e.g., physical, financial, etc.) to attain those experiences (Zuckerman, 2009). Extreme sensation-seekers are more likely to not use condoms (Kalichman & Cain, 2004), to have a greater number of sexual partners (e.g., McCoul & Haslam, 2001), and to use substances before or during their sexual encounters (e.g., McCoul & Haslam, 2001; Teva et al., 2010). Impulsive people react in the moment whether or not they recognize the risks associated with their behaviours (Kahn, Kaplowitz, Goodman, & Emans, 2002). Highly impulsive persons are more likely to participate in sexual activity without a condom, to use drugs and alcohol before or during sexual encounters, and to have a history of STIs (e.g., Kahn et al., 2002; Winters, Botzet, Fahnhorst, Baumel, & Lee, 2009).

Personality factors associated with distress may also be risk factors for contracting HIV or STIs. For example, social anxiety or anxiety about being evaluated in social situations is associated with sexual risk behaviour among gay and bisexual men (Hart & Heimberg, 2005; Hart, James, Purcell, & Farber, 2008).

Socio-cultural Factors

Socio-cultural and demographic factors also play an important role in risky sexual behaviour. Some minority groups, specifically Black and Latina women, represent a disproportionate number of new US cases of STIs and HIV (CDC, 2011b). However, racial and ethnic differences may not be the reason for the increased incidence rate among these groups. In fact, persons with lower income experience more stress and are more likely to participate in unsafe sexual practices (e.g., Capaldi, Stoolmiller, Clark, & Owen, 2002; Ickovics et al., 2002). Moreover, poverty is more common among African-American and Latina women than among Caucasian women (Ickovics et al., 2002). Furthermore, religious affiliation, rather than ethnicity, is associated with a higher likelihood of participating in vaginal sex without a condom. Catholic, non-Catholic Christian, and non-religious or agnostic students are more likely to have vaginal intercourse without a condom compared to students who are Muslim or who practise East Asian religions (e.g., Buddhism, Hinduism) (James et al., 2011). Other possible factors that may explain the higher incidence rate of STIs among minority groups include unequal power between partners (e.g., Teitelman, Tennille, Bohinski, Jemmott, & Jemmott, 2011) and age differences of six or more years between sexual partners (e.g., Hurt et al., 2010).

Psychology of Living with HIV/STIs

Stressors

Stigmatizing

Stigmatizing is the devaluing or discrediting of an individual (or group) who has an undesirable attribute, such as a physical characteristic or behaviour (Brown, Macintyre, & Trujillo, 2003). One of the main attributes shared by diseases with the highest level of stigma (Goffman, 1963) is that persons with the disease are viewed as being responsible for having it. Therefore, people living with HIV and incurable STIs, such as herpes and hepatitis B, may experience high levels of stigmatization. Some members of society hold the belief that the ill person is to blame for contracting the disease due to morally reprehensible or irresponsible decisions or actions (Herek, 1999). Discrimination as a result of the stigma attached to HIV may be perceived as coming from society in general or from specific sources such as

family members, friends, employers, colleagues, or even health-care professionals. Almost half of people living with HIV report being treated negatively due to their HIV status, and about half are concerned about HIV stigmatization (Whetten, Reif, Whetten, & Murphy-MacMillan, 2008). This concern about stigma among people living with HIV appears to be justified, because almost one-third of Americans report that, if possible, they would avoid interacting with someone with HIV (Herek, Capitanio, & Widaman, 2002). Furthermore,

PHOTO 11.5 | Earvin "Magic" Johnson, retired NBA player, announced in November 1991 that he was HIV positive. To prevent his HIV infection from progressing to AIDS, Johnson takes daily antiretroviral medications. He has been active in campaigns to educate others about HIV and has raised money to provide free testing and treatment for HIV.

over one-third mistakenly believe that HIV transmission is possible via coughing, sneezing, or sharing a glass (CDC, 2000). The stigma of HIV may impact employers' hiring decisions, leading to higher unemployment rates and greater poverty among people living with HIV (Liu, Canada, Shi, & Corrigan, 2012).

HIV stigmatization has been associated with poorer mental health among people living with HIV. People who experience greater stigmatization have higher levels of anxiety (Ivanova, Hart, Wagner, Aljassem, & Loutfy, 2012; Wagner et al., 2010), more severe depressive symptoms, and are more likely to seek psychiatric care (Vanable, Carey, Blair, & Littlewood, 2006). Similarly, people who experience or who internalize HIV stigmatization show greater levels of depression, anxiety, and hopelessness than those who do not (Ivanova et al., 2012; Lee, Kochman, & Sikkema, 2002).

The stigmatizing of HIV may also contribute indirectly to the severity of the HIV epidemic. Perceiving HIV as a stigma is associated with lower quality of life in general (Holzemer et al., 2009), and people living with HIV who perceive greater stigmatization from health-care providers are less likely to visit their physician (Kinsler, Wong, Sayles, Davis, & Cunningham, 2007). HIV stigmatization is also associated with poorer medication adherence (see review by Whetten et al., 2008), and some individuals may fear taking medication in public for fear their HIV status will be discovered by others (Golin, Isasi, Bontempi, & Eng, 2002). The stigmatizing of HIV may inhibit

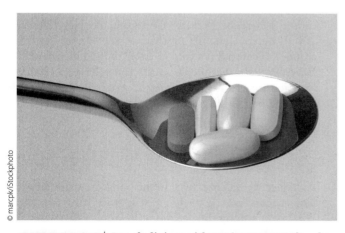

© marcpk/iStockphoto

PHOTO 11.6 | People living with HIV/AIDS must closely adhere to a daily antiretroviral medication schedule in order to benefit from treatment. Many recent regimens involve fewer pills but adherence must be carefully maintained.

people from getting tested for HIV (Ma et al., 2007; Obermeyer & Osborn, 2007), either by delaying HIV testing (Chesney & Smith, 1999) or by avoiding testing altogether (Fortenberry et al., 2002), thus perpetuating the epidemic. Fearing stigmatization also is associated with a lower likelihood of being tested for other STIs, such as gonorrhea and chlamydia (Fortenberry et al., 2002; Balfe et al., 2010). People who experience discrimination as a result of HIV may be less likely to disclose their HIV status to sex partners (Calin, Green, Hetherton, & Brook, 2007; Simbayi et al., 2007).

HIV Disclosure and the Law

In the US, there is no overarching federal law mandating that people living with HIV must disclose their HIV status prior to engaging in behaviour likely to result in HIV transmission (i.e., unprotected sex, sharing needles). In some states, there is no legislation surrounding HIV disclosure, and in others non-disclosure has been deemed a criminal offence (American Civil Liberties Union, 2008), and punishment ranges from monetary fines to imprisonment. In some states, the same laws apply equally to the disclosure of HIV and of other STIs and infectious diseases. In Canada, federal law states that an HIV-positive status must be disclosed prior to engaging in any sexual activity that poses a significant risk of HIV transmission to one's partner. The punishment for non-disclosure in Canada can result in a charge of aggravated assault that carries a maximum sentence of life imprisonment. Many individuals charged under this law engaged in behaviour not generally considered to pose a significant risk for HIV transmission, such as having oral sex (Canadian HIV/AIDS Legal Network, 2011). However, the Joint United Nations AIDS Programme on HIV/AIDS (UNAIDS) recommends that criminal law should only apply to non-disclosure if there is malicious intent and transmission actually occurs (UNAIDS, 2008). When a health professional discovers that an HIV-positive patient is having unprotected sex, he or she may feel in a dilemma as to whether the patient's right to confidentiality supersedes the professional's legal duty to warn the individual(s) at risk. Currently, no universal standard practice exists regarding one's duty to warn someone in the case of risk of HIV transmission. Depending on the jurisdiction, local laws may conflict with professional codes of ethics so that the professional is placed in a potential lose-lose situation (Alghazo, Upton, & Cioe, 2011). Health professionals must navigate this complex ethical issue on a case-by-case basis with great care, weighing legal obligation, patient confidentiality, and duty to warn.

Diagnoses

The prevalence of some types of mental disorders (e.g., depression, anxiety, schizophrenia, and substance-use disorders) is higher among people living with HIV than among the general population (Owe-Larsson, Säll, Salamon, & Allgulander, 2009). It is not clear whether this is because certain types of mental disorders put people at greater risk of contracting HIV or whether having HIV puts people at greater risk of suffering from mental disorders.

Depression

The prevalence of major depression among people living with HIV is higher than among the general adult population of the US (Ciesla & Roberts, 2001; Treisman & Angelino, 2007), with estimates ranging from 10 per cent to 20 per cent, as compared to 5 per cent to 10 per cent in the general population (Klinkenberg & Sacks, 2004). Estimates for the prevalence of lifetime depressive disorder among people living with HIV range from 30 per cent to 50 per cent, as compared to 6 per cent to 17 per cent in the general population (Klinkenberg & Sacks, 2004). Among people living with HIV, there is a higher prevalence of depression among women than among men (Evans et al., 2002; Ickovics et al., 2001). Depression is sometimes difficult to accurately diagnose in this population because some of the physiological symptoms of depression are also associated with HIV: fatigue, weight loss, and decreased appetite and sex drive (Rabkin, 1996).

The higher prevalence of depression among people living with HIV does not necessarily mean that HIV causes depression. Depression and HIV interact in complex ways and may be interrelated. For example, people with depression may be more likely to have unprotected sexual intercourse, putting them at greater risk for contracting HIV or other STIs. Alternatively, HIV may damage subcortical brain structures (i.e., parts of the brain beneath the cerebral cortex), thus leading to a sense of hopelessness that is often seen among people who are depressed (Treisman & Angelino, 2007), and depression may result from HIV-related events such as HIV infection, side effects of antiretroviral medications, and opportunistic infections (Goforth, Cohen, & Murrough, 2008).

Depression negatively impacts the immune system functioning of people living with HIV and is associated with disease progression (Evans et al., 2002) and with higher mortality rates (Mayne, Vittinghoff, Chesney, Barrett, & Coates, 1996). Depression is associated with poor medication adherence (Treisman & Angelino, 2007; Whetten et al., 2008).

Anxiety

Some of the physical symptoms of anxiety are similar to the physical symptoms of HIV/AIDS and medication side effects, so particular attention must be given to determine whether people living with HIV are experiencing effects of the disease and its management, or whether they are experiencing anxiety, for which treatment is available (Hofman & Nelson, 2006). People with high anxiety may tend to avoid stressors associated with HIV such as taking medication, accessing health care, and thinking about the diagnosis. This avoidance negatively impacts disease management and may lead to a worsening of symptoms and a more rapid decline in health (Antoni, 2003). Anxiety among people living with HIV is associated with poorer medication adherence (Ammassari et al., 2002; Van Servellen, Chang, Garcia, & Lombardi, 2002).

Post-Traumatic Stress Disorder (PTSD)

The prevalence of PTSD diagnoses among people living with HIV ranges from 13 per cent among adolescents and young adults (Radcliffe et al., 2007) to 30 per cent among gay men (Theuninck, Lake, & Gibson, 2010) and 64 per cent among individuals who have problems with medication adherence (Safren, Gershuny, & Hendriksen, 2003). By contrast, the prevalence of PTSD among US adults is about 6.8 per cent (Kessler, Berglund, Demler, Jin, & Walters, 2005). Theuninck and colleagues (2010) reported that half of HIV-infected gay men mentioned receiving an HIV diagnosis as a traumatic event. PTSD is also associated with poorer HIV medication adherence (Boarts, Sledjeski, Bogart, & Delahanty, 2006).

Substance Use

A higher prevalence of current substance use problems occurs among people living with HIV (44 per cent) than among the general population (11 per cent) (Klinkenberg & Sacks, 2004). Klinkenberg and Sacks also reported a higher prevalence of lifetime alcohol and drug use disorders among people living with HIV as compared to the general population: 26–60 per cent versus 14–24 per cent for alcohol use disorders and 23–56 per cent versus 6–12 per cent for drug use disorders.

HIV-Associated Dementia

Advanced HIV infection has been shown to impact the central nervous system, and is associated with neuropsychological deficits such as declines in cognitive and behavioural functioning (e.g., Owe-Larsson et al., 2009; Sperber & Shao, 2003). This decline, known as HIV-associated dementia (HAD), typically occurs during late stages of HIV infection once CD4+ T-lymphocyte counts drop to low levels (Sperber & Shao, 2003). Symptom severity increases over time as disease progression moves from asymptomatic to symptomatic HIV infection, then onto late symptomatic HIV disease (Owe-Larsson et al., 2009). In developed countries where combination antiretroviral therapy is available, the prevalence of HAD decreased from 20 per cent to about 10 per cent of people with advanced AIDS (Brew & Gonzalez-Scarano, 2007; Geraci & Simpson, 2001). Some common symptoms of HAD are memory problems, difficulty concentrating, impaired fine motor movements, apathy, social withdrawal, and decreased interest in sex, and in some cases, mania, psychosis, and tremors (Sperber & Shao, 2003; Geraci & Simpson, 2001).

Coping with HIV

People living with HIV routinely face a number of serious problems simultaneously, such as stigmatization, mental illness, physical health problems, and the stress of living with a chronic and potentially fatal disease. Lazarus and Folkman (1984), pioneers in the field of coping research, identified two main types of coping: problem-focused and emotion-focused (see also Chapter 5). Problem-focused coping involves dealing with the stressor itself by removing, working around, or confronting it, whereas emotion-focused coping is an attempt to reduce or eliminate the emotional distress associated with the stressor (e.g., Siegel & Schrimshaw, 2000). People who use a problem-focused coping style tend to be better adjusted to living with HIV. The emotion-focused coping style involves both active (i.e., having a fighting spirit) and passive (i.e., avoiding thinking about problems) strategies. People who use active strategies are better adjusted to living with HIV, whereas those who use more passive strategies have greater distress than those who use other approaches and coping styles (Pakenham & Rinaldis, 2001). Another form of coping is through the social support of friends, family, and others. People living with HIV who are more satisfied with social support report less increase in HIV-related physical health problems over time such as CD4+ T-cell count, diarrhea, fever, night sweats, or persistent fatigue (Ashton et al., 2005).

The attitudes people adopt towards their illness may impact their adjustment to living with HIV and STIs. Evidence that an optimistic attitude is associated with improved adjustment to living with HIV is conflicting (e.g., Anderson, 1995; Peterson, Folkman, & Bakeman, 1996; Taylor et al., 1992). In light of these conflicting results, it has been proposed that situational optimism (a person's optimism in a specific situation) is associated with improved adjustment whereas dispositional optimism (a person's long-term level of optimism across many situations) is unrelated to adjustment (Pakenham & Rinaldis, 2001).

Medication Adherence

People living with HIV who have low adherence to HIV medications have a five-fold increase in risk of HIV disease progression compared to those with moderate or high adherence (Kitahata et al., 2004), and adherence levels must often be as high as 95 per cent in order to fully benefit from these medications (Paterson et al., 2000). It is therefore extremely important to adhere to medication schedules (see Chapter 3 for additional discussion of medication adherence). Many factors are associated with poor medication adherence among people living with HIV, such as mental disorders (e.g., anxiety, depression) (Ammassari et al., 2002; Boarts et al., 2006), substance use (Begley, McLaws, Ross, & Gold, 2008), HIV stigmatization (Rintamaki, Davis, Skripkauskas, Bennett, & Wolf, 2006; Vanable et al., 2006), and sexual dysfunction in males (Miguez-Burbano, Espinoza, & Lewis, 2008).

Assessment of HIV/STI Risk Behaviour and Medication Adherence

Although health psychologists working in clinical settings with people who are at risk for or who are living with HIV and STIs tend to use similar measures to assess personality, psychopathology, and other clinically relevant variables, two additional types of measures have been created when working with these populations. The first type of measures assesses risk behaviour that predisposes a person to contract HIV and STIs. Sexual behaviour is typically assessed via self-report, such as number of instances of unprotected vaginal or anal intercourse in the past three months (e.g., Koblin et al., 2003). There are also standardized sexual risk behaviour assessments, such as the Risk Assessment Battery (Navaline et al., 1994). Injection risk behaviour is also assessed, especially for people at risk for HIV and hepatitis B and C. Injection risk behaviour is also assessed via self-report. Self-report measures, while potentially subject to social desirability, are necessary because of the ethical problems involved with directly observing an individual's sexual or drug-use risk behaviour, or doing frequent biomedical assessment of evidence of risk behaviour of clients or patients (e.g., conducting vaginal or rectal swabs to assess for presence of semen; drug screening via blood draws).

Medication adherence is also frequently assessed for people living with STIs or HIV. Medication adherence can be assessed via self-report using standardized measures such as the Adherence to Anti-Retroviral Medications Questionnaire (Chesney et al., 2000) or via patient interviews (e.g., Catz, Kelly, Bogart, Benotsch, & McAuliffe, 2000). Other, more objective measures may also be used, such as pharmacy reports of medication refills, evidence of biological outcomes such as amount of medication in the blood, amount of bacteria or virus in the blood, or in the case of HIV, number of CD4$^+$ T-cells in the blood, which would be expected to increase with proper medication adherence. Another innovative method is the use of electronic pill caps, or Medication Event Monitoring Systems (MEMS; Aprex Corporation, Fremont, Calif.). These pill caps contain a chip that records the date and time of each instance a pill bottle is opened. Although MEMS are typically used to assess rather than improve medication adherence, it has been proposed that treatment providers could use MEMS data to provide feedback and counselling to patients in order to help those who wish to increase their medication adherence (Rosen, Ryan, & Rigsby, 2002).

PHOTO 11.7 | HIV prevention interventions may be provided individually or in small groups, and may be delivered in a variety of settings, including schools, community-based organizations, health centres, and sexual health clinics.

Mauricio Jordan De Souza Coelho

Evidence-Based Treatments and Other Interventions

Many psychological interventions have been developed for HIV and STI prevention as well as to support or treat people living with HIV and STIs. The term "intervention" is used as opposed to "treatment" because many clinicians working in the field of HIV and STIs, such as in public health clinics, may also be working to prevent new cases among people at higher risk. With the advancement of research on behavioural interventions, public health agencies such as the CDC developed

standards to assess interventions that reduce risk behaviours. The CDC developed the Tiers of Evidence framework for classifying interventions to distinguish those that have been efficacious and produced changes in behaviour. Tiers 1 and 2 include interventions that are supported by empirical evidence and produce a decrease in risk behaviours, viral load, and medication adherence. Tiers 3 and 4 include interventions that are theoretically supported but have not satisfied the criteria for tiers 1 and 2. The last category includes interventions that have not been evaluated (CDC, 2011d).

Although most of these interventions are rooted in psychological models, they typically view any psychological changes (e.g., decreases in sexual risk behaviour, increases in medication adherence) through the lens of the biopsychosocial model. For example, sexual risk reduction interventions for people living with HIV are biopsychosocial because they may discuss the societal effects of HIV stigma or focus on specific demographic or social groups (socio-cultural) and help them to change their attitudes and behaviours (psychological). These interventions consider biomedical factors because the purpose of the interventions is to reduce HIV and STI incidence and HIV transmission. Most interventions focus on the individual psychological and behavioural problems that contribute to HIV transmission risk; however, greater attention is being drawn to the broader systemic problems that contribute to HIV transmission, such as poverty and discrimination (Newman & Poindexter, 2010).

Theoretical Frameworks Used in Evidence-Based Interventions

Several theoretical frameworks, such as social cognitive theory (Bandura, 1998), the health belief model (Rosenstock, 1974), and the transtheoretical model (Prochaska & Velicer, 1997; see Chapter 4), provide a foundation for evidence-based interventions. Other theoretical models commonly used for planning sexual health promotion interventions include the theory of reasoned action (Ajzen & Fishbein, 1980), the theory of planned behaviour (Ajzen, 1991), and the information, motivation, and behavioural skills model (Fisher & Fisher, 1992).

Theory of Reasoned Action and Theory of Planned Behaviour (TPB)

These theories assert that behavioural intention is the best predictor of a behaviour, which is influenced by the attitude towards performing the behaviour and the subjective norms associated with the behaviour (see Chapter 1). Attitudes are determined by individual beliefs regarding outcomes or characteristics of performing the behaviour. Likewise, subjective norms are based on normative beliefs (e.g., approval/disapproval of performing the behaviour) and the individual's motivation to comply with norms. The theory of planned behaviour also includes perceived control with regard to performing a behaviour as an additional variable that may predict behavioural intentions. Both theories have been used to successfully predict behaviours with which individuals demonstrate substantial control, including behaviours and intentions of substance use, sexual behaviour, and health service utilization (Montaño & Kasprzyk, 2008). Regarding HIV and STI risk behaviours, the theory of reasoned action and theory of planned behaviour have been applied to explaining condom use. In a study with university students in Ghana, Bosompra (2001) found that participants had greater intentions of using condoms when the intervention targeted positive attitudes towards using condoms and the potential for protection against HIV and STIs, as well as perceptions that condom use would be acceptable to their sexual partners and peers.

Information, Motivation, and Behavioural Skills Model

Developed by Fisher and Fisher (1992), this model is recommended by the Canadian Guidelines for Sexual Health Education (PHAC, 2008). The core principles of the model include information (e.g., knowledge regarding STI transmission), motivation (e.g., to change risky behaviour), and behavioural skills (e.g., performing preventative behaviours, such as negotiating condom use). The information, motivation, and behavioural skills model specifies that HIV prevention information and motivation independently affect preventive behaviour, as well as through improved behavioural skills. In addition, the model requires that elicitation research (i.e. exploring the most appropriate information, motivation, and behavioural skills for the target populations) should be conducted prior to developing the intervention. This model has been used effectively to reduce sexual risk behaviours for a variety of populations, including minority youth, young adults, and low-income women (PHAC, 2008). The model has also been used outside of HIV, such as to improve glycemic control among people with diabetes (Osborn & Egede, 2010).

Methods of Delivering Interventions

Interventions for preventing HIV/STIs and supporting individuals living with HIV/STIs may be approached through one or several levels. The social-ecological approach for health promotion acknowledges that health is influenced through the interplay of factors related to people, their immediate surroundings (e.g., family and friends), and broader social structures (e.g., organizations and communities) (Bartholomew, Parcel, Kok, & Gottlieb, 2006). Individual-level interventions are delivered in one-on-one counselling sessions, and interpersonal interventions may use a small group format. Community-level interventions adopt a systems approach to changing the behaviour of a population and may be delivered through multiple venues and outreach activities. Interventions operating at multiple social-ecological levels (e.g., individual and community levels) may be more effective in producing long-term behaviour change than those that focus on a single level (Sallis, Owen, & Fisher, 2008).

Interventions to Prevent HIV and STI Transmission

Interventions that focus on preventing HIV and STIs are delivered in a variety of settings, including educational institutions, community-based organizations, health centres, and sexual health clinics. Such sexual health promotion programs focus largely on providing information regarding risk factors for contracting HIV and STIs and on resources to health services in local communities that provide testing and contraceptives.

Behavioural interventions addressing condom use skills and motivational training can be effective in reducing the risk of contracting HIV and STIs among youth. A recent meta-analysis on interventions for adolescents concluded that programs focused on sexual behaviour beyond an abstinence-only approach (one that encourages adolescents to abstain from sex), such as encouraging condom use, were more successful in reducing risky sex in the long term than were abstinence-only approaches (Johnson, Scott-Sheldon, Huedo-Medina, & Carey, 2011). Abstinence-only education may not have a significant effect on reducing engagement in unprotected sex or on postponing sexual activity (Kohler, Manhart, & Lafferty, 2008). In addition, abstinence-only approaches to sexual health education do not prepare youth to use condoms when they decide to become sexually active (Johnson et al., 2011), and these approaches may violate individuals' rights to access complete sexual health information (Santelli et al., 2006).

Examples of Interventions

The Study to Reduce Intravenous Exposures is a group level intervention designed for injection drug users who are HIV-negative and are living with hepatitis C. This intervention is delivered over six sessions in groups of 5–9 participants and two facilitators. It uses a harm reduction approach, which seeks to minimize the harmful consequences associated with illegal or stigmatized behaviours, to promote safer injection behaviours, and to reduce hepatitis C transmission. The sessions focus on improving knowledge, skills building, managing hepatitis C, and peer mentoring to engage other injection drug users in safer injection behaviours (Latka et al., 2008). The Mpowerment Project is a community-level HIV prevention program aimed at young men who have sex with men. The intervention included peer outreach activities in venues frequented by young men who have sex with men, peer-led groups offered in community settings, and a social marketing campaign (Kegeles, Hays, & Coates, 1996).

Treatments and Interventions Involving People Living with HIV/STIs

Prevention Interventions

Most of the focus in HIV prevention has been on working with HIV-negative populations to reduce sexual and drug-use risk behaviours. However, over the past decade the benefits of working with people living with HIV to reduce HIV transmission have increasingly been recognized (CDC, 2003). In a review of research related to prevention with people living with HIV, interventions delivered to individuals and/or groups were found to decrease HIV risk behaviours (Gilliam & Straub, 2009). Although many of the interventions were delivered by health-care providers, a recent trend is the use of peer facilitators who themselves are living with HIV. Peer-delivered interventions have been used for HIV prevention with various populations and have been successful in improving HIV knowledge and condom use, as well as in reducing the sharing of drug-use equipment among injection drug users (Medley, Kennedy, O'Reilly, & Sweat, 2009). In addition to providing support to clients, peer interventions have been beneficial to the educators themselves through reciprocal support, learning, and empowerment (Marino, Simoni, & Bordeaux Silverstein, 2007).

One intervention with a focus on people living with HIV is called Healthy Relationships. Based on social cognitive theory, Healthy Relationships is a group-level intervention delivered through five two-hour sessions over two and a half weeks, and is offered for groups of 6–10 participants. The goals of Healthy Relationships are to develop coping skills related to HIV and situations of sexual risk, improve self-efficacy for decisions to disclose HIV status, and develop and maintain safer sex behaviours. The intervention uses role-playing activities, videos, skills-building exercises, and personalized feedback reports based on the risky behaviours they reported prior to the intervention (Kalichman et al., 2001). At six-month follow-up, participants had lower rates of sexual risk behaviours than those in the comparison intervention, including reduced unprotected intercourse with HIV-negative partners and increased condom use (Kalichman, Rompa, & Cage, 2005).

Recently there has been increased interest in "treatment as prevention," which is the use of combination antiretroviral therapy to decrease the chances of transmitting HIV via reducing the amount of virus in the body of an individual living with HIV (Williams et al., 2011). Thus, in addition to helping people living with HIV maintain their health, this approach could help to reduce HIV transmission on a large scale. Combination antiretroviral therapy can be used as a preventative measure by reducing the rate of transmission between partners who are serodiscordant (opposite HIV status) and from mother to child (Granich et al., 2010). Given that some may continue to engage in unprotected sex even when on combination antiretroviral therapy, HIV prevention should include evidence-based behavioural interventions to reduce HIV risk behaviours in addition to the use of combination antiretroviral therapy (WHO, 2008). Research into the implementation of this method for HIV prevention is ongoing.

⦿ IN FOCUS

The Role of Evidence in Policy Development: Spotlight on Insite

Injection drug use is associated with high risk for the transmission of HIV, hepatitis C, and other blood-borne illnesses (Hagan & Des Jarlais, 2000). Many of these negative health outcomes result from limited access to sterile injection equipment and fear of legal prosecution. Harm reduction programs address the needs of injection drug users by providing access to syringes, needles, and other safer drug-use equipment (e.g., tourniquets, sterile water, alcohol swabs, cookers, etc.). Since the 1980s, about 40 cities have opened safe injection facilities across the globe to provide injection drug users with a safe environment where they can inject drugs under the supervision of health-care providers (Hedrich, 2004).

In 2003, the first North American safe injection facility was opened in Vancouver, Canada. The safe injection facility, called Insite, began operations after receiving a special exemption from the Canadian federal government (Dooling & Rachlis, 2010). The

exemption was provided for a three-year period and required an external scientific program evaluation (Wood, Tyndall, Montaner, & Kerr, 2006). Since the first two months of service, Insite has consistently had an average of about 500 visits per day. Nursing staff and addiction counsellors provide injection drug users with access to safer drug-use equipment and first aid, offer counselling and referrals to treatment programs, and assist in cases of overdose (Wood et al., 2006).

Within the initial three-year phase, 22 peer-reviewed studies have been published demonstrating the effectiveness of Insite, such as reductions of HIV risk behaviour, decreased injections in public places (Kerr, Tyndall, Li, Montaner, & Wood, 2005), and increased engagement in drug treatment programs (Wood, Tyndall, Zhang, Montaner, & Kerr, 2007). Using mathematical modelling, researchers calculated that Insite prevents between 2 to 12 deaths due to overdose per year (Milloy, Kerr,

The Canadian Press/Jonathan Hayward

PHOTO 11.8 | The innovative but controversial Insite program offers free needles and a safe and sanitary area to use injection drugs. The purpose of this evidence-supported program is to reduce the risk of transmitting HIV and other diseases for people who are dependent on injection drugs.

(Continued)

Tyndall, Montaner, & Wood, 2008). Insite's services were not associated with increased relapse among former drug users and did not have a negative effect on those attempting to discontinue drug use (Kerr et al., 2006). Further, there was a significant decrease in crime, public injecting, and litter related to drug use (Wood, Tyndall, Zhenguo, et al., 2006). Insite was also found to be a cost-effective program (Bayoumi & Zaric, 2008).

Although Insite was granted an additional three-year extension, the continuation of the safe injection facility was questioned once there was a change in political parties in the Canadian federal government. Despite the various health benefits to drug users as well as to the community, the federal government believed it encouraged injection drug use and continued to oppose Insite. This government opposition led to the federal health agency, Health Canada, removing funding for the evaluation of the program in 2006 (CBC, 2009).

Following several short-term extensions for exemptions and three years of legal proceedings in the British Columbia Supreme Court and the Supreme Court of Canada, the Supreme Court announced on 30 September 2011 that Insite should be allowed to continue its operations (CBC, 2011). The case of Insite demonstrates the challenges of implementing evidence-based policy for addressing the HIV and hepatitis C epidemics via reducing the harms associated with illicit drug use. This case also demonstrates the relevance of the biopsychosocial model for injection drug users: There are legal challenges rooted in societal attitudes that prevent access to harm-reduction services that need to be addressed for the Insite program to run (socio-cultural factors), the program allows changes in behaviour such as use of clean needles (psychological factors), and the purpose of the program is to reduce HIV transmission among drug users and the larger community (biomedical factors).

Psychotherapeutic Treatments

Most psychotherapy is offered one-on-one or in small-group format. The treatments offered to people living with HIV or incurable STIs like herpes are typically the same as those offered to people in the general population.

Research-supported psychological treatments, specifically useful for people living with HIV, are available. For example, the Life-Steps intervention (Safren, Otto, & Worth, 1999) is a single-session treatment that incorporates cognitive behavioural and motivational interviewing, and problem-solving techniques designed to improve medication adherence (see In Practice box). For clients with co-morbid problems such as substance use and homelessness or severe mental health problems, more than one session may be needed. A brief follow-up phone call is scheduled one week after the intervention to review strategies and cues that were identified during the session.

More intensive treatments may also combine health psychology techniques with techniques from clinical psychology, such as cognitive behavioural therapy for adherence and depression among HIV-infected individuals (Safren et al., 2009). Another example is a brief risk-reduction intervention developed by Sikkema and colleagues (2011) designed for men who have sex with men recently diagnosed with HIV. This intervention comprises three 60-minute sessions within one month

of diagnosis and involves developing a personalized risk-reduction plan, increasing motivation for transmission risk reduction, and developing behavioural skills to protect the individual's health. This brief intervention is more effective than standard care procedures at reducing risk behaviour, alcohol use, STI symptoms, and traumatic stress as well as increasing use of clinical services (Sikkema et al., 2011).

Future Directions

Although much research has already been conducted examining risk factors for STIs and HIV, less research has examined factors that protect uninfected people against these infections. Similarly, there is a lack of research that examines which factors are associated with positive mental health and well-being among people living with HIV and other incurable STIs. Regarding interventions to prevent HIV and STIs and to promote better HIV and STI health outcomes, most of these interventions may need to be administered face-to-face, which may limit the ability of health psychology programs to reach people from rural populations or others who are unable to attend weekly counselling sessions. It has been recommended, therefore, that health psychologists increase the use of the Internet to increase access for marginalized populations (Hart & Hart, 2010).

⊞ IN PRACTICE
HIV and Depression

Mark is a 30-year-old heterosexual man who presented to the HIV clinic at the local hospital to get more of the combination antiretroviral treatment medications to control the amount of HIV virus in his body. Mark's combination antiretroviral treatment regimen helped change his diagnosis from a possible death sentence to a chronic but manageable disease. He has been living with HIV for five years now, and after a period of two years during which Mark was too sick to work, he is back at work as a server at a restaurant. Mark was referred to the psychologist at the HIV clinic, Dr Jimenez, because he has been experiencing depressed mood, irritability, and sleep problems over the last two months.

Dr Jimenez has extensive expertise working at the HIV clinic, and knows that people living with HIV are more likely to suffer from depression than people in the general population. Dr Jimenez also knows that depression is associated with increased risk of death from HIV and difficulties taking medications as prescribed. Mark has informed his psychologist that he has skipped a few doses of his medications because he has been feeling too tired and apathetic. Dr Jimenez therefore views Mark's depression as being dangerous not only for mental health reasons, but also because it may affect Mark's physical health.

Dr Jimenez, who is aware of the latest treatments available for people living with HIV, provided a psychological treatment called Life-Steps (Safren, Otto, & Worth, 1999) to help Mark reduce his depression and become more adherent to his HIV medications. Life-Steps is a single-session treatment in which the therapist and client proceed through 11 informational, problem-solving, and cognitive behavioural steps in order to help the client identify and develop strategies to overcome problems with medication adherence. Some examples of steps addressed in treatment are: obtaining medication, coping with side effects, cues for pill-taking, and responses to slips in adherence (Safren et al., 1999). Dr Jimenez follows up this initial session with eight sessions of cognitive behavioural treatment for medication adherence and depression, which aim to reduce Mark's depressive symptoms while continuing to increase his medication adherence (Safren et al., 2009).

SUMMARY

HIV and STIs are of psychological interest because they are transmitted largely through sexual behaviour. In the case of HIV, another common route is through injection drug-use behaviours. These infections are also psychological because psychological factors like personality traits and beliefs predict someone's susceptibility to engaging in risky behaviour. Living with STIs and HIV can also have psychological consequences, such as poor mental health outcomes due to societal stigmatization. Fortunately, health psychologists and other researchers and health providers operating within the biopsychosocial model have created psychological interventions that promote improved sexual health outcomes, reduce sexual risk behaviours, and help people living with STIs and especially people living with HIV to live longer and fuller lives.

Critical Thought Questions

1. Which psychological factors may explain why younger adults may be more at risk for STIs than older adults?
2. How would you respond to a friend who does not understand why psychologists would study STIs and HIV?
3. What role do you think you would have if you were a health psychologist working in a clinic for clients with HIV?

Recommended Reading

Cohen, M.A., & Gorman, J.M. (2008). *Comprehensive textbook of AIDS psychiatry.* Toronto: Oxford University Press.

Wolitski, R.J., Stall, R., & Validserri, R.O. (2008). *Unequal opportunity: Health disparities affecting gay and bisexual men in the United States.* Toronto: Oxford University Press.

Acknowledgements

T.G. Tulloch, N.L. Stratton, and S. Ing are supported through Canada Graduate Scholarships. T.A. Hart is supported through a Career Scientist Award from the Ontario HIV Treatment Network. The authors would like to thank the staff at the HIV Prevention Lab at Ryerson University for their help with this chapter.

Multiple Sclerosis and Other Chronic Neurological Diseases

DANIELLE BLACKMORE | JENNA ALBIANI | TAE HART

Learning Objectives

In this chapter you will:

- Be provided with an overview of multiple sclerosis (MS), including information about its prevalence, specific types, common symptoms, and risk factors that have been identified.

- Learn about psychological problems commonly associated with MS.

- Gain an understanding of how psychologists and other mental health practitioners assess psychological and physical difficulties in people with MS, such as depression, anxiety, fatigue, sexual dysfunction, and cognitive function.

- Learn about the treatments being successfully used to target both the physical and psychological symptoms of MS.

- Be presented with an overview of some other chronic neurological diseases, such as Huntington's disease and amyotrophic lateral sclerosis (ALS).

Background on Multiple Sclerosis (MS), Symptoms, and Prevalence

MS is a chronic disease that affects the central nervous system (CNS), which includes the brain, the spinal cord, and the optic nerves. Most experts believe that MS is an autoimmune disease, meaning that the body's immune system mistakenly attacks and destroys healthy body tissue. In MS, the body attacks the protective covering, called myelin, surrounding nerve cells of the CNS. This process is called **demyelination**. When demyelination occurs, plaques (also called **lesions**) are formed along the myelin and interrupt or distort the nerve signals moving through them. The symptoms that occur in MS are a result of this damage to the nerve cells (MS Society, 2012).

Prevalence and Risk Factors

Approximately 2.5 million people worldwide have been diagnosed with MS, with more than 500,000 MS individuals living in the United States and 75,000 in Canada (MS Society, 2012; Pugliatti, Sotgiu, & Rosati, 2002; Rosati, 2002). Although MS can occur at any age, it is most commonly diagnosed in young adulthood (25–32 years of age), when people typically are beginning careers and starting families (WHO, 2008).

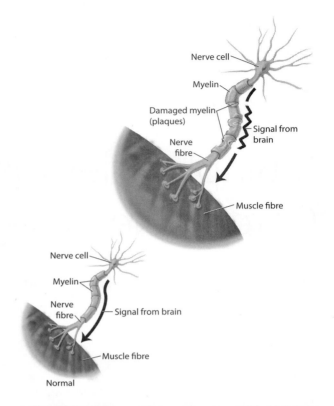

FIGURE 12.1 | Image of myelin damage in MS.

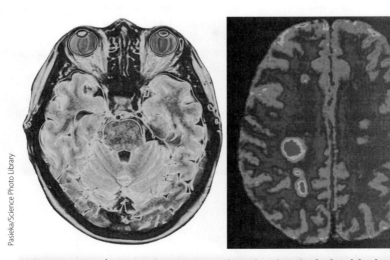

PHOTO 12.1 | Magnetic resonance imaging (MRI) of a healthy brain and a brain with MS.

⊚ IN FOCUS

MS: From Unexplained Symptoms to Present-Day Diagnosis

Sir Augustus d'Esté (1794–1848), grandchild of King George III, had the first known case of MS. At 28, Augustus d'Esté noticed the first symptom, a disturbance in his vision. He reported, "my eyes were so attacked that when fixed upon minute objects, indistinctness of vision was the consequence." He later experienced other symptoms of MS, including loss of motor control, pain, fatigue, and incontinence. In his diary, he wrote of the attempts by physicians to cure him. In one entry he wrote, "Dr Kissock supposed bile to be the cause: I was twice blooded from the temple by leeches." Augustus d'Esté passed away without any relief from treatments offered at the time (Landtblom, Fazio, Fredrikson, & Granieri, 2010).

Today, reality TV star Jack Osbourne (son of rock legend Ozzy Osbourne) is one of many young adults living with MS. While younger (age 26) than Augustus d'Esté when he developed MS, Jack's future is more hopeful. Like d'Esté, Jack underwent medical testing after experiencing blindness and struggled with the diagnosis, saying, "I'd just had a baby, work was going great—I kept thinking: 'Why now?'" However, Jack is now learning to live with the new reality of his illness, taking advantage of the many treatment options available: "Adapt and overcome is my new motto." While MS still has no known cure, there have been dramatic improvements in knowledge about MS (Arpe, 2012; BBC, 2012) and promising new research. For some in the limelight who have been stricken with the disease, such as Osbourne and country musician Clay Walker, there is hope. Actress, singer, and Disney legend Annette Funicello, who

PHOTO 12.2 | Jack Osbourne, reality television star and son of Ozzy Osbourne, was recently diagnosed with multiple sclerosis (Arpe, 2012).

died in 2013 at the age of 70 from complications caused by MS, following many years of struggle and deterioration, developed the disease before new medications that slow its progression were available.

It is one of the most common causes of disability in young adults.

Although the specific cause is not yet known, current research suggests that MS is likely the result of a complex interplay between environmental exposure and genetic factors. Certain factors appear to increase the likelihood of developing MS. For example, MS has an uneven gender distribution, with women being diagnosed three times more often than men (MS Society, 2012). In addition, MS prevalence rates generally increase the farther one travels from the equator in either hemisphere (Pugliatti et al., 2002). MS is most commonly seen in Caucasians (Koch-Henriksen & Sørensen, 2010; MS Society, 2012). The risk of developing MS is higher in relatives of individuals with MS than in the general population (Compston & Coles, 2008).

Prevalence of multiple sclerosis (per 100, 000)

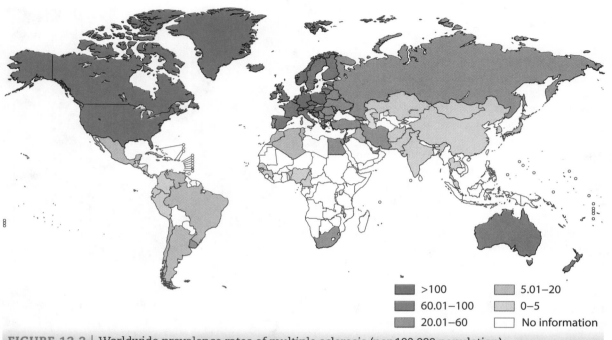

▓ >100	▓ 5.01–20
▓ 60.01–100	▓ 0–5
▓ 20.01–60	☐ No information

FIGURE 12.2 | Worldwide prevalence rates of multiple sclerosis (per 100,000 population).

PHOTO 12.3 | Country musician Clay Walker was diagnosed with relapsing-remitting MS in 1996, at the age of 26. In 2003 he started the Band Against MS Foundation to support education, awareness, and research into multiple sclerosis.

Types of MS

Depending on the pattern of symptom presentation, MS can be categorized in one of five disease subtypes (MS Society, 2012):

1. *Benign MS* is the mildest form of MS, which typically produces minimal disability even after many years of being diagnosed. However, some people can eventually develop more progressive disease.
2. *Relapsing-remitting MS* is characterized by a pattern of flare-ups followed by incomplete or full symptom resolution. Relapsing-remitting MS occurs in 75–90 per cent of newly diagnosed patients.
3. *Primary progressive MS* afflicts 10–15 per cent of patients and causes an unrelenting progression of MS symptoms without relapses.
4. *Secondary progressive MS* typically develops following many years of relapsing-remitting MS. In this form of MS, neurologic deficits gradually and steadily worsen over time.
5. *Progressive relapsing MS* (not shown in Figure 12.3) is uncommon. It is found in about 5 per cent of cases. Those with this type of MS face a continuous increase in symptoms along with symptom flare-ups.

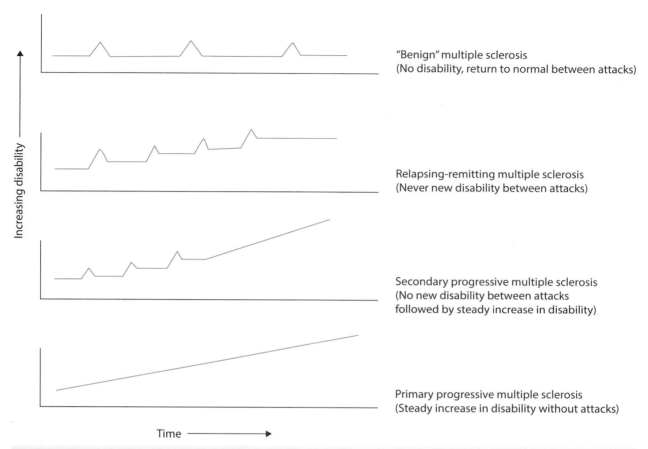

FIGURE 12.3 | Typical illness course for different types of MS.

Medical Interventions and Symptom Management Strategies

There is no known cure for MS, but various treatments help to manage acute attacks, prevent new attacks, and cope with existing symptoms.

PHOTO 12.4 | Avonex Pen (interferon beta-1a) used by some MS patients to deliver treatment.

Source: Used with the permission of Biogen Idec.

Managing Acute Attacks

During a symptom flare-up, patients often are given **corticosteroids** (or steroids) over a period of a few days to help manage their symptoms (Compston & Coles, 2008). Corticosteroids can be delivered via tablet or intravenously. Although corticosteroids are effective in the short term for speeding up the recovery from a relapse, they do not appear to have a significant impact on the long-term course of MS.

Preventing New Attacks

Disease-modifying therapies (also called immunomodulatory therapies) are taken regularly for the purpose of targeting the inflammatory process of MS, thereby preventing relapses. Although these therapies are effective in slowing down the progression of MS, they do not stop it.

Managing Existing Symptoms of MS

A variety of treatments are available to address various MS-related symptoms or functional deficits. For example, bladder problems, muscle spasticity, and pain tend to be quite responsive to medication (Compston & Coles, 2008). Physical activity has recently been shown to be an effective strategy for managing a variety of MS-related symptoms. For example, exercise has been shown to help individuals with MS improve their fatigue, quality of life, and mood (Stroud & Minahan, 2009). It is, however, important that exercise be carefully monitored by a trained professional as overworking and/or overheating during exercise can trigger a symptom flare-up.

Complementary and Alternative Medicine

Complementary and alternative medicine (CAM) therapies are commonly used by MS patients. Treatments such as acupuncture, **cooling therapy**, guided imagery, massage, reflexology, Tai Chi, and yoga are frequently used to manage MS-related symptoms. In general, research supporting the efficacy of these treatments is limited; however, these forms of CAM appear to be of low risk and are tolerated well by individuals with MS (Bowling, 2011).

Emerging Treatment

Liberation therapy has garnered a tremendous amount of media attention. This procedure is based on the premise that impaired venous drainage from the CNS, termed chronic cerebrospinal venous insufficiency (CCSVI), contributes to MS (Zamboni et al., 2009). Liberation therapy involves completing an endovascular angioplasty (i.e., a medical procedure that uses stenting to improve blood flow in specific veins) in MS patients with CCSVI. This procedure has received criticism due to the potential for serious complications and deaths to occur as side effects. In addition, the research in this area is currently limited and the benefits of liberation therapy are yet to be conclusively proven (Khan et al., 2010; Qiu, 2010). Research in this area is continuing.

Psychological Factors in MS

Those diagnosed with MS face an increased risk of psychological co-morbidity due to MS-related illness processes and stress. Yet, despite the heightened prevalence rates for many psychological disorders, not all people with MS will develop such conditions.

Depression

Depression is very common among those living with MS, with a lifetime prevalence rate of 40–60 per cent (Vattakatuchery, Rickards, & Cavanna, 2011). Several factors have been proposed to explain this high occurrence among those with MS. First, it has been theorized that MS lesions, and possibly their location, may play a role in the onset of depression (Arnett & Strober, 2011). Second, immune system disturbances seen in those with MS may also predispose individuals to depression (Vattakatuchery et al., 2011). Negative beliefs about MS and one's ability to cope, as well as engaging in avoidance behaviours (such as avoiding social interaction), are associated with increased rates of depression (Arnett & Strober, 2011; Vattakatuchery et al., 2011). Nonetheless, having good psychological coping strategies has been found to decrease rates of depression.

Anxiety

Compared to research for depression, research into anxiety among those with MS is less extensive. The lifetime prevalence of anxiety disorders in MS is 36 per cent; greater than seen in healthy populations (Arnett & Strober, 2011; Chwastiak & Ehde, 2009). Generalized anxiety disorder, obsessive compulsive disorder, and panic disorder are the most commonly occurring anxiety disorders (Haussleiter, Brüne, & Juckel, 2009). Anxiety in MS is associated with poor social support, illness progression, and increased social stressors (Chwastiak & Ehde, 2009; Haussleiter et al., 2009). Finally, anxiety about injecting immunomodulatory medications (which are often required for the treatment of MS) can become problematic, with 18 per cent of MS patients in a recent study reporting injection anxiety (Dennison & Moss-Morris, 2010; Mohr, Boudewyn, Likosky, Levine, & Goodkin, 2001). More research is necessary to help uncover the complex role of stress, illness symptoms, neurological changes, and social support in the onset and maintenance of anxiety.

Fatigue

Fatigue is very frequent and one of the most disruptive symptoms of MS (Bol, Duits, Hupperts, Vlaeyen, & Verhey, 2009). It has been defined as "a subjective lack of physical and/or mental energy" (Shah, 2009). In fact, as many as 74 per cent of individuals with MS may suffer from fatigue (Hadjimichael, Vollmer, & Oleen-Burkey, 2008). Fatigue can be broken down into primary and secondary fatigue. Primary fatigue results from the illness itself, such as damage to the CNS or dysregulation of the

© Fitzer/iStockphoto

PHOTO 12.5 | Fatigue is highly prevalent and one of the most disruptive symptoms of MS.

immune system (Braley & Chervin, 2010). Secondary fatigue is associated with consequences of MS, such as side effects from medication, decreased physical activity, co-morbid depression, anxiety, and sleep disorders, as well as physical symptoms such as pain (Braley & Chervin, 2010; Krupp, Serafin, & Christodoulou, 2010; Shah, 2009). Fatigue often results in difficulties working, lowered quality of life, and increased use of health-care services (Krupp et al., 2010).

Sexual Dysfunction

Men and women with MS suffer from sexual dysfunction at rates of 50–90 per cent and 40–80 per cent, respectively (Kessler, Fowler, & Panicker, 2009). Sexual dysfunction in MS may best be explained by a three-part model of primary, secondary, and tertiary sexual dysfunction (Foley & Werner, 2004; Kessler et al., 2009). Primary sexual dysfunction directly results from neurological consequences of the illness (such as erectile difficulties or loss of feeling in the genital region) (Miller, Bourdette, Ritvo, & Stuart, 1994; Zivadinov et al., 1999; Zorzon et al., 1999). Secondary sexual dysfunction results from illness symptoms, such as fatigue or loss of bladder and bowel control, which lead to difficulties engaging in sexual intercourse. Finally, tertiary sexual dysfunction results from psychological or social issues, which arise from living with MS and directly impact intimate relations (Foley & Werner, 2004).

Cognitive Function

Changes in cognitive functioning are often associated with MS. Some level of cognitive deterioration has been estimated in 40–60 per cent of individuals with MS (Amato, Zipoli, & Portaccio, 2006; Arnett & Strober, 2011). While the actual changes in cognition typically are small, they can have a negative effect on a person's day-to-day life, such as limiting ability to work, negatively impacting relationships, and decreasing quality of life (Amato et al., 2006; Arnett & Strober, 2011). Typical cognitive impairment can include difficulties with planning, recalling information, or concentration (Amato et al., 2006; Arnett & Strober, 2011; Ghaffar & Feinstein, 2007). As with other MS symptoms, there are thought to be primary and secondary cognitive factors. Primary causes stem from neurological changes due to MS, which result in cognitive decline (Arnett & Strober, 2011). Secondary causes refer to cognitive decline stemming from other psychological issues, such as anxiety and depression (Arnett & Strober, 2011).

Stress, Appraisal, and Coping

MS can create stress and uncertainty, as it can be an invasive illness with the potential for physical disability, troubling symptoms, and an unpredictable course. A theory by Lazarus and Folkman (see Chapter 5) helps explain the importance of coping strategies in adapting to the challenges presented by MS. A person examines each source of stress and looks at how much he or she can control the event. When an event is out of a person's control, using a strategy that focuses on emotional coping is a better fit (e.g., seeking emotional support). However, if the stressful event is controllable, using strategies such as problem-solving (e.g., brainstorming best possible options) can be most useful (Lazarus, 1993). Use of effective coping strategies can decrease the stress associated with MS (Dennison, Moss-Morris, & Chalder, 2009; Mitsonis, Potagas, Zervas, & Sfagos, 2009). In addition, those who hold the belief that they can control some aspect of their illness have better psychological adjustment compared to those who believe the illness is out of their control (Mitsonis et al., 2009). Moreover, those who perceive their illness as more uncertain, view events as more stressful, and feel higher levels of helplessness in dealing with their MS suffer worse emotional adjustment than those who experience lower amounts of uncertainty, stress, and helplessness (Dennison, Moss-Morris, & Chalder, 2009).

Other Psychological Factors in MS

Those with MS frequently have sleep disturbance, with prevalence estimates ranging from 36 to 62 per cent (Arnett & Strober, 2011). Sleep disturbance often worsens with MS-related neurological changes and physical symptoms (Arnett & Strober, 2011). Pain is also a common symptom of MS, with prevalence rates of 29–86 per cent. Pain among those with MS is associated with various negative repercussions such as increased rates of depression, worse physical adjustment, and lower quality of life (O'Connor, Schwid, Herrmann, Markman, & Dworkin, 2008).

Along with difficulties with pain and sleep, a host of other psychological issues are associated with MS disease progression and medications. For instance, higher rates of bipolar disorder, characterized by the presence of mania (i.e., a mood that is unusually high or agitated that causes problems for the person) or hypomania (i.e., similar to mania, but shorter-lasting and does not cause as significant problems for the person), exist among those with MS (APA, 2013). The prevalence of bipolar disorder has been estimated to be two to three times that of the general population (Lacovides & Andreoulakis, 2011). It is thought that corticosteroids used to treat MS flare-ups may cause mania (Brown & Chandler, 2001; Kenna, Poon, de los Angeles, & Koran, 2011; Lacovides & Andreoulakis, 2011). In addition, mania can be caused by brain lesions or other damage associated with MS (Lacovides & Andreoulakis, 2011). Finally, in some cases there may be a genetic predisposition to developing both MS and bipolar disorder (Bozikas et. al., 2003; Lacovides & Andreoulakis, 2011). Neurological damage due to MS can also create excessive laughing or crying in about 10 per cent of those with MS. More research is needed to clarify exactly what type of damage creates these symptoms (Arnett & Strober, 2011; Feinstein, 2004; Ghaffar & Feinstein, 2007).

Psychological Assessment in People with MS

The assessment of psychological problems or disorders in individuals with MS can be a challenging process, primarily due to the substantial overlap between MS symptoms and the symptoms of various psychological disorders. For example, depression is characterized by low mood or loss of interest and it is accompanied by the presence of somatic symptoms such as decreased energy and motor retardation, and cognitive features such as lack of concentration (American Psychiatric Association, 2013). But in MS patients, some of these symptoms (e.g., fatigue, difficulty concentrating) can be specifically due to the disease of MS and may not be associated with depression (Bakshi et al., 2000). Therefore, clinicians treating those with MS must be aware of the potential overlap between MS-related symptoms and symptoms of a psychological condition.

The Assessment of Depression and Anxiety

The ideal method for identifying depression or anxiety disorders is the use of a diagnostic interview, for example, the Structured Clinical Interview for DSM Diagnosis (SCID) (First, Spitzer, Gibbon, & Williams, 1996), conducted by a qualified mental health professional. However, such interviews are time-consuming and are often impractical. Consequently, depression and anxiety are commonly assessed using self-report measures.

Two of the most frequently used self-report questionnaires to assess depressive symptoms are the Beck Depression Inventory (BDI) (Beck, Ward, Mendelson, Mock, & Erbaugh, 1961) and the Center for Epidemiologic Studies of Depression Scale (CES-D) (Radloff, 1977). However, due to the symptom overlap between depression and MS, these scales do not distinguish whether a specific symptom arises from a depressive disorder or from MS. Measures have been developed to assess depression symptoms among individuals with medical conditions. For example, the Beck Fast Screen for Medically Ill Populations (B-FS) (Beck, Steer, & Brown, 2000) has been validated for use in assessing the severity of depression among MS patients (Benedict et al., 2003).

Assessment of anxiety in MS patients has received significantly less attention than depression, but questionnaires are available to measure anxiety severity among individuals with MS. For example, the State-Trait Anxiety Inventory (STAI) (Spielberger, 1985) measures both the short-term, situation-based "state" anxiety and the long-term, more stable, "trait" anxiety. Another option, the Hospital Anxiety and Depression Scale (Zigmond & Snaith, 1983), is designed for use in medically ill patients and has the advantage of assessing anxiety and depression together in one measure.

The Assessment of Fatigue

MS-related fatigue is typically assessed with self-report questionnaires, such as the Modified Fatigue Impact Scale (MFIS) (Multiple Sclerosis Council for

Clinical Practice Guidelines, 1998) and the Fatigue Severity Scale (FSS) (Krupp, LaRocca, Muir-Nash, & Steinberg, 1989). The MFIS assesses multiple dimensions of fatigue, including cognitive, psychological, and physical components. The FSS, on the other hand, examines the severity of fatigue and the impact it has on one's life.

The Assessment of Sexual Dysfunction

Discussing sexual functioning can be difficult for many individuals. One of the simplest methods is to include a question about sexual functioning when conducting the initial assessment interview and, if warranted, to initiate a discussion about the sexual problems the patient is experiencing. Research shows the majority of MS patients are grateful when topics of sexuality are directly discussed by health professionals (Foley, 2006). Alternatively, patients can be given a self-report questionnaire that screens for sexual dysfunction. For example, the MS Intimacy and Sexuality Questionnaire–19 (MSISQ–19) (Sanders et al., 2000) assesses primary, secondary, and tertiary components of sexual dysfunction in both men and women.

The Assessment of Cognitive Function

An assessment of cognitive functioning typically includes multiple measures and methods. Often, clinicians will ask patients about subjective changes they have noticed in their own memory, attention, decision-making skills, etc. It is also common for clinicians to speak to family members, friends, employers, or other informants to inquire about any changes they have noticed in the cognitive functioning of the person with MS.

Clinicians should also conduct objective tests with batteries to screen for cognitive dysfunction in MS. The Screening Examination for Cognitive Impairment (Beatty et al., 1995), for example, was designed as a quick testing procedure to assess for cognitive functions frequently affected by MS. The entire battery can be administered in approximately 30 minutes. However, it is often beneficial or necessary to conduct a full neuropsychological battery to gain a more comprehensive assessment of a patient's cognitive function. Neuropsychological batteries include many tests that examine several different cognitive functions, such as general intellectual ability, attention and concentration, memory, language skills, dexterity, processing speed, and conceptual reasoning (LaRocca & Caruso, 2006).

Treatment of Psychological Issues in MS

The Treatment of Depression and Anxiety

As mentioned earlier, people with MS face a heightened risk of developing various psychological disorders, but not all individuals develop these problems. Therefore, it is important to remember that while there is an increased risk of psychological co-morbidity within this group, it is not a certainty. Moreover, promising new treatments, including medications and psychological therapies, have shown beneficial results.

The most extensively studied psychotherapy among individuals with MS is cognitive behavioural therapy (CBT) (Beck, 2005). CBT is aimed to help people appraise their symptoms in adaptive ways and to lead more productive and rewarding lives despite their health condition. Most research on CBT has focused on its effectiveness in treating depression; indeed, CBT seems to alleviate depression in those with MS (Mohr & Cox, 2001). Moreover, telephone-delivered CBT has been found to be effective in treating depression among this group (Mohr et al., 2005). Research indicates that CBT produces the most significant improvement in depression among those with MS (i.e., Mohr & Cox, 2001; Mohr et. al., 2005).

There have been very few studies of CBT for anxiety in those with MS; however, limited research to date suggests that CBT can be effective in treating anxiety in this group (Mohr & Cox, 2001). Moreover, there is also some early evidence that CBT can be used to treat anxiety about injecting immunomodulatory medications (Dennison & Moss-Morris, 2010). Generally speaking, therapies that focus on bolstering coping skills are most beneficial for those with MS (Mohr & Goodkin, 1999). CBT can also be used to improve coping and stress management techniques among those without a psychological diagnosis (Mohr & Goodkin, 1999).

Pharmacotherapy is the other most commonly used form of treatment for symptoms of depression among those with MS (Mohr, Boudewyn, Goodkin, Bostrom, & Epstein, 2001). For example, antidepressants such as sertraline (e.g., Zoloft) and fluoxetine (e.g., Prozac) are frequently used (Mohr, Boudewyn, Goodkin, et al., 2001; Thompson, Toosy, & Ciccarelli, 2010), though these and other antidepressants have numerous potential side effects. Antidepressants have shown promising effects in reducing depression in MS

⊞ IN PRACTICE
Beginning to Cope with a Diagnosis of Multiple Sclerosis

Jessica is a 28-year-old woman with a high-stress corporate job. She has recently started seeing a psychologist to help her cope better with her stress. Six months ago, she experienced optic neuritis, a neurological symptom that caused a complete loss of vision in her right eye. After an MRI of her head and neck ordered by her neurologist, she was diagnosed with multiple sclerosis. Currently, she has extreme fatigue and sleep problems affecting her ability to work. She is feeling very anxious about her future and the medications she is taking to prevent further worsening of her symptoms. She feels her friends cannot relate to her now that she has to cope with a chronic illness and uncertain future. Jessica also worries about whether her boyfriend of nine months will leave her if her health worsens. The psychologist administers a structured clinical interview and the Hospital Anxiety and Depression Scale to Jessica, and finds that Jessica has clinically elevated levels of depression and anxiety. Cognitive behavioural therapy (a type of therapy that focuses on changing unhelpful thoughts and behaviour in order to improve one's mood and mental health) will be used to treat Jessica's anxiety and depression (Beck, 2005).

MS symptoms typically occur in acute episodes, commonly referred to as "relapses," "exacerbations," "attacks," or "flare-ups," which can last for days, weeks, or even months and are followed by periods of time with reduced or no symptoms (called "remissions") (MS Society, 2012). Because nerves in any part of the CNS may be affected, people with MS can experience symptoms in many different parts of the body. For example, they may experience physical symptoms such as muscle weakness, muscle spasms, loss of balance or co-ordination, numbness, tingling or pricking sensations in the body, difficulty moving arms or legs, or problems walking. In addition, bowel and bladder difficulties, sexual dysfunction, problems with speech or swallowing, and visual problems such as double vision or vision loss are common. Cognitive impairment and emotional changes, particularly depression, are also frequently observed in individuals with MS. One of the most common and bothersome symptoms reported by people with MS is fatigue (MS Society, 2012). All of these are issues Jessica, with the help of her psychologist, will aim to deal with over the coming weeks and months.

(Mohr, Boudewyn, Goodkin, et al., 2001), but research has been quite limited and needs further investigation. Little research has examined the efficacy of pharmacotherapy for anxiety among those with MS.

The Treatment of Fatigue

While several treatment options for MS-related fatigue are available, it is important to rule out other possible causes of the fatigue (e.g., depression, sleep disturbance due to pain or symptom discomfort) (Krupp et al., 2010). If fatigue persists, some preliminary evidence indicates that CBT can reduce MS-related fatigue (Krupp et al., 2010). In addition, regular exercise and techniques to conserve energy show promise in improving fatigue among those with MS (Krupp et al., 2010). Medications such amantadine (Symmetrel) and modafinil (e.g., Alertec, Provigil) are also prescribed for the management of fatigue, but further research into their mechanisms and efficacy is needed (Braley & Chervin, 2010).

The Treatment of Sexual Dysfunction

The treatment of sexual dysfunction varies for men and women with MS. For men, one common treatment is the prescription of medications, such as Viagra, but the efficacy has shown mixed results in drug trials among men with MS (Kessler et al., 2009). Vacuum constriction devices and localized injections into the penis can also be used to achieve an erection (Kessler et al., 2009). For women, medication has not been found to be as effective as compared to men. However, medications to treat symptoms such as spasticity of muscles, bladder dysfunction, and bowel dysfunction, as well as behavioural techniques to manage these symptoms, can aid in treating secondary sexual dysfunction (Bronner, Elran, Golomb, & Korczyn, 2010; Kessler et al., 2009). Moreover, counselling can be important to help individuals and couples find alternative methods or helpful techniques for sexual expression, as well as activities such as sensate-focused exercises, a sex therapy technique used to increase emotional and physical connection between partners. These treatments and counselling techniques can assist individuals and couples in maintaining their sexual satisfaction, despite their MS-related symptoms (Bronner et al., 2010; Kessler et al., 2009).

Management of Cognitive Symptoms

To manage cognitive dysfunction or problems, memory aids (like agendas) or other external cues (e.g., written notes) can be used, accommodations in the workplace can be given (such as working in a quieter room), and education of patients and family members can be conducted. These strategies can aid in understanding what MS-related cognitive changes look like, what to expect, and how to adapt (Mohr & Cox, 2001). A few studies have examined the impact of cognitive rehabilitation techniques for people with MS, such as the use of memory strategies (Lyros, Messinis, Papageorgiou, & Papathanasopoulos, 2010; Mohr & Cox, 2001). Some research has also been conducted on the use of specific activities to strengthen memory; however, research in this field is limited and has produced conflicting findings. While various medications have been tested, with some success, research in this field is still in early stages and often provides mixed conclusions. Additional research is needed, with larger studies and improved methodology, before the influence of medications can be properly assessed (Lyros et al., 2010).

Treating Other Psychological and Physical Symptoms

Those with MS face other psychological and physical consequences due to their illness. Two common symptoms are pain and sleep disturbance. Medications can be used to alleviate pain, but more MS-specific drug trials are needed (O'Connor et al., 2008). A dearth of research prevails on the use of CBT for MS-related pain, despite its successful use for other pain conditions (Kerns, Kassirer, & Otis, 2002). Various treatments for sleep, on the other hand, are better researched. Sleep disruption can often result from physical discomfort or from other MS-related symptoms or psychological issues. In such cases the treatments of the primary symptom (instead of the sleep problem) would be warranted (Caminero & Bartolomé, 2011). Sleep disorders that are co-morbid with MS have various promising treatments. For example, insomnia can be treated with therapies such as sleep restriction (i.e., decreasing time spent in bed to lead to more efficient sleep), medication, or CBT for insomnia. Often, the previously noted forms

of psychotherapy alone are effective and lead to lasting results (Caminero & Bartolomé, 2011). Some people with MS may experience excessive crying or laughing that is out of context to the situation. Individuals who experience these neurological disruptions are aware that their affect does not match their mood, and often report frustration or embarrassment as a result. Medication can be used to treat this condition. As with many drug trials in MS, research is still limited, but antidepressants (specifically selective serotonin reuptake inhibitors, or SSRIs) along with other medications have been found to be useful.

As noted earlier, mania and hypomania can be induced due to corticosteroid treatment used to treat MS flare-ups. This medication-induced mood change would not be considered bipolar disorder, as it is considered a temporary reaction that resolves after medication is discontinued (Brown & Chandler, 2001; Kenna et al., 2011). Before treatment is initiated for mania, hypomania, or bipolar disorder, a careful and thorough assessment to determine whether the symptoms are due to a medication, direct consequences of neurological changes from the illness, or co-morbid MS and bipolar disorder is crucial. If medication treatment is appropriate, mood-stabilizing medications such as lithium are often recommended (Lacovides & Andreoulakis, 2011).

Other Chronic Neurological Diseases: Huntington's Disease and ALS

Although the focus of this chapter has been MS, there are numerous other types of chronic neurological diseases. Two of the most notable of such diseases are amyotrophic lateral sclerosis (ALS or Lou Gehrig's disease) and Huntington's disease.

Huntington's Disease

Huntington's disease is an inherited degenerative brain disorder that causes cells in specific parts of the brain to die. The worldwide prevalence of Huntington's disease is between five and seven individuals per 100,000 (Walker, 2007). Huntington's disease is a genetic disorder that is inherited in an **autosomal dominant** manner, which means that if a parent carries the gene responsible for Huntington's disease, there is a 50 per cent chance that each child will be affected. Females and males are equally likely to be diagnosed with the disease. Every person who carries that gene will develop Huntington's disease. The onset of the disease typically begins in middle age, between the ages of 30 and 50 (Harper, 1996).

Huntington's disease is progressive, slowly impacting an individual's mental and physical abilities. People with Huntington's disease experience involuntary muscle movements and lack of co-ordination, muscle stiffness, impaired initiation of movement, and speech and swallowing difficulties (Walker, 2007). Moreover, the disease impacts cognitive abilities, causing forgetfulness, lack of concentration, and decreased short-term memory. The disease is fatal and there is no known cure (Kent, 2004; Walker, 2007). The average length of time from diagnosis of the disease to death is 20 years (Walker, 2007). Individuals with Huntington's disease also exhibit a number of psychological and psychiatric features, such as irritability, aggressiveness, and emotional lability. Mood disorders are common, with major depression being reported in approximately 40 per cent of individuals with Huntington's disease (Peyser & Folstein, 1990). Suicidal ideation is frequently reported, and one study estimated that over 25 per cent of individuals with Huntington's disease attempt suicide at least once during the course of their illness (Farrer, 1986). Manic symptoms and psychosis also have been reported (Ranen, 2002).

The symptoms of Huntington's disease are most commonly managed through pharmacological interventions; however, these drugs only partially relieve a small amount of the difficulties encountered by patients (van Vugt & Roos, 1999). Researchers and practitioners have also highlighted the importance of utilizing the services of professionals from multiple disciplines such as psychology, physical therapy, speech therapy, and social work to help maximize the patient's level of functioning and well-being. Finally, because the gene for Huntington's disease has been identified, it is possible to test whether a person is a carrier of this gene. As such, genetic counsellors play a very important role in the lives of patients with Huntington's disease and their families.

ALS

ALS is a progressive neurodegenerative disease in which nerve cells die, leaving voluntary muscles paralyzed. The disease is characterized by muscle weakness and atrophy, muscle spasticity, speech difficulties, difficulty swallowing, and a decline in breathing function (Mitchell & Borasio, 2007). Although the disease does not usually affect the individual's mental abilities, some ALS patients may experience cognitive difficulties (Mitchell & Borasio, 2007). ALS is fatal and there is no known cure. Symptoms generally progress over a two- to four-year period, typically resulting in death from respiratory failure (Borasio & Miller, 2001).

The worldwide prevalence rate of ALS is estimated to be six per 100,000. ALS most commonly occurs between the ages of 40 and 70. In approximately 10 per cent of cases, ALS demonstrates a hereditary pattern; however, in the remaining 90 per cent of cases, the cause of ALS is unknown (Mitchell & Borasio, 2007). Men are affected at a higher rate than females; in fact, men have a 50 per cent greater risk of developing ALS compared to women (Migliore and Coppede, 2009).

Considering that ALS is a fatal disease, it has surprised researchers to discover that the rates of psychological disorders in this population appear to be quite low. For example, it is estimated that the prevalence of depression among ALS patients is only slightly higher than that of the general non-medicalized population, with depression rates ranging between 9 and 13 per cent (Ganzini, Johnston, & Hoffman, 1999; Rabkin et al., 2000). However, some controversy exists as to whether these findings reflect an accurate representation of the distress experienced by this population or whether diagnostic and measurement issues are suppressing the findings. To date, no specific psychological interventions have been developed for individuals with ALS.

Future Directions

While great strides have been made in the understanding of symptoms such as depression in people with MS, much work is needed. Specifically, studies that examine the effect of psychological treatments such as CBT for anxiety and pain among those with MS are still required. Moreover, research into interventions that may help ameliorate cognitive symptoms in this group has been limited. Further, research on the use of psychopharmacology to treat mood disorders, anxiety, fatigue, and cognitive issues in this population is a developing area of study. There have been many promising advances in the understanding of psychological symptoms and their corresponding treatment in MS, Huntington's, and ALS. Continued research into psychological and pharmacological treatments for these individuals will aid in improving quality of life among those diagnosed with these challenging illnesses.

SUMMARY

MS is an autoimmune disease, which is usually diagnosed in early adulthood. Common MS-related physical and neurological problems include fatigue, sexual dysfunction, cognitive dysfunction, pain, and sleep disturbance. Because MS typically has a relapsing and remitting nature, it can create a great deal of stress and uncertainty about the future. Not surprisingly, rates of depression and anxiety are higher for those with MS as compared to the general population. A number of established subjective and objective measures exist to assess both the psychological and physical problems associated with MS. For psychological problems, cognitive behavioural therapy and pharmacotherapy have been most frequently examined. For physical problems, a number of behavioural and pharmacological treatment options exist to reduce MS-related fatigue, sexual dysfunction, cognitive dysfunction, pain, and sleep disturbance. Huntington's disease and ALS are chronic neurological diseases diagnosed in adulthood, but differ from MS in that both progress more quickly and are fatal. Huntington's disease is a genetic disorder causing severe neurological symptoms; depression and anxiety are common reactions to the illness. ALS, on the other hand, is not typically genetic and causes death within a few years. Surprisingly, compared to MS and Huntington's disease, rates of psychological disorders among those with ALS are not significantly higher than they are for the general population.

Critical Thought Questions

1. What are the most common physical symptoms that people diagnosed with MS may develop?
2. Is depression caused by MS or do people become depressed as a psychological reaction to having MS?
3. What are the similarities and differences among MS, Huntington's disease, and ALS?

Recommended Reading

DeLuca, J., & Nocentini, U. (2011). Neuropsychological, medical and rehabilitative management of persons with multiple sclerosis. *NeuroRehabilitation, 29*, 197–219.

Dennison, L., Moss-Morris, R., & Chalder, T. (2009). A review of psychological correlates of adjustment in patients with multiple sclerosis. *Clinical Psychology Review 29*, 141–153.

Giesser, B.S. (2011). *Primer on multiple sclerosis.* New York: Oxford University Press.

Cohen, J.A., & Rudick, R.A. (2011). *Multiple sclerosis therapeutics.* Cambridge: Cambridge University Press.

Mohr, D.C. (2010). *The stress and mood management program for individuals with multiple sclerosis: Workbook.* New York: Oxford University Press.

13

Obstetric and Gynecological Conditions

PAMELA A. GELLER   ALEXA BONACQUISTI

Learning Objectives

In this chapter you will:

- Learn about common mental health symptoms that are associated with ob/gyn conditions.

- Understand the role of health psychologists working with women who have ob/gyn conditions.

- Learn about health behaviour changes during pregnancy.

- Become familiar with the application of health psychology principles to clinical cases of two women with ob/gyn conditions.

Introduction

Many women receive primary and preventive health-care services within obstetrical and gynecological (ob/gyn) settings. Women can present with a wide range of needs and concerns spanning prenatal and postpartum care, sexual health and functioning, chronic pelvic pain, perimenopause/menopause, and genitourinary cancers. In addition to assessment and treatment of gynecological conditions and supervision of pregnancy, women may receive contraception, immunizations, routine screenings, and management of chronic and benign disease. A number of variables influence the experiences of women in ob/gyn settings, and various mental health conditions often emerge around pregnancy and childbearing and are **co-morbid** with other ob/gyn concerns (Curbow, Khoury, & Weisman, 1998; Farr, Bitsko, Hayes, & Dietz, 2010). A role for clinical health psychologists with expertise in women's health to work with women receiving ob/gyn care is emerging.

Following a brief discussion of contextual issues and the role of health psychologists in ob/gyn care, we discuss mental health issues that commonly appear within ob/gyn settings for women during the childbearing years and beyond. We begin with a discussion of the psychological experiences and management of infertility. Following this, we provide an overview of mental health issues surrounding pregnancy, childbirth, pregnancy loss, and menopause. Potential mental health symptoms and health behaviour changes required for such issues as gestational diabetes and prenatal smoking cessation are commonly addressed by health psychologists. For each area discussed, the specific psychological and psychiatric consequences are described along with prevalence rates and relevant information on psychological intervention.

Psychosocial/Contextual Factors

Many reproductive health concerns are associated with mental health issues such as depression and anxiety, relationship challenges, shame and body image, and specific challenges related to women's roles and phase of life. In addition to ob/gyn conditions, understanding a woman's life phase and the interaction of **contextual factors** (i.e., relevant to culture, spirituality, politics, economics, biology, psychology, family and social relationships, as well as history of stressful life events such as trauma and work stress) are critical in order to provide the best treatment for women (Striepe & Coons, 2002). Women face unique psychosocial and mental health challenges, including stress from multiple roles (e.g., employee, spouse, mother) combined with primary caregiving responsibilities for children, elderly parents, and relatives. The demands of caregiving can have a significant impact on the caregiver. Health problems related to mood, sleep, eating, and blood pressure, as well as financial problems, and increased risk of chronic disease and mortality have been noted (Aranda & Knight, 1997; Berg, 2011; Pavalko & Woodbury, 2000; Remennick, 2001; Robinson, 1988). The health impact for lower-income, minority, or immigrant women with limited access to social resources, such as daycare centres and home-care attendants, is especially damaging (Aranda & Knight, 1997; Remennick, 2001).

Between two and four million women in the US (Tjaden & Thoennes, 1998; 2000), and more than 100,000 women in Canada (Sinha, 2012) are at risk for intimate partner violence each year (Mechanic, Weaver, & Resick, 2008). Low-income women, especially those who are unemployed and have low levels of social support, are more likely to experience symptoms of post-traumatic stress disorder (PTSD) (Hughes & Jones, 2000). In turn,

PHOTO 13.1 | Women face unique psychosocial challenges, such as stress from multiple roles (e.g., employee, spouse, mother), often combined with primary caregiving responsibilities for children, elderly parents, and relatives.

© Courtney Keating/iStockphoto

women who screen positive for PTSD tend to report more co-morbid anxiety disorders and depression, as well as domestic violence, during their lifetimes (Dobie et al., 2004). These clinical signs can also lead to drug and alcohol abuse and even suicide (Hughes & Jones, 2000). Women with histories of sexual trauma, including childhood sexual abuse, tend to experience routine ob/gyn visits and prenatal care visits as distressing. They also may have fears about pregnancy and childbirth because of traumatic memories that may be triggered (Issokson, 2004).

As with other populations discussed in this textbook, the theory underlying the research and clinical application of work with women is based on the biopsychosocial model, which forms the general foundation of health psychology theories. Using this theoretical model, health psychologists are increasingly present in women's health-care settings and are navigating multiple roles as provider, liaison, and educator to enhance team-based, comprehensive care (Geller, Nelson, Kornfield, & Silverman, 2014; see Table 13.1). They may conduct brief cognitive screens as well as more in-depth psychological assessments, consultation, facilitation of patient–provider communication, triage (prioritizing patients based on severity of symptoms), crisis management, and referrals for medication or to specialty inpatient or outpatient mental health treatment settings. Whether health psychologists are present as on-site providers in medical offices or as outpatient practitioners, responsibilities can include evidence-based treatment of individuals, couples, and families, developing strategies to promote treatment adherence and lifestyle modifications, and leading psycho-educational therapy groups. Helping women

to cope with infertility, perinatal loss, and postpartum depression are additional services within the purview of health psychologists. Further, they can provide training and consultation to staff, students, and medical residents and facilitate access to resources such as shelters and referrals, for example, for legal and financial counselling for patients experiencing domestic violence. Health psychologists can play a pivotal role in empowering female patients as they navigate the complex medical and emotional aspects of potentially stressful ob/gyn concerns.

Infertility

While many women become pregnant and go on to have successful pregnancies and births, some women are unable to conceive or to continue a pregnancy to full term without medical assistance. **Infertility**—the inability of a couple to achieve pregnancy after at least 12 months of consistent, unprotected intercourse—occurs in approximately 7.4 per cent of American couples (Chandra, Martinez, Mosher, Abma, & Jones, 2005), and in 11.5–15.7 per cent of Canadian couples (Bushnik, Cook, Yuzpe, Tough, & Collins, 2012). The most common treatment is in vitro fertilization (IVF), which involves fertilization of an ovum outside the body, followed by the transfer of viable embryos into the woman's uterus. Other treatment options include ovulation induction, surgeries, intrauterine insemination, and procedures involving third parties (e.g., surrogates) (Office on Women's Health, 2009). These treatments offer variable and unpredictable success rates, often less than

---

TABLE 13.1 | Role of Health Psychologists in Obstetrical and Gynecological Care

- Assess mental health symptoms, such as depressed mood and anxiety
- Evaluate risk factors, such as inadequate social support, stressful life events, mental health history
- Facilitate communication with medical providers and family/friends, as needed
- Provide psychological intervention to address mental health symptoms and risk factors for individuals, couples, and families
- Offer psycho-education and facilitate support groups
- Specific targets for intervention may include:
  - *Infertility*: development of coping strategies; treatment adherence
  - *Pregnancy*: education on pregnancy and mood; fears associated with childbirth; adherence to prescribed modified lifestyle regimens
  - *Postpartum*: promotion of exercise, sleep, nutrition; education on postpartum mood fluctuations; maternal–child attachment
  - *Pregnancy loss*: grief; maintaining connections to partners and existing children; anxiety associated with future pregnancies

50 per cent (Prince & Domar, 2013). Moreover, they are costly and invasive, and can have many side effects.

Mental Health Issues

Given the demands associated with identifying, coping with, and treating infertility, the experience can be extremely distressing (Prince & Domar, 2013). A diagnosis of infertility often results in a range of psychological consequences, with adjustment and anxiety disorders among the most prevalent. Among women presenting for infertility treatment, Chen and colleagues (2004) found that 40 per cent met diagnostic criteria for a psychiatric disorder, with anxiety and depressive disorders being common; however, depression may be seen more often among women with a history of depressive symptoms (Burns, 2007). Among women who endure treatment failures or loss of pregnancies that result from infertility treatment, grief is common, making it important to differentiate normative grieving from depression. In addition, women who experience infertility also experience stress related to interpersonal, romantic, and sexual relationships; feelings of inadequacy; loss of control; and loss of hope for becoming a parent in the

---

⊞ IN PRACTICE
Anxiety about Fertility

Amy is a 37-year-old woman who currently lives with Dominic, her husband of 14 years. Amy is a defence attorney, and Dominic is a partner at an accounting firm. While Amy is satisfied with many aspects of her life, she and Dominic have been struggling with infertility for the past five years. They delayed childbearing to focus on their careers, but then had difficulty becoming pregnant. After two years of trying, they decided to use assisted reproductive technologies and were successful in achieving pregnancy twice, but both pregnancies ended in miscarriages. Recently, their last cycle of IVF failed, requiring them to decide to initiate another cycle or to explore other options, including remaining childless.

Amy's primary reason for seeking mental health treatment is that she has been plagued with excessive worry for approximately the past eight months. She reported that she has been a perfectionist and a "worrier" her whole life, but that recently the anxiety has become "unbearable" and has resulted in physical symptoms. Amy stated that she worries about everything, including her work performance, her relationship with Dominic, and her inability to have children. She reported regret regarding past decisions related to childbearing, worrying that she had done something to compromise her ability to have children, and has had physical symptoms, including restlessness, difficulty concentrating, irritability, and sleep disturbances.

Amy reported that her worries have become excessive in that she cannot concentrate at work and finds herself arguing with Dominic and her family and friends because of her irritability and lack of sleep. She indicated she is increasingly upset with Dominic, as he does not seem to want a child with the same intensity as she does, and she reported that this makes her feel alone and unsupported. She feels consumed by the anxiety, as if it were out of control. She is concerned that if she and Dominic attempt another round of IVF, she will be unable to become pregnant or carry a baby to term. She is stricken with anxiety at the thought of remaining child-free, and has continual worries related to her future and who will care for her and Dominic in their old age if they do not have children. Though self-described as a lifelong "worrier," Amy denied a history of any mental disorders. Still, there is evidence that she may have suffered from considerable anxiety during her early twenties when she was applying to law school. It seems that her worries are exacerbated in times of stress. She denied past or current suicidal ideation.

Clinical Impressions

It appears that Amy is experiencing significant anxiety symptoms and excessive worry, primarily centred on her struggles with infertility, but potentially encompassing other areas of her life as well. The infertility diagnosis, failed IVF cycles, and miscarriages were extremely traumatic and stressful for her, which explains the exacerbation of her worries and anxious thoughts. Given Amy's history and the symptoms she described, she may meet criteria for an anxiety disorder. A health psychologist could help Amy cope with and overcome her anxiety and stress.

future (Burns, 2007), all of which can influence psychological adjustment and coping. Verhaak et al. (2005) demonstrated that the emotional adjustment of women following an unsuccessful IVF treatment cycle is significantly better for those with social support, highlighting that support may be an important protective factor.

Accurate psychological assessments are critical in identifying women's potential responses, including coping strategies and treatment adherence. This is especially important among women with prior histories of mental disorders, as they may be at greater risk for psychological symptoms surrounding an infertility diagnosis (Burns, 2007). Specific measures, such as the Fertility Problem Inventory (Newton, Sherrard, & Glavac, 1999) and the Fertility Quality of Life tool (Boivin, Takefman, & Braverman, 2011) have been developed for the assessment of infertility-related distress. Psychological intervention can target symptom reduction and encourage women to engage their social support system to improve psychological outcomes.

Pregnancy

Pregnancy includes the fertilization and development of one or more embryos in a woman's uterus. Childbirth occurs on average approximately 38 weeks after conception, or 40 weeks from the start of the last menstrual period. This time frame is divided into three phases, or trimesters, which refer to the different stages of prenatal development. The first trimester carries the highest risk of miscarriage (natural death of embryo or fetus) and physical symptoms, such as nausea and fatigue (Attard et al., 2002). Early diagnostic testing (e.g., chorionic villus sampling) that may identify genetic abnormalities may be conducted at this time. During the second trimester, the development of the fetus can be monitored more easily via sonography, and diagnostic testing may be conducted by amniocentesis. The point when the fetus can survive outside of the mother's uterus (with or without medical assistance) begins early in the third trimester.

In addition to excitement and joy, some women may experience a range of concerns, fears, and even mental health symptoms around the time of childbearing. Depression can occur during the **antenatal** and **postnatal** periods regardless of the outcome of the pregnancy (see Figure 13.1). Having a healthy pregnancy may

PHOTO 13.2 | Excitement and joy are common responses to pregnancy.

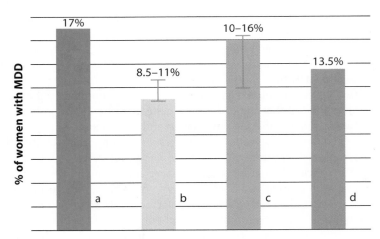

Note: This graph provides estimates of MDD as a relative comparison; it is a compilation of findings from various studies with differences in measurement and sample size.

⊢——⊣ = range

FIGURE 13.1 | Estimated prevalence of major depressive disorder (MDD) among childbearing women.
Sources: a: Chen et al. (2004); b: Gaynes et al. (2005); c: Austin et al. (2010); O'Hara & Swain (1996); d: Kessler et al. (1993).

require lifestyle or health behaviour changes, which can contribute to stress. When pregnancy spontaneously ends in miscarriage or stillbirth, grief may result. Clinical health psychologists have the opportunity to assist in the prevention, assessment, and treatment of adverse reactions during and following pregnancy, and can aid women in preparing for childbirth and adjusting to subsequent life changes and challenges.

Prenatal Mental Health Issues

During the major hormonal and psychosocial changes that happen during the time of pregnancy and child-bearing, depressive and anxiety symptoms can occur or worsen for many women (e.g., Glover, 2011; Vesga-Lopez et al., 2008). Similar to same-aged non-childbearing women, 8.5 per cent to 11 per cent of pregnant women suffer from depressive disorders in the antenatal period (Gaynes et al., 2005; Koleva, Stuart, O'Hara, & Bowman-Reif, 2011). However, the potential negative consequences to fetal development, birth outcomes, and maternal health make antenatal depression distinctive. While severe depression appears less often in the prenatal period than postpartum (Jones & Cantwell, 2010), risk increases for pregnant women with personal and family histories of mood disorders (Jones & Craddock, 2001; Viguera et al., 2011). Risk for depression during pregnancy may be further increased for women who stop taking antidepressant medication due to pregnancy (Cohen et al., 2006).

General anxiety symptoms frequently occur with depressive symptoms during pregnancy, particularly for first-time mothers (Buist, Gotman, & Yonkers, 2011). Specific anxiety disorders such as obsessive-compulsive disorder (OCD) and panic disorder also appear or worsen throughout the **perinatal period** (e.g., Abramowitz et al., 2010; Austin et al., 2010; Mauri et al., 2010). Some pregnant women experience anticipatory anxiety about childbirth. Women who previously experienced a delivery that was particularly painful, traumatic, and/ or involved medical complications or neonatal death may express their fears of childbirth in the form of PTSD or OCD symptoms (Abramowitz et al., 2010; Saisto, Salmela-Aro, Nurmi, Könönen, & Halmesmäki, 2001).

Maternal anxiety has been associated with various pregnancy complications and outcomes, such as preterm delivery, low birth weight, pre-eclampsia (high blood pressure and excess protein in urine), emergency Caesarean section, postpartum depression, and problems with infant–maternal attachment (Berle et al., 2005). Of growing concern is that some women attempt to avoid the experience and fears associated with vaginal delivery by requesting a Caesarean delivery without a valid medical reason. Given the substantial risks associated with Caesarean deliveries as well as the financial costs, recovery time, and ethical issues raised, these deliveries remain controversial (MacDorman, Menacker, & Declercq, 2008).

Health psychologists working within ob/gyn settings can evaluate pregnant women for risk factors and current depressive and anxiety symptoms during their prenatal and six-week postpartum visits. More frequent assessments can be completed for women with notable risk factors (e.g., a personal history of a psychiatric disorder and/or stopping psychotropic medication during pregnancy), and preventive interventions can be implemented (Novick & Flynn, 2013). Early identification of symptoms allows for earlier treatment. Treatment options effective during non-reproductive times are effective during pregnancy and help reduce potential pregnancy-related complications (Gossier, 2010; Kuehn, 2010; Sockol, Epperson, & Barber, 2011). Traditional cognitive behavioural approaches and interpersonal psychotherapy (IPT), a therapy targeting relational issues, have been shown to be effective with childbearing women (O'Hara, Stuart, Gorman, & Wenzel, 2000; Sockol et al., 2011).

Health psychologists can educate women and families that, while some anxiety in the perinatal period may be normal, moderate or severe symptoms of depression or anxiety that interfere with functioning are serious concerns. Psychologists can promote adherence to prescribed lifestyle changes while also managing the emotional and physical challenges associated with pregnancy and pending parenthood. Psychologists also can work with women and their partners to develop realistic plans for labour and delivery. Furthermore, teaching couples to incorporate relaxation and guided imagery techniques has been associated with anxiety reduction, fewer Caesarean deliveries, and shorter durations of labour (Saisto et al., 2001; Sjögren & Thomassen, 1997).

Health Behaviour Changes during Pregnancy

Pregnancy often requires maternal health behaviour changes to safeguard the health of the fetus and to promote the woman's physical health. Motivation to make health behaviour changes may be greater during pregnancy due to the mother's attachment to her unborn child (Alhusen, Gross, Hayat, Woods, & Sharps, 2012).

Nonetheless, initiating and maintaining health behaviour changes during pregnancy can be difficult and stressful. Moreover, conditions that require behaviour modification during pregnancy (such as those discussed below) may result in future health problems, further adding to a mother's stress during pregnancy (Geller, 2004).

Gestational Diabetes Mellitus

Gestational diabetes mellitus (GDM) is defined as glucose intolerance of varying degrees and severity that is identified during pregnancy (WHO, 1999; also see Chapter 10). The health risks associated with GDM can be dangerous for both mother and child, making a diagnosis particularly distressing for pregnant women (Geller, 2004). Women with GDM may be more likely to develop type 2 diabetes later in life (Canadian Diabetes Association, 2012). **Macrosomia**, or excessive birth weight, is a significant risk for infants born to mothers with GDM, resulting in an increased risk for obesity and type 2 diabetes (American Diabetes Association, 2012; Canadian Diabetes Association, 2012). To reduce the risk of negative health outcomes, significant behavioural changes are recommended during pregnancy, including adherence to a specific diet, scheduled physical activity, daily blood glucose monitoring, and insulin injections (American Diabetes Association, 2012). Adherence may be challenging during pregnancy when women are already confronted with a number of other physical and emotional changes. Lydon et al. (2012) found that relative to women without GDM, those with GDM experienced more pregnancy "hassles," depressive symptoms, and elevated levels of diabetes-related stress, suggesting that psychological distress is more prevalent in women with GDM. Health psychologists can contribute to the implementation of behavioural interventions to reduce the prevalence of GDM among women at risk (see Chapter 10).

Smoking Cessation

It is estimated that 18 per cent of adult American women and 20 per cent of Canadian women aged 15 and older currently smoke cigarettes (Schiller, Lucas, Ward, & Peregoy, 2012; Health Canada, 2002). Of these, 10.7 per cent of American women and 11 per cent of Canadian women smoked during at least one pregnancy (Martin et al., 2007; Health Canada, 2002). During pregnancy, tobacco smoking causes significant health risks for mothers and infants. Severe health effects from smoking include coronary heart disease, stroke, lung cancer, chronic obstructive lung diseases, and death

(CDC, 2012). Negative pregnancy and infant outcomes include low birth weight, miscarriage, preterm birth, and fetal growth retardation (Lumley et al., 2009). These risks make smoking cessation a significant public health concern. Most importantly, smoking is a modifiable behaviour; its negative health effects on mothers and infants are potentially preventable (Lumley et al., 2009). Women may be more likely to cease smoking during pregnancy (Curry, McBride, Grothaus, Lando, & Pirie, 2001). Moreover, health-care providers may have multiple opportunities to emphasize smoking cessation during the interaction pregnant women have with the health-care system and may more easily succeed with women experiencing increased motivation to ensure the health of their infant (DiClemente, Dolan-Mullen, & Windsor, 2000). Despite these considerations, pregnant women still may struggle with an addictive habit. Psychological symptoms, such as depression, may pose an obstacle for those who attempt to quit (Blalock, Fouladi, Wetter, & Cinciripini, 2005). Therefore, interventions should address the perceived barriers to smoking cessation, and should promote smoking cessation as early in pregnancy as possible (DiClemente et al., 2000). Non-pharmacological interventions that have demonstrated effectiveness are often individual-based, and include cognitive behaviour therapy, motivational interviewing, support and encouragement, incentives corresponding to cessation, and advice and counselling using written or electronic resources, or telephone calls (Lumley et al., 2009).

Pregnancy Loss

Regardless of whether a pregnancy is planned or wanted, the experience of a perinatal loss is stressful and may significantly impact mental health. Spontaneous abortion (miscarriage) refers to the death of a fetus prior to 20 weeks of completed gestation. Miscarriage occurs in approximately 15 per cent of clinically recognized pregnancies, with risk of miscarriage increasing by maternal age (Andersen, Wohlfahrt, Christens, Olsen, & Melbye, 2000). Stillbirth, defined as fetal death after 20 weeks of completed gestation, occurs in approximately 1 per cent of pregnancies where there is a single fetus and much more frequently in **multiple pregnancies** (i.e., twins, triplets, or more fetuses) (Evans, Ayoub, Shalhoub, Feldman, & Yaron, 2002). Overall, Black women have a 2.2 times greater risk of stillbirth compared to White women, with specific factors that contribute to risk varying by race and gestational age (Willinger, Ko, & Reddy, 2009).

Pregnancy loss is an unanticipated and often traumatic experience that can result in considerable pain and discomfort for many women. In some cases, it may even be life-threatening (Grimes, 2006; Saraiya, Green, Berg, Hopkins, Koonin, & Atrash, 1999). Sadness, grief, guilt, anger, and self-reproach, as well as fears about one's ability to have a baby in the future, can result from this experience (Toedter, Lasker, & Janssen, 2001; Borg & Lasker, 1981).

Pregnancy losses frequently are minimized or not acknowledged by society. The experience of **disenfranchised grief**, combined with the fact that women and their partners may grieve differently (incongruent grief), may further contribute to social isolation and distress. Even medical providers may not fully recognize the loss or the range of responses a woman might experience, particularly with early miscarriage. As such, they may not be prepared to provide the needed support, information, or referrals, and when pressured for time, may not formally evaluate a woman's individual psychological responses (Geller, Psaros, & Kornfield, 2010).

In addition to grief, depressive reactions are also evident following pregnancy loss (see Klier, Geller, & Ritsher, 2002). Controlled studies have clearly documented that miscarriage is a risk factor for depressive symptoms and disorders (e.g., Janssen, Cuisinier, Hoogduin, & de Graauw, 1996; Neugebauer et al., 1997). History of depression increases risk for a recurrent episode following pregnancy loss, as does having no other living children at the time of the loss.

Feelings of anxiety may be increased by a pregnancy loss. For example, concerns about continued bleeding/discharge, potential undetected medical illness, or underlying genetic factors can be worrisome and alarming. Studies employing comparison groups suggest that anxiety levels may be even more elevated than depressive symptoms immediately after loss, and that the elevation may be sustained for at least four months (e.g., Lee & Slade, 1996; Thapar & Thapar, 1992). Elevated risks for a recurrent episode of OCD (Geller, Klier, & Neugebauer, 2001) and for PTSD (e.g., Engelhard, van den Hout, & Arntz, 2001) following loss also have been documented.

Approximately half of women experiencing perinatal loss become pregnant again within one year, with these subsequent pregnancies involving heightened maternal anxiety relative to first pregnancies (Armstrong & Hutti, 1998; Theut, Pedersen, Zaslow, & Rabinovich, 1988). Children born under these circumstances have been referred to as "shadow children," as they live in the shadow of siblings they never knew and who may be continuously idealized and mourned by their parents (e.g., Hughes, Turton, Hopper, McGauley, & Fonagy, 2001).

Clinical health psychologists can assist women with maintaining intimate connection to their partners and existing children, as well as attachment to future children. Women may be responsive to opportunities to promote healing through meaning-making and creation of mementos and rituals to connect, grieve, and remember. Women also may need to address feelings of self-blame and of anger towards others who are pregnant. Discussing options regarding what and how to communicate the loss experience to extended family members, friends, and co-workers, and helping women anticipate and plan for psychological responses in the year(s) following the loss—particularly on the due date or on the anniversary of the loss—can be beneficial (Jaffe & Diamond, 2011).

Better communication with health-care providers may increase women's satisfaction with care after loss (Geller, Psaros, & Kornfield, 2010). Care providers

PHOTO 13.3 | Couples' therapy is sometimes used to assist people in coping with perinatal loss.

© ilkeryuksel-/iStockphoto

can validate a woman's loss as real and her grief as legitimate, as well as discuss physiological changes that can occur after the pregnancy loss, the cause of the pregnancy loss (if known), and implications for future reproductive plans. Moreover, evaluating psychological symptoms and providing referrals for treatment when needed may prevent lasting psychological consequences and may reduce anxiety in subsequent pregnancies.

Individualized interventions may take the form of individual or couples cognitive behavioural therapy, such as mindfulness-based approaches or IPT. Participation in bereavement support groups can be helpful. Internet resources can be a source of information for women as well as for care providers, and social media may be a source of support (e.g., Geller, 2012; Geller, Psaros, & Kerns, 2006; Gold, Boggs, Mugisha, & Palladino, 2011). Greater understanding of ethnic-racial and cultural differences in coping following pregnancy loss, as well as the role of factors such as religion and spirituality, would help psychologists better tailor interventions (e.g., Mann, McKeown, Bacon, Vesselinov, & Bush, 2008). The National Board for Certification of Hospice and Palliative Nurses in the US recently developed the first certification examination for professionals (including psychologists) providing perinatal loss care, which demonstrates a growing recognition of the special needs of this population.

Postpartum Responses

From a mental health perspective, dysphoria, postpartum depression (PPD), and psychosis are the most common postnatal responses, usually beginning within 30 days following childbirth (Austin et al., 2010; Llewellyn, Stowe, & Nemeroff, 1997; O'Hara & Swain, 1996). Postpartum dysphoria, or "the baby blues," is mild and temporary, with symptoms of tearfulness and depressed mood peaking about five days after childbirth. Primarily attributed to hormonal fluctuations, 26 per cent to 85 per cent of all mothers appear to experience postpartum blues regardless of socio-cultural context or environmental factors (Henshaw, 2003; Kumar, 1994). The wide range can be attributed to differing assessment techniques used across studies (Austin et al., 2010; O'Hara, Schlechte, Lewis, & Varner, 1991; Wisner, Parry, & Piontek, 2002).

PPD resembles other forms of major depressive disorder in its symptoms, severity, and persistence, although there can be a greater frequency of anxiety, somatic complaints, and sleep disturbances (Yonkers, Vigod, & Ross, 2011). Occurring in 10–16 per cent of women in the first six months postpartum, onset usually is within two weeks following childbirth (Austin et al., 2010; O'Hara & Swain, 1996). Community-based surveys—many of which employed the Edinburgh Postnatal Depression Scale (EPDS) (Cox, Holden, & Sagovsky, 1987)—reveal that rates of PPD are similar in different countries (Kumar, 1994). When other assessment tools are used, and depending on how the time frame of the postnatal period is defined, estimates vary. The incidence of PPD is greater in women who are economically disadvantaged (Gaynes et al., 2005).

Following childbirth, particularly after the birth of the first child, major physiological changes occur and women must adjust to changing social and personal circumstances. Other life events, limited social support, and personality factors also may play a role (O'Hara & Swain, 1996; Robertson, Grace, Wallington, & Stewart, 2004). Unrealistic expectations for oneself and about motherhood, such as the belief that maternal–infant bonding occurs instantly and is immediately positive and fulfilling, also may contribute to PPD (Lee, 1998). In addition to psychosocial

© MachineHeadz/iStockphoto

PHOTO 13.4 | Postpartum depression sometimes follows childbirth.

⊞ IN PRACTICE

Postpartum Depression

Crystal is a 26-year-old single mother who gave birth to her first child, Timothy, six weeks ago. During her postpartum medical appointment, Crystal completed the Edinburgh Postnatal Depression Scale (EPDS) in the waiting room. She scored 22 out of 30, indicating possible depression. Crystal's physician reviewed her results, and asked how she had been feeling since Timothy's birth. Crystal said that her mood has been low; most of the time she "doesn't want to get out of bed" and she "is tired all the time." Crystal is concerned because she finds herself crying frequently, but cannot articulate a specific reason for her sadness. She indicated that she no longer wants to see her friends, watch TV, or go shopping, which are activities she usually enjoys. While she reported commitment to caring for Timothy's physical needs, she does not feel the "instant love that every mother should feel for her child." In addition, she stopped breast-feeding her son much earlier than she had intended, and reported that she often feels frustrated and has several bouts of tearfulness nearly every day where she feels hopeless and cannot identify the cause. During these times, she reported difficulty caring for Timothy and is fearful of being alone with him.

Most of Crystal's day is spent in bed or lying on the couch. She stated that she rarely feels hungry and has to force herself to eat. She noted that friends have commented how quickly she has lost the weight gained during pregnancy. She expressed difficulty concentrating and feels that she is "not a good mother." Though she denied suicidal ideation or a history of suicide attempts, she stated that lately she has been thinking a lot about death and "what it would be like." Crystal denied having a specific plan to kill herself, saying she is too tired.

Crystal reported that her symptoms began shortly after giving birth. She described the initial symptoms as mild sadness, which then progressed to more significant and severe symptoms within four weeks postpartum. Crystal is distressed because she believes her symptoms impair her ability to feel excited about motherhood and to care for Timothy. Because of her loss of interest and her fatigue, Crystal has withdrawn socially from friends and family, and remains unemployed and reluctant to leave her home. This is problematic for a number of reasons, but particularly considering her status as a new mother, it is important for Crystal to adhere to medical appointments and to remain motivated to bond with and care for her son.

Clinical Impressions

It appears that Crystal is experiencing significant depressive symptoms that are impacting her ability to function and influencing her thoughts and feelings about motherhood. It is important to consider that the onset of these symptoms was shortly after birth, but that symptoms progressively worsened, becoming most severe approximately four weeks after delivery. The nature of the symptoms and the time frame would suggest that Crystal is experiencing postpartum depression. Another psychosocial factor to consider is Crystal's inadequate social support system and how that may be relevant to address her current diagnosis. A health psychologist could assist Crystal in overcoming her depression and improving her quality of life.

stressors and hormonal shifts, personal psychiatric history is a significant and well-documented risk factor. A prior episode of PPD or depression during a previous pregnancy elevates a women's risk of PPD by approximately 50–62 per cent, and 20–30 per cent of women with a history of major depressive disorder prior to conception go on to develop PPD (O'Hara & Swain, 1996; Viguera et al., 2011).

Many psychopharmacological interventions may be appropriate for a subset of women. Some options are deemed safe for women who are breast-feeding in addition to alternative approaches (Gossier, 2010; Marchand & Thatcher, 2008). Cognitive behavioural interventions and therapies taking a relational approach can be quite effective (O'Hara et al., 2000; Sockol et al., 2011). In addition to standard means of evaluating depressive symptoms, clinical psychologists might also employ the EPDS or Beck and Gable's (2000) Postpartum Depression Screening Scale (Boyd, Le, & Somberg, 2005). As an alternative or adjunct to individual treatment, support groups to assist women with overall adjustment to motherhood or specific parenting challenges can help to improve functioning.

Occurring in one to two of every 1,000 deliveries, postpartum psychosis is the rarest yet most severe of

© zergkind/iStockphoto

PHOTO 13.5 | Following childbirth, major physiological changes occur and adjustment associated with changing social and personal circumstances is required, particularly after the birth of the first child.

causing harm to her fetus or infant. Differing from postpartum psychosis, women with OCD recognize the thoughts as unreasonable and unwanted and avoid acting on them, although fear, anxiety, and sometimes avoidance or refusal to care for the newborn is evident (Ross & McLean, 2006). Notably, independent of OCD or postpartum psychosis, over 40 per cent of women with PPD and 34–65 per cent of new parents in healthy community samples report experiencing obsessive thoughts about causing inadvertent or intentional harm to their newborns (Abramowitz et al., 2010; Jennings, Ross, Popper, & Elmore, 1999; Wisner, Peindl, Gigliotti, & Hanusa, 1999).

In addition to limited maternal attachment in the postpartum period, the postnatal responses described above can have negative consequences for the developing child. These negative consequences affect the child's eating and sleeping (Righetti-Veltema, Conne-Perréard, Bousquet, & Manzano, 2002; Swanson, Flynn, Wilburn, Marcus, & Armitage, 2010), as well as promoting cognitive deficits and emotional and behavioural disturbances (O'Connor, Heron, Golding, Beveridge, & Glover, 2002; West & Newman, 2003). When compared to women without mental health complications, women experiencing postnatal mood and/or anxiety symptoms are less likely to initiate and more likely to stop breast-feeding early in infancy (Field, Hernandez-Reif, & Feijo, 2002; Watkins, Meltzer-Brody, Zolnoun, & Stuebe, 2011), more likely to delay or avoid vaccination of their children (Turner, Boyle, & O'Rourke, 2003), and more likely to skip pediatrician visits and to require acute outpatient or emergency room care for the baby (Flynn, Davis, Marcus, Cunningham, & Blow, 2004).

Menopause

Menopause refers to a woman's final menstrual period, signifying the end of fertility and childbearing years. On average, women reach menopause between ages 40

the postpartum conditions that occur across all societies (Kendell, Chalmers, & Platz, 1987; Kumar, 1994; Yonkers et al., 2011). Onset typically occurs within the first 72 hours to two weeks after childbirth, but risk remains high for several months (Kendell et al., 1987). Although prognosis is much more positive, symptoms mirror those of schizophrenia, with the content of hallucinations and delusions often thematically associated with pregnancy, childbirth, or the newborn. Thoughts of suicide or of harming one's infant are not uncommon, but homicide is rare. As with PPD, a personal or family history of mental disorder places one at risk for postpartum psychosis. An episode of postpartum psychosis places a woman at greater risk during future pregnancies, and over half of women with postpartum psychosis also meet criteria for PPD (Kendell et al., 1987). Inpatient psychiatric treatment is frequently required, which can be particularly challenging for women with newborns and their families.

Symptoms of anxiety also may be evident in the postnatal period, including obsessive thoughts that may heighten and require diagnostic intervention. With OCD, intrusive thoughts often revolve around the mother and 60. However, prior to the cessation of menstruation, women experience perimenopause, which is characterized by a process of physiological and psychological changes that accompany aging. Definitions of menopause and the transitional period of perimenopause are somewhat inconsistent. Researchers have attempted to determine standard definitions and stages, but the experience of menopause varies widely among women (Derry & Dillaway, 2013).

During menopause women may experience a variety of physical and psychological health issues and changes. Common signs and symptoms of menopause have been noted across racial-ethnic groups, including physiological menopausal symptoms, such as hot flashes, night sweats, weight gain, insomnia, fatigue, and sexual changes, and psychological symptoms, such as depression and mood changes (Avis et al., 2001). Women must also cope with stress that may result from managing these symptoms. Psychologically, women may confront their feelings about the cessation of fertility and what it means to move to the next stage in their life. Often this process is influenced by negative societal and cultural attitudes about aging (Derry & Dillaway, 2013).

Health psychologists can assist women during and following the transition to menopause by providing information on what to expect during menopause, by "normalizing" the experience, and by helping women manage their symptoms using cognitive behavioural approaches (Derry & Dillaway, 2013). In addition, health psychologists can promote coping by helping women explore their own perceptions, appraisals, and attitudes surrounding menopause. Women with more negative attitudes towards menopause report more symptoms (Ayers, Forshaw, & Hunter, 2010), suggesting that psychological well-being may play an important role in women's adjustment and transition to menopause.

Future Directions

Despite the prevalence of psychological distress and concerns among women receiving ob/gyn care, psychological and behavioural interventions with this population have been understudied. Further research using larger sample sizes, randomized designs, and consistent assessment tools is warranted. Moreover, applying empirical research to practice is essential to advancing treatment options in this field. Additional research regarding the psychological responses of fathers to events such as childbirth or pregnancy loss, for example, would be beneficial. For women experiencing severe perinatal mental health issues, further development and implementation of comprehensive treatment programs that provide efficacious treatment and facilitate women's connection with their newborns and social networks—such as the first North American Perinatal Psychiatry Inpatient Unit, at the University of North Carolina (see Vogel, 2011)—hold great promise to reduce the burden of adverse mental health responses during this important life phase.

SUMMARY

Health psychologists increasingly address psychological issues associated with reproductive health and other ob/gyn conditions across the lifespan of women. A number of psychosocial variables influence the experiences of women receiving ob/gyn care, and mental health conditions often emerge around pregnancy and childbirth. Infertility and pregnancy loss, as well as the time during pregnancy and postpartum, can be particularly stressful and give rise to symptoms in a subset of women. Health psychologists can provide valuable services to promote medical adherence and behavioural management of various conditions during the perinatal period. The many psychological, social, and contextual factors that are relevant to successful treatment and management of women's reproductive health and well-being can be targets of psychological intervention. This stage of life further highlights the significant potential contributions of health psychologists to improve medical outcomes, patient satisfaction with medical care, and quality of life for women and families.

Critical Thought Questions

1. What are some ways in which health psychologists can work with women receiving ob/gyn care?
2. What are common psychological responses to various ob/gyn-related conditions such as infertility or pregnancy loss?

3. What types of mental health issues may arise during pregnancy? In the postnatal period?

Recommended Reading

Geller, P.A., Nelson, A.R., Kornfield, S.L., & Silverman, D.G. (2014). Women's health: Obstetrics & gynecology. In C.M. Hunter, C.L. Hunter, & R. Kessler (Eds.), *Handbook of clinical psychology in medical settings: Evidence-based assessment and intervention*. New York: Springer.

Jaffe, J., & Diamond, M. (2011).*Reproductive trauma: Psychotherapy with infertility and pregnancy loss clients*. Washington: American Psychological Association.

Spiers, M.V., Geller, P.A., & Kloss, J.D. (Eds.). (2013). *Women's health psychology*. New York: John Wiley & Sons.

Wenzel, A. (2010). *Anxiety in childbearing women: diagnosis and treatment*. Washington: American Psychological Association.

14

Asthma and Chronic Obstructive Pulmonary Disease

THOMAS RITZ | THOMAS JANSSENS

Learning Objectives

In this chapter you will:

- Gain basic information about the two most common chronic respiratory conditions, asthma and chronic obstructive pulmonary disease (COPD).

- Acquire knowledge about different ways psychological factors can impact asthma and COPD, either by direct influences on airway functioning or by indirect influences on health behaviour.

- Find an inventory of different instruments that are available to assess psychological aspects of asthma and COPD.

- Learn about treatment strategies for asthma and COPD from a biopsychosocial perspective.

Asthma

Definition, Prevalence, and Medical Treatment

Marcel Proust, the early twentieth-century French novelist, documented in his writings his multiple physical symptoms. However, the manifestation of his airway problems suggests a diagnosis of asthma, an illness with an organic basis that creates substantial suffering (see In Focus box). The assessment of his father, who was a physician, reflected a prominent struggle in the acceptance of asthma as an organic disease—in its extreme, it was interpreted as a nervous affliction that would require only psychotherapy. This notion was alive in some of the psychoanalytical approaches to asthma (for a review, see Weiner, 1977), most prominently moulded by Alexander (1950), who interpreted asthma as the "suppressed cry for the mother." Contemporary academics in health psychology, pulmonology, and allergy have moved far beyond these early views by using rigorous empirical methods. They are uncovering an ever-evolving picture of a complex organic disorder that is affected by psychological factors both in its pathophysiology and its management.

Disease Manifestation and Physiology

Asthma is a common chronic inflammatory disease of the airways that is characterized by a variety of recurring respiratory symptoms and pathophysiological changes that include obstruction, inflammation, hyper-responsiveness, and remodelling of the airways (NHLBI/NAEPP, 2007; GINA, 2010). Of these phenomena, **airway inflammation** is thought to be the central pathophysiological process, although airway obstruction is most readily perceived by patients. It impedes proper airflow through the lungs and, thus, generates **dyspnea**, the characteristic unpleasant breathlessness. The bronchi are also hyper-responsive, showing more vigorous **bronchoconstriction** (narrowing of the bronchi) in response to a range of **triggers**, such as allergens, physical exercise, air pollutants or airborne irritants, certain drugs (e.g., Aspirin), gastric reflux, cold air, upper airway infections, or psychological stress and emotions.

Inflammation that persists for years can lead to *airway remodelling*, which consists of changes in airway structure that are at least partly irreversible, such as a greater smooth muscle mass, enlargement and

IN FOCUS

Marcel Proust: From Letters to His Mother

"An attack of asthma of unbelievable violence and tenacity—such is the depressing balance sheet of my night, which it obliged me to spend on my feet in spite of the early hour at which I got up yesterday. Heaven knows what sort of day I shall have! ... There's some dust or other in my room, and an odour as well left no doubt by the hairdresser, which have nothing to do with this dreadful attack, but set it going every time I want to go in." (pp. 121–122)

"By the way, as they wanted to bring me back to the car, Constantin said it was all my imagination that cold air was bad for me, because Papa told everyone that there was nothing wrong with me and that asthma was purely imaginary. I know only too well when I awake here in the morning that it is very real, and it would be very nice of you if you could put something in your next letter like this: 'Your father was furious when he heard you'd been in a motor-car. You know how few the things are that are bad for you, but nothing is worse than a rush of cold air for your asthma.'" (p. 100)

Source: From *Marcel Proust: Letters to His Mother* by Marcel Proust (translated by George D. Painter). Published by Rider and Company. Reprinted by permission of The Random House Group Limited, and Edition PLON.

hyper-secretion of mucus glands, excessive blood vessel growth, and damage of the epithelium and underlying tissues. Failure to manage the condition adequately can lead to life-threatening situations or even death.

Asthma is increasingly viewed as a disease with heterogeneous manifestations and underlying physiological mechanisms. Traditionally, a childhood onset type with a stronger allergic background is distinguished from an adulthood onset type linked more with respiratory infections. Allergic processes are recognized as an important characteristic of asthma, but less than half of the patients actually show a hypersensitivity to specific allergens (Pearce, Pekkanen, & Beasley, 1999). Beyond that, exercise-associated, aspirin-sensitive, steroid-resistant, and severe phenotypes have been described. The causes of asthma are still poorly understood, but there is a consensus that specific interactions of genetic risk and environmental factors need to be considered

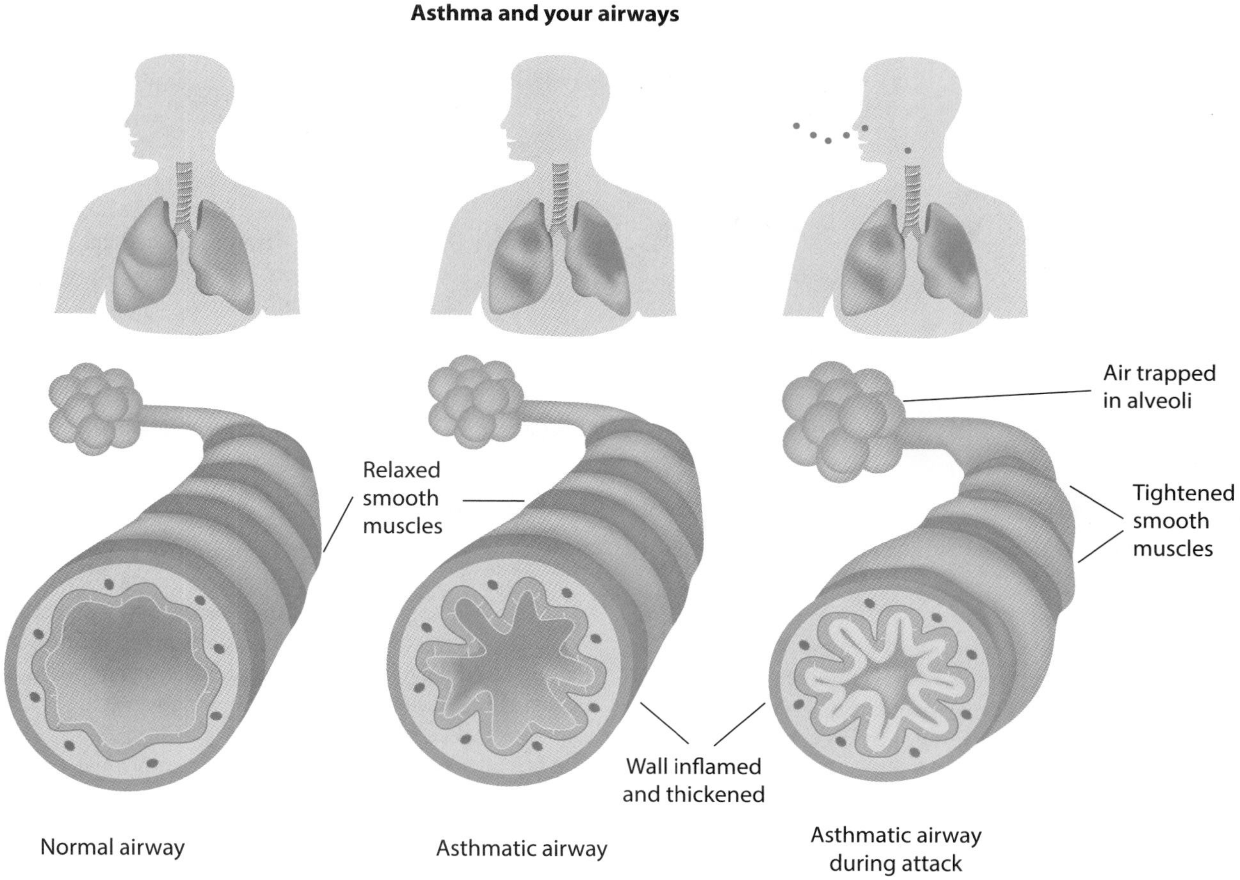

Asthma and your airways

FIGURE 14.1 | Airways in asthma are inflamed and thickened, mucus builds up, and smooth muscles contract, which narrows the airway passages. This causes symptoms of shortness of breath, chest tightness, coughing, and wheezing.

Source: Alila Medical Media/Shutterstock

(NHLBI/NAEPP, 2007). A number of genetic characteristics have been linked to asthma development and management outcomes, but, as with many other diseases, a complex interplay of a number of genes and environmental factors must be assumed (Vercelli, 2010).

Prevalence

Asthma can affect individuals of all ages, although a clear diagnosis is difficult in the first five years of life (Bush, 2007). It is now among the most common of chronic conditions in adult populations, and in children it is the most common chronic condition and among the most frequent reasons for hospital admissions. The prevalence of asthma has increased markedly in the last few decades, now affecting an estimated 300 million individuals worldwide, 30 million of these in the United States and 2.8 million in Canada (Braman, 2006; Statistics Canada, 2010). Asthma is more prevalent among low-income inner-city residents and in minority populations, in particular in African-American and Puerto Rican communities.

Medical Treatment

The first line of asthma treatment is pharmacological (NHLBI/NAEPP, 2007). Daily anti-inflammatory medication, mostly inhaled corticosteroids, is required for treatment of persistent asthma. This treatment often is combined with long-acting beta-adrenergic bronchodilators that mimic the effects of epinephrine on the airways and help prevent bronchoconstriction for 12–14 hours, particularly throughout the night. In addition to this maintenance medication, short-acting

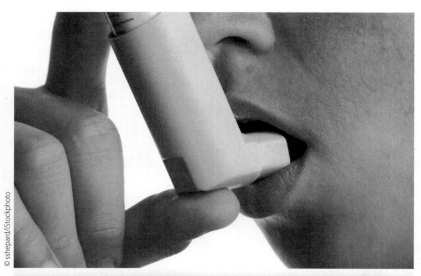

© sshepard/iStockphoto

PHOTO 14.1 | Inhalers are used in the management of asthma.

Direct Influences by Altered Nervous System Activity

Central nervous system activity can directly alter airway pathophysiology by immune, endocrine, or autonomic nervous systems pathways. Negative emotions have been shown to constrict the airways, exacerbate airway inflammation, and produce symptoms (Chen, Chim, Strunk, & Miller, 2007; Ritz, 2012). Various mechanisms have been considered for such influences, including parasympathetic discharge that constricts the airway smooth muscles and stress hormones leading to an immune system shift that emphasizes over-responding to allergens. Longitudinal research has also shown that, in children, negative life events predict asthma exacerbations within days (Sandberg, Jarvenpaa, Penttinen, Paton, & McCann, 2004). Hospitalizations and deaths from asthma have been associated with adverse life events and depression (Kolbe, Fergusson, Vamos, & Garrett, 2002; Miller & Strunk, 1989). Strong emotional expression, such as laughing or crying, may also trigger asthma symptoms through abrupt changes in breathing that irritate or dry out the hyper-reactive airways (Liangas, Morton, & Henry, 2003; Weinstein, 1984).

beta-adrenergic inhalers are used as rescue medication that relieves acute episodes of bronchoconstriction for 6–8 hours. Other types of medication are sometimes added to the maintenance medication schedule. These medications reduce allergic inflammation, bronchoconstriction, and hyper-responsiveness of the airways. High doses of oral or injected corticosteroids may be required in severe cases or disease **exacerbation**.

Asthma varies in severity from intermittent to severe and persistent. With greater severity, patient distress about symptoms and limitations in daily functioning can be considerable. Regardless of severity, the overarching aim of treatment is **asthma control**, which ideally is achieved with the right dose and combination of medications. However, despite substantial progress in the medical treatment and comprehensive guideline efforts for diagnosis and management (NHLBI/NAEPP, 2007; GINA, 2010), overall asthma control remains unsatisfactory. It is estimated that the overall cost of asthma in the US is $18.3 billion annually, which includes health care and lost productivity costs.

A sizable proportion of asthma patients (20–40 per cent) are also susceptible to bronchoconstrictive suggestions: when they inhale a substance that is suggested to induce bronchoconstriction, they will show clinically significant airway narrowing (Isenberg, Lehrer, & Hochron, 1992). Positive or negative suggestions (including placebo administrations or hypnosis) can also dampen or enhance airway hyper-reactivity to pharmacological substances, to allergens, or to exercise (Ritz, 2012). A higher prevalence of co-morbid psychological disorders, such as anxiety disorders, depression, and schizophrenia, have been shown in patients with asthma (Goodwin, Jacobi, & Thefeld, 2003; Lavoie, Boudreau, Plourde, Campbell, & Bacon, 2011; Pedersen, Benros, Agerbo, Børglum, & Mortensen, 2012). In addition to these direct influences on existing asthma, longitudinal epidemiological studies indicate that psychological factors contribute to the onset of asthma (Wright, 2010). For example, mothers' anxiety during pregnancy (Cookson, Granell, Joinson, Ben-Shlomo, & Henderson, 2009), early life adversity (Klinnert et al., 2001), or psychopathology (particularly panic disorder) in the first 20 years (Hasler et al., 2005) predict asthma onset.

Psychological Factors in Asthma

The empirical literature abounds with examples of the psychological impact on asthma (Lehrer, Isenberg, & Hochron, 1993). Commonly, psychological factors that directly influence the pathophysiology of asthma through altered nervous system activity are distinguished from indirect factors that influence asthma through health behaviours and disease management.

Indirect Influences by Altered Health Behaviour

The patient's day-to-day management of asthma is viewed as critical in achieving optimal asthma control. Interference with asthma management can thus exert indirect influences on asthma status. Across studies, 50 per cent of patients are estimated to show insufficient **adherence** to maintenance medication schedules and self-monitoring of signs of the disease (such as increases in symptoms and decline in lung function as monitored by diaries) (Bender, Milgrom, & Apter, 2003). Perception of critical symptoms and, thus, initiation of emergency measures are also compromised in a sizable number of patients by emotions, learning, focus of attention, and the environmental context (Janssens, Verleden, De Peuter, Van Diest, & Van den Bergh, 2009). Both over-perception and under-perception of symptoms can have adverse consequences, such as overuse or underuse of medication and health-care services. Imaging studies also suggest that perceptual deficits are manifested in altered central nervous system activity (von Leupoldt et al., 2009).

Illness perception and interpretation can also exert a powerful impact on asthma management efforts (Kaptein, Klok, Moss-Morris, & Brand, 2010): most prominently, misconceptions about medications (catastrophizing of benign side effects) or about the character of the disease as temporary. Urban minority populations have demonstrated substantial disparities in asthma treatment outcomes (Leong, Ramsey, & Celedón, 2012) due to multiple factors, including low socio-economic status, educational level, air pollution, psychosocial stressors, racial/ethnic discrimination, and, most likely, culture-specific biases in perceiving and managing asthma. African Americans tend to focus more on upper airway sensations when describing their symptoms (Hardie, Janson, Gold, Carrieri-Kohlman, & Boushey, 2000) and Puerto Rican communities tend to favour traditional home and herbal remedies for asthma (Koinis Mitchell et al., 2008). Poor general health behaviours, such as lack of physical activity, smoking, and suboptimal diet (obesity), also contribute to suboptimal asthma management outcomes in various ways (Eneli, Skybo, & Camargo, 2008; Millard, 2003; Thomson & Chaudhuri, 2009).

COPD

Definition, Prevalence, and Medical Treatment

Chronic obstructive pulmonary disease (COPD) is a respiratory condition characterized by persistent **airflow** **limitation** and lung inflammation (GOLD, 2011). The airflow limitation is caused by a combination of destruction of lung tissue (*emphysema*) and small airway disease (*obstructive bronchiolitis*), which often causes air to become trapped inside the airways (*airway hyperinflation*). It is associated with airway inflammation in response to exposure to noxious agents and is not fully reversible. COPD is often progressive, leading to increasing airflow limitation and worsening symptoms over time.

Dyspnea, the unpleasant sensation of breathlessness, is the cardinal physical symptom associated with COPD (Banzett et al., 2000; GOLD, 2011). It is a key determinant of quality of life in patients with COPD, due to its frightening unpleasantness and its limiting influence on daily activities (Banzett, Dempsey, O'Donnell, & Wamboldt, 2000; Hajiro et al., 1999). Other major symptoms are chronic cough and increased sputum (coughed-up lower airway mucus) production (GOLD, 2011). Symptom levels

PHOTO 14.2 | An oxygen concentrator is a medical device that produces oxygen-rich air by taking room air and concentrating it to approximately 95 per cent pure oxygen. The use of supplemental oxygen therapy is advised for patients with COPD who suffer from severely low oxygen levels.

are usually stable, although patients with COPD may experience episodes of *symptom exacerbation*. Frequent exacerbations are a risk factor for faster progression of the disease (Donaldson, Seemungal, Bhowmik, & Wedzicha, 2002).

Currently, COPD is the fifth leading cause of mortality worldwide (Mathers & Loncar, 2006), with a prevalence in adults age 40 or older of approximately 10 per cent, although self-reported diagnosis of COPD is about 6 per cent, suggesting under-diagnosis (Buist et al., 2007; GOLD, 2011). Prevalence rates increase with age and smoking history. Longitudinal studies show that prevalence of COPD is increasing (Gershon, Wang, Wilton, Raut, & To, 2010), and the World Health Organization has projected that by 2030 COPD will be the fourth leading cause of mortality (Mathers & Loncar, 2006).

Tobacco smoke is a major risk factor for the development of COPD, but other environmental exposures such as dusts, chemical agents and fumes, and fumes from biomass fuel stoves also are risk factors, as are genetic predispositions, pre-existing conditions such as

asthma, and the occurrence of severe respiratory infections in early childhood (GOLD, 2011).

Pharmacological treatment of COPD consists of bronchodilator medication, which reduces airway smooth muscle tone, airway hyperinflation, and dyspnea. Other types of medication, such as antibiotics and inhaled corticosteroids, are also used. In severe cases of COPD, oxygen therapy, lung volume reduction surgery, or lung transplantation may be necessary. Pharmacological and surgical treatments are often complemented by pulmonary rehabilitation to form a multidisciplinary rehabilitation program with an emphasis on physical exercise (Troosters, Casaburi, Gosselink, & Decramer, 2005).

Psychological Factors in COPD

Depression and anxiety are highly prevalent in patients with COPD. Clinical anxiety affects 10–19 per cent and clinical depression is found in 10–42 per cent of COPD patients (Maurer et al., 2008). Both anxiety and depression are associated with worse COPD outcomes such as lower exercise capacity and exercise tolerance (as measured by six-minute walking distance and ergometer peak workload), increased physical symptoms and functional limitations, and/or reductions in treatment adherence and quality of life (Eisner et al., 2010; Giardino et al., 2010b; von Leupoldt, Taube, Lehmann, Fritzsche, & Magnussen, 2011). Anxiety and depression also have been associated with greater risks of exacerbation and hospitalization (Dahlén & Janson, 2002; Xu et al., 2008). A recent meta-analysis suggests this may be limited to depression or co-morbid anxiety and depression, whereas anxiety is more associated with exacerbations treated outside the hospital (Laurin, Moullec, Bacon, & Lavoie, 2012). Subclinical states of dyspnea-related anxiety and specific catastrophic beliefs about dyspnea are also associated with stronger dyspnea in COPD (Carrieri-Kohlman et al., 2001; Janssens et al., 2011).

Several mechanisms have been proposed to account for such associations. Anxiety and depression may change the affective quality and perceived intensity of dyspnea. Negative affect increases dyspnea, both in patients and healthy populations (Bogaerts et al., 2005; von Leupoldt, Taube, Henkhus, Dahme, & Magnussen, 2010). Moreover, patients with COPD and co-morbid panic disorder show higher dyspnea ratings than patients with COPD without panic disorder and healthy controls when confronted with standardized resistors that restrict their airflow (Giardino et al., 2010a). The higher intensity and unpleasantness of

PHOTO 14.3 | Exercise training is an essential component of pulmonary rehabilitation in COPD.

Andersen Ross/Getty Images

dyspnea may adversely impact daily life activities and exercise performance of COPD patients. Furthermore, the increased perception of dyspnea in patients with co-morbid COPD and anxiety may explain the increased likelihood of symptom-based exacerbations (Laurin et al., 2012), although the role of symptom perception in these outcomes has not been formally tested.

Anxiety and depression may also influence COPD outcomes by dysregulation of the hypothalamic-pituary-adrenal (HPA) axis. HPA dysregulation due to chronic stress has been associated with elevated inflammation and increased susceptibility to respiratory infections (Miller, Cohen, & Ritchey, 2002). The latter is also a key trigger for exacerbations in COPD (Mallia & Johnston, 2006; Papi et al., 2006), but more research is needed to consolidate this pathway in COPD. Finally, individuals with anxiety and depression may also show a range of adverse health behaviours, such as unsuccessful attempts to quit smoking, less physical exercise, a less healthy diet, and less adherence to medication regimens (Bourbeau & Bartlett, 2008; Burgess, Kunik, & Stanley, 2005; Glassman et al., 1990).

Patient beliefs or attitudes about COPD have also been shown to influence COPD outcomes (Kaptein et al., 2008). Most research on these illness representations has been carried out within the framework of the self-regulation theory (Leventhal, Meyer, & Nerenz, 1980), which posits *illness representations* as determinants of illness experience and illness behaviour. In particular, studies have shown an association between perceived control over COPD and better self-management and medication adherence (Dowson, Town, Frampton, & Mulder, 2004; George, Kong, Thoman, & Stewart, 2005), increased participation in pulmonary rehabilitation (Fischer et al., 2009), and fewer emergency room return visits (Stehr, Klein, & Murata, 1991). Furthermore, higher quality of life has been shown to be associated with more positive beliefs about symptoms; the duration and chronicity of COPD; associated physical, psychological, and social outcomes; emotional impact; and attributions about the cause of COPD (Scharloo et al., 2007).

Psychological Assessment of Patients with Asthma and COPD

No single test allows for an unequivocal asthma diagnosis, because each disease characteristic can be present in other conditions. Clinical pulmonologists and allergists use a number of somatic indicators that make a diagnosis more likely, such as basal lung function, reversibility of airway obstruction by bronchodilator medication, skin hypersensitivity to a range of allergens, and airway hyper-reactivity to pharmacological agents that mimic aspects of the allergic reaction or physical triggers (exercise, cold air). Nevertheless, in clinical practice, the patients' self-report of disease history and manifestations will always take centre stage. A thorough *medical history* includes information on types and patterns of symptoms, perceived triggers, development and past treatment, history of exacerbations, impact on patient functioning and family, social history (including education, social support, social barriers to management), and assessment of patient's and family's illness perceptions (NHLBI/NAEPP, 2007). Although psychometrically validated instruments have been published for some of these aspects (for examples, see the In Focus box below), in practice, much of this information will be collected using ad-hoc designed clinical report forms. Current guidelines also provide key example questions that help to narrow down the diagnosis, but their psychometric status is not established.

Central to the clinical assessment of asthma and COPD is the assessment of impairment and exacerbation risk. Short questionnaires determining *impairment* have been developed (see In Focus box). In asthma, current guidelines categorize patients based on impairment as well controlled, not well controlled, or very poorly controlled, using cut-off scores of these questionnaires or clinician ratings of daytime asthma symptoms, nocturnal awakenings, frequency of short-acting bronchodilator use, and limitations in daily activities combined with lung function testing (NHLBI/NAEPP, 2007). Assessment of *exacerbation risk* has remained less standardized. In asthma, it comprises information on systemic corticosteroid use, unscheduled emergency care, hospitalization, or intensive care admissions; in COPD, exacerbation risk is usually determined based on the severity of airflow limitation. A validated indicator for future exacerbations of asthma and COPD is the occurrence of two or more severe exacerbations during the previous year (GINA, 2010; GOLD, 2011).

Assessment of **health-related quality of life (HRQL)** can be used to gauge the impact of the disease on several aspects of life (Apfelbacher, Hankins, Stenner, Frew, & Smith, 2011; Guyatt, Feeny, & Patrick, 1993) (see In Focus box). HRQL measures usually incorporate aspects of multiple constructs such as

◉ IN FOCUS

Selected Questionnaire Instruments Validated for the Psychological Assessment of Asthma and COPD Patients

Omnibus Clinical Outcome Measures

Clinical Control and Impairment

Asthma Control Test (Nathan et al., 2004)

Asthma Control Questionnaire (Juniper, O'Byrne, Guyatt, Ferrie, & King, 1999b)

COPD Assessment Test (Jones et al., 2009)

Health-Related Quality of Life

Asthma Quality of Life Questionnaire (Marks, Dunn, & Woolcock, 1992)

Mini Asthma Quality of Life Questionnaire (Juniper, Guyatt, Cox, Ferrie, & King, 1999a)

Living with Asthma Questionnaire (Hyland, Kenyon, Taylor, & Morice, 1993)

Chronic Respiratory Disease Questionnaire (CRQ) (Guyatt, Berman, Townsend, Pugsley, & Chambers, 1987)

St. George's Respiratory Questionnaire (SGRQ) (Jones, Quirk, & Baveystock, 1991).

Short Form-36 (Ware, 2000).

Measures of Individual Constructs

Symptoms and Symptom Distress

Asthma Symptom Questionnaire (Steen et al., 1994)

Asthma Symptom Checklist (Kinsman, Luparello, O'Banion, & Spector, 1973)

Borg Scale (Wilson & Jones, 1989)

Multidimensional Dyspnea Profile (MDP) (Meek et al., 2012).

Triggers

Asthma Trigger Inventory (Ritz, Steptoe, Bobb, Harris, & Edwards, 2006; Wood et al., 2007)

Illness Perception and Coping

Perceived Control of Asthma Questionnaire (Katz, Yelin, Eisner, & Blanc, 2002)

Brief Illness Perception Questionnaire (Broadbent, Petrie, Main, & Weinman, 2006)

Breathlessness Beliefs Questionnaire (BBQ) (De Peuter et al., 2011)

Knowledge, Attitude, and Self-Efficacy Asthma Questionnaire (Wigal et al., 1993)

Asthma Specific Coping Scale (Aalto, Harkapaa, Aro, & Rissanen, 2002)

---

symptoms, triggers, social and physical activity limitations, and emotional functioning. Although most measures of HRQL lack reference to explicit conceptual models of quality of life, they may serve as convenient overall measures of patients' perceived impact of the disease. Other questionnaires have been developed around distinct concepts, which allow a more detailed assessment of patient functioning and support a more concept-oriented health psychology perspective.

Established generic instruments can be administered to capture aspects of HRQL (Ware, 2000), stress, life events, and mood (Kopp et al., 2010). Due to high co-morbidity of respiratory disease with mood disorders, a structured diagnostic assessment guided by a contemporary version of the Diagnostic Statistical Manual may be indicated (First, Gibbon, Spitzer, & Williams, 2002). However, in practice, limited resources will only allow short screening questionnaire measures, such as the

Primary Care Evaluation of Mental Disorders (PRIME-MD) (Spitzer et al., 1994) or the Hospital Anxiety and Depression Scale (HADS) ((Zigmond & Snaith, 1983). The HADS is particularly suitable for measuring persistent anxious and depressed mood states because of its lack of overlap of the physical symptoms of mood states with respiratory symptoms (Zigmond & Snaith, 1983).

Psychological Interventions for Patients with Asthma and COPD

Psychological interventions for asthma and COPD are adjunctive in that they support or add to the necessary medical treatment. Types of interventions may directly focus on patients' pathophysiology or aim to alleviate symptoms, improve quality of life, and reduce disease progression through self-management training and education, physical exercise and lifestyle change, individualized psychotherapy, or psychosocial interventions (Ritz Meuret, Trueba, Fritzsche, & von Leupoldt, 2013; von Leupoldt, Fritzsche, Trueba, Meuret, & Ritz, 2012). Thus, interventions may range from brief, limited skills training administered by psychologists to large-scale interventions that may include multiple experts in interdisciplinary teams, including social and community workers.

Self-Management and Education

It is generally accepted that successful treatment of asthma and COPD depends on patients taking charge of the day-to-day management of their disease (NHLBI/NAEPP, 2007; GINA, 2010; Bourbeau & van der Palen, 2009). For asthma, self-management includes regular maintenance medication intake, monitoring symptoms and/or lung function, avoiding trigger exposure, and taking the necessary steps in case of exacerbations or emergencies. Patients often are ill-prepared to deal with the complexity of monitoring and managing asthma adequately. The episodic character of asthma, with symptom-free intervals implying change, reduces the perceived urgency of managing the condition (e.g., Halm, Mora, & Leventhal, 2006). Asthma **self-management** and education programs vary widely in their intensity and formats, but overall have been shown efficacious in improving asthma control. Often, multi-session group formats are used, although individualized tailoring of at least some elements (written action plans to guide individual adjustments of medication in case of symptoms) are often preferred by patients. Administering single components, such as trigger avoidance advice, in individual sessions can also improve aspects of asthma control (e.g., Bobb, Ritz, Rowlands, & Griffiths, 2010), but little is known about the effects of most components in isolation. Improving medication adherence is one of the major goals of training, but programs that have focused on this goal selectively have had mixed success (Bender et al., 2003). Studying adherence adequately in daily life is challenging and requires advanced electronic monitoring techniques. Techniques based on *motivational interviewing* (a counselling approach aimed at behaviour change) have been implemented more recently to enhance asthma self-management (Halterman et al., 2011). Although hospital or practice-based settings have dominated asthma self-management training, implementation of school programs (e.g., Bruzzese et al., 2011) or administration over telephone or Internet (McLean et al.,

2011) has shown promising results. Implementing asthma self-management training and education in a multicultural society also require adaptations to make programs culturally sensitive (see Chapter 19 for a discussion of cross-cultural issues). Well-controlled studies have shown superiority of programs adapted directly to African-American, Hispanic, or South Asian cultural contexts (Bailey et al., 2009.

In COPD treatment, self-management interventions help patients gain perceived control over their disease, which includes gains in knowledge and skills to carry out medication and exercise regimens and necessary measures in episodes of exacerbation. Programs vary in content, and may also include interventions aimed at coping with the daily impact of COPD (e.g., coping with stress and impairment, and impact of COPD on social relationships), and the adoption or maintenance of a healthy lifestyle (Peytremann-Bridevaux et al., 2008). However, little is known about the efficacy of individual components of self-management interventions.

Self-management programs for COPD reduce hospitalizations, shorten hospital stays, and reduce emergency medical consultations. Patients participating in self-management programs show reductions in dyspnea as well as improvements in exercise capacity and quality of life (Effing et al., 2007; Peytremann-Bridevaux, Staeger, Bridevaux, Ghali, & Burnand, 2008). Optimal programs go beyond patient education in that they take place in a collaborative format that includes problem-solving and change of current behaviour that may interfere with improving COPD outcomes (Bourbeau & van der Palen, 2009).

Psychophysiological Control Interventions

This type of intervention primarily targets experiences and behaviours that may impact physiology or perception of the illness directly. Improving perception of airway obstruction has been attempted by *interoception (internal sensation) training* using a series of devices (standardized resistors) that obstruct airflow to varying degrees. Findings have been encouraging (Stout, Kotses, & Creer, 1997), but little is known about the overall impact on asthma control. Relaxation, biofeedback, and breathing training interventions have been devised to improve lung function, reduce airway hyper-reactivity and inflammation, and, thus, reduce symptoms and exacerbations. The literature has remained inconsistent regarding the efficacy of various relaxation and biofeedback techniques (Huntley, White, & Ernst, 2002; Posadzki & Ernst, 2011; Ritz, Dahme, & Roth,

2004). The psychophysiological rationale for muscle relaxation is questionable, given that muscle activation reduces parasympathetic activity and thus dilates the airways (Ritz et al, 2013). So far, among the biofeedback techniques, only *heart rate variability feedback* has demonstrated some success in reducing medication needs and improving some aspects of lung function (Lehrer et al., 2004), although the exact mechanism of influence is not yet known. In this training, participants follow visual (screen displays) or auditory cues (tone signals changing in pitch) to increase fluctuations of their heart rate related to breathing in and out. This is achieved particularly by breathing more deeply and slowly (down to six breaths per minute), until heart rate fluctuations due to blood pressure regulation start overlapping with fluctuations due to breathing.

Slow abdominal breathing is also common in various forms of breathing training. Recent clinical trials have shown success of such training techniques in improving mood, symptoms, and quality of life, but not the underlying physiology (Bruton & Thomas, 2011). Another form of breathing training targets hyperventilation, a disturbance in gas exchange (low levels of CO_2 or *hypocapnia*) that comes from breathing more than required for the activity level of the organism. A substantial portion of asthma patients show symptoms of over-breathing and/or exaggerated ventilation (Meuret & Ritz, 2010), which can lead to bronchoconstriction and symptoms. *Hypoventilation training* involves prescriptions to reduce breathing by taking slower and shallower breaths, as well as breath-holding. It has been associated with improvements in medication needs and quality of life, but studies demonstrating the critical role of CO_2 are missing. Overall, the current state of clinical trials suggests that slow breathing techniques can help reduce symptoms and medication needs, but physiology of the airways remains largely unaltered.

In COPD, various novel strategies have been suggested to reduce dyspnea and improve COPD treatment. These strategies include positive mood induction during exercise, humour and laughter, or singing, which may work by reducing hyperinflation and/or by distracting from the negative quality of dyspnea (Lebowitz, Suh, Diaz, & Emery, 2011; Lord et al., 2012; von Leupoldt et al., 2010).

Lifestyle Interventions and Rehabilitation

The fact that heavier physical activity leads to bronchoconstriction in many patients with asthma has made patients reluctant to exercise. However, reduced fitness levels can

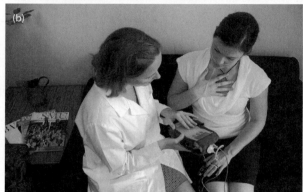

PHOTO 14.4 | Teaching breathing techniques has been shown to improve asthma patients' well-being.

Source: SMU. Used by permission of Alicia Meuret.

make patients more symptomatic and affect general cardiovascular health adversely. Patients can safely exercise with the necessary precautions (specific warm-up trainings or pre-exercise bronchodilators), and such programs have generally shown improvements in cardiopulmonary fitness without side effects (Carson et al., 2013).

In COPD treatment, physical exercise is the main component of pulmonary rehabilitation, a treatment strategy that aims to reduce the impact of COPD on physical activity by strengthening skeletal muscle function, limiting deconditioning, and increasing exercise capacity (Troosters et al., 2005; Troosters, Gosselink, Janssens, & Decramer, 2010). Most pulmonary rehabilitation programs are multidisciplinary and include education and self-management components, nutritional interventions, and psychosocial support or psychotherapy. Overall, these interventions result in improved exercise tolerance, reduced exacerbations of COPD, and improved symptoms and quality of life.

Pulmonary rehabilitation programs consistently reduce anxiety and depression in COPD (Coventry, 2009). Experience with physical exercise during the pulmonary rehabilitation program may act in a similar way as exposure therapy and reduce exercise-related anxiety and fears (Brenes, 2003). Pulmonary rehabilitation has indeed been shown to reduce the unpleasantness of exercise-induced dyspnea (Carrieri-Kohlman et al., 2001) and individuals with high levels of dyspnea-related fear show a reduction in dyspnea and greater exercise tolerance after rehabilitation (Janssens et al., 2011). Because most pulmonary rehabilitation interventions include both physical exercise and some form of psychotherapy or counselling, it may be difficult to separate effects of these components. However, two trials have shown that a combination of exercise and psychotherapy is more effective at reducing anxiety and depression compared to only psychotherapy or only exercise and education (de Godoy & de Godoy, 2003; Emery, Schein, Hauck, & MacIntyre, 1998).

An avoidable trigger of asthma symptoms is tobacco smoke, yet the prevalence of smoking in asthma patients is comparable to the general population (Zimmerman et al., 2004), with adverse consequences for both general and asthma-specific health (Thomson & Chaudhuri 2009). The few available studies of smoking cessation training adapted for asthma have demonstrated improvements in asthma pathophysiology. Reducing environmental tobacco smoke in homes of children with asthma is also an important preventative measure, but programs have so far shown mixed success.

Tobacco smoke is the main risk factor for COPD onset and progression (GOLD, 2011). Key intervention targets are therefore the prevention or cessation of smoking. Changes in tobacco-related policies are associated with a reduction of COPD prevalence (Polednak, 2010). Successful smoking cessation is associated with improvements in pulmonary function and respiratory symptoms, a decreased exacerbation rate, and slower progression of COPD (Anthonisen, Connett, & Murray, 2002). Nevertheless, a large proportion of patients with COPD continue to smoke after diagnosis (Watson et al., 2006). Programs to help patients stop smoking range from low-intensity (advice, information, self-help materials) to higher-intensity (telephone counselling, group counselling) interventions and are incorporated in many self-management or pulmonary rehabilitation programs (Tønnesen et al., 2007). However, the success rate of smoking cessation is lower compared to similar interventions in persons without COPD. On average, only 5–35 per cent of COPD patients succeed in cessation

after an intervention (Tønnesen et al., 2007), and even COPD patients who undergo lung transplantation have a high probability of resuming smoking (Vos et al., 2010).

Given the worldwide rise in obesity rates and associated complications in asthma pathophysiology and management, weight-loss and dietary interventions have gained greater importance (Eneli et al., 2008). In addition, supplementation with a range of foods (fruit, vegetables, Mediterranean diet) and nutrients (e.g., vitamin D, magnesium) has been recommended for improvements in asthma pathophysiology and control (Nurmatov, Devereux, & Sheikh, 2011). Although initial findings are encouraging, more efforts are needed in development and evaluation of programs that address the complex network of developmental, pathophysiology, lifestyle, and social factors involved in effects of physical activity, smoking, and diet on asthma.

Psychotherapy

Co-morbid psychological disorders may make psychotherapy relevant, but interventions require tailoring to accommodate the needs of patients with asthma. For example, interoceptive exposure in panic disorder treatment, in which patients are instructed to hyperventilate to voluntarily produce their feared symptoms (as a means of getting used to these symptoms), is not advisable in asthma because of the risk of bronchoconstriction. In general, extra care must be taken to distinguish symptoms elicited by asthma from those specific to the disorder. Cognitive behaviour therapy (CBT) tailored to individuals with asthma and anxiety disorders has shown improvement of both anxiety and asthma outcomes (e.g., Lehrer et al., 2008), but larger and better-controlled studies are needed.

More elementary strategies with relevance to psychotherapy have also been tested in asthma, such as expressive writing and suggestive techniques including hypnosis. Symptomatic improvement has been shown with as little as three sessions of writing about emotionally unpleasant life events (Warner et al., 2006). Suggestions, placebo, and hypnosis have also shown to improve aspects of lung function (Isenberg et al., 1992; Hackman, Stern, & Gershwin, 2000; Joyce, Jackevicius, Chapman, McIvor, & Kesten, 2000), but such effects have not yet been harnessed systematically for psychotherapy interventions. It should be noted that suggestion effects on asthma do not imply that the disease is all imaginary (see In Focus box), rather that some aspects of symptoms and lung function may be

⊞ IN PRACTICE
Trying to Gain Control of Asthma

Illness history and manifestation

A 30-year-old female patient, Claire, presents with a history of episodes of severe breathlessness since her first years of life. In childhood, symptoms were triggered by running and other sports activities, but also crying or loud and prolonged laughing. Symptoms were worse in spring and after Sunday nature walks with her parents. Asthma was diagnosed formally around eight years of age and symptoms were controlled with regular low-dose inhaled corticosteroids and as-needed beta-adrenergic bronchodilators. Following a number of relatively symptom-free years Claire experienced a strong exacerbation of symptoms at the age of 15, which required a trip to the hospital emergency room. Claire's life situation was difficult during this time due to relocation of the family to another part of the country and the inevitable transition to another school, where she suffered in a fiercely competitive environment. In the days leading up to the exacerbation, she complained about having pressure on her chest and used her bronchodilator multiple times during the day without finding great symptom relief.

Medical and adjunctive psychological treatment

Although the emergency treatment and a subsequent trial of oral corticosteroids helped her by reducing breathlessness severity, symptoms of chest tightness returned episodically during the day. Subsequent allergy skin-testing by a specialist revealed sensitization to dust mites and multiple pollens, grasses, and moulds. At this point, Claire was provided with asthma management training, which included a plan to avoid overexposure to outdoor allergens and improvement of indoor environment by pollen filters and mould eradication. Because symptoms persisted a clinical health psychology consultation was scheduled, which uncovered a generalized anxiety disorder and occasional panic attacks. Feelings of helplessness were accompanied by hyperventilation, which led to strong symptoms of shortness of breath, chest tightness, and dizziness. Symptoms sometimes spiralled out of control as she feared suffering from an asthma attack. Hyperventilation then made asthma symptoms worse by leading to reflex airway constriction. Bronchodilators were only partly effective in relieving these symptoms.

The suggested treatment when, as a 30-year-old woman, she sought help was an eight-week course of cognitive behaviour therapy combined with breathing exercises. Claire received training in cognitive restructuring, problem-solving, realistic goal-setting, and reinterpreting physical symptoms of hyperventilation as products of dysfunctional breathing under stress. Breathing exercises focused on a slow, abdominal, and shallow breathing pattern that she practised both with the therapist and in homework assignments. Particularly helpful was feedback from a device that measured her gas exchange during therapist-led sessions. Using that device she learned how changes in her breathing pattern increased exhaled carbon dioxide levels, which are low in hyperventilation. She also learned to de-catastrophize symptoms of breathlessness and chest tightness, which were not due to low oxygen saturation but often caused by hyperventilation. In subsequent months, asthma control improved and Claire experienced fewer symptoms, initiating breathing exercises whenever feeling anxious or stressed.

---

improved with such adjunctive intervention elements while the underlying asthma still requires guideline-informed medical treatment.

CBT interventions have been adapted for specific problems faced by patients with COPD and co-morbid anxiety or depression, with a focus on the modification of negative or catastrophic thoughts and beliefs related to symptoms and COPD in general, as well as on modification of symptom- and illness-related behaviour (Coventry & Gellatly, 2008). Significant but small overall effects on anxiety and depression resulting from CBT for COPD have been demonstrated (Baraniak & Sheffield, 2010).

Pulmonary Rehabilitation

Endurance training: exercise aimed at improving overall fitness

Strength training: exercise aimed at improving strength of specific muscles e.g., upper/lower body strength training, respiratory muscle training

Cognitive-Behavioural Therapy

Cognitive Interventions:
e.g., challenging symptom- and illness-related negative or catastrophic thoughts

Behaviour Modification:
e.g., response prevention, behaviour activation, exposure to feared situations, problem-solving techniques, breathing exercises, relaxation techniques

Self-Management Interventions: interventions aimed at putting the patient in charge of the management of the disease
e.g., development of a personal action plan, training of inhaler use, training of cough techniques, practising ways to cope with impact of COPD on daily life

Patient Education: giving the patient information about the disease and treatment

FIGURE 14.2 | A combination of strategies are used for the management of respiratory conditions.

A four-session CBT intervention has also been deployed to prevent onset of panic disorder in patients with COPD (Livermore, Sharpe, & McKenzie, 2010). Future research into the development of anxiety and depression may lead to interventions that can be implemented at earlier stages of COPD treatment and may help prevent the poor outcomes that are associated with anxiety and depression.

Psychosocial Interventions

Given that self-management of asthma for children is usually embedded in the family context, the particular emotional challenges arising from this shared burden have sometimes been addressed by family therapy. Research has shown that this type of intervention improves children's functioning and aspects of airway pathophysiology, as well as children's and parents' asthma-related self-efficacy (Yorke & Shuldham, 2005; Ng et al., 2008). Interventions have also been implemented on the community level with a major focus on addressing multiple disadvantages of urban communities and disparities in asthma care. Visitations by community or social workers, nurses, and specialists aim to increase asthma control by improving aspects of the home environment (e.g., identification and elimination of triggers) and removal of barriers to adequate management (e.g.,

help with implementation of self-management plans, medication refills). Benefits have been shown for a wide range of asthma outcomes, including reduction in costly emergency care (Postma, Karr, & Kieckhefer, 2009).

Future Directions

Interventions, including those with psychological components, have already been developed to complement medical therapy in both asthma and COPD. These interventions contribute to improvements in clinical outcome and quality of life. However, larger clinical trials are needed in many areas, as are critical evaluations of individual treatment components in multi-component interventions. Furthermore, interdisciplinary research is required to further examine pathways of influence and to translate these findings into interventions with a strong basis in psychobiology. Finally, in asthma, progress has also been made in adapting programs to the needs of disadvantaged urban communities and minorities, who share a large part of the burden of uncontrolled asthma. Rather than being only a specialty niche of psychosocial intervention research, community-directed initiatives and culturally sensitive versions of interventions should ideally become part of every treatment development.

SUMMARY

Asthma and COPD are chronic respiratory disorders and are leading causes of morbidity and mortality worldwide. Psychological factors are important in the course and management of these conditions, although our knowledge in this area is constantly evolving. The co-morbidity of psychological disorders, in particular anxiety and depression, and asthma or COPD is well established and is associated with poorer treatment outcomes and increased risk of exacerbations. In asthma, associations of negative affect with airway obstruction, inflammation, and patient-reported symptoms are well documented, whereas in COPD associations of negative mood and catastrophic beliefs with elevated symptoms have been documented. Interference of these factors with disease management and quality of life has been widely observed.

Patients with asthma and COPD profit from treatments informed by clinical and health psychology.

A number of interventions have been devised that are complementary to the necessary medical treatment of these patients and with the ultimate goal of improving control of the disease and patients' quality of life. A strong focus is on self-management training and education that seek to enhance disease-related health behaviours and ideally draw on research on health beliefs, illness representations, and behaviour change. Physical activity, often an integral part of pulmonary rehabilitation, is beneficial in reducing symptoms and improving general health. The transfer of gains of these interventions to the daily life of patients requires particular attention. CBT interventions have also been customized for asthma and COPD patients with co-morbid anxiety or depression and initial findings are promising. For treatment of patients with asthma and COPD, health psychologists are ideally embedded in a multidisciplinary team.

Critical Thought Questions

1. Psychosocial effects on asthma can be divided into direct and indirect influences, depending on how directly they influence airway pathophysiology through nervous system processes. How well can individual psychological interventions be distinguished along these lines?

2. Self-management, pulmonary rehabilitation, and CBT interventions for COPD patients aim to increase quality of life and to reduce impact of COPD on day-to-day activities. What are key differences among these approaches? To which intervention would you refer patients with COPD based on which patient characteristics?

3. Do asthma and COPD require different psychological treatment approaches? What are the similarities and differences between health psychology treatments for asthma and for COPD?

Recommended Reading

National Heart, Lung, and Blood Institute (NHLBI)/ National Asthma Education and Prevention Program (NAEPP). (2007). *Expert panel report: Guidelines for the diagnosis and management of asthma* (NIH Publication No. 07–4051). Bethesda, Md: National Institutes of Health.

Parshall, M.B., Schwartzstein, R.M., Adams, L., Banzett, R.B., Manning, H.L., Bourbeau, J. American Thoracic Society Committee on Dyspnea. (2012). An official American Thoracic Society statement: Update on the mechanisms, assessment, and management of dyspnea. *American Journal of Respiratory and Critical Care Medicine, 185*, 435–452.

Ritz, T., Meuret, A.E., Trueba, A.F., Fritzsche, A., & von Leupoldt, A. (2013). Psychosocial factors and behavioral medicine interventions in asthma. *Journal of Consulting and Clinical Psychology, 81*(2), 231–250.

von Leupoldt, A. Fritzsche, A., Trueba, A.F., Meuret, A.E., & Ritz, T. (2012). Behavioral medicine approaches to chronic obstructive pulmonary disease. *Annals of Behavioral Medicine, 44*, 52–65.

15

Gastrointestinal Conditions

SARAH K. BALLOU │ RACHEL C. LAWTON │ LAURIE KEEFER

Learning Objectives

In this chapter you will:

- Learn the difference between irritable bowel syndrome (IBS) and inflammatory bowel disease (IBD).

- Understand the different medical treatments for IBS and IBD.

- Discover the psychosocial factors and behavioural factors associated with chronic gastrointestinal disorders.

- Read about psychological treatments used with people who suffer from gastrointestinal conditions.

This chapter provides an introduction to two important gastrointestinal diagnoses for which there is the most evidence supporting the work of health psychologists in patient care: **irritable bowel syndrome (IBS)** and **inflammatory bowel disease (IBD)**. More information is available on IBS because it is more commonly seen in health psychology settings and there is also more psychosocial research on this condition. However, most of the information presented in this chapter applies across gastrointestinal conditions.

To understand the application of health psychology to IBS and IBD, we must first review an important concept within health psychology: the biopsychosocial model. As indicated elsewhere in this volume (e.g., see Chapter 1), the biopsychosocial model posits that a complex blend of biological (e.g., genetic), psychological (e.g., thoughts and behaviours), and social (e.g., environmental) factors contribute to the clinical presentation of a disease (Engel, 1977). This model is commonly applied to gastrointestinal diseases such as IBS and IBD and is especially important in the study of health psychology (see Figure 15.1).

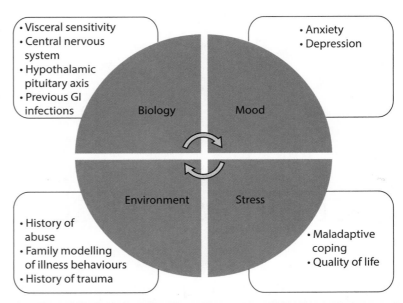

FIGURE 15.1 | Biopsychosocial influences on GI diseases. According to the biopsychosocial model, numerous and complex biological (e.g., genetic), psychological (e.g., cognitions and behaviours), and social (e.g., environmental) factors contribute to the clinical presentation of gastrointestinal diseases.

Introduction to Gastrointestinal Conditions: IBS and IBD

Irritable Bowel Syndrome: A Functional Syndrome of the Gastrointestinal Tract

Irritable bowel syndrome is a common syndrome of the gastrointestinal tract, affecting between 10–15 per cent of the population in North America (Hungin, Chang, Locke, Dennis, & Barghout, 2005; Thompson, Irvine, Pare, Ferrazzi, & Rance, 2002). It is classified as a **functional gastrointestinal disorder (FGID)**, meaning that its symptoms are not associated with any structural or biochemical abnormalities in the gut (also known as "organic abnormalities") and that there are no imaging or laboratory tests that can confirm IBS.

Primary Symptoms and Diagnosis

Symptoms of IBS are characterized by abdominal pain and/or discomfort associated with diarrhea, constipation, or

PHOTO 15.1 | Irritable bowel syndrome is often characterized by crampy abdominal pain, diarrhea, constipation, and bloating.

TABLE 15.1 | Rome III Criteria

Recurrent abdominal pain or discomfort at least three days per month in the last three months associated with two or more of the following:

1. Improvement with defecation
2. Onset associated with change in frequency of stool
3. Onset associated with change in form (appearance of stool)

both (Longstreth et al., 2006; Remes-Troche et al., 2009). IBS can be classified into three distinct subtypes: diarrhea-predominant (IBS-D); constipation-predominant (IBS-C); or mixed-type (IBS-M). Since there is not currently a biological marker or test for IBS, a diagnostic symptom checklist is available to physicians and researchers. The **Rome III criteria** (see Table 15.1) comprise the most up-to-date diagnostic tool for clinicians who suspect that a patient may have IBS (Longstreth et al., 2006).

IBS is also associated with many co-morbid symptoms, that is, symptoms or health conditions that occur at the same time as another disease but that are not diagnostically related to the disease. These symptoms may be related to gastrointestinal functioning or unrelated (i.e. "extraintestinal"). Approximately 65 per cent of patients with IBS have **extraintestinal co-morbid symptoms** (Riedl et al., 2008). Examples of some common co-morbid symptoms and disorders reported by IBS patients are: fibromyalgia (Sperber et al., 1999), back pain (Smith, Russell, & Hodges, 2008), urogenital problems (Francis,

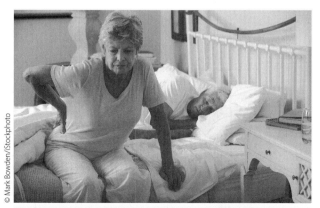

© Mark Bowden/iStockphoto

PHOTO 15.2 | Back pain is a common co-morbid symptom reported by IBS patients.

Duffy, Whorwell, & Morris, 1997; Guo et al., 2010), sleep problems (Heitkemper et al., 2005), and anxiety and depression (Gros, Antony, McCabe, & Swinson, 2009; Sykes, Blanchard, Lackner, Keefer, & Krasner, 2003).

Etiology of Irritable Bowel Syndrome

The biological factors of IBS have been widely researched in pursuit of a physical explanation for this functional disorder and they are particularly important for health psychologists to understand when treating patients with these conditions. The pathophysiology of IBS is believed to lie in alterations in the **brain–gut axis**, which refers to neural and hormonal influences between the central nervous system and the GI tract (see In Focus box). When the brain–gut axis becomes dysregulated, patients with IBS may experience increased pain and stress symptoms in response to normal activity in their gut (Fukudo, Nomura, Muranaka, & Taguchi, 1993). This process is called **visceral hypersensitivity**, and is believed to be a result of amplified pain signals originating in the neurons of the gut. For example, in a study evaluating discomfort by using rectal balloon distension (i.e. a procedure that involves inserting and then inflating a balloon inside the rectum), patients with IBS reported lower thresholds for colonic discomfort than healthy controls in the same balloon distension condition (Schmulson, Chang, Naliboff, Lee, & Mayer, 2000).

The role of the brain–gut axis in IBS symptoms has also been demonstrated by functional brain-imaging studies (i.e. functional magnetic resonance imaging, fMRI). These studies have shown that IBS patients have increased brain activation in the anterior cingulate cortex (a region of the brain that is involved in pain perception

◎ IN FOCUS

The Brain–Gut Axis

The brain–gut axis is a common term in the field of neurogastroenterology, or the study of the relationship between the central nervous system and the gut. The brain–gut axis refers to the connection between the digestive system and the central nervous system via neurons that start in the gut and travel through the spinal cord to the brain. Therefore, there is communication between the gut and the brain. For example, a signal in the gut might trigger an emotional response in the brain and vice versa.

and emotion) when they feel abdominal pain or discomfort (Mertz et al., 2000). This activation can cause patients to feel more pain, be more fearful, or experience more stress as a result of—or in anticipation of—abdominal discomfort (Berman et al., 2008). In addition, the experience of stress or negative emotion is known to *cause* increased pain sensitivity and increased gut motility (the way food and waste move through the tract) in IBS patients (Murray et al., 2004).

Finally, the hypothalamic pituitary adrenal axis (HPA axis) is involved in hormonal regulation of digestion, stress, emotion, and mood. The HPA axis consists of the pituitary gland, located in the brain, and the adrenal glands, located on the kidneys. These glands secrete hormones into the blood, which regulate many bodily functions. Corticotropic releasing hormone (CRH), for example, modulates gut motility, stress levels, and sensitivity to pain. Increased levels of stress trigger the release of CRH, which increases bowel motility and metabolic functions. Therefore, increased sensitivity to stress (or excessive exposure to stress) in some patients with IBS may cause abnormal bowel responses. Furthermore, some patients with IBS may have abnormal baseline levels of HPA hormones (Chang et al., 2009).

In sum, many of the key brain structures and endocrine axes involved in the expression of IBS are also involved in regulation of emotion, stress, and fear. This complicated overlap between emotion and gut

functioning may contribute to the high co-morbidity between IBS and certain psychological disorders, which is described later in this chapter.

Medical Management

Given the *functional* nature of IBS, medical treatments for this condition are relatively ineffective and often provide only partial relief of symptoms (Brandt et al., 2009; Lesbros-Pantoflickova, Michetti, Fried, Beglinger, & Blum, 2004). Thinking back to the definition of FGIDs, this should make some sense. Without a clear understanding of what causes IBS, it is difficult to target the symptoms with medical interventions. Patients with IBS may experience a wide array of abdominal or bowel symptoms (i.e., diarrhea and/or constipation) with poorly defined "triggers" or causes for those symptoms.

Several treatments are aimed at reducing *specific* IBS symptoms. For example, some medications treat abdominal pain, some treat constipation, some treat diarrhea, and so on. Literature reviews and **meta-analyses** (a statistical method of comparing results from different studies) have evaluated the efficacy of medical treatments for IBS (Lesbros-Pantoflickova, Michetti, Fried, Beglinger, & Blum, 2004; Tillisch & Chang, 2005). Unfortunately, the various studies often produce mixed results that are due to inconsistencies in research methods across different studies. The main types of IBS treatments included in meta-analyses are described in Table 15.2.

TABLE 15.2 | Main Types of IBS Treatments

Treatment	Symptom Treated	Example
Bulking agents	Constipation	Dietary fibre
Anti-diarrheals	Diarrhea	Loperamide
Probiotics	Abdominal pain/bloating/diarrhea	Bifidobacterium
Laxatives	Constipation	Polyethylene Glycol 3350 (e.g., Miralax™)
Antibiotics	Bloating, diarrhea (especially traveller's diarrhea), bacterial overgrowth in small intestine	Rifaximin (Xifaxin™)
Seratonergic agents: Serotonin antagonists Serotonin agonists	Diarrhea Constipation	Alosetron (Lotronex™) Tergaserod (Zelnorm™)
Antidepressants	Abdominal pain associated with diarrhea	Amitryptaline (Elavil®)

(Continued)

TABLE 15.2 | (*Continued*)

Treatment	Symptom Treated	Example
Tricyclic antidepressants SSRIs	Abdominal pain associated with constipation	Fluoxetine (Prozac®), Citalopram (Celexa®)
Antispasmodics	Abdominal pain	Dicyclomine (Bentyl®), peppermint oil
Dietary changes	Not recommended	n/a
Herbal remedies	Not enough evidence	n/a
Acupuncture	Not enough evidence	n/a

Irritable Bowel Syndrome: Psychosocial Factors

Approximately 40–60 per cent of IBS patients have co-morbid psychiatric diagnoses, compared to about 20 per cent of people without IBS (Drossman, Camilleri, Mayer, & Whitehead, 2002). In particular, IBS has been associated with the presence of anxiety disorders, mood disorders, and general neuroticism (a personality trait characterized by anxiety, instability, and worry) (Cohen et al., 2006; Gros et al., 2009; Lee et al., 2009). Patients with IBS are also more likely to report low quality of life (Hahn, Kirchdoerfer, Fullerton, & Mayer, 1997; Koloski, Talley, & Boyce, 2000) and up to 38 per cent of IBS patients in tertiary care settings have contemplated suicide as a result of their symptoms (Miller, Hopkins, & Whorwell, 2004). These psychological co-morbidities tend to remain stable over time and often precede IBS (Sykes et al., 2003).

Anxiety

Up to 58 per cent of IBS patients have a co-morbid anxiety disorder (Gros et al., 2009) and IBS patients are five times more likely than healthy people to have a diagnosis of generalized anxiety disorder (GAD) (a condition characterized by excessive anxiety and worry about a variety of domains) (Lee et al., 2009). In addition, the prevalence of panic disorder in IBS patients is 25–30 per cent, which is higher than in the general population (Lydiard, 2005). It has been suggested that IBS patients may monitor and worry about their GI symptoms in a manner similar to anxiety disorder patients who often monitor their bodies (see Chapter 6) for somatic symptoms (Naliboff et al., 1997; Verne, Robinson, & Price, 2001). This worry is referred to as gastrointestinal-specific anxiety (GSA), which can create an unhealthy cycle of increased attention to symptoms, worry about symptoms, and increased perception of symptoms (see Figure 15.2).

Stress/Traumatic Experiences

As you read this chapter, you may be noticing that stress plays an important role in the expression of IBS symptoms. This may be caused by increased reactivity to stress or by chronic exposure to stress, such as trauma or abuse. For example, women with a history of sexual and/or physical abuse are more likely than women who have not been abused to report GI symptoms (Leserman, 2007; Leserman & Drossman, 2007) and war veterans with post-traumatic stress disorder (PTSD) are more likely to report IBS symptoms than veterans without PTSD (White et al., 2010).

Depression

Up to 50 per cent of patients who have IBS also report a lifetime mood disorder, such as depression (Mykletun et al., 2010; Osterberg et al., 2000), and depressive symptoms are more common in IBS patients than in patients with organic gastrointestinal diseases such as inflammatory bowel disease (Kovacs & Kovacs, 2007).

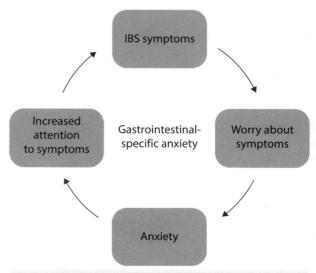

FIGURE 15.2 | Gastrointestinal-specific anxiety.

When treating an IBS patient who also suffers from depression, it is important to assess the impact of IBS symptoms on the patient's mood. While we know that increased stress and depression may influence gut functioning via the brain–gut axis, it is also important to know how the patient's gut symptoms may influence his or her mood. In the case provided in the In Practice box, the clinician must consider the patient's cognitions about her illness, how she has modified her behaviours to accommodate for her symptoms, and how this may relate to any co-morbid depression.

Inflammatory Bowel Disease: An Organic Gastrointestinal Tract Condition

Inflammatory bowel diseases (IBDs) are chronic, relapsing and remitting gastrointestinal conditions associated with persistent and chronic intestinal inflammation. They are considered "organic disorders" because they are classified by structural changes (e.g., inflammation) in the bowels and are detectable through laboratory tests and imaging procedures. The prevalence of IBD is estimated at 396 cases per 100,000 worldwide, affecting up to 1.4 million people in the US and 170,000 people in Canada (Lakatos, 2006; Bernstein et al., 2006). The two most common forms of IBD are Crohn's disease (CD) and ulcerative colitis (UC). Although there are key differences between CD and UC, both illnesses share several specific commonalities. These include:

- Uncontrolled inflammation within the gastrointestinal tract.
- Diagnosis most commonly in teenager/young adult years (ages 13–26) or in middle age (55–65).
- Unknown cause of disease but genetic and environmental factors likely are influential.
- Controlled both medically and surgically (Baumgart and Sandborn, 2012; Ordás, Eckmann, Talamini, Baumgart, & Sandborn, 2012).

Primary Symptoms and Diagnosis

A diagnosis of IBD can be made only after a full clinical evaluation (including a physical examination) and assessment of travel history, medications, smoking status, family history, stool frequency/consistency, urgency, rectal bleeding, abdominal pain, fever, fatigue, weight loss, and presence of other extraintestinal manifestations, which may include joint pain, ocular (eye) inflammation, liver problems, rashes and other dermatological changes, and ulcerations in the mouth (Carter, Lobo, & Travis, 2004). Confirmation of inflammation must be corroborated through imaging and laboratory tests and other causative agents, such as bacterial infections and other infectious agents, must be ruled out (Carter et al., 2004). While IBD can be diagnosed at any age, it most commonly presents in adolescence to early adulthood with a spike in diagnosis again in the fourth and fifth decades.

Medical Management

The management of IBD is multi-faceted. Typically, the two primary medical goals are induction of remission and maintenance. Induction of remission involves a process whereby a patient must initiate or increase a medication or therapy in order to transition from active disease to inactive or remissive disease. Maintenance of remission is a process by which a patient maintains inactive disease, which usually requires some form of medication. The management in this stage is meant to decrease the likelihood of relapse.

The medical treatment options for IBD are diverse (Cottone, Renna, Orlando, & Mocciaro, 2011). Table 15.3 presents the primary types of medication that are frequently used throughout the course of treatment.

Most of the medications used to treat and control IBD have considerable side effects—the most benign side effects include weight gain, "moon face" (round or puffy face), and insomnia, and the most significant include serious infection or cancer (Ashworth et al., 2012). This said, the risks associated with untreated active IBD are often substantially more likely to occur and thus represent a greater risk (Bousvaros, Morley-Fletcher, Pensabene, & Cucchiara, 2008).

Inflammatory Bowel Disease: Psychosocial Factors

IBD has the capacity to influence a patient's life in many ways. Chronic physical illness, potentially embarrassing symptom presentation, and a complex treatment regimen place the patient at risk for psychological stress and symptoms. The two most common psychological conditions in people with IBD are anxiety and depression.

TABLE 15.3 | Primary Types of Frequently Used Medication throughout the Course of IBD Treatment

Medication Type	Medical Goal	Route	Possible Side Effects
Corticosteroids	Induction of remission	Oral, rectal, and Intravenous	Weight gain, mood swings, acne, osteopenia/osteoporosis
Antibiotics	Induction and maintenance of remission	Oral and intravenous	Peripheral neuropathy
Anti-inflammatory	Induction and maintenance of remission	Oral and rectal	Pancreatitis, rash, and abdominal pain
Immunosuppressive	Maintenance of remission	Oral and subcutaneous	Pancreatitis, increased risk of infection, and certain types of cancer (lymphomas)
Biologic	Induction and maintenance of remission	Intravenous	Increased risk of infection and certain types of cancer (lymphomas)

Anxiety and Depression

While the literature suggests a minimal relationship between psychological symptoms and disease status (Mikocka-Walus et al., 2008), a complex relationship occurs between the presence of psychological symptoms and IBD (Goodhand et al., 2012; Mittermaier et al., 2004). Severe and active disease is a primary risk factor for the development of anxiety and depression (Nahon et al., 2012). There are also comparable rates of psychopathology among patients with Crohn's disease and those with ulcerative colitis (Goodhand et al., 2012). The etiology of these psychological symptoms appears to differ between the two conditions.

Depression and anxiety influence the course of inflammatory disease activity in a negative way by worsening symptoms, increasing disability, reducing quality of life, and interfering with self-management (Mittermaier et al., 2004). Anxiety about the treatment itself may be due to insufficient information and education provided about their disease (Baars et al., 2010). Understanding the relationship between IBD and coexisting psychological conditions, therefore, is an important part of comprehensive patient care. Any perception of illness-related stigma also increases the likelihood of psychological symptoms, including depression and anxiety, and is correlated with increasingly negative clinical outcomes (Taft, Keefer, Leonhard, & Nealon-Woods, 2009).

Health Behaviours Affecting Disease Outcomes

While health behaviours are important in the self-management of any psychological or physical problem, patients with IBD face unique challenges. First, IBD patients who have difficulty adapting to disease-related demands report more bowel and systemic symptoms, more pain, less engagement in activities, higher

PHOTO 15.3 | Mood disorders, such as depression and anxiety, can impact the course of both IBS and IBD.

© MJDigitalArt/iStockphoto

perceived stress, and higher health-system use (Kiebles, Doerfler, & Keefer, 2010).

Medication adherence. Medication adherence in IBD is notably poor, with as many as 50 per cent of patients reporting partial non-adherence (regularly missing doses) and 12 per cent who are completely non-adherent (Kane & Shaya, 2008). An annual relapse rate between 58 and 89 per cent is expected for UC patients who do not follow their maintenance regimen (Misiewicz, Lennard-Jones, Connell, Baron, & Avery Jones, 1965; Wright, O'Keefe, Cuming, & Jaskiewicz, 1993). Consequently, helping patients reduce barriers to adherence can have a direct impact on outcome. Adherence research in IBD suggests that the level of involvement patients believe they have in their treatment plan (Sewitch, Leffondre, & Dobkin, 2004), their amount of perceived stress, and their perceptions of poor health may affect adherence to medical regimens (Sewitch et al., 2003). (See Chapter 3 for a more detailed discussion of adherence.)

Smoking. Smoking is known to have considerable impact on the health status of the IBD patient (Mahid, Minor, Soto, Hornung, & Galandiuk, 2006). Interestingly, the effect of smoking among patients with UC is quite different from its influence on patients with Crohn's disease. It appears that smoking may be a protective factor for individuals with UC. More specifically, smoking decreases both the likelihood of developing UC and the risk for colectomy, although the reasons for this phenomenon remain unknown (Karban & Eliakim, 2007). In contrast, individuals who have CD and who smoke have an increased incidence of flare-up, steroid dependence, and multiple surgeries (Mahid et al., 2006).

Stress. The relationship between stress and IBD involves a complex interplay among the biological factors in the individual, including neuroendocrine functioning (the relationship between the nervous system and hormones) and stressful experiences or trauma (Collins, 2001). Animal studies have clarified the potential for stress to contribute to disease flare-ups. For example, the cotton-top tamarin and Siamang gibbons, both primates, are at increased risk for developing ulcerative-type colitis when they are held in captivity—when they are returned to their natural habitat, they almost immediately experience full remission, suggesting that such stress can directly affect disease onset and course (Wood et al., 2000; Stout & Snyder, 1969).

In humans, the occurrence of significant life events consistently appears to be a trigger for relapse in UC (Bitton et al., 2001; Mardini, Kip, & Wilson, 2004). For example, UC patients who perceive more stress in their lives are more likely to experience a flare-up within two years than are less-stressed UC patients (Levenstein, 2002). Regardless of the evidence linking stress and IBD, 75 per cent of IBD patients identify psychological stress as a direct trigger for disease flares (Moser et al., 1995). The first goal of a health psychologist assessing an IBS or IBD patient is to understand the complex interplay of disease characteristics and psychological concerns through psychosocial assessment.

© Mac99/iStockphoto

PHOTO 15.4 | Smoking status is known to exert considerable influence on the health status of the IBD patient.

Psychological Assessment of Patients with Gastrointestinal Conditions

Psychological evaluation of IBS/IBD often begins with a detailed clinical interview with each patient. This interview is not meant to diagnose IBS/IBD, but rather to lead to a better understanding of the individual factors associated with the development and maintenance of the condition. The clinical interview usually involves a screening for co-morbid psychiatric disorders, which should follow either the *Diagnostic and Statistical Manual* (DSM) criteria or the International Classification of Diseases (ICD) diagnostic criteria for mental and behavioural disorders (American Psychiatric Association, 2013; WHO, 2008). The results of this section of the interview can help to determine whether a patient may fall within the clinical range for conditions such as depression or anxiety (among many others).

The rest of the clinical interview usually involves the following components: (1) inquiry into the onset of symptoms (i.e., any precipitating factors that may have led to the presentation of the illness); (2) the effect of IBS/IBD on current functioning (work/family/social functioning); (3) the overall effect of IBS/IBD on daily life (i.e., self-esteem, body image); and (4) ways in which the patient has modified his or her daily routine to accommodate for IBS/IBD symptoms (i.e., mapping out bathroom locations, avoiding certain foods, avoiding long car rides, etc).

After the clinical interview, patients often complete a series of questionnaires in order to quantitatively assess their current symptoms and/or functioning. At this point, clinicians can determine which evidence-based psychological interventions would be most appropriate. Assessment results help the psychologist design and implement the best possible therapy. Research has suggested that cognitive behaviour therapy and its derivatives and gut-directed hypnotherapy are particularly useful in modifying symptoms and improving quality of life (Ford, Talley, Schoenfeld, Quigley, & Moayyedi, 2009).

Psychological Interventions for Patients with Gastrointestinal Conditions

In light of the impact of stress on inflammatory bowel disease and irritable bowel syndrome, as well as the high psychological co-morbidities in IBS, a considerable amount of research has been devoted to understanding the utility of psychologically based interventions in GI patients. In this section we introduce and briefly describe several primary psychological interventions that are used among patients with IBS and, to some extent, IBD. Finally, we explore the preliminary empirical evidence and relative efficacy of each intervention.

Cognitive Behavioural Therapy

Using cognitive behavioural therapy (CBT) techniques, the therapist attempts to alter an individual's affect by changing the substance of his or her behaviours and cognitions (thoughts). Within the context of IBD and IBS, CBT has been applied to both direct and indirect clinical symptoms. A direct approach to management of symptoms attempts to control clinical features of disease via

CBT psychotherapy. In contrast, an indirect approach to management of symptoms attempts to control secondary features of disease, namely depression and anxiety, via CBT psychotherapy (see In Practice box).

CBT has been successfully applied in multiple settings with the IBS patient population (Blanchard et al., 2007; Drossman et al., 2003; Lackner et al., 2008). This approach has been associated with decreased pain, decreased bowel symptoms, and improved psychological status (Lackner et al., 2006; Grover & Drossman, 2011). Among those who initiate therapy, early positive response to CBT sessions (within the first four weeks of therapeutic initiation) is predictive of maintained, long-term, positive outcome (Lackner et al., 2010).

Gut-Directed Hypnotherapy

Hypnotherapy is a technique in which a qualified clinician guides a patient to a state of deep and focused relaxation in order to decrease stress and even increase healing. During approximately 30 minutes, patients undergo four "steps": induction, deepening, metaphors and post-hypnotic suggestions, and re-alerting. The utility of hypnotherapy in the treatment of IBS has garnered support (Palsson, 2010). Among adults with IBS, hypnotherapy studies suggest a decrease in symptoms and an increase in quality of life among patients who received hypnotherapy treatment (Lindfors et al., 2012). More specifically, hypnotherapy has been associated with decreased somatization and psychological distress within this patient population (Palsson, Turner, Johnson, Burnett, & Whitehead, 2002). Broadly speaking, hypnotherapy has also been associated with markedly decreased gastrointestinal symptoms, improved psychological health, and decreased presence of co-morbid symptoms (Whorwell, 2008). Long-term follow-up studies suggest that therapeutic gains remain for up to five years and can be generalized as well to other gastrointestinal problems including heartburn, difficulty swallowing, non-cardiac chest pain, and peptic ulcer disease with similar effects (Palsson, 2010). More recently, hypnotherapy has been tried in IBD, although results are mixed as to whether it influences disease course or alters quality of life (Keefer & Keshavarzian, 2007; Mawdsley, Jenkins, Macey, Langmead, & Rampton, 2008).

Self-Management

Self-management describes the process in which patients take an active role learning about disease education, dietary guidelines, treatment adherence, and/or

🞖 IN PRACTICE

Cognitive Behavioural Therapy for IBS

Early in treatment, Dr Digestion and Jane discuss the physiology of IBS and the tendency of some people to have overactive bowels and increased pain sensitivity in response to normal bowel movements, resulting in diarrhea and pain. Dr Digestion also introduces the concept of the brain–gut connection and the influence of stress on symptoms. It is identified that Jane has a stressful job working as a teacher, which may contribute to her symptoms. On top of that, her symptoms have increased her level of stress—creating an unwanted cycle of stress and symptoms. In fact, Jane has modified her life to such an extent that she is increasingly controlled by her IBS symptoms.

Dr Digestion and Jane work to help Jane decrease worry about her symptoms. They do this by changing the way Jane thinks about her symptoms. While she used to think "Oh no, I feel my stomach starting to cramp. I should leave, just in case!" she eventually becomes able to think "OK. I am having a symptom, but this is just a little pain and I can work through it. If this gets worse, or if I need to go to the bathroom, I will excuse myself." They also work on her thoughts about what other people are thinking. While she used to think, "This is so embarrassing, what will they think if I leave again," she now thinks "If I have to go, I have to go; this is part of life. People will understand." Furthermore, Dr Digestion and Jane work on exposing her to her symptoms, so that she decreases physical reactions to the symptoms themselves. They can do this by using deep breathing exercises while Jane has abdominal pain, or helping her to physically relax in response to pain. This technique helps Jane to stay physically calm during her symptoms, thereby decreasing the likelihood of physical tension, which may exacerbate symptoms.

Finally, Dr Digestion and Jane discuss her tendency to cancel plans or stay home in anticipation of symptoms. This behaviour only increases Jane's attention to her symptoms and may also increase her likelihood to worry or feel depressed. Together, they begin to conduct "experiments" in which Jane does not cancel plans and then observes what happens while she is out of the home. Sometimes she does not have any symptoms, which is great. Other times she does have symptoms, but she is still able to enjoy herself. And just a few times, Jane has symptoms and leaves to go home. Through this experiment, Jane realizes that there is a good chance that she will be able to manage her symptoms if she goes out with her friends and that it is OK if she becomes symptomatic and has to go home—she'll go out with them again soon!

stress reduction (Jarrett et al., 2009). The ability of a patient to employ some self-management is critical in conditions such as IBD, where symptom monitoring is important in identifying early stages of a flare-up and strict medication adherence is necessary in preventing a flare-up. Comprehensive models of self-management often include skills training, CBT techniques, and relaxation therapy (Heitkemper et al., 2004). Self-management models of intervention have been applied to both IBD and IBS.

Among patients with CD and UC, self-management training is correlated with improved quality of life, altered disease course, and increased treatment adherence (Hommel et al., 2012; Keefer, Doerfler, & Artz, 2012). Similar effects have been found within the IBS patient population. Within this patient group, investigators have reported decreased symptoms, improved quality of life, increasing functionality, and stress

reduction following self-management directed intervention (Deechakawan, Cain, Jarrett, Burr, & Heitkemper, 2011; Hsueh et al., 2011; Heitkemper et al., 2004; Ringstrom, Storsrud, & Simren, 2012).

Future Directions

In this chapter, we discussed two prominent gastrointestinal conditions. IBS has received the most attention from health psychology research and ongoing investigations are beginning to explore how psychological treatments work for IBS patients, for which subsets of patients they work, and how to incorporate this information into the medical decision-making model.

While there has been increased focus on IBD as a target for psychological assessment and treatment, controversy exists around the type of psychological support needed, how stress and psychological co-morbidity might impact the disease (and vice versa), who is likely to benefit from a psychosocial approach, and whether psychological treatments for IBD have any effect on disease outcomes. Further, it is likely that interventions targeting health behaviour change (smoking cessation, stress management) rather than psychological distress may improve care for IBD patients (Keefer et al., 2012). While most of the research to date has been in the areas of irritable bowel syndrome and inflammatory bowel disease, health psychologists have also started to make an impact in other areas of gastroenterology. For example, there is some new interest in identifying the psychosocial factors influencing outcome in chronic pancreatitis (Braganza, Lee, McCloy, & McMahon, 2011) and hepatitis C (Rifai, Gleason, & Sabouni, 2010; Silberbogen, Ulloa, Janke, & Mori, 2009). Psychological assessment and treatment techniques have also been modified to assist with functional heartburn, non-cardiac chest pain (Chiarioni, Palsson, & Whitehead, 2008; Palsson & Whitehead, 2006), dysphagia (difficulty swallowing), globus (the persistent feeling of having a lump in one's throat) (Kiebles, Kwiatek, Pandolfino,

Kahrilas, & Keefer, 2010), eosiniphilic esophagitis (Taft, Ballou, & Keefer, 2012; Taft, Kern, Keefer, Burstein, & Hirano, 2011), and the growing problem of fecal incontinence in older adults (Whitehead, 2002; Whitehead et al., 2009).

Future research in psychosocial gastroenterology will likely focus on a few topics. First, research is currently ongoing to identify psychosocial "phenotypes" that allow for streamlined medical care. For example, patients who do not respond to traditional medical treatments may have psychosocial factors that undermine the efficacy of their treatment. Identifying these could positively impact care, including reducing health costs from unnecessary testing and ineffective treatment. Another likely future direction will be to improve on research that has demonstrated differences in brain function in patients with functional gastrointestinal diseases and to focus on better characterizing the importance of the brain–gut axis. Along these lines, it is likely that psychologists will become more involved in identifying medical targets of treatment by clarifying the role of psychosocial factors in the functioning of the gastrointestinal system.

SUMMARY

Health psychologists have an important role in the assessment and treatment of gastrointestinal conditions. The gastrointestinal tract interacts with the environment more than most other organ systems, and therefore lifestyle is an important consideration in gastrointestinal health. Health psychologists are well equipped to provide treatments likely to benefit gastrointestinal motility, decrease pain and discomfort, improve quality of life, and teach chronic disease self-management skills.

Critical Thought Questions

1. We discussed the importance of visceral hypersensitivity in irritable bowel syndrome. What role does visceral hypersensitivity play in inflammatory bowel disease?
2. Cognitive behavioural therapy is an evidence-based therapy for IBS. How might a health psychologist adapt CBT for IBS to patients with Crohn's disease or ulcerative colitis?
3. Would you advise a patient with ulcerative colitis to quit smoking? Why or why not?

Recommended Reading

Barney, P., Weisman, P., Jarrett, M., Levy, R.L., & Heitkemper, M. (2010). *Master your IBS: An 8-week plan proven to control the symptoms of irritable bowel syndrome*. Bethesda, Md: AGA Press.

Drossman, D.A. (2006). *Rome III: The functional gastrointestinal disorders* (3rd ed.). McLean, Virginia: Degnon Associates.

Gershon, M.P. (1999). *The second brain: A groundbreaking new understanding of nervous disorders of the stomach and intestine*. New York: Harper Perennial.

Lackner, J.M. (2007). *Controlling IBS the drug-free way: A 10-step plan for symptom relief*. New York: Stewart, Tabori and Chang.

16

The Renal and Urological Systems: Focus on Kidney Disease

KONSTADINA GRIVA

Learning Objectives

In this chapter you will:

- Learn the basic functions of renal and urinary systems and diseases that affect these systems.

- Learn about the different renal replacement treatments (dialysis and transplantation) available for people with kidney disease.

- Gain an understanding of the key issues around psychosocial adjustment and functioning that are central to the experience of kidney disease for both the adult and pediatric patients.

- Appreciate the importance of psychological interventions in the context of kidney disease.

Introduction

The case presented in the accompanying In Practice box illustrates some of the difficulties that individuals with kidney disease face. In this chapter the psychosocial context of kidney disease is highlighted. Discussion of associated treatments is also included.

The Renal and Urinary System

The urinary system is made up of two kidneys, which drain via the ureters into the urinary bladder. The urethra carries urine from the bladder to the outside of the body. In men, the prostate (which is just below the bladder), the penis, and scrotum (containing the testicles) also make up part of the urinary system (Figure 16.1). Besides kidney disease, a range of urological conditions (e.g., urinary tract infections, prostate enlargement, bladder/prostate cancer, urinary incontinence, erectile dysfunction, bladder stones, and prostate cancer) can also occur. These conditions have been shown to have a significant effect on quality of life

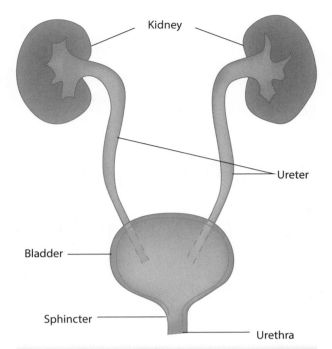

FIGURE 16.1 | Urinary system.

⊞ IN PRACTICE

Dealing with Dialysis

Life for 55-year-old Chris was a lot different before he found himself in need of dialysis because he developed kidney disease secondary to his poorly controlled diabetes. He has always been careless over diabetes care and has had trouble keeping his blood glucose in check. Over time, the persistently high levels of glucose damaged his kidneys, causing a second serious condition for him to cope with on a daily basis. He now spends three days a week in a hemodialysis centre for treatment. He is limited in his consumption of liquids to about one-half litre per day. That includes drinks and foods with high water content like watermelons. He had to rearrange his life—working hours, visits with friends, grocery shopping—around dialysis. He now becomes bored sitting on the dialysis chair every other day. It is uncomfortable sitting for three and a half hours with his arm held out straight. His shoulder and elbow cramp but he cannot bend it or turn it and he feels drained at the end of the procedure and too tired to spend time with his partner or to meet friends. He considers dialysis day to be a wasted day.

Chris had to cut back on his working hours and is now struggling to make his mortgage payment and pay for many of his expenses. Due to his poor health he cannot be considered a transplant candidate and, after hearing of several patients from his dialysis centre who died, he now believes that he has no hope of getting his normal life back and very little to look forward to. He has stopped taking his medication and watching his diet and fluid intake. He also missed two dialysis sessions last month. Doing so nearly cost him his life as he became seriously ill and had to be rushed to hospital emergency. He took this as a wake-up call. He has requested referral to a psychologist and has now been regularly attending sessions structured around a cognitive behavioural plan aiming to increase his tolerance of physical symptoms through pacing of activities and relaxation and to challenge his maladaptive beliefs related to treatment outcomes and course of illness. Using goal-setting and self-monitoring, his dietary and fluid control has improved. He has been able to resume some activities and, although he continues to have physical difficulties, his quality of life and outlook have improved.

(QOL) as they cause bothersome symptoms (e.g., pain, discomfort) and interfere with activities of daily living (e.g., Heijnsdijk et al., 2012). Psychosocial programs used as adjunct to medical treatments tend to improve symptoms and QOL in patients with lower urinary tract symptoms, localized prostate cancer (Brown et al., 2007; Penedo et al., 2006), and potentially other urological conditions (Penedo & Dahn, 2004). Nonetheless, the primary focus of this chapter is kidney disease.

Kidney Disease

The kidneys act as vital filters and perform many complex homeostatic functions essential to life: removal of unwanted products of metabolism and excess water through urine; release of hormones that control production of red blood cells and regulate blood pressure; and maintenance of the correct levels of chemicals in our body, which help the heart and muscles to function properly. Kidney disease denotes conditions characterized by reduction or loss in the ability of kidneys to perform these functions. Loss of kidney function can be progressive and gradual (**chronic kidney disease**) or sudden (**acute kidney injury**).

Acute Kidney Injury

Acute kidney injury (AKI), also known as acute renal failure, is a life-threatening condition that relates to loss of kidney function that develops rapidly over the course of hours or days. It usually happens as a result of a disorder that directly affects the kidney, its blood supply, or urine flow from it. In some cases it can be due to toxicity (e.g., adverse reactions to drugs or exposure to chemicals), infections, or injury. AKI is common among hospitalized patients, with older adults being particularly affected. Although AKI is often reversible with complete recovery of kidney function, survivors may be left with lasting damage that could lead to a progressive decline in kidney function in the future and lower QOL (Basile, 2008).

Chronic Kidney Disease

When one's kidneys are failing in a gradual and permanent manner, the person has chronic kidney disease (CKD). A chronic loss of kidney function may be caused by a number of factors including diabetes, glomerulonephritis (a condition where the immune system mistakenly attacks tissue in the kidneys), hypertension, and familial polycystic renal disease (an inherited condition where cysts start to form in the kidneys and slowly grow).

Detection and management of CKD have been facilitated in recent years by clinical practice guidelines developed under the National Kidney Foundation's Kidney Disease Outcomes Quality Initiative (National Kidney Foundation, 2002), which classifies CKD into five stages (with stage 5 being the most severe) of increasing disease severity based on glomerular filtration rate (GFR), an index of kidneys' filtering capacity.

Progression from early (stages 1 to 3) to advanced stages of CKD with the decline of kidney function is related to a gradual accumulation of metabolic waste products and typically is accompanied by several symptoms (most notably fatigue and lethargy, muscle weakness, generalized itching, loss of appetite, nausea, and vomiting). Stage 5 CKD is also referred to as kidney failure or **end-stage renal disease (ESRD)**, wherein there is total or near-total loss of kidney function. Water, waste, and toxic substances accumulate to dangerous levels so that most individuals in this stage need dialysis or **transplantation** to stay alive.

CKD has emerged as a global public health problem with rates and demand for renal replacement therapy rising rapidly among adults, due mainly to an aging population and a worldwide epidemic of obesity and diabetes. Data from the National Health and Nutrition Examination Surveys (NHANES) indicate that up to 13.1 per cent of the US cohort may have CKD (Coresh et al., 2007), and surveys in Australia, Europe, and Japan show the prevalence of CKD to be 6–16 per cent of their respective populations (Hallan et al., 2006). The frequency of CKD increases with age and is more common in particular ethnic groups (i.e., Hispanic, African-American, or South-Asian) (USRDS, 2011) and among individuals with lower socio-economic standing (Couser, Remuzzi, Mendis, & Tonelli, 2011).

In 2011 the UN High Level Meeting on Prevention and Control of Non-communicable Diseases designated CKD as one of the leading non-communicable diseases that necessitate global health action (United Nations, 2011). Moreover, the declaration of World Kidney Day, to be observed annually on 8 March, sends a clear message that "*CKD is common, harmful, and treatable.*"

The economic burden of CKD in terms of direct health-care costs and loss of productivity is very large. For instance, Medicare expenditures on CKD patients in the United States exceeded $60 billion in 2007 and represented 27 per cent of the total Medicare budget (Collins, Chen, Gilbertson, & Foley, 2009). In Canada, the cost for hemodialysis is approximately $60,000 per patient per year and each kidney transplantation incurs a one-time cost of approximately $23,000, with $6,000 added annually for necessary medication (CIHI, 2011a).

Moreover, CKD is associated with extremely high morbidity and mortality even in its earlier stages (Couser et al., 2011). International data from the Dialysis Outcomes and Practice Patterns Study (DOPPS) and the Canadian Institute of Health Information (CIHI) indicate 15.6 per cent, 6.6 per cent, 15.6 per cent, and 21.7 per cent year mortality rates for dialysis patients in Europe, Japan, Canada, and the US, respectively (Goodkin et al., 2003; CIHI, 2011b). Although ESRD is rarely a cause of death in itself, it increases the risk of other mortality causes such as cardiovascular disease (Muntner, He, Hamm, Loria, & Whelton, 2002). Cardiovascular disease, including stroke, sudden cardiac death, coronary heart disease, acute myocardial infarction, and congestive heart failure, accounts for premature death in about 50 per cent of dialysis patients in Europe and North America (Foley, Parfrey, & Sarnak, 1998).

Treatment for CKD

CKD is an irreversible and progressive disease. Renal functioning can only be stabilized and preserved but cannot recover. Once CKD is diagnosed, the aim of treatment is, therefore, to slow further damage to kidneys so as to delay the commencement of dialysis while reducing cardiovascular risks and relieving symptoms. Management of early-stage CKD involves blood pressure control, diet and nutritional management, multiple medications, and careful monitoring through regular appointments with health-care providers. When relevant, better management of underlying conditions causing kidney damage, such as diabetes, is also paramount.

Early detection and proactive management are essential to improve prognosis. This has led to calls for primary-care screening and surveillance programs to identify individuals at risk and to raise awareness, which is less than 20 per cent even at advanced CKD stages. Once in ESRD, patients may be treated with **renal replacement therapy (RRT)** (kidney transplant, dialysis) or supportive non-dialytic therapy, referred to as conservative care. Health disparities (see Chapter 19) in access to transplantation, reluctance to engage with health services, miscommunication, and poorer treatment outcomes (i.e., meeting clinical targets or lower adherence)

have been reported in non-Caucasian patients and ethnic minority groups (e.g., Aboriginal patients), a finding that highlights the need for patient-centred, culturally sensitive health care throughout all stages of CKD. Providing health services to minority cultural groups is challenging because of access as well as the need to negotiate cultural differences in the context of medical consultations and health-care services.

Transplantation

Renal transplantation is associated with the greatest longevity and the highest quality of life (QOL) as well as reduced medical costs (Sayin, Mutluay, & Sindel, 2007; Wolfe et al., 1999). Kidney transplants may come from a deceased donor or from a living donor following extensive evaluation and preparation of the recipient and donor. There are risks to donor yet the rates of complications are low and, interestingly, donors often report improved psychological well-being and QOL after the

PHOTO 16.1 | Comedian George Lopez underwent kidney transplantation in 2005.

transplantation (Clemens et al., 2006). Several medical criteria are considered when selecting potential transplant candidates/donors and all recipients are screened to ensure suitability. Biological age per se is not a barrier, yet co-morbidities may limit accessibility of transplantation to older patients. Despite mandated evaluation of all dialysis patients for transplant eligibility in Medicare, disparities remain in relation to access to and waiting times for transplantation for racial and ethnic groups (i.e., African-American and Hispanic patients relative to Caucasian patients). Socio-economic factors (e.g., access to care, insurance, income), geographical considerations (e.g., distance to transplant centre), and patient or physical preferences are thought to underline these differences (Joshi, Gaynor, & Ciancio, 2012).

In North America, first-year survival rates with a functioning graft after deceased-donor transplantation now exceeds 90 per cent, but rates decrease over time (USRDS, 2011). In Canada, for example, survival rate at five years falls to 79 per cent, mainly due to cardiovascular disease and infection (CIHI, 2011b).

The limited availability of organ donors and the unsuitability of some patients for surgery mean that the majority of patients are maintained on long-term dialysis. In the United States and Canada, only 2.5 and 3.5 out of every 100 dialysis patients, respectively, receive a deceased-donor kidney transplant in a year (USRDS, 2011; CIHI, 2011b). Furthermore, all transplants have a definite limitation, with most grafts eventually failing through a process of chronic rejection and subsequent resumption of dialysis. This makes dialysis the most prevalent form of treatment for ESRD worldwide.

Dialysis

Hemodialysis (HD) and **peritoneal dialysis (PD)** are the two types of dialysis. They differ in technical procedures yet provide equivalent survival benefits and clinical efficacy (Mehrotra, Chiu, Kalantar-Zadeh, Bargman, & Vonesh, 2011). Hemodialysis is usually performed in an outpatient dialysis facility three times a week for three to five hours, and trained nurses and technicians

PHOTO 16.2 | Woman undergoing dialysis.

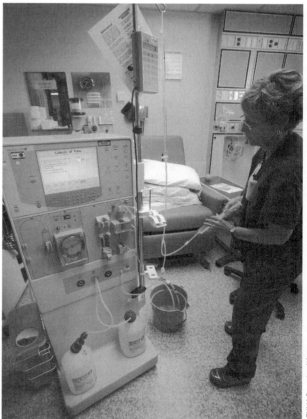

PHOTO 16.3 | A hemodialysis unit.

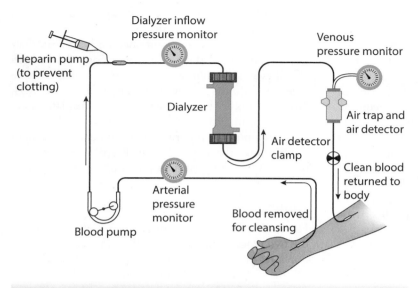

FIGURE 16.2 | Illustration of hemodialysis procedure.

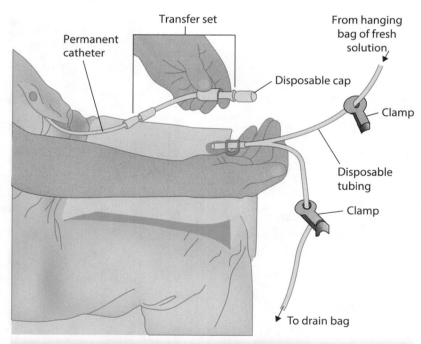

FIGURE 16.3 | Illustration of peritoneal dialysis procedure.

a surgically modified blood vessel that is created by connecting an artery to a vein), graft, or catheter, so that blood can flow out to the HD machine for filtering and then back into the body (see Figure 16.2).

Peritoneal dialysis (PD) uses the peritoneum (a thin membrane lining the abdomen area) as the filtering surface. A permanent catheter is used for daily repeated instillation into the abdomen and drainage of dialysate (a special liquid that attracts metabolic waste and excess fluid) and is administered by the patient and/or caregiver, typically three or four times a day (continuous ambulatory PD [CAPD]), or performed automatically overnight by a machine while the patient sleeps (automated PD) (see Figure 16.3). PD offers patients the convenience of home-based care and continuous clearance but requires a daily commitment and a greater level of involvement by patient and/or caregiver, with scrupulous attention to hygiene to avoid infection to the peritoneum.

Although the delivery of satisfactory pre-dialysis education is the subject of international guidelines and most patients may be medically suitable for either PD or HD, HD is the norm in most settings (USRDS, 2011). PD utilization rates remain low worldwide with the exception of settings (e.g., Hong Kong) that implement a PD-first policy. The proportion of ESRD patients on HD and PD in the United States is 65.1 per cent and 4.8 per cent, respectively (USRDS, 2011), and in Canada 48.4 per cent and 10.7 per cent (CIHI, 2011b) (see Table 16.1).

Decision-Making Process in CKD

The decision-making process in the context of CKD involves several parties (patients, families, and health-care providers) and a complex interplay of organizational/socio-economic structures (e.g., reimbursement or medical insurance policies) as well as patient/provider preferences

carry out the prescribed treatment using a dialysis machine under the direction of a physician. Home HD programs allow patients to dialyze at home following training. Hemodialysis requires establishing access to the blood stream through an arteriovenous fistula (i.e.,

TABLE 16.1 | RRT Distribution for Prevalent Population (in Percentages)

	Transplant	HD	PD
United States	30.1	65.1	4.8
Canada	40.9	48.4	10.7
United Kingdom	46.8	45.3	7.9
Australia	44.2	44.9	10.9
New Zealand	37.8	40.4	21.8

Sources: Canada, 2010 data: (CIHI, 2012); US, 2009 data: (USRDS, 2011); UK, 2010 data: (ERA EDTA, 2010); Australia and New Zealand, 2010 data: (Briggs & Hurst, 2011; Grace & Hurst, 2011).

and clinical needs. Lifestyle and psychosocial considerations are pivotal in guiding decision-making on dialysis modality and often are ranked higher than medical considerations (Murray et al., 2009). These psychosocial considerations include availability of social support, preference for autonomy and control over treatment, fear of needling and/or infections, concerns about body image and/or geographical location of dialysis centres. Likewise, decisions on whether to pursue kidney transplantation involve considerations of the risks and benefits of transplantation and of the transplantation referral and evaluation process, which are variable across centres and regions.

Patients may face multiple treatment-related decisions as treatment transitions are frequent in CKD. These decisions may regard the commencement of dialysis, a switch from one treatment type to another (as in the case of patients receiving a kidney transplant), patients withdrawing from dialysis or converting from PD to HD, and/or a return back to dialysis after graft failure. It is anticipated that each form of therapy (i.e., HD, PD, or transplantation) may have a role to play during the lifetime of patients with CKD.

Conservative Management

More than 95 per cent of ESRD cases begin RRT via one of the dialysis modalities. However, for patients with poor functional status and high levels of co-morbidity, there is no guarantee that initiating dialysis will prolong life or improve QOL (Smith et al., 2003). It is therefore reasonable for some patients to choose, in consultation with their renal team, to have conservative (non-dialytic) management, and the numbers of such patients are increasing steadily. In Australia, about 14 per cent of pre-dialysis patients referred for education select conservative management (Morton, Turner, Howard, Snelling, & Webster, 2012) whereas comparable numbers in North America are approximately 5 per cent (Mendelssohn et al., 2009). A Canadian study demonstrated that a very high (61 per cent) percentage of people on dialysis regretted their decision to start on dialysis, stating that the commencement of dialysis was their physician's decision. Moreover, 90 per cent of dialysis patients reported never having discussed advanced-care planning with their nephrologists (Davison, 2010).

Risk of withdrawal or opting out of dialysis is higher in older patients (Leggat, Bloembergen, Levine, Hulbert-Shearon, & Port, 1997). Conservative management can only be palliative, aiming to control symptoms and complications, avoiding factors that can accelerate the deterioration of renal function, providing advanced-care planning, and addressing psychosocial and spiritual needs of patients and their families.

CKD in Children

Unlike in adults, for whom diabetes and hypertension are the main causes of CKD, congenital causes (e.g., urological malformations, glomerulonephritis) are responsible for the greatest percentage of CKD cases in children. Pediatric CKD patients still constitute a small percentage of CKD populations and are mostly treated with transplantation (see Chapter 17 for a discussion of pediatric health psychology). Dialysis is generally commenced as an interim option while awaiting a transplant. Due to the complexities with HD in maintaining vascular access in children as well as their inherent cardiovascular instability, PD is usually the modality of choice. Despite renal replacement therapy, death rates for children with CKD remain 30 times higher than for children without kidney disease (McDonald & Craig, 2004).

Depression, anxiety, behavioural problems, difficulties in social relationships and schooling, delayed growth, and impaired cognitive development have also been identified in this population (Tong, Lowe, Sainsbury, & Craig, 2008). Long-term social consequences such as unemployment and dependency on caregivers have also been reported in young adults who underwent long-term dialysis during childhood (Diseth, Tangeraas, Reinfjell, & Bjerre, 2011; Groothoff et al., 2005).

Psychological Problems and Quality of Life

The psychological impact of CKD is a function of the disruptive and permanent consequences of the disease and treatment on patients' physical health, identity, emotions, family, lifestyle, relationships, and employment. Patients are required to make ongoing psychological adjustments over the course of their illness: accepting the life-threatening diagnosis and need for lifelong treatment, learning the techniques of dialysis, integrating treatment into their lives, and coping with treatment transitions/failures, related side effects, and complications.

Quality of Life (QOL)

QOL is increasingly recognized as an important measure of treatment outcome. QOL is broadly defined as a person's sense of physical and emotional well-being and ability to function productively in daily life. In the field of ESRD and CKD there has been a rapid increase in the number of studies investigating patients' QOL using several condition-specific QOL measures developed to assess overall physical and emotional well-being alongside functioning in kidney-specific domains: Kidney Disease Quality of Life (Hays, Kallich, Mapes, Coons, & Carter, 1994); CHOICE Health Experience Questionnaire (Wu et al., 2001); and Transplant Effects Questionnaire (Ziegelmann et al., 2002).

ESRD patients, compared with the general population, have poor QOL, particularly as measured by its physical components such as physical functioning or vitality; in addition, lower QOL is associated with increased risk of mortality and hospitalizations (Finkelstein, Wuerth, & Finkelstein, 2009). The extent to which QOL is impaired appears to be related to disease severity, burden of co-morbid conditions and symptoms, and affect, such as depressive symptoms and perceived stress (Chan

et al., 2012). The way people think about their CKD or treatment may be another important influence on QOL. Negative perceptions about controllability of illness or treatment/illness intrusiveness are associated with worse QOL (Griva, Jayasena, Davenport, Harrison, & Newman, 2009).

QOL improves following kidney transplantation (Cameron, Whiteside, Katz, & Devins, 2000), yet transplantation may not fully restore QOL to levels seen in the general population. Transplant failure can also have profound effects on well-being, often resulting in diminished QOL and increased levels of depression (Christensen, Turner, Smith, Holman, & Gregory, 1991; Griva, Davenport, Harrison, & Newman, 2012).

QOL outcomes between dialysis modalities are mostly comparable when sample differences are adjusted for (Boateng & East, 2011; Cameron et al. 2000). Nonetheless, some differences emerge on specific QOL subscales, such as dietary restrictions, dialysis access problems, ability to travel in favour of PD or sexual functioning favouring HD, reflecting the procedural differences between the modalities (Wu et al., 2004).

Neurocognitive Function

Everyday function and QOL are intimately linked to cognition. Decreased cognitive abilities, such as the ability to acquire, understand, retain, and retrieve knowledge, may impact many aspects of patients' lives, including work and school as well as tasks related to disease management and medical decision-making (e.g., selecting a treatment modality).

© csakist/iStockphoto

PHOTO 16.4 | A large portion of dialysis patients experience cognitive symptoms in domains such as attention and memory.

Cognitive dysfunction is a well-known complication of CKD. It has been shown that cognitive impairment is relative to the severity of CKD (Kurella, Chertow, Luan, & Yaffe, 2004) and that the prevalence of cognitive deficits is particularly high in ESRD patients. An estimated 30–60 per cent of dialysis patients experience cognitive impairment, yet the nature of these deficits is under debate, with some research highlighting global declines and other research noting impairments in specific domains such as memory, executive function, psychomotor speed, and attention (Koushik, McArthur, & Baird, 2010).

Cognitive function varies significantly during the HD cycle, being worst during HD and best the day after (Griva et al., 2003; Murray et al., 2007). These acute changes mirror the intermittent nature of conventional three-times-a-week hemodialysis that allows for the accumulation of toxins. By comparison, PD patients have not been shown to exhibit fluctuations in their cognitive abilities, yet rates of cognitive impairments are comparable to those in HD (Griva et al., 2003).

With successful kidney transplantation cognitive functioning improves, particularly with respect to memory, with more recent studies documenting beneficial effects on attention and concentration, too (Madero, Gul, & Sarnak, 2008). These data indicate that the cognitive deficits while on dialysis are to some extent reversible. The use of immunosuppressive medications following kidney transplantation, however, may adversely affect cognitive functioning. Their long-term use has been linked with hippocampal atrophy (Brown et al., 2004; Cukor, Rosenthal, & Kimmel, 2010), which is associated with memory problems.

Research on clinical implications of cognitive dysfunction is not well developed but cognitive impairment can be associated with an increased risk of mortality (Griva, Stygall, et al., 2010) and may impact treatment adherence and the ability to resume work (Gelb, Shapiro, Hill, & Thornton, 2008). More research is, therefore, warranted to explore the value of cognitive enhancement interventions for CKD patients.

Emotional Distress

Depression is common in CKD patients although reported prevalence varies due to differences in the assessment and criteria for the diagnosis of depression. Inherent difficulties in assessing depression in dialysis patients occur because the symptoms of depression and symptoms of the kidney disease overlap (e.g., fatigue, loss of appetite, sleep disorders) (Hedayati & Finkelstein, 2009). Most studies use questionnaire assessments that identify "possible" or "probable" depression but a diagnostic interview is required to confirm the presence of clinically significant depression. Reported prevalence rates of depression range from 19 per cent of those diagnosed with CKD meeting the criteria for depression, using a structured diagnostic interview (Watnick, Wang, Demadura, & Ganzini, 2005), to 47 per cent who scored on the depressed range of self-report questionnaires (Chilcot, Wellsted, & Farrington, 2010).

Successful transplantation is associated with lower rates of depression than is dialysis (Cameron et al., 2000). Nonetheless, the impact of dialysis on the prevalence of depression has yielded contradictory findings. It has been suggested that depression is significantly lower in patients receiving PD as compared to those on HD (Kalender, Ozdemir, Dervisoglu, & Ozdemir, 2007), mainly due to PD affording greater opportunities for control and autonomy and the convenience of home-based treatment (Wuerth et al., 2002). Conversely, the burden of self-care and daily commitment of PD have been shown to adversely affect emotional well-being, especially in CAPD patients and those with more co-morbid conditions (Eitel, Hatchett, Friend, Griffin, & Wadhwa, 1995; Griva, Davenport, Harrison, & Newman, 2010).

Depression is associated with poor QOL and adverse clinical outcomes. The Dialysis Outcomes and Practice Patterns Study has shown a strong correlation of mortality, withdrawal from therapy, and hospitalization rates with depressive symptoms in a large cohort of HD patients (Lopes et al., 2002), whereas high levels of depressive symptoms were associated with increased risk of cardiovascular events in the Choices for Healthy Outcomes in Caring for End-Stage Renal Disease Study (Boulware et al., 2006).

Depression may affect clinical outcomes via a number of pathways. First, depressed mood may be associated with increases in a variety of health-risk behaviours (e.g., low adherence to medication, skipping dialysis sessions, poor diet and/or malnutrition). Neuroendocrine dysregulation represents another plausible pathway whereby depressed mood influences prognosis and survival. That is, elevations in cortisol, catecholamines, and inflammatory cytokines (i.e., proteins that control responses to foreign antigens and germs) are commonly observed in depressed persons and have been associated with immune dysfunction and poor health (Kimmel, Cukor, Cohen, & Peterson, 2007). Recent evidence also shows that withdrawal from dialysis, as a cause of death, increases dramatically in patients with depressive symptoms (Lacson et al., 2012).

In contrast to depression, anxiety disorders have received little attention in CKD patients (Cukor, Cohen,

Peterson, & Kimmel, 2007). According to a review, 38 per cent (range: 12 per cent to 52 per cent) of ESRD patients report substantial anxiety symptoms (Murtagh et al., 2007).

Studies evaluating interventions to ameliorate emotional dysfunction in CKD are few. Evidence suggests that depression and anxiety may be under-treated in this population (Chilcot et al., 2010). Pharmacological therapy can improve outcomes yet there are concerns as to whether the side effects of antidepressant medication can be tolerated well by ESRD patients. More recent work indicates that cognitive behavioural therapy might be an efficacious, acceptable, and practical treatment for depressive symptoms in dialysis patients (Duarte, Miyazaki, Blay, & Sesso, 2009).

Treatment-Related Stress

ESRD patients face new, unexpected adjustments and challenges that extend far beyond the direct consequences of their illness (Cukor et al., 2007). General distress (e.g., depression) may be related to or accompanied by treatment-specific concerns. Dialysis regimens are understandably sources of significant stress as they entail intrusive and time-consuming treatment schedules, dependency on others, reliance on technology for survival, unpleasant side effects and complications, lifelong behavioural changes, and considerable limitations on patients' lives (Yeh & Chou, 2007). In some settings where geographical distances to dialysis facilities are long, the access to dialysis can be economically, psychologically, and physiologically stressful for patients and their families. There seems to be an increased risk of death and low QOL with longer time to travel to dialysis centres (Moist et al., 2008).

The transplantation process, which ranges from pre-transplant evaluation and waiting for graft/donation to operation and recovery, also brings about pervasive psychosocial effects. These include emotions related to transplant and act of donation, such as fear of transplant failure, guilt, indebtedness, or concerns towards donor's well-being (Griva et al., 2002). Other stressors revolve around the need for constant vigilance and ongoing medical management, the side effects and post-transplant complications, as well as struggling to regain a sense of normality and to resume activities (Orr, Willis, Holmes, Britton, & Orr, 2007).

Challenges also extend to kidney donors. Although most donors view donation as a rewarding and positive experience, they, too, renegotiate their identity, roles and responsibilities, and relationships following donation with some reports of emotional distress and low QOL (Tong et al., 2012). Other issues pertaining specifically to living donor transplantation include ambivalence and conflict related to donation that may strain family relationships (Franklin & Crombie, 2003).

Other Psychological Factors

Social Support

Social support has been defined as the perception that an individual is a member of a complex network in which one can give and receive affection, aid, and obligation (House, Landis, & Umberson, 1988). Social support, from a spouse, family members, friends, colleagues, or the community, has been linked to better outcomes in CKD such as lower symptoms of depression, higher QOL and life satisfaction, and better adherence to treatment (Cohen et al., 2007). Lack of social support or social isolation has also been found to be associated with increased risk of mortality (Untas et al., 2011). Besides clinical outcomes and adaptation, family members or friends may influence a patient's treatment modality decision. A patient selecting home dialysis (i.e., PD) may reverse this decision if he or she does not feel supported by family. ESRD patients are concerned about the effects of dialysis therapy on their families and seek/value family involvement in and acceptance of their modality choice (Morton, Tong, Howard, Snelling, & Webster, 2010). Research suggests that contact and support from physicians is also important for patient satisfaction and adherence (Plantinga et al., 2004).

Illness and Treatment Beliefs

Patient perceptions of illness and treatment are strongly associated with psychosocial and health-related outcomes. Illness perceptions are conceptualized within a framework of self-regulation (common-sense model) (Leventhal, Brissette, & Leventhal, 2003) where, following the onset of disease, patients develop an organized set of beliefs that determine how they cope with, understand, and manage the illness. Research examining the role of illness beliefs in CKD shows considerable impact on QOL, depression, and adherence. These associations are particularly strong for patients' beliefs about the extent to which the illness and treatment are disruptive and for the amount of control they feel they have over their disease (Griva et al., 2009; O'Connor, Jardine, & Millar, 2008). Illness beliefs have also been linked to survival rates (Chilcot, Wellsted, & Farrington, 2011).

Adherence

Managing CKD and ESRD are considerable challenges. The majority of patients are diagnosed in late adulthood when health behaviours are firmly established and thereby harder to change. Moreover, most patients present with such coexisting illnesses as diabetes and hypertension, which complicate regimens.

Even when not complicated by co-morbidities, CKD and ESRD involve a complex and demanding behavioural regimen above and beyond dialysis. This includes continual nutritional management (e.g., restriction of dietary intake of phosphate and potassium-rich foods, and reduced salt and fluid intake), multiple medications to facilitate management of blood pressure, anemia, and other problems related to co-morbidities, and recommendations about exercise. Kidney transplantation releases patients from the daily constraints of dialysis but requires strict adherence to immunosuppressive medication, known to be associated with many side effects (e.g., mood swings, sleep problems, and sexual dysfunction, to name a few).

Non-adherence is a profound problem in ESRD patients, owing to its prevalence within the population as well as to its impact on health outcomes, namely increased risk of mortality, hospitalization (Saran et al., 2003), and transplant rejection (Butler, Roderick, Mullee, Mason, & Peveler, 2004). Rates for non-adherence to the dialysis prescription, including medication, fluid intake, diet regimen, and medical appointments are substantial, ranging from 2 to 99 per cent depending on methods and criteria used to define non-adherence (Denhaerynck, Manhaeve, Dobbels, Garzoni, Nolte, & De Geest, 2007; Griva, Lai, Lim, Yu, Foo, & Newman, 2014). Non-adherence to immunosuppressive medication among transplant recipients also is common (Butler et al., 2004; Denhaerynck et al., 2005), with rates being substantially higher than those in recipients of other types of organ transplant (Dew et al., 2007). See also Chapter 3 for discussion of adherence with medical regimens.

Patient characteristics, such as educational level and socio-economic status, may create literacy and financial barriers to adherence. Research indicated that non-adherence is more likely in younger patients, those with lower income and inadequate prescription coverage, some ethnic minority groups, and patients with transportation challenges (Browne & Merighy, 2010). The strongest associations, however, are reported between adherence and health beliefs, lack of self-efficacy, and lack of social support (Karamanidou, Clatworthy, Weinman, & Horne, 2008).

Psychological Assessment in CKD

Psychological assessment in CKD has shifted from making selections (e.g., transplant candidacy) to guiding clinical care. Assessment clarifies the patient's needs and identifies problems so that appropriate support can be rendered. Assessors gather information on the patient's lifestyle, personality, coping patterns, understanding of the illness, perception of treatment regimens, recent life stresses or changes, and other issues related to the disease/treatment.

Assessment may also involve diagnostic interviews and/or neuropsychological testing to diagnose cognitive impairment or signs of psychopathology (e.g., major depressive disorder or dementia). Several test batteries and standardized instruments are available and widely used with CKD patients (see review by Danquah, Wasserman, Meininger, & Bergstrom, 2010).

Psychological Interventions

Psychologists can make significant contributions to the care of patients with CKD, from assessment to intervention and provision of psychological care. Some of these interventions may be informed rather than conducted by psychologists, through education/training of healthcare staff who deliver clinic-integrated programs and consultancy.

A variety of interventions have been developed and used with ESRD patients to decrease distress and support adherence with the hope of enhancing QOL and improving clinical outcomes.

Self-management interventions drawing on social cognitive theory (Bandura, 1997) have become increasingly popular in recent years (also see Chapter 1). Self-management has been described as an individual's ability to manage his or her symptoms, treatment regimen, and lifestyle changes inherent in living with a chronic condition (Barlow, Wright, Sheasby, Turner, & Hainsworth, 2002). Typically, these programs incorporate informational/educational components to impart knowledge and skills, along with a variety of psychological methods to empower patients to change behaviour. The multi-component approach has been underlined by the recognition that knowledge alone is not a sufficient precondition of change. These interventions are designed to enhance goal-setting, problem-solving, coping, stress management, social support, and self-motivation.

Interventions in the context of CKD can improve adherence to diet, fluid control, and medication (Matteson & Russell, 2010; Sharp, Wild, & Gumley, 2005). They can also lead to increased survival (Mason, Khunti, Stone, Farooqi, & Carr, 2008) and lower hospitalization rates, and can delay the progression of CKD (Chen et al., 2011). Although it appears that conducting these multi-component interventions in group formats may offer optimal efficacy and cost efficiency, future work needs to address the various components of the interventions to better understand the mechanisms of action. In addition to psycho-educational interventions, appropriately supervised exercise-only programs have been shown to improve important dimensions of dialysis patients' QOL and functioning (Johansen, 2008).

Future Directions

Despite the growing body of research, issues remain that warrant further work. These include the role of interventions in earlier stages of CKD and in children. Prevention of CKD through behavioural/public health interventions is also a worthy field of research to complement the existing rehabilitation efforts.

SUMMARY

The rate of CKD (Chronic Kidney Disease) and subsequent ESRD (End Stage Renal Disease) is rising worldwide. CKD is conventionally assessed in terms of overall renal function and is classified into early stage CKD (stages 1–3) and advanced stage CKD and ESRD (stages 4 and 5). ESRD is managed by dialysis, renal transplant, or conservative non-dialytic management, which is essentially end-of-life care. Patients may face multiple treatment transitions across the trajectory of CKD such as receipt or failure of kidney transplant or withdrawal from treatment. Transplantation of a kidney from a living or dead donor is the best treatment for ESRD in terms of QOL and survival. However, disadvantages to transplantation include the need for lifelong medication, the constant threat of rejection, and increased risk of complications. Transplant failure is also a psychological blow that may cause emotional distress and poor QOL.

Hemodialysis (HD) and peritoneal dialysis (PD) are the two principal forms of dialysis used to correct the effect of CKD. The dialysis regimen is relentless and complex, and involves invasive and painful procedures alongside strict fluid and diet restrictions and the need to manage multiple medications. Poor adherence is common in both dialysis and transplantation, with dire consequences in terms of patient or graft survival and hospitalization. Dialysis patients experience profound psychological consequences, including increased stress and symptoms of anxiety, depression, and impaired quality of life that have implications for disease management and prognosis. Interventions can improve adjustment and adherence outcomes, especially when didactic education is combined with psychological methods to change behaviour and treat depression if needed.

Critical Thought Questions

1. How might different psychological factors influence decisions related to treatment modality for patients with ESRD?

2. Discuss how to improve adherence with treatment recommendations for patients on dialysis and for kidney transplant recipients.

3. What are the main difficulties faced by patients with CKD and ESRD?

Recommended Reading

Chilcot, J., Wellsted, D., & Farrington, K. (2010). Depression in end-stage renal disease: Current advances and research. *Seminars in Dialysis, 23,* 74–82.

Finkelstein, F.O., Wuerth, D., & Finkelstein, S.H. (2009). Health-related quality of life and the CKD patient: Challenges for the nephrology community. *Kidney International, 7*(9), 946–952.

Matteson, M.L., & Russell, C. (2010). Interventions to improve hemodialysis adherence: A systematic review of randomized-controlled trials. *Hemodialysis International, 14,* 370–382.

Part III

Special Populations

17

Pediatric Psychology

CHRISTINE T. CHAMBERS

Learning Objectives

In this chapter, you will:

- Learn how children and their families cope with being diagnosed with chronic medical conditions.

- Discover the role of pediatric psychologists in helping children and their families adhere to pediatric treatment regimens and cope with painful medical procedures.

- Understand common parenting challenges in young children, including sleeping, feeding, and toileting issues, and the role of pediatric psychology in addressing these issues.

- Consider future directions in the field of pediatric psychology, including the use of technology in delivery of pediatric psychology services and the unique needs of children with medical conditions transitioning to adult care.

What Is Pediatric Psychology?

Up to 25 per cent of children and adolescents in North America have a diagnosed chronic illness or potentially life-limiting medical condition, such as asthma, diabetes, or cancer (Bethell et al., 2011; Canadian Institute of Child Health, 2001). Figure 17.1 shows the percentages of children reported to have various common health conditions. With advances in modern medicine a range of available medical treatments now can reduce condition-related symptoms and improve quality of life. These medical treatments, however, are often complex and multi-faceted in nature, including medications, dietary restrictions, and physical therapy. Further, as a result of improvements in medical treatments, children now live longer or survive what would previously have been life-threatening illnesses associated with high mortality. For example, in the case of pediatric acute lymphoblastic leukemia, the most common cancer diagnosed in children, survival rates have improved dramatically, from 70 per cent in the 1980s to nearly 90 per cent in recent years (Pui, Mullighan, Evans, & Relling, 2012). Children with medical conditions and their families often experience psychological effects associated with their conditions and multiple interactions with the health-care system, and they can also experience cognitive and psychological effects as a direct result of their treatments (e.g., radiation, chemotherapy) (Jannoun & Chessels, 1987; Rubenstein, Varni, & Katz, 1990). This means that millions of children and adolescents in North America now live with chronic illnesses and medical conditions that can contribute to significant emotional and behavioural difficulties and negatively impact treatment adherence and child and family adjustment. Furthermore, it has been shown that chronic medical conditions in childhood can be associated with psychological issues in adulthood (Pless, Power, & Peckham, 1993).

The field of **pediatric psychology** was developed to address the needs of patients in pediatric settings and brings together several areas within psychology, including health, clinical, and developmental psychology. The term "pediatric psychology" was first coined in 1967 by Logan Wright in the article "The pediatric psychologist: A role model," and was defined as "dealing primarily with children in a medical setting which is non-psychiatric in nature" (Wright, 1967). Today, the field of pediatric psychology is acknowledged as a specialized field within health psychology that integrates both scientific research and clinical practice to

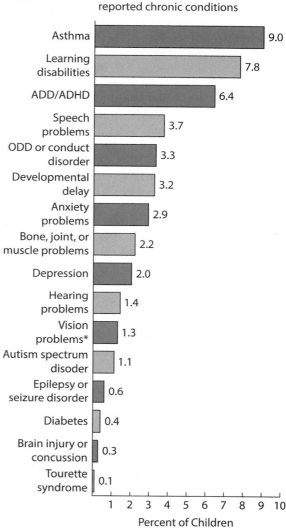

Percent of children with reported chronic conditions

Condition	Percent
Asthma	9.0
Learning disabilities	7.8
ADD/ADHD	6.4
Speech problems	3.7
ODD or conduct disorder	3.3
Developmental delay	3.2
Anxiety problems	2.9
Bone, joint, or muscle problems	2.2
Depression	2.0
Hearing problems	1.4
Vision problems*	1.3
Autism spectrum disoder	1.1
Epilepsy or seizure disorder	0.6
Diabetes	0.4
Brain injury or concussion	0.3
Tourette syndrome	0.1

Percent of Children

*Includes only vision problems that cannot be corrected with glasses or contact lenses.

FIGURE 17.1 | Percentage of children with reported chronic conditions by health condition.
Source: US Department of Health and Human Services. (2009).

address the psychological aspects of children's medical conditions and the promotion of health behaviours in children and their families. For example, pediatric psychologists might be called upon to help children with diabetes manage their treatment regimen, help children with cancer and their families cope with their diagnosis, or teach a child psychological strategies to deal with a painful medical procedure.

The professional face for the field of pediatric psychology is the Society of Pediatric Psychology (SPP), which is Division 54 of the American Psychological Association (APA) (see www.apadivisions.org/division-54/index.aspx). The Society aims to promote the health and psychological well-being of children, youth, and their families through science and an evidence-based approach to practice, education, training, advocacy, and consultation. SPP publishes a journal, the *Journal of Pediatric Psychology*, which was founded in 1976; however, research studies in pediatric psychology are published in a broad range of journals, including general psychological and medical journals. The role of psychological factors in children's health is generally recognized as important by all medical specialty and subspecialty groups.

Despite the varied nature of health conditions in children, pediatric psychologists deal with a number of cross-cutting themes that are described throughout this chapter. These include **coping** with chronic medical conditions, adherence to pediatric treatment regimens, coping with medical procedures, pediatric **chronic pain**, and pediatric **palliative care**. Furthermore,

PHOTO 17.1 | Journal of Pediatric Psychology.

By permission of Oxford University Press.

pediatric psychologists have expertise in dealing with a number of health issues unique to childhood that often present as significant parenting challenges, including sleeping, feeding, and toileting problems. The impact of pediatric chronic medical conditions on parents and siblings is also addressed by pediatric psychologists. Further, there are many exciting future directions in pediatric psychology, including innovative models of delivery of health services, such as use of electronic and mobile health interventions, and addressing the needs of youth with medical conditions transitioning from pediatric to adult care. Each of these topics is described in this chapter.

Coping with Chronic Medical Conditions

How a child copes with a chronic medical condition is related to patient outcomes and can play an important role in health behaviour and health-care utilization in children (Feeney, 2000). The study of coping with chronic medical conditions is challenging in pediatrics as a result of the unique developmental and familial contexts in which children with medical conditions live and are dependent (Compas, Jaser, Dunn, & Rodriguez, 2012). Diagnosis of a chronic medical condition can cause significant stress for the whole family and affect children's functioning across multiple domains and points in time. Typically, a chronic medical condition begins with a sudden onset of medical symptoms (e.g., fatigue, pain, fever), which prompts the family to seek initial medical consultation and care. In most cases this initial phase concludes with diagnosis of a specific medical condition and identification and implementation of an appropriate medical management plan. However, for some children and their families, a clear medical diagnosis and accompanying management plan may not always be immediate or evident, as in the case of children experiencing some forms of chronic pain, which is discussed further below. This uncertainty can create considerable additional stress for the child and family. Provided an appropriate diagnosis and management plan are identified, the child and family enter a longer-term phase where they gradually adjust to the impact of the medical condition and management on their day-to-day lives. Further, many children with chronic medical conditions and their families must learn to deal with an uncertain course associated with their condition. For example, many medical conditions experienced by children, such as inflammatory bowel disease and arthritis, are associated with flares or crises that may be unpredictable.

Children with chronic medical conditions face a range of stressors associated with their conditions and management. These stressors are in addition to the typical stressors associated with normal development (e.g., challenges with peer relationships, school transitions) experienced by all children (Olson, Johansen, Powers, Pope, & Klein, 1993). As an example, Rodriguez et al. (2012) surveyed children with cancer and their parents regarding perceptions of stressors associated with childhood cancer. The three most common areas of stressors identified by children included: (1) interruptions in daily role functioning (e.g., missing school days, falling behind in school work, not being able to do the things they used to do); (2) physical effects associated with treatment (e.g., feeling sick or nauseous from treatments, pain from medical procedures); and (3) uncertainty about the cancer (e.g., concerns about their future health or about length of life). The study revealed that children reported interruptions in their daily role functioning (i.e., interruptions in their school and social activities) as the most frequently experienced stressor, and as more stressful than uncertainty about disease/chance for survival, indicating that it is the disruption of typical activities and tasks associated with childhood, rather than the specific limitations imposed by a medical condition itself, that is most problematic for children. Parents, on the other hand, reported cancer caregiving (e.g., effects of treatment, not knowing if child's cancer will get better) as most stressful (Rodriguez et al., 2012). They also reported high levels of stress associated with interruptions in daily role functioning (e.g., paying bills, having less time for other children) and cancer communication (e.g., talking with child or others about cancer). Parents who expressed high levels of stress in the areas of cancer caregiving and cancer communication were more likely to report post-traumatic stress symptoms as a result of their child's condition.

The extent to which a stressor is perceived as stressful depends on a number of internal and external factors associated with the child, parent, and the specific medical condition. Not all coping responses are equally effective. Considerable attention has been given in the theoretical and empirical literature to conceptualizations of children's coping with medical conditions and medical stressors (for reviews, see Compas et al., 2012; Rudolph, Dennig, & Weisz, 1995; Schmidt, Peterson, & Bullinger, 2003; Thompson & Gustafson, 1996). The majority of this work has generally examined the fit between appraisal of medically related stressful events and corresponding coping responses. A variety of developmental and familial factors that can affect how a child copes, and how a child generally approaches a stressful event, are typically addressed in these models. Coping with medical conditions in children is intertwined with development. As children get older, coping approaches change and become more sophisticated. For example, use of behavioural strategies (e.g., **distraction**) is more common in early childhood, and evolves into more complex cognitive strategies (e.g., cognitive restructuring) in later childhood. It is important to note that medical conditions differ considerably in their level of associated symptoms and challenges across conditions (e.g., treatment regimens, life expectancy) and these variables are typically considered in theoretical conceptualizations of children's coping with medical conditions (Thompson & Gustafson, 1996).

Several specific theoretical models to guide the understanding and study of how children can and do cope in the context of medical conditions have been put forward in the literature, including Wallander and Varni's disability-stress-coping model of adjustment (Wallander & Varni, 1992) and Thompson's stress and coping model of adjustment (Thompson, Gustafson, Hamlett, & Spock, 1992). A recent review of coping with chronic illness in childhood and adolescence was published by Compas and colleagues (2012). They present a control-based model of coping that includes primary control or active coping (i.e., efforts to act on the source of stress or one's emotions), secondary control or accommodative coping (i.e., efforts to adapt to the source of stress), and disengagement or passive coping (i.e., efforts to avoid or deny the stressor). Research has shown that children with a variety of medical conditions including diabetes, chronic pain, and cancer, and who engage in secondary control coping, generally adjust and cope better than children who use disengagement coping (Compas et al., 2012). While there are many common elements across the various theoretical models of children's coping with medical conditions that have been proposed, the lack of a universal conceptual model for guiding research has been a challenge for those conducting work in this area.

An additional challenge in the study of children's coping with medical conditions is the difficulty associated with appropriate assessment (Blount et al., 2008). Measures of stress and coping in children typically require them to rate the extent to which they find various aspects of their medical condition stressful (as done in the study by Rodriguez et al. (2012) and the degree to which they engage in a variety of coping strategies, such as problem-solving, distraction, social support, and catastrophizing. Most of what we know about the assessment of children's medical stress and coping is in the area of children's pain (e.g., the Pain Coping Questionnaire) (Reid, Gilbert, & McGrath, 1998). The best-known coping questionnaire that has been used across various childhood medical conditions and in children ranging in age from 7 to 16 years is the Kidcope (Spirito, Stark, & Williams, 1988). Similar to other coping measures, children rate commonly used coping strategies (e.g., problem-solving, distracting), but also the degree of anxiety, unhappiness, and anger experienced in dealing with stressful situations related to their condition. Children's questionnaire responses can be analyzed separately by specific subscale or in two categories of coping: positive/approach or negative/avoidance. The review by Blount et al. (2008) was helpful in identifying coping and stress measures that can be used both in research and in clinical practice with children with medical conditions. This paper has also made important contributions to the field by highlighting the importance of improving assessment of children's coping in order to advance the field and to test the efficacy of interventions aimed to improve children's coping.

The development and evaluation of interventions to improve children's abilities to cope with the range of stressors they may experience as a result of their medical condition have been a focus in pediatric psychology for a long time. Progress in the area has been hindered in part by the challenging measurement issues and lack of a universal theoretical model. Regardless, psychological interventions to improve coping have taken many forms, ranging from simple provision of written materials to more intensive individual or group interventions (for example, see an outline of a group-based intervention in Table 17.1). Interventions are increasingly making use of technological advances such as the Internet and mobile phones (described below). These psychological interventions are often referred to as psycho-educational in nature because they typically include basic information about disease management in addition to providing instruction in specific cognitive-behavioural coping skills (e.g., relaxation, problem-solving, communication skills) to address psychosocial aspects of living with a chronic medical condition. (The accompanying In Focus box provides a sample relaxation script.) The strongest research support is for the efficacy of psycho-educational interventions that incorporate cognitive behavioural techniques in improving a range of outcomes, including self-efficacy,

 IN FOCUS

Relaxation Script for Children

You are lying down on your back.... Start to take slow, deep breaths into your belly. Make your belly bigger as you breathe in, and let it flatten down as you breathe out. [Perhaps the child wants to place a small stuffed animal on his or her belly.] Don't worry about your breathing. Just let it happen. You can feel your whole body begin to relax with each breath ... breathing out stress and worry ... breathing in relaxation and calm. Centring yourself ... inwardly smile. Deep breathing, relaxing ... now imagine a warm ball of light in your belly. Every time you take a breath in, the warm ball of light climbs up the front of your body, becoming bigger, expanding. It is now in your chest, making it feel warm and light ... with another inhalation, it travels up into your throat and neck ... each time you breathe in, the warm ball of light grows bigger ... it is filling you....

Your face is now filled with this warm light and your jaw loosens ... let your mouth open slightly.... The ball of light reaches the top of your head ... relaxing your scalp ... it travels with each inward breath down the back of your head to your spine ... warming and relaxing your entire back ... softening each bone in your back. The ball of light rolls slowly down both arms ... then to your hands ... making them heavy and warm.... This warm flow slowly moves into each of your legs ... travelling to your knees ... ankles ... softly on to your feet ... warming you ... each toe and bone in your foot is relaxed ... softened. This is everywhere. Keep breathing and let all your tension and worry be gone ... quiet ... melted away. Go back to any area that has any tightness and bring the warm ball of healing light back to it. Take your time. You are warm, relaxed, happy, and safe. Your body is heavy and comfortable ... filled with relaxation.

TABLE 17.1 | Overview of a Six-Week Cognitive Behavioural Treatment Program for Children with Recurrent Abdominal Pain and Their Parents

	Sessions for Parents	Sessions for Children
Week 1	How Does Pain Work?	How Does Pain Work?
Week 2	Behaviour and Pain	Relaxation
Week 3	Relaxation	Imagery, Distraction, and Pain
Week 4	Thoughts, Feelings, and Pain	Thoughts, Feelings, and Pain
Week 5	Daily Living	Thoughts, Feelings, and Pain (continued)
Week 6	Review and Relapse Prevention	Review and Relapse Prevention

Source: Based on Noel, Petter, Parker, & Chambers (2012).

self-management of disease, family functioning, general psychosocial well-being, reduced isolation, social competence, knowledge, and hope (Barlow & Ellard, 2004). Furthermore, these interventions can produce improvements in a number of disease-specific outcomes for various medical conditions, including reduced pain (for headache), improved pulmonary function (for asthma), and improved metabolic control (for diabetes) in the short and long terms (Beale, 2006).

Adherence to Pediatric Treatment Regimens

Chapter 3 provides a broad discussion of adherence with medical treatments. In this section, the focus is on issues particular to children.

Most parents struggle to get their children to complete simple tasks of daily living like brushing teeth or making their beds. Getting children to adhere to treatment regimens can seem overwhelming, yet there are potentially life-threatening outcomes associated with failure to comply (Modi et al., 2012). High rates of non-adherence to treatment have been reported across numerous pediatric conditions (Kahana, Drotar, & Frazier, 2008) with an estimated overall non-adherence rate of 50 per cent for pediatric patients across various medical conditions (Modi et al., 2012). Similar to adult outcomes, non-adherence is known to be associated with increased morbidity, use of the health system, and mortality (Modi et al., 2012).

Numerous variables have been associated with adherence to treatment in children (Modi et al., 2012). These include child age, child emotional development, family factors, and disease- and treatment-specific considerations. Adolescents are at particularly high risk for non-adherence to prescribed medical regimens, potentially due to less parental involvement and other developmental aspects of adolescence. Family relationships and parental beliefs about medical conditions and treatment demonstrate consistent relationships with treatment adherence (Drotar & Bonner, 2009). Across medical conditions, greater levels of both child and parental involvement in condition management have been associated with improved adherence and better outcomes. More complex treatment regimens generally are associated with lower levels of adherence then simpler regimens (Modi et al., 2012). Identification of factors associated with treatment adherence is important in enhancing treatments to improve adherence.

A variety of creative interventions have been developed to improve adherence. Reinforcement-based interventions, such as the use of simple sticker charts or other forms positive reinforcement can be very powerful for children (Luersen et al., 2012). Figure 17.2 shows a sample rewards chart used with children. A range of additional behaviour management techniques have also been applied with children, including monitoring, goal-setting, contingency contracting, problem-solving, and linking medication with established routines (La Greca & Race Mackey, 2009). More complex regimens typically require more intensive education and intervention, such as instruction in social support and family-based problem-solving (La Greca & Race Mackey, 2009). Education efforts alone generally are insufficient to promote adherence; adding a behavioural management component enhances adherence-related outcomes (Dean, Walters, & Hall, 2010; Kahana et al.,

Privileges Chart

☆	To be on GOLD STAR LEVEL I must:	GOLD STAR PRIVILEGES	"I did it!" check marks
☆	To be on SILVER STAR LEVEL I must:	SILVER STAR PRIVILEGES	
☆	To be on BRONZE STAR LEVEL I must:	BRONZE STAR PRIVILEGES	
	No Privileges		Oops!

FIGURE 17.2 | Sample reward chart commonly used with children as positive reinforcement.

Source: Rewards for Kids: Ready to Use Charts and Activities for Positing Parenting, Virginia Shiller PhD. APA Press 2003, p. 127.

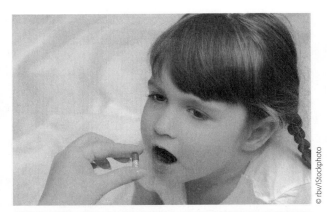

PHOTO 17.2 | One area of children's health that is effectively managed with behavioural intervention by a pediatric psychologist is pill-swallowing.

2008). Multi-component interventions, which typically incorporate some variety of social skills training or family therapy, are also effective (Kahana et al., 2008). Successful interventions usually target adherence to a narrow age range, include the family, and improve access to care (Modi et al., 2012). More customized interventions are needed to target adherence in children who have established poor adherence and children who are at different developmental stages.

Addressing barriers to adherence to treatment regimens is important. For example, many parents of children struggle with basic issues related to condition management. A simple problem such as an inability to swallow pills may cause considerable stress for families. Up to 20 per cent of children have difficulty swallowing pills (Meltzer, Welch, & Ostrom, 2006), and it is reasonable to assume that these difficulties could lead to some degree of avoidance and/or inappropriate medication use and health-care use. Many parents receive extensive coaching from health professionals and pharmacists in how to

"hide" medication (e.g., in foods) rather than in the best methods for teaching their children how to swallow pills. Pill-swallowing is an excellent example of application of a children's health intervention based on basic behavioural principles (e.g., modelling, shaping, and reinforcement) (see In Practice box). Although there have been no large-scale randomized trials, numerous published case studies and single case designs have revealed success rates in the range of 75–90 per cent with excellent maintenance at three months and longer in children with a variety of health issues (e.g., cancer, autism, attention deficit hyperactivity disorder) (Beck, Cataldo, Slifer, Pulbrook, & Ghuman, 2005; Blount, Dahlquist, Baer, & Wuori, 1984; Cruz-Arrieta, 2008; Funk, Mullins, & Olson, 1984; Ghuman, Cataldo, Beck, & Slifer, 2004; Reitman & Passeri, 2008; Walco, 1986). Research has shown that pill-swallowing training improved adherence to antiretroviral medication treatment in pediatric patients with HIV/AIDS (Garvie, Lensing, & Rai, 2007). Pill-swallowing is just one example of the unique contributions that pediatric psychologists can make in applying psychological principles and interventions to address health issues in children.

Coping with Medical Procedures

Needle procedures, such as immunizations and **venepuncture**, and the pain associated with such procedures are frequently cited as among the most feared experiences of children, including healthy children and children with chronic medical conditions (Broome, Bates, Lillis, & McGahee, 1990). These fears tend to persist over time and can cause considerable distress not only for the child, but also for his/her parents, siblings,

🔲 IN PRACTICE

Practice in Pill-Swallowing

Case Description

Mark is a seven-year-old boy recently diagnosed with ulcerative colitis by the gastroenterology clinic at the local pediatric health centre. The medical team recommends an oral medication, and these can sometimes be very large tablets that need to be taken two to four times per day. The family panics. As the parents try to process the impact of this significant diagnosis on their child's health and future, they become anxious as they realize that Mark has never had to swallow a pill before. The clinic sends the family home with some oral medication and a pill-swallowing cup, which is purported to be able to help individuals learn how to swallow pills without stress. The family spends a nerve-wracking evening trying to help Mark learn to swallow pills. They try using the cup but with no luck. They try to encourage him to swallow the pills, but by this time Mark and his parents are agitated and stressed. "Did you swallow it?" "No, it's still on his tongue." "Try again." "Try!" "Yes you can. It's important." "It's going to help your belly." The pill is dissolving in his mouth. Mark cries and storms off, indicating that he will never be able to swallow pills. The parents wonder how they can ever make this happen. How will the babysitter or grandparents manage? They place an exasperated call to the gastronterology clinic, and a referral to the pediatric psychology service for assistance with pill-swallowing is made.

Treatment Description

The psychological intervention used for pill-swallowing is based on principles of behaviour therapy, primarily "shaping," in which successive approximations to the desired behaviour are rewarded. Children are initially taught to swallow very small cake decorations (e.g., chocolate sprinkles) and once this task is mastered, the child is offered larger and larger candies, and then placebo tablets and capsules of varying sizes. The hospital pharmacy and the local candy store are helpful resources for psychologists who need to create a pill-swallowing placebo kit. It is important that the psychologist always check with parents first regarding any potential allergies or concerns they might have about the use of different types of placebo pills/candies. Children are provided with praise and reinforcement (e.g., a sticker) for effort and eventual mastery of each step. Treatment can also include behavioural modelling, with the therapist demonstrating and the child trying in a game-like manner, and relaxation strategies (e.g., deep breathing). For children with disruptive or inattentive behaviours, basic behaviour management principles (e.g., ignoring, time-out) may need to be integrated into the session.

Source: Modified from Chambers (2012).

and any health professionals working with the child. Children with significant fears towards medical procedures are likely to avoid seeking appropriate health care in the future (Taddio et al., 2009). It is estimated that one in 10 adults avoids medical procedures, such as immunization, due to severe needle-related fears or phobias (Taddio et al., 2009).

Painful medical procedures unfortunately are commonplace even for healthy children, who now undergo up to as many as 20 routine immunizations by age five. Preterm infants who spend time in the neonatal intensive care unit (NICU) are at particular risk of experiencing repeated painful medical procedures (Craig, Whitfield, Grunau, Linton, & Hadjistavropoulos, 1993; Stevens, Johnston, Petryshen, & Taddio, 1996). Unfortunately,

the majority of children undergoing painful medical procedures receive no pain-relieving interventions. For example, a recent survey of **procedural pain** management practices at eight children's hospitals across Canada showed that 80 per cent of hospitalized children experienced at least one painful procedure over the last 24 hours (the average was six procedures per child) and more than two-thirds of these procedures had *no* documented pain management intervention (either pharmacological, psychological, or physical) (Stevens et al., 2011). In the past it was believed by many health professionals that young infants did not feel pain and as a result they were often denied appropriate pain management. This situation is troubling because poorly managed painful procedures early in childhood have

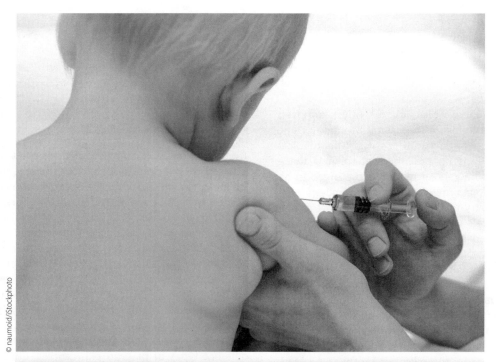

PHOTO 17.3 | Medical interventions involving needles are often reported as children's most feared experiences.

been shown to be related to later increased pain sensitivity (Grunau, Whitfield, Petrie, & Fryer, 1994; Porter, Grunau, & Anand, 1999; Taddio, Goldbach, Ipp, Stevens, & Koren, 1995; Taddio, Katz, Ilersich, & Koren, 1997). A recent study showed that, after controlling for a range of clinical factors, the frequency of painful medical procedures was related to impaired brain development in a sample of preterm infants hospitalized in the NICU (Brummelte et al., 2012).

An impressive body of literature highlights the importance of family factors in children's responses to painful medical procedures (Birnie, Uman, & Chambers, 2013; Chambers, 2003). Numerous studies in the field have documented a strong relationship between certain parent behaviours (e.g., use of reassurance) and increased child pain and distress, while other behaviours (e.g., use of distraction, humour) have been associated with child coping when used by mothers, fathers, and health professionals (Blount et al., 1989; Blount et al., 1997; Chambers, Craig, & Bennett, 2002; Moon, Chambers, & McGrath, 2011). The counterintuitive relationship between adult reassurance and child pain and distress is one that has begun to receive considerable support in the literature. It has been suggested that parental reassurance

likely serves as a signal to children that the parent is nervous or worried (McMurtry, McGrath, & Chambers, 2006; McMurtry, McGrath, Asp, & Chambers, 2007; McMurtry, Chambers, McGrath, & Asp, 2010). A study by McMurtry et al. (2010) involved a pairing of clinical and lab-based methodologies in children undergoing blood work to provide a detailed examination of the complexities of adult reassurance during painful medical procedures. They solicited children's impressions of their parents' reassurance via asking children to rate emotional context associated with clips of their own parents reassuring them during a blood draw. Children also rated parental reassurance in a series of videotaped vignette clips where parental facial expression, vocal tone, and verbal content during children's painful procedures. Results supported that children do indeed perceive their parents as more fearful and less happy when they reassure, and that this was particularly the case for reassurance spoken in a rising vocal tone (indicative of uncertainty) (McMurtry et al., 2010).

Pain as a subjective experience can be challenging to assess in children due to communication problems or children too upset or distressed to report on their pain. Children above the age of five years are generally

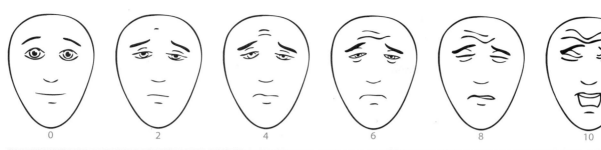

FIGURE 17.3 | Faces Pain Scale–Revised.

Source: Faces Pain Scale – Revised, © 2001, International Association for the Study of Pain.

able to provide self-reports of their pain using validated self-report tools such as the Faces Pain Scale–Revised (Figure 17.3) (Hicks, von Baeyer, Spafford, van Korlaar, & Goodenough, 2001). Children use these scales to point to the face that best shows how much hurt or pain they have. It is important that scales for pain assessment begin with a relatively neutral face, as is the case in the FPS–R. Research has shown that faces that begin with a smiling face instead of a neutral face can confound more general distress with pain and make pain self-report more challenging for children (Chambers & Craig, 1998; Chambers, Giesbrecht, Craig, Bennett, & Huntsman, 1999; Chambers, Hardial, Craig, Court, & Montgomery, 2005). When children are unable to provide self-reports of pain, pain can be assessed using a variety of validated behavioural measures that assess either broad-band behaviours (e.g., flailing) or fine-grained facial movements (e.g., eye squeeze, nasolabial furrow) that quantify pain. Parents and health professionals can also be asked to provide an observer report of children's pain, although research has shown that these observer reports generally tend to underestimate children's pain (Chambers, Reid, Craig, McGrath, & Finley, 1998; Zhou, Roberts, & Horgan, 2008).

A variety of pharmacological, psychological, physical, and combined pain management strategies can significantly reduce procedure-related pain in children. This research evidence has been gathered in the form of randomized clinical trials and summarized in comprehensive meta-analyses and systematic reviews (e.g., for immunizations: Chambers, Taddio, Uman, & McMurtry, 2009; Shah, Taddio, & Rieder, 2009; Taddio, Ilersich, Ipp, Kikuta, & Shah, 2009), and for painful procedures in general (Chambers et al., 2009; Uman, Chambers, McGrath, & Kisely, 2006; Uman, Chambers, McGrath, & Kisely, 2008). In the case of psychological interventions specifically, strong evidence supports the use of cognitive behavioural strategies for decreasing pain and distress associated with medical procedures (Powers & Rubenstein,

1999; Uman et al., 2006; Uman et al., 2008). These reviews conclude that the psychological interventions with the most support include distraction, **hypnosis**, and some combination of cognitive behavioural interventions (e.g., deep breathing combined with positive self-statements).

Despite the compelling evidence showing the efficacy of a variety of pain-relieving interventions in children, a significant gap looms between what is known in the research literature about pain management for procedures and what is happening for children and their families in the real world (Taddio et al., 2009). Barriers to proper pain management are present at many levels, including the level of the patient, primary caregiver, health-care provider, and the health-care system (Cohen & MacLaren, 2007; Craig, Lilley, & Gilbert, 1996). Incorporating information about evidence-based pain management in children, in the case of immunization for example, has been distilled into clinical practice guidelines directed towards health professionals (Taddio et al., 2010). These guidelines have identified simple, cost-effective, evidence-based pain-relieving interventions for immunization pain management, which included breast-feeding (for infants), sweet-tasting solutions (i.e., sucrose, for infants), sitting position (vs lying down), use of topical anesthetic creams (e.g., eutectic mixture of local anesthetics; EMLA), use of parent-led distraction, coaching, and deep breathing by the child. It is hoped that the publication and dissemination of clinical practice guidelines will support practice changes at the health professional and institutional levels.

It is also important that parents have the opportunity to access important information about pain-relieving interventions directly, so they are in a position to advocate for and implement these strategies on behalf of their child (see Table 17.2). Guidance from health professionals regarding how parents can best prepare and provide information to children about forthcoming medical procedures is critical. It is generally

TABLE 17.2 | Behavioural Management Tips for Parents for Procedural Pain Management

- Prepare yourself and stay calm.
- Prepare your child by using age-appropriate words and be honest; children five years old and up should be told about the procedure at least one day in advance.
- Distract your child using age-appropriate strategies, such as toys, books, or music or videos.
- Encourage your child to take slow, deep breaths, for example, with bubbles or pinwheels.
- Avoid words that focus on the pain or the procedures, such as "It'll be over soon" and "You'll be okay"; it's better to talk about things not related to the procedure.
- Use other age-appropriate pain-relieving interventions, such as breast-feeding or sucrose for infants or topical anesthetic creams.
- After the procedure, praise your child for a job well done.

Source: Birnie, Boerner, & Chambers (2013), p.113. By permission of Oxford University Press.

recommended that children above the age of five years receive at least a five-day notice for procedures, although this will vary depending on the age and temperament of the child and the severity of the procedure (Jaaniste, Hayes, & von Baeyer, 2007). Jaaniste et al. (2007) provide a useful review and summary of how to best provide children with information about forthcoming medical procedures. They note the importance of including both sensory and procedural information, of giving advice on coping skills, and of informing the child of whether the procedure is going to be painful, in neutral language.

While many to most children experience some distress around medical procedures and can benefit from instructions in basic coping skills (e.g., deep breathing) that can be parent-directed, children with more severe needle phobias often require more in-depth therapeutic support from a pediatric psychologist. For these children, coping skills interventions to decrease procedural pain and distress are often folded into a more general psychological treatment protocol for specific phobia, which typically includes desensitization via exposure, contingency management, modelling, and self-control procedures.

Pediatric Chronic Pain

Chronic pain is a serious health concern that affects a surprisingly large number of children and adolescents (see Chapter 7 for a broader discussion of pain). A population-based survey of Canadian adolescents aged 13–17 years found that approximately 20 per cent of adolescents report experiencing weekly or more frequent chronic pains such as headaches, stomach aches, or backaches (Stanford, Chambers, Biesanz, & Chen,

2007). Many other studies from around the world yield similar prevalence rates and provide further support for the commonplace nature of chronic pains in children and adolescents (King et al., 2011). These chronic pains can occur as a result of associated medical conditions or in the absence of any identifiable organic pathology. It is important to note that not all children who experience chronic pains are significantly disabled by this pain. It is a subgroup of children (estimated at around 5 per cent) who experience significant pain-related interference (Huguet & Miro, 2008). However, for these children the negative consequences of their pain are far-reaching, affecting emotional functioning, school performance, peer relationships, sleep, and family functioning (Palermo, 2000). Pain was once viewed by scientists and clinicians as a purely biological phenomenon, but it is now understood that pain is a complex experience where psychological factors play an important role (Hadjistavropoulos et al., 2011). There is evidence that as many as two-thirds of children with chronic pain continue to experience chronic pain as adults, and psychological factors have been shown to play an important role in predicting this trajectory (Walker, Sherman, Bruehl, Garber, & Smith, 2012).

A variety of measures have been developed to assess chronic pain and pain-related outcomes in children. Core outcome domains for assessment of pediatric chronic pain include not only pain intensity, but also physical functioning, emotional functioning, role functioning, and sleep (McGrath et al., 2008). A recent review by Eccleston et al. (2012) summarizes the efficacy of psychological interventions, primarily cognitive behavioural therapy, for improving pain, disability, and mood in children with chronic pain.

The type of psychological interventions tested in the studies in the review included relaxation, hypnosis, coping skills training, biofeedback, and cognitive behavioural therapy, which were delivered individually, by group, or by Internet. These interventions were applied to a variety of chronic pain conditions, which for the purposes of the review were grouped as either headache or non-headache (i.e., recurrent abdominal pain, fibromyalgia, sickle cell disease, and arthritis). The review found that psychological treatments were effective in reducing pain intensity associated with both headache and non-headache pain, both in the short term and in follow-up; there was limited evidence for the effects of psychological interventions on mood and disability (Eccleston et al., 2012).

While psychological interventions delivered on their own can certainly be helpful for some children, many children with chronic pain require more

© pzRomashka/iStockphoto

PHOTO 17.4 | Some children experiencing chronic pain require more intensive interventions and are treated by a multidisciplinary team through inpatient and outpatient clinics specializing in chronic pain.

intensive, multidisciplinary interventions and are seen in clinics specializing in chronic pain (Eccleston, Malleson, Clinch, Connell, & Sourbut, 2003; Logan et al., 2012). Treatments offered in these clinics usually include a combination of medication, nursing support, and physical therapy, in addition to psychological interventions and support with school-based modifications. These treatment programs are delivered as outpatient programs, or in some settings they are offered as inpatient or residential programs.

Pediatric Palliative Care

Over the last 20 years there has been tremendous growth in the field of pediatric palliative care, which originated within oncology but is now beneficially applied to children with other medical conditions, including conditions where curative treatments have failed or that require intensive long-term treatment aimed at maintaining quality of life (Moody, Siegel, Scharbach, Cunningham, & Cantor, 2011). That said, pediatric palliative care has significantly lagged behind care provided to adults with life-threatening illnesses. It is estimated that only 10 per cent of dying children each year receive hospice or palliative services (Moody et al., 2011). The goals of pediatric palliative care are multi-faceted and include establishing goals of care, symptom (e.g., pain, fatigue) management, and advanced-care planning, as well as ethical and legal considerations. Pediatric palliative care is different from adult care in that the types of medical conditions experienced by children, their needs for education and support, their family environment, and their understanding of death and dying all differ significantly from those of adults (McCulloch, Comac, & Craig, 2008). The potential or impending death of a child can have a huge impact on a family; parents of children with life-threatening illnesses require unique support (Bergstraesser, 2012).

Pediatric psychologists involved in caring for dying children typically work as part of an interdisciplinary palliative care team that provides comprehensive physical, psychological, and spiritual support. There is evidence that involvement of pediatric palliative care can significantly improve the quality of children's remaining lifetime and address other palliative care goals, such as pain (Moody et al., 2011).

Common Parenting Challenges: Sleeping, Feeding, Toileting

In addition to their expertise in dealing with children with chronic medical conditions, pediatric psychologists also have considerable knowledge in dealing with several common parenting challenges that are often problematic in healthy children as well as in children with medical conditions. These common challenges include difficulties in the areas of sleeping, feeding, and toileting.

Sleep problems are very common among young children and are associated with a range of emotional and behavioural issues (Meltzer & Mindell, 2009; Meltzer, Johnson, Crosette, Ramos, & Mindell, 2010; Meltzer & Montgomery-Downs, 2011). Sleep problems are a very strong correlate of emotional and behavioural issues, and children's sleep problems are known to exacerbate their emotional and behavioural problems (Coulombe, Reid, Boyle, & Racine, 2010; Reid, Hong, & Wade, 2009). Sleep problems are a greater issue for children with medical conditions (Lewandowski, Ward, & Palermo, 2011). The most common sleep difficulties in childhood include bedtime resistance and night wakings. Most often related to a parental lack of education about appropriate sleep habits for children and inappropriate reliance on parental intervention (e.g., rocking, feeding, staying in the room or bed with the child), these negative sleep habits have their roots in early infancy (Meltzer & Montgomery-Downs, 2011). They are likely to persist throughout childhood without intervention, although the specific nature or presentation of the sleep problem can change over the course of development (Meltzer & Montgomery-Downs, 2011). There is very strong

support for the efficacy of behavioural interventions for pediatric sleep (Mindell et al., 2006), most often involving gradual reduction of parental involvement and attention using principles of graduated or full extinction, in order to promote independent sleep and self-soothing. Many pediatric sleep problems can be managed effectively using basic principles of sleep hygiene, such as deciding on appropriate bed and wake times and eliminating television and other screen use while in bed (see Table 17.3) (Mindell et al., 2006).

Feeding issues are a common concern of parents of young children. Common challenges reported by parents include trying to get children to eat food at assigned, structured mealtimes (versus snacking or on the go) and encouraging children to try new foods (those who will not are referred to as "picky eaters") (Crist & Napier-Phillips, 2001). Mealtime lengths greater than 30 minutes are often associated with feeding problems (Crist & Napier-Phillips, 2001). Children's eating behaviours are influenced by a host of factors. Some factors are related to overeating, such as food responsiveness, enjoyment of food, and emotional overeating, while other dimensions relate to under-eating, such as slowness in eating, fussiness, or refusal of new foods (Birch & Fisher, 1995; Birch & Fisher, 1998). Parent attitudes show significant relationships with children's nutritional behaviours, including their food intake and eating motivations (Birch & Fisher, 1995; Birch & Fisher, 1998). Parents create environments for children that may foster the development of healthy eating behaviours and weight, or that may promote overweight and aspects of disordered eating. These dietary habits acquired in early childhood are likely to persist through to adulthood (Birch & Fisher, 1995; Birch &

TABLE 17.3 | Sleep Tips for Parents

	Core concept	Details and Recommendations
A	**Age appropriate**	It is important that children go to bed and wake up at times that ensure that they receive an age-appropriate amount of sleep. For children who have outgrown naps (which usually occurs during the preschool age period), napping during the day could be an indication that children are not getting sufficient quality and/or quantity of sleep at night.
B	**Bedtimes**	Set bedtimes and wake times, as well as routines in the evening and morning are key to good sleep. It is recommended that bedtimes be no later than 9 p.m. across childhood.
C	**Consistency**	It is very important that these bedtimes and wake times are consistent, even on weekends (i.e., no more than a 30–60-minute difference between weekday and weekend bedtimes and wake times).

TABLE 17.3 | (*Continued*)

	Core concept	Details and Recommendations
S	**Schedule**	The child's schedule in general is important—in addition to having routines at bedtime and wake time, it is also important that they have consistency throughout their day, including the timing of homework, extracurricular activities, etc.
L	**Location**	It is important that the child's location for sleep includes a comfortable bed, the room is quiet, dark, and cool, and the location remains consistent and familiar. Also, the child's bedroom should only be used for sleeping—children should not be sent to their bedroom for a time out. Their bedroom also should not be too exciting or distracting, and should be conducive to relaxation.
E	**No Electronics in the bedroom or before bed**	The use of electronics, including both the timing of use and the location, should also be considered—children should not be using stimulating electronic devices (i.e., iPods, cell phones, laptops, etc.) too close to bedtime (most commonly defined as one hour prior to going to bed), and it is recommended that these items not be placed in the bedroom.
E	**Exercise and diet**	Exercise and diet are both important factors that should be considered when evaluating sleep hygiene—physical activity during the day is important to healthy sleep, but should not be undertaken too close to bedtime (defined in the literature as anywhere from 1 hour to 4 hours prior to bedtime). The child's day should be organized so that there is time for a "cool down" period before bedtime, where he or she slowly comes down from the regular level of activity into a quiet, more restful state. Diet includes things like caffeine consumption—children should limit or totally eliminate caffeine consumption (i.e., caffeinated soft drinks)—as well as the timing of meals. Children should not be going to bed hungry, but they also should not be consuming a large meal right before bedtime. A healthy balanced diet is also important to the child's sleep as well as to his/her overall health.
P	**Positivity**	Positivity surrounding sleep is also an important aspect of sleep hygiene. Parents should have a positive attitude towards sleep and the bedtime/wake time routine, and the atmosphere in the house should be positive, in order to be conducive to creating a positive mood in the child. It is important that this positive mood is relaxing and calming, rather than fun and exciting—we want the child to be winding down before bedtime. Also, doing frustrating activities right before bed (i.e., math problems for a child who struggles with math) is not recommended, as this may interfere with the child's ability to fall asleep.
I	**Independence when falling asleep**	Independence is also important. Once the child reaches an age where he or she is capable of settling into sleep without the presence of a parent, independence when falling asleep should be encouraged, in order to discourage dependence on someone else in order to fall asleep. For children, independence means no calling out and no getting out of bed, and for parents, no responding to their child calling out and returning the child to the bedroom if he/she does get out of bed.
N	**Needs met during the day**	Finally, the needs of the child should be met throughout the day. This refers to both the child's emotional needs (i.e., love, support, hugs, etc.), as well as basic physiological needs (i.e., thirst, hunger, etc.).
G	**All of the above equals a Great sleep!**	

Adapted from: Bessey, J., Coulombe, A., & Corkum, P. Sleep hygiene in children with ADHD: Research findings and clinical recommendations. *The ADHD Report*. (Acronym created by M. Gendron, Project Coordinator, Corkum LABS).

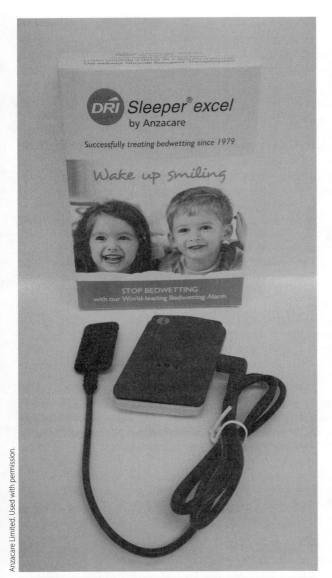

PHOTO 17.5 | A modern version of a urine alarm, a small, ultra-lightweight alarm that can be comfortably attached to a child's pajamas.

Fisher, 1998). Behavioural interventions for pediatric feeding issues, which include setting reasonable expectations, removing attention from undesired behaviours, and providing reinforcement for desired behaviours, are well supported in the literature (Kerwin, 1999).

Enuresis and **encopresis** are two common yet often poorly understood toileting-related issues that occur in childhood and are often treated by pediatric psychologists (Christopherson, 2010). Encopresis is defined as the passage of feces in inappropriate places, such as clothing. For the vast majority of these children (>90 per cent), this soiling occurs as the direct result of overflow incontinence, which is involuntary and results from constipation. A variety of predisposing biopsychosocial factors may make a child likely to get constipation, which is typically then followed by painful defecation and withholding. The colon walls stretch and this leads to an accumulation of stool, creating a vicious cycle that can result in frequent soiling incidents. Encopresis is an extremely frustrating problem for children and their families and is a frequent source of conflict (Christopherson, 2010; Culbert & Banez, 2007). Evidence-based treatment for encopresis includes education about the nature of constipation and soiling, disimpaction using some sort of laxative medication (in order to prevent constipation and make it easier for children to have bowel movements), followed by maintenance laxative therapy and behavioural treatment to reinforce frequent toilet sitting and compliance with medication (Culbert & Banez, 2007).

Nocturnal enuresis (bedwetting) is also a common disorder and affects as many as 5–10 per cent of five-year-olds, decreasing in frequency with age, although 1 per cent of older adolescents are estimated to continue to struggle with enuresis (Christopherson, 2010). It is more common in boys than girls. While the specific mechanisms that produce bedwetting are not well understood, there is strong empirical evidence in support of the urine alarm as the most effective intervention. These alarms, worn in undergarments or pajamas, alert the child when he/she starts to urinate, and after consistent usage most children begin to be able to rouse themselves prior to urination. Use of the urine alarm results in complete resolution of bedwetting in up to 80 per cent of patients (Brown, Pope, & Brown, 2010; Christopherson, 2010). Despite this compelling evidence, this treatment approach is relatively unknown to parents and is used less commonly by physicians than medications, even though medications for enuresis are generally less effective and any improvements cease following discontinuation of the medication (von Gontard, 2003; von Gontard, Baeyens, Van Hoecke, Warzak, & Bachmann, 2011). Pediatric psychologists assist with providing education about the urine alarm, assessing for factors that may influence the success of this treatment (e.g., child motivation, ability of child to awake independently) and providing support to increase the effectiveness once it is implemented (e.g., charting, reinforcement of effort, over-learning to prevent relapse).

Impact on Family

In addition to the impact on the child, parenting a child with a chronic or life-limiting illness can have a major negative impact on the child's parents and family. For example, taking care of a child with chronic illness can impact a parent's ability to go to work, have social life, care for other children, and accomplish necessary chores around the house. A healthy family environment is critical in supporting children's physical and mental health and development (Repetti, Taylor, & Seeman, 2002). Recently, research has focused on developing psychological interventions specifically directed at parents of children with medical conditions. A systematic review identified 26 studies for six common childhood chronic illnesses (pain, cancer, diabetes, asthma, traumatic brain injury, and eczema) (Eccleston, Palermo, Fisher, & Law, 2012). Four types of psychological interventions directed towards parents were examined: cognitive behavioural therapy, family therapy, problem-solving therapy, and multi-systemic therapy. Cognitive behavioural therapy was found to be associated with improvements in the child's medical symptoms, while problem-solving therapy improved parents' distress and their ability to solve problems.

The needs of siblings of children with medical conditions have also been acknowledged. Frequently, having a child with a medical condition in the family can pull attention and resources away from other children. However, research on the psychological impact of having a sibling with a medical condition has yielded mixed findings and can vary depending on the specific medical condition of the child. For example, O'Brien, Duffy, and Nicholl (2009) studied three different sibling groups—siblings of children with autism, cancer, and Down's syndrome—and found that siblings of children with Down's syndrome were well adjusted but siblings of children with cancer and autism were more likely to experience difficulties. Intervention programs have been developed to address the psychosocial needs of siblings (O'Brien et al., 2009). These interventions, usually group-based, typically include developmentally appropriate information regarding the sibling's condition, coping skills training, and the opportunity to meet others with similarly ill siblings. Prchal and Landolt (2009) reviewed literature on interventions with siblings of pediatric cancer patients and found that this type of treatment can effectively reduce psychological maladjustment and improve knowledge about medical aspects of cancer.

Future Directions

Several exciting new themes are emerging in the field of pediatric psychology. One includes the use of technology to improve both assessment and interventions. For example, in the case of pain, electronic pain diaries (using iPhones or other Internet sites; see Figure 17.4) are being used to capture real-time data (Stinson, 2009). Telemedicine delivery of pediatric psychology services, with families participating in assessment and treatment from their own communities through an interactive phone or video interface, has shown comparable outcomes to face-to-face treatments (Van Allen, Davis, & Lassen, 2011). Delivering psychological interventions to families via the Internet can be more flexible and can address important barriers to psychological treatment for children and families, such as cost, transportation, and missed time from school or work. The literature on Internet interventions is rapidly growing, but systematic reviews of Internet-based self-management interventions for youth with health conditions found that these interventions are effective in improving symptoms across a range of common pediatric health conditions (e.g., asthma, recurrent pain, encopresis, traumatic brain injury, and obesity) (Stinson, Wilson, Gill, Yamada, & Holt, 2009). That said, unique ethical issues are associated with these types of interventions and research (e.g., informed consent, privacy, and participant safety) that require special consideration (Henderson, Rosser, Keogh, & Eccleston, 2012).

Another emerging theme in pediatric psychology is the need to properly anticipate and meet the needs of children with medical conditions as they progress into adolescence and young adulthood and require transition to adult-oriented care for continued management. Adolescence is a challenging developmental period that has not been extensively studied in pediatric psychology. Co-ordinated transition to adult care is associated with improved health, better disease management, and more appropriate use of health-care services (Schwartz, Tuchman, Hobbie, & Ginsberg, 2011). Attention to the transition process of these young adults, their unique psychological and social needs, their transition readiness, planning, and transfer of care are all important variables in facilitating this important process (Schwartz et al., 2011).

Further, there will be a continued need for pediatric psychologists with expertise in dealing with the unique psychosocial issues faced by children

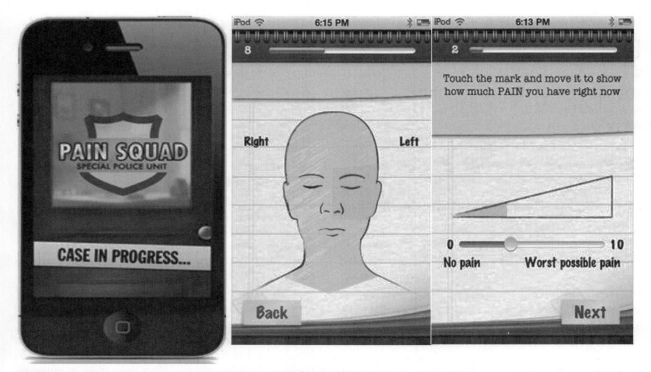

FIGURE 17.4 | A series of screen shots from an iPhone application originally developed for children with cancer pain.

Source: The Hospital for Sick Children/Cundari.

with health conditions and their families. A Society of Pediatric Psychology task force has made recommendations for the continued training of pediatric psychologists (Spirito et al., 2003). The underlying principles of these recommendations include that clinical child psychology is the foundation for developing skills and expertise in pediatric psychology, and that training should include: lifespan developmental psychology and psychopathology; child, adolescent, and family assessment; intervention strategies, research methods, and systems evaluation; professional, ethical, and legal issues; cultural diversity; the role of different disciplines in service delivery systems; social issues affecting children and families; consultation liaison; and disease process and management (Spirito et al., 2003).

SUMMARY

Pediatric psychology is a specialized field in health psychology that integrates both scientific research and clinical practice to address the psychological aspects of medical conditions and the promotion of health behaviours in children and their families. The field addresses the unique needs of patients in pediatric settings and their families. Areas of major focus in pediatric psychology include coping with medical conditions; adherence to pediatric treatment regimens; coping with medical procedures; pediatric chronic pain; pediatric palliative care; common parenting challenges in the areas of sleeping, feeding, and toileting; and the impact of pediatric health conditions on the family. Pediatric psychologists make important contributions to supporting children with health conditions and their families.

Critical Thought Questions

1. What can explain the continued failure to appropriately manage children's pain from procedures despite the availability of numerous evidence-based interventions to reduce this pain?

2. How can we better use modern technology to deliver needed interventions to children with medical conditions and their parents?

Recommended Reading

Drotar, D. (2006). *Psychological interventions in childhood chronic illness*. Washington: American Psychological Association.

Roberts, M.C., & Steele, R.G. (2009). *Handbook of pediatric psychology*. New York: Guilford Press.

Spirito, A., & Kazak, A.E. (2006). *Effective and emerging treatments in pediatric psychology*. New York: Oxford University Press.

18

Health Geropsychology

REBECCA S. ALLEN │ CASEY B. AZUERO │ THOMAS HADJISTAVROPOULOS

Learning Objectives
In this chapter you will:

- Learn about the demographics of aging in relation to health in North America and to theories that reflect individuals' response to chronic illness, stress, and coping.

- Familiarize yourself with common health issues (e.g., pain, falls) affecting older adults and the role of health psychologists in the management of these health issues.

- Come to know behavioural interventions used to enhance long-term care residents' response to chronic illness and enhance their health and quality of life.

- Learn about interventions designed to improve the quality of life of older adults who live independently in the community.

Introduction

Older adults represent the fastest-growing segment of the US and Canadian populations, with the leading edge of the baby boomers turning 65 in 2011. Approximately 40 million adults in the United States are 65 years of age and older, and the portion of those over the age of 85 is increasing especially rapidly (Werner, 2011). In Canada, the numbers of seniors are expected to increase from 4.2 million to 9.8 million between 2005 and 2036 (Statistics Canada, 2013).

The prevalence of most types of **disability** (e.g., problems in mobility, agility, hearing, vision, and pain) increases with age, with the highest rates occurring in those aged 75 and older. Pearson, Bhat-Schelbert, and Probst (2012) examined the prevalence of nine chronic illnesses in the US: angina/coronary heart disease, arthritis, asthma, cancer, diabetes, heart attack, hypertension, obesity, and stroke. All conditions except for obesity and asthma increase across the lifespan. By age 70, 7 per cent of the population have hypertension and 55 per cent have arthritis. Similar patterns of chronic illness are seen across the lifespan of Canadian adults (Health Canada, 2003; PHAC, 2011; 2012; 2009a; 2009b). Prevalence rates of asthma (PHAC, 2012) and obesity decrease as age increases, with obesity rates being the highest in adults 55–64 years old (PHAC, 2009b) and asthma being greatest in children 12 and younger (PHAC, 2012). At the age of 75 and older, 23 per cent of Canadians have cardiovascular disease (PHAC, 2009a).

Health disparities (see Chapter 19) reduce the ability to achieve the best health outcomes among minority groups, including people of colour, women, those with low education and income, and rural-dwelling individuals (Centers for Disease Control, 2012). Health disparities arise due to poverty, poor access to health care, and educational differences. Notably, lifespan and health are determined by both genetic and environmental or lifestyle influences, with genetics accounting for roughly 35 per cent and health behaviours (e.g., smoking, poor diet, inactivity) accounting for the largest percentage. These health behaviours may be changed through culturally competent educational programs.

Ability to decrease risk factors is important for health geropsychology, but the childhood and adult obesity epidemic threatens longevity and health for people as they grow older. Overweight individuals are at increased risk for heart disease, type 2 diabetes, high blood pressure, stroke, osteoarthritis, respiratory problems, and some cancers. Interventions to increase physical activity and promote self-management of chronic illness are needed for the benefit of public health in North America.

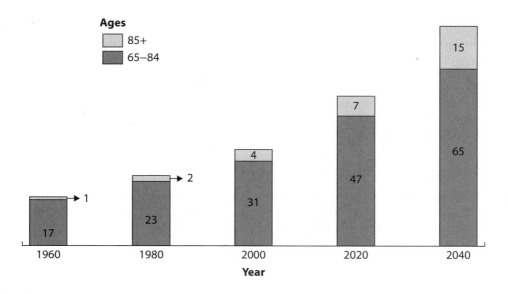

FIGURE 18.1 | Number of older Americans, 1960–2040 (in millions).

Source: Urban Institute. Data source: US Census Bureau (2004a, 2004b, 2004c). Used with permission.

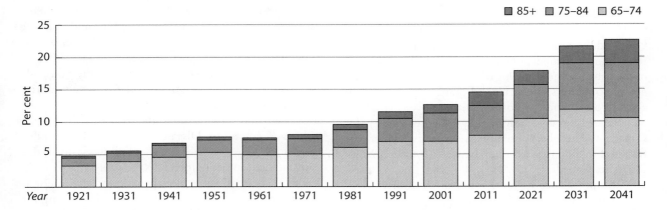

FIGURE 18.2 | Seniors by age subgroups, as % of the total population, Canada, 1921–2041.

Working with Older Adults with Chronic Illnesses

Approximately 75 million people in the US have more than one chronic condition (Parekh & Barton, 2010). Poor health outcomes associated with multiple chronic illnesses include increased hospitalizations, complicated medication schedules, duplicated medical tests, conflicting medical advice, increased disability, and death. Research findings are often slow to reach and to be applied in clinical practice. This is because research studies usually include only people with one illness, so applying treatments developed in research to people with multiple chronic illnesses in a practice setting may not work. Moreover, health professionals are less likely to use research findings about treatments that work in research studies with older adults because seniors are seen as a more complex age group.

Interdisciplinary and Collaborative Care

Chronic conditions often are accompanied by psychological disorders (Solano, Gomes, & Higginson, 2006), such as depression and anxiety (Scherrer, 2003). This has led to the development of integrated health programs that combine mental health screening (Scogin & Shah, 2006) and services into medical care settings treating patients with chronic conditions. This form of health care is called **collaborative care** (Scherrer, 2003), an approach in which physicians and mental health-care providers work together in an organized way to manage

common mental disorders and chronic disease. These programs are practical and apply principles of chronic disease management, including establishing and sustaining effective communication and teamwork among primary care, mental health–care providers, and care managers (Boyd et al., 2005). This collaboration supports systematic diagnosis and health or mental health outcomes tracking. It also facilitates adjustment of treatments based on these outcomes (Scogin, Hanson, & Welsh, 2003; Thielke, Vannoy, & Unützer, 2007). Collaborative care represents best clinical practice, particularly given the multiple chronic conditions experienced by many older adults (Parekh & Barton, 2010).

Family Caregiving and Chronic Illness

Family members are often the ones providing care to people living with chronic illness in the community (Family Caregiver Alliance, 2006). Despite the many positive aspects of caregiving, providing care to an older family member with a chronic illness can be associated with psychological distress and feelings of caregiver burden (Aneshensel, Pearlin, Mullan, Zarit, & Whitlach, 1995; Family Caregiver Alliance, 2006). For example, family caregivers of individuals approaching the end of life are at risk for stress, depression, and health problems (McMillan, 2005; McMillan et al., 2006), especially when there have not been previous discussions of the dying person's wishes for medical care at the end of life. In ethnic minority groups, inclusion of family in medical decision-making is common, for example, among Hispanics and African Americans

⬜ IN PRACTICE

The Need to Understand Cognitive Impairment

Mrs Land, living at her daughter's home, is an 82-year-old widow receiving palliative care for congestive heart failure. She has suffered a series of strokes, leaving her with moderate cognitive impairment. She is morbidly obese and confined to her bed. Her daughter, a substitute middle-school teacher, occasionally leaves Mrs Land at home alone when she substitute teaches. She always leaves the house telephone within her mother's reach and alerts her neighbour to the possibility that her mother will call during the school day if the need arises. The consulting health psychologist has been educating the daughter regarding caregiving issues and the potential need for respite care.

On one occasion, the home health aide arrived to find Mrs Land had become incontinent of bowel and was covered in her own feces. Mrs Land reported that she had called out for her daughter, but that her daughter did not appear to be home. The telephone sat beside Mrs Land on a bed stand.

The home health aide provided continence care and bathed Mrs Land. Upon returning to the home health agency, the aide reported the incident to her supervisor. After consulting with the interdisciplinary team, the medical director of the home health agency reported the incident to Adult Protective Services.[1] The daughter continued her work with the health psychologist but the relationship with the medical director was irreparable and the services of another home health agency were engaged.

[1]Legislation and regulations concerning reporting of such incidents vary from jurisdiction to jurisdiction. Individuals are advised to be familiar with the laws and regulations of their jurisdiction. For health professionals, any decision concerning reporting must be in accordance with professional standards and ethics codes adopted by their discipline.

where, culturally, the use of family to communicate the wishes of the patient is often seen as more relevant than a written directive (Volker, 2005). Chapter 19 provides a detailed discussion of cross-cultural issues.

In the context of caregiving, family behaviours and communication patterns are important in the overall outcomes of patients living with chronic health problems. Critical, overprotective, controlling, and distracting family responses to illness management have been associated with negative patient outcomes (Rosland, Heisler, & Piette, 2012). Therefore, interventions aimed at improving chronic illness outcomes should emphasize increased family use of attentive coping techniques and family support for the patient's autonomous motivation.

The Caregiver Stress–Health Model (Monin & Schulz, 2009) suggests ways in which an older adult's suffering (as displayed through physical and emotional symptoms) may influence family members' emotion regulation and, thus, provision of care. Two possible family member response patterns are proposed: **cognitive empathy** and **conditioned emotional responses**. Cognitive empathy refers to the shared or complementary emotional experience of the family member in response to the older adult's physical and emotional suffering. Conditioned emotional responses may occur when the family member has paired certain emotions with past experiences of the older person's suffering (i.e., becoming angry when the older relative displays fatigue or pain) and can cause defensive emotions (e.g., denial, fatalism) and withdrawal from the older patient. Health geropsychologists and other health professionals consider the history of the relationship and long-term familial coping patterns when designing family-based interventions for care of chronic illness in the home.

As the In Practice box above illustrates, family members of people with chronic illnesses may be inadequately prepared for caregiving tasks and require intervention and education in order to provide care at home. For example, the adult daughter described in the case study may not have understood the impact of cognitive impairment on an individual's ability to meet his or her needs, such as calling a neighbour for help when in distress. Effectively educating this caregiver about respite care and sitter services may have prevented the episode and subsequent involvement of Adult Protective Services; this type of caregiver education can be facilitated by health geropsychologists.

Chronic Pain

According to the Core Curriculum for Pain Education published by the International Association for the Study of Pain (IASP) (Charlton, 2005), chronic pain affects at least 50 per cent of older adults who live in the community and as many as 80 per cent of seniors who live in long-term care (LTC) facilities.

A detailed discussion of the experience of pain and health psychologists' role in its assessment and management has been included in Chapter 7. In this section, we focus on special issues pertaining to pain in older adults.

Older Adults Who Live Independently in the Community

Although there are many similarities between the way psychologists assess and treat younger and older pain patients, there are also unique challenges to working with older persons. Gauthier and Gagliese (2010) have discussed some of the issues specific to pain assessment and have pointed out that some commonly seen age-related changes (e.g., changes in visual acuity, auditory impairments) may make it more difficult for older adults to complete psychological questionnaires and to participate in clinical interviews. Accommodations, such as use of larger type on written materials, are often needed. Aside from such practical considerations, a complicating factor relates to commonly held false beliefs such as the idea that pain is an inevitable part of aging that must be endured (e.g., Martin, Williams, Hadjistavropoulos, Hadjistavropoulos, & MacLean, 2005). Pain is not the result of aging per se but the result of pathology that ought to be treated irrespective of a person's age. Beliefs that pain in old age is natural may make older persons less likely to seek assessment and treatment of their pain and contribute to the under-treatment of pain that is often seen in this population (Herr, 2010).

Although a wide variety of tools are available to assess the pain experience and co-morbid psychological concerns, only a small portion of these have been validated in older populations. As such, it is critical that psychologists select their assessment tools carefully and that they ensure these have been appropriately researched with older persons (Hadjistavropoulos, Herr, et al., 2007).

Cognitive behaviour therapy (CBT) is frequently employed in the psychological management of chronic pain. The CBT methods used with older adults are similar to those employed with younger persons, although the

focus may be different. For example, older adults often present with inaccurate beliefs about pain and aging such as the aforementioned idea that pain is inevitable in old age and must be endured. The psychologist will challenge such beliefs with Socratic dialogue. In other words, the psychologist queries the client regarding the logic underlying inaccurate beliefs about pain experienced by older adults. Moreover, the types of stressors that older adults face (and consequently are addressed in therapy) often are different from those typically seen among younger persons (e.g., younger persons are concerned about their ability to perform the duties of their occupation whereas retired older persons are more likely to be preoccupied with such issues as widowhood and empty nest).

As discussed in Chapter 7, CBT has been found to be effective in the management of pain (Butler, Chapman, Forman, & Beck, 2006), and several studies have investigated its effectiveness specifically with older persons (e.g., Lunde, Nordhus, & Pallesen, 2009; Green, Hadjistavropoulos, Hadjistavropoulos, Martin, & Sharpe, 2009). Lunde, Nordhus, and Pallesen (2009) found CBT to be moderately effective, with demonstrated benefit on self-reported pain but not on physical function, depression, or patterns of medication use. Psychologists have also developed bibliotherapy interventions (i.e., self-help treatments involving the use of books and manuals) to help older adults deal with chronic pain (Hadjistavropoulos & Hadjistavropoulos, 2008), although the effectiveness of such programs requires further study (Hadjistavropoulos, 2012).

Older Adults with Dementia Who Live in Long-Term Care Facilities

While pain tends to be under-treated in older adults in general (Herr, 2010), this under-treatment is an even more significant concern when focusing specifically on older adults who live in LTC facilities. There is evidence that older persons who live in LTC in both the US (e.g., Horgas, Nichols, Schapson, & Vietes, 2007; Morrison & Siu, 2000; Robinson, 2007) and Canada (Martin, Williams, Hadjistavropoulos, Hadjistavropoulos, & MacLean, 2005; Hadjistavropoulos et al., 2009) suffer from unnecessary pain. One of the factors contributing to this under-treatment is the communication challenge (Hadjistavropoulos et al., 2011) associated with advanced **dementia**.

Dementia rates in the US and Canada are similar, demonstrating a significant public health need in older populations. For older adults, at least 71 years of age, 13.9 per cent of the population has a diagnosis of dementia and 9.7 per cent have a diagnosis of Alzheimer's disease (AD) (Canadian Study of Health and Aging Working Group, 1994). Advanced AD and other dementias are associated with major impairments in judgement and language abilities. As a result, older adults with dementia often do not report their pain. Given subjectivity in the experience of pain and fluctuations in pain intensity, underlying physical problems may be missed when pain is not self-reported. Health psychologists and other professionals have played an active role in trying to solve the problem of pain under-reporting by developing behavioural observation assessment methods, emphasizing non-verbal pain behaviours (e.g., vocalizations, grimaces). Such automatic, reflexive pain behaviours tend to be less affected by advanced dementia

PHOTO 18.1 | Falls represent a frequent cause of injury in older persons.

compared to self-report. As such, observational procedures focusing on such behaviours have been shown to be helpful in identifying pain and its fluctuations. One of the most effective methods for identifying pain in this population is the Pain Assessment Checklist for Seniors with Limited Ability to Communicate[1] (PACSLAC) (Fuchs-Lacelle, Hadjistavropoulos, & Lix, 2008; Lints-Martindale, Hadjistavropoulos, Lix, & Thorpe, 2012) and the PACSLAC-II (Chan, Hadjistavropoulos, Williams, & Lints-Martindale, in press), which require health-care personnel to observe the patient and evaluate him or her for pain behaviours (for more detailed assessment protocols, see Hadjistavropoulos, Fitzgerald, & Marchildon, 2010; Hadjistavropoulos et al., 2007). Increasingly, LTC facilities are employing observational pain assessment procedures such as the PACSLAC, although challenges remain (e.g., nursing staff may be unfamiliar with such procedures).[1]

Untreated pain in long-term care can lead to behavioural disturbances (e.g., aggression, loud vocalizations), which can easily be misattributed to psychiatric conditions and can lead to unnecessary and risky pharmacological therapies (Balfour & O'Rourke, 2003; Ballard et al., 2009). In response to this, psychologists increasingly are involved in the development of

appropriate interventions designed to identify and modify the sources of behavioural disturbance (e.g., whether or not the disturbance is due to pain). For example, psychologist Jane Fisher and her colleagues developed the Functional Analytic Model of Intervention (Fisher, Drossel, Ferguson, Cherup, & Sylvester, 2008). This model recognizes that all behaviours are influenced by a person's psychological and physiological history and his or her current social and physical context. Through appropriate assessment (e.g., observing the antecedents and consequences of a behaviour), sources of distress are identified and managed through a variety of integrated approaches, including behavioural interventions (e.g., Cohen-Mansfield, 2001; Opie, Doyle, & O'Connor, 2002), structured activities, and environmental design. More research is needed to determine the extent to which such interventions are effective in the management of pain in seniors who reside in LTC facilities.

Falls

Falls represent one of the most frequent sources of painful injury among older adults. Approximately one in three older persons experiences a fall, with roughly half of these individuals falling more than once per year (Hawk, Hyland, Rupert, Colonvega, & Hall, 2006). Such falls are a leading cause of injury and hospitalization, with hospitalization rates doubling in seniors above age 75 (Rubenstein, 2006). In an American study, Stevens et al. (2008) found that 31 per cent of falls reported over one

1 Disclosure of conflict of interest: Thomas Hadjistavropoulos, who is a co-author of this chapter, is also one of the developers of the PACSLAC and the PACSLAC-II.

year resulted in at least one medical visit and at least one day of restricted activity. In a Canadian six-month longitudinal study (i.e., a study in which information is collected from the same people over relatively long periods of time) involving 571 older adults over age 69, Hadjistavropoulos, Martin, et al. (2007) found that 199 falls occurred with 50 per cent of these falls leading to significant injury and 22 per cent leading to pain lasting more than a few days. Moreover, 18 per cent of the falls resulted in seeking medical attention.

While a variety of medical factors increase the risk of falling (e.g., visual problems, significant orthopedic diagnosis, use of medications that affect balance), psychological factors also increase the risk of falling. This is consistent with biopsychosocial models of health discussed throughout this volume. For example, depression (e.g., Ivziku, Matarese, & Pedone, 2011) and excessive fear of falling can predict future falls (e.g., Hadjistavropoulos, Martin, et al., 2007). It is often assumed that fear of falling leads to excessive avoidance of activity, which in turn leads to loss of muscle tone and fitness, which then leads to falls (e.g., Brummel-Smith, 1989), but this is not necessarily the case. Specifically, in their longitudinal investigation, Hadjistavropoulos, Martin, and colleagues (2007) did not find an association between fear-related avoidance of activity and future falls and speculated that fear of falling may have a direct negative effect on balance. This has now been confirmed (i.e., older people walk in a less stable way when they become anxious) (Delbaere, Sturnieks, Crombez, &

Lord, 2009; Feltner, MacRae, & McNitt-Gray, 1994; Hadjistavropoulos et al., 2012). These changes in gait are less likely to appear when people are not anxious.

Educational interventions often focus on preventing falls (e.g., by recommending appropriate footwear and environmental modifications), but given the association between fear of falling—as well as depression—and increased fall risk, it is not surprising that CBT has also been employed in this context. CBT has been found to be effective in reducing fear of falling and recurrent falls, especially when it is combined with an appropriately supervised physical exercise program (Zijlstra, Van Haastreght, Van Rossum, Van Eijk, Yardley, & Kempen, 2007; Zijlstra et al., 2009). CBT interventions aim to increase self-efficacy beliefs regarding falls as well as the sense of control over falling. An emphasis is also placed on correcting misconceptions about the view of falls and fall risk, setting realistic goals for safely increasing physical activity and changing the home environment to reduce risk (Zijlstra et al., 2009). In cases where physical exercise is involved in preventing falls, it is appropriate and usually necessary for psychologists to collaborate with other treating professionals such as physical therapists.

Behavioural Interventions in Long-Term Care

Many options for sheltered housing are available to older individuals, including independent senior housing with services, assisted living facilities (ALFs), continuing care retirement communities, and skilled nursing facilities (Stone & Reinhard, 2007). Transition to any residential care may result in depression and loneliness (Rossen, 2007). Six to 25 per cent of LTC residents have a diagnosis of major depression, 12–25 per cent suffer from mild depressive disorders, and 30–50 per cent display significant depressive symptoms (e.g., Parmelee, Katz, & Lawton, 1992; Teresi, Abrams, Holmes, Ramirez, & Eimicke, 2001). Transitions to LTC often are precipitated by increasing physical or cognitive impairments, which are associated with decreased quality of life in multiple domains, such as privacy, individuality, relationship, and mood (Abrahamson, Clark, Perkins, & Arling, 2012). Passage of

PHOTO 18.2 | Meaningful activity is an important component of quality of life.

© FredFroese/iStockphoto

the Nursing Home Reform Act as part of the Omnibus Budget Reconciliation Act of 1987 in the United States mandated that adequate care in skilled nursing facilities include psychosocial and quality-of-life assessments (Fields, Kramer, & Lubin, 1993) and required certified LTC facilities to employ activities personnel (e.g., activities director, recreation therapist). Engagement in pleasant and meaningful activity is a fundamental component of quality of life (Colombo, Della Buono, Smania, Raviola, & De Leo, 2006; Glass, de Leon, Bassuk, & Berkman, 2006; Moos & Björn, 2006) and has been used as an intervention for improving mood and decreasing symptoms of depression (Glass et al., 2006; Lawton, 1997).

Behavioural Activation in Long-Term Care

The Brief Behavioural Activation Treatment for Depression (BATD) (Lejuez, Hopko, & Hopko, 2001) focuses on unique environmental contingencies that maintain depressed behaviour across settings. The intervention seeks to increase participation in meaningful events through goal-setting and activity-planning. A modified version of BATD with inpatients in a geropsychiatric facility involving eight sessions over a four-week period improved depression in patients (Snarski et al., 2011).

Animal-assisted therapy in LTC has health benefits. It can improve psychological states and self-worth, and increase morale (Beck & Katcher, 2003). Nursing home residents have demonstrated improvements in physical functioning, self-care, depression and anxiety, cognitive functioning, social functioning, and life satisfaction after taking care of a canary in comparison with caring for a plant or doing nothing. The canary group also demonstrated significant decreases in somatic complaints compared to the control group and significant decreases in anxiety and psychotic symptoms compared to the plant group (Colombo et al., 2006).

The amount of total activity, including group and individual activities, is positively related to interest and pleasure among nursing home residents. Residents vary greatly in terms of the activities that generate positive affect, and for some residents, participation in an activity increased negative affect. Depressed residents are less likely to engage in informal spontaneous activities and may benefit from more structured activities (Meeks, Young, & Looney, 2007). Thus, particularly for depressed residents, individually tailored activity programs are needed to increase their engagement in activities that are meaningful to them. It would be important for health geropsychologists and other mental health

professionals to consider LTC settings as a primary practice arena. When mental health consultants have worked with LTC residents and staff to evaluate individualized activity plans and then implemented interventions engaging residents in pleasurable activities, both residents and staff reported satisfaction with this intervention (Meeks & Depp, 2002; Meeks, Looney, Van Haitsma, & Teri, 2008).

Reminiscence Therapy

Although older adults experience declines in episodic memory with advancing age (Radvansky, 2011), considerable evidence demonstrates that **life review** and **reminiscence** interventions are effective in reducing symptoms of depression in this population (Bohlmeijer, Smit, & Cuijpers, 2003; Haight, Michel, & Hendrix, 2000; Haight & Webster, 1995; Scogin, Welsh, Hanson, Stump, & Coates, 2005), improving social interaction, quality of life, and aspects of

PHOTO 18.3 | Reminiscence interventions are often effective in reducing symptoms of depression in older persons.

well-being (Haber, 2006; Moos & Björn, 2006), and assisting in the integration, maintenance, or development of the self (Haber, 2006; Moos & Björn, 2006). Haber (2006) clearly differentiates reminiscence, the universal, passive recall of memories from life review, a structured, potentially multi-session interview focused around one or more life themes such as family, work, major turning points, the impact of historical events, the arts, aging, dying and death, and socialization issues

⊚ IN FOCUS

The Legacy Project

The Legacy Project (Allen, Hilgeman, Ege, Shuster, & Burgio, 2008), conducted with palliative care patients and their informal family caregivers living in the community, combined reminiscence with creative activity. Both the individual with chronic illness and a member of his or her family were active participants in the intervention.

"You told me, you said, 'If you can't go forward, don't go backward. Stand still.' And that meant a whole lot to me."—Mrs J, caregiver and Legacy Project participant (2004).

This 70-year-old African-American woman, Mrs M, was living with chronic kidney disease in a rural community and receiving dialysis three times per week. Her lifelong friend (Mrs J) had taken up the task of caregiving, providing instrumental and emotional support on a daily basis. Mrs M was struggling with a desire for **primary control** over her chronic illness (she wanted her illness to be cured), but her advanced-stage kidney disease left her in a position of vulnerability and in need of help from her friend (her chronic illness could not be cured and she needed to receive care).

Mrs M displayed significant symptoms of depression related to her diminished physical function and need for care. In a despondent tone, she stated, "I'm just not worth nothin'. I'm so sorry I'm putting you through all of this!" Mrs J response, quoted above, was a reminder that Mrs M had been a source of comfort and support in the past when Mrs J was in need. Mrs J emphasized their lifelong connection and stated it was time she repaid the favour. The two of them continued to work together in the Legacy Project to reminisce and to create a cookbook of recipes from Mrs M's family.

such as meaning, values, and purpose in life. We discuss reminiscence therapy in relation to three different populations: older adults in community, LTC residents, and persons in palliative care settings. Notably, across settings, incorporation of volunteer-delivered interventions incorporating schoolchildren, a folklorist/oral historian, or same-aged peer may be effective means of improving accessibility of reminiscence interventions to older adults with chronic illness; (Allen et al., 2014 Kazdin & Blaise, 2011).

Treatments in the Community

Reminiscence has received support as an evidence-based treatment for depression among community-dwelling older adults. Using specific coding criteria developed by the Committee on Science and Practice of the Society for Clinical Psychology (Division 12) of the American Psychological Association, Scogin and colleagues (Scogin et al., 2005) found life review to be one of six treatments that are beneficial in reducing geriatric depression, and it is the only intervention developed specifically for older adults. Advanced-practice psychiatric nurses have been shown to effectively deliver life review and reminiscence therapy in the community with depressed patients and to decrease their anxiety, denial, despair, and isolation (McDougall, Buxen, & Suen, 1997).

Treatments in Long-Term Care

In 28 studies, published between 1990 and 2003, using life review with nursing home patients with mild to moderate dementia, benefits were found in self-esteem and self-integration, quality of life, and modification of problematic behaviour (Moos & Björn, 2006). Specifically, the individuals with mild to moderate dementia appeared to benefit most in the five interventions that targeted self-integration (e.g., Bourgeois, Dijkstra, Burgio, & Allen-Burge, 2001; Burgio et al., 2001) in comparison with the nine interventions targeting general quality-of-life outcomes and 11 targeting specific behaviour change. The features of the interventions associated with an enhanced sense of identity were: (1) a thorough and encompassing treatment of the individual's life story; (2) the translation of the life story into care interactions with nursing home staff (e.g., mutual reminiscence); and (3) active encouragement of the residents' meaningful activity. Kitwood (1997) has argued that the emphasis on personhood and subjectivity in dementia care is in the process of being adopted as a best practice within LTC, with a humanistic emphasis on seeing the person with dementia as a person capable of having experiences within physical, social, and cultural contexts. However, Moos and Björn (2006) note several methodological problems within life review studies, including inadequate information on the staging of dementia, limitations of personalized content as a result of group sessions, and poor documentation of unprompted or spontaneous recall of memories or events.

A relatively new intervention not included in these reviews was conducted by Cohen-Mansfield and colleagues (Cohen-Mansfield, Parpura-Gill, & Golander, 2006) based on their prior work in developing the Self-Identity in Dementia Questionnaire (Cohen-Mansfield, Golander, & Arnheim, 2000). Older persons with dementia most frequently report the following salient identity roles, in order of prevalence: (1) family heritage; (2) success of a relative; (3) academic achievement; (4) occupations; (5) traits; and (6) survival. Notably, better cognitive functioning was shown to be consistently related to a greater saliency of identity role in their sample (Cohen-Mansfield et al., 2000).

Using the Self-Identity in Dementia Questionnaire (Cohen-Mansfield et al., 2000), meaningful activity interventions were individualized for 93 older persons with severe dementia. Individuals with moderate dementia provided more salient input regarding their prior roles; the saliency of caregiver input increased as the severity of dementia within an individual increased. In all cases, interventions were designed to match the demographics and cognitive abilities of the person with dementia while still providing purposeful or meaningful activity (Cohen-Mansfield et al., 2006). A family role intervention, for example, involved the creation of a family tree using family photographs or watching videos from close family members. Self-identity awareness, affect, involvement, agitation, well-being, cognitive functioning, and provision of activities were assessed before and during the intervention. In comparison with usual care, the treatment group showed a significant increase in interest, pleasure, and involvement with activities, fewer agitated behaviours, and increased orientation during the treatment period (Cohen-Mansfield et al., 2006). Notably, feedback was not systematically gathered from family members about their impressions of the effectiveness of this intervention.

A product called "CIRCA" was developed by Scottish computer designers and psychologists to support reminiscence among individuals with dementia working with family and professional caregivers in adult daycare settings. It is a touch-screen interface to support reminiscence. Opinions of potential users and their caregivers are elicited and a guided system design uses an iterative (i.e., recurrent trial and error) approach. The interface was designed to be attractive and as simple as possible, with command prompts at the bottom of the screen to lessen fatigue. The system contains 10 videos, 23 music items, and 80 historic photographs of the local city organized into three themes: (1) recreation; (2) entertainment; and (3) city life. In comparison with traditionally administered reminiscence therapy, CIRCA sessions are more conversational with more varied topics and materials (Alm et al., 2007).

Although longitudinal intervention outcome studies are scarce, Haight, Michel, and Hendrix (2000) examined the potential therapeutic effects of a face-to-face structured life review with a therapeutic listener over three years. Half of the residents in this study received the life review intervention whereas the other half received a friendly visit. Measures consisted of life satisfaction, well-being, self-esteem, depression, hopelessness, and suicide intent. Results indicated that the life review intervention was beneficial. Scores on the baseline and post-test measures stayed the same in the intervention group but went down in the friendly visit control group, indicating that the life review intervention helped residents maintain stability in affect and identity over three years.

Treatment for Individuals Approaching the End of Life

Two intervention models using reminiscence and life review with individuals with advanced, chronic illness and either health-care professionals or family caregivers have been applied in palliative care settings: (1) Chochinov's Dignity Therapy (Chochinov, 2012; Chochinov et al., 2011); and (2) the Legacy Project (Allen, 2009; Allen et al., 2008). Chochinov's Dignity Therapy (Chochinov, 2012; Chochinov et al., 2011) is a combination treatment approach that borrows elements from supportive therapy with its emphasis on empathy and connectedness; existential psychotherapy with engagement of issues such as meaning, hope, and mortality; and life review. One component of Chochinov's (2012) dignity-conserving repertoire is "generativity or legacy," an exercise that attempts to provide comfort through the telling of the life story and sense that one's life will transcend death. In the Dignity intervention (Chochinov et al., 2011), treatment was delivered individually over three to four sessions to terminally ill cancer patients in the hospital and those receiving home-based palliative care. A semi-structured interview was administered individually and the interviews were transcribed verbatim and edited by the treatment team to end with the patient's overall life message. After the therapist read the transcript to the patient, who could edit the life narrative, the patient could then share the life story transcript with his or her family. Results indicated that Dignity Therapy was effective in improving positive affect and was perceived by patients and families as beneficial (Chochinov et al., 2011). Moreover, patients' belief that the Dignity interviews would be helpful to family members was associated with perceptions that life is more meaningful.

As mentioned in the case of Mrs M, the Legacy Project (Allen et al., 2008) was found to decrease caregiving stress and increase positive affect and family communication as the patient was approaching the end of life. Specifically, caregivers show reduced caregiving stress and patients report increased religious meaning and decreased difficulty breathing. Caregivers and

patients report greater perceived social interaction in the care recipient. And they both report that completing the Legacy Project improved family communication (Allen et al., 2008).

A review of supportive interventions to improve psychological and physical health of informal caregivers and those with terminal illness found 11 randomized controlled trials. These research projects involved 1,836 caregivers (and some patients). The review authors concluded that there is weak evidence that supportive interventions with caregivers of individuals with terminal illness may reduce caregiving distress; however, more evidence is needed.

To summarize, reminiscence and life-review interventions have yielded mostly successful outcomes and promoted successful aging among community-dwelling and institutionalized older adults as well as those approaching the end of life. However, very few studies have assessed outcomes of the life-review process on caregivers as well as patients, and greater research attention is needed in this area (Candy, Jones, Drake, Leurent, & King, 2011).

Cognitive Rehabilitation

Cognitive decline frequently is conceptualized as a part of normal aging. Cognitive processing speed slows with age, and is, sometimes, further slowed by cognitive impairment that sometimes occurs (Lezak, Howieson, & Loring, 2004). Poor decision-making is a consequence of cognitive decline among some older persons without Alzheimer's disease (i.e., those widely considered cognitively healthy) (Boyle et al., 2012). Divided attention is the ability to pay attention to multiple streams of information simultaneously, or to ignore competing information or stimulation while concentrating on a task. Divided attention is slightly compromised by age, and more so by cognitive impairments (Lezak et al., 2004). Wilson (1997) defined **cognitive rehabilitation** as "any intervention strategy or technique which intends to enable clients or patients, and their families, to live with, manage, by-pass, reduce or come to terms with deficits precipitated by injury to the brain." Some examples of this that can improve encoding (use of context and existing knowledge to understand and store information) are providing instruction about activities at a slower pace, controlling the environment to cut down on distractions, and providing instruction in multiple modalities (i.e., demonstrating the task, then explaining the task in words) (Lezak et al., 2004).

PHOTO 18.4 | Harvey Chochinov of the University of Manitoba developed Dignity Therapy.

Used with the permission of Harvey Chochinov.

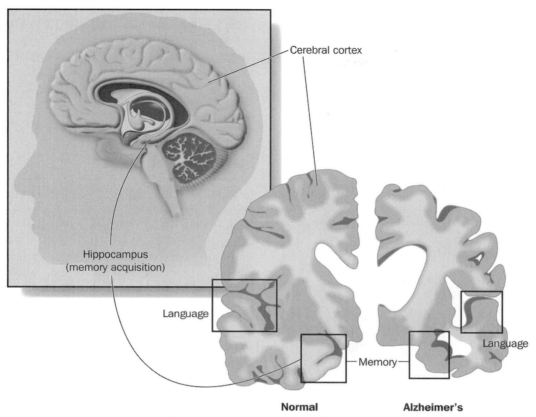

FIGURE 18.3 | Neuronal loss associated with Alzheimer's disease results in atrophy of the affected brain regions. A cure for Alzheimer's disease has yet to be found.

Other strategies can facilitate encoding by improving engagement, thereby increasing attention to the activity. Examples of such strategies include providing activities that have high levels of initial success and using adaptive or supportive environments and assistive devices (e.g., provision of electronic reminders) as needed (Camp, Cohen-Mansfield, & Capezuti, 2002). This intermediate strategy is important because Sperling and colleagues (2011) found that older persons who exhibit cognitive decline, but do not yet meet accepted criteria for mild cognitive impairment (MCI) or Alzheimer's disease (AD), may be most likely to benefit from early intervention and offer a unique opportunity to reduce the public health burden posed by AD.

There is growing evidence that cognitive training may be beneficial (Aguire et al., 2010; Willis et al., 2006). Plassman and colleagues (2009) reviewed factors associated with risk and possible prevention of cognitive decline and found insufficient evidence for most factors but acknowledged some promise for exercise,

cognitive training, and certain nutritional patterns (i.e., a Mediterranean diet and fruits and vegetables). Yamaguchi, Maki, and Yamagami (2010) recommend a new approach to maintaining cognitive function called brain-activation rehabilitation. They recommend that activities designed to maintain cognitive function should include five principles: (1) enjoyable and comfortable activities; (2) activities that promote two-way communication; (3) efforts to enhance motivation among patients; (4) engagement in social roles that tap lifelong interests and abilities; and (5) pleasant environmental settings that are patient-centred.

Dementia

The available evidence is limited and there are no significant benefits of cognitive training in individuals with early stage AD or vascular dementia (Clare & Woods, 2003). This is attributed to a lack of randomized control trials in cognitive rehabilitation studies (Clare &

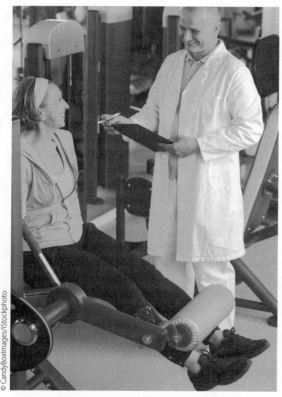

PHOTO 18.5 | Appropriately supervised physical exercise can have many benefits for older adults.

Woods, 2003). In 2012, a clinical study examining cognitive rehabilitation also demonstrated no effect on the everyday functioning of participants with early-onset dementia (Kurz et al., 2012). Therefore, at this time, the efficacy of this treatment lacks scientific support in individuals with early-onset or vascular dementia (i.e., dementia related to problems in the flow of blood to the brain).

Future Directions

In addition to funding more graduate training in gerontology and geriatric medicine, professional organizations must focus continuing education efforts for currently practising professionals on the needs of older adults in North America. Practitioners interested in focusing assessment and intervention efforts on the needs of older adults with chronic illness need to be proactive in identifying their competencies and training needs (Karel et al., 2010; Knight, Karel, Hinrichsen, Qualls, & Duffy, 2009). Technology-based continuing education opportunities such as "webinars" are becoming increasingly available to meet the training needs of a diverse workforce. Through interdisciplinary collaboration and increased focus on health geropsychology, it is possible that the public health crisis in caring for older adults with chronic illness faced by the United States and Canada can be met in an effective manner.

SUMMARY

In this chapter, we considered the prevalence of chronic illness among older people in the United States and Canada, clinical needs in working with these patients (e.g., considerations of multi-morbidity, the need for interdisciplinary teams, and a focus on the family), the impact of pain and falls, and how individuals cope with chronic illness. Moreover, we considered specific areas of intervention, including behavioural interventions in

LTC, reminiscence therapy, and cognitive rehabilitation. Because the numbers of older adults are growing rapidly, the public health burden of chronic disease and multi-morbidity will impact health-care costs, policy, and employment opportunities for the foreseeable future. A multi-faceted approach is critical to train the numbers of health geropsychologists needed to meet this burgeoning need.

Critical Thought Questions

1. Considering the different health-care systems operating within the United States and Canada, how might health geropsychologists structure their practice to best meet the needs of older clients with chronic illness?

2. What are the barriers and facilitators to collaborative or stepped care in different practice settings (i.e., community, primary care, LTC)?

3. How might the training needs of practising professionals and current health geropsychology students be met within technology-based workshops on working with older adults with chronic illness?

Recommended Reading

Aldwin. C.M., Park, C.L., & Spiro, A. (Eds.). (2007). *Handbook of health psychology and aging.* New York: Guilford Press.

Laidlaw, K., & Knight, B. (2008). *Handbook of emotional disorders in later life: Assessment and treatment.* New York: Oxford University Press.

Lichtenberg, P.A. (Ed.). (2010). *Handbook of assessment in clinical gerontology* (2nd ed.). Burlington, Mass.: Elsevier.

Mast, B.T. (2011). *Whole person dementia assessment.* Baltimore: Health Professions Press.

19

Cross-Cultural Issues in Health Psychology

JAIME WILLIAMS   CHANTELLE RICHMOND

Learning Objectives

In this chapter you will:

- Discover how culture influences health and how people respond to illness and use support or treatment.

- Recognize how culture may function in a biopsychosocial model to explain better the etiology of illness, as well as to improve illness prevention and management strategies.

- Learn to describe key causes of disparities in health outcomes among different cultural groups and the key health disparities that exist in North America.

- Become familiar with the cross-cultural presentation of mental disorders, treatment implications, and the relationship to physical conditions.

Introduction: The Importance of Cross-Cultural Issues in Health Psychology

Our society is becoming increasingly multicultural and globally conscious. In recent years, the cultural composition of North America has shifted. In the United States in 2001, 25–30 per cent of people self-reported as being of minority status; this statistic increased to 34 per cent in 2010 and is expected to rise to approximately 50 per cent by the year 2050 (US Census Bureau, 2001; 2011). In Canada, visible minority persons (of non-Aboriginal descent) constituted approximately 16 per cent of the population in 2006 and this portion is projected to double by 2031 (Statistics Canada, 2008). Aboriginal persons (i.e., First Nations, Métis, Inuit) comprised approximately 3 per cent of the population in 2001 and almost 4 per cent in 2006; the Aboriginal population is growing at a pace exceeding that of other Canadian ethnic groups (Statistics Canada, 2003; 2005).

Shifting demographics have a direct impact on the practice of health psychologists (Keefe & Blumenthal, 2004). We work with clients from many different cultural backgrounds and contexts and this is reflected in the current training and practice of psychology. Professional associations, researchers, and training programs recognize the importance of becoming culturally competent by understanding how different groups respond to physical and psychological symptoms and view medical services (Dana, 2002; Yali & Revenson, 2004). This chapter serves as a primer for the study of culture and health in psychology, with a focus on North American people of non-European/Western cultural backgrounds. In this chapter, we draw from a biopsychosocial model to describe and explain health disparities that exist among North Americans of differing cultures. This model is useful as it enables for the accounting of cultural differences and the ways these differences affect health. Such understanding allows for insight into the psychological impact of illness, responses to illness, challenges, and strengths that affect people of all ethnic and cultural backgrounds.

What Is Diversity? Distinguishing among Race, Ethnicity, and Culture

The terms **race**, **ethnicity**, and **culture**, although related, can also be distinguished from one another. Originally, the term "race" was intended to capture differences in biological substrates through physical characteristics such as skin colour and hair type (APA, 2002; Watt & Norton, 2004). However, the genetic and/or biological basis of race has been debated and the term is contentious, given current understanding of genetics (Watt & Norton, 2004). Watt and Norton stress that genetic differences contributing to health and disease among various racial groups should not be dismissed. However, Mountain and Risch (2004) found that genetics only contribute to racial group differences in physical traits, complex diseases, and behaviour to a limited extent. They concluded that "we are far from characterizing the contribution of genes to between-group variation (racial group differences) of any complex trait and are likely to continue struggling in the future" (p. s52). Nevertheless, the term "race" still reflects how others assign individuals to categories (or how people self-identify) (Helms & Talleyrand, 1997). Some argue that underlying concepts referenced by the term "race" (e.g., belonging, ownership, citizenship, and racism) have important implications for identity among African Americans (Airhihenbuwa & Liburd, 2006).

Some authors do not distinguish between the terms "race" and "ethnicity" or they use them interchangeably (e.g., Kressin, Raymond, & Manze, 2008; Skrentny, 2008). Kaplan and Bennett (2003) note that the term "race," as opposed to "ethnicity," however, is almost always linked to the idea of biological variation between groups. The American Psychological Association (APA) describes ethnicity as "the acceptance of the group mores and practices of one's culture of origin and the concomitant sense of belonging" (APA, 2002, p. 9), thereby recognizing the subjectivity and self-reflective nature of the concept, which is often captured through self-report measures. The APA further states that individuals may hold more than one ethnic identity with varying salience at different times (APA, 2002). Unfortunately, even among researchers, there is no consistency, with some arguing for the term "ethnicity" to encompass both of the terms "race" and "culture" (Kaplan & Bennett, 2003).

The term "culture" generally refers to a set of values, ideals, beliefs, and assumptions about life that are shared among a particular group of people (Alarcon, Westermeyer, Foulks, & Ruiz, 1999). Culture is "indicated by ideas that are transmitted generation to generation, rarely with explicit instruction, by members of the older generation" (Brisline, 1990, p. 12). These ideas may include implicitly and explicitly learned assumptions about individualism, equality, and health and illness (Yali & Revenson, 2004). Language is also considered a fundamental aspect of culture and its transmission (Marshall et al., 2011). Airhihenbuwa and Liburd (2006) note that culture as "collective consciousness" is reinforced through society. Society may promote health-supporting (protective) or health-hindering values, beliefs, and behaviours. Further, Stephens (2011) notes that representations of illness, appropriate responses to illness, the relationship between the mind and body, and the role of medical knowledge may all be culturally transmitted. Given that culture is primarily learned, it remains dynamic, ever-changing, and responsive to new situations depending on resources that are available versus required, and our roles and responsibilities (Andrews & Boyle, 1995; Watt & Norton, 2004). Of particular note in these definitions is the inclusivity of the term; all persons from all racial and ethnic origins are cultural producers and consumers (APA, 2002).

Hofstede's Value Dimensions of Culture

A highly influential framework for considering how values may vary across cultures was developed by Dutch social psychologist, Geert Hofstede, and is referred to as **Hofstede's value dimensions of culture** (Hofstede, 2001; Taras & Kirkman, 2010). Hofstede conducted a pioneering study on how values in the workplace are influenced by culture through survey data from 88,000 IBM employees in 40 countries (20 languages) during the 1960s and 1970s (Hofstede, 2001; Taras & Kirkman, 2010). His framework originally included four dimensions of culture, with a fifth dimension being added later (Figure 19.1) (Hofstede & Bond, 1988). The first, *individualism–collectivism*, refers to the degree to which people within a society act individually rather than as part of a group, depending on how close or loose their interpersonal frameworks are. The second, *power distance*, refers to societal acceptance of the equal or unequal distribution of power within institutions. Third, *uncertainty avoidance* involves the ability of societies to tolerate ambiguity, as indicated by the presence or absence of clear rules. *Masculinity–femininity* is the extent to which a society values assertiveness and monetary acquisition ("ego-oriented" or "masculine") as opposed to co-operation, position security, and a friendly atmosphere ("relationship-oriented" or "feminine"). The fifth dimension, *Confucian dynamism* (long-term versus short-term orientation), refers to future-oriented values (e.g., persistence) as compared with present/past orientation (e.g., traditions, social engagements). Both in Hofstede's original research (1980) and in more recent cross-cultural re-examinations of those dimensions (Fernandez et al., 1997), inter-country differences have been found. Fernandez et al. (1997) examined differences in Hofstede's dimensions using a sample of respondents from nine countries. Overall, they found several differences, of note being that people from Western countries (e.g., the US, Germany) score higher on individualism and those from non-Western cultures (e.g., Japan, China, Russia) were found to be more collectivist in orientation.

Studies of Hofstede's theories were compiled and meta-analyzed (i.e., statistically combined) by Taras and Kirkman (2010). In their review of 598 empirical investigations, several hypotheses were tested concerning the predictive power of Hofstede's cultural dimensions for individual traits such as emotional responses and attitudes. They found that the cultural dimensions predict most strongly participants' emotional responses (e.g., depression, anxiety) rather than their attitudes (e.g., religiosity, perceived justice, life satisfaction) or job satisfaction. This cultural trend was especially true for managers and employees, men, and those of higher levels of education. They concluded that cultural values are useful in predicting emotional responses (Taras & Kirkman, 2010). There have also been criticisms of Hofstede's work (Jones, 2007; McSweeney, 2002; Moulettes, 2007; Yeh, 1988). McSweeney (2002) notes the core assumption of Hofstede's view of culture is that

FIGURE 19.1 | Hofstede's value dimensions of culture.

it is implicit, causal, territorially unique, and shared. McSweeney further notes that this idea of culture has been debated at length. In other words, Hofstede's work has been criticized for minimizing the possibility of many cultures operating simultaneously within a country and also for assuming that national boundaries demarcate different cultural orientations (Jones, 2007). Moulettes (2007) provides a critique of the cultural value dimensions by asking whether the theory overall engenders Westernized, patriarchial structures. Moulettes and others raise their questions using **postcolonial theory**, which makes an attempt to understand the process and problems stemming from European colonization (Culler, 1997).

Cultural Factors and a Biopsychosocial Formulation of Health

Although past medical models and traditional views of health have somewhat neglected cultural differences in health and illness, this is changing. Alternatively, within health psychology the biopsychosocial formulation posits that biological, psychological, and social processes interact and contribute reciprocally to health and illness (Suls & Rothman, 2004); people's psychological and social experiences and behaviours are proposed to be interconnected with their biological processes. Culture and ethnicity have increasingly been recognized within a biopsychosocial formulation of health as important for the causation, prevention, and management of illness (Suls & Rothman, 2004). It is important to consider all the influences that culture exerts on health, including coping styles, economic resources, appraisals of and exposure to stress, and illness exposure (Suls & Rothman, 2004). Diversity is accelerating in multiple contexts, including social, religious, educational, and economic spheres (Keefe & Blumenthal, 2004), and these, in turn, have been shown to impact on health and mental health through such factors as language barriers and access to health insurance and health care (Yali & Revenson, 2004).

To illustrate, Marshall and colleagues (2011) demonstrate how culture may be a central consideration within a biopsychosocial model of health for patients diagnosed with cancer and for their families. They emphasize socio-cultural and family-systems models in which culture, family, and social class interconnect and influence the trajectory of cancer illness. Although they recognize

Photo by Anastasia Knyazeva. Used with the permission of Capital Health.

PHOTO 19.1 | Susan Mogae (far left), diversity co-ordinator for Public Health, helped co-ordinate a Multicultural Fair that provided newcomers to Canada and service providers an opportunity to share information and learn about different resources supporting the health of Nova Scotians. To encourage interaction, volunteer interpreters trained by the Immigrant Settlement and Integration Service interpretation program were on hand to provide simultaneous interpretation in several languages.

the role of biology in cancer, they present evidence suggesting that differences between groups of patients in the rates of cancers and recovery can be accounted for, at least in part, by socio-cultural factors. They describe, for example, findings that link cancer outcome disparities to low economic class, culture, and injustice, concluding that poverty, in particular, has strong explanatory power. Their model considers the "cancer experience" and treatment to involve all members of the family, rather than just the patient to the exclusion of his or her support people. They stress the personal influence of culture on individuals and families and, in turn, the individual's role as a producer of culture. Finally, Marshall and colleagues (2011) describe how cancer education may become more responsive to culture by considering language, transportation, finances, flexible care provision (e.g., time of treatments, setting), family-friendly treatment settings, and appropriate follow-up.

Health Beliefs Expressed Cross-Culturally

Within a biopsychosocial approach, health psychologists often focus on the *health beliefs* of the patient (e.g., Abraham, Sheeran, & Johnston, 1998; Rabia, Knauper, & Miquelon, 2006). The health beliefs model of social cognition (also see Chapter 1) explains how beliefs interact to produce behavioural effects (health behaviours) (Rosenstock, 1974; Rosenstock, Strecher, & Becker, 1988). It is based on the assumption that people are motivated to be healthy (value) and that they hold beliefs about the helpfulness of their behaviours (expectancy) (hence, *value expectancy* theory). The likelihood that behaviours will occur depends on how effective a person believes that behaviour will be and his or her perceived level of risk for an illness (Strecher & Rosenstock, 1997). Culture may affect people's health beliefs about disease and wellness, feelings about medical treatment and providers, and use of traditional medicines (Vaughn, Jacquez, & Baker, 2009).

Similarly, culture may affect *attributions* about health, which are causal explanations people assign to illness and wellness. For instance, Kottak (2011) describes three different styles of health attributions that may differ cross-culturally. Naturalistic theories (most characteristic of Western medicine) seek to explain illness scientifically, systematically, and impersonally. This approach is contrasted with personalistic theories that attribute illness to sorcerers, spirits, and ghosts, and emotionalistic theories that ascribe illness to extreme states of emotion. Some research has suggested that individuals from developing countries may more likely attribute causes of illness (mental and physical) to spiritual, social, and supernatural beliefs whereas those from more developed countries make attributes based on naturalistic, individual-centred theories of illness (e.g., Mulatu & Berry, 2001; Teferra & Shibre, 2012; Tenkorang, Gyimah, Maticka-Tyndale, & Adiei., 2011), although it is difficult to make generalizations (Kirmayer & Sartorius, 2007). Health beliefs and health attributions have a reciprocal relationship wherein attributions influence the development of health beliefs, which in turn affect how people make attributions (Vaughn et al., 2009). Health beliefs and attributions provide information to the patient about the meaning and seriousness of symptoms and influence health behaviours.

One may begin to gain insight into cross-cultural differences in health beliefs through the examination of values associated with systems of non-Western medicine (Gurung, 2011). Gurung (2011) describes a number of culturally based systems of medicine that are likely to influence health beliefs. For example, in traditional Chinese medicine (TCM), practitioners work *holistically* with the human body and environment. Opposing forces in the body (yin and yang), along with pairings of organs and *qi* (chee; energy circulating in bodies, which is popularly conceptualized as bioelectric) are central in health and illness (Yang, 1997). Health is viewed as optimizing balance between states and the illness occurs from unbalance (Figure 19.2). Food is principle for balancing the body and optimizing the flow of *qi*.

As a second example, Cohen (2003) notes that among Native Americans medicine is more akin to healing than to curing and focuses on restoring well-being and harmony to the body. Gurung (2011) notes that many elements of Native American medicine are similar to TCM, and that the values of both contrast with values in Western medicine. Elements of the natural world are considered alongside the human world wherein everything is connected. Healers co-ordinate medical practices and work with patients to find connections among their life experiences and their illness. Ritual, ceremony, and the spirit world are also often given consideration (Gurung, 2011).

Within Western medicine, many of these traditional systems of healing are being incorporated into complementary and alternative approaches to treating illness, perhaps reflecting the changing health beliefs of our multicultural society. Although many people use the terms "alternative" and "complementary" medicine interchangeably, the National Center for Complementary and Alternative Medicine (NCCAM) in the US distinguishes between the two. It defines alternative medicine as non-mainstream approaches to health that are used *in place of* conventional medicine whereas complementary approaches refer to the use of non-mainstream approaches *in conjunction with* conventional medicine (NCCAM, 2013). It is further noted that the array of specific approaches can be divided into natural products and mind–body practices. Several mind–body practices are adaptations from non-Western medicine, such as meditation, yoga, Tai Chi, and qigong. Some empirical evidence supports the use of complementary and alternative approaches for the management of some health conditions. Although not perfectly consistent across studies, for example, some investigations have led to the conclusion that yoga has beneficial effects for patients with musculoskeletal pain problems (Cramer, Lauche, Langhorst, & Dobos, 2013; Ward, Stebbings, Cherkin, & Baxter, 2013).

Despite their potential importance, it is not easy to examine etiological (i.e., concerning the origins or causes) and other beliefs about physical and mental disorders cross-culturally (Kirmayer & Sartorius, 2007; Vaughn et al., 2009), and many have cautioned against the categorical measurement of ethnicity or race as proxy for culture (e.g., Ford & Kelly, 2005; Rudell & Diefenbach, 2008). For these reasons, few summative statements can be made concerning differences in health beliefs cross-culturally. For example, Sheikh and Furnham (2000) examined health beliefs among three cultural groups (community

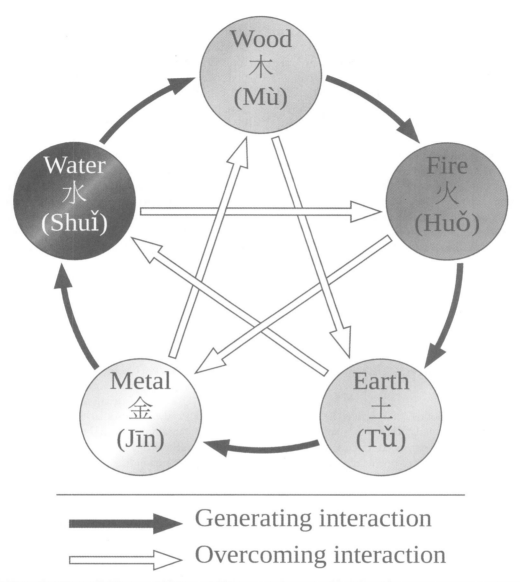

FIGURE 19.2 | The five elements of traditional Chinese medicine.

Source: Wikipedia/Ju gatsu mikka based on works of Benoît Stella

sample, total N = 287) including British Western, Asian British (Indo-Asian background residing in Britain), and Pakistani (residing in Pakistan) persons, expecting that Asian British and Pakistani people would endorse more non-Western and fewer Western health beliefs compared to British Western individuals. Although they found these expected patterns for Asian British and Western British participants, Pakistani participants scored higher on measures of Western attributions of illness as well as non-Western attributions of illness than British Western participants. The authors admitted this was unexpected

and suggested speculatively that plurality within the Pakistani medical system may explain the differences.

Health Disparities among Cultural Groups

Health disparities refer to the gap between the incidence (i.e., number of new cases of an illness in a given time period) and prevalence (i.e., number of total cases of an illness in a given time period) rates of illness and death among different groups of people, for example, socio-economic status groups, cultural groups, older adults, and gay, lesbian, and transgendered persons (Carter-Pokras & Baquet, 2002; CDC, 2011). These differences can be evaluated quantitatively and qualitatively in terms of *inequality* (i.e., an unequal condition) and also *inequity* (i.e., an unequal condition deemed to be unfair or unjust) (Carter-Pokras & Baquet, 2002). Although significant health disparities exist among Caucasian people and visible minority populations, Aboriginal people, and Hispanic and Latino people, the relationship between health disparities and ethnic status is not straightforward; it generally is considered to be mostly mediated. Mediation occurs when a third variable accounts for the measured relationship between two variables, such as socio-economic status and health behaviours (Carter-Pokras & Baquet, 2002; CDC, 2011). To understand health disparities, researchers use multiple health-related outcomes/indicators including health status (e.g., life expectancy), subjective self-rated health, disease presence (e.g., diabetes), health-care access and use, and health behaviours (e.g., smoking) (Frohlich, Ross, & Richmond, 2006).

Significant Health Disparities in North America

Frohlich, Ross, and Richmond (2006) review the evidence for health disparities in Canada. They note that although some health disparities have narrowed, Canada still shows clear differences among groups of people regardless of the indicators used (e.g., health status, health behaviours, disease outcomes). Most notably, Canada's Aboriginal peoples fare much worse than the majority of Canadians on indicators such as life expectancy and infant mortality, chronic disease outcomes, and health behaviours (Frohlich et al., 2006). For example, Aboriginal men living off reserve have a life expectancy of 72.1 years whereas the general Canadian population has a life expectancy of 76 years. For Aboriginal women, life expectancy is 77.7 years off reserve compared to 81.5 years for the general population. When Aboriginal persons living on reserves are considered, this gap widens to nearly 9 years for men and 8.5 years for women. Smylie, Fell, and Ohlsson (2010) examined infant mortality rates among Aboriginal people in Canada, noting that these rates are important indicators of the overall level of health of a population. They found sizable and persistent elevations in infant mortality rates among First Nations people residing both on and off reserve as well as among Inuit people compared to the general population of Canada. Infant mortality is an important indicator of health disparity, reflecting several

underlying mechanisms, such as maternal health, quality of health care, socio-economic conditions, and public health practices (MacDorman & Mathews, 2011). The Inuit of Quebec have a rate of infant mortality greater than five times that of the general Canadian population (23.1 deaths/1,000 vs 4.4 deaths/1,000). Similar findings have been reported for life expectancy and infant mortality for Indigenous populations in the US, Australia, and New Zealand (Smylie et al., 2010).

Regarding specific illness outcomes, diabetes and its complications are particularly problematic for Aboriginal persons. Health Canada has reported that rates of diabetes among First Nations persons living on reserve are 3–5 times higher than among other Canadians (Health Canada, 2011): 19.7 per cent of First Nations people are diagnosed with diabetes, compared to 5.2 per cent in the general population. Although rates of diabetes are somewhat lower among Métis and First Nations persons living off reserve (Reading & Wien, 2009), health disparities are still present and Health Canada (2011) expects these rates to increase due to a significant presence of risk factors, such as obesity and physical inactivity. In the United States, Native Americans and Alaska Natives are more than twice as likely to have a diagnosis of diabetes as their non-Hispanic White counterparts (American Diabetes Association, 2012). The American Diabetes Association (2012) notes that there have been steady increases in diabetes over the past 15 years, especially among youth. For more information about Indigenous knowledge and patterns of health in Canada, see the accompanying In Focus box.

In the United States, health disparities among African-American and other ethnic groups are of particular note (e.g., CDC, 2011; Mensah, Mokdad, Ford, Greenlund, & Croft, 2005). The health disparities between African-American men and other groups in the US have been described as "staggering" (Xanthos, Treadwell, & Braithwaite Holden, 2010, p. 11). The CDC (2011) reported that in terms of life expectancy, African Americans live 6–10 years less than non-Hispanic White Americans and have twice the infant mortality rate (13.35 per 1,000 live births compared to 5.58 per 1,000). Cardiovascular health and cardiovascular risk factors are other key outcomes that pose a particular problem for African-American men and women (Keenan & Shaw, 2011; Mensah et al., 2005). Cardiovascular disease mortality in general and premature death rates from cardiovascular disease and stroke are highest among African Americans compared to all other ethnic groups, including non-Hispanic White, Hispanic, American Indian/Alaskan Native, and Asian/Pacific Islander (Keenan & Shaw, 2011; Mensah et al.,

2005). Keenan and Shaw (2011) in their literature review also examined health disparities for cardiovascular disease risk factors and found that major disparities exist among younger individuals aged 23–25. With regard to these risk factors, obesity (especially among women) and hypertension are particularly problematic for African Americans compared to other ethnic groups (Mensah et al., 2005). However, concerning ethnic group differences in cardiovascular disease and risk, Mensah et al. (2005) note that these relationships are complex. Similar to other conclusions about health disparities, they stress the importance of mediating variables such as education level and poverty.

Among the US Hispanic population, there are several notable health disparities. Vega, Rodriguez, and Gruskin (2009) describe diabetes, certain types of cancer, liver disease, and human immunodeficiency virus (HIV) as being particularly problematic. Regarding diabetes, Hispanic people living in the US experience greater disparities in risk, greater complications from diabetes, and both men and women experience higher diabetes-related mortality rates (Osborn, de Groot, & Wagner, 2013; Vega et al., 2009). Moreover, these mortality rates are increasing at a greater rate than in the general population (Vega et al., 2009). Specific types of cancers, especially cervical cancer among women and stomach and liver cancers among men, also reflect disparities among US Hispanics, although the overall cancer rates are not elevated within this population (Vega et al., 2009). Moreover, there are disparities in the rates of mortality

 IN FOCUS

Cultural Loss, Environmental Change, and Contemporary Patterns of Health

Indigenous knowledge (IK) is understood as the knowledge held by local people concerning their everyday realities of living in, and as part of, their environments and greater ecosystems (Cajete, 1999; Ermine, Nilson, Sauchyn, Sauve, & Smith, 2005). Indigenous knowledge refers to the cultural traditions, values, and belief systems that have enabled many generations of Aboriginal people to have nourishing relationships with their natural and social environments, thereby allowing them not only to survive, but to flourish (Battiste & Henderson, 2000). Traditionally, IK has been expressed through oral tradition—language and stories—about the ways Indigenous peoples live their lives (Battiste & Henderson, 2000). Over time, processes of environmental dispossession have altered the maintenance and transmission of IK. Environmental dispossession refers to the processes by which Indigenous people's access to their traditional lands and resources is reduced or severed (see Richmond & Ross, 2009; Luginaah, Smith, & Lockridge, 2010). This occurs through direct and indirect forms. Direct forms of environmental dispossession involve physical processes that block use of land, such as contamination events or industrial development, which physically sever ties to traditional foods or resources required for sustaining daily activities. Indirect forms of dispossession occur as a result of policies intended to sever links to the environment, such as the residential school system, which was regulated under Canada's Indian Act, and which forcibly removed 150,000 Aboriginal children from their homes. Because of the special links between First Nations people and their physical environments (Richmond, Elliott, Mathews, & Elliott, 2005; Parlee, Berkes, & Gwich'in, 2005; Wilson, 2003), environmental dispossession has had disastrous implications for the health and well-being of affected communities (Gracey & King, 2009; Adelson, 2005; Guimond & Cooke, 2008; Richmond & Ross, 2009).

In contemporary times, these processes manifest in the health of the population as social upheaval, mental illness, violence, crime, suicide, disease (Adelson, 2005), and culture stress, which is often apparent in societies that have undergone massive, imposed, or uncontrollable change. Berry (1990) states that cultural change may occur on a number of levels, including physical, biological, political, economic, cultural, relational, and psychological. In cultures under stress, people tend to lose confidence in what they know to be true, and they also begin to question their own value as human beings (Bartlett, 2003). The effects of culture stress have been particularly prominent among Canada's Aboriginal youth population, leading to a disproportionate incidence of accidents, violence, substance/drug abuse, and suicide, as well as lower high school completion rates and reduced workforce participation (Adelson, 2005; Chandler, Lalonde, Sokol, & Hallet, 2003; Richmond, 2007; Richmond & Ross, 2008; Gideon, Gray, Nicholas, & Ha, 2008; Browne, Smye, & Varcoe, 2005; Wilson & Rosenberg, 2002).

due to liver disease among the Hispanic population, although the rates of these conditions are not elevated (Vega et al., 2009). It is somewhat unclear why these disparities occur, although several secondary variables (e.g., patterns of alcohol consumption, obesity, socioeconomic status) may be responsible (see Determinants of Health Disparities below). Finally, HIV mortality reflects an important health disparity among the US Hispanic population, although this gap has narrowed (Henao-Martinez & Castillo-Mancilla, 2013; Vega et al., 2009). Despite progress in this area, mortality rates from HIV among Hispanics are almost three times the rate for White people (Vega et al., 2009). Moreover, the number of new cases of HIV is disproportionately large among Hispanic people, and those being infected are on average younger than White non-Hispanics (Vega et al., 2009).

Determinants of Health Disparities

Carter-Pokras and Baquet (2002) note that health disparities are not thought to occur due to ethnicity/race/culture per se but rather because of a complex chain of secondary, mediating variables (e.g., health-care access) contributing to disease outcomes (e.g., recovery from illness) (Carter-Pokras & Baquet, 2002; CDC, 2011). These secondary variables can be described as *health-care disparities* (i.e., differences that exist among people of various cultures regarding access to health-care services, facilities, and providers). Therefore, determining and predicting health status among groups of people requires the examination of multiple factors. These multi-dimensional approaches to understanding health disparities are in accordance with biopsychosocial perspectives of health.

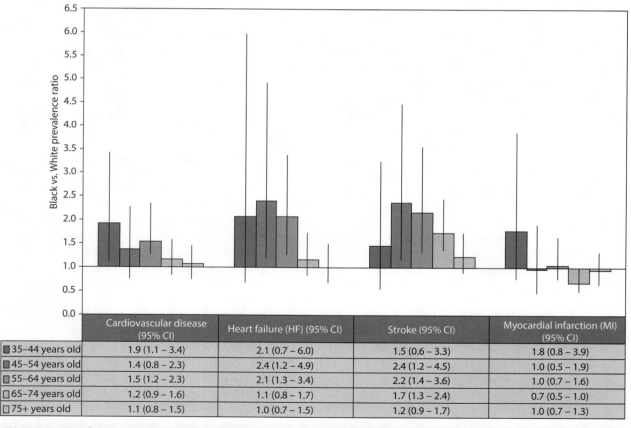

FIGURE 19.3 | Prevalence ratios of self-reported cardiovascular disease, congestive heart failure, myocardial infarction, and stroke for Black and White adults by age categories, National Health and Nutrition Examination Survey, 1999–2006.
Source: © 2010 Elsevier Inc.

Government agencies responsible for researching population health often identify *determinants* that are given priority within a health-care platform. **Determinants of health** can be defined as the range of factors (i.e., personal, socio-economic, environmental) that account for the health status of groups of people (WHO, 1998). The US Department of Health and Human Services (HealthyPeople.gov, 2012) groups determinants of health into policy-making, social factors, health services, individual behaviour, and biology and genetics. Health Canada (2011) considers 12 key determinants of health, 11 of which are socially based and one that recognizes "biological and genetic endowment." The full list includes income and social status, social support

networks, education and literacy, employment/working conditions/social environments, physical environments, personal health practices and coping skills, healthy child development, biology and genetic endowment, health services, gender, and culture. Although ethnicity (i.e., "culture") is included, Health Canada emphasizes that the risks to health evident through group membership are due to the socio-economic environment in which dominant cultural values serve to marginalize, devalue, and reduce health-care access. Indeed, when considering why health disparities occur among different ethnic groups, one must account for the entire set of determinants (Reading & Wien, 2009), including processes such as colonialism, racism, and discrimination. As

Used with the permission of Health Canada

PHOTO 19.2 | Then Canadian federal Minister of Health, Leona Aglukkaq (left), signs an agreement on 13 October 2011 ensuring a new First Nations health governance structure. This structure ensures a major role for the First Nations of British Columbia in the management and planning of health services for First Nations. Also pictured are BC Minister of Health, Michael de Jong (sitting, second from left), members of the BC First Nations Health Council and the BC First Nations Health Society, and Assembly of First Nations National Chief, Shawn A-in-chut Atleo (standing, second from right).

Adelson (2005) notes, Aboriginal health disparities are related to economic, political, and social disparities—not to any inherent Aboriginal trait—and exist because of the limited autonomy Aboriginal peoples have in determining and addressing their health needs.

Socio-Economic Status: A Critical Determinant of Health Disparity

Socio-economic status (SES), which is generally established through a combination of education, income, and work status, is emphasized as a leading cause of health disparities (e.g., APA, 2007; Brawley, 2007). Brawley (2007), the chief medical officer of the American Cancer Society, notes that it is appropriate to define disparities in socio-economic terms rather than racial terms, given the substantial numbers of disadvantaged persons of all ethnicities who are at increased risk for health problems. Nevertheless, there are many complexities when examining the relationships among culture/race/ethnicity, socio-economic status, and health. Socio-economic status does not account for all disparities in health;

some ethnic health disparities persist at similar levels of SES (Xanthos et al., 2010).

The APA's Task Force on Socioeconomic Status (APA, 2007) describes three conceptualizations of SES: materialist, gradient, and social class perspectives. The materialist perspective uses education, income, and occupation to explain varying levels of *access to resources*, which is the primary explanatory mechanism of disparities. A gradient perspective considers the *relative gap* between groups of people as important for health and often focuses on mediating pathways (e.g., coping styles, belief structures) as explanatory mechanisms. The social class perspective considers aspects of society that promote closed perpetuation of wealth and power. Unequal access to resources is viewed as important for understanding health, but unlike a materialist perspective, the focus is on a broad societal level. The APA (2007) notes that only recently have researchers focused on systematic factors within broader societal systems that reinforce inequality and disparities.

Overall, a well-known positive association exists between health and SES; those of higher status tend

© Eric Fowke/Alamy

PHOTO 19.3 | The National School Lunch Program, administered by the US Department of Agriculture, promotes nutrition and prevents hunger for approximately 31 million students throughout the US through federal assistance to schools and child-care centres.

to have better health (Adler & Ostrove, 1999; Ram, 2006). People of lower SES are more likely to suffer from diseases, to experience lowered functioning due to illness, to have higher physical and cognitive impairment, and to have higher mortality rates (e.g., Adler & Ostrove, 1999; Anderson, Bulatao, & Cohen, 2004; Zheng, 2009). Visible minorities, Aboriginal people, and Hispanic and Latino persons are over-represented among those living in poverty (Statistics Canada, 2008; US Census Bureau, 2011). In the United States and Canada, adults of African descent are over-represented in the lowest income bracket and under-represented in the highest brackets (Attewell, Kasinitz, & Dunn, 2010). Attewell et al. (2010) further note that Black households have significantly lower household income than White households and that these income gaps "are not simply a matter of educational differences or differences in household composition between Blacks and Whites in each country. After controlling for education and the other factors, the racial income gaps remain substantial, and of roughly similar magnitude in Canada and the US" (Attewell et al., 2010, p. 484). In Canada, Aboriginal people are among the poorest in the country and the income gap has not substantially closed since 1996 (Wilson & Macdonald, 2010). Morales, Lara, Kington, and Valdez (2002) note that socio-economic status for Hispanic Americans is comparable to African Americans and much lower than among non-Hispanic Whites, although this finding varies by Hispanic sub-group (e.g., Puerto Rican, Cuban, Mexican).

To illustrate the relationships among race, socio-economic status, and health, consider that African-American men are disadvantaged economically compared to Caucasian men as evidenced through lower earnings, higher unemployment, and greater representation in lower-income jobs; and these economic factors contribute to social disadvantages such as poorer neighbourhood conditions and environmental hazards (Xanthos et al., 2010). As previously discussed, African-American men also experience disparities in health in many regards in comparison to men from other ethnic groups, including Caucasians (CDC, 2011; Mensah et al., 2005). Xanthos et al. (2010) note that lower SES has been linked to poorer health in this population through a stress-related mechanism, which may result from reduced opportunities (e.g., educational, occupational, health). However, socio-economic conditions do not account for all the differences between African Americans and other groups, with disparities in health remaining after SES has been controlled for (Hayward, Miles, Crimmins, & Yang, 2000; Xanthos et al., 2010). Xanthos et al. (2010) recommend

examination of other social conditions (related to SES) to further understand health disparities, specifically racial discrimination and elevated incarceration rates among Black (young especially) males, and call for these social conditions to be examined in conjunction with their effects on health behaviours in order to begin to close the gap in health outcomes for Black men.

The Effect of Acculturation

When people relocate to another culture, they undergo a socio-cultural process of **acculturation** wherein they adapt to and take on characteristics (i.e., behavioural, lifestyle) of the "new" culture via continual contact (Hazuda, Haffner, Stern, & Eifler, 1988; Kazarian & Evans, 2001; Morales et al., 2002). Some argue that characteristics from the first culture are lost during acculturation whereas others maintain that aspects of both cultures can be held concomitantly (Morales et al., 2002). A useful theory for understanding acculturation is Berry's (1997) two-factor model of acculturation (Figure 19.4) in which levels of identification with the native and host cultures are considered. Four outcomes are possible: (1) *marginalization* occurs when there is low affiliation with either culture; (2) *separation* occurs when an individual has a high affiliation with the culture of origin but a low identification with the new culture; (3) *assimilation* involves a low affiliation with the culture of origin but a high affiliation with the new culture and; (4) *integration* involves high affiliation with both cultures. More recent theories consider a multi-dimensional view in defining and measuring

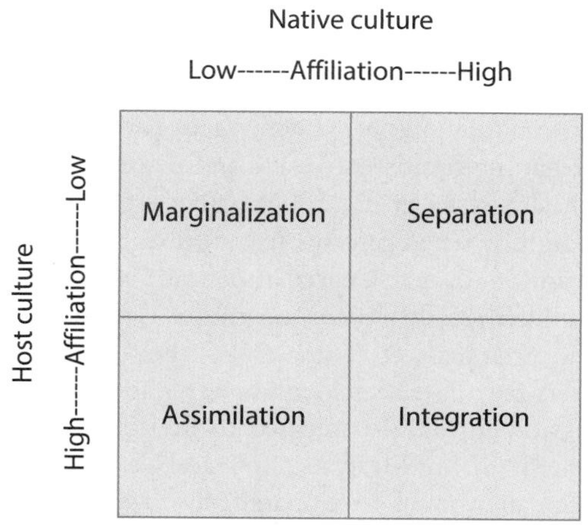

Native culture

Low------Affiliation------High

Marginalization	Separation
Assimilation	Integration

Host culture
High------Affiliation------Low

FIGURE 19.4 | Model of acculturation.
Source: Adapted from Berry (1997).

acculturation (Lopez-Class, Castro, & Ramirez, 2011). Acculturation is not necessarily a straightforward process, but rather occurs in stages across several domains such as language and socio-economic status, and the characteristics of acculturation and the degree to which changes manifest depend on the differences between the two cultures (Lopez-Class et al., 2011).

Acculturation is important for explaining variation in health behaviours as well as discrepancies in health conditions within cultural groups (e.g., Lara, Gamboa, Kahramanian, Morales, & Hayes Bautista, 2005). Morales et al. (2002) note that acculturation can have positive or negative effects on health behaviours depending on the frequency of the behaviour in the original and new cultures. For example, if reliance on fast food is more common in the new culture, acculturation would have a negative effect evidenced through increased consumption of fast food. Conversely, if rates of obesity were higher in the original culture, acculturation may exert a positive influence.

Consider the effect of acculturation on the Hispanic population living in the US. It has been observed that indicators of health such as age-adjusted mortality rates and birth outcomes are *more* favourable among Hispanic persons compared to other groups (including Caucasians) and compared to what would be expected given their levels of poverty (Lara et al., 2005); this is sometimes referred to as the *Hispanic Paradox* (Cutler, Lleras-Muney, & Vogl, 2008). Acculturation has been examined as a factor in this discrepancy. Morales et al. (2002) found that acculturation had a positive impact on some behaviours and a negative impact on others. Specifically, acculturation to mainstream America resulted in increased alcohol consumption. Concerning diet, acculturation can have both negative and positive effects, but overall the effects tend to be more negative (i.e., traditional diets are protective and a typical North American diet may lead to health deterioration). Acculturation's *positive* effects for Latinos seem to be with regard to health-system use and perceptions of one's own health (Lara et al., 2005). However, the Hispanic population is heterogeneous (e.g., Cuban, Puerto Rican, Mexican, South and Central American) and health outcomes differ greatly among subgroups (Ortega, Feldman, Canino, Steinman, & Alegria, 2006). For example, infant mortality rates have been found to be higher among Puerto Rican women (8.01) compared to non-Hispanic White women (5.58), but Mexican, South and Central American, and Cuban women have marginally lower infant mortality rates (5.34, 4.52, and 5.08 per 1,000, respectively) (MacDorman & Mathews, 2011), underscoring the complexities in understanding health disparities and the importance of considering mediating variables.

Mental Health Issues and Health

The APA (2012) describes clinical health psychologists as working at the intersection between physical and emotional conditions. In order to treat clients, they need to have knowledge of how diseases affect the body physically and psychologically and how psychological states may affect physical well-being. They must also be aware of how culture, race, and ethnicity affect both physical illnesses and mental disorders, which may be co-morbid (Scott, McGee, Schaaf, & Baxter, 2008). Although the relationship between mental disorders and physical conditions has been well established, possible cross-cultural differences have not often been researched despite significant impetus to do so (Scott et al., 2008). Researching cross-cultural differences may provide insight into the mechanisms linking physical and psychological conditions more generally, and health disparities could be narrowed (Scott et al., 2008). At this point, more research into the area is needed.

Scott and colleagues (2008) conducted one of only a few studies examining patients presenting with mental and physical health co-morbidities. They examined a general population survey ($N = 7435$) in New Zealand, focusing on cultural groups (Indigenous Maōri, Pacific Islanders, and those of European descent), physical conditions (chronic pain, cardiovascular disease, diabetes, and respiratory disease), and psychological difficulties. Few differences were found based on cultural/ethnic group. The only noteworthy finding was that the association between respiratory disease and mood disorders was stronger for the Pacific group, but the authors were unable to explain this finding (Scott et al., 2008).

In another study, Scott, Kokaua, and Baxter (2011) found that having a physical condition resulted in *increased* help-seeking behaviour for mental health problems. This finding was strongest for Pacific Islanders. However, Pacific Islanders, in the absence of a physical problem, were *less* likely to seek mental health treatment compared to other ethnic groups. Ortega et al. (2006) analyzed health survey data on concurrent physical and psychological problems from four US Latino groups (Puerto Ricans, Cubans, Mexicans, and other Latinos). Differences between the groups emerged, with Puerto Ricans faring the worst: the highest levels of concurrent psychiatric and physical conditions; higher lifetime prevalence for any psychiatric disorders; the highest rate of more than one disorder; and the highest level of having a depressive disorder or an anxiety disorder. However, their findings overall suggested that Latinos do not have significant depression co-occurring with cardiovascular disorders or diabetes, which is contrary to previous findings that indicated these associations (Anderson, Freedland, Clouse, & Lustman, 2001; Möller-Leimkühler, 2007; Ortega et al., 2006). Nonetheless, there is limited evidence of different patterns of co-occurrence of physical and mental conditions among different cultural groups.

In the context of the co-occurrence between physical and psychological disorders, it is important to note that immigrants in general across countries have increased rates of psychological disorders compared to native populations (Bhugra & Jones, 2001). In addition, Canadian First Nations people have been found to have higher rates of suicide (some estimates indicate twice the rate), alcoholism, and incidences of violence (e.g., Health Canada, 2008; Kirmayer, 1994; Kirmayer et al., 1993; Royal Commission on Aboriginal Peoples, 1995). For example, Frideres (2011, p. 128) notes that "For the past decade, over one-third of all First Nation deaths have resulted from accidents and violence, compared to 8 per cent for non-First Nations deaths." Moreover, minority populations in North America have fewer psychological services available to them and have difficulty accessing these services; they have a lower likelihood of seeking out, receiving, and retaining services, and there is less probability they will receive high-quality care and obtain benefits of therapy (e.g., Saha, Arbelaez, & Cooper, 2003; Shin et al., 2005; Smedley, Stith, & Nelson, 2002).

Cross-Cultural Presentation of Psychological Symptoms and Disorders

Much of the mental health research conducted in North America and Europe primarily focuses on Caucasian populations. Although this research has relevance to minority groups, there is also evidence that rates of mental disorders, patterns of psychopathology, and presentation of symptoms are influenced by cultural factors (Blumentritt, Angle, & Brown, 2004; Kirmayer, 2001; Thakker & Ward, 1998; Weisz et al., 1993). Also, some physical and psychological conditions are specific to various cultures. These are referred to as **culture-bound syndromes**, which have been described as recurrent patterns of abnormal behaviour and troubling experience that occur specifically to a local culture/community (American Psychiatric Association, 2000; Vaughn et al., 2009). Both symptom presentation and culture-bound syndromes may be important for clinicians to understand to improve assessment, diagnosis, and treatment (Vaughn et al., 2009).

Cultural factors have been investigated within many categories and types of mental disorders such as anxiety disorders, mood disorders, schizophrenia, and conduct disorder, as well as general symptoms of distress (Kim et al., 1993; Muris, Schmidt, Engelbrecht, & Perold, 2002; Oates et al., 2004). To illustrate, consider a research investigation on postpartum depression (Oates et al., 2004). The researchers describe the universality of feelings of distress and unhappiness following childbirth in women in 11 countries as diverse as France, Uganda, Japan, and the United States. Using a qualitative approach, they found that women from all countries attributed insufficient sleep and fatigue to unhappiness following delivery. Women from all the countries recognized the phenomenon of morbid unhappiness (i.e., postpartum depression). However, the term "postnatal depression" was not consistently used and not all of the cultural groups considered these feelings abnormal and requiring professional treatment.

As another example, Lewis-Fernández et al. (2009) reviewed the cross-cultural literature on anxiety disorders, including panic attacks, panic disorder, agoraphobia, specific phobia, social anxiety disorder, obsessive compulsive disorder, and generalized anxiety disorder. They found that research studies supported the importance of cultural factors in the expression of panic disorder, social anxiety disorder (SAD), and generalized anxiety disorder especially. With regard to SAD, prevalence rates were found to be higher in US populations compared to other countries such as Japan and Mexico. The situation within the US was more complex. There, higher prevalence of SAD was associated with being American Indian and lower prevalence associated with being Asian, Latino, African American, or Caribbean Black; however, these associations varied depending on other variables such as education, age, and immigration status. In terms of cultural variation within symptom presentation, Lewis-Fernandéz et al. (2009) describe a cultural variant of social anxiety, *Taijin kyofusho*, a culture-bound syndrome, although the distinct status of *Taijin kyofusho* from SAD has been debated (American Psychiatric Association, 2000; Suzuki, Takei, Kawai, Minabe, & Mori, 2003). In Japan and South Korea, a subgroup of patients who have fear of social situations and avoidance express concerns that are not typically found among North American samples. Specifically, these individuals have social fears of doing something that will embarrass *the other person*. These concerns may involve staring at another person's body parts inappropriately, having offensive body odour, or appearing physically offensive.

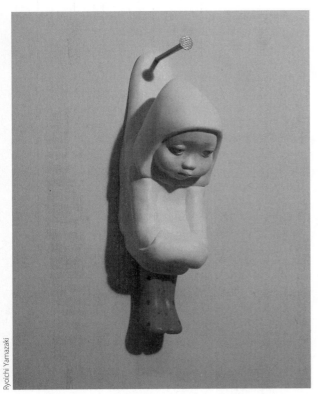

Ryoichi Yamazaki

PHOTO 19.4 | Japanese artist Ryoichi Yamazaki creates diminutive ceramic sculptures that explore the culture-bound syndrome, *hikikomori*, such as in the above example entitled, "Nobody helps me". *Hikikomori* is described as extreme social isolation and withdrawal of Japanese youth to their bedrooms within their parents' homes and is often associated with extreme apathy.

Empirically Supported Therapies with Cultural Groups

Of particular interest in the cross-cultural clinical psychology literature is the effectiveness of evidence-based therapy for people of various cultural/ethnic groups. It has been noted that the evidence-based therapy literature and the literature on multicultural therapies have developed separately and, unfortunately, minority groups have been under-represented in most psychotherapy studies (Bernal & Scharrón-Del-Río, 2001; Hall, 2001; Morales & Norcross, 2010). Furthermore, these studies give little formal consideration to the external validity (i.e., whether the results of a study can be generalized/extended to other settings, populations, or conditions) of the intervention relevant to people from diverse cultures (i.e., cultural, interpretative, population, ecological, and construct validities) (Bernal & Scharrón-Del-Río, 2001). Nevertheless, newer commentary by Morales and Norcross (2010) notes that the gap between evidence-based practice and multicultural interventions has closed. Beginning in 2002, they describe a proliferation of national conferences, federal initiatives, and discipline-specific guidelines highlighting the need for cultural inclusion in empirically based practice (Morales & Norcross, 2010). They note that the APA has a definition of empirically based practice that is culturally inclusive, i.e., empirically based practice is "the integration of the best available research with clinical expertise in the context of patient characteristics, culture, and preferences" (APA Task Force, 2006, p. 273).

Cultural Competence

Cultural competence, as it relates to psychotherapists' ability to provide interventions to clients from diverse ethnic backgrounds, is necessary in our multicultural society (APA, 2002). Both the APA and the Canadian Psychological Association (CPA) have incorporated diversity training into their professional training standards (Trilateral Forum on Professional Psychology, 2000). Sue, Zane, Nagayama Hall, and Berger (2009) define competence as having the required training, experience, and qualifications to adequately complete a task. When individuals from different cultures are considered, a therapist's degree of competence may shift, as different client groups often require differing approaches to treatment (Sue et al., 2009). "Competence" and "cultural competence" are related constructs sharing common ingredients, such as empathy and therapeutic alliance, but there is also evidence that cultural competence predicts client satisfaction with therapy beyond competence alone (Fuertes & Brobst, 2002; Fuertes, Costa, Mueller, & Hersh, 2005). Cultural competence then can be described as care that acknowledges the importance of culture at multiple levels, is sensitive to differences in cultural dynamics, and adapts services to meet the client's culturally unique needs (Danish, Forneris, & Wilder Schaaf, 2007). A culturally responsive psychologist must understand both general psychopathology and his or her client's specific cultural background and should be proficient at navigating the specificities of ethnic groups in practice (Sue, 1998).

Cultural competence can be further distinguished from two related terms, "cultural sensitivity" and "patient-centred cultural sensitivity." Cultural sensitivity refers to a general, ongoing awareness of and responsiveness to cultural differences and similarities (Majumdar, Browne, Roberts, & Carpio, 2004). Patient-centred cultural sensitivity is a more specific term applied to health-care workers. It comprises several characteristics, including sensitivity wherein professionals provide care that indicates respect for the patient's culture. It considers the provider and patient as partners in care and is oriented towards empowering the patient (Tucker, Marsiske, Rice, Jones, & Herman, 2011). Cultural competence may be conceptualized as the outcome of the process a professional has undergone in order to be both culturally sensitive and to provide patient-centred culturally sensitive care.

Several prominent scholars have proposed theoretical models of multicultural counselling competencies that stress three components: *cultural awareness and beliefs, cultural knowledge*, and *cultural skills* (Constantine & Ladany, 2000; Kitaoka, 2005; Purnell, 2002; Sue, 2001; Sue et al., 2009). The therapist must be aware of his or her own assumptions, values, and biases associated with racism, sexism, disability, and ageism, and the way this affects his or her practice. He or she must strive to understand that the world views of clients are culturally diverse. This may occur through empathetic practice, but, more importantly, through a learning process aimed to uncover the scope and nature of the client's background

🔲 IN PRACTICE

Adapting Practice to Meet Client Needs

Mr L. (82 years of age) has been referred to Dr W. for support in caring for his wife, who has moderate dementia. Mrs L. (79 years of age) was diagnosed with Alzheimer's disease approximately four years ago and since this time Mr L. has cared for her in their home. Mr L. reported that his wife's memory difficulties and level of impairment remained fairly minimal for the first three years following diagnosis. However, in the past year, her illness progressed more quickly and she has deteriorated in her level of independence and ability to communicate. She also started to resist some aspects of personal care. Mr L. reported feelings of depression and frustration, stating that he "does not know what to do" any more.

Mr and Mrs L., along with their young son, immigrated to Canada from China in 1956. Although their son had little trouble adjusting to life in Canada, Mr L. reported that he and his wife had always felt isolated from those outside their own cultural circle and had little interaction with other cultural groups. Upon assessment, Mr L. spoke English somewhat brokenly and reported sometimes having trouble finding the right words to describe his situation. He stated that his wife is still quite limited in speaking and understanding English and that they speak their native language in the home. Mr L. describes both himself and his wife as traditional and their Chinese heritage of primary importance. Mr L. also noted that he specifically asked for a referral to a Chinese therapist.

Dr W. (age 36) is fourth-generation Canadian and until recently felt little cultural affiliation with the Chinese community. Dr W. recently began learning about his Chinese culture and ancestry to provide culturally responsive psychotherapy. This has resulted in increased referrals of Asian clients. To support his new expertise, Dr W. regularly seeks consultation from a more experienced therapist to ensure he is appropriately attending to cultural issues.

Following their initial interview, Dr W. offered the services of an experienced translator, but Mr L. declined, stating they could communicate in English. In the first treatment session, Dr W. clarified his and Mr L.'s roles and the two discussed some differences and similarities in their world views. They jointly established the treatment goals of improved mood, more home care support, and more behavioural strategies for aiding Mrs L. Throughout the weeks, Dr W. tailored the content of the sessions to facilitate Mr L.'s goals. He further discussed the process of therapy in his consultation sessions, focusing on language barriers, cultural dissimilarities (e.g., views on receiving professional support for adjustment difficulties), and differing social roles. Through these discussions, Mr L. reported feeling respected and understood specifically in regard to his culture. This provided a portal for communication and enhanced rapport, which facilitated the success of the psychotherapy. Mr L. improved substantially in terms of his mood and noted improved ability to assist his wife. Upon termination of therapy, Dr W. referred Mr L. to a support group for family caregivers of seniors with dementia. He acknowledged Mr L.'s ongoing need for support and thus left the door to therapy "ajar," indicating that Mr. L. could make additional appointments if necessary.

and daily experiences through cultural encounters (Campinha-Bacote, 1999). Based on this knowledge, the therapist works with the client to develop appropriate interventions. Therapists who assume that their mode of therapy may be applied to everyone, regardless of culture, do not account for the fact that interactions require approaches consistent with the person's life experiences (Purnell, 2002; Sue, Ivey, & Pederson, 1996). Some view cultural competence as similar to other skill-based competencies in that the therapist can use specific strategies to improve cultural competence (Whaley & Davis, 2007). However, Sue et al. (2009) note that it is difficult to isolate and operationalize (i.e., assigning specific indicators) components of cultural competence and, thus, these models still require empirical grounding.

Racial/ethnic similarities between client and therapist are important for culturally responsive care, with "race" used as a proxy for "shared cultural experiences" (Maramba & Hall, 2002). Early efforts examined therapists and clients of the same or different racial/ethnic backgrounds and, despite some mixed evidence (Flaskerud, 1990; Shin et al., 2005), found that ethnic matching was related to better client outcomes (Flaskerud, 1990; Gamst, Dana, Der-Karaberian, & Kramer, 2000; Smith & Glass, 1977). However, it has been argued that racial or ethnic match is not necessarily a good indicator of cultural match, which would include, for instance, shared language, understanding of the client's cultural background, and an openness to modify and match treatment approach (Jacob & Kuruvilla, 2012; Sue, Fujino, Hu, Takeuchi, & Zane, 1991). It is important to note, however, that clients' preferences and perceptions about the importance of the ethnicity of their therapist may differ, including both positive and negative appraisals of ethnic match or mismatch (Chang & Yoon, 2011).

Future Directions

Research that compares ethnic or cultural groups in terms of group averages is ill suited to capture this process of cultural shaping of illness experience. The majority of epidemiological studies that report on ethnoracial blocs ... cannot shed much light on the impact of culture on psychopathological processes. Specifying ethnicity more precisely does not get at the real issue, which is the heterogeneity within even well-defined ethnic groups.... For research to advance on cultural variations in psychopathology, we need to go beyond conventional group labels to examine the specific biological, psychological, or social mediators of cultural difference. (Kirmayer & Sartorius, 2007, p.832)

Adequate representation of different cultural groups is important in health psychology research and the importance of such representation has been emphasized by research-governing bodies in both Canada and the United States (Government of Canada, 2011; National Institutes of Health, 2012). There are both ethical and scientific reasons for representing minority groups in research. Rudell and Diefenbach (2008) note that accounting for cultural factors in research may enrich theories of health behaviour and aid in the interpretation of research findings. They caution that it is not sufficient to rely solely on proxy variables when defining culture (i.e., nationality, race, ethnicity), but rather, the interplay among varying cultures, cultural change, and potentially the degree of immersion in a second culture must be examined. It has been suggested that in research, race be defined in social-psychological and social-political terms, including factors such as perception of racism, level of acculturation, and socio-economic status (Ford & Kelly, 2005; Kao, Hsu, & Clark, 2004).

It has been widely noted that ethnic minority groups are under-represented in health-care research, although there has been improvement, and it is somewhat unclear why this under-representation occurs (e.g., Corbie-Smith, Thomas, & St George, 2002; Fisher & Kalbaugh, 2011; Wendler et al., 2005; Yancey, Ortega, & Kumanyika, 2006). Historically, researchers thought under-representation likely occurs because of minority distrust of the research community, biases and negative attitudes among the gatekeepers to research participation, decreased access to health-care research, and less willingness to participate (Corbie-Smith, Thomas, Williams, & Moody-Ayers, 1999; Corbie-Smith et al., 2002; Fisher & Kalbaugh, 2011). Researchers often cite the Tuskegee Syphilis Study (1932–72) as a contributing factor to distrust of research by African Americans (Gamble, 1997). In this study, 399 African-American men who had previously contracted syphilis were enrolled in a research study and were told they would receive medical care for their "bad blood" (CDC, 2011; Gamble, 1997). They were not told they had syphilis and were deliberately denied treatment so the researchers could document the natural progression of the disease. Even after penicillin was found to effectively treat syphilis in the 1940s, these men were not treated.

However, Wendler et al. (2005) noted that it does not appear minorities are less willing to participate or have negative attitudes towards research; rather, health-care access functions as the primary barrier to recruitment and retention of minority research participants. For example, Fisher and Kalbaugh (2011) examined the distribution of minority participants among phase I, II, and

PHOTO 19.5 | Canada is a multicultural society.

III clinical trials. They note that minority research participants, while under-represented in phase III clinical trials (the treatment phase considered to have the most potential for benefit and a low risk of harmful side effects), are actually over-represented in phase I trials (safety studies that provide monetary compensation, but have a lower probability of providing benefit and greater risk of adverse effects). They note that this finding is not consistent with the literature, which cites distrust, attitudes, and access as reasons for under-representation. Instead, they point to broader (structural) socio-economic and political concerns, such as the greater amount of money paid for participation in a phase I trial. Fisher and Kalbaugh (2011, p. 2221) conclude that "minorities share a disproportionately greater risk and enjoy disproportionately fewer benefits (from a health and disease standpoint) from participating in clinical trials."

Kao and colleagues (2004) describe a number of strategies researchers can employ to integrate better the concept of culture into their study designs. They advocate for mixed-methods research, combining quantitative and qualitative approaches in order to understand cultural aspects from multiple perspectives. They stress that culture needs to be deeply integrated into the research paradigm; when cultural factors are eliminated because they are not expected to exert an effect, the reason for the omission should be thoroughly explored. Kao et al. (2004) state that instruments and frameworks should be carefully chosen to ensure they are *culturally sensitive* (i.e., valid, reliable, and appropriate) for the research participant. They note the importance of dialogue with communities throughout the stages of research to better understand an "emic" (cultural insider) perspective. It is also of value to consider historical contexts for populations. Finally, they state that interventions need to be replicated across populations to improve their ecological validity and determine their clinical applicability for individuals from different cultural backgrounds.

SUMMARY

Shifting demographics in Canada and the US have resulted in an increased focus on cultural issues in health psychology training, research, and clinical work. It is important that distinctions among the terms "race," "culture," and "ethnicity" be acknowledged. While "race" denotes a biological basis for some obvious difference (e.g., skin colour), "ethnicity" accounts for the subjectivity of self-report in group identification, and "culture" focuses on shared ideologies. Researchers have emphasized the importance of incorporating culture, including health beliefs and attributions, into a biopsychosocial framework to help explain health disparities in the general population. Aboriginal and African-American populations are at particular risk for experiencing several negative health outcomes, including lower life expectancy, higher infant mortality rates, diabetes among Aboriginal people, and heart disease among African Americans. It must be stressed that health disparities are *not* a consequence of group membership or ethnicity, but rather, they are the result of a chain of events and other determinants of health, such as socio-economic status, racial discrimination, health-care access and treatment quality, and health behaviour, all of which can be influenced by acculturation. When considering the influence of culture on mental disorders that may be co-morbid with physical disorders, differing cross-cultural symptom presentations may be relevant. Consideration of the literature on psychological therapies with different cultural groups and cultural competence in clinical work are also important. We provide relevant considerations for people who may work with minority populations, urging for the appropriate application of terminology (e.g., "race," "ethnicity," "culture") and noting the distinctions among these terms. Finally, we place emphasis on the need for multi-dimensional conceptualizations of culture.

Critical Thought Questions

1. In what ways might it be possible to research health disparities that are present among different cultural groups *without* directly assessing race or ethnicity and how would you justify the decision *not* to assess these constructs?
2. The Tuskegee Syphilis Study is often cited as an example of how a historical occurrence may continue to influence attitudes towards research among African Americans. What other North American historical occurrences continue to exert their influence on health variables within cultural groups and through what mechanisms?

Recommended Reading

Frohlich, K.L., Ross, N., & Richmond, C. (2006). Health disparities in Canada today: Some evidence and a theoretical framework. *Health Policy, 79*, 132–143.

Hall, G.C.N. (2001). Psychotherapy research with ethnic minorities: Empirical, ethical, and conceptual issues. *Journal of Consulting and Clinical Psychology, 69*, 502–510.

Morales, E., & Norcross, J.C. (2010). Evidence-based practices with ethnic minorities: Strange bedfellows no more. *Journal of Clinical Psychology, 66*, 821–829.

US Department of Health and Human Services, Centers for Disease Control and Prevention. (2011). *CDC health disparities and inequalities report—United States 2011* (Morbidity and Mortality Weekly Report, No. 60).

Yali, A.M., & Revenson, T.A. (2004). How changes in population demographics will impact health psychology: Incorporating a broader notion of cultural competence into the field. *Health Psychology, 23*, 147–155.

Glossary

Acculturation: A socio-cultural process that occurs when people relocate to another culture wherein they adapt to and take on characteristics (i.e., behavioural, belief, and lifestyle) of the "new" second culture via continual contact.

Acute kidney injury (AKI): Acute renal failure, a life-threatening condition that develops rapidly over the course of hours or days.

Acquired immunodeficiency syndrome (AIDS): A disease that occurs when an individual infected with HIV can no longer fight the infection. It takes on average more than 10 years to progress from HIV infection to AIDS.

Adherence (*in the context of health care*): Observance of medication or treatment schedules in accordance with the prescription by health-care personnel.

Adrenal glands: Two small glands located near the kidneys that release a number of hormones involved in the stress response.

Aerobic exercise: Any physical activity that increases heart rate and breathing. It strengthens the heart and lungs, increases the rate at which we burn calories (metabolism), tones muscles, lowers blood pressure, and can help with weight loss.

Airflow limitation: A reduction in the amount of air that can pass through the airways in a certain time.

Airway inflammation: Immune response in the airways characterized by increased temperature, redness, and a proliferation of white blood cells.

Angina: A symptom of ischemic heart disease characterized by chest, shoulder, jaw, or neck pain; occurs when part of the heart muscle does not receive enough oxygen.

Antenatal: During pregnancy.

Appraisal support: Helping someone identify a stressor and potential coping options.

Asthma control: A key variable in the assessment of treatment outcome in asthma, which includes assessment of long-term control of the manifestations of asthma (daytime and nighttime symptoms, reliever medication use, activity limitations, and lung function) and the risk of future exacerbations.

Autonomic nervous system: The portion of the peripheral nervous system involved in control of organs that support muscle activity and behaviour (the heart, lungs, etc.).

Autosomal dominant: When a gene carried by one parent has a 50 per cent chance of being transmitted to and expressed by the offspring.

Avoidant coping: Ignoring or trying to ignore a problem and its resulting consequences and emotions.

Bacteria: Single-celled microorganisms that can multiply given ideal environments. Antibiotic medications are most commonly used to treat bacterial infections.

Behavioural medicine: "The field concerned with the development of behavioral-science knowledge and techniques relevant to the understanding of physical health and illness and the application of this knowledge and these techniques to diagnosis, prevention, treatment and rehabilitation. Psychosis, neurosis and substance abuse are included only insofar as they contribute to physical disorders as an end point" (Schwartz & Weiss, 1977).

Beveridge systems: Health systems financed through general taxation that involve a government overseeing the co-ordination and integration of a broad range of health services; named after William Beveridge, the civil servant whose recommendations led to the creation of the National Health Service in the United Kingdom.

Biofeedback: A procedure that helps clients become more aware of specific physiological functions (e.g., muscle tension) using psychophysiological measuring instruments.

Biopsychosocial model: Model that proposes that health is a function of biological, psychological, and social factors, which interact.

Biopsychosocial models of pain: These models tend to be consistent with the gate control theory of pain. While they recognize the importance of biological/physiological factors (e.g., tissue damage) in the pain experience, they also stress and describe the role of psychological and social (cultural) influences on pain.

Blood glucose: The amount of sugar in the bloodstream.

Brain–gut axis: Neural and hormonal influences between the central nervous system and the gastrointestinal tract.

Breast-conserving surgery: Surgical treatment for breast cancer that removes the cancerous tumour along with a margin of normal tissue. Accompanying radiation therapy over several weeks often is used to eliminate any remaining cancer cells.

Bronchoconstriction: Narrowing of the airways (bronchi), which causes airflow limitation.

Buffering hypothesis: The notion that social support leads to better health outcomes by buffering or protecting the individual from the negative effects of stress.

Carcinogen: An environmental factor that increases the risk of developing cancer.

Cardiovascular rehabilitation: A comprehensive secondary prevention program, providing risk factor modification through education, counselling (for health behaviours such as pharmacological therapy adherence, nutrition and weight management, smoking cessation, etc.) and individualized exercise training.

Cartesian dualism: The idea that mind and body are separate entities and explanations for illness can be found in the body alone.

Cause (*as related to illness representation*): Beliefs about what caused one's illness.

Centers for Disease Control and Prevention (CDC): Part of the US Department of Health and Human Services with a mission to protect public health, often through statistical analyses and epidemiological research.

Chronic kidney disease (CKD): A long-term condition described as the gradual loss of kidney function over time.

Chronic pain: Recurrent and frequent pain (e.g., headaches, stomach aches, backaches). Chronic pain is common in children and adolescents, as well as in older people, and can occur as a result of an associated medical condition or in the absence of any identifiable organic pathology.

Clinical health psychology: Subfield of health psychology focused on applying or translating knowledge from health psychology into practices that promote health, prevent and treat illness or disability, and improve the health system.

Cognitive behavioural therapy (CBT): A structured psychological intervention of short duration that involves the identification and modification of maladaptive cognitive patterns and behaviours that contribute to a patient's psychological distress.

Cognitive empathy: Shared or complementary emotional experience in response to another person's physical and emotional suffering.

Cognitive rehabilitation: Any intervention strategy or technique intended to enable clients or patients, and their families, to live with, manage, bypass, reduce, or come to terms with deficits precipitated by injury or other damage to the brain.

Collaborative care: An approach in which physicians and mental health-care providers work together to manage common mental disorders and chronic disease.

Combination antiretroviral therapy (cART): A type of drug therapy in which a combination of multiple antiretroviral drugs is used to treat HIV and other retroviruses. This combination treatment is sometimes also known as Highly Active Antiretroviral Therapy (HAART).

Community health psychology: Subspecialty of health psychology focused on health status, health needs, and health-care systems to effect change and to promote access and cultural competence within those systems.

Co-morbid: Different physical or mental health conditions occurring at the same time in the same individual.

Conditioned emotional responses: When the family member has paired certain emotions with past experiences of the older person's suffering (i.e., becoming angry when the older relative displays fatigue or pain), which can cause defensive emotions and withdrawal from the older patient.

Confirmatory bias: When individuals with anxiety tend to focus on information that confirms their fears and ignore information that disconfirms their fears.

Consequences (*as related to illness representation*): Beliefs about how illness impacts one's everyday life (e.g., self-care, household responsibilities, family, work).

Contextual factors: Different areas or aspects of a person's life, such as culture, spirituality, and social networks, that allow for a more comprehensive understanding of the individual.

Controlability (*as related to illness representation*): Beliefs about whether we have control over our illness and how efficacious treatment will be.

Cooling therapy: A medical intervention that attempts to decrease MS-related symptoms by lowering body temperature.

Coping: The ability to manage a chronic medical condition or how a person responds to medical procedures. Coping responses include simple behavioural strategies (e.g., distraction, deep breathing) as well as more complex cognitive strategies (e.g., cognitive restructuring) and vary by the person's age and development. Effective coping skills are related positively with many patient outcomes.

Corticosteroids: Medications to suppress the immune system, often used to treat MS symptom flare-ups.

Cortisol: A key adrenal hormone that increases blood glucose and has numerous effects on metabolism and immune function.

Cultural competence: Having the required training, experience, and qualifications to provide care to clients from different cultural backgrounds by acknowledging the importance of culture at multiple levels, being sensitive to differences in cultural dynamics, and adapting services to meet the client's culturally unique needs.

Culture: A set of values, ideals, beliefs, and assumptions about life shared among a particular group of people and transmitted generationally, rarely with implicit instruction.

Culture-bound syndromes: A recurrent pattern of abnormal behaviour and experience, specifically in relation to a local culture/community that may or may not be linked to a recognized category of mental disorders (e.g., anxiety disorders).

Dementia: Cognitive loss beyond what would be expected as a result of normal aging. Among the most common types of dementia are Alzheimer's disease and vascular dementia.

Demyelination: The action whereby the myelin sheath (a structure of the central nervous system that carries messages to the body) is damaged.

Determinants of health: The range of personal, socioeconomic, and environmental factors that determine the health status of people or groups of people. Government agencies often prioritize sets of determinants within a healthcare platform.

Diabetes self-efficacy: Confidence in one's ability to be successful in managing the demands of diabetes self-care.

Disability: A condition that limits an individual's mobiliy, senses, speech or activities.

Disenfranchised grief: Grief that is not acknowledged by society.

Distraction: A widely used and effective behavioural coping strategy involving directing one's attention away from a painful stimulus (e.g., blowing bubbles, listening to music, talking with others, humour). Distraction is often used to deal with acute pain, such as a medical procedure, and can be self-led or parent/other-led.

Distress: A negative form of stress in which demands outweigh resources, which can lead to negative health outcomes.

Dyspnea: The unpleasant sensation of breathlessness.

Emotional support: Providing encouragement and empathy.

Emotion-focused coping: A type of coping in which one addresses and regulates the negative emotions caused by stressful events.

Encopresis: A problem of toileting that involves the passage of feces in inappropriate places (e.g., clothing) and occurs as the direct result of involuntary overflow incontinence, resulting from constipation.

End-stage renal disease (ESRD): The terminal stage of CKD when treatment with renal replacement therapy (dialysis or transplant) becomes necessary to sustain life.

Endocrine system: Glands that release hormones into the bloodstream to influence different aspects of physiology.

Enuresis: A problem of toileting that involves the involuntary passage of urine, most often during the night (e.g., bedwetting).

Ethnicity: Subjectively identifying with a group by accepting group customs and practices from one's culture of origin in conjunction with a feeling a belonging.

Eustress: A positive form of stress when situations do not overwhelm resources, and so it can lead to mastery and a sense of meaning.

Exacerbation (*within the context of a disease*): An increase in disease severity.

Extraintestinal symptoms: Symptoms that occur outside of the gastrointestinal tract.

Functional gastrointestinal disorder (FGID): A gastrointestinal disorder in which symptoms are not associated with any structural or biochemical abnormalities. There are no imaging or laboratory tests to confirm functional disorders.

Gate control theory: Theory that conceptualizes pain as a complex psychological phenomenon and postulates that there is a gating mechanism at the level of the spinal cord that either blocks potentially painful ascending signals or allows them to continue travelling to the brain. Signals travelling via small nerve fibres tend to open the "gate" whereas signals of large-diameter fibres tend to close the "gate." The "gate" can also be opened and closed through descending messages from the brain. This theory provides an explanation for the important role of social and psychological factors in the pain experience.

General Adaptation Syndrome: Selye's term for the general response of the body to all threats; also known as the fight-or-flight response.

Genetic counsellor: A professional (usually with a Master of Science degree) certified to provide information on hereditary conditions, their health and familial implications, preventive options and management, and possible genetic testing to determine mutation carrier status. Genetic counsellors are experts in educating patients and translating complex medical information.

Glucose control: A term that means blood glucose levels are properly controlled and generally remain in the normal or "prescribed" range.

Health anxiety: The experience of anxiety about one's present or future health.

Health belief model: Model postulating that readiness to take action in relation to health problems is a function of people's beliefs and their perception of the benefits of taking action in order to prevent health problems.

Health disparities: Preventable differences in the burden of disease, injury, violence, and opportunities to achieve optimal health experienced by socially disadvantaged populations.

Health psychology: A discipline-specific descriptor within the broad interdisciplinary field of behavioural medicine; discipline of psychology focused on the promotion and maintenance of health, the prevention and treatment of illness, and the identification of etiologic and diagnostic correlates of health, illness, and related dysfunction.

Health-related quality of life (HRQL): The patient's evaluation of various aspects of his/her daily life as these are related to health and disease.

Health system: The complex array of governance, funding, administrative, and service delivery arrangements established to deliver personal and population-based health services, all in an effort to improve health and health-care outcomes.

Heart failure: The heart's inability to adequately pump enough blood with oxygen and nutrients to meet the needs of the body.

Hemodialysis (HD): A form of renal replacement therapy that uses an artificial dialyzer to filter the blood; usually performed in hospital under medical supervision.

Hemoglobin A1c: The average of a person's blood glucose levels over the prior 2–3 months.

Hofstede's value dimensions of culture: A framework of five cultural dimensions that may vary across cultures including: individualism–collectivism; power distance; uncertainty avoidance; masculinity–femininity; and Confucian dynamism (long- vs short-term orientation).

Human immunodeficiency virus (HIV): A virus that attacks the immune system, resulting in a chronic progressive illness that leaves individuals vulnerable to opportunistic infections and cancers.

Hyperglycemia: A condition where blood glucose levels are chronically elevated.

Hypochondriasis: Extreme health anxiety based on misinterpretation of bodily symptoms that persists despite medical reassurance, and results in significant distress and/or disability for at least six months

Hypnosis: A psychological intervention involving a disassociation from a painful experience through suggestion, which has been shown to be effective in decreasing pain and distress associated with medical procedures.

Hypoglycemia: A condition where blood glucose levels drop too low.

Identity: Beliefs about the distinctive characteristics of one's illness.

Immune system: A system involving organs and circulating blood cells devoted primarily to protecting the body from foreign substances.

Immunosurveillance: The immune system's detection and destruction of cancerous cells.

Infertility: The failure of a couple to achieve pregnancy after at least 12 months of consistent, unprotected intercourse.

Inflammation: A co-ordinated reaction of the body especially in response to injury or infection. Specifically, in response to injury, blood vessel dilation and migration of fluid and immune cells occur in order to seal the area and speed healing.

Inflammatory bowel disease: A group of autoimmune conditions that target the gastrointestinal tract.

Informational support: Providing valuable information relevant to addressing a stressful situation.

Instrumental support: Providing tangible goods and services.

Insulin: A hormone produced by the pancreas that is necessary for cells to remove, break down, and use glucose.

Irritable bowel syndrome: A functional syndrome of the gastrointestinal tract.

Ischemic heart disease: Restriction of blood flow through circulatory vessels depriving heart muscle tissues of blood supply and hence access to oxygen and nutrients, which may lead to myocardial infarction.

Job stress: Generally thought to be not so much a function of a particular position, but instead having job demands without sufficient authority, autonomy, or rewards.

Ketoacidosis: A condition where the body does not have enough insulin and this prevents glucose metabolism. The body is then forced to break down fat for energy, which produces dangerously high levels of ketones.

Ketones: Poisonous acids that the body makes when it breaks down fat instead of sugar for energy.

Lesions: Damage resulting from demyelination.

Liberation therapy: A new and controversial therapy that attempts to relieve MS symptoms by draining excess fluid from the central nervous system through a procedure called endovascular angioplasty.

Life review: A structured, potentially multi-session interview focused around one or more life themes such as family, work, major turning points, the impact of historical events, the arts, aging, dying and death, and socialization issues such as meaning, values, and purpose in life.

Lymphedema: Buildup of lymphatic fluid in a limb, often as a result of surgery or radiation treatment; a chronic and progressive problem resulting in swelling, aching, pain, and hardening of tissue.

Macrosomia: Excessive birth weight.

Macrovascular complications: Diseases involving the large blood vessels, including cardiovascular diseases such as coronary artery disease, peripheral arterial disease, and stroke.

Main effects model: An approach to stress and health positing that social support is generally beneficial to well-being, whether we are carefree or stress-ridden.

Mastectomy: Surgical treatment for breast cancer that removes the entire breast.

Medical cost offset: The net savings in medical costs resulting from an intervention.

Meta-analysis: A statistical method that considers the results of multiple studies within a single analysis.

Metastasis: The ability of malignant neoplasm cells to spread to distant parts of the body and grow at those sites.

Microvascular complications: Diseases of the small blood vessels including diabetic retinopathy, nephropathy, and neuropathy.

Moderate exercise: Any exercise where you're working hard enough to raise your heart rate and break a sweat. One way to tell if you're working hard enough is that you'll be able to talk, but not sing the words to your favourite song.

Multiple pregnancies: A pregnancy of two or more fetuses (e.g., twins).

Myocardial infarction (MI): A complete blockage of an artery causing the death of heart muscle in the surrounding area due to the deprivation of oxygen and nutrients to the tissues.

Neuromatrix model: Model complementary to the gate control theory of pain positing that the multi-dimensional pain experience is associated with a "neurosignature" or pattern of nerve impulses generated by a widely distributed neural network in the brain (the body–self neuromatrix).

Neuroticism: A tendency to experience negative emotions and emotional instability; also referred to as negative affectivity or trait anxiety.

Nociception: The activity of nociceptors (sensory receptors that respond to stimulation) that has the potential to be perceived as painful.

Obesity: Having too much body fat. Obesity happens over time when you eat more calories than you use.

Occupational health psychology: A subspecialty of health psychology focused on the prevention and management of occupational stress, the prevention of injury, and the maintenance of workers' health.

Opportunistic infection: An infection caused by pathogens that usually do not cause disease in a host with a healthy immune system, but can cause disease in an individual with a compromised immune system.

Overdiagnosis (*in the context of cancer*): The detection and diagnosis, for example, of a tumour that will not become malignant or is slow growing enough that it is unlikely to be the cause of death.

Pain: According to the International Association for the Study of Pain, an unpleasant sensory and emotional experience associated with actual or potential tissue damage, or described in terms of such damage.

Palliative care: Care provided to those who have been diagnosed with a range of medical conditions where curative treatments have failed or to those who require intensive long-term treatment aimed at maintaining quality of life.

Parasympathetic nervous system: The portion of the autonomic nervous system that usually reduces cardiac and smooth muscle activity.

Patient navigator: Lay person or health-care professional who assists patients at all stages of cancer care. While first conceived as a role to help under-served patients obtain early diagnosis and treatment, navigators now guide patients through coping with diagnosis, treatment, and making the transition to survivorship.

Pediatric psychology: A specialized psychological field, which encompasses areas of health, clinical, and developmental psychology and integrates both scientific research and clinical practice to address the psychological aspects of children's medical conditions and the promotion of health behaviours in children and their families.

Perinatal period: Period surrounding childbirth.

Peripheral nervous system: Neurons that lie outside the central nervous system (brain and spinal cord) that allow the brain to influence physiology.

Peritoneal dialysis (PD): A home-based form of renal replacement therapy that uses the peritoneum membrane in the abdomen as a natural filter to cleanse the blood. Patients or caregivers are responsible for performing treatment at home.

Pharmacotherapy: Therapy with medication to treat physical illness or mental disorders.

Postcolonial theory: Literary and cultural theory that attempts to understand the process and problems stemming from European colonization and its effects. It is often noted that historical texts represent the perspectives of the colonizers with little acknowledgement of the experiences of those who were colonized.

Postnatal: Following pregnancy and childbirth.

Prediabetes: A condition in which blood glucose levels are higher than normal but not high enough to meet criteria for a diabetes diagnosis.

Primary appraisal: A determination of whether a situation presents a threat, and the magnitude of that threat.

Primary care: First level of personal care for common conditions, focused on both prevention and treatment, from which access to specialized care is co-ordinated.

Primary control: An individual's attempts to maintain equilibrium and a sense of efficacy by using active, problem-focused coping strategies to change environmental circumstances.

Private health insurance systems: Health systems in which the majority of payments are made through individual or employment-based private insurance contracts.

Problem-focused coping: A type of coping in which one takes specific actions to address the demands of the stressful situation.

Procedural pain: Pain experienced as a result of a medical treatment or procedure (e.g., venepuncture, immunizations, intravenous tube placement, etc.)

Quality of life: An individual's general well-being, including emotional, social, and physical aspects of one's life. Health-related quality of life may be impacted by numerous illnesses and diseases, such as CVD.

Race: A term intended to capture differences in biological substrates based on physical characteristics such as skin colour and hair type. However, the term is contentious, given current understandings of genetics.

Regular physical activity: Either 150 minutes of moderate exercise or 75 minutes of vigorous exercise a week, plus muscle-strengthening activities for all major muscle groups at least two days a week.

Reminiscence: The universal, passive recall of memories.

Renal replacement therapy (RRT): Treatments (dialysis or transplantation) to sustain line in ESRD patients.

Revascularization: A medical procedure performed in a hospital to restore blood flow to the heart tissues; includes percutaneous coronary intervention (e.g., stents) and coronary artery bypass graft (CABG) surgery.

Rome III criteria: The most up-to-date diagnostic tool for clinicians who suspect that a patient may have inflammatory bowel syndrome.

Rumination: Dwelling on the events that caused acute stress so that the stress becomes chronic.

Safety behaviours: Behaviours that anxious individuals engage in because they believe they will keep them safe, such as information-seeking, reassurance-seeking, body-checking, and cleaning, but that, in fact, serve to increase anxiety.

Secondary appraisal: A determination of whether one has sufficient resources to cope with the threat. If resources are sufficient, then the situation can be viewed as a challenge rather than a threat, and it will be less damaging to the system.

Secondary care: Health-care services provided by medical specialists and other health professionals who generally do not have first contact with patients.

Self-management: The situation whereby the patient gains control or perceived control over a chronic condition, such as asthma.

Sexually transmitted infections (STIs): Infections spread primarily through intimate person-to-person contact.

Social cognitive theory: Theory that emphasizes the importance of self-efficacy beliefs (developed through personal experiences, observing others, and social experiences as well any internal experiences) as a determinant of health behaviour. Personal factors, environmental influences and behaviour are believed to interact.

Social health insurance systems: Health systems financed largely through compulsory employer–employee insurance contributions regulated by the state.

Social support: A social network in which others care about one's well-being and provide help and assistance.

Somatic nervous system: The portion of the peripheral nervous system involved in control of voluntary, striated muscle activity.

Specificity theory: View based on the idea that there is a one-to-one correspondence between pain and tissue damage.

Stress management: Any method or activity that helps a person manage stress, such as deep breathing, meditation, yoga, visualizing a calming place, exercising, or seeking support from a friend.

Sympathetic nervous system: The portion of the autonomic nervous system that often stimulates cardiac and smooth muscle activity.

Tend-and-befriend: The hypothesis put forth by Taylor and colleagues suggesting that women's stress response is marked by efforts at social bonding and caring for offspring.

10,000 steps a day: A method for gaining and maintaining good health (this is equal to walking about five miles).

Tertiary care: Care provided in a facility that has specialized personnel and facilities for advanced medical investigation and treatment.

Theory of planned behaviour: A view of behaviour as determined by three types of beliefs: behavioural, normative, and control beliefs.

Timeline (*as related to illness representation*): Beliefs about how long an illness will last and whether the illness will fluctuate or persist over time.

Transplantation (of kidney): The form of renal replacement therapy that confers best outcomes and involves either a deceased or living related or unrelated donor.

Triggers (*within the context of a health condition*): Substances or states that initiate symptoms or worsens a health problem.

Venepuncture: Intravenous access for the purpose of blood sampling, performed by a phlebotomist or other health professional. It is one of the most routinely performed invasive procedures.

Viruses: Submicroscopic organisms that require a host to survive—they can only reproduce by taking over the host cell's cellular machinery. Vaccines and antiviral medications aid in the treatment and prevention of viral infections.

Visceral hypersensitivity: Amplified pain signals in the neurons of the gut that result in increased pain and stress symptoms in response to normal changes in the gut.

References

Chapter 1

Ajzen, I. (1991). The theory of planned behavior. *Organizational Behavior and Human Decision Processes, 50,* 179–211.

Ajzen, I. (n.d.). *Constructing a theory of planned behaviour questionnaire.* Retrieved from people.umass.edu/aizen/pdf/tpb.measurement.pdf

Ajzen, I., & Fishbein, M. (1980). *Understanding attitudes and predicting social behavior.* Englewood Cliffs, NJ: Prentice-Hall.

Allen, J.K., Becker, D.M., & Swank, R.T. (1990). Factors related to functional status after coronary artery bypass surgery. *Heart & Lung: The Journal of Critical Care, 19,* 337–343.

American Psychological Association (2011). *Public description of clinical health psychology.* Retrieved from www.apa.org/ed/graduate/specialize/health.aspx

American Psychological Association Division 38 (2014). *Health psychology.* Retrieved from www.health-psych.org/CompetenciesinResearch.cfm

Antoni, M.H., August, S., LaPerriere, A., Baggett, H.L., Klimas, N., Ironson, G., … Fletcher, M.A. (1990). Psychological and neuroendocrine measures related to functional immune changes in anticipation of HIV-1 serostatus notification. *Psychosomatic Medicine, 52,* 496–510.

Armitage, C.J., & Conner, M. (2001). Efficacy of the theory of planned behaviour: A meta-analytic review. *British Journal of Social Psychology, 40,* 471–499.

Bandura, A. (1986). *Social foundations of thought and action: A social cognitive theory.* Englewood Cliffs, NJ: Prentice-Hall.

Bandura, A. (1991a). Self-efficacy mechanism in physiological activation and health-promoting behavior. In J. Madden IV (Ed.), *Neurobiology of learning, emotion and affect* (pp. 229–270). New York: Raven.

Bandura, A. (1991b). Self-regulation of motivation through anticipatory and self-regulatory mechanisms. In R.A. Dienstbier (Ed.), *Perspectives on motivation: Nebraska symposium on motivation* (Vol. 38, pp. 69–164). Lincoln: University of Nebraska Press.

Bandura, A. (1998). Health promotion from the perspective of social cognitive theory. *Psychology and Health, 13,* 623–649.

Bastone, E.C., & Kerns, R.D. (1995). Effects of self-efficacy and perceived social support on recovery-related behaviours after coronary artery bypass graft surgery. *Annals of Behavioral Medicine, 17,* 324–330.

Beckham, J.C., Burker, E.J., Lytle, B.L., Feldman, M.E., & Costakis, M.J. (1997). Self-efficacy and adjustment in cancer patients: A preliminary report. *Behavioural Medicine, 23,* 138–142.

Belar, C. (1997). Clinical health psychology: A specialty for the 21st century. *Health Psychology, 16,* 411–416.

Belar, C.D., Mendonca McIntyre, T.M., & Matarazzo, J.D. (2003). Health psychology. In D.K. Freedheim (Ed.), *Handbook of psychology* (pp. 451–464). Hoboken, NJ: John Wiley & Sons.

Brus, H., van de Laar, M., Taal, E., Rasker, J., & Wiegman, O. (1999). Determinants of compliance with medication in patients with rheumatoid arthritis: The importance of self-efficacy expectations. *Patient Education and Counseling, 36,* 57–64.

Centers for Disease Control and Prevention. (2012). Occupational health psychology. Retrieved from www.cdc.gov/niosh/topics/ohp/

Champion, V.L., & Skinner, C.S. (2008). The health belief model. In K. Glanz, B.K. Rimer, & K. Viswanath (Eds.), *Health behavior and health education* (pp. 45–65). San Francisco: John Wiley & Sons.

Child, N. (2000). The limits of the medical model in child psychiatry. *Clinical Child Psychology and Psychiatry, 5,* 11–21.

Cutrona, C.E., & Troutman, B.R. (1986). Social support, infant temperament, and parenting self-efficacy: A mediational model of postpartum depression. *Child Development, 57,* 1507–1518.

De Geest, S., Borgermans, L., Gemoets, H., Abraham, I., Vlaminck, H., Evers, G., & Vanrenterghem, Y. (1995). Incidence, determinants, and consequences of subclinical noncompliance with immunosuppressive therapy in renal transplant recipients. *Transplantation, 59,* 340–347.

De La Cancela, V., Lau Chin, J., & Jenkins, Y.M. (1998). What is community health psychology? Empowerment for diverse communities. In V. De La Cancela, J. Lau Chin, & Y.M. Jenkins (Eds.), *Community health psychology: Empowerment for diverse communities.* New York: Routledge.

Devins, G.M., Binik, Y.M., Borman, P., Dattel, M., McCloskey, B., Oscar, G., & Briggs, J. (1982). Perceived self-efficacy, outcome expectancies, and negative mood states in end-stage renal disease. *Journal of Abnormal Psychology, 91,* 241–244.

Duncan, T.E., & McAuley, E. (1993). Social support and efficacy cognitions in exercise adherence: A latent growth curve analysis. *Journal of Behavioral Medicine, 16,* 199–218.

Engel, G.L. (1977). The need for a new medical model: A challenge for biomedicine. *Science, 196,* 129–136.

France, C. (2011, spring). The future of APA division 38. *Health Psychologist, 33.* Retrieved from www.health-psych.org/PDF/Spring2011.pdf

Gatchel, R.J., Baum, A., & Krantz, D.S. (1989). *An introduction to health psychology*. New York: Random House.

Glanz, K., & Bishop, D.B. (2010). The role of behavioral science theory in development and implementation of public health interventions. *Annual Review of Public Health, 31,* 399–418.

Grey, M., Boland, E.A., Davidson, M., Li, J., & Tamborlane, W.V. (2002). Coping skills training for youth with diabetes mellitus has long-lasting effects on metabolic control and quality of life. *Journal of Pediatrics, 137,* 107–113.

Grover, N., Kumaraiah, V., Prasadrao, P.S., & D'souza, G. (2002). Cognitive behavioural intervention in bronchial asthma. *Journal of the Association of Physicians of India, 50,* 896–900.

Gruber, B.L., Hall, N.R., Hersh, S.P., & Dubois, P. (1988). Immune system and psychological changes in metastatic cancer patients using relaxation and guided imagery: A pilot study. *Scandinavian Journal of Behaviour Therapy, 17,* 25–46.

Guze, S.B., Matarazzo, J.D., & Saslow, G. (1953). A formulation of principles of comprehensive medicine with special reference to learning theory. *Journal of Clinical Psychology, 9,* 127–136.

Haran, M.L., Kim, K.K., Gendler, P., Froman, R.D., & Patel, M.D. (1998). Development and evaluation of the osteoporosis self-efficacy scale. *Research in Nursing & Health, 21,* 395–403.

Hunsley, J. (2003). Cost effectiveness and medical cost-offset considerations in psychological service provision. *Canadian Psychology, 44,* 61–73.

Janz, N.K., & Becker, M.H. (1984). The health belief model: A decade later. *Health Education Quarterly, 11,* 1–47.

Kiecolt-Glaser, J., Glaser, R., Strain, E.C., Stout, J.C., Tarr, K.L., Holliday, J.E., & Speicher, C.E. (1986). Modulation of cellular immunity in medical students. *Journal of Behavioral Medicine, 9,* 5–21.

Larson, E.B., Olsen, E., Cole, W., & Shortell, S. (1979). The relationship of health beliefs and a postcard reminder in influenza vaccination. *Journal of Family Practice, 8,* 1207–1211.

Lipsitt, D. (1999). A century of psychosomatic medicine: Successes and failures. In M. Dinis (Ed.), *Reflexões sobre psicossomatica* [Reflections on psychosomatics] (pp. 11–22). Lisbon, Portugal: Sociedade Portuguesa de Psicossomatica [Portuguese Society of Psychosomatics].

Lopez-Olivo, M.A., Landon, G.C., Siff, S.J., Edelstein, D., Pak, C., Kallen, M.A., … Suarez-Almazor, M.E. (2011). Psychosocial determinants of outcomes in knee replacement. *Annals of the Rheumatic Diseases, 70,* 1775–1781.

Lyons, A.C., & Chamberlain, K. (2006). *Health psychology: A critical introduction*. New York: CambridgeUniversity Press.

McAlister, A.L., Perry, C.L., & Parcel, G.S. (2008). How individuals, environments and health behaviors interact: Social cognitive theory. In K. Glanz, B.K. Rimer, & K. Viswanath (Eds.), *Health behavior and health education* (pp. 45–65). San Francisco: John Wiley & Sons.

McCracken, L.M., & Turk, D.C. (2002). Behavioral and cognitive-behavioral treatment for chronic pain: Outcome, predictors of outcome, and treatment process. *Spine, 27,* 2564–2573.

McGregor, B.A., Antoni, M.H., Boyers, A., Alferi, S.M., Blomberg, B.B., & Carver, C.S. (2002). Cognitive-behavioral stress management increases benefit finding and immune function among women with early-stage breast cancer. *Journal of Psychosomatic Research, 56,* 1–8.

Major, B., Mueller, P., & Hildebrandt, K. (1985). Attributions, expectations, and coping with abortion. *Journal of Personality and Social Psychology, 48,* 585–599.

Matarazzo, J.D. (1980). Behavioral health and behavioral medicine: Frontiers for a new health psychology. *American Psychologist, 35,* 807–817.

Matarazzo, J.D. (1982). Behavioral health's challenge to academic, scientific, and professional psychology. *American Psychologist, 37,* 1–14.

Miller, G., Chen, E., & Cole, S.W. (2009). Health psychology: Developing biologically plausible models linking the social world and physical health. *Annual Review of Psychology, 60,* 501–524.

Munro, S., Lewin, S., Swart, T., & Volmink, J. (2007). A review of health behaviour theories: How useful are these for developing interventions to promote long-term medication adherence for TB and HIV/AIDS? *BMC Public Health, 7,* 1–16.

Rosenstock, I.M. (1974). The health belief model and preventive health behavior. *Health Education Monographs, 2,* 354–386.

Rozanski, A., Blumenthal, J.A., & Kaplan, J. (1999). Impact of psychological factors on the pathogenesis of cardiovascular disease and implications for therapy. *Clinical Cardiology: New Frontiers, 99,* 2192–2217.

Salyer, J., Schubert, C.M., & Chiaranai, C. (2012). Supportive relationships, self-care confidence, and heart failure self-care. *Journal of Cardiovascular Nursing, 27*(5), 384–393.

Schlesinger, H.J., Mumford, E., Glass, G.V., Patrick, C., & Sharfstein, S. (1983). Mental health treatment and medical care utilization in a fee-for-service system: Outpatient mental health treatment following the onset of a chronic disease. *American Journal of Public Health, 73,* 422–429.

Schneiderman, N., Antoni, M.H., Saab, P.G., & Ironson, G. (2001). Health psychology: Psychosocial and biobehavioral aspects of chronic disease management. *Annual Review of Psychology, 52,* 555–580.

Schwartz, G.E., & Weiss, S.M. (1977). What is behavioral medicine? *Psychosomatic Medicine, 39,* 377–381.

Segerstrom, S.C., & Miller, G.E. (2004). Psychological stress and the human immune system: A meta-analytic study of 30 years of inquiry. *Psychological Bulletin, 130,* 601–630.

Simpson, J.S.A., Carlson, L.E., & Trew, M.E. (2001). Effect of group therapy for breast cancer on healthcare utilization. *Cancer Practice, 9,* 19-26.

Smith, T.W., Orleans, C.T., & Jenkins, C.D. (2004). Prevention and health promotion: Decades of progress, new challenges, and an emerging agenda. *Health Psychology, 23,* 115–118.

Smith, T.W., & Ruiz, J.M. (2002). Psychosocial influences on the development and course of coronary heart disease: Current status and implications for research and practice. *Journal of Consulting and Clinical Psychology, 70,* 548–568.

Smith Fawzi, M.C., Eustache, E., Oswald, C., Louis, E., Surkan, P.J., Scanlan, F., … Mukherjee, J.S. (2012). Psychosocial support intervention for HIV-affected families in Haiti: Implications for programs and policies for orphans and vulnerable children. *Social Science & Medicine, 74,* 1494–1503.

Straub, R.O. (2007). *Health psychology: A biopsychological approach* (2nd ed.). New York: Worth Publishers.

Suls, J., & Rothman, A. (2004). Evolution of the biopsychosocial model: Prospects and challenges for health psychology. *Health Psychology, 23*, 119–125.

Turner, L.W., Hunt, S.B., Dibrezzo, R., & Jones, C. (2009). Design and implementation of an osteoporosis prevention program using the health belief model. In J.A. Hayden (Ed.), *Introduction to health behavior theory* (pp. 37–42). Wayne, NJ: Jones and Bartlett.

Vallance, J.K., Lavallee, C., Culos-Reed, N.S., & Trudeau, M.G. (2012). Predictors of physical activity among rural and small town breast cancer survivors: An application of the theory of planned behaviour. *Psychology, Health, & Medicine, 17*(6), 685–697.

Welsh, D., Lennie, T.A., Marcinek, R., Biddle, M.J., Abshire, D., Bentley, B., & Moser, D.K. (2013). Low-sodium diet self-management intervention in heart failure: Pilot study results. *European Journal of Cardiovascular Nursing, 12*(1), 87–95.

Chapter 2

Abdel-Sater, K.A., Abdel-Daiem, W.M., & Sayyed Bakheet, M. (2012). The gender difference of selective serotonin reuptake inhibitor, fluoxetine in adult rats with stress-induced gastric ulcer. *European Journal of Pharmacology, 688*, 42–48.

Ader, R., & Cohen, N. (1975). Behaviorally conditioned immunosuppression. *Psychosomatic Medicine, 37*, 333–340.

Alexander, F. (1939). Psychoanalytic study of a case of essential hypertension. *Psychosomatic Medicine, 1*, 139–152.

Andersen, B.L., Yang, H.C., Farrar, W.B., Golden-Kreutz, D.M., Emery, C.F., Thornton, L.M., & Carson, W.E. (2008). Psychologic intervention improves survival for breast cancer patients: A randomized clinical trial. *Cancer, 113*, 3450–3458.

Aoyama, N., Kinoshita, Y., Fujimoto, S., Himeno, S., Todo, A., Kasuga, M., & Chiba, T. (1998). Peptic ulcers after the Hanshin-Awaji earthquake: Increased incidence of bleeding gastric ulcers. *American Journal of Gastroenterology, 93*, 311–316.

Ax, A.F. (1953). The physiological differentiation between fear and anger in humans. *Psychosomatic Medicine, 15*, 433–442.

Benschop, R.J., Jacobs, R., Sommer, B., Schurmeyer, T.H., Raab, J.R., Schmidt, R.E., & Schedlowski, M. (1996). Modulation of the immunologic response to acute stress in humans by beta-blockade or benzodiazepines. *FASEB, 10*, 517–524.

Bernatova, I., Puzserova, A., & Dubovicky, M. (2010). Sex differences in social stress-induced pressor and behavioral responses in normotensive and prehypertensive rats. *General Physiology and Biophysics, 29*, 346–354.

Bonga, S.E.W. (1997). The stress response in fish. *Physiological Reviews, 77*, 591–625.

Bracha, H.S. (2004). Freeze, flight, fight, fright, faint: Adaptationist perspectives on the acute stress response spectrum. *CNS Spectrums, 9*, 679–685.

Brady, J.V., Porter, R.W., Conrad, D.G., & Mason, J.W. (1958). Avoidance behavior and the development of gastroduodenal ulcers. *Journal of the Experimental Analysis of Behavior, 1*, 69–72.

Cannon, W.B. (1929). *Bodily changes in pain, hunger, fear, and rage*. Oxford, UK: Appleton.

Cannon, W.B. (1942). "Voodoo" death. *American Anthropologist, 44*, 169–181.

Chen, E., Miller, G.E., Walker, H.A., Arevalo, J.M., Sung, C.Y., & Cole, S.W. (2009). Genome-wide transcriptional profiling linked to social class in asthma. *Thorax, 64*, 38–43.

Choy, D.S.J., & Ellis, R. (1998). Multiple hearts in animals other than Barosaurus. *Lancet, 352*, 744.

Cohen, S. (2005). Keynote presentation at the Eight International Congress of Behavioral Medicine: The Pittsburgh common cold studies: Psychosocial predictors of susceptibility to respiratory infectious illness. *International Journal of Behavioral Medicine, 12*, 123–131.

Cohen, S., Janicki-Deverts, D., Doyle, W.J., Miller, G.E., Frank, E., Rabin, B.S., & Turner, R.B. (2012). Chronic stress, glucocorticoid receptor resistance, inflammation, and disease risk. *Proceedings of the National Academy of Sciences of the United States of America, 109*, 5995–5999.

Cole, S.W., Hawkley, L.C., Arevalo, J.M., Sung, C.Y., Rose, R.M., & Cacioppo, J.T. (2007). Social regulation of gene expression in human leukocytes. *Genome Biology, 8*, R189.

Darwin, C.R. (1872). *The expression of emotions in man and animals*. London: John Murray.

Davies, S.A., Overend, G., Sebastian, S., Cundall, M., Cabrero, P., Dow, J.A., & Terhzaz, S. (2012). Immune and stress response "cross-talk" in the Drosophila Malpighian tubule. *Journal of Insect Physiology, 58*, 488–497.

Diehl, R.R. (2005). Vasovagal syncope and Darwinian fitness. *Clinical Autonomic Research, 15*, 126–129.

Ditto, B., Gilchrist, P.T., & Holly, C.D. (2012). Fear-related predictors of vasovagal symptoms during blood donation: It's in the blood. *Journal of Behavioral Medicine, 35*, 393–399.

Dutour, A., Boiteau, V., Dadoun, F., Feissel, A., Atlan, C., & Oliver, C. (1996). Hormonal response to stress in brittle diabetes. *Psychoneuroendocrinology, 21*, 525–543.

Epel, E.S., McEwen, B., Seeman, T., Matthews, K., Castellazzo, G., Brownell, K.D., Ickovics, J.R. (2000). Stress and body shape: Stress-induced cortisol secretion is consistently greater among women with central fat. *Psychosomatic Medicine, 62*, 623–632.

Fink, G. (2011). Stress controversies: Post-traumatic stress disorder, hippocampal volume, gastroduodenal ulceration. *Journal of Neuroendocrinology, 23*, 107–117.

Fitch, D.R., & Rippert, E.T. (1992). Syncope in military formations: A persistent problem. *Military Medicine, 157*, 577–578.

Folino, A.F. (2006). Cerebral autoregulation in neurally mediated syncope: Victim or executioner? *Heart, 92*, 724–726.

Giese-Davis, J., Collie, K., Rancourt, K.M., Neri, E., Kraemer, H.C., & Spiegel, D. (2011). Decrease in depression symptoms is associated with longer survival in patients with metastatic breast cancer: A secondary analysis. *Journal of Clinical Oncology, 29*, 413–420.

Glaser, R. (2005). Stress-associated immune dysregulation and its importance for human health: A personal history of psychoneuroimmunology. *Brain, Behavior, and Immunity, 19*, 3–11.

Graham, D.T., Kabler, J.D., & Lunsford, L., Jr. (1961). Vasovagal fainting: A diphasic response. *Psychosomatic Medicine, 23*, 493–507.

Harkness, E.F., Abbot, N.C., & Ernst, E. (2000). A randomized trial of distant healing for skin warts. *American Journal of Medicine, 108*, 448–452.

Ishigami, T. (1919). The influence of psychic acts on the progress of pulmonary tuberculosis. *American Review of Tuberculosis, 2*, 470–484.

Kiecolt-Glaser, J.K., Garner, W., Speicher, C., Penn, G.M., Holliday, J., & Glaser, R. (1984). Psychosocial modifiers of immunocompetence in medical students. *Psychosomatic Medicine, 46*, 7–14.

Kin, N.W., & Sanders, V.M. (2006). It takes nerve to tell T and B cells what to do. *Journal of Leukocyte Biology, 79*, 1093–1104.

Leserman, J., Petitto, J.M., Gu, H., Gaynes, B.N., Barroso, J., Golden, R.N., & Evans, D.L. (2002). Progression to AIDS, a clinical AIDS condition and mortality: Psychosocial and physiological predictors. *Psychological Medicine, 32*, 1059–1073.

Levenson, R.W., & Ditto, W.B. (1981). Individual differences in ability to control heart rate: Personality, strategy, physiological and other variables. *Psychophysiology, 18*(2), 91–100.

Levenstein, S. (2000). The very model of a modern etiology: A biopsychosocial view of peptic ulcer. *Psychosomatic Medicine, 62*, 176–185.

Miller, G.E., Cohen, S., & Ritchey, A.K. (2002). Chronic psychological stress and the regulation of pro-inflammatory cytokines: A glucocorticoid-resistance model. *Health Psychology, 21*, 531–541.

Ost, L.G. (1992). Blood and injection phobia: Background and cognitive, physiological, and behavioral variables. *Journal of Abnormal Psychology, 101*, 68–74.

Pereira, D.B., Antoni, M.H., Danielson, A., Simon, T., Efantis-Potter, J., Carver, C.S., O'Sullivan, M.J. (2003). Life stress and cervical squamous intraepithelial lesions in women with human papillomavirus and human immunodeficiency virus. *Psychosomatic Medicine, 65*, 427–434.

Regecova, V., & Kellerova, E. (1995). Effects of urban noise pollution on blood pressure and heart rate in preschool children. *Journal of Hypertension, 13*(4), 405–412.

Sapolsky, R.M. (2000). Glucocorticoids and hippocampal atrophy in neuropsychiatric disorders. *Archives of General Psychiatry, 57*, 925–935.

Sapolsky, R.M. (2004). *Why zebras don't get ulcers* (3rd ed). New York: Holt.

Schneider, R.H., Alexander, C.N., Staggers, F., Orme-Johnson, D.W., Rainforth, M., Salerno, J.W., & Nidich, S.I. (2005). A randomized controlled trial of stress reduction in African Americans treated for hypertension for over one year. *American Journal of Hypertension, 18*, 88–98.

Schuster, J.P., Limosin, F., Levenstein, S., & Le Strat, Y. (2010). Association between peptic ulcer and personality disorders in a nationally representative US sample. *Psychosomatic Medicine, 72*, 941–946.

Segerstrom, S.C., & Miller, G.E. (2004). Psychological stress and the human immune system: A meta-analytic study of 30 years of inquiry. *Psychological Bulletin, 130*, 601–630.

Selye, H. (1956). *The stress of life*. New York: McGraw-Hill.

Sinha, R., Lovallo, W.R., & Parsons, O.A. (1992). Cardiovascular differentiation of emotions. *Psychosomatic Medicine, 54*, 422–435.

Sontag, S. (1978). *Illness as metaphor*. New York: Farrar, Straus, & Giroux.

Spanos, N.P., Williams, V., & Gwynn, M.I. (1990). Effects of hypnotic, placebo, and salicylic acid treatments on wart regression. *Psychosomatic Medicine, 52*, 109–114.

Sternberg, E. M. (2002). Walter B. Cannon and "Voodoo Death": A perspective from 60 years on. *American Journal of Public Health, 92*, 1564–1566.

Sweet, E., McDade, T.W., Kiefe, C.I., & Liu, K. (2007). Relationships between skin color, income, and blood pressure among African Americans in the CARDIA Study. *American Journal of Public Health, 97*, 2253–2259.

Taylor, S.E., Gonzaga, G.C., Klein, L.C., Hu, P., Greendale, G.A., & Seeman, T.E. (2006). Relation of oxytocin to psychological stress responses and hypothalamic-pituitary-adrenocortical axis activity in older women. *Psychosomatic Medicine, 68*, 238–245.

Tomfohr, L., Cooper, D.C., Mills, P.J., Nelesen, R.A., & Dimsdale, J.E. (2010). Everyday discrimination and nocturnal blood pressure dipping in Black and White Americans. *Psychosomatic Medicine, 72*, 266–272.

van Kempen, E., & Babisch, W. (2012). The quantitative relationship between road traffic noise and hypertension: A meta-analysis. *Journal of Hypertension, 30*, 1075–1086.

Weiss, J.M., Pohorecky, L.A., Salman, S., & Gruenthal, M. (1976). Attenuation of gastric lesions by psychological aspects of aggression in rats. *Journal of Comparative and Physiological Psychology, 90*, 252–259.

Chapter 3

Abramson, J.S., Oshea, T.M., Ratledge, D.L., Lawless, M.R.,& Givner, L.B. (1995). Development of a vaccine tracking system to improve the rate of age-appropriate primary immunization in children of lower socioeconomic-status. *Journal of Pediatrics, 126*, 583–586.

Alemayehu, B., & Warner, K.E. (2004). The lifetime distribution of health care costs. *Health Services Research, 39*, 627–642.

American Psychiatric Association. (2013). *Diagnostic and statistical manual of mental disorders* (5th ed.). Washington: Author.

Barsky, A.J., Peekna, H.M., & Borus, J.F. (2001). Somatic symptom reporting in women and men. *Journal of General Internal Medicine, 16*, 266–275.

Belar, C.D. (1997). Clinical health psychology: A specialty for the 21st century. *Health Psychology, 16*, 411–416.

Blackwell, D.L., Martinez, M.E., Gentleman, J.F., Sanmartin, C., & Berthelot, J.M. (2009). Socioeconomic status and utilization of health care services in Canada and the United States: Findings from a binational health survey. *Medical Care, 47*, 1136–1146.

Burau, V., & Blank, R.H. (2006). Comparing health policy: An assessment of typologies of health systems. *Journal of Comparative Policy Analysis, 8*, 63–76.

Burgess, D.J., Ding, Y., Hargreaves, M., van Ryn, M., & Phelan, S. (2008). The association between perceived discrimination and underutilization of needed medical and mental health care in a multi-ethnic community sample. *Journal of Health Care for the Poor and Underserved, 19*, 894–911.

Chiles, J.A., Lambert, M.J., & Hatch, A.L. (1999). The impact of psychological interventions on medical cost offset: A meta-analytic review. *Clinical Psychology-Science and Practice, 6*, 204–220.

Collins, K.A., Westra, H.A., Dozois, D.J.A., & Burns, D.D. (2004). Gaps in accessing treatment for anxiety and depression: Challenges for the delivery of care. *Clinical Psychology Review, 24*, 583–616.

Davidson, K.W., Gidron, Y., Mostofsky, E., & Trudeau, K.J. (2007). Hospitalization cost offset of a hostility intervention for coronary heart disease patients. *Journal of Consulting and Clinical Psychology 75*, 657–662.

Deacon, B., Lickel, J., & Abramowitz, J.S. (2008). Medical utilization across the anxiety disorders. *Journal of Anxiety Disorders, 22*, 344–350.

DiMatteo, M.R. (2004). Social support and patient adherence to medical treatment: A meta-analysis. *Health Psychology, 23*, 207–218.

DiMatteo, M.R., Giordani, P.J., Lepper, H.S., & Croghan, T.W. (2002). Patient adherence and medical treatment outcomes—A meta-analysis. *Medical Care, 40*, 794–811.

DiMatteo, M.R., Haskard-Zolnierek, K.B., & Martin, L.R. (2012). Improving patient adherence: a three-factor model to guide practice. *Health Psychology Review, 6*, 74-91.

Figueras, J., McKee, M., Lessof, S., Duran, A., & Menabde, N. (2008). *Health systems, health and wealth: Assessing the case for investing in health systems*. Copenhagen: WHO on behalf on the European Observatory on Health Systems and Policies.

Flood, C.M., & Archibald, T. (2001). The illegality of private health care in Canada. *Canadian Medical Association Journal, 164*, 825–830.

Frank, G., McDaniel, S.H., Bray, J.H., & Heldring, M. (2004). *Primary care psychology*. Washington: American Psychological Association.

Freeman, R., & Frisina, L. (2010). Health care systems and the problem of classification. *Journal of Comparative Health Policy Analysis, 12*, 163–178.

Gray, B.H. (2006). The rise and decline of the HMO: A chapter in U.S. health-policy history. In R. Stevens, C.E. Rosenberg, & L.R. Burns (Eds.), *History and health policy in the United States: Putting the past back in* (pp. 309–440). Piscataway, NJ: Rutgers University Press.

Gray, V., Lowery, D., & Godwin, E.K. (2007). The political management of managed care: Explaining variations in state health maintenance organization regulations. *Journal of Health Politics, Policy and Law, 32*, 457–495.

Hacke, W., Donnan, G., Fieschi, C., Kaste, M., von Kummer, R., Broderick, J. P., ... Hamilton, S. (2004). Association of outcome with early stroke treatment: Pooled analysis of ATLANTIS, ECASS, and NINDS rt-PA stroke trials. *Lancet, 363*, 768–774.

Hacker, J. S. (2002). *The divided welfare state: The battle over public and private social benefits in the United States*. New York: Cambridge University Press.

Hagger, M.S., & Orbell, S. (2003). A meta-analytic review of the common-sense model of illness representations. *Psychology & Health, 18*, 141–184.

Hagger, M.S., Wood, C., Stiff, C., & Chatzisarantis, N.L.D. (2009). The strength model of self-regulation failure and health-related behaviour. *Health Psychology Review, 3*, 208–238.

Hand, M., Brown, C., Horan, M., & Simons-Morton, D. (1998). The National Heart Attack Alert Program: Progress at 5 years in educating providers, patients, and the public and future directions. *Journal of Thrombosis and Thrombolysis, 6*, 9–17.

Hunsley, J. (2003). Cost-effectiveness and medical cost-offset considerations in psychological service provision. *Canadian Psychology, 44*, 61–73.

Ingersoll, K.S., & Cohen, J. (2008). The impact of medication regimen factors on adherence to chronic treatment: A review of literature. *Journal of Behavioral Medicine, 31*, 213–224.

Kainth, A., Hewitt, A., Sowden, A., Duffy, S., Pattenden, J., Lewin, R., ... Thompson, D. (2004). Systematic review of interventions to reduce delay in patients with suspected heart attack. *Emergency Medicine Journal, 21*, 506–508.

Kimerling, R., Ouimette, P.C., Cronkite, R.C., & Moos, R.H. (1999). Depression and outpatient medical utilization: A naturalistic 10-year follow-up. *Annals of Behavioral Medicine, 21*, 317–321.

Kraft, S., Puschner, B., Lambert, M.J., & Kordy, H. (2006). Medical utilization and treatment outcome in mid- and long-term outpatient psychotherapy. *Psychotherapy Research, 16*, 241–249.

LaVeist, T.A., Isaac, L.A., & Williams, K.P. (2009). Mistrust of health care organizations is associated with underutilization of health services. *Health Services Research, 44*, 2093–2105.

Luepker, R.V., Raczynski, J.M., Osganian, S., Goldberg, R.J., Finnegan, J.R., Hedges, J.R., ... Grp, R.S. (2000). Effect of a community intervention on patient delay and emergency medical service use in acute coronary heart disease—The Rapid Early Action for Coronary Treatment (REACT) trial. *Journal of the American Medical Association, 284*, 60–67.

McDonald, H.P., Garg, A.X., & Haynes, R.B. (2002). Interventions to enhance patient adherence to medication prescriptions—Scientific review. *Journal of the American Medical Association, 288*, 2868–2879.

Marchildon, G.P. (2013). *Health systems in transition: Canada* (2nd ed.). Toronto: University of Toronto Press.

Marchildon, G.P., & Lockhart, W. (2012). Common trends in public stewardship in health care. In B. Rosen, A. Israeli, & S. Shortell (Eds.), *Accountability and responsibility in health care: Issues in addressing an emerging global challenge* (pp. 255–276). Hackensack, NJ: World Scientific.

Moser, D.K., Kimble, L.P., Alberts, M.J., Alonzo, A., Croft, J.B., Dracup, K., ... Zerwic, J.J. (2007). Reducing delay in seeking treatment by patients with acute coronary syndrome and stroke: A scientific statement from the American Heart Association Council on Cardiovascular Nursing and Stroke Council. *Journal of Cardiovascular Nursing, 22*, 326–343.

Nicassio, P.M., Meyerowitz, B.E., & Kerns, R.D. (2004). The future of health psychology interventions. *Health Psychology, 23*, 132–137.

Noyes, R., Happel, R.L., & Yagla, S.J. (1999). Correlates of hypochondriasis in a nonclinical population. *Psychosomatics, 40*, 461–469.

Organisation for Economic Co-operation and Development (OECD). (2011). *Health at a glance: OECD indicators*. Paris: OECD.

Quan, H., Fong, A., De Coster, C., Wang, J.L., Musto, R., Noseworthy, T.W., & Ghali, W.A. (2006). Variation in health services utilization among ethnic populations. *Canadian Medical Association Journal, 174*, 787–791.

Rawles, J. (1996). Magnitude of benefit from earlier thrombolytic treatment in acute myocardial infarction: New evidence from Grampian region early anistreplase trial (GREAT). *British Medical Journal, 312*, 212–215.

Rodin, J., & Janis, I.L. (1979). The social power of health-care practitioners as agents of change. *Journal of Social Issues, 35*, 60–81.

Romanow, R.J., & Marchildon, G.P. (2003). Psychological services and the future of health care in Canada. *Canadian Psychology, 44*, 283–295.

Roter, D.L., Hall, J.A., & Aoki, Y. (2002). Physician gender effects in medical communication: A meta-analytic review. *Journal of the American Medical Association, 288*, 756–764.

Saltman, R.B., & Dubois, H.F.W. (2004). The historical and social base of social health insurance systems. In R.B. Saltman, R. Busse, & A. Figueras (Eds.), *Social health insurance systems in Europe* (pp. 33–80). Maidenhead, UK: Open University Press for European Observatory on Health Systems and Policies.

Saltman, R.B., & Ferroussier-Davis, O. (2000). The concept of stewardship in health policy. *Bulletin of the World Health Organization, 78*, 732–739.

Scheppers, E., van Dongen, E., Dekker, J., Geertzen, J., & Dekker, J. (2006). Potential barriers to the use of health services among ethnic minorities: A review. *Family Practice, 23*, 325–348.

Schoen, C. (2011). New 2011 survey of patients with complex care needs in 11 countries finds that care is often poorly coordinated. *Health Affairs 30*, 2437–2448.

Schoen, C., Osborn, R., Doty, M.M., Squires, D., Peugh, J., & Applebaum, S. (2009). A survey of primary care physicians in eleven countries, 2009: Perspectives on care costs, and experiences. *Health Affairs web exclusive, 28*, w1171–w1183.

Sitzia, J., & Wood, N. (1997). Patient satisfaction: A review of issues and concepts. *Social Science & Medicine, 45*, 1829–1843.

Smith, E., & Stark, K. (2012, June 28). By the numbers: Health insurance. *CNN Politics*. Retrieved from: www.cnn.com/2012/06/27/politics/btn-health-care/index.html

Smith, T.W., Orleans, C.T., & Jenkins, C.D. (2004). Prevention and health promotion: Decades of progress, new challenges, and an emerging agenda. *Health Psychology, 23*, 126–131.

Starr, P. (2011). *Remedy and reaction: The peculiar American struggle over health care reform*. New Yaven: Yale University Press.

Suls, J., & Rothman, A. (2004). Evolution of the biopsychosocial model: Prospects and challenges for health psychology. *Health Psychology, 23*, 119–125.

Tomenson, B., McBeth, J., Chew-Graham, C.A., Macfarlane, G., Davies, I., Jackson, J., ... Creed, F.H. (2012).

Somatization and health anxiety as predictors of health care use. *Psychosomatic Medicine, 74*, 656–664.

Tovian, S.M. (2004). Health services and health care economics: The health psychology marketplace. *Health Psychology, 23*, 138–141.

World Health Organization (WHO). (2000). *The World Health Report 2000: Health systems: improving performance*. Geneva: WHO.

Worthington, C. (2005). Patient satisfacton with health care: Recent theoretical developments and implications for evaluation practice. *Canadian Journal of Program Evaluation, 20*, 41–63.

Xiao, H., & Barber, J.P. (2008). The effect of perceived health status on patient satisfaction. *Value in Health, 11*, 719–725.

Zolnierek, K.B., & DiMatteo, M.R. (2009). Physician communication and patient adherence to treatment: A meta-analysis. *Medical Care, 47*, 826–834.

Chapter 4

Abrams, D.B., Herzog, T.A., Emmons, K.M., & Linnan, L. (2000). Stages of change versus addiction: A replication and extension. *Nicotine & Tobacco Research, 2*, 223–229.

Aveyard, P., Cheng, K.K., Almond, J., Sherratt, E., Lancashire, R., Lawrence, T., ... Evans, O. (1999). Cluster randomized controlled trial of expert system based on the transtheoretical ("stages of change") model for smoking prevention and cessation in schools. *British Medical Journal, 319*, 948–953.

Bandura, A. (1982). Self-efficacy mechanism in human agency. *American Psychologist, 37*, 122–147.

Blissmer, B., Prochaska, J.O., Velicer, W.F., Redding, C.A., Rossi, J.S., Greene, G.W., ... Robbins, M.L. (2010). Common factors predicting long-term changes in multiple health behaviours. *Journal of Health Psychology, 15*, 201–214.

Centers for Disease Control and Prevention (CDC), AIDS Community Demonstration Projects Research Group. (1999). Community-level HIV intervention in 5 cities: Final outcome data from the CDC AIDS community demonstration projects. *American Journal of Public Health, 89*, 336–345.

DiClemente, C.C., & Prochaska, J.O. (1982). Self-change and therapy change of smoking behaviour: A comparison of processes of change in cessation and maintenance. *Addictive Behaviour, 7*, 133–142.

DiClemente, C.C., Prochaska, J.O., Fairhurst, S.K., Velicer, W.F., Valesquez, M.M., & Rossi, J.S. (1991). The processes of smoking cessation: An analysis of precontemplation, contemplation, and preparation stages of change. *Journal of Consulting and Clinical Psychology, 59*, 295–304.

Dijkstra, A., Conijm, B., & De Vries, H. (2006). A match-mismatch test of a stage model of behaviour change in tobacco smoking. *Addiction, 101*, 1035–1043.

Edington, D.W. (2001). Emerging research: A view from one research center. *American Journal of Health Promotion, 15*, 341–349.

Etter, J.F., Perneger, T.V., & Ronchi, A. (1997). Distributions of smokers by stage: International comparison and association with smoking prevalence. *Preventive Medicine, 26*(4), 580–585.

Evers, K.E., Prochaska, J.O., Van Marter, D.F., Johnson, J.L., & Prochaska, J.M. (2007). Transtheoretical-based bullying prevention effectiveness trials in middle schools and high schools. *Education Research, 49*, 397–414.

Farkas, A.J., Pierce, J.P., Zhu, S.H., Rosbrook, B., Gilpin, E.A., Berry, C., & Kaplan, R.M. (1996). Addiction versus stages of change models in predicting smoking cessation. *Addiction, 91*, 1271–1280.

Goldstein, M.G., Pinto, B.M., Marcus, B.H., Lynn, H., Jette, A.M., Rakowski, W., ... Tennstedt, S. (1999). Physician-based physical activity counseling for middle-aged and older adults: A randomized trial. *Annals of Behavioural Medicine, 21*, 40–47.

Hall, J.S., & Rossi, J.S. (2008). Meta-analytic examination of the strong and weak principles across 48 health behaviours. *Preventive Medicine, 46*, 266–274.

Herzog, T.A., Abrams, D.B., Emmons, K.A., Linnan, L., & Shadel, W.G. (1999). Do processes of change predict stage movements? A prospective analysis of the transtheoretical model. *Health Psychology, 18*, 369–375.

Hoffman A., Redding, C.A., Goldberg, D.N., Añel, D., Prochaska, J.O., Meyer, P.M., & Pandey, D. (2006). Computer expert systems for African American smokers in physicians' offices: A feasibility study. *Preventive Medicine, 43*, 204–211.

Hollis, J.F., Polen, M.R., Whitlock, E.P., Lichtenstein, E., Mullooly, J., Velicer, W.F., & Redding, C.A. (2005). Teen REACH: Outcomes from a randomized controlled trial of a tobacco reduction program for teens seen in primary medical care. *Pediatrics, 115*, 981–989.

Janis, I.L., & Mann, L. (1977). *Decision making: A psychological analysis of conflict, chance and commitment*. London: Cassil & Collier Macmillan.

Johnson, J.L., Regan, R., Maddock, J.E., Fava, J.L., Velicer, W.F., Rossi, J.S., & Prochaska, J.O. (2000). What predicts stage of change for smoking cessation? *Annals of Behavioural Medicine, 22*, S173. (Abstract).

Johnson, S.S., Paiva, A.L., Cummins, C.O., Johnson, J.L., Dyment, S.J., Wright, J.A., ... Sherman, K. (2008). Transtheoretical model-based multiple behaviour intervention for weight management: Effectiveness on a population basis. *Preventive Medicine, 46*, 238–246.

Johnson, S.S., Paiva, A., Mauriello, L., Prochaska, J.O., Redding, C.A., & Velier, W.F. (2013, November 25). Coaction in multiple behavior change interventions: Consistency across multiple studies on weight management & obesity prevention. *Health Psychology*. (E-publication ahead of print).

Khaw, K.T., Wareham, N., Bingham, S., Welch, A., Luben, R., & Day, N. (2008). Combined impact of health behaviours and mortality in men and women: The EPIC-Norfolk Prospective Population Study. *PLoS Med 5*, e12.

Kreuter, M.W., Strecher, V.J., & Glassman, B. (1999). One size does not fit all: The case for tailoring print materials. *Annals of Behavioural Medicine, 21*, 276–283.

Mauriello, L.M., Ciavatta, M.M.H., Paiva, A.L., Sherman, K.J., Castle, P.H., Johnson, J.L., and Prochaska, J.M. (2010). Results of a multi-media multiple behaviour obesity prevention program for adolescents. *Preventive Medicine, 51*, 451–456.

Mauriello, L.M., Sherman, K.J., Driskell, M.M., & Prochaska, J.M. (2007). Using interactive behaviour change technology to intervene on physical activity and nutrition with adolescents. *Adolescent Medicine, 8*, 383–399. PMID: 18605653.

Noar, S.M., Benac, C., & Harris, M. (2007). Does tailoring matter? Meta-analytic review of tailored print health behaviour change interventions. *Psychological Bulletin, 133*, 673–693.

Norman, G.J., Adams, M.A., Calfas, K.J., Covin, J., Sallis, J.F., Rossi, J.S.,...Patrick, K. (2007). A randomized controlled trial of a multicomponent intervention for adolescent sun protection behaviours. *Archives of Pediatric & Adolescent Medicine, 161*, 146–152.

Paiva, A.L., Prochaska, J.O., Hui-Qing Yin, H., Redding, C.R., Rossi, J.S., Blissmer, B., ... Horiuchi, S. (2012). Treated individuals who progress to action or maintenance for one behavior are more likely to make similar progress on another behavior: Coaction results of a pooled data analysis of three trials. *Preventive Medicine, 54*, 331–334.

Peterson, A.V., Kealey, K.A., Mann, S.L., Marek, P.M., & Sarason, I.G. (2000). Hutchinson Smoking Prevention Project: Long-term randomized trial in school-based tobacco use prevention—results on smoking. *Journal of the National Cancer Institute, 92*, 1979–1991.

Prochaska, J.J., Velicer, W.F., Prochaska, J.O., Delucchi, K., & Hall, S.M. (2006). Comparing intervention outcomes in smokers treated for single versus multiple behavioural risks. *Health Psychology, 25*, 380–388.

Prochaska, J.M., Prochaska, J.O., Cohen, F.C., Gomes, S.O., Laforge, R.G., & Eastwood, A. (2004). The transtheoretical model of change for multi-level interventions for alcohol abuse on campus. *Journal of Alcohol and Drug Education, 47*, 34–50.

Prochaska, J.O. (1979). *Systems of psychotherapy: A transtheoretical analysis*. Pacific Grove, Calif.: Brooks-Cole. (7th ed., 2009).

Prochaska, J.O., Butterworth, S., Redding, C.A., Burden, V., Perrin, N., Leo, M., ... Prochaska, J.M.(2008). Initial efficacy of MI, TTM tailoring and HRI's with multiple behaviours for employee health promotion. *Preventive Medicine, 45*, 226–231.

Prochaska, J.O., & DiClemente, C.C. (1983). Stages and processes of self-change of smoking: Toward an integrative model of change. *Journal of Consulting and Clinical Psychology, 51*, 390–395.

Prochaska, J.O., DiClemente, C.C., Velicer, W.F., Ginpil, S., & Norcross, J.C. (1985). Predicting change in smoking status for self-changers. *Addictive Behaviours, 10*, 407–412. PMID: 4091072.

Prochaska, J.O., Evers, K.E., Castle, P.H., Johnson, J.L., Prochaska, J.M., Rula, E.Y., ... Pope, J.E. (2012). Enhancing multiple domains of well-being by decreasing multiple health risk behaviours: A randomized clinical trial. *Population Health Management, 15*, 276–286.

Prochaska, J.O., & Velicer, W.F. (1996). On models, methods and premature conclusions. *Addictions, 91*, 1281–1283.

Prochaska, J.O., & Velicer, W.F. (1997). The transtheoretical model of health behaviour change. *American Journal of Health Promotion, 12*, 38–48.

Prochaska, J.O., Velicer, W.F., Fava, J.L., Ruggiero, L., Laforge, R.G., Rossi, J.S., … Lee, P.A. (2001). Counselor and stimulus control enhancements of a stage-matched expert system intervention for smokers in a managed care setting. *Preventive Medicine, 32*, 23–32.

Prochaska, J.O., Velicer, W.F., Guadagnoli, E., Rossi, J.S., & DiClemente, C.C. (1991). Patterns of change: Dynamic typology applied to smoking cessation. *Multivariate Behavioural Research, 26*, 83–107.

Prochaska, J.O., Velicer, W.F., Redding, C.A., Rossi, J.S., Goldstein, M., DePue, J., … Plummer, B.A. (2005). Stage-based expert systems to guide a population of primary care patients to quit smoking, eat healthier, prevent skin cancer, and receive regular mammograms. *Preventive Medicine, 41*, 406–416.

Prochaska, J.O., Velicer, W.F., Rossi, J.S., Goldstein, M.G., Marcus, B.H., Rakowski, W., … Rossi, S.R. (1994). Stages of change and decisional balance for twelve problem behaviours. *Health Psychology, 13*, 39–46.

Prochaska, J.O., Velicer, W.F., Rossi, J.S., Redding, C.A., Greene, G.W., Rossi, S.R., … Plummer, B.A. (2004). Impact of simultaneous stage-matched expert system interventions for smoking, high fat diet, and sun exposure in a population of parents. *Health Psychology, 23*, 503–516.

Prochaska, J.O., Wright, J.A., & Velicer, W.F. (2008). Evaluating theories of health behaviour change: A hierarchy of criteria applied to the transtheoretical model. *Applied Psychology: An International Review, 57*, 561–588.

Pronk, N.P., Lowry, M., Kottke, T.E., Austin, E., Gallagher, J., & Katz, A. (2010). The association between optimal lifestyle adherence and short-term incidence of chronic conditions among employees. *Population Health Management, 13*, 289–295.

Rakowski, W.R., Ehrich, B., Goldstein, M.G., Rimer, B.K., Pearlman, D.N., Clark, M.A., … Woolverton, H. (1998). Increasing mammography among women aged 40–74 by use of a stage-matched, tailored intervention. *Preventive Medicine, 27*, 748–756.

Redding, C.A., Maddock, J.E., & Rossi, J.S. (2006). The sequential approach to measurement of health behaviour constructs: Issues in selecting and developing measures. *Californian Journal of Health Promotion, 4*, 83–101.

Reeves, M.J., & Rafferty, A.P. (2005). Healthy lifestyle characteristics among adults in the United States, 2000. *Archives of Internal Medicine, 165*, 854–857.

Rosen, C.S. (2000). Is the sequencing of change processes by stage consistent across health problems? A meta-analysis. *Health Psychology, 19*, 593–604.

Rossi, J.S. (1992a). Stages of change for 15 health risk behaviours in an HMO population. Paper presented at 13th meeting of the Society for Behavioural Medicine, New York.

Rossi, J.S. (1992b). Common processes of change across nine problem behaviours. Paper presented at 100th meeting of American Psychological Association, Washington.

Ruggiero, L., Glasgow, R., Dryfoos, J.M., Rossi, J.S., Prochaska, J.O., Orleans, C.T., … Johnson, S. (1997). Diabetes self-management: Self-reported recommendations and patterns in a large population. *Diabetes Care, 20*, 568–576.

Skinner, C.S., Campbell, M.D., Rimer, B.K., Curry, S., & Prochaska, J.O. (1999). How effective is tailored print communication? *Annals of Behavioural Medicine, 21*, 290–298.

Snow, M.G., Prochaska, J.O., & Rossi, J.S. (1992). Stages of change for smoking cessation among former problem drinkers: A cross-sectional analysis. *Journal of Substance Abuse, 4*, 107–116.

Sun, X., Prochaska, J.O., Velicer, W.F., & Laforge, R.G. (2007). Transtheoretical principles and processes for quitting smoking: A 24-month comparison of a representative sample of quitters, relapsers and non-quitters. *Addictive Behaviours, 32*, 2707–2726.

US Department of Health and Human Services (USDHHS). (1990). *The health benefits of smoking cessation: A report of the Surgeon General* (DHHS Publication No. CDC 90-8416). Washington: US Government Printing Office.

van den Brandt, P.A. (2011). The impact of a Mediterranean diet and healthy lifestyle on premature mortality in men and women. *American Journal of Clinical Nutrition, 94*, 913–920.

Velicer, W.F., Fava, J.L., Prochaska, J.O., Abrams, D.B., Emmons, K.M., & Pierce, J. (1995). Distribution of smokers by stage in three representative samples. *Preventive Medicine, 24*, 401–411.

Velicer, W.F., Prochaska, J.O., Bellis, J.M., DiClemente, C.C., Rossi, J.S., Fava, J.L., & Steiger, J.H. (1993). An expert system intervention for smoking cessation. *Addictive Behaviours, 18*, 269–290.

Velicer, W.F., Redding, C.A., Paiva, A.L., Mauriello, L.M., Blissmer, B., Oatley, K., … & Fernandez, A.C. (2013). Multiple behavior interventions to prevent substance abuse and increase energy balance behaviors in middle school students. *Translational Behavioral Medicine: Practice, Policy and Research, 3*(1), 82–93.

Velicer, W.F., Redding, C.A., Sun, X., & Prochaska, J.O. (2007). Demographic variables, smoking variables, and outcome across five studies. *Health Psychology, 26*, 278–287.

Voorhees, C.C., Stillman, F.A., Swank, R.T., Heagerty, P.J., Levine, D.M., & Becker, D.M. (1996). Heart, body, and soul: Impact of church-based smoking cessation interventions on readiness to quit. *Preventive Medicine, 25*, 277–285.

Wewers, M.E., Stillman, F.A., Hartman, A.M., & Shopland, D.R. (2003). Distribution of daily smokers by stage of change: Current population survey results. *Preventive Medicine, 36*, 710–720.

Yang, G., Ma, J., Chen, A., Zhang, Y., Samet, J.M., Taylor, C.E., & Becker, K. (2001). Smoking cessation in China: Findings from the 1996 national prevalence survey. *Tobacco Control, 10*, 170–174.

Chapter 5

Alexander, F. (1939). Emotional factors in essential hypertension. *Psychosomatic Medicine, 1*, 173–179.

American Psychiatric Association (2013). *Diagnostic and statistical manual of mental disorders* (5th ed.). Arlington, Va.: American Psychiatric Publishing.

Arora, N., Rutten, L., Gustafson, D., Moser, R., & Hawkins, R. (2007). Perceived helpfulness and impact of social support provided by family, friends, and health care providers to women newly diagnosed with breast cancer. *Psycho-Oncology, 16*, 474–486.

Banerjee, B., Vadiraj, H.S., Ram, A., Rao, R., Jayapal, M., Gopinath, K.S., & Prakash Hande, M. (2007). Effects of an integrated yoga program in modulating psychological stress and radiation-induced genotoxic stress in breast cancer patients undergoing radiotherapy. *Integrated Cancer Therapy, 6*, 242–250.

Barefoot, J.C., Dodge, K.A., Peterson, B.L., Dahlstrom, W.G., & Williams, R.B. (1989). The Cook-Medley Hostility Scale: Item content and ability to predict survival. *Psychosomatic Medicine, 51*, 46–57.

Brady, J.V. (1958). Ulcers in executive monkeys. *Scientific American, 199*, 95–100.

Brady, J.V., Porter, R.W., Conrad, D.G., & Mason, J.W. (1958). Avoidance behavior and the development of duodenal ulcers. *Journal of the Experimental Analysis of Behavior, 1*, 69–72.

Brondolo, E., Grantham, K.I., Karlin, W., Taravella, J., Mencía-Ripley, A., Schwartz, J.E., … Contrada, R.J. (2009). Trait hostility and ambulatory blood pressure among traffic enforcement agents: The effects of stressful social interactions. *Journal of Occupational Health Psychology, 14*, 110–121.

Brown, G.W, & Harris, T.O. (1978). *Social origins of depression: A study of psychiatric disorder in women.* New York: Free Press.

Brummett, B.H., Maynard, K.E., Haney, T.L., Siegler, I.C., & Barefoot, J.C. (2000). Reliability of interview-assessed hostility ratings across mode of assessment and time. *Journal of Personality Assessment, 75*, 225–236.

Bryant, R.A., Harvey, A.G., Dang, S.T., Sackville, T., & Basten, C. (1998). Treatment of acute stress disorder: A comparison of cognitive-behavioral therapy and supportive counseling. *Journal of Consulting and Clinical Psychology, 66*, 862–866.

Buss, A.H., & Perry, M. (1992). The aggression questionnaire. *Journal of Personality and Social Psychology, 63*, 452–459.

Butler, A.C., Chapman, J.E., Forman, E.M., & Beck, A.T. (2006). The empirical status of cognitive-behavioral therapy: A review of meta-analyses. *Clinical Psychology Review, 26*, 17–31.

Cannon, W.C (1929). *Bodily changes in pain, hunger, fear, and rage.* New York: Appleton-Century-Crofts.

Carver, C.S., Scheier, M.F., & Weintraub, J.K. (1989). Assessing coping strategies: A theoretically based approach. *Journal of Personality and Social Psychology, 56*, 267–283.

Chafin, S., Christenfeld, N., & Gerin, W. (2008). Improving cardiovascular recovery from stress with brief poststress exercise. *Health Psychology, 27*(1 Suppl), S64–72.

Chandra, V., Szklo, M., Goldberg, R., & Tonascia, J. (1983). The impact of marital status on survival after an acute myocardial infarction: A population-based study. *American Journal of Epidemiology, 117*, 320–325.

Christenfeld, N., Glynn, L.M., Phillips, D.P., & Shrira, I. (1999). New York City as a risk factor for heart attack mortality. *Psychosomatic Medicine, 61*, 740–743.

CIA World Factbook. (2012). Retrieved from www.cia.gov/library/publications/the-world-factbook/

Clarke, H.F., Dalley, J.W., Crofts, H.S., Robbins, T.W., & Roberts, A.C. (2004). Cognitive inflexibility after prefrontal serotonin depletion. *Science, 304*, 878–880.

Cohen, S., Doyle, W.J., Skoner, D.P., Rabin, B.S., & Gwaltney, J.M., Jr. (1997). Social ties and susceptibility to the common cold. *Journal of the American Medical Association, 277*, 1940–1944.

Cohen, S., & Wills, T.A. (1985). Stress, social support, and the buffering hypothesis. *Psychological Bulletin, 98*, 310–357.

Cook, W.W., & Medley, D.M. (1954). Proposed hostility and pharisaic virtue scales for the MMPI. *Journal of Applied Psychology, 38*, 414–418.

Coverman, S. (1989). Role overload, role conflict, and stress: Addressing consequences of multiple role demands. *Social Forces, 67*, 965–982.

Coyne, J.C., Rohrbaugh, M.J., Shoham, V., Sonnega, J.S., Nicklas, J.M., & Cranford, J.A. (2001). Prognostic importance of marital quality for survival of congestive heart failure. *American Journal of Cardiology, 88*, 526–529.

Cutrona, C.E., Russell, D.W., Brown, P.A., Clark, L.A., Hessling, R.M., & Gardner, K.A. (2005). Neighborhood context, personality, and stressful life events as predictors of depression among African American women. *Journal of Abnormal Psychology, 114*, 3–15.

D'Atri, D.A., Fitzgerald, E.F., Kasl, S.K., & Ostfeld, A.M. (1981). Crowding in prison: The relationship between changes in housing mode and blood pressure. *PsychosomaticMedicine, 43*, 95–105.

Dressier, W.W. (1990). Lifestyle, stress, and blood pressure in a southern Black community. *Psychosomatic Medicine, 52*, 182–198.

Dressier, W.W. (1991). Social support, lifestyle incongruity, and arterial blood pressure in a southern Black community. *Psychosomatic Medicine, 53*, 608–620.

Edwards, K.M., Burns, V.E., Reynolds, T., Carroll, D., Drayson, M., & Ring, C. (2006). Acute stress exposure prior to influenza vaccination enhances antibody response in women. *Brain, Behavior, and Immunity, 20*, 159–168.

Eibner, C., & Evans, W.N. (2005). Relative deprivation, poor health habits, and mortality. *Journal of Human Resources, 40*, 592–620.

Ellis, A. (1962). *Reason and emotion in psychotherapy.* New York: L. Stuart.

Epel, E.S., Blackburn, E.H., Lin, J., Dhabhar, F.S., Adler, N.E., Morrow, J.D., & Cawthon, R.M. (2004). Accelerated telomere shortening in response to life stress. *Proceedings of the National Academies of Science, 101*, 17312–17315.

Eysenck, H.J. (1991). Type A behaviour and coronary heart diesase: The third stage. In M.J. Strube (Ed.) *Type A behavior.* Newbury Park, Calif.: Sage.

Folkman, S., & Lazarus, R.S. (1980). An analysis of coping in a middle-aged community sample. *Journal of Health and Social Behavior, 21*, 219–239.

Folkman, S., Lazarus, R.S., Dunkel-Schetter, C., DeLongis, A., & Gruen, R.J. (1986). Dynamics of a stressful encounter: Cognitive appraisal, coping, and encounter outcomes. *Journal of Personality and Social Psychology, 50*, 992–1003.

Folkow, B. (1978). Cardiovascular structural adaptation: Its role in the initiation and maintenance of primary hypertension. *Clinical Science and Molecular Medicine, 55* (Suppl. 4), IV-3–IV-22.

Francis, M.E., & Pennebaker, J.W. (1992). Putting stress into words: The impact of writing on physiological, absentee, and self-reported emotional well-being measures. *American Journal of Health Promotion, 6*, 280–287.

Frankenhaeuser, M. (1983). The sympathetic-adrenal and pituitary-adrenal response to challenge: Comparison between the sexes. In T.M. Dembroski, T.H. Schmidt, & G. Blomchen (Eds.), *Biobehavioral bases of coronary heart disease* (pp. 91–105). Basel, Switzerland: Karger.

French, J.R., Caplan, R.D., & Harrison, R.V. (1982). *The mechanisms of job stress and strain*. Chichester, UK: Wiley.

Friedman, M., & Rosenman, R. (1959). Association of specific overt behaviour pattern with blood and cardiovascular findings. *Journal of the American Medical Association, 169*, 1286–1296.

Garrison, R.J., Gold, R.S., Wilson, P.W.F., & Kannel, W.B. (1993). Educational attainment and coronary heart disease risk: The Framingham Offspring Study. *Preventive Medicine, 22*, 54–64.

Geary, D.C., & Flinn, M.V. (2002). Sex differences in behavioral and hormonal response to social threat: Commentary on Taylor et al. (2000). *Psychological Review, 109*, 745–750.

Gerin, W., Zawadzki, M., Brosschot, J., Thayer, J., Christenfeld, N., Campbell, T.S., & Smyth, J.M. (2012). Rumination as a mediator of chronic stress effects on hypertension: A causal model. *International Journal of Hypertension*.

Gerstel, N., Riessman, C.K., & Rosenfield, S. (1985). Explaining the symptomatology of separated and divorced women and men: The role of material conditions and social networks. *Social Forces, 64*, 84–101.

Glynn, L.M., Christenfeld, N., & Gerin, W. (1999). Gender, social support, and cardiovascular responses to stress. *Psychosomatic Medicine, 61*, 234–242.

Glynn, L.M., Christenfeld, N., & Gerin, W. (2002). The role of rumination in recovery from reactivity: Cardiovascular consequences of emotional states. *Psychosomatic Medicine, 64*, 714–726.

Goodwin, J.S., Hunt, W.C., Key, C.R., & Samet, J.M. (1987). The effect of marital status on stage, treatment, and survival of cancer patients. *Journal of the American Medical Association, 258*, 3125–3130.

Green, C.A., & Pope, C.R. (1999). Gender, psychosocial factors and the use of medical services: A longitudinal analysis. *Social Science & Medicine, 48*, 1363–1372.

Helgeson, V.S., Cohen, S., Schulz, R., & Yasko, J. (2000). Group support interventions for women with breast cancer: Who benefits from what? *Health Psychology, 19*, 107–114.

Hemingway, H., & Marmot, M. (1999). Clinical evidence: Psychosocial factors in the etiology and prognosis of coronary heart disease: Systematic review of prospective cohort studies. *Western Journal of Medicine, 171*, 342–350.

Holahan, C.J., & Moos, R.H. (1986). Personality, coping, and family resources in stress resistance: A longitudinal analysis. *Journal of Personality and Social Psychology, 51*, 389–395.

Holmes, D.S., & Houston, B.K. (1974). Effect of avoidant thinking and reappraisal for coping with threat involving temporal uncertainty. *Journal of Personality and Social Psychology, 30*, 382–388.

Holmes, T.H., & Rahe, R.H. (1967). The Social Readjustment Rating Scale. *Journal of Psychosomatic Research, 11*, 213–218.

Irvine, J., Garner, D.M., Craig, H.M., & Logan, A.G. (1991). Prevalence of Type A behavior in untreated hypertensive individuals. *Hypertension, 18*, 72–78.

Jacobs, G.D. (2001). Clinical applications of the relaxation response and mind–body interventions. *Journal of Alternative and Complementary Medicine, 7* (Suppl 1), S93–101.

Jain, S., Shapiro, S.L., Swanick, S., Roesch, S.C., Mills, P.J., Bell, I., & Schwartz, G.E. (2007). A randomised controlled trial of mindfulness meditation versus relaxation training: Effects on distress, positive states of mind, rumination, and distraction. *Annals of Behavioral Medicine, 33*, 11–21.

Jones, S. (1996). The association between objective and subjective caregiver burden. *Archives of Psychiatric Nursing, 10*, 77–84.

Kabat-Zinn, J., Massion, A.O., Kristeller, J., Peterson, L.G., Fletcher, K., Pbert, L., ... Santorelli, S.F. (1992). Effectiveness of a meditation-based stress reduction program in the treatment of anxiety disorders. *American Journal of Psychiatry, 149*, 936–943.

Kanner, A.D., Coyne, J.C., Schaefer, C., & Lazarus, R.S. (1981). Comparison of two modes of stress measurement: Daily hassles and uplifts versus major life events. *Journal of Behavioral Medicine, 4*, 1–39.

Karasek, R.A., Theorell, T., Schwartz, J.E., Schnall, P.L., Pieper, C.F., & Michela, J.L. (1988). Job characteristics in relation to the prevalence of myocardial infarction in the U.S. Health Examination Survey (HES) and the Health and Nutrition Examination Survey (HANES). *American Journal of Public Health, 78*, 910–918.

Kelly, J.A., Murphy, D.A., Bahr, G.R., Kalichman, S.C., Morgan, M.G., Stevenson, L.Y., ... Bernstein, B.M. (1993). Outcome of cognitive-behavioral and support group brief therapies for depressed, HIV-infected persons. *American Journal of Psychiatry, 150*, 1679–1686.

Kenny, D.T. (2006). A systematic review for treatments of music performance anxiety. *Anxiety, Stress, & Coping, 18*, 183–208.

Kiecolt-Glaser, J.K., & Newton, T.L. (2001). Marriage and health: His and hers. *Psychological Bulletin, 127*, 472–503.

Kivimaki, M., Leino-Arjas, P., Luukkonen, R., Riihimäki, H., Vahtera, J., & Kirjonen, J. (2002). Work stress and risk of cardiovascular mortality: Prospective cohort study of industrial employees. *British Medical Journal, 325*, 857–860.

Kreutzer, J.S., Serio, C.D., & Bergquist, S. (1994). Family needs after brain injury: A quantitative analysis. *Archives of Physical Medicine and Rehabilitation, 73*, 771–778.

Kulik, J.A., & Mahler, H.I. (1987). Effects of preoperative roommate assignment on preoperative anxiety and recovery from coronary-bypass surgery. *Health Psychology, 6*, 525–543.

Kulik, J.A., & Mahler, H.I. (1989). Social support and recovery from surgery. *Health Psychology, 8*, 221–238.

Lanska, D.J., & Kuller, L.H. (1995). The geography of stroke mortality in the United States and the concept of a Stroke Belt. *Stroke, 26*, 1145–1149.

Larsen, B.A., & Christenfeld, N.J.S. (2009). Cardiovascular disease and psychiatric comorbidity: The potential role of perseverative cognition. *Cardiovascular Psychiatry and Neurology*.

Lawton, M.P., Moss, M., Kleban, M.H., Glicksman, A., & Rovine, M. (1991). A two-factor model of caregiving appraisal and psychological well-being. *Journal of Gerontology, 46*, 181–189.

Lazarus, R.S. (1966). *Psychological stress and the coping process.* New York: McGraw-Hill.

Lazarus, R.S., & Folkman, S. (1984). *Stress, appraisal and coping.* New York: Springer.

Le Fevre, M., Matheny, J., & Kilt, G. (2003). Eustress, distress, and interpretation in occupational stress. *Journal of Managerial Psychology, 18*, 726–744.

Lleras-Muney, A. (2005). The relationship between education and adult mortality in the United States. *Review of Economic Studies, 72*, 189–221.

Luepker, R.V., Rosamond, W.D., Murphy, R., Sprafka, J.M., Folsom, A.R., McGovern, P.G., & Blackburn, H. (1993). Socioeconomic status and coronary heart disease risk factor trends. *Circulation*, SS(Part 1), 2172–2179.

McEwen, B.S. (1998). Protective and damaging effects of stress mediators. *New England Journal of Medicine, 338*, 1771–1779.

McNutt, L., Strogatz, D.S., Coles, F.B., & Fehrs, L.J. (1994). Is the high ischemic heart disease rate in New York State just an urban effect? *Public Health Reports, 109*, 567–577.

McCrae, R.R. (1990). Controlling neuroticism in the measurement of stress. *Stress Medicine, 6*, 237–241.

Matschinger, H., Siegrist, J., Siegrist, K., & Dittmann, K.H. (1986). Type A as a coping career: Towards a conceptual and methodological redefinition. In T.H. Schmidt, T.M. Dembroski, & G. Blümchen (Eds.), *Biological and psychological factors in cardiovascular disease* (pp. 104–126). Berlin: Springer.

Maurin, J., & Boyd, C. (1990). Burden of mental illness on the family: A critical review. *Archives of Psychiatric Nursing, 4*, 99–107.

Nijboer, C., Triemstra, M., Tempelaar, R., Sanderman, R., & Van den Bos, G. (1999). Determinants of caregiving experiences and mental health of partners of cancer patients. *Cancer, 86*, 577–88.

Nolan, M., Grant, G., & Ellis, N. (1990). Stress is in the eye of the beholder: Reconceptualizing the measurement of career burden. *Journal of Advanced Nursing, 15*, 544–555.

Nolen-Hoeksema, S. (2000). The role of rumination in depressive disorders and mixed anxiety/depressive symptoms. *Journal of Abnormal Psychology, 109*, 504–511.

Norris, R., Carroll, D., & Cochrane, R. (1992). The effects of physical activity and exercise training on psychological stress and well-being in an adolescent population. *Journal of Psychosomatic Research, 36*, 55–65.

Obrist, P. (1981). *Cardiovascular psychophysiology: A perspective.* New York: Plenum Press.

Oparil, S. (1995). Hypertension in postmenopausal women: Pathophysiology and management. *Current Opinion inNephrology and Hypertension, 4*, 438–442.

O'Sullivan, G. (2010). The relationship between hope, eustress, self-efficacy, and life satisfaction among undergraduates. *Social Indicators Research, 101*, 155–172.

Padesky, C.A., & Hammen, C.L. (1981). Sex differences in depressive symptom expression and help-seeking among college students. *Sex Roles, 7*, 309–320.

Penedo, F.J., & Dahn, J.R. (2005). Exercise and well-being: A review of mental and physical health benefits associated with physical activity. *Current Opinion in Psychiatry, 18*, 189–193.

Pennebaker, J.W., Colder, M., & Sharp, L.K. (1990). Accelerating the coping process. *Journal of Personality and Social Psychology, 58*, 528–537.

Pennebaker, J.W., & Seagal, J.D. (1999). Forming a story: The health benefits of narrative. *Journal of Clinical Psychology, 55*, 12431254.

Pérez-Stable, E.J., Marín, G., & Marín, B.V. (1994). Behavioral risk factors: A comparison of Latinos and non-Latino Whites in San Francisco. *American Journal of Public Health*, 84, 971–976.

Petrie, K.J., Booth, R.J., Pennebaker, J.W., Davison, K.P., & Thomas, M.G. (1995). Disclosure of trauma and immune response to a hepatitis B vaccination program. *Journal of Consulting and Clinical Psychology, 63*, 787–792.

Rabkin, J.G., & Struening, E.L. (1976). Life events, stress, and illness. *Science, 194*, 1013–1020.

Repetti, R.L., & Wood, J. (1997). Effects of daily stress at work on mothers' interaction with preschool children. *Journal of Family Psychology, 11*, 90–108.

Rosengren, A., Orth-Gomer, K., Wedel, H., & Wilhelmsen, L. (1993). Stressful life events, social support, and mortality in men born in 1933. *British Medical Journal, 307*, 1102–1105.

Sandlund, E.S., & Norlander, T. (2000). The effects of Tai Chi Chuan relaxation and exercise on stress responses and well-being: An overview of research. *International Journal of Stress Management, 7*, 139–149.

Sapolsky, R.M. (2004). *Why zebras don't get ulcers: The acclaimed guide to stress, stress related diseases, and coping* (3rd rev. ed.). New York: W.H. Freeman.

Saunders, T., Driskell, J.E., Johnston, J.H., & Salas, E. (1996). The effect of stress inoculation training on anxiety and performance. *Journal of Occupational Health Psychology, 1*, 170–186.

Schell, F.J., Allolio, B., & Schonecke, O.W. (1994). Physiological and psychological effects of Hatha-Yoga exercise in healthy women. *International Journal of Psychosomatics, 41*, 46–52.

Schulz, R., & Beach, S.R. (1999). Caregiving as a risk factor for mortality. *Journal of the American Medical Association, 282*, 2215–2219.

Seligman, M.E.P., & Maier, S.F. (1967). Failure to escape traumatic shock. *Journal of Experimental Psychology, 74*, 1–9.

Selye, H. (1976). *The stress of life* (rev. ed.). New York: McGraw-Hill.

Shakespeare, W. (2003). *Hamlet* (The New Folger Library Shakespeare). New York: Simon & Schuster, New Folger Edition.

Siegrist, J. (1996). Adverse health effects of high-effort/low reward conditions. *Journal of Occupational Health Psychology, 1*, 27–41.

Smyth, J.M., Stone, A.A., Hurewitz, A., & Kaell, A. (1999). Effects of writing about stressful experiences on symptom reduction in patients with asthma or rheumatoid arthritis: A randomized trial. *Journal of the American Medical Association, 281*, 1304–1309.

Son, J., Erno, A., Shea, D.G., Femia, E.E., Zarit, S.H., & Parris Stephens, M.A. (2007). The caregiver stress process and health outcomes. *Journal of Aging and Health, 19*, 871–887.

Spiegel, D., Bloom, J.R., & Yalom, I. (1981). Group support for patients with metastatic cancer. A randomized outcome study. *Archives of General Psychiatry, 38*(5), 527–533.

Spielberger, C.D., Johnson, E.H., Russell, S.F., Crane, R.J., Jacobs, G.A., & Worden, T.I. (1985). The experience and expression of anger: Construction and validation of an anger expression scale. In M.A. Chesney & R.H. Rosenman (Eds.), *Anger and hostility in cardiovascular and behavioral disorders*. New York: Hemisphere/McGraw-Hill.

Stone, A.A., & Neale, J.M. (1984). New measure of daily coping. Development and preliminary results. *Journal of Personality and Social Psychology, 46*, 892–906.

Stringhini, S., Dugravot, A., Shipley, M., Goldberg, M., Zins, M., Kivimäki, M., … Singh-Manoux, A. (2011). Health behaviours, socioeconomic status, and mortality: Further analyses of the British Whitehall II and the French GAZEL prospective cohorts. *PLoS Med 8*, e1000419.

Szanton, S.L., Rifkind, J.M., Mohanty, J.G., Miller, E.R., Thorpe, R.J., Nagababu, E., … Evans, M.K. (2011). Racial discrimination is associated with a measure of red blood cell oxidative stress: A potential pathway for racial health disparities. *International Journal of Behavioral Medicine*, September.

Taylor, S.E., Klein, L.C., Gruenewald, T.L., Gurung, R.A., & Taylor, S.F. (2003). Affiliation, social support, and biobehavioral responses to stress. In J.M. Suls & K.A. Wallston (Eds.), *Social psychological foundations of health and illness* (pp. 314–332). Boston: Blackwell.

Taylor, S.E., Klein, L.C., Lewis, B.P., Gruenewald, T.L., Gurung, R.A., & Updegraff, J.A. (2000). Biobehavioral responses to stress in females: Tend-and-befriend, not fight-or-flight. *Psychological Review, 107*, 411–429.

Teel, C.S., & Press, A.N. (1999). Fatigue among elders in caregiving and noncaregiving roles. *Western Journal of Nursing Research, 21*(4), 498–520.

Tennant, C. (2001). Work-related stress and depressive disorders. *Journal of Psychosomatic Research, 51*, 697–704.

Theorell, T., DeFaire, U., Johnson, J., Hall, E., Perski, A., & Stewart, W. (1991). Job strain and ambulatory blood pressure profiles. *Scandinavian Journal of Work Environment and Health, 17*, 380–385.

Timio, M., Verdecchia, P., Venanzi, S., Gentili, S., Ronconi, M., Francucci, B., … & Bichisao, E. (1988). Age and blood pressure changes: A 20-year follow-up study in nuns in a secluded order. *Hypertension, 12*, 457–61.

Tomaka, J., Blascovich, J., Kelsey, R.M., & Leitten, C.L. (1993). Subjective, physiological, and behavioral effects of threat and challengeappraisal. *Journal of Personality and Social Psychology, 65*, 248–260.

Uchino, B.N., Cacioppo, J.T, & Kiecolt-Glaser, J.K. (1996). The relationship between social support and physiological processes: A review with emphasis on underlying mechanisms and implications for health. *Psychological Bulletin, 119*, 488–531.

Umberson, D. (1987). Family status and health behaviors: Social control as a dimension of social integration. *Journal of Health and Social Behavior, 28*, 306–319.

Verhaeghe, S., Defloor, T., & Grypdonck, M. (2005). Stress and coping among families of patients with traumatic brain injury: A review of the literature. *Journal of Clinical Nursing, 14*, 1004–1012.

Wareham, S., Fowler, K., & Pike, A. (2007). Determinants of depression severity and duration in Canadian adults: The moderating effects of gender and social support. *Journal of Applied Social Psychology, 37*, 2951–2979.

Weiss, J.M. (1968). Effects of coping responses on stress. *Journal of Comparative and Physiological Psychology, 65*, 251–260.

Williams, D.R., Neighbors, H.W., & Jackson, J.S. (2003). Racial/ethnic discrimination and health: findings from community studies. *American Journal of Public Health, 93*, 200–208.

Williams, R.B., & Barefoot, J.C. (1988). Coronary-prone behavior: The emerging role of the hostility complex. In B.K. Houston & C.R. Snyder (Eds.), *Type A behavior Pattern—Research, theory, and intervention* (pp. 189–211). New York: Wiley.

Wills, T.A. (1990). Social support and interpersonal relationships. In M.S. Clark (Ed.), *Prosocial Behavior* (pp. 265–289). Thousand Oaks, Calif.: Sage.

Chapter 6

Abramowitz, J.S., & Braddock, A.E. (2008). *Psychological treatment of health anxiety and hypochondriasis: A biopsychosocial approach*. Ashland, Ohio: Hogrefe & Huber.

Abramowitz, J.S., & Moore, E.L. (2007). An experimental analysis of hypochondriasis. *Behaviour Research and Therapy, 45*, 413–424.

American Psychiatric Association. (2013). Diagnostic and statistical manual of mental disorders (5th ed.). Washington: Author.

Arntz, A., Rauner, M., & Vandenhout, M. (1995). If I feel anxious, there must be danger—Ex-consequentia reasoning in inferring danger in anxiety disorders. *Behaviour Research and Therapy, 33*, 917–925.

Asmundson, G.J., Taylor, S., & Cox, B.J. (Eds.). (2001). *Health anxiety: Clinical and research perspectives on hypochondriasis and related conditions*. New York: Wiley.

Avia, M.D., Ruiz, M., Olivares, M., Crespo, M., Guisado, A.B., Sánchez, A., & Varela, A. (1996). The meaning of psychological symptoms: Effectiveness of a group intervention with hypochondriacal patients. *Behaviour Research and Therapy, 34*, 23–31.

Baker, L., Wagner, T.H., Singer, S., & Bundorf, M.K. (2003). Use of the Internet and e-mail for health care information—Results from a national survey. *Journal of the American Medical Association, 289*, 2400–2406.

Barsky, A.J., & Ahern, D.K. (2004). Cognitive behavior therapy for hypochondriasis: A randomized controlled trial. *Journal of the American Medical Association, 291*, 1464–1470.

Barsky, A.J., Frank, C.B., Cleary, P.D., Wyshak, G., & Klerman, G. (1991). The relation between hypochondriasis and age. *American Journal of Psychiatry, 148*, 923–928.

Barsky, A.J., Wyshak, G., Klerman, G., & Latham, K. (1990). The prevalence of hypochondriasis in medical outpatients. *Social Psychiatry and Psychiatric Epidemiology, 25*, 89–94.

Bijsterbosch, J., Scharloo, M., Visser, A.W., Watt, I., Mieulenbelt, I., Huizinga, T. W. J., … Kloppenburg, M. et al. (2009). Illness perceptions in patients with osteoarthritis: Change over time and association with disability. *Arthritis & Rheumatism—Arthritis Care & Research, 61,* 1054–1061.

Birley, A.J., Gillespie, N.A., Heath, A.C., Sullivan, P.F., Boomsma, D.I., & Martin, N.G. (2006). Heritability and nineteen-year stability of long and short EPQ-R neuroticism scales. *Personality and Individual Differences, 40,* 737–747.

Block, A.R., Kremer, E.F., & Gaylor, M. (1980). Behavioral treatment of chronic pain—The spouse as a discriminative cue for pain behavior. *Pain, 9,* 243–252.

Bourgault-Fagnou, M.D., & Hadjistavropoulos, H.D. (2009). Understanding health anxiety among community dwelling seniors with varying degrees of frailty. *Aging & Mental Health, 13,* 226–237.

Buwalda, F.M., Bouman, T., & van Duijn, M.A. (2007). Psychoeducation for hypochondriasis: A comparison of a cognitive-behavioural approach and a problem-solving approach. *Behaviour Research and Therapy, 45,* 887–899.

Cameron, L.D., & Jago, L. (2008). Emotion regulation interventions: A common-sense model approach. *British Journal of Health Psychology, 13,* 215–221.

Cannon, N. (Producer). (2012a, April 2). *NCredible health hustle: Episode 1.* [Video file] Retrieved from www.youtube.com/watch?v=jSTyfZUX2ps

Cannon, N. (Producer). (2012b, May 10). *Ncredible health hustle: Episode 6.* [Video file] Retrieved from www.essence.com/2012/05/10/must-see-nick-cannons-ncredible-health-hustle-episode-6/

Cannon, N. (Producer). (2012c, May 15). *NCredible health hustle: Episode 7.* [Video file] Retrieved from www.youtube.com/watch?v=RAEVrcPHIMc

Charles, S.T., Gatz, M., Kato, K., & Pedersen, N.L. (2008). Physical health 25 years later: The predictive ability of neuroticism. *Health Psychology, 27,* 369–378.

Clark, D.M., Salkovskis, P. M., Hackmann, A., Wells, A., Fennell, M., Ludgate, J., … Gelder, M. (1998). Two psychological treatments for hypochondriasis: A randomised controlled trial. *British Journal of Psychiatry, 173,* 218–225.

Costa, P.T., & Mccrae, R.R. (1985). Hypochondriasis, neuroticism, and aging—When are somatic complaints unfounded? *American Psychologist, 40,* 19–28.

Cousins, N. (1976). Anatomy of an illness as perceived by the patient. *New England Journal of Medicine, 295,* 1458–1463.

Craig, K.D., & Weiss, S.M. (1971). Vicarious influences on pain-threshold determinations. *Journal of Personality and Social Psychology, 19,* 53–57.

Croyle, R.T., & Uretsky, M.B. (1987). Effects of mood on self-appraisal of health status. *Health Psychology, 6,* 239–253.

Dahlquist, L.M., Gil, K.M., Armstrong, F.D., Delawyer, D.D., Greene, P., & Wuori, D. (1986). Preparing children for medical examinations—The importance of previous medical experience. *Health Psychology, 5,* 249–259.

de Zubiria Salgado, A., & Herrera-Diaz, C. (2012). Lupus nephritis: An overview of recent findings. *Autoimmune Diseases, 2012,* 849684.

Diefenbach, M.A., & Leventhal, H. (1996). The common-sense model of illness representation: Theoretical and practical considerations. *Journal of Social Distress and the Homeless, 5,* 11–38.

Faravelli, C., Salvatori, S., Galassi, F., Aiazzi, L., Drei, C., & Cabras, P. (1997). Epidemiology of somatoform disorders: A community survey in Florence. *Social Psychiatry and Psychiatric Epidemiology, 32,* 24–29.

Ferguson, E. (2009). A taxometric analysis of health anxiety. *Psychological Medicine, 39,* 277–285.

Fischer, M., Scharloo, M., Abbink, J., van't Hul, A., van Ranst, D., Rudolphus, A., … Kaptein, A.A. (2010). The dynamics of illness perceptions: Testing assumptions of Leventhal's common-sense model in a pulmonary rehabilitation setting. *British Journal of Health Psychology, 15,* 887–903.

Ford, D., Zapka, J., Gebregziabher, M., Yang, C.W., & Sterba, K. (2010). Factors associated with illness perception among critically ill patients and surrogates. *Chest, 138,* 59–67.

Fulton, J.J., Marcus, D.K., & Merkey, T. (2011). Irrational health beliefs and health anxiety. *Journal of Clinical Psychology, 67,* 527–538.

Furer, P., Walker, J.R., & Stein, M.B. (2007). *Treating health anxiety and fear of death: A practitioner's guide.* New York: Springer Science + Business Media.

Gil, K.M., Carson, J.W., Porter, L.S., Scipio, C., Bediako, S.M., & Orringer, E. (2004). Daily mood and stress predict pain, health care use, and work activity in African American adults with sickle-cell disease. *Health Psychology, 23,* 267–274.

Gillespie, N.A., Zhu, G., Heath, A., Hickie, I., & Martin, N. (2000). The genetic aetiology of somatic distress. *Psychological Medicine: A Journal of Research in Psychiatry and the Allied Sciences, 30,* 1051–1061.

Greeven, A., van Balkom, A.J., Visser, S., Merkelbach, J.W., van Rood, Y.R., van Dyck, R., … Spinhoven, P. (2007). Cognitive behavior therapy and paroxetine in the treatment of hypochondriasis: A randomized controlled trial. *American Journal of Psychiatry, 164,* 91–99.

Grewal, K., Stewart, D.E., & Grace, S.L. (2010). Differences in social support and illness perceptions among South Asian and Caucasian patients with coronary artery disease. *Heart & Lung, 39,* 180–187.

Griva, K., Jayasena, D., Davenport, A., Harrison, M., & Newman, S.P. (2009). Illness and treatment cognitions and health related quality of life in end stage renal disease. *British Journal of Health Psychology, 14,* 17–34.

Hadjistavropoulos, H.D., Janzen, J.A., Kehler, M.D., Leclerc, J.A., Sharpe, D., & Bourgault-Fagnou, M.D. (2012). Core cognitions related to health anxiety in self-reported medical and non-medical samples. *Journal of Behavioural Medicine, 35,* 167–178.

Hagger, M.S., & Orbell, S. (2003). A meta-analytic review of the common-sense model of illness representations. *Psychology & Health, 18,* 141–184.

Hedman, E., Andersson, G., Andersson, E., Ljotsson, B., Ruck, C., Asmundson, G.J., & Lindefors, N. (2011). Internet-based cognitive-behavioural therapy for severe health anxiety: Randomised controlled trial. *British Journal of Psychiatry, 198,* 230–236.

Hedman, E., Ljotsson, B., Andersson, E., Ruck, C., Andersson, G., & Lindefors, N. (2010). Effectiveness and cost offset analysis of group CBT for hypochondriasis delivered in a psychiatric setting: An open trial. *Cognitive Behaviour Therapy, 39*, 239–250.

Henselmans, I., Sanderman, R., Helgeson, V.S., de Vries, J., Smink, A., & Ranchor, A.V. (2010). Personal control over the cure of breast cancer: Adaptiveness, underlying beliefs and correlates. *Psycho-Oncology, 19*, 525–534.

Jessop, D.C., & Rutter, D.R. (2003). Adherence to asthma medication: The role of illness representations. *Psychology & Health, 18*, 595–612.

Jimenez, S., Cervera, R., Font, J., & Ingelmo, M. (2003). The epidemiology of systemic lupus erythematosus. *Clinical Reviews in Allergy and Immunology, 25*, 3–12.

Landrine, H., & Klonoff, E.A. (1992). Culture and health-related schemas—A review and proposal for interdisciplinary integration. *Health Psychology, 11*, 267–276.

Lawson, V.L., Bundy, C., Lyne, P.A., & Harvey, J.N. (2004). Using the IPQ and PMDI to predict regular diabetes care-seeking among patients with type 1 diabetes. British *Journal of Health Psychology, 9*, 241–252.

Leventhal, H., Meyer, D., & Nerenz, D. (1980). The common sense representation of illness danger. In S. Rachman (Ed.), *Contributions to medical psychology* (Vol. II, pp. 7–30). New York: Pergamon Press.

Looper, K.J., & Kirmayer, L.J. (2001). Hypochondriacal concerns in a community population. *Psychological Medicine, 31*, 577–584.

McSharry, J., Moss-Morris, R., & Kendrick, T. (2011). Illness perceptions and glycaemic control in diabetes: A systematic review with meta-analysis. *Diabetic Medicine, 28*, 1300–1310.

Moss-Morris, R., Weinman, J., Petrie, K.J., Horne, R., Cameron, L.D., & Buick, D. (2002). The revised Illness Perception Questionnaire (IPQ-R). *Psychology & Health, 17*, 1–16.

Noyes, R., Happel, R.L., & Yagla, S.J. (1999). Correlates of hypochondriasis in a nonclinical population. *Psychosomatics, 40*, 461–469.

Olatunji, B.O., Etzel, E.N., Tomarken, A.J., Ciesielski, B.G., & Deacon, B. (2011). The effects of safety behaviors on health anxiety: An experimental investigation. *Behaviour Research and Therapy, 49*, 719–728.

Owens, K.M.B., & Antony, M. (2011). *Overcoming health anxiety: Letting go of your fear of illness.* Oakland, Calif.: New Harbinger.

Pennebaker, J.W. (1982). The psychology of physical symptoms. New York: Springer-Verlag.

Petrie, K.J., Cameron, L.D., Ellis, C.J., Buick, D., & Weinman, J. (2002). Changing illness perceptions after myocardial infarction: An early intervention randomized controlled trial. *Psychosomatic Medicine, 64*, 580–586.

Pollard, T.M., & Schwartz, J.E. (2003). Are changes in blood pressure and total cholesterol related to changes in mood? An 18-month study of men and women. *Health Psychology, 22*, 47–53.

Rachman, S. (2012). Health anxiety disorders: A cognitive construal. *Behaviour Research and Therapy, 50*, 502–512.

Radomsky, A.S., Shafran, R., Coughtrey, A.E., & Rachman, S. (2010). Cognitive-behavior therapy for compulsive checking in OCD. *Cognitive and Behavioral Practice, 17*, 119–131.

Salkovskis, P.M., & Warwick, H.M.C. (1986). Morbid preoccupations, health anxiety and reassurance—A cognitive behavioral approach to hypochondriasis. *Behaviour Research and Therapy, 24*, 597–602.

Seivewright, H., Green, J., Salkovskis, P., Barrett, B., Nur, U., & Tyrer, P. (2008). Cognitive-behavioural therapy for health anxiety in a genitourinary medicine clinic: Randomised controlled trial. *British Journal of Psychiatry, 193*, 332–337.

Shafran, R., & Rachman, S. (2004). Thought-action fusion: A review. *Journal of Behavior Therapy and Experimental Psychiatry, 35*, 87–107.

Shapiro, M.F., Ware, J.E., Jr., & Sherbourne, C.D. (1986). Effects of cost sharing on seeking care for serious and minor symptoms: Results of a randomized controlled trial. *Annals of Internal Medicine, 104*, 246–251.

Sorensen, P., Birket-Smith, M., Wattar, U., Buemann, I., & Salkovskis, P. (2011). A randomized clinical trial of cognitive behavioural therapy versus short-term psychodynamic psychotherapy versus no intervention for patients with hypochondriasis. *Psychological Medicine: A Journal of Research in Psychiatry and the Allied Sciences, 41*, 431–441.

Stein, M.B., Jang, K.L., & Livesley, W. (1999). Heritability of anxiety sensitivity: A twin study. *American Journal of Psychiatry, 156*, 246–251.

Taylor, S., & Asmundson, G.J.G. (2004). *Treating health anxiety: A cognitive-behavioral approach.* New York: Guilford Press.

Taylor, S., Asmundson, G.J., & Coons, M.J. (2005). Current directions in the treatment of hypochondriasis. *Journal of Cognitive Psychotherapy, 19*, 285–304.

Tomenson, B., McBeth, J., Chew-Graham, C.A., Macfarlane, G., Davies, I., Jackson, J., … Creed, F.H. (2012). Somatization and health anxiety as predictors of health care use. *Psychosomatic Medicine, 74*, 656–664.

Torgerson, S. (1986). Genetics of somatoform disorders. *Archives of General Psychiatry, 43*, 502–505.

Tyrer, P., Cooper, S., Crawford, M., Dupont, S., Green, J., Murphy, D., … Tyrer, H. (2011). Prevalence of health anxiety problems in medical clinics. *Journal of Psychosomatic Research, 71*, 392–394.

Vilchinsky, N., Dekel, R., Leibowitz, M., Reges, O., Khaskia, A., & Mosseri, M. (2011). Dynamics of support perceptions among couples coping with cardiac illness: The effect on recovery outcomes. *Health Psychology, 30*, 411–419.

Warwick, H.M., Clark, D.M., Cobb, A.M., & Salkovskis, P.M. (1996). A controlled trial of cognitive-behavioural treatment of hypochondriasis. *British Journal of Psychiatry, 169*, 189–195.

Warwick, H.M., & Salkovskis, P.M. (1990). Hypochondriasis. *Behaviour Research and Therapy, 28*, 105–117.

Wattar, U., Sorensen, P., Buemann, I., Birket-Smith, M., Salkovskis, P.M., Albertsen, M., & Strange, S. (2005). Outcome of cognitive-behavioural treatment for health anxiety (hypochondriasis) in a routine clinical setting. *Behavioural and Cognitive Psychotherapy, 33*, 165–175.

Weinman, J., Petrie, K.J., Moss Morris, R., & Horne, R. (1996). The illness perception questionnaire: A new method for assessing the cognitive representation of illness. *Psychology & Health, 11*, 431–445.

Yohannes, A.M., Yalfani, A., Doherty, P., & Bundy, C. (2007). Predictors of drop-out from an outpatient cardiac rehabilitation programme. *Clinical Rehabilitation, 21*, 222–229.

Zolnierek, K.B., & DiMatteo, M.R. (2009). Physician communication and patient adherence to treatment: A meta-analysis. *Medical Care, 47*, 826–834.

Chapter 7

Bair, M.J., Robinson, R.L., Katon, W., & Kroenke, K. (2003). Depression and pain comorbidity. *Archives of Internal Medicine, 163*, 2433–2445.

Boothby, J.L., Thorn, B.E., Overduin, L.Y., & Ward, L.C. (2004). Catastrophizing and perceived partner responses to pain. *Pain, 109*, 500–506.

Breau, L.M., Finley, G.A., McGrath, P.J. & Camfield, C.S. (2002). Validation of the non-communicating children's pain checklist—post operative version. *Anesthesiology, 96*, 528–535.

Breivik, H., Collett, B., Ventafridda, V., Cohen, R., & Gallacher, D. (2006). Survey of chronic pain in Europe: Prevalence, impact on daily life, and treatment. *European Journal of Pain 10*, 287–333.

Bruehl, S., & Chung, O.Y. (2004). Interactions between the cardiovascular systems: An updated review of mechanisms and possible alterations in chronic pain. *Neuroscience and Biobehavioral Reviews, 28*, 395–414.

Burckhardt, C.S. (1985). The impact of arthritis on quality of life. *Nursing Research, 34*, 11–18.

Canadian Pain Society (2011). *Call to action: The need for a national pain strategy for Canada*. Toronto: Author.

Chambers, C.T., Craig, K.D., & Bennett, S.M. (2002). The impact of maternal behavior on children's pain experiences: An experimental analysis. *Journal of Pediatric Psychology, 27*, 293–301.

Cimmino, M.A., Ferrone, C., & Cutolo, M. (2011). Epidemiology of chronic musculoskeletal pain. *Best Practice and Research Clinical Rheumatology, 25*, 173–183.

Covic, T., Adamson, B., & Hough, M. (2000). The impact of passive coping on rheumatoid arthritis pain. *Rheumatology, 39*, 1027–1030.

Craig, K.D. (1986). Social modeling influences: Pain in context. In R.A. Sternbach (Ed.), *The psychology of pain* (2nd ed., pp. 67–96). New York: Raven Press.

Craig, K.D., & Weiss, S.M. (1972). Verbal reports of pain without noxious stimulation. *Perceptual and Motor Skills, 34*, 943–948.

Day, M.A., Thorn, B.E., & Burns, J.W. (2012). The continuing evolution of biopsychosocial interventions for chronic. *Journal of Cognitive Psychotherapy, 26*, 114–129.

Dube, A.A., Duquette, M., Roy, M., Lepore, F., Duncan, G., & Rainville, P. (2009). Brain activity associated with the electrodermal reactivity to acute heat pain. *NeuroImage, 45*, 169–180.

Dubuisson, D., & Melzack, R. (1976). Classification of clinical pain descriptions by multiple group discriminant analysis. *Experimental Neurology, 51*, 480–487.

Eccleston, C., Williams, A.C.D.C., & Morley S. (2009). Psychological therapies for the management of chronic pain (excluding headache) in adults. *Cochrane Database of Systematic Reviews*, UK: John Wiley & Sons.

Facco, E., Casiglia, E., Masiero, S., Tikhonoff, V., Giacomello, M., & Zanette, G. (2011). Effects of hypnotic focused analgesia on dental pain threshold. *International Journal of Clinical and Experimental Hypnosis, 59*, 454–68.

Faucett, J.A., & Levine, J.D. (1991). The contributions of interpersonal conflict to chronic pain in the presence or absence of organic pathology. *Pain, 44*, 35–43.

Flor, H., Knost, B., & Birbaumer, N. (2002). The role of operant conditioning in chronic pain: An experimental investigation. *Pain, 95*, 111–118.

Fordyce, W.E. (1976). *Behavioral methods for chronic pain and illness*. St Louis: Mosby.

Fordyce, W.E., Shelton, J.L., & Dundore, D.E. (1982). The modification of avoidance learning pain behaviors. *Journal of Behavioral Medicine, 5*, 405–414.

Fritz, J.M., George, S.Z., & Delitto, A. (2001). The role of fear-avoidance beliefs in acute low back pain: Relationships with current and future disability and work status. *Pain, 94*, 7–15.

Gerrig, R.J., Zimbardo, P.G., Desmarais, S., & Ivanco, T. (2010). *Psychology and life*. Toronto: Pearson.

Guerriere, D.N., Choiniere, M., Dion, D., Peng, P., Stafford-Coyte, E., Zagorski, B., … Ware, M. (2010). The Canadian STOP-PAIN project—Part 2: What is the cost of pain for patients on waitlists of multidisciplinary pain treatment facilities? Canadian Journal of Anesthesia, 57, 549–558.

Gureje, O., Von Korff, M., Simon, G.E., & Gater, R. (1998). Persistent pain and well-being. *Journal of the American Medical Association, 280*, 147–151.

Hadjistavropoulos, H.D., Thompson, M., Ivanov, M., Drost, C., Butz, C.J., Klein, B., & Austin, D.W. (2011). Considerations in the development of a therapist-assisted Internet cognitive behavior therapy service. *Professional Psychology: Research and Practice, 42*, 463–471.

Hadjistavropoulos, T. (1999). Chronic pain on trial: The influence of compensation and litigation on chronic pain syndromes. In A.R. Block, E.F. Kremer, & E. Fernandez (Eds.), *Handbook of pain syndromes: Biopsychosocial perspectives* (pp. 59–76). Mahwah, NJ: Lawrence Erlbaum.

Hadjistavropoulos, T., Breau, L.M., & Craig, K.D. (2011). Assessment of pain in adults and children with limited ability to communicate. In D.C. Turk and R. Melzack (Eds.), *Handbook of pain assessment* (3rd ed., pp. 260–280). New York: Guilford.

Hadjistavropoulos, T., & Craig, K.D. (2002). A theoretical framework for understanding self-report and observational measures of pain: A communications model. *Behaviour Research and Therapy, 40*, 551–570.

Hadjistavropoulos, T., & Craig, K.D. (Eds.). (2004). *Pain: Psychological perspectives*. Mahwah, NJ: Lawrence Erlbaum.

Hadjistavropoulos, T., Craig, K.D., Duck, S., Cano, A., Goubert, L., Jackson, P., … Dever Fitzgerald, T. (2011).

A biopsychosocial formulation of pain communication. *Psychological Bulletin, 137*, 910–939.

Hadjistavropoulos, T., LaChapelle, D., Hale, C., & MacLeod, F. (2000). Age- and appearance-based stereotypes about patients undergoing a painful medical procedure. *Pain Clinic, 12*, 25–34.

Hadjistavropoulos, T., LaChapelle, D., MacLeod, F., Hale, C., O'Rourke, N., & Craig, K.D. (1998). Cognitive functioning and pain reactions in hospitalized elders. *Pain Research and Management, 3*, 145–151.

Hadjistavropoulos, T., McMurtry, B., & Craig, K.D. (1996). Beautiful faces in pain: Biases and accuracy in the perception of pain. *Psychology and Health, 11*, 411–420.

Hadjistavropoulos, T., von Baeyer, C., & Craig, K.D. (2001). Pain assessment in persons with limited ability to communicate. In D.C. Turk and R. Melzack (Eds.), *Handbook of pain assessment* (2nd ed., pp. 134–149). New York: Guilford.

Hale, C., & Hadjistavropoulos, T. (1997). Emotional components of pain. *Pain Research and Management, 2*, 217–225.

Hayes, S.C., & Wilson, K.G. (1994). Acceptance and commitment therapy: Altering the verbal support for experiential avoidance. *Behavior Analyst, 17*, 289–303.

Haythornthwaite, J.A., Clark, M.R., Pappagallo, M., & Raja, S.N. (2003). Pain coping strategies play a role in the persistence of pain in post-herpetic neuralgia. *Pain, 106*, 453–460.

Henschke, N., Ostello, R.W.J.G., val Tulder, M.W., Vlaeyen, J.W.S., Morley, S., Assendelft, W.J.J., & Main, C.J. (2010). Behavioural treatment for chronic low-back pain. *Cochrane Database of Systematic Reviews*, UK: John Wiley & Sons.

Institute of Medicine, Committee on Advancing Pain Research, Care, and Education. (2011). *Relieving pain in America: Blue for transforming prevention, care, education, and research.* Washington: National Academies Press.

Jackson, P.L., Meltzoff, A.N., & Decety, J. (2005). How do we perceive the pain of others? A window into the neural processes involved in empathy. *NeuroImage, 24*, 771–779.

Jackson, P.L., Rainville, P., & Decety, J. (2006). To what extent do we share the pain of others? Insight from the neural bases of pain empathy. *Pain, 125*, 5–9.

Jolliffe, C.D., & Nicholas, M.K. (2004). Verbally reinforcing pain reports: An experimental test of the operant model of chronic pain. *Pain, 107*, 167–175.

Kabat-Zinn, J. (1990). *Full catastrophe living: Using the wisdom of your body and mind to face stress, pain and illness.* New York: Delta.

Kiecolt-Glaser, J.K., Page, G.G., Marucha, P.T., & MacCallum, R.C. (1998). Psychological influences on surgical recovery: Perspectives from psychoneuroimmunology. *American Psychologist, 53*, 1209–1218.

Li, A., Montaño, Z., Chen, V.J., & Gold, J.I. (2011). Virtual reality and pain management: Current trends and future directions. *Pain Management, 1*, 147–157.

Linton, S.J. (2005). Do psychological factors increase the risk for back pain in the general population in both a cross-sectional and prospective analysis? *European Journal of Pain, 9*, 355–361.

Lints-Martindale, A.C., Hadjistavropoulos, T., Lix, L.M., & Thorpe, L. (2012). A comparative investigation of observational pain assessment tools for older adults with dementia. *Clinical Journal of Pain, 28*, 226–237.

Loeser, J.D., & Melzack, R. (1999). Pain: an overview. *Lancet, 353*, 1607–1609.

McCracken, L.M. (2005). Social context and acceptance of chronic pain: The role of solicitous and punishing responses. *Pain, 113*, 155–159.

Macea, D.D., Gajos, K., Daglia Calil, Y.A., & Fregni, F. (2010). The efficacy of web-based cognitive behavioral interventions for chronic pain: A systematic review and meta-analysis. *Journal of Pain, 11*, 917–929.

McGrath, P. (1998). We all failed the Latimers. *Journal of Paediatrics and Child Health, 2*, 153–154.

MacLeod, F., LaChapelle, D., Hadjistavropoulos, T., & Pfeifer, J. (2001). The effect of disability claimants' coping styles on judgments of pain, disability and compensation. *Rehabilitation Psychology, 46*, 417–435.

Melzack, R. (1975). The McGill Pain Questionnaire: Major properties and scoring methods. *Pain, 1*, 277–299.

Melzack, R. (2001). Pain and the neuromatrix in the brain. *Journal of Dental Education, 65*, 1378–1382.

Melzack, R. (2005). Evolution of the neuromatrix theory of pain. The Prithvi Raj lecture: presented at the Third World Congress of World Institute of Pain, Barcelona 2004. *Pain Practice, 5*, 85–94.

Melzack, R., & Casey K.L. (1968). Sensory, motivational and central control determinants of pain. In D.R. Kenshalo (Ed.), *The skin senses* (pp. 423–439). Springfield, Ill.: Charles C. Thomas.

Melzack, R., & Katz, J. (2004). The gate control theory: Reaching for the brain. In T. Hadjistavropoulos & K.D. Craig (Eds.), *Pain: psychological perspectives* (pp. 13–34). Mahwah, NJ: Lawrence Erlbaum.

Melzack, R., Terrence, C., Fromm, G., & Amsel, R. (1986). Trigeminal neuralgia and atypical facial pain: Use of the McGill Pain Questionnaire for discrimination and diagnosis. *Pain, 27*, 297–302.

Melzack, R., & Wall, P.D. (1965). Pain mechanisms: A new theory. *Science, 150*, 971–979.

Melzack, R., & Wall, P.D. (2004). *The challenge of pain.* London: Penguin Global.

Merskey, H., & Bogduk, N. (Eds.). (1994). *Classification of chronic pain: Descriptions of chronic pain syndromes and definitions of pain terms.* Seattle: IASP Press.

Meulders, A., Vansteenwegen, D., & Vlaeyen, J.W.S. (2011). The acquisition of fear of movement-related pain and associative learning: A novel pain-relevant human fear conditioning paradigm. *Pain, 152*, 2460–2469.

Miller, L.R., & Cano, A. (2009). Comorbid chronic pain and depression: Who is at risk? *Journal of Pain, 10*, 619–627.

Morasco, B.J., Corson, K., Turk, D.C., & Dobscha, S.K. (2011). Association between substance use disorder status related function following 12 months of treatment in primary care patients with musculoskeletal pain. *Journal of Pain, 12*, 352–359.

Morley, S., Eccleston, C., & Williams, A. (1999). Systematic review and meta-analysis of randomized controlled trials of cognitive behaviour therapy and behaviour therapy for chronic pain in adults, excluding headache. *Pain, 80*, 1–13.

Moseley, G.L. (2011). A new direction for the fear avoidance model? *Pain, 152*, 2447–2428.

Murphy, S., Creed, F., & Jayson, M.I. (1988). Psychiatric disorder and illness behaviour in rheumatoid arthritis. *British Journal of Rheumatology, 27*, 357–363.

National Center for Health Statistics (2006). *Health, United States, 2006. With chartbook on trends in the health of Americans.* Hyattsville, Md: Author.

Nayak, S., Shiflett, S.C., Eshun, S., & Levine, F.M. (2000). Culture and gender effects in pain beliefs and the prediction of pain tolerance. *Cross-Cultural Research, 34*, 135–151.

Paulsen, J.S., & Altmaier, E.M. (1995). The effects of perceived versus enacted social support on the discriminative cue function of spouses for pain behaviors. *Pain, 60*, 103–110.

Phillips, C.J., & Schopflocher, D. (2008). The economics of chronic pain. In S. Rashiq, D. Schopflocher, P. Taenzer, & E. Jonsson (Eds.), *Chronic pain: A health policy perspective* (pp. 41–50). Weinheim, Germany: Wiley.

Picavet, H.S., Vlaeyen, J.W., & Schouten, J.S. (2002). Pain catastrophizing and kinesiophobia: Predictors of chronic low back pain. *American Journal of Epidemiology, 156*, 1028–1034.

Piva, S.R., Fitzgerald, G.K., Wisniewski, S. & Delitto, A. (2009). Predictors of pain and function outcome in patients with patellofemoral pain syndrome. *Journal of Rehabilitation Medicine, 8*, 604–612.

Price, D.D. (2000). Psychological and neural mechanisms of the affective dimension of pain. *Science, 288*, 1769–1772.

Prkachin, K.M., & Craig, K.D. (1994). Expressing pain: The communication and interpretation of facial pain signals. *Journal of Nonverbal Behavior, 19*, 191–205.

Rainville, P. (2002). Brain mechanisms of pain affect and pain modulation. *Current Opinion in Neurobiology, 12*, 195–204.

Romano, J.M., & Turner, J.A. (1985). Chronic pain and depression: Does the evidence support a relationship? *Psychological Bulletin, 97*, 18–34.

Rosenthal, R. (1982). Conducting judgement studies. In K. Scherer & P. Ekman (Eds.), *Handbook of methods in nonverbal behavior research* (pp. 287–361). New York: Cambridge University Press.

Ruskin, D.A., Amaria, K.A., Warnock, F.F., & McGrath, P.A. (2001). Assessment of pain in infants, children, and adolescents. In D.C. Turk & R. Melzack (Eds.), *Handbook of pain assessment* (3rd ed., pp. 213–241). New York: Guilford Press.

Schopflocher, D., Taenzer, P., & Jovey, R. (2011). The prevalence of chronic pain in Canada. *Pain Research and Management, 16*, 445–450.

Sessle, B. (2011). Unrelieved pain: A crisis. *Pain Research and Management, 16*, 16–20.

Sharp, T.J. (2001). Chronic pain: A reformulation of the cognitive-behavioural model. *Behaviour Research and Therapy, 39*, 787–800.

Skinner, M., Wilson, H.D., & Turk, D.C. (2012). Cognitive-behavioral perspective and cognitive-behavioral therapy for people with chronic pain—Distinctions, outcomes, & innovations. *Journal of Cognitive Psychotherapy, 26*, 93–113.

Stanford, E.A., Chambers, C.T., Biesanz, J.C., & Chen, E. (2008). The frequency, trajectories and predictors of adolescent recurrent pain: A population-based approach. *Pain, 138*, 11–21.

Staud, R., Craggs, J.G., Robinson, M.E., Perlstein, W.M., & Price, D.D. (2007). Brain activity related to temporal summation of c-fibre evoked pain. *Pain, 129*, 130–142.

Sullivan, M.J.L., Bishop, S.R., & Pivik, J. (1995). The pain catastrophizing scale: Development and validation. *Psychological Assessment, 7*, 524–532.

Sullivan, M.J.L., Feuerstein, M., Gatchel, R., Linton, S.J., & Pransky, G. (2005). Integrating psychosocial and behavioral interventions to achieve optimal rehabilitation outcomes. *Journal of Occupational Rehabilitation, 15*, 475–489.

Tsang, A., Von Korff, M., Lee, S., Alonso, J., Karam, E., Angermeyer, M.C., … Watanabe, M. (2008). Common chronic pain conditions in developed and developing countries: Gender and age differences and comorbidity with depression-anxiety disorders. *Journal of Pain, 9*, 883–891.

Turk, D.C., Meichenbaum, D., & Genest, M. (1987). *Pain and behavioral medicine: A cognitive-behavioral perspective.* New York: Guilford Press.

Turk, D.C., & Melzack, R. (2011). The measurement of pain and the assessment of people experiencing pain. In D.C. Turk & R. Melzack (Eds.), *Handbook of pain assessment* (3rd ed., pp. 242–259). New York: Guilford Press.

Turk, D.C., Wilson, H.D., & Cahana, A. (2011). Treatment of chronic non-cancer pain. *Lancet, 377*, 2226–2235.

Turner, R.J., & Noh, S. (1988). Physical disability and depression: A longitudinal analysis. *Journal of Health and Social Behavior, 29*, 23–37.

Veehof, M.M., Oskam, M.J., Schreurs, K.M., & Bohlmeijer, E.T. (2011). Acceptance-based interventions for the treatment of chronic pain: A systematic review and meta-analysis. *Pain, 152*, 533–542.

Vlaeyen, J.W.S., & Linton, S.J. (2000). Fear-avoidance and its consequences in chronic musculoskeletal pain: A state of the art. *Pain, 85*, 317–332.

Waddell, G. (1987). A new clinical model for the treatment of low-back pain. *Spine, 12*, 632–644.

Waddell, G. (1991). Low back disability. A syndrome of Western civilization. *Neurosurgery Clinics of North America, 2*, 719–738.

Waddell, G. (1992). Biopsychosocial analysis of low back pain. *Clinical Rheumatology, 6*, 523–557.

Waddell, G., Newton, M., Henderson, I., Somerville, D., & Main, C.J. (1993). A fear-avoidance beliefs questionnaire (FABQ) and the role of fear-avoidance in chronic low back pain and disability. *Pain, 52*, 157–168.

Chapter 8

Adler, N.E., & Page, A.E.K. (Eds.), Institute of Medicine Committee on Psychosocial Services to Cancer Patients/Families in a Community Setting. (2008). *Cancer care for the whole patient: Meeting psychosocial and health needs.* Washington: National Academies Press.

Ahmed, R.L., Thomas, W., Yee, D., & Schmitz, K.H. (2006). Randomized controlled trial of weight training and lymphedema in breast cancer survivors. *Journal of Clinical Oncology, 24*, 2765–2772.

Altekruse, S.F., Kosary, C.L., Krapcho, M., Neyman, N., Aminou, R., Waldron, W., … & Edwards, B.K. (2010). *SEER cancer statistics review, 1975–2007*. Bethesda, Md: National Cancer Institute.

American Cancer Society (ACS). (2011). *Cancer facts & figures 2011*. Atlanta: ACS.

American Cancer Society (ACS). (2012). *Cancer facts & figures 2012*. Atlanta: ACS.

Andersen, B.L., Farrar, W.B., Golden-Kreutz, D., Kutz, L.A., MacCallum, R., Courtney, M.E., & Glaser, R. (1998). Stress and immune responses after surgical treatment for regional breast cancer. *Journal of the National Cancer Institute, 90*, 30–36.

Ando, M., Morita, T., Akechi, T., & Okamoto, T. (2010). Efficacy of short-term life-review interviews on the spiritual well-being of terminally ill cancer patients. *Journal of Pain and Symptom Management, 39*, 993–1002.

Antoni, M.H., Lutgendorf, S.K., Cole, S.W., Dhabhar, F.S., Sephton, S.E., McDonald, P.G., … Sood, A.K. (2006). The influence of bio-behavioural factors on tumour biology: Pathways and mechanisms. *Nature Reviews Cancer, 6*, 240–248.

Benson, J.R., & Liau, S.-S. (2010). The nature and development of cancer. In D.A. Warrell, T.M. Cox, & J.D. Firth (Eds.), *Oxford textbook of medicine* (5th ed., Vol. 1. pp. 333–357). New York: Oxford.

Bleiker, E.M.A., Hendriks, J.H.C.L., Otten, J.D.M., Verbeek, A.L.M., & van der Ploeg, H.M. (2008). Personality factors and breast cancer risk: A 13-year follow-up. *Journal of the National Cancer Institute, 100*, 213–218.

Booth, C.M., Li, G., Zhang-Salomons, J., & Mackillop, W.J. (2010). The impact of socioeconomic status on stage of cancer at diagnosis and survival. *Cancer, 116*, 4160–4167.

Brett, J., Bankhead, C., Henderson, B., Watson, E., & Austoker, J. (2005). The psychological impact of mammographic screening: A systematic review. *Psycho-Oncology, 14*, 917–938.

Brewer, N.T., Salz, T., & Lillie, S.E. (2007). Systematic review: The long-term effects of false-positive mammograms. *Annals of Internal Medicine, 146*, 502-510. Retrieved from annals.org/article.aspx?volume=146&page=502

Brown, J.C., Huedo-Medina, T.B., Pescatello, L.S., Pescatello, S.M., Ferrer, R.A., & Johnson, B.T. (2011). Efficacy of exercise interventions in modulating cancer-related fatigue among adult cancer survivors: A meta-analysis. *Cancer Epidemiology, Biomarkers & Prevention, 20*, 123–133.

Canadian Cancer Society (CCS), Steering Committee on Cancer Statistics. (2011). *Canadian cancer statistics 2011*. Toronto: CCS.

Canadian Cancer Society (CCS), Steering Committee on Cancer Statistics. (2012a). *Canadian cancer statistics 2012*. Toronto: CCS.

Canadian Cancer Society (CCS). (2012b). General cancer information. In *Canadian cancer encyclopedia*. Retrieved from info.cancer.ca/cce-ecc/default.aspx?Lang=E&toc=1

Canadian Cancer Society (CCS), Steering Committee on Cancer Statistics. (2013). *Canadian cancer statistics 2013*. Toronto: CCS.

Canadian Task Force on Preventive Health Care (CTF). (2011). Recommendations on screening for breast cancer in average-risk women aged 40–74 years. *Canadian Medical Association Journal, 183*, 1991–2001.

Champion, V.L., & Skinner, C.S. (2003). Differences in perceptions of risk, benefits, and barriers by stage of mammography adoption. *Journal of Women's Health, 12*, 277–286.

Chida, Y., Hamer, M., Wardle, J., & Steptoe, A. (2008). Do stress-related psychosocial factors contribute to cancer incidence and survival? *Nature Clinical Practice Oncology, 5*, 466–475.

Classen, C.C., Kraemer, H.C., Blasey, C., Giese-Davis, J., Koopman, C., Palesh, O.G., … Spiegel, D. (2008). Supportive-expressive group therapy for primary breast cancer patients: A randomized prospective multicenter trial. *Psycho-Oncology, 17*, 438–447.

Clegg, L.X., Reichman, M.E., Miller, B.A., Hankey, B.F., Singh, G.K., Dan Lin, Y., … Edwards, B.K. (2009). Impact of socioeconomic status on cancer incidence and stage at diagnosis: Selected findings from the surveillance, epidemiology, and end results: National Longitudinal Mortality Study. *Cancer Causes and Control, 20*, 417–435.

Costanzo, E.S., Lutgendorf, S.K., Sood, A.K., Andersen, B., Sorosky, J., & Lubaroff, D.M. (2005). Psychosocial factors and interleukin-6 among women with advanced ovarian cancer. *Cancer, 104*, 305–313.

Costanzo, E.S., Sood, A.K., & Lutgendorf, S.K. (2011). Biobehavioral influences on cancer progression. *Immunology and Allergy Clinics of North America, 31*, 109–132.

Curtis, E., Quale, C., Haggstrom, D., & Smith-Bindman, R. (2008). Racial and ethnic differences in breast cancer survival: How much is explained by screening, tumor severity, biology, treatment, comordities, and demographics? *Cancer, 112*, 171–180.

De Faye, B.J., Wilson, K.G., Chater, S., Viola, R.A., & Hall, P. (2006). Stress and coping with advanced cancer. *Palliative and Supportive Care, 4*, 239–249.

Dunn, G.P., Koebel, C.M., & Schreiber, R.D. (2006). Interferons, immunity and cancer immunoediting. *Nature Reviews Immunology, 6*, 836–848.

Edelman, S., & Kidman, A.D. (1999). Description of a group cognitive behaviour therapy programme with cancer patients. *Psycho-Oncology, 8*, 306–314.

Engel, G.L. (1977). The need for a new medical model: A challenge for biomedicine. *Science, 196*, 129–136.

Franks, H.M., & Roesche, S.C. (2006). Appraisals and coping in people with cancer: A meta-analysis. *Psycho-Oncology, 15*, 1027–1037.

Glaser, R., & Kiecolt-Glaser, J.K. (2005). Stress-induced immune dysfunction: Implications for health. *Nature Reviews Immunology, 5*, 243–251.

Hart, S.L., Hoyt, M.A., Diefenbach, M., Anderson, D.R., Kilbourn, K.M., Craft, L.L., … Stanton, A.L. (2012). Meta-analysis of efficacy of interventions for elevated depressive symptoms in adults diagnosed with cancer. *Journal of the National Cancer Institute, 104*, 990–1004.

Helgeson, V.S., & Cohen, S. (1996). Social support and adjustment to cancer: Reconciling descriptive, correlational, and intervention research. *Health Psychology, 15*, 135–148.

Holland, J.M., & Gooen-Piels, J. (2003). Psycho-oncology. In D.W. Kufe, R.E. Pollock, R.R. Weichselbaum, et al. (Eds.), *Holland-Frei cancer medicine* (6th ed.). Retrieved from www.ncbi.nlm.nih.gov/books/NBK12537/

Jorgensen, K.J., Keen, J.D., & Gøtzsche, P.C. (2011). Is mammographic screening justifiable considering its substantial overdiagnosis rate and minor effect on mortality? *Radiology, 260*, 621–627.

Kawachi, I., & Kroenke, C. (2006). Socioecomonic disparities in cancer incidence and mortality. In D. Schottenfeld & J.F. Fraumeni, Jr. (Eds.), *Cancer epidemiology and prevention* (3rd ed., pp. 174–188). New York: Oxford University Press.

Keegan, T.H.M., Gomez, S.L., Clarke, C.A., Chan, J.K., & Glaser, S.L. (2007). Recent trends in breast cancer incidence among 6 Asian groups in the Greater Bay Area of Northern California. *International Journal of Cancer, 120*, 1324–1329.

Kolonel, L.N., & Wilkens, L.R. (2006). Migrant studies. In D. Schottenfeld & J.F. Fraumeni, Jr. (Eds.), *Cancer epidemiology and prevention* (3rd ed., pp. 189–201). New York: Oxford University Press.

Kroenke, C.H., Kubzansky, L.D., Schernhammer, E.S., Holmes, M.D., & Kawachi, I. (2006). Social networks, social support, and survival after breast cancer diagnosis. *Journal of Clinical Oncology, 24*, 1105–1111.

Lerner, B.H. (2001). *The breast cancer wars.* New York: Oxford University Press.

Levav, I., Kohn, R., Iscovich, J., Abramson, J.H., Tsai, W.Y., & Vigdorovich, D. (2000). Cancer incidence and survival following bereavement. *American Journal of Public Health, 90*, 1601–1607.

Levin, B., & Prorock, P.C. (2006). Principles of screening. In D. Schottenfeld & J.F. Fraumeni, Jr. (Eds.), *Cancer epidemiology and prevention*, (3rd ed., pp. 1310–1317). New York: Oxford University Press.

Levy, S.M., Heberman, R.B., Whiteside, T., Sanzo, K., Lee, J., & Kirkwood, J. (1990). Perceived social support and tumor estrogen/progesterone receptor status as predictors of natural killer cell activity in breast cancer patients. *Psychosomatic Medicine, 52*, 73–85. Retrieved from www.psychosomaticmedicine.org/content/52/1/73.long

Lillberg, K., Verkasalo, P.K., Kaprio, J., Teppo, L., Helenius, H., & Koskenvuo, M. (2003). Stressful life events and risk of breast cancer in 10,808 women: A cohort study. *American Journal of Epidemiology, 157*, 415–423.

Lutgendorf, S.K., Johnsen, E.L., Cooper, B., Anderson, B., Sorosky, J.I., Buller, R.E., & Sood, A.K. (2002). Vascular endothelial growth factor and social support in patients with ovarian carcinoma. *Cancer, 95*, 808–815.

Lutgendorf, S.K., & Sood, A.K. (2011). Biobehavioral factors and cancer progression physiological pathways and mechanisms. *Psychosomatic Medicine, 73*, 724–730.

Manne, S., Rini, C., Rubin, S., Rosenblum, N., Bergman, C., Edelson, M., … Rocereto, T. (2008). Long-term trajectories of psychological adaptation among women diagnosed with gynecological cancers. *Psychosomatic Medicine, 70*, 677–687.

Massie, M.J. (2004). Prevalence of depression in patients with cancer. *Journal of the National Cancer Institute Monographs, 32*, 57–71.

Matloff, E., & Caplan, A. (2008). Direct to confusion: Lessons learned from marketing BRCA testing. *American Journal of Bioethics, 8*, 5–8.

Miller, S.J., O'Hea, E.L., Block Lerner, J., Moon, S., & Foran-Tuller, K.A. (2011). The relationship between breast cancer anxiety and mammography: Experiential avoidance as a moderator. *Behavioral Medicine, 37*, 113–118.

Moyer, A., Goldenberg, M., Hall, M.A., Knapp-Oliver, S.K., Sohl, S.J., Sarma, E.A., & Schneider, S. (2012). Mediators of change in psychosocial interventions for cancer patients: A systematic review. *Behavioral Medicine, 38*, 90–114.

Moyer, A., Sohl, S.J., Knapp-Oliver, S.K., & Schneider, S. (2009). Characteristics and methodological quality of 25 years of research investigating psychosocial interventions for cancer patients. *Cancer Treatment Reviews, 35*, 475–484.

National Cancer Institute (NCI). (2009, April 29). BRCA1 and BRCA2: Cancer risk and genetic testing. Retrieved from www.cancer.gov/cancertopics/factsheet/Risk/BRCA

National Cancer Institute (NCI). (2012a, February 6). What is cancer? Retrieved from cancer.gov/cancertopics/cancerlibrary/what-is-cancer

National Cancer Institute (NCI). (2012b, January 24). PDQ cancer screening overview (health professional version). Retrieved from www.cancer.gov/cancertopics/pdq/screening/overview/HealthProfessional

National Center for Health Statistics (NCHS). (2012). *Health, United States, 2011 with special feature on socioeconomic status and health.* Hyattsville, Md.

Nelson, H.D., Tyne, K., Naik, A., Bougatsos, C., Chan, B.K., & Humphrey, L. (2009). Screening for breast cancer: An update for the U.S. Preventive Services Task Force. *Annals of Internal Medicine, 151*, 727–737.

Nicholas, D.R., & Veach, T.A. (2000). The psychosocial assessment of the adult cancer patient. *Professional Psychology: Research and Practice, 31*, 206–215.

Ogedegbe, G., Cassells, A.N., Robinson, C.M., DuHamel, K., Tobin, J.N., Sox, C.H., & Dietrich, A.J. (2005). Perceptions of barriers and facilitators of cancer early detection among low-income minority women in community health centers. *Journal of the National Medical Association, 97*, 162–170. Retrieved from www.ncbi.nlm.nih.gov/pmc/articles/PMC2568778/

Palesh, O., Butler, L.D., Koopman, C., Giese-Davis, J., Carlson, R., & Spiegel, D. (2007). Stress history and breast cancer recurrence. *Journal of Psychosomatic Research, 63*, 233–239.

Parkin, D.M., & Bray, F.I. (2006). International patterns of cancer incidence and mortality. In D. Schottenfeld & J.F. Fraumeni, Jr. (Eds), *Cancer epidemiology and prevention* (3rd ed., pp. 101–138). New York: Oxford University Press.

Penninx, B.W.J.H., Guralnik, J.M., & Havlik, R.J. (1998). Chronically depressed mood and cancer risk in older persons. *Journal of the National Cancer Institute, 90*, 1888–1893.

Petticrew, M., Bell, R., & Hunter, D. (2002). Influence of psychological coping on survival and recurrence in people with cancer: A systematic review. *British Medical Journal, 325*, 1–10.

Pinquart, M., & Duberstein, P.R. (2010). Associations of social networks with cancer mortality: A meta-analysis. *Critical Reviews in Oncology/Hematology, 75*, 122–137.

Pinquart, M., Fröhlich, C., & Silbereisen, R.K. (2007). Optimism, pessimism, and change of psychological well-being in cancer patients. *Psychology, Health, & Medicine, 12*, 421–432.

Puetz, T.W., & Herring, M.P. (2012). Differential effects of exercise on cancer-related fatigue during and following treatment: A meta-analysis. *American Journal of Preventive Medicine, 43*, e1–e24.

Rawl, S.M., Champion, V.L., Menon, U., & Foster, J.L. (2000). The impact of age and race on mammography practices. *Health Care for Women International, 21*, 583–597.

Reiche, E.M.V., Nunes, S.O.V., & Morimoto, H.K. (2004). Stress, depression, immune system, and cancer. *Lancet Oncology, 5*, 617–625.

Reynolds, P., Hurley, S., Torres, M., Jackson, J., Boyd, P., & Chen, V.W. (2000). Use of coping strategies and breast cancer survival: Results from the Black/White Cancer Survival Study. *American Journal of Epidemiology, 152*, 940–949.

Reynolds, P., & Kaplan, G.A. (1990). Social connections and risk for cancer: Prospective evidence from the Alameda County study. *Behavioral Medicine, 16*, 101–110.

Rosenbaum, E.H., & Rosenbaum, I.R. (2005). Genetics and cancer. In E.H. Rosenbaum & I. Rosenbaum (Eds.), *Everyone's guide to cancer supportive care: A comprehensive handbook for patients and their families* (pp. 9–15). Kansas City: Andrews McMeel.

Rosenbaum, E.H., Rosenbaum, I.R., Margolis, L., Meyler, T.S., Haas-Kogan, D., Benz, C., & Hawn, M. (2005). Cancer therapy. In E.H. Rosenbaum & I. Rosenbaum (Eds.), *Everyone's guide to cancer supportive care: A comprehensive handbook for patients and their families* (pp. 9–15). Kansas City: Andrews McMeel.

Rosenstock, I.M., Strecher, V.J., & Becker, M.H. (1988). Social learning theory and the Health Belief Model. *Health Education and Behavior, 15*(2), 175–183.

Sarma, E.A. (2013) Barriers to screening mammography. *Health Psychology Review.* doi: 10.1080/17437199.2013.766831

Satin, J.R., Linden, W., & Phillips, M.J. (2009). Depression as a predictor of disease progression and mortality in cancer patients: A meta-analysis. *Cancer, 115*, 5349–5361.

Schneider, S., Moyer, A., Knapp-Oliver, S., Sohl, S., Cannella, D., & Targhetta, V. (2010). Pre-intervention distress moderates the efficacy of psychosocial treatment for cancer patients: A meta-analysis. *Journal of Behavioral Medicine, 33*, 1–14.

Segerstrom, S.C., & Miller, G.E. (2004). Psychological stress and the human immune system: A meta-analytic study of 30 years of inquiry. *Psychological Bulletin, 130*, 601–630.

Shields, M., & Wilkins, K. (2009). An update on mammography use in Canada. *Statistics Canada Health Reports, 20*, 1–13. Retrieved from www5.statcan.gc.ca/access_acces/archive.action?loc=/pub/82-003-x/2009003/article/10873-eng.pdf

Sklar, L.S., & Anisman, H. (1981). Stress and cancer. *Psychological Bulletin, 89*, 369–406.

Spiegel, D., & Giese-Davis, J. (2003). Depression and cancer: Mechanisms and disease progression. *Society of Biological Psychiatry, 54*, 269–282.

Sprehn, G.C., Chambers, J.E., Saykin, A.J., Konski, A., & Johnstone, P.A. (2009). Decreased cancer survival in individuals separated at time of diagnosis: Critical period for cancer pathophysiology? *Cancer, 115*, 5108–5116.

Stanton, A.L., Danoff-Burg, S., Cameron, C.L., Bishop, M., Collins, C.A., Kirk, S.B., ... Twillman, R. (2000). Emotionally expressive coping predicts psychological and physical adjustment to breast cancer. *Journal of Consulting and Clinical Psychology, 68*, 875–882.

Stanton, A.L., Luecken, L.J., Mackinnon, D.P., & Thompson, E.H. (2012). Mechanisms in psychosocial interventions for adults living with cancer: Opportunity for integration of theory, research, and practice. *Journal of Consulting and Clinical Psychology, 81*(2), 318–325.

Statistics Canada. (2011, November 1). Leading causes of death. Retrieved from www.statcan.gc.ca/daily-quotidien/111101/t111101b1-eng.htm

Surveillance Epidemiology and End Results (SEER). (2012). Retrieved from seer.cancer.gov/statfacts/

Swerdlow, A.J., Peto, R., & Doll, R.S. (2010). Epidemiology of cancer. In D.A. Warrell, T.M. Cox, & J.D. Firth (Eds.), *Oxford textbook of medicine* (5th ed., Vol. 1, pp. 299–332). New York: Oxford University Press.

Tamagawa, R., Garland, S., Vaska, M., & Carlson, L.E. (2012). Who benefits from psychosocial interventions in oncology? A systematic review of psychological moderators of treatment outcome. *Journal of Behavioral Medicine.* Advance online publication.

Taylor, S.E., & Lobel, M. (1989). Social comparison activity under threat: Downward evaluation and upward contacts. *Psychological Review, 96*, 569–575.

US Preventive Services Task Force (USPSTF). (2009, December). *Report of the USPSTF onscreening for breast cancer.* Retrieved from www.uspreventiveservicestaskforce.org/uspstf/uspsbrca.htm

van't Spijker, A., Trijsburg, R.W., & Duivenvoorden, H.J. (1997). Psychological sequelae of cancer diagnosis: A meta-analytical review of 58 studies after 1980. *Psychosomatic Medicine, 59*, 280–293. Retrieved from www.psychosomaticmedicine.org/content/59/3/280.long

Watson, M., Haviland, J.S., Greer, S., Davidson, J., & Bliss, J.M. (1999). Influence of psychological response on survival in breast cancer a population-based cohort study. *Lancet, 354*, 1331–1336.

Watson, M., & Kissane, D. (Eds.). (2011). *Handbook of psychotherapy in cancer care.* Hoboken, NJ: John Wiley & Sons.

Wilt, T.J., Brawer, M.K., Jones. K.M., Barry, M.J., Aronson, W.J., Fox, S., ... Wheeler, T. (Prostate Cancer Intervention versus Observation Trial (PIVOT) Study Group). (2012). Radical prostatectomy versus observation for localized prostate cancer. *New England Journal of Medicine, 367*, 203–13.

Wood, J.V., Taylor, S.E., & Lichtman, R.R. (1985). Social comparison in adjustment to breast cancer. *Journal of Personality and Social Psychology, 49*, 1169–1183.

Woods, L.M., Rachet, B., & Coleman, M.P. (2006). Origins of socio-economic inequalities in cancer survival: A review. *Annals of Oncology, 17*, 5–19.

World Health Organization (WHO). (2012). Cancer. Retrieved from www.who.int/cancer/en/

Wortman, C.B., & Dunkel-Schetter, C. (1979). Interpersonal relationships and cancer: A theoretical analysis. *Journal of Social Issues, 35*, 120–155.

Yaffe, M.J., & Mainprize, J.G. (2011). Risk of radiation-induced breast cancer from mammographic screening. *Radiology, 258*, 98–105.

Ziegler, R.G., Hoover, R.N., Pike, M.C., Hildesheim, A., Nomura, A.M.Y., West, D.W., ... Hyer, M.B. (1993). Migration patterns and breast cancer risk in Asian-American women. *Journal of the National Cancer Institute, 85*, 1819–1827.

Chapter 9

Aboa-Éboulé, C., Brisson, C., Blanchette, C., Maunsell, E., Bourbonnais, R., ... Dagenais, G.R. (2011). Effort-reward imbalance at work and psychological distress: A validation study of post-myocardial infarction patients. *Psychosomatic Medicine, 73*, 448–455.

Aboa-Éboulé, C., Brisson, C., & Maunsell, E. (2011). Effort-reward imbalance at work and recurrent coronary heart disease events: A 4-year prospective study of post-myocardial infarction patients. *Psychosomatic Medicine, 73*, 436–447.

Aboa-Éboulé, C., Brisson, C., Maunsell, E., Mâsse, B., Bourbonnais, R., Vézina, M., ... Dagenais, G.R. (2007). Job strain and risk of acute recurrent coronary heart disease events. *Journal of American Medical Association, 298*, 1652–1660.

Agarwal, M., Dalal, A.K., Agarwal, D.K., & Agarwal, R.K. (1995). Positive life orientation and recovery from myocardial infarction. *Social Science & Medicine, 40*, 125–130. Retrieved from www.sciencedirect.com/science/article/pii/0277953694E0058Z

Ahmadi, N., Hajsadeghi, F., Mirshkarlo, H.B., Budoff, M., Yehuda, R., & Ebrahimi, R. (2011). Post-traumatic stress disorder, coronary atherosclerosis, and mortality. *American Journal of Cardiology, 108*, 29–33.

Albert, C.M., Chae, C.V., Rexrode, K.M., Manson, J.E., & Kawachi, I. (2005). Phobic anxiety and risk of coronary heart disease and sudden cardiac death among women. *Circulation, 111*, 480–487.

Aldwin, C.M. (1994). *Stress, coping, and development: An integrative perspective.* New York: Guilford Press.

Alter, D.A., Ko, D.T., Tu, J.V., Stukel, T.A., Lee, D.S., Laupacis, A., ... & Austin, P.C. (2012). The average lifespan of patients discharged from hospital with heart failure. *Journal of General Internal Medicine, 27*, 1171–79.

American Heart Association. (2012). Warning signs of heart attack, stroke & cardiac arrest. Retrieved from www.heart.org/HEARTORG/Conditions/Conditions_UCM_305346_SubHomePage.jsp

Barefoot, J.C., Peterson, B.L., & Harrell, F.E. (1989). Type A behaviour and survival: A follow-up study of 1,467 patients with coronary artery disease. *American Journal of Cardiology, 64*, 427–432.

Barth, J., Schumacher, M., & Herrmann-Lingen, C. (2004). Depression as a risk factor for mortality in patients with coronary heart disease: A meta-analysis. *Psychosomatic Medicine, 66*, 802–813.

Baumeister, H., Hutter, N., & Bengel, J. (2011). Psychological and pharmacological interventions for depression in patients with coronary artery disease. *Cochrane Database of Systematic Reviews*, Issue 9, Art. No.: CD008012.

Berkman, L.F., Blumental, J., Burg, M., Carney, R.M., Catellier, D., Cowan, M.J., ... Schneiderman, N. (2003). Effects of treating depression and low perceived social support on clinical events after myocardial infarction: The Enhancing Recovery in Coronary Heart Disease Patients (ENRICHD) Randomized Trial. *Journal of the American Medical Association, 289*, 3106–3116.

Blumenthal, J.A., Sherwood, A., Babyak, M.A., Babyak, M.A., Watkins, L.L., Waugh, R., Georgiades, A., ... Hinderliter, A. (2005). Effects of exercise and stress management training on markers of cardiovascular risk in patients with ischemic heart disease: A randomized controlled trial. *Journal of the American Medical Association, 293*, 1626–1634.

Blumenthal, J.A., Wang, J.T., Babyak, M., Watkins, L., Kraus, W., Miller, P., ... Sherwood, A. (2010). Enhancing standard cardiac rehabilitation with stress management training: Background, methods, and design for the enhanced study. *Journal of Cardiopulmonary Rehabilitation and Prevention, 30*, 77–84.

Broadwell, S.D., & Light, K.C. (1999). Family support and cardiovascular responses in married couples during conflict and other interactions. *International Journal of Behavioural Medicine, 6*, 40–63.

Bunker, S.J., Colquhoun, D.M., Esler, M.D., Hickie, I.B., Hunt, D., Jelinek, V.M., ... Tennant, C.C. (2003). "Stress" and coronary heart disease: Psychosocial risk factors. *Medical Journal of Australia, 178*, 272–276. Retrieved from: www.mja.com.au/journal/2003/178/6/stress-and-coronary-heart-disease-psychosocial-risk-factors

Burg, M.M., Barefoot, J., Berkman, L., Catellier, D.J., Czajkowski, S., Saab, P., ... Taylor, C.B. (2005). Low perceived social support and post-myocardial infarction prognosis in the enhancing recovery in coronary heart disease clinical trial: The effects of treatment. *Psychosomatic Medicine, 67*, 879–888.

Buselli, E.F., & Stuart, E.M. (1999). Influence of psychosocial factors and biopsychosocial interventions on outcomes after myocardial infarction. *Journal of Cardiovascular Nursing, 13*, 60–72.

Carney, R.M., Blumenthal, J.A., Freedland, K.E., Youngblood, M., Veith, R.C., Burg, M.M., ... Jaffe, A.S. (2004). Depression and later mortality after myocardial infarction in the Enhancing Recovery in Coronary Heart Disease (ENRICHD) study. *Psychosomatic Medicine, 66*, 466–474.

Centers for Disease Control and Prevention (CDC). (2011). Heart disease and stroke prevention. Addressing the nation's leading killers: At a glance 2011. Retrieved from www.cdc.gov/chronicdisease/resources/publications/AAG/dhdsp.htm

Chan, I.W.S., Lai, J.C.L., & Wong, K.W.N. (2006). Resilience is associated with better recovery in Chinese people diagnosed with coronary artery disease. *Psychology & Health, 21*, 335–349.

Chida, Y., & Steptoe, A. (2009). The association of anger and hostility with future coronary heart disease: A meta-analytic review of prospective evidence. *Journal of the American College of Cardiology, 53*, 936–946.

Cossette, S., Frasure-Smith, N., & Lespérance, F. (2001). Clinical implications of a reduction in psychological distress on cardiac prognosis in patients participating in a psychosocial intervention program. *Psychosomatic Medicine, 63*, 257–266. Retrieved from www.psychosomaticmedicine.org/content/63/2/257

Cowan, M.J., Freedland, K.E., Burg, M.M., Saab, P.G., Youngblood, M.E., Cornell, C.E., & Czajkowski, S.M. (2008). Predictors of treatment response for depression and inadequate social support—The ENRICHD randomized clinical trial. *Psychotherapy and Psychosomatics, 77*, 27–37.

Davies, E., Moxham, T.I., Rees, K., Singh, S., Coats, A.S., Ebrahim, S., ... Taylor, R.S. (2010). Exercise training for systolic heart failure: Cochrane systematic review and meta-analysis. *European Journal of Heart Failure, 12,* 706–715.

de Jonge, P., Ormel, J., van den Brink, R.H., van Melle, J.P., Spikerman, T.A., Kuijper, A., ... Schene, A.H. (2006). Symptom dimensions of depression following myocardial infarction and their relationship with somatic health status and cardiovascular prognosis. *American Journal of Psychiatry, 163,* 138–144.

Denollet, J. (2005). DS14: Standard assessment of negative affectivity, social inhibition, and Type D personality. *Psychosomatic Medicine, 67,* 89–97.

Denollet, J., & Brutsaert, D.L. (1998). Personality, disease severity, and the risk of long-term cardiac events in patients with a decreased ejection fraction after myocardial infarction. *Circulation, 97,* 167–173.

de Voogd, J.N., Sanderman, R., & Coyne, J.C. (2012). A meta-analysis of spurious associations between type D personality and cardiovascular disease endpoints. *Annals of Behavioral Medicine, 44,* 136–137.

Dickens, C.M., McGowan, L., Percival, C., Douglas, J., Tomenson, B., Cotter, L., ... Creed, F.H. (2004). Lack of a close confidant, but not depression, predicts further cardiac events after myocardial infarction. *Heart, 90,* 518–522.

Eaker, E.D., Sullivan, L.M., Kelley-Hayes, M., D'Agostino, R.B., & Benjamin, E.J. (2007). Marital status, marital strain, and risk of coronary heart disease of total mortality: The Framingham Offspring Study. *Psychosomatic Medicine, 69,* 509–513.

Feinstein, M., Ning, H., Kang, J., Bertoni, A., Carnethon, M., & Lloyd-Jones, D.M. (2012). Racial differences in risks for first cardiovascular events and noncardiovascular death: The Atherosclerosis Risk in Communities study, the Cardiovascular Health Study, and the Multi-Ethnic Study of Atherosclerosis. *Circulation, 126:* 50–59.

Ferris, P.A, Kline, T.J., & Bourdage, J.S.(2012). He said, she said: Work, biopsychosocial, and lifestyle contributions to coronary heart disease risk. *Health Psychology, 31,* 503–511.

Fiedorowicz, J.G., He, J., & Merikangas, K.R. (2011). The association between mood and anxiety disorders with vascular diseases and risk factors in a nationally representative sample. *Journal of Psychosomatic Research, 70,* 145–154.

Fleet, R., Lavoie, K., & Beitman, B.D. (2000). Is panic disorder associated with coronary artery disease? A critical review of the literature. *Journal of Psychosomatic Research, 48,* 347–356.

Frasure-Smith, N., & Lespérance, F. (2003). Depression and other psychological risks following myocardial infarction. *Archives of General Psychiatry, 60,* 627–636.

Frasure-Smith, N., & Lespérance, F. (2008). Depression and anxiety as predictors of 2-year cardiac events in patients with stable coronary artery disease. *Archives of General Psychiatry, 65,* 62–71.

Frasure-Smith, N., Lespérance, F., & Talajic, M. (1995a). Depression and 18-month prognosis after myocardial infarction. *Circulation, 91,* 999–1005.

Frasure-Smith, N., Lespérance, F., & Talajic, M. (1995b). The impact of negative emotions on prognosis following myocardial infarction: Is it more than depression? *Health Psychology, 14,* 388–398. Retrieved from psycnet.apa.org/journals/hea/14/5/388/

Freedland, K.E., Skala, J.A., Carney, R.M., Raczynski, J.M., Taylor, C.B., Mendes de Leon, C.F., ... Veith, R.C. (2002). The Depression Interview and Structured Hamilton (DISH): Rationale, development, characteristics, and clinical validity. *Psychosomatic Medicine, 64,* 897–905.

Friedman, M., & Rosenman, R.H. (1959). Association of specific overt behaviour pattern with blood and cardiovascular findings: Blood cholesterol level, blood clotting time, incidence of arcussenilis, and clinical coronary artery disease. *Journal of the American Medical Association, 169,* 1286–1296.

Friedmann, E., & Thomas, A. (1995). Pet ownership, social support, and one-year survival after acute myocardial infarction in the cardiac arrhythmia suppression trial (CAST). *American Journal of Cardiology, 76,* 1213–1217.

Gilbody, S., House, A., & Sheldon, T. (2005). Screening and case finding instruments for depression. *Cochrane Database of Systematic Reviews,* Issue 4, Art. No.: CD002792.

Gilbody, S., Sheldon, T., & House, A. (2008). Screening and case-finding instruments for depression: A meta-analysis. *Canadian Medical Association Journal, 178,* 997–1003.

Glassman, A.H., O'Connor, C.M., Califf, R.M., Swedberg, K., Schwartz, P., Bigger, J.T., ... McIvor, M.(2002). Sertraline treatment of major depression in patients with acute MI or unstable angina. *Journal of the American Medical Association, 288,* 701–709.

Goulding, L., Furze, G., & Birks, Y. (2012). Randomized controlled trials of interventions to change maladaptive illness beliefs in people with coronary heart disease: Systematic review. *Journal of Advanced Nursing, 66,* 946–961.

Grace, S.L., Abbey, S.E., Pinto, R., Shnek, Z.M., Irvine, J., & Stewart, D.E. (2005). Longitudinal course of depressive symptomology after a cardiac event: Effects of gender and cardiac rehabilitation. *Psychosomatic Medicine, 67,* 52–58.

Grande, G., Romppel, M., Vesper, J.M., Schubmann, R., Glaesmer, H., & Herrmann-Lingen, C. (2011). Type D personality and all-cause mortality in cardiac patients—Data from a German cohort study. *Psychosomatic Medicine, 73,* 548–556.

Griggs, R.A. (2012). *Psychology: A concise introduction.* New York: Worth.

Gulliksson, M., Burell, G., Vessby, B., Lundin, L., Toss, H., & Svärdsudd, K. (2011). Randomized controlled trial of cognitive behavioural therapy vs. standard treatment to prevent recurrent cardiovascular events in patients with coronary artery disease: Secondary Prevention in Uppsala Primary Health Care project (SUPRIM). *Archives of Internal Medicine, 171,* 134–140.

Haley, W.E., Roth, D.L., Howard, G., & Safford, M.M. (2010). Caregiving strain and estimated risk for stroke and coronary heart disease among spouse caregivers: Differential effects by race and sex. *Stroke, 41,* 331–336.

Haupt, C.M., Alte, D., Dorr, M. Robinson, D.M., Felix, S.B., John, U., & Völzke, H. (2008). The relation of exposure to shift work with atherosclerosis and myocardial infarction in a general population. *Atherosclerosis, 201,* 205–211.

Heart & Stroke Foundation of Canada. (2012). Statistics. Retrieved from www.heartandstroke.com/site/c.ikIQLcM-WJtE/b.3483991/k.34A8/Statistics.htm

Hemingway, H., & Marmot, M. (1999). Evidence-based cardiology: Psychosocial factors in the aetiology and prognosis of coronary artery disease: Systematic review of prospective cohort studies. *British Medical Journal, 318,* 1460–1467. Retrieved from www.ncbi.nlm.nih.gov/pmc/articles/PMC1115843/

Heran, B.S., Chen, J.M., Ebrahim, S., Moxham, T., Oldridge, N., Rees, K., … Taylor, R.S. (2011). Exercise-based cardiac rehabilitation for coronary heart disease. *Cochrane Database of Systematic Reviews,* Issue 7, Article No.: CD001800.

Heron, M.P., Hoyert, D.L., Murphy, S.L., Xu, J.Q., Kochanek, K.D., & Tejada-Vera, B. (2009). Deaths: Final data for 2006. *National Vital Statistics Reports 57*(14). Hyattsville, Md: National Center for Health Statistics.

Herrmann, C., Brand-Driehorst, S., Buss, U., & Ruger, U. (2000). Effects of anxiety and depression on 5-year mortality in 5,057 patients referred for exercise testing. *Journal of Psychosomatic Research, 48,* 455–462.

Honig, A., Kuyper, A.M., Schene, A.H., van Melle, J.P., de Jonge, P., Tulner, D.M., … Ormel, J. (2007). Treatment of post-myocardial infarction depressive disorder: A randomized, placebo-controlled trial with mirtazapine. *Psychosomatic Medicine, 69,* 606–613.

Hunt, S.A., Abraham, W.T., Chin, M.H., Feldman, A.M., Francis, G.S., Ganiats, T.G., … Heart Rhythm Society. (2005). ACC/AHA 2005 guideline update for the adult: A report of the American College of Cardiology/American Heart Association Task Force on Practice Guidelines (Writing Committee to Update the 2001 Guidelines for the Evaluation and Management of Heart Failure): developed in collaboration with the American College of Chest Physicians and the International Society for Heart and Lung Transplantation: endorsed by the Heart Rhythm Society. *Circulation, 112,* e154–e235.

Hunt-Shanks, T., Blanchard, C., Reid, R., Fortier, M., & Cappelli, M. (2010). A psychometric evaluation of the Hospital Anxiety and Depression Scale in cardiac patients: Addressing factor structure and gender invariance. *British Journal Health Psychology, 15,* 97–114.

Johnson, J.L. (1991). Learning to live again: The process of adjustment following a heart attack. In J.M. Morse & J.L. Johnson (Eds.), *The illness experience: Dimensions of suffering.* Newbury Park, Calif.: Sage.

Johnson-Lawrence, V., Kaplan, G., & Galea, S. (2013). Socioeconomic mobility in adulthood and cardiovascular disease mortality. *Annals of Epidemiology,* 167–171. doi: 10.1016/j.annepidem.2013.02.004

Kaprio, J., Koskenvuo, M., & Rita, H. (1987). Mortality after bereavement: A prospective study of 95,647 persons. *American Journal of Public Health, 77,* 283–287.

Karasek, R., & Theorell, T. (1990). *Healthy work: Stress, productivity, and the reconstruction of working life.* New York: Basic Books.

Kario, K., McEwen, B.S., & Pickering, T.G. (2003). Disasters and the heart: A review of the effects of earthquake-induced stress on cardiovascular disease. *Hypertension Research, 26,* 355–367.

Kawachi, I., Colditz, G.A., Ascherio, A., Rimm, E.B., Giovonnucci, E., Stampfer, M.J., & Willett, W.C. (1994). Prospective study of phobic anxiety and risk of coronary heart disease in men. *Circulation, 89,* 1992–1997.

Kawachi, I., Colditz, G.A., Stampfer, M.J., Willett, W.C., Manson, J.E., Speizer, F.E., & Hennekens, C.H. (1995). Prospective study of shift work and risk of coronary heart disease in women. *Circulation, 92,* 3178–3182.

Kessler, R.C., Chiu, W.T., Demler, O., & Walters, E.E. (2005). Prevalence, severity, and comorbidity of twelve-month DSM-IV disorders in the National Comorbidity Survey Replication (NCS-R). *Archives of General Psychiatry, 62,* 617–627.

Kroenke, K., Spitzer, R.L., & Williams, J.B. (2003). The Patient Health Questionnaire-2: Validity of a two-item depression screener. *Medical Care, 32,* 1284–1292.

Kuper, H., Singh-Manoux, A., Siegrist, J., & Marmot, M. (2002). When reciprocity fails: Effort-reward imbalance in relation to coronary heart disease and health functioning within the Whitehall II study. *Occupational Environmental Medicine, 59,* 777–784.

Lane, D., Caroll, D., Ring, C., Beevers, D.G., & Lip, G.Y. (2000). Mortality and quality of life 12 months after myocardial infarction: Effects of depression and anxiety. *Psychosomatic Medicine, 63,* 221–230. Retrieved from www.psychosomaticmedicine.org/content/63/2/221.long

Leedham, B., Meyerowitz, B.E., Muirhead, J., & Frist, W.H. (1995). Positive expectations predict health after heart transplantation. *Health Psychology, 14,* 74–79. Retrieved from psycnet.apa.org/journals/hea/14/1/74/

Leifheit-Limson, E.C., Reid, K.J., Kasl, S.V., Lin, H., Jones, P.G., Buchanan, D.M., … Lichtman, J.H. (2010). The role of social support in health status and depressive symptoms after acute myocardial infarction: Evidence for a stronger relationship among women. *Circulation: Cardiovascular Quality and Outcomes, 3,* 143–150.

Lespérance, F., Frasure-Smith, N., Koszycki, D., Laliberte, M.A., van Zyl, L.T., Baker, B., … Guertin, M.C. (2007). Effects of citalopram and interpersonal psychotherapy on depression in patients with coronary artery disease: The Canadian Cardiac Randomized Evaluation of Antidepressant and Psychotherapy Efficacy (CREATE) trial. *Journal of the American Medical Association, 297,* 367–379.

Lespérance, F., Frasure-Smith, N., Talajic, M., & Bourassa, M.G. (2002). Five-year risk of cardiac mortality in relation to initial severity and one-year changes in depression symptoms after myocardial infarction. *Circulation, 105,* 1049–1053.

Linden, W., Phillips, M.J., & Leclerc, J. (2007). Psychological treatment of cardiac patients: A meta-analysis. *European Heart Journal, 28,* 2972–2984.

Low, C.A., Thurston, R.C., & Matthews, K.A. (2010). Psychosocial factors in the development of heart disease in women: Current research and future directions. *Psychosomatic Medicine, 72,* 842–854.

Martikainen, P., & Valkonen, T. (1996). Mortality after the death of a spouse: Rates and causes of death in a large Finnish cohort. *American Journal of Public Health, 86,* 1087–1093.

Matthews, K.A., Räikkönen, K., Sutton-Tyrrell, K., & Kuller, L.H. (2004). Optimistic attitudes protect against progression of carotid atherosclerosis in healthy middle-aged women. *Psychosomatic Medicine, 66,* 640–644.

Mensah, G.A., Mokdad, A.H., Ford, E.S., Greenlund, K.J., & Croft, J.B. (2005). State of disparities in cardiovascular health in the United States. *Circulation, 111,* 1233–1241.

Milani, R.V., & Lavie, C.J. (2009). Reducing psychosocial stress: A novel mechanism of improving survival from exercise training. *American Journal of Medicine, 122,* 931–938.

Mitchell, P.H., Powell, L., Blumenthal, J., Norten, J., Ironson, G., Pitula, C.R., ... Berkman, L.F. (2003). A short social support measure for patients recovering from myocardial infarction: The ENRICHD Social Support Inventory. *Journal of Cardiopulmonary Rehabilitation, 23,* 398–403.

Moser, D.K., & Dracup, K. (1996). Is anxiety early after myocardial infarction associated with subsequent ischemic and arrhythmic events? *Psychosomatic Medicine, 58,* 395–401. Retrieved from www.psychosomaticmedicine.org/content/58/5/395.long

National Institute of Health (NIH), NHLBI Working Group. (2004). Assessment and treatment of depression in patients with cardiovascular disease." Retrieved from www.nhlbi.nih.gov/meetings/workshops/depression/index.htm

Ormel, J., Von Korff, M., Burger, H., Scott, K., Demyttenaere, K., Huang, Y.Q., ... Kessler, R. (2007). Mental disorders among persons with heart disease—Results from World Mental Health surveys. *General Hospital Psychiatry, 29,* 325–334.

Orth-Gomer, K., Rosengren, A., & Wilhelmsen, L.(1993). Lack of social support and incidence of coronary heart disease in middle-aged Swedish men. *Psychosomatic Medicine, 55,* 37–43. Retrieved from www.psychosomaticmedicine.org/content/55/1/37

Orth-Gomer, K., Wamala, S.P., Horsten, M., Schenck-Gustafsson, K.C., Schneiderman, N., & Mittleman, M.A. (2000). Marital stress worsens prognosis in women with coronary heart disease: The Stockholm Female Coronary Risk Study. *Journal of the American Medical Association, 284,* 3008–3014.

O'Shea, J.C., Wilcox, R.G., Skene, A.M., Stebbins, A.L., Granger, C.B., Armstrong, P.W., ... Ohman, E.M. (2002). Comparison of outcomes of patients with myocardial infarction when living alone versus those not living alone. *American Journal of Cardiology, 90,* 1374–1377. Retrieved from dx.doi.org/10.1016/S0002-9149(02)02876-X

Parker, G.B., Owen, C.A., Brotchie, H.L., & Hyett, M.P. (2010). The impact of differing anxiety disorders on outcome following an acute coronary syndrome: Time to start worrying? *Depression and Anxiety, 27,* 302–309.

Plüss, C.E., Karlsson, M.R., Wallen, N.H., Billing, E., & Held, C. (2008). Effects of an expanded cardiac rehabilitation programme in patients treated for an acute myocardial infarction or a coronary artery by-pass graft operation. *Clinical Rehabilitation, 22,* 306–318.

Prior, P.L., Francis, J., Reitav, J., & Stone, J.A. (2009). Behavioural, psychological and functional issues in cardiovascular disease and cardiac rehabilitation. In J.A. Stone, H.M. Arthur, & N.G. Suskin (Eds.), *Canadian guidelines for cardiac rehabilitation and cardiovascular disease prevention: Translating knowledge into action.* Winnipeg: Canadian Association for Cardiac Rehabilitation.

Public Health Agency of Canada. (2009). 2009 Tracking heart disease and stroke in Canada. Retrieved from www.phac-aspc.gc.ca/publicat/2009/cvd-avc/report-rapport-eng.php

Rodriguez, C.J., Elkind, M.S., Clemow, L., Jin, Z., Di Tullio, M., Sacco, R.L., ... Boden-Albala, B. (2011). Association between social isolation and left ventricular mass. *American Journal of Medicine, 124,* 164–170.

Roger, V.L., Go, A.S., Lloyd-Jones, D.M., Adams, R.J., Berry, J.D., Brown, T.M., ... Wylie-Rosett, J. (2011). Heart disease and stroke statistics--2011update: A report from the American Heart Association. *Circulation, 123,* e18–e209.

Rosengren, A., Hawken, S, Ounpuu, S., Sliwa, K., Zubaid, M., Almahmeed, W.A., ... Yusuf, S. (2004). Association of psychosocial risk factors with risk of myocardial infarction in 11119 cases and 13648 controls from 52 countries (the INTERHEART study: Case control study). *Lancet, 364,* 953–962.

Roth, D.L., Perkins, M., Wadley, V.G., Temple, E., & Haley, W.E. (2009). Family caregiving and emotional strain: Associations with psychological health in a national sample of community-dwelling middle-aged and older adults. *Quality of Life Research, 18,* 679–688. Retrieved from www.ncbi.nlm.nih.gov/pmc/articles/PMC2855243/

Rozanski, A., Bairey, C.N., Krantz, D.S., Friedman, J., Resser, K.J., Morell, M., ... Berman, D.S. (1988). Mental stress and the induction of silent myocardial ischemia in patients with coronary artery disease. *New England Journal of Medicine, 318,* 1005–1012.

Rozanski, A., Blumenthal, J.A., & Davidson, K.W. (2005) The epidemiology, pathophysiology, and management of psychosocial risk factors in cardiac practice: The emerging field of behavioural cardiology. *Journal of the American College of Cardiology, 45,* 637–651.

Rozanski, A., Blumenthal, J.A., & Kaplan, J. (1999). Impact of psychological factors on the pathogenesis of cardiovascular disease and implication for therapy. *Circulation, 99,* 2192–2217.

Rozanski, A., & Kubzansky, L.D. (2005). Psychologic functioning and physical health: A paradigm of flexibility. *Psychosomatic Medicine, 67,* S47–S53.

Rugulies, R. (2002). Depression as a predictor for coronary heart disease: A review and meta-analysis. *American Journal of Preventive Medicine, 23,* 51–61. Retrieved from www.sciencedirect.com/science/article/pii/S0749379702004397

Ryan, T.J., Anderson, J.L., Antman, E.M., Braniff, B.A., Brooks, N.H., Califf, R.M., ... Weaver, D. (1996). ACC/AHA guidelines for the management of patients with acute myocardial infarction: Executive summary. A report of the American College of Cardiology/American Heart Association Task Force on Practice Guidelines (Committee on Management of Acute Myocardial Infarction). *Circulation, 94,* 2341–2350.

Scheier, M.F., Matthews, K.A., Owens, J.F., Schulz, R., Bridges, M.W., Magovern, G.J., & Carver, C.S. (1999). Optimism and rehospitalization after coronary artery bypass surgery. *Archives of Internal Medicine, 159,* 829–835.

Schmaltz, H.N., Southern, D., Ghali, W.A., Jelinski, S.E., Parsons, G.A., King, K.M., & Maxwell, C.J. (2007). Living alone, patient sex and mortality after acute myocardial infarction. *Society of General Internal Medicine, 22,* 572–578.

Shankar, A., McMunn, A., Banks, J., & Steptoe, A. (2011). Loneliness, social isolation, and behavioural and biological health indicators in older adults. *Health Psychology, 30*, 377–385.

Siegrist, J. (2010). Effort-reward imbalance at work and cardiovascular disease. *International Journal of Occupational Medicine and Environmental Health, 23*, 279–285.

Siegrist, J., Starke, D., Chandola, T., Gordon, I., Marmot, M., Niedhammer, I., & Peter, R. (2004). The measurement of effort-reward imbalance at work: European comparisons. *Social Science &Medicine, 58*, 1483–1499.

Simon, G.E., & Von Korff, M. (2006). Medical co-morbidity and validity of DSM-IV depression criteria. *PsychologicalMedicine, 36*, 27–36.

Smith, T., & Ruiz, J. (2002). Psychosocial influences on the development and course of coronary heart disease: Current status and implications for research and practice. *Journal of Consulting and Clinical Psychology, 70*, 548–568.

Smith, T.W., Uchino, B.N., Berg, C.A., Florsheim, P., Pearce, G., Hawkins, M., … Olsen-Cerny, C. (2009). Conflict and collaboration in middle-aged and older couples: II. Cardiovascular reactivity during marital interaction. *Psychological Aging, 24*, 274–286.

Statistics Canada. (2011). Mortality, summary list of causes (2008 numbers: CVD).

Stone, J.A., & Mancini, G.M.J. (2009). The pathophysiology of atherosclerosis and cardiovascular disease. In J.A. Stone, H.M. Arthur, & N.G. Suskin (Eds.), *Canadian guidelines for cardiac rehabilitation and cardiovascular disease prevention: Translating knowledge into action*. Winnipeg: Canadian Association for Cardiac Rehabilitation.

Strik, J.J., Denollet, J., Lousberg, R., & Honig, A. (2003). Comparing symptoms of depression and anxiety as predictors of cardiac events and increased health care consumption after myocardial infarction. *Journal of the American College of Cardiology, 42*, 1801–1807.

Tedeschi, R.G., Park, C.L., & Calhoun, L.G. (1998). Posttraumatic growth: Positive change in the aftermath of crisis. Mahwah, NJ: Lawrence Erlbaum.

Thombs, B.D., Bass, E.B., Ford, D.E., Stewart, K.J., Tsilidis, K.K., Patel, U., … Ziegelstein, R.C. (2006). Prevalence of depression in survivors of acute myocardial infarction. *Journal General Internal Medicine, 21*, 30–38.

Thombs, B.D., de Jonge, P., Coyne, J.C., Whooley, M.A., Frasure-Smith, N., Mitchell, A.J., … Ziegelstein, R.C. (2008). Depression screening and patient outcomes in cardiovascular care: A systematic review. *Journal of the American Heart Association, 300*, 2161–2171.

Todaro, J.F., Shen, B.J., Raffia, S.D., Tilkemeir, P.L., & Niaura, R. (2007). Prevalence of anxiety disorders in men and women with established coronary artery disease. *Journal of Cardiopulmonary Rehabilitation and Prevention, 27*, 86–91.

Vaglio, J., Conard, M., Poston, W., O'Keefe, J., Haddock, K., House, J., & Spertus, J.A. (2004). Testing the performance of the ENRICHD Social Support Instrument in cardiac patients. *Health & Quality of Life Outcomes, 2*, 24–29.

Van der Kooy, K., van Hout, H., Marwijk, H., Marten, H., Stewouwer, C., & Beekman, A. (2007). Depression and the risk for cardiovascular diseases: A systematic review and meta-analysis. *International Journal of Geriatric Psychiatry, 22*, 613–626.

van Harten, A.E., Scheeren, T.W, & Absalom, A.R. (2012). A review of postoperative cognitive dysfunction and neuroinflammation associated with cardiac surgery and anaesthesia. *Anaesthesia, 67*, 280–293.

van Melle, J.P., de Jonge, P., Spijkerman, T.A., Tijssen, J.G., Ormel, J., van Veldhuisen, D.J., … van den Berg, M.P. (2004). Prognostic association of depression following myocardial infarction with mortality and cardiovascular events: A meta-analysis. *Psychosomatic Medicine, 66*, 814–822.

Watkins, L.L., Blumenthal, J.A., Davidson, J.R., Babyak, M.A., McCants, C.B., & Sketch, M.H. (2006). Phobic anxiety, depression, and risk of ventricular arrhythmias in patients with coronary heart disease. *Psychosomatic Medicine, 68*, 651–656.

Wulsin, L., & Singal, B. (2003). Do depressive symptoms increase the risk for the onset of coronary disease? A systematic quantitative review. *Psychosomatic Medicine, 65*, 201–210.

Yohannes, A.M., Doherty, P., Bundy, C., & Yalfani, A. (2010). The long-term benefits of cardiac rehabilitation on depression, anxiety, physical activity and quality of life. *Journal of Clinical Nursing, 19*, 2806–2813.

Zen, A.L., Whooley, M.A., Zhao, S., & Cohen, B.E. (2012). Post-traumatic stress disorder is associated with poor health behaviors: Findings from the heart and soul study. *Health Psychology, 31*, 194–201.

Ziegelstein, R.C., Thombs, B.D., Coyne, J.C., & de Jonge, P. (2009). Routine screening for depression in patients with coronary heart disease never mind. *Journal of the American College of Cardiology, 54*, 886–890.

Chapter 10

Ahmad, L.A., & Crandall, J.P. (2010). Type 2 diabetes prevention: A review. *Clinical Diabetes, 28*, 53–59.

Åkerblom, H.K., Vaarala, O., Hyöty, H., Ilonen, J., & Knip, M. (2002). Environmental factors in the etiology of type 1 diabetes. *American Journal of Medical Genetics, 115*, 18–29.

American Diabetes Association (ADA). (2009). *Toolkit no. 2: All about insulin resistance*. Retrieved from professional.diabetes.org/admin/UserFiles/file/Reducing%20 Cardiometabolic%20Risk_%20Patient%20 Education%20Toolkit/English/ADA%20CMR%20 Toolkit_2Insulin.pdf

American Diabetes Association (ADA). (2012). Clinical practice recommendations. *Diabetes Care, 35*(Suppl. 1), S1–E113.

American Diabetes Association. (n.d.). *Genetics of diabetes*. Retrieved from www.diabetes.org/diabetes-basics/genetics-of-diabetes.html

Anderson, B.J., Vangsness, L., Connell, A., Butler, D., Goebel-Fabbri, A., & Laffel, M.B. (2002). Family conflict, adherence, and glycaemic control in youth with short duration type 1 diabetes. *Diabetic Medicine, 19*, 635–642.

Anderson, R.J., Freedland, K.E., Clouse, R.E., & Lustman, P.J. (2001). The prevalence of comorbid depression in adults with diabetes: A meta-analysis. *Diabetes Care, 24*, 1069–1078.

Beckman, J.A., Creager, M.A., & Libby, P. (2002). Diabetes and atherosclerosis: Epidemiology, pathophysiology, and management. *Journal of the American Medical Association, 287*, 2570–2581.

Bennett, W.L., Maruthur, N.M., Singh, S., Segal, J.B., Wilson, L.M., Chatterjee, R., … Bolen, S. (2011). Comparative effectiveness and safety of medications for type 2 diabetes: An update including new drugs and 2-drug combinations. *Annals of Internal Medicine, 154*(9): 602–13.

Black, P.H. (2003). The inflammatory response is an integral part of the stress response: Implications for atherosclerosis, insulin resistance, type II diabetes and metabolic syndrome X. *Brain, Behavior, and Immunity, 17*, 350–364.

Buchwald, H., Estok, R., Fahrbach, K., Banel, D., Jensen, M.D., Pories, W.J., … Sledge, I. (2009). Weight and type 2 diabetes after bariatric surgery: Systematic review and meta-analysis. *American Journal of Medicine, 122*, 248–256.

Bykowski, C.A., Sacco, W.P., & Mayhew, L. (2009). The effect of psychological interventions on glycemic control in diabetics: A meta-analysis. Presented at the annual meeting of the American Psychosomatic Society, March, Chicago. (citation poster).

Canadian Diabetes Association Clinical Practice Guidelines Expert Committee. (2008). Canadian Diabetes Association 2008 clinical practice guidelines for the prevention and management of diabetes in Canada. *Canadian Journal of Diabetes, 32*, S1–S201.

Canadian Diabetes Association (CDA) & Diabetes Quebec. (2011). Diabetes: Canada at the tipping point—Charting a new path. Retrieved from www.diabetes.ca/documents/get-involved/WEB_Eng.CDA_Report_pdf

Cardona-Morrell, M., Rychetnik, L. Morrell, S.L., Espinel, P.T., & Bauman, A. (2010). Reduction of diabetes risk in routine clinical practice: Are physical activity and nutrition interventions feasible and are the outcomes from reference trials replicable? A systematic review and meta-analysis. *BMC Public Health, 10*, 653–669.

Centers for Disease Control and Prevention (CDC). (2011). *National diabetes fact sheet: National estimates and general information on diabetes and prediabetes in the United States, 2011*. Atlanta.

Centers for Disease Control and Prevention, National Center for Health Statistics, Division of Health Interview Statistics (CDC). (2012). *Crude and age-adjusted percentage of civilian, noninstitutionalized adults with diagnosed diabetes, United States, 1980–2010*. Retrieved from www.cdc.gov/diabetes/statistics/prev/national/figage.htm

Charmandari, E., Tsigos, C., & Chrousos G. (2005). Endocrinology of the stress response. *Annual Review of Physiology, 67*, 259–284.

Ciechanowski, P.S., Katon, W.J., & Russo, J.E. (2000). Depression and diabetes: Impact of depressive symptoms on adherence, function, and costs. *Archives of Internal Medicine, 160*, 3278–3285.

Cochran, J., & Conn, V.S. (2008). Meta-analysis of quality of life outcomes following diabetes self-management training. *Diabetes Educator, 34*, 815–823.

Collins, M.M., Corcoran, P., & Perry, I.J. (2009). Anxiety and depression symptoms in patients with diabetes. *Diabetic Medicine, 26*, 153–161.

Deakin, T., McShane, C.E., Cade, J.E., & Williams, R.D. (2005). Group-based training for self-management strategies in people with type 2 diabetes mellitus. *Cochrane Database of Systematic Reviews, 18*, 1–88.

de Groot, M., Anderson, R., Freedland, K.E., Clouse, R.E., & Lustman, P.J. (2001). Association of depression and diabetes complications: A meta-analysis. *Psychosomatic Medicine, 63*, 619–630.

Delamater, A.M. (2006). Improving patient adherence. *Clinical Diabetes, 24*, 71–77.

Diabetes Prevention Program Research Group (DPRG). (2002). Reduction in the incidence of type 2 diabetes with lifestyle intervention or metformin. *New England Journal of Medicine, 46*, 393–403.

Diabetes Prevention Program Research Group (DPRG). (2009). 10-year follow-up of diabetes incidence and weight loss in the Diabetes Prevention Program Outcomes Study. *Lancet, 374*, 1677–1686.

Duangdao, K.M., & Roesch, S.C. (2008). Coping with diabetes in adulthood: A meta-analysis. *Journal of Behavioral Medicine, 31*, 291–300.

D'Zurilla, T.J., & Nezu, A.M. (2010). Problem-solving therapy. In K.S. Dobson (Ed.), *Handbook of cognitive-behavioral therapies* (3rd ed., pp. 197–225). New York: Guilford Press.

Egede, L.E., Nietert, P.J., & Zheng, D. (2005). Depression and all-cause and coronary heart disease mortality among adults with and without diabetes. *Diabetes Care 28*, 1339–1345.

Farmer, A.J., Perera, R., Ward, A., Heneghan, C., Oke, J., Barnett, A.H., … O'Malley, S. (2012). Meta-analysis of individual patient data in randomised trials of self monitoring of blood glucose in people with non-insulin treated type 2 diabetes. *British Medical Journal, 344*, e486.

Fisher, E.B., Thorpe, C.T., DeVellis, B.M., & DeVellis, R.F. (2007). Healthy coping, negative emotions, and diabetes management: A systematic review and appraisal. *Diabetes Educator, 33*, 1080–1103.

Florez, J.C., Hirschhorn, J., & Altshuler, D. (2003). The inherited basis of diabetes mellitus: Implications for the genetic analysis of complex traits. *Annual Review of Genomics and Human Genetics, 4*, 257–291.

Frier, B.M. (2009). The incidence and impact of hypoglycemia in type 1 and type 2 diabetes. *International Diabetes Monitor, 21*, 210–218.

Gherman, A., Schur, J., Montgomery, G., Sassu, R., Veresiu, I., & David, D. (2011). How are adherent people more likely to think? A meta-analysis of health beliefs and diabetes self-care. *Diabetes Educator, 37*, 392–408.

Glasgow, R.E., McKay, H.G., Piette, J.D., & Reynolds, K.D. (2001). The RE-AIM framework for evaluating interventions: What can it tell us about approaches to chronic illness management? *Patient Education and Counseling, 44*, 119–127.

Golden, S.H., Lazo, M., Carnethon, M., Bertoni, A.G., Schreiner, P.J., Roux, A.V.D., … Lyketsos, C. (2008). Examining a bidirectional association between depressive symptoms and diabetes. *Journal of the American Medical Association, 299*, 2751–2759.

Gollwitzer, P.M., & Sheeran, P. (2006). Implementation intentions and goal achievement: A meta-analysis of effects and processes. *Advances in Experimental Social Psychology, 38*, 69–119.

Graue, M., Wentzel-Larsen, T., Bru, E., Hanestad, B.R., & Søvik, O. (2004). The coping styles of adolescents with type 1 diabetes are associated with degree of metabolic control. *Diabetes Care, 27*, 1313–1317.

Harris, M.I. (2001). Frequency of blood glucose monitoring in relation to glycemic control in patients with type 2 diabetes. *Diabetes Care, 24*, 979–982.

Harvey, J.N., & Lawson, V.L. (2009). The importance of health belief models in determining self-care behaviour in diabetes. *Diabetic Medicine, 26*, 5–13.

Henry, J.L., Wilson, P.H., Bruce, D.G., Chisholm, D.J., & Rawling, P.J. (1997). Cognitive-behavioural stress management for patients with non-insulin dependent diabetes mellitus. *Psychology, Health & Medicine, 2*, 109–118.

Hettema, H., Steele, J., & Miller, W.R. (2005). Motivational interviewing. *Annual Review of Clinical Psychology, 1*, 91–111.

Hopper, I., Billah, B., Skiba, M., & Krum, H. (2011). Prevention of diabetes and reduction in major cardiovascular events in studies of subjects with prediabetes: A meta-analysis of randomized controlled clinical trials. *European Journal of Cardiovascular Prevention & Rehabilitation, 18*, 813–823.

Inzucchi, S.E., Bergenstal, R.M., Buse, J.B., Diamant, M., Ferrannini, E., Nauck, M., ... Matthews, D.R. (2012). Management of hyperglycemia in type 2 diabetes: A patient-centered approach: Position statement of the American Diabetes Association (ADA) and the European Association for the Study of Diabetes (EASD). *Diabetes Care, 35*, 1364–1379.

Ismail, K., Winkley, K., & Rabe-Hesketh, S. (2004). Systematic review and meta-analysis of randomised controlled trials of psychological interventions to improve glycaemic control in patients with type 2 diabetes. *Lancet, 363*, 1589–1597.

JDRF. (2011, December). General diabetes facts, 2012. Retrieved from www.jdrf.org/index.cfm?page_id=102586

Katon, W.J., Russo, J.E., Heckbert, S.R., Lin, E.H.B., Ciechanowski, P., Ludman, E., ... Von Korff, M. (2010). The relationship between changes in depression symptoms and changes in health risk behaviors in patients with diabetes. *International Journal of Geriatric Psychiatry, 25*, 466–475.

Kenardy, J., Mensch, M., Bowen, K., Green, B., Walton, J., & Dalton, M. (2001). Disordered eating behaviours in women with type 2 diabetes mellitus. *Eating Behaviors, 2*, 183–192.

Knol, M.J., Heerdink, E.R., Egberts, A.C.G., Geerlings, M.I., Gorter, K.J., Numans, M.E., ... Burger, H. (2007). Depressive symptoms in subjects with diagnosed and undiagnosed type 2 diabetes. *Psychosomatic Medicine, 69*, 300–305.

Knol, M.J., Twisk, J.W.R., Beekman, A.T.F., Heine, R.J., Snoek, F.J., & Pouwer, F. (2006). Depression as a risk factor for the onset of type 2 diabetes mellitus. A meta-analysis. *Diabetolgia, 49*, 837–845.

Koro, C.E., Bowlin, S.J., Bourgeois, N., & Fedder, D.O. (2004). Glycemic control from 1988 to 2000 among U.S. adults diagnosed with type 2 diabetes: A preliminary report. *Diabetes Care, 27*, 17–20.

Li, C., Barker, L., Ford, E.S., Zhang, X., Strine, T.W., & Mokdad, A.H. (2008). Diabetes and anxiety in US adults: Findings from the 2006 Behavioral Risk Factor Surveillance System. *Diabetic Medicine, 25*, 878–881.

Li, Y., Qi, Q., Workalemahu, T., Hu, F.B., & Qi, L. (2012). Birth weight, genetic susceptibility, and adulthood risk of type 2 diabetes. *Diabetes Care, 35*, 2479–2484.

Lipska, K.J., Warton, E.M., Huang, E.S., Moffet, H.H., Inzucchi, S.E., Krumholz, H.M., & Karter, A.J. (2013). HbA1c and risk of severe hypoglycemia in type 2 diabetes: The Diabetes and Aging Study. *Diabetes Care, 36*, 3535–3542.

McCowen, K.C., Malhorta, A., & Bistrian, B.R. (2001). Stress-induced hyperglycemia. *Critical Care Clinics, 17*, 107–124.

Manzoni, G.M., Pagnini, F., Castelnuovo, G., & Molinari, E. (2008). Relaxation training for anxiety: A ten-year systematic review with meta-analysis. *BMC Psychiatry, 8*.

Martin, A.L. (2012). Changes and consistencies over five years: Results of the 2010 national diabetes education practice survey. *Diabetes Educator, 38*, 35–46.

Martins, R.K., & McNeil, D.W. (2009). Review of Motivational Interviewing in promoting health behaviors. *Clinical Psychology Review, 29*, 283–293.

May, A.L., Kuklina, E.V., & Yoon, P.W. (2012). Prevalence of cardiovascular disease risk factors among US adolescents, 1999–2008. *Pediatrics, 129*, 1035–1041.

MedlinePlus. (2012, April 2). Endocrine diseases Retrieved from www.nlm.nih.gov/medlineplus/endocrinediseases.html

Mezuk, B., Eaton, W.W., Albrecht, S., & Golden, S.H. (2008). Depression and type 2 diabetes over the lifespan: A meta-analysis. *Diabetes Care, 31*, 2383–2390.

Miller, W.R., & Rose, G.S. (2009). Toward a theory of Motivational Interviewing. *American Psychologist, 64*, 527–537.

Mokdad, A.H., Bowman, B.A., Ford, E.S., Vinicor, F., Marks, J.S., & Koplan, J.P. (2001). The continuing epidemics of obesity and diabetes in the United States. *Journal of the American Medical Association, 286*, 1195–1200.

Nathan, D.M. (1993). Long-term complications of diabetes mellitus. *New England Journal of Medicine, 328*, 1676–1685.

Norris, S.L., Lau, J., Smith, S.J., Schmid, C. H., & Engelgau, M.M. (2002). Self-management education for adults with type 2 diabetes: A meta-analysis of the effect on glycemic control. *Diabetes Care, 25*, 1159–1171.

Padgett, D.A., & Glaser, R. (2003). How stress influences the immune response. *TRENDS in Immunology, 24*, 444–448.

Pan, A., Lucas, M., Sun, Q., van Dam, R.M., Franco, O.H., Manson, J.E., ... Hu, F.B. (2010). Bidirectional association between depression and type 2 diabetes mellitus in women. *Archives of Internal Medicine, 170*, 1884–1891.

Peng, H., & Hagopian, W. (2006). Environmental factors in the development of type 1 diabetes. *Reviews in Endocrine and Metabolic Disorders, 7*, 149–162.

Peyrot, M.F., & McMurry, J.F. (1992). Stress buffering and glycemic control. *Diabetes Care, 15*, 842–846.

Peyrot, M., McMurry, J.F., & Kruger, D. F. (1999). A biopsychosocial model of glycemic control in diabetes: Stress, coping, and regimen adherence. *Journal of Health and Social Behavior, 40*(2), 141–158.

Peyrot, M., & Rubin, R.R. (2007). Behavioral and psychosocial interventions in diabetes. *Diabetes Care, 30*, 2433–2440.

Peyrot, M., Rubin, R.R., Lauritzen, T., Snoek, F.J., Matthews, D.R., & Skovlund, S.E. (2005). Psychosocial problems and barriers to improved diabetes management: Results of the cross-national Diabetes Attitudes, Wishes, and Needs study. *Diabetic Medicine, 22*, 1379–1385.

Public Health Agency of Canada (PHAC). (2009). Report from the National Diabetes Surveillance System: Diabetes in Canada, 2009. Retrieved from www.phac-aspc.gc.ca/publicat/2009/ndssdic-snsddac-09/index-eng.php

Public Health Agency of Canada (PHAC). (2011). Diabetes in Canada: Facts and figures from a public health perspective.

Rabi, D.M., Edwards, A.L., Southern, D.A., Svenson, L.W., Sargious, P.M., Norton, P., ... Ghali, W.A. (2006). Association of socio-economic status with diabetes prevalence and utilization of diabetes care services. *BMC Health Services Research, 6*(1), 124–130.

Renn, B.N., Feliciano, L., & Segal, D.L. (2011). The bidirectional relationship of depression and diabetes: A systematic review. *Clinical Psychology Review, 31*, 1239–1246.

Resnicow, K.D., Dilorio, C., Soet, J.E., Borrelli, B.H., Hecht, J., & Ernst, D. (2002). Motivational Interviewing in health promotion: It sounds like something is changing. *Health Psychology, 21*, 444–451.

Rosenstock, I.M., Strecher, V.J., & Becker, M.H. (1988). Social learning theory and the health belief model. *Health Education & Behavior, 15*, 175–183.

Rosmond, R. (2005). Role of stress in the pathogenesis of the metabolic syndrome. *Psychoneuroendocrinology, 30*, 1–10.

Ruzic, L., Sporis, G., & Matkovic, B.R. (2008). High volume-low intensity exercise camp and glycemic control in diabetic children. *Journal of Paediatrics and Child Health, 44*, 122–128.

Sacco, W.P., & Beck, A.T. (1995). Cognitive theory and therapy. In E.E. Beckham & W.R. Leber (Eds.), *Handbook of depression* (2nd ed., pp. 329–351). New York: Guilford Press.

Sacco, W.P., & Bykowski, C.A. (2010). Depression and hemoglobin A1c in type 1 and type 2 diabetes: The role of self-efficacy. *Diabetes Research and Clinical Practice, 90*, 141–146.

Sacco, W.P., Malone, J.I., Morrison, A.D., Friedman, A.L., & Wells, K.J. (2009). Effect of a brief, regular telephone intervention by paraprofessionals for type 2 diabetes. *Journal of Behavioral Medicine, 32*, 349–359.

Sacco, W.P., Wells, K.J., Friedman, A., Matthew, R., Perez, S., & Vaughan, C.A. (2007). Adherence, body mass index, and depression in adults with type 2 diabetes: The mediational role of diabetes symptoms and self-efficacy. *Health Psychology, 26*, 693–700.

Saydah, S., & Lochner, K. (2010). Socioeconomic status and risk of diabetes-related mortality in the U.S. *Public Health Reports, 125*(3), 377–388.

SEARCH for Diabetes in Youth Study Group. (2006). The burden of diabetes mellitus among US youth: Prevalence estimates from the SEARCH for diabetes in youth study. *Pediatrics, 118*, 1510–1518.

Shaw, J.E., Sicree, R.A., & Zimmet, P.Z. (2010). Global estimates of the prevalence of diabetes for 2010 and 2030. *Diabetes Research and Clinical Practice, 87*, 4–14.

Snoek, F.J., Kersch, N.Y., Eldrup, E., Harman-Boehm, I., Hermanns, N., Kokoszka, A., ... Skovlund, S.E. (2011). Monitoring of individual needs in diabetes (MIND): Baseline data from the Cross-National Diabetes Attitudes, Wishes, and Needs (DAWN) MIND study. *Diabetes Care, 34*(3): 601–603.

Spitzer, R., Kroenke, K., & Williams, J. (1999). Validation and utility of a self-report version of PRIME-MD: The PHQ Primary Care Study. *Journal of the American Medical Association, 282*, 1737–1744.

Stetler, C., & Miller, G.E. (2011). Depression and hypothalamic-pituitary-adrenal activation: A quantitative summary of four decades of research. *Psychosomatic Medicine, 73*, 114–126.

Statistics Canada. (2010). Canadian Community Health Survey, 2010. Retrieved from www.statcan.gc.ca/pub/82-625-x/2011001/article/11459-eng.htm

Strom, J.L., & Egede, L.E. (2012). The impact of social support on outcomes in adult patients with type 2 diabetes: A systematic review. *Current Diabetes Reports, 12*, 1–13.

Suh, S., & Kim, K. (2011). Diabetes and cancer: Is diabetes causally related to cancer? *Diabetes and Metabolism Journal, 35*, 193–198.

TODAY Study Group (2012). A clinical trial to maintain glycemic control in youth with type 2 diabetes. *New England Journal of Medicine, 366*, 2247–2256.

Tsigos, C., & Chrousos, G.P. (2002). Hypothalamic-pituitary-adrenal axis, neuroendocrine factors, and stress. *Journal of Psychosomatic Research, 53*, 865–871.

US Department of Health and Human Services, National Institutes of Health, National Institute of Diabetes and Digestive and Kidney Diseases. (2011). *The A1C test and diabetes*. (NIH Publication No. 11–7816). Retrieved from diabetes.niddk.nih.gov/dm/pubs/A1CTest/

van Dam, H.A., van der Horst, F.G., Knoops, L., Ryckman, R.M., Crebolder, H.F., & van den Borne, B.H. (2005). Social support in diabetes: A systematic review of controlled intervention studies. *Patient Education and Counseling, 59*, 1–12.

Weinger, K., Beverly, E.A., Lee, Y., Sitnokov, L., Ganda, O.P., & Caballero, A.E. (2011). The effect of a structured behavioral intervention on poorly controlled diabetes. *Archives of Internal Medicine, 171*, 1990–1999.

Welch, G.W., Jacobson, A.M., & Polonsky, W.H. (1997). The Problem Areas in Diabetes Scale: An evaluation of its clinical utility. *Diabetes Care, 20*, 760–766.

Wellen, K.E., & Hotamisligil, G.S. (2005). Inflammation, stress, and diabetes. *Journal of Clinical Investigation, 115*, 1111–1119.

Whooley, M.A., Avins, A.L., Miranda, J., Browner, W.S. (1997). Case-finding instruments for depression: Two questions are as good as many. *Journal of General Internal Medicine, 12*, 439–445.

Winkley, K., Landau, S., Eisler, I., & Ismail, K. (2006). Psychological interventions to improve glycaemic control in patients with type 1 diabetes: Systematic review and meta-analysis of randomised controlled trials. *British Medical Journal, 333*, 1–5.

Wysocki, T. (2006). Behavioural assessment and intervention in pediatric diabetes. *Behavior Modification, 30*, 72–92.

Young-Hyman, D.L., & Davis, C.L. (2010). Disordered eating behavior in individuals with diabetes: Importance of context, evaluation, and classification. *Diabetes Care, 33*, 683–68.

Chapter 11

Ajzen, I. (1991). The theory of planned behavior. *Organizational Behavior and Human Decision Processes, 50*, 179–211.

Ajzen, I., & Fishbein, M. (1980). *Understanding attitudes and predicting social behavior*. Englewood Cliffs, NJ: Prentice-Hall.

Alghazo, R., Upton, T.D., & Cioe, N. (2011). Duty to warn versus duty to protect confidentiality: Ethical and legal considerations relative to individuals with AIDS/HIV. *Journal of Applied Rehabilitation Counseling, 42*, 1, 43–49.

American Civil Liberties Union. (2008). Lesbian & Gay Rights Project AIDS Project: State criminal statutes on HIV transmission—2008. Retrieved from www.aclu.org/files/images/asset_upload_file292_35655.pdf

Ammassari, A., Trotta, M.P., Murri, R., Castelli, F., Narciso, P., Noto, P., … Antinori, A. (2002). Correlates and predictors of adherence to highly active antiretroviral therapy: Overview of published literature. *Journal of Acquired Immune Deficiency Syndromes, 31*, S123–S127.

Anderson, S.E.H. (1995). Personality, appraisal, and adaptational outcomes in HIV seropositive men and women. *Research in Nursing and Health, 18*, 303–312.

Antoni, M.H. (2003). Stress management effects on psychological, endocrinological and immune functioning in men with HIV infection: Empirical support for a psychoneuroimmunological model. *Stress, 6*, 173–188.

Ashton, E., Vosvick, M., Chesney, M., Gore-Felton, C., Koopman, C., O'Shea, K., … Spiegel, S. (2005). Social support and maladaptive coping as predictors of the change in physical health symptoms among persons living with HIV/AIDS. *AIDS Patient Care and STDs, 19*, 587–598.

AVERT. (2012). HIV structure and life cycle. Retrieved from www.avert.org/hiv-virus.htm

Balfe, M., Brugha, R., O'Connell, E., McGee, H., O'Donovan, D., & Vaughan, D. (2010). Why don't young women go for chlamydia testing? A qualitative study employing Goffman's stigma framework. *Health, Risk & Society, 12*, 131–148.

Bandura, A. (1998). Health promotion from the perspective of social cognitive theory. *Personality and Social Psychology, 13*, 623–649.

Bartholomew, L.K, Parcel, G.S., Kok, G, & Gottlieb, N.H. (2006). *Planning health promotion programs: An intervention mapping approach*. San Francisco: Jossey-Bass.

Bayoumi, A.M., & Zaric, G.S. (2008). The cost-effectiveness of Vancouver's supervised injection facility. *Canadian Medical Journal Association, 179*, 1143–1151.

BC Centre for Disease Control. (2012). Sexually transmitted infections (STIs). Retrieved from www.bccdc.ca/dis-cond/a-z/_s/SexuallyTransmittedInfections/default.htm

Begley, K., McLaws, M.-L., Ross, M.W., & Gold, J. (2008). Cognitive and behavioural correlates of non-adherence to HIV anti-retroviral therapy: Theoretical and practical insight for clinical psychology and health psychology. *Clinical Psychologist, 12*, 9–17.

Boarts, J.M., Sledjeski, E.M., Bogart, L.M., & Delahanty, D.L. (2006). The differential impact of PTSD and depression on HIV disease markers and adherence to HAART in people living with HIV. *AIDS and Behavior, 10*, 253–261.

Bosompra, K. (2001). Determinants of condom use intentions of university students in Ghana: An application of the theory of reasoned action. *Social Science & Medicine, 52*, 1057–1069.

Brew, B.J., & Gonzalez-Scarano, F. (2007). HIV-associated dementia: An inconvenient truth. *Neurology, 68*, 324–325.

Brown, J.L., & Vanable, P.A. (2007). Alcohol use, partner type, and risky sexual behaviour among college students: Findings from an event-level study. *Addictive Behaviors, 32*, 2940–2952.

Brown, L., Macintyre, K., & Trujillo, L. (2003). Interventions to reduce HIV/AIDS stigma: What have we learned? *AIDS Education and Prevention, 15*, 49–69.

Calin, T., Green, J., Hetherton, J., & Brook, G. (2007). Disclosure of HIV among Black African men and women attending a London HIV clinic. *AIDS Care, 19*, 385–391.

Canadian Broadcasting Corporation (CBC). (2009). Timeline: Insite. Retrieved from www.cbc.ca/fifth/2008-2009/staying_alive/timeline.html

Canadian Broadcasting Corporation (CBC). (2011). Vancouver's Insite drug injection clinic will stay open: Top court rules on clinic's exemption from federal drug laws. Retrieved from www.cbc.ca/news/canada/british-columbia/story/2011/09/29/bc-insite-supreme-court-ruling-advancer.html

Canadian HIV/AIDS Legal Network. (2011). Criminalization of HIV non-disclosure: Current Canadian law. Retrieved from www.aidslaw.ca/publications/interfaces/downloadFile.php?ref=1887

Capaldi, D.M., Stoolmiller, M., Clark, S., & Owen, L.D. (2002). Heterosexual risk behaviors in at-risk young men from early adolescence to young adulthood: Prevalence, prediction, and association with STD contraction. *Developmental Psychology, 38*, 394–406.

Catz, S.L., Kelly, J.A., Bogart, L.M., Benotsch, E.G., & McAuliffe, T.L. (2000). Patterns, correlates, and barriers to medication adherence among persons prescribed new treatments for HIV disease. *Health Psychology, 19*, 124–133.

Centers for Disease Control and Prevention (CDC). (2000). HIV-related knowledge and stigma—United States. *Morbidity and Mortality Weekly Report, 49*, 1062–1064.

Centers for Disease Control and Prevention (CDC). (2003). Incorporating HIV prevention into the medical care of persons living with HIV. *Morbidity and Mortality Weekly Report, 52*, 1–24.

Centers for Disease Control and Prevention (CDC). (2008). Revised surveillance case definitions for HIV infection among adults, adolescents, and children aged <18 months and for HIV infection and AIDS among children aged 18 months to <13 years—United States, 2008. *Morbidity and Mortality Weekly Report, 57*, 1–8.

Centers for Disease Control and Prevention (CDC). (2009a). Hepatitis A information for the public. Retrieved from www.cdc.gov/hepatitis/A/aFAQ.htm#overview

Centers for Disease Control and Prevention (CDC). (2009b). Hepatitis B. Retrieved from www.cdc.gov/hepatitis/B/bFAQ.htm#overview

Centers for Disease Control and Prevention (CDC). (2010a). Parasites—Lice—Pubic "crab" lice. Retrieved from www.cdc.gov/parasites/lice/pubic/gen_info/faqs.html

Centers for Disease Control and Prevention (CDC). (2010b). Parasites: Scabies. Retrieved from www.cdc.gov/parasites/scabies/gen_info/faqs.html

Centers for Disease Control and Prevention (CDC). (2011a). 10 ways STDs impact women differently from men. Retrieved from www.cdc.gov/nchhstp/newsroom/docs/STDs-Women-042011.pdf

Centers for Disease Control and Prevention (CDC). (2011b). Sexually transmitted diseases surveillance: 2010. Retrieved from www.cdc.gov/std/stats10/surv2010.pdf

Centers for Disease Control and Prevention (CDC). (2011c). Condoms and STDs: Fact sheet for public health personnel. Retrieved from www.cdc.gov/condomeffectiveness/latex.htm.

Centers for Disease Control and Prevention (CDC). (2011d). Tiers of evidence: A framework for classifying HIV behavioral interventions. Retrieved from www.cdc.gov/hiv/topics/research/prs/tiers-of-evidence.htm

Centers for Disease Control and Prevention (CDC). (2012a). Sexually transmitted diseases (STDs): Reportable STDs in young people 15–24 years of age, by state. Retrieved from www.cdc.gov/Std/stats/by-age/15-24-all-STDs/default.htm

Centers for Disease Control and Prevention (CDC). (2012b). African Americans and sexually transmitted diseases. Retrieved from www.cdc.gov/nchhstp/newsroom/docs/AAs-and-STD-Fact-Sheet.pdf

Centers for Disease Control and Prevention (CDC). (2012c). STD fact sheets. Retrieved from www.cdc.gov/std/healthcomm/fact_sheets.htm

Centers for Disease Control and Prevention (CDC). (2012d). HIV incidence. Retrieved from www.cdc.gov/hiv/topics/surveillance/incidence.htm

Centers for Disease Control and Prevention (CDC). (2012e). Hepatitis C. Retrieved from www.cdc.gov/hepatitis/C/cFAQ.htm#overview

Centers for Disease Control and Prevention (CDC). (2012f). Sexually transmitted diseases (STDs): Chlamydia. Retrieved from www.cdc.gov/std/chlamydia/STDFact-Chlamydia.htm

Centers for Disease Control and Prevention (CDC). (2012g). HIV surveillance—epidemiology of HIV infection (through 2010). Retrieved from www.cdc.gov/hiv/topics/surveillance/resources/slides/general/index.htm

Centers for Disease Control and Prevention (CDC). (2012h). STDs in racial and ethnic minorities. Retrieved from www.cdc.gov/std/stats11/minorities.htm

Centers for Disease Control and Prevention (CDC). (2013). Genital HPV infection. Retrieved from www.cdc.gov/std/HPV/STDFact-HPV.htm

Chesney, M.A., Ickovics, J.R., Chambers, D.B., Gifford, A.L., Neidig, J., Zwickl, B., & Wu, A.W. (2000). Self-reported adherence to antiretroviral medications among participants in HIV clinical trials: The AACTG adherence instruments. AIDS Care, 12, 255–266.

Chesney, M.A., & Smith, A.W. (1999). Critical delays in HIV testing and care: The potential role of stigma. American Behavioral Scientist, 42, 1162–1174.

Ciesla, J.A., & Roberts, J.E. (2001). Meta-analysis of the relationship between HIV infection and risk for depressive disorder. American Journal of Psychiatry, 158, 725–730.

Cohen, D., Scribner, R., Bedimo, R., & Farley, T.A. (1999). Cost as a barrier to condom use: The evidence for condom subsidies in the United States. American Journal of Public Health, 89, 567–568.

Crosby, R.A., DiClemente, R.J., Wingood, G.M., Cobb, B.K., Harrington, K., Davies, S.L., … Oh, M.K. (2002). Condom use and correlates of African American adolescent females' infrequent communication with sex partners about preventing sexually transmitted diseases and pregnancy. Health Education & Behavior, 29, 219–231.

DeLonga, K., Torres, H.L., Kamen, C., Evans, S.N., Lee, S., Koopman, C., & Gore-Felton, C. (2011). Loneliness, internalized homophobia, and compulsive Internet use: Factors associated with sexual risk behaviour among a sample of adolescent males seeking services at a community LGBT center. Sexual Addiction & Compulsivity, 18, 61–74.

Dew, B.J., & Chaney, M.P. (2005). The relationship among sexual compulsivity, internalized homophobia, and HIV at-risk sexual behaviour in gay and bisexual male users of Internet chat rooms. Sexual Addiction & Compulsivity, 12, 259–273.

DiIorio, C., Dudley, W.N., Kelly, M., Soet, J.E., Mbwara, J., & Potter, J.S. (2001). Social cognitive correlates of sexual experience and condom use among 13- through 15-year-old adolescents. Journal of Adolescent Health, 29, 208–216.

Dooling, K., & Rachlis, M. (2010). Vancouver's supervised injection facility challenges Canada's drug laws. Canadian Medical Association Journal, 182, 1440–1444.

Drumright, L.N., Patterson, T.L., & Strathdee, S.A. (2006). Club drugs as causal risk factors for HIV acquisition among men who have sex with men: A review. Substance Use & Misuse, 41, 1551–1601.

Eaton, D.K., Kann, L., Kinchen, S., Shanklin S., Flint, K.H., Hawkins, J., … Centers for Disease Control and Prevention (CDC). (2012). Youth risk behavior surveillance—United States, 2011. MMWR Surveillance Summaries, 61, 1–162.

Evans, D.L., Ten Have, T.R., Douglas, S.D., Gettes, D.R., Morrison, M., Chiappini, M.S., … Pettito, J.M. (2002). Association of depression with viral load, CD8 T lymphocytes, and natural killer cells in women with HIV infection. American Journal of Psychiatry, 159, 1752–1759.

Farmer, M.A., & Meston, C.M. (2006). Predictors of condom use self-efficacy in an ethnically diverse university sample. Archives of Sexual Behavior, 35, 313–326.

Fisher, J.D., & Fisher, W.A. (1992). Changing AIDS-risk behavior. Psychological Bulletin, 111, 455–474.

Fortenberry, J.D., McFarlane, M., Bleakley, A., Bull, S., Fishbein, M., Grimley, D.M., … Stoner, B.P. (2002). Relationships of stigma and shame to gonorrhea and HIV screening. American Journal of Public Health, 92, 378–381.

Geraci, A.P., & Simpson, D.M. (2001). Neurological manifestations of HIV-1 infection in the HAART era. Comprehensive Therapy, 27, 232–241.

Gilliam, P.P., & Straub, D.M. (2009). Prevention with positives: A review of published research, 1998–2008. Journal of the Association of Nurses in AIDS Care, 20, 92–109.

Global Initiative to Fight Human Trafficking (GIFHT). (2013). Human trafficking and HIV/AIDS. Retrieved from www.ungift.org/knowledgehub/en/about/human-trafficking-and-hiv-aids.html

Goffman, E. (1963). Stigma: Notes on the management of spoiled identity. Englewood Cliffs, NJ: Prentice-Hall.

Goforth, H.W., Cohen, M.A., & Murrough, J. (2008). Mood disorders. In M.A. Cohen & J.M. Gorman (Eds.), *Comprehensive textbook of AIDS psychiatry*. New York: Oxford University Press.

Golin, C., Isasi, F., Bontempi, J.B., & Eng, E. (2002). Secret pills: HIV-positive patients' experiences taking antiretroviral therapy in North Carolina. *AIDS Education and Prevention, 14*, 318–329.

Granich, R., Crowley, S., Vitoria, M., Smyth, C., Kahn, J.G., Bennett, R., ... Williams, B. (2010). Highly active antiretroviral treatment as prevention of HIV transmission: Review of scientific evidence and update. *Current Opinion in HIV and AIDS, 5*, 298–304.

Grimley, D.M., Annang, L., Houser, S., & Chen, H. (2005). Prevalence of condom use errors among STD clinic patients. *American Journal of Health Behavior, 29*, 324–330.

Hagan, H., & Des Jarlais, D.C. (2000). HIV and HCV infection among injecting drug users. *Mount Sinai Journal of Medicine, 67*, 423–428.

Hart, T.A., & Hart, S.L. (2010). The future of cognitive behavioral interventions within behavioral medicine. *Journal of Cognitive Psychotherapy, 24*, 344–353.

Hart, T.A., & Heimberg, R.G. (2005). Social anxiety as a risk factor for unprotected intercourse among gay and bisexual male youth. *AIDS and Behavior, 9*, 505–512.

Hart, T.A., James, C.A., Purcell, D.W., & Farber, E. (2008). Social anxiety and HIV transmission risk among HIV-seropositive male patients. *AIDS Patient Care and STDs, 22*, 879–886.

Hedrich, D. (2004). *European report on drug consumption rooms*. Luxembourg: European Monitoring Centre for Drugs and Drug Addiction.

Herek, G.M. (1999). AIDS and stigma. *American Behavioral Scientist, 42*, 1102–1112.

Herek, G.M., Capitanio, J.P., & Widaman, K.F. (2002). HIV-related stigma and knowledge in the United States: Prevalence and trends, 1991–1999. *American Journal of Public Health, 92*, 371–377.

Hofman, P., & Nelson, A.M. (2006). The pathology induced by highly active antiretroviral therapy against human immunodeficiency virus: An update. *Current Medicinal Chemistry, 13*, 3121–3132.

Holzemer, W.L., Human, S., Arudo, J., Rosa, M., Hamilton, M.J., Corless, I., ... Maryland, M. (2009). Exploring HIV stigma and quality of life for persons living with HIV infection. *Journal of the Association of Nurses in AIDS Care, 20*, 161–168.

Hurt, C.B., Matthews, D.D., Calabria, M.S., Green, K.A., Adimora, A.A., Golin, C.E., & Hightow-Weidman, L. (2010). Sex with older partners is associated with primary HIV infection among men who have sex with men in North Carolina. *Journal of Acquired Immune Deficiency Syndromes, 54*, 185–190.

Ickovics, J.R., Beren, S.E., Grigorenko, E.L., Morrill, A.C., Druley, J.A., & Rodin, J. (2002). Pathways of risk: Race, social class, stress, and coping as factors predicting heterosexual risk behaviors for HIV among women. *AIDS and Behavior, 6*, 339–350.

Ickovics, J.R., Hamburger, M.E., Vlahov, D., Schoenbaum, E.E., Schuman, P., Boland, R.J., & Moore, J. (2001). Mortality, CD4 count decline, and depressive symptoms among HIV-seropositive women: Longitudinal analysis from the HIV epidemiology research study. *Journal of the American Medical Association, 285*, 1466–1474.

Ivanova, E.L., Hart, T.A., Wagner, A.C., Aljassem, K., & Loutfy, M.R. (2012). Correlates of anxiety in women living with HIV of reproductive age. *AIDS and Behavior, 16*, 2181–2191.

James, C.A., Hart, T.A., Roberts, K.E., Ghai, A., Petrovic, B., & Lima, M.D. (2011). Religion versus ethnicity as predictors of unprotected vaginal intercourse among young adults. *Sexual Health, 8*, 363–371.

Johnson, B.T., Scott-Sheldon, L.A., Huedo-Medina, T.B., & Carey, M.P. (2011). Interventions to reduce sexual risk for human immunodeficiency virus in adolescents. *Archives of Pediatrics & Adolescent Medicine, 165*, 77–84.

Kahn, J.A., Kaplowitz, R.A., Goodman, E., & Emans, S.J. (2002). The association between impulsiveness and sexual risk behaviors in adolescent and young adult women. *Journal of Adolescent Health, 30*, 229–232.

Kalichman, S.C., & Cain, D. (2004). A prospective study of sensation seeking and alcohol use as predictors of sexual risk behaviors among men and women receiving sexual transmitted infection clinic services. *Psychology of Addictive Behaviors, 18*, 367–373.

Kalichman, S.C., Rompa, D., & Cage, M. (2005). Group intervention to reduce HIV transmission risk behavior among persons living with HIV/AIDS. *Behavior Modification, 29*, 256–285.

Kalichman, S.C., Rompa, D., Cage, M., DiFonzo, K., Simpson, D., Austin, J., ... Graham, J. (2001). Effectiveness of an intervention to reduce HIV transmission risks in HIV-positive people. *American Journal of Preventive Medicine, 21*, 84–92.

Kashubeck-West, S., & Szymanski, D.M. (2008). Risky sexual behaviour in gay and bisexual men: Internalized heterosexism, sensation seeking, and substance use. *Counseling Psychologist, 36*, 595–614.

Kegeles, S.M., Hays, R.B., & Coates, T.J. (1996). The Mpowerment Project: A community-level HIV prevention intervention for young gay men. *American Journal of Public Health, 86*, 1129–1136.

Kerr, T., Stoltz, J., Tyndall, M., Li, K., Zhang, R., Montaner, J., & Wood, E. (2006). Impact of a medically supervised safer injection facility on community drug use patterns: A before and after study. *British Medical Journal, 332*, 220–222.

Kerr, T., Tyndall, M., Li, K., Montaner, J.S., & Wood, E. (2005). Safer injecting facility use and syringe sharing in injection drug users. *Lancet, 366*, 316–318.

Kessler, R.C., Berglund, P., Demler, O., Jin, R., & Walters, E.E. (2005). Lifetime prevalence and age-of-onset distributions of *DSM-IV* disorders in the national comorbidity survey replication. *Archives of General Psychiatry, 62*, 593–602.

Kinsler, J.J., Wong, M.D., Sayles, J.N., Davis, C., & Cunningham, W.E. (2007). The effect of perceived stigma from a health care provider on access to care among a low-income HIV-positive population. *AIDS Patient Care and STDs, 21*, 584–592.

Kitahata, M.M., Reed, S.D., Dillingham, P.W., Van Rompaey, S.E., Young, A.A., Harrington, R.D., & Holmes, K.K. (2004). Pharmacy-based assessment of adherence to HAART predicts virologic and immunologic treatment response and clinical progression to AIDS and death. *International Journal of STD & AIDS, 15*, 803–810.

Klinkenberg, W.D., & Sacks, S. (2004). Mental disorders and drug abuse in persons living with HIV/AIDS. *AIDS Care, 16,* S22–S42.

Koblin, B.A., Chesney, M.A., Husnik, M.J., Bozeman, S., Celum, C.L., Buchbinder, S., … Coates, T.J. (2003). High-risk behaviors among men who have sex with men in 6 US cities: Baseline data from the EXPLORE study. *American Journal of Public Health, 93,* 926–932.

Kohler, P.K., Manhart, L.E., & Lafferty, W.E. (2008). Abstinence-only and comprehensive sex education and the initiation of sexual activity and teen pregnancy. *Journal of Adolescent Health, 42,* 344–351.

Kulig, J. (2003). Condoms: The basics and beyond. *Adolescent Medicine Clinics, 14,* 633–645.

Latka, M.H., Hagan, H., Kapadia, F., Golub, E.T., Bonner, S., Campbell, J.V., … Strathdee, S.A. (2008). A randomized intervention trial to reduce the lending of used injection equipment among injection drug users infected with hepatitis C. *American Journal of Public Health, 98,* 853–861.

Lazarus, R.S., & Folkman, S. (1984). *Stress, appraisal, and coping.* New York: Springer.

Lee, R.S., Kochman, A., & Sikkema, K.J. (2002). Internalized stigma among people living with HIV-AIDS. *AIDS and Behavior, 6,* 309–319.

Liu, Y., Canada, K., Shi, K., & Corrigan, P. (2012). AIDS care: Psychological and socio-medical aspects of AIDS/HIV. *AIDS Care, 24,* 129–135.

Logan, T.K., Cole, J., & Leukefeld, C. (2002). Women, sex, and HIV: Social and contextual factors, meta-analysis of published interventions, and implications for practice and research. *Psychological Bulletin, 128,* 851–885.

Ma, W., Detels, R., Feng, Y., Wu, Z., Shen, L., Li, Y., … Liu, T. (2007). Acceptance of and barriers to voluntary HIV counselling and testing among adults in Guizhou Province, China. *AIDS, 21,* S129–S135.

McCoul, M.D., & Haslam, N. (2001). Predicting high risk sexual behaviour in heterosexual and homosexual men: The roles of impulsivity and sensation seeking. *Personality and Individual Differences, 31,* 1303–1310.

Marino, P., Simoni, J.M., & Bordeaux Silverstein, L. (2007). Peer support to promote medication adherence among people living with HIV/AIDS: The benefits to peers. *Social Work in Health Care, 45,* 67–80.

Mayne, T.J., Vittinghoff, E., Chesney, M.A., Barrett, D.C., & Coates, T.J. (1996). Depressive affect and survival among gay and bisexual men infected with HIV. *Archives of Internal Medicine, 156,* 2233–2238.

Medley, A., Kennedy, C., O'Reilly, K., & Sweat, M. (2009). Effectiveness of peer education interventions for HIV prevention in developing countries: A systematic review and meta-analysis. *AIDS Education and Prevention, 21,* 181–206.

Miguez-Burbano, M.J., Espinoza, L., & Lewis, J.E. (2008). HIV treatment adherence and sexual functioning. *AIDS and Behavior, 12,* 78–85.

Milloy, M.J.S., Kerr, T., Tyndall, M., Montaner, J., & Wood, E. (2008). Estimated drug overdose deaths averted by North America's first medically-supervised safer injection facility. *PLoS ONE, 3:* e3351.

Montaño, D.E., & Kasprzyk, D. (2008). The theory of reasoned action, the theory of planned behavior, and the integrated behavioral model. In K. Glanz, B.K. Rimer, & K. Viswanath (Eds.), *Health behavior and health education: Theory, research and practice* (pp. 67–96). San Francisco: Jossey-Bass.

National Institute of Allergy and Infectious Diseases (NIAID). (2012). *HIV replication cycle: Steps in HIV replication cycle.* Retrieved from www.niaid.nih.gov/topics/HIVAIDS/ Understanding/Biology/pages/hivreplicationcycle.aspx

Navaline, H.A., Snider, E.C., Petro, C.J., Tobin, D., Metzger, D., Alterman, A.I., & Woody, G.E. (1994). Preparations for AIDS vaccine trials. An automated version of the Risk Assessment Battery (RAB): Enhancing the assessment of risk behaviors. *AIDS Research and Human Retroviruses, 10,* S281–S283.

Newcomb, M.E., & Mustanski, B. (2011). Moderators of the relationship between internalized homophobia and risky sexual behaviour in men who have sex with men: A meta-analysis. *Archives of Sexual Behavior, 40,* 189–199.

Newman, P.A., & Poindexter, C.C. (2010). HIV prevention innovations and challenges. In P.A. Newman & C.C. Poindexter (Eds.), *Handbook of HIV and social work: Principles, practice, and populations* (pp. 183–196). Hoboken, NJ: John Wiley & Sons.

Obermeyer, C.M., & Osborn, M. (2007). The utilization of testing and counseling for HIV: A review of the social and behavioral evidence. *American Journal of Public Health, 97,* 1762–1774.

Osborn, C.Y., & Egede, L.E. (2010). Validation of an information-motivation-behavioral skills model of diabetes self-care (IMB-DSC). *Patient Education and Counseling, 79,* 49–54.

Owe-Larsson, B., Säll, L., Salamon, E., & Allgulander, C. (2009). HIV infection and psychiatric illness. *African Journal of Psychiatry, 12,* 115–128.

Pakenham, K.I., & Rinaldis, M. (2001). The role of illness, resources, appraisal, and coping strategies in adjustment to HIV/AIDS: The direct and buffering effects. *Journal of Behavioral Medicine, 24,* 259–279.

Paterson, D.L., Swindells, S., Mohr, J., Brester, M., Vergis, E. N., Squier, C., … Singh, N. (2000). Adherence to protease inhibitor therapy and outcomes in patients with HIV infection. *Annals of Internal Medicine, 133,* 21–30.

Peterson, J.L., Folkman, S., & Bakeman, R. (1996). Stress, coping, HIV status, psychosocial resources, and depressive mood in African gay, bisexual, and heterosexual men. *American Journal of Community Psychology, 24,* 461–487.

Poulin, C., & Graham, L. (2001). The association between substance use, unplanned sexual intercourse and other sexual behaviours among adolescent students. *Addiction, 96,* 607–621.

Prochaska, J.O., & Velicer, W.F. (1997). The transtheoretical model of health behavior change. *American Journal of Health Promotion, 12,* 38–48.

Public Health Agency of Canada (PHAC). (2007). STI—Sexually transmitted infections. Retrieved from www.phac-aspc.gc.ca/ publicat/std-mts/index-eng.php

Public Health Agency of Canada (PHAC). (2008). *Canadian guidelines for sexual health education.* Ottawa: Sexual Health & Sexually Transmitted Infections Section, Community Acquired Infections Division, Public Health Agency of Canada.

Public Health Agency of Canada (PHAC). (2009a). Hepatitis A. Retrieved from www.phac-aspc.gc.ca/tmp-pmv/info/hepa-eng.php

Public Health Agency of Canada (PHAC). (2009b). Hepatitis C. Retrieved from www.phac-aspc.gc.ca/hepc/faq-eng.php

Public Health Agency of Canada (PHAC). (2010). Hepatitis B—Get the facts. Retrieved from www.phac-aspc.gc.ca/hcai-iamss/bbp-pts/hepatitis/hep_b-eng.php

Public Health Agency of Canada (PHAC). (2011a). Reported cases and rates of chlamydia by province/territory and sex, 1991 to 2009. Retrieved from www.phac-aspc.gc.ca/std-mts/sti-its_tab/chlamydia_pts-eng.php

Public Health Agency of Canada (PHAC). (2011b). Reported cases and rates of gonorrhea by province/territory and sex, 1980 to 2009. Retrieved from www.phac-aspc.gc.ca/std-mts/sti-its_tab/gonorrhea_pts-eng.php

Public Health Agency of Canada (PHAC). (2011c). Reported cases and rates of infectious syphilis by province/territory and sex, 1993 to 2009. Retrieved from www.phac-aspc.gc.ca/std-mts/sti-its_tab/syphilis_pts-eng.php

Public Health Agency of Canada (PHAC). (2012a). Executive summary—Report on sexually transmitted infections in Canada: 2009. Retrieved from www.phac-aspc.gc.ca/sti-its-surv-epi/sum-som-eng.php

Public Health Agency of Canada (PHAC). (2012b). At a glance: HIV and AIDS in Canada: Surveillance report to December 31st, 2010. Retrieved from www.phac-aspc.gc.ca/aids-sida/publication/survreport/2010/dec/index-eng.php

Public Health Agency of Canada (PHAC). (2012c). Summary: Estimates of HIV prevalence and incidence in Canada, 2011. Retrieved from www.phac-aspc.gc.ca/aids-sida/publication/survreport/assets/pdf/estimat2011-eng.pdf

Rabkin, J.G. (1996). Prevalence of psychiatric disorders in HIV illness. *International Review of Psychiatry, 8*, 157–166.

Radcliffe, J., Landau Fleisher, C., Hawkins, L.A., Tanney, M., Kassam-Adams, N., Ambrose, C., & Rudy, B.J. (2007). Posttraumatic stress and trauma history in adolescents and young adults with HIV. *AIDS Patient Care and STDs, 21*, 501–508.

Rathus, S.A., Nevid, J.S., Fichner-Rathus, L., Herold, E.S., & McKenzie, S.W. (2007). Sexually transmitted infections. In S.A. Rathus, J.S. Nevid, & L. Fichner-Rathus (Eds.), *Human sexuality in a world of diversity* (2nd Canadian ed., pp. 406–439). Toronto: Pearson.

Rickman, R.L., Lodico, M., DiClemente, R.J., Morris, R., Baker, C., & Huscroft, S. (1994). Sexual communication is associated with condom use by sexually active incarcerated adolescents. *Journal of Adolescent Health, 15*, 383–388.

Rintamaki, L.S., Davis, T.C., Skripkauskas, S., Bennett, C.L., & Wolf, M.S. (2006). Social stigma concerns and HIV medication adherence. *AIDS Patient Care and STDs, 20*, 359–368.

Rosen, M.I., Ryan, C., & Rigsby, M. (2002). Motivational enhancement and MEMS review to improve medication adherence. *Behaviour Change, 19*, 183–190.

Rosenstock, I.M. (1974). The health belief model and preventive health behavior. *Health Education Monographs, 2*, 354–386.

Rotermann, M. (2012). Sexual behavior and condom use of 15- to 24-year-olds in 2003 and 2009/2012. *Statistics Canada: Health Reports, 23*, 1–5.

Safren, S.A., Gershuny, B.S., & Hendriksen, E. (2003). Symptoms of posttraumatic stress and death anxiety in persons with HIV and medication adherence difficulties. *AIDS Patient Care and STDs, 17*, 657–664.

Safren, S.A., O'Cleirigh, C., Tan, J.Y., Raminani, S.R., Reilly, L.C., Otto, M.W., & Mayer, K.H. (2009). A randomized controlled trial of cognitive behavioral therapy for adherence and depression (CBT-AD) in HIV-infected individuals. *Health Psychology, 28*, 1–10.

Safren, S.A., Otto, M.W., & Worth, J.L. (1999). Life-steps: Applying cognitive-behavioral therapy to HIV medication adherence. *Cognitive and Behavioral Practice, 6*, 332–341.

Sallis, J.F., Owen, N., & Fisher, E.B. (2008). Ecological models of health behavior. In K. Glanz, B.K. Rimer, & K. Viswanath (Eds.), *Health behavior and health education: Theory, research and practice* (pp. 465–485). San Francisco: Jossey-Bass.

Santelli, J., Ott, M.A., Lyon, M., Rogers, J., Summers, D., & Schleifer, R. (2006). Abstinence and abstinence-only education: A review of U.S. policies and programs. *Journal of Adolescent Health, 38*, 72–81.

Seeley, J., Watts, C.H., Kippax, S., Russell, S., Heise, L., & Whiteside, A. (2012). Addressing the structural drivers of HIV: A luxury or necessity for programmes? *Journal of the International AIDS Society, 15*(Suppl. 1), 1–4.

Shiely, F., Horgan, M., & Hayes, K. (2009). Increased sexually transmitted infection incidence in a low risk population: Identifying the risk factors. *European Journal of Public Health, 20*, 207–212.

Siegel, K., & Schrimshaw, E.W. (2000). Coping with negative emotions: The cognitive strategies of HIV-infected gay/bisexual men. *Journal of Health Psychology, 5*, 517–530.

Sikkema, K.J., Hansen, N.B., Kochman, A., Santos, J., Watt, M.H., Wilson, P.A., … Mayer, G. (2011). The development and feasibility of a brief risk reduction intervention for newly HIV-diagnosed men who have sex with men. *Journal of Community Psychology, 39*, 717–732.

Simbayi, L.C., Kalichman, S., Strebel, A., Cloete, A., Henda, N., & Mqeketo, A. (2007). Internalized stigma, discrimination, and depression among men and women living with HIV/AIDS in Cape Town, South Africa. *Social Science & Medicine, 64*, 1823–1831.

Small, E., Weinman, M.L., Buzi, R.S., & Smith, P.G. (2009). Risk factors, knowledge, and attitudes as predictors of intent to use condoms among minority female adolescents attending family planning clinics. *Journal of HIV/AIDS & Social Services, 8*, 251–268.

Sperber, K., & Shao, L. (2003). Neurologic consequences of HIV infection in the era of HAART. *AIDS Patient Care and STDs, 17*, 509–518.

Springer, Y.P., Samuel, M.C., & Bolan, G. (2010). Socioeconomic gradients in sexually transmitted diseases: A geographic information system-based analysis of poverty, race/ethnicity, and gonorrhea rates in California, 2004–2006. *American Journal of Public Health, 100*, 1060–1067.

Tapert, S.F., Aarons, G.A., Sedlar, G.R., & Brown, S.A. (2001). Adolescent substance use and sexual risk-taking behaviour. *Journal of Adolescent Health, 28*, 181–189.

Taylor, S.E., Kemeny, M.E., Aspinwall, L.G., Schneider, S.G., Rodriguez, R., & Herbert, M. (1992). Optimism, coping, psychological distress, and high-risk sexual behaviour among men at risk for acquired immunodeficiency syndrome (AIDS). *Journal of Personality and Social Psychology, 63,* 460–473.

Teitelman, A.M., Tennille, J., Bohinski, J.M., Jemmott, L.S., & Jemmott, J.B. (2011). Unwanted unprotected sex: Condom coercion by male partners and self-silencing of condom negotiation among adolescent girls. *Advances in Nursing Science, 34,* 243–259.

Teva, I., Bermudez, M.P., & Buela-Casal, G. (2010). Sexual sensation seeking, social stress, and coping styles as predictors of HIV/STD risk behaviors in adolescents. *Youth & Society, 42,* 255–277.

Theuninck, A.C., Lake, N., & Gibson, S. (2010). HIV-related posttraumatic stress disorder: Investigating the traumatic events. *AIDS Patient Care and STDs, 24,* 458–491.

Treisman, G., & Angelino, A. (2007). Interralation between psychiatric disorders and the prevention and treatment of HIV infection. *Clinical Infectious Diseases, 45,* S313–S317.

UNAIDS. (2008). Criminalization of HIV transmission: Policy brief. Retrieved from data.unaids.org/pub/basedocument/2008/20080731_jc1513_policy_criminalization_en.pdf

UNAIDS. (2012). *Global fact sheet.* Retrieved from www.unaids.org/en/media/unaids/contentassets/documents/epidemiology/2012/gr2012/20121120_FactSheet_Global_en.pdf

Vanable, P.A., Carey, M.P., Blair, D.C., & Littlewood, R.A. (2006). Impact of HIV-related stigma on health behaviors and psychological adjustment among HIV-positive men and women. *AIDS and Behavior, 10,* 473–482.

van Servellen, G., Chang, B., Garcia, L., & Lombardi, E. (2002). Individual and system-level factors associated with treatment nonadherence in human immunodeficiency virus-infected men and women. *AIDS Patient Care and STDs, 16,* 269–281.

Wagner, A.C., Hart, T.A., Mohammed, S., Ivanova, E., Wong, J., & Loutfy, M.R. (2010). Correlates of HIV stigma in HIV-positive women. *Archives of Women's Mental Health, 13,* 207–214.

Whetten, K., Reif, S., Whetten, R., & Murphy-MacMillan, L.K. (2008). Trauma, mental health, distrust, and stigma among HIV-positive persons: Implications for effective care. *Psychosomatic Medicine, 70,* 531–538.

Williams, B., Wood, R., Dukay, V., Delva, W., Ginsburg, D., Hargrove, J., … Welte, A. (2011). Treatment as prevention: Preparing the way. *Journal of the International AIDS Society, 14,* S6.

Winters, K.C., Botzet, A.M., Fahnhorst, T., Baumel, L., & Lee, S. (2009). Impulsivity and its relationship to risky sexual behaviors and drug abuse. *Journal of Child & Adolescent Substance Abuse, 18,* 43–56.

Wood, E., Tyndall, M.W., Montaner, J.S., & Kerr, T. (2006). Summary of findings from the evaluation of a pilot medically supervised safer injecting facility. *Canadian Medical Association Journal, 175,* 1399–1404.

Wood, E., Tyndall, M.W., Zhang, R., Montaner, J.S.G., & Kerr, T. (2007). Rate of detoxification service use and its impact among a cohort of supervised injection facility users. *Addiction, 102,* 916–919.

Wood, E., Tyndall, M.W., Zhenguo, Q., Zhang, R., Montaner, J.S.G., & Kerr, T. (2006) Service uptake and characteristics of injection drug users utilizing North America's first medically supervised safer injecting facility. *American Journal of Public Health, 96,* 770–773.

World Health Organization (WHO). (2007). WHO case definitions of HIV for surveillance and revised clinical staging and immunological classification of HIV-related disease in adults and children. Retrieved from www.who.int/hiv/pub/guidelines/HIVstaging150307.pdf

World Health Organization (WHO). (2008). Essential prevention and care interventions for adults and adolescents living with HIV in resource-limited settings. Retrieved from www.who.int/hiv/pub/prev_care/OMS_EPP_AFF_en.pdf

World Health Organization (WHO). (2012). Fact sheet 1 HIV/AIDS: The infection. Retrieved from www.who.int/hiv/abouthiv/en/fact_sheet_hiv.htm

World Health Organization (WHO). (2013a). Sexually transmitted infections. Retrieved from www.who.int/mediacentre/factsheets/fs110/en/index.html

World Health Organization (WHO). (2013b). Gender, women and health. Retrieved from www.who.int/gender/hiv_aids/en/

Zuckerman, M. (2009). Sensation seeking. In M.R. Leary & R.H., Hoyle (Eds.), *Handbook of individual differences in social behavior* (pp. 455–465). New York: Guilford.

Chapter 12

Amato, M.P., Zipoli, V., & Portaccio, E. (2006). Multiple sclerosis-related cognitive changes: A review of cross-sectional and longitudinal studies. *Journal of the Neurological Sciences, 245,* 41–46.

American Psychiatric Association (APA). (2013). *Diagnostic and statistical manual of mental disorders* (5th ed.). Arlington, Va.

Arnett, P.A., & Strober, L.B. (2011). Cognitive and neurobehavioral features in multiple sclerosis. *Expert Review of Neurotherapeutics, 11,* 411–424.

Arpe, Malene. (2012). Jack Osbourne "really, really angry" after multiple sclerosis diagnosis. *Toronto Star,* 18 June. Retrieved from www.thestar.com/entertainment/stargazing/article/1212966--jack-osbourne-really-really-angry-after-multiple-sclerosis-diagnosis

Bakshi, R., Shaikh, Z.A., Miletich, R.S., Czarnecki, D., Dmochowski, J., Henschel, K., … Kinkel, P.R. (2000). Fatigue in multiple sclerosis and its relationship to depression and neurologic disability. *Multiple Sclerosis, 6,* 181–185.

BBC News. (2012). Jack Osbourne diagnosed with MS, Ozzy and Sharon reveal, 17 June. Retrieved from www.bbc.co.uk/news/entertainment-arts-18478530

Beatty, W.W., Paul, R.H., Wilbanks, S.L., Hames, K.A., Blanco, C.R., & Goodkin, D.E. (1995). Identifying multiple sclerosis patients with mild or global cognitive impairment using the Screening Examination for Cognitive Impairment (SEFCI). *Neurology, 45,* 718–723.

Beck, A.T. (2005). The current state of cognitive therapy: A 40-year retrospective. *Archives of General Psychiatry, 62,* 953–959.

Beck, A.T., Steer, R.A., & Brown, G.K. (2000). *BDI-fast screen for medical patients manual.* San Antonio: Psychological Corporation.

Beck, A.T., Ward, C.H., Mendelson, M., Mock, J., & Erbaugh, J. (1961). An inventory for measuring depression. *Archives of General Psychiatry, 4*, 561–571.

Benedict, R.H.B., Fishman, I., McClellan, M.M., Bakshi, R., & Weinstock-Guttman, B. (2003). Validity of the Beck Depression Inventory-Fast Screen in multiple sclerosis. *Multiple Sclerosis, 9*, 393–396.

Bol, Y., Duits, A.A., Hupperts, R.M.M., Vlaeyen, J.W.S., & Verhey, F.R.J. (2009). The psychology of fatigue in patients with multiple sclerosis: A review. *Journal of Psychosomatic Research, 66*, 3–11.

Borasio, G.D., & Miller, R.G. (2001). Clinical characteristics and management of ALS. *Seminars in Neurology 21*, 155–166.

Bowling, A.C. (2011). Complementary and alternative medicine and multiple sclerosis. *Neurologic Clinics, 29*, 465–580.

Bozikas, V.P., Anagnostouli, M.C., Petrikis, P., Sitzoglou, C., Phokas, C., Tsakanikas, C., & Karavatos, A. (2003). Familial bipolar disorder and multiple sclerosis: A three-generation HLA family study. *Progress in Neuro-Psychopharmacology & Biological Psychiatry, 27*, 835–839.

Braley, T.J., & Chervin, R.D. (2010). Fatigue in multiple sclerosis: Mechanisms, evaluation, and treatment. *Sleep: Journal of Sleep and Sleep Disorders Research, 33*, 1061–1067.

Bronner, G., Elran, E., Golomb, J., & Korczyn, A.D. (2010). Female sexuality in multiple sclerosis: The multidimensional nature of the problem and the intervention. *Acta Neurologica Scandinavica, 121*, 289–301.

Brown, E.S., & Chandler, P.A. (2001). Mood and cognitive changes during systemic corticosteroid therapy. *Primary Care Companion to the Journal of Clinical Psychiatry, 3*, 7–21.

Caminero, A., & Bartolomé, M. (2011). Sleep disturbances in multiple sclerosis. *Journal of the Neurological Sciences, 309*, 86–91.

Chwastiak, L.A., & Ehde, D.M. (2007). Psychiatric issues in multiple sclerosis. *Psychiatric Clinics of North America, 30*, 803–817.

Compston, A., & Coles, A. (2008). Multiple sclerosis. *Lancet, 372*, 1502–1517.

Dennison, L., & Moss-Morris, R. (2010). Cognitive-behavioral therapy: What benefits can it offer people with multiple sclerosis? *Expert Review of Neurotherapeutics, 10*(9), 1383–1390.

Dennison, L., Moss-Morris, R., & Chalder, T. (2009). A review of psychological correlates of adjustment in patients with multiple sclerosis. *Clinical Psychology Review, 29*, 141–153.

Farrer, L.A. (1986). Suicide and attempted suicide in Huntington disease: Implications for preclinical testing of persons at risk. *American Journal of Medical Genetics, 24*, 305–311.

Feinstein, A. (2004). The neuropsychiatry of mental illness. *Canadial Journal of Psychiatry, 49*, 157–163.

First, M.B., Spitzer, R.L., Gibbon, M., & Williams, J.B. (1996). *Structured clinical interview for DSM-IV axis I disorders (SCID-I)—Clinician Version*. Washington: American Psychiatric Press.

Foley, F.W. (2006). Sexuality. In R.C. Kalb (Ed.), *Multiple sclerosis: A guide for families* (3rd ed., 53–80). New York: Demos Medical Publishing.

Foley, F.W., & Werner, M.A. (2004). Sexuality. In R.C. Kalb (Ed.), *Multiple sclerosis: The questions you have the answers you need* (3rd ed., pp.297–327). New York: Demos Medical Publishing.

Ganzini, L., Johnston, W.S., & Hoffman, W.F. (1999). Correlates of suffering in amyotrophic lateral sclerosis. *Neurology, 52*, 1434–1440.

Ghaffar, O., & Feinstein, A. (2007). The neuropsychiatry of multiple sclerosis: A review of recent developments. *Current Opinion in Psychiatry, 20*, 278–285.

Hadjimichael, O., Vollmer, T., & Oleen-Burkey, M. (2008). Fatigue characteristics in multiple sclerosis: The North American Research Committee on Multiple Sclerosis (NARCOMS) survey. *Health and Quality of Life Outcomes, 6*.

Harper, P.S. (Ed.). (1996). *Huntington's disease: Major problems in neurology*, Vol 31. London: W.B. Saunders.

Haussleiter, I.S., Brüne, M., & Juckel, G. (2009). Psychopathology in multiple sclerosis: Diagnosis, prevalence and treatment. *Therapeutic Advances in Neurological Disorders, 2*, 13–29.

Kenna, H.A., Poon, A.W., de los Angeles, C.P., & Koran, L.M. (2011). Psychiatric complications of treatment with corticosteroids: Review with case report. *Psychiatry and Clinical Neurosciences, 65*, 549–560.

Kent, A. (2004). Huntington's disease. *Nursing Standard, 18*, 45–53.

Kerns, R.D., Kassirer, M., & Otis, J. (2002). Pain in multiple sclerosis: A biopsychosocial perspective. *Journal of Rehabilitation Research and Development, 39*, 225–232.

Kessler, T.M., Fowler, C.J., & Panicker, J.N. (2009). Sexual dysfunction in multiple sclerosis. *Expert Review of Neurotherapeutics, 9*, 341–350.

Khan, O., Filippi, M., Freedman, M., Barkhof, F., Dore-Duffy, P., Lassmann, H., … Lisak, R. (2010). Chronic cerebrospinal venous insufficiency and multiple sclerosis. *Annals of Neurology, 67*, 286–290.

Koch-Henriksen, N., & Sørensen, P.S. (2010). The changing demographic pattern of multiple sclerosis epidemiology. *Lancet Neurology, 9*, 520–532.

Krupp, L.B., LaRocca, N.G., Muir-Nash, J., & Steinberg, A.D. (1989). The fatigue severity scale: Application to patients with multiple sclerosis and systematic lupus erythematosus. *Archives of Neurology, 46*, 1121–1123.

Krupp, L.B., Serafin, D.J., & Christodoulou, C. (2010). Multiple sclerosis-associated fatigue. *Expert Review of Neurotherapeutics, 10*, 1437–1447.

Lacovides, A., & Andreoulakis, E. (2011). Bipolar disorder and resembling special psychopathological manifestations in multiple sclerosis: A review. *Current Opinion in Psychiatry, 24*, 336–340.

Landtblom, A., Fazio, P., Fredrikson, S., & Granieri, E. (2010). The first case history of multiple sclerosis: Augustus d'Esté (1794–1848). *Neurological Sciences, 31*, 29–33.

LaRocca, N., & Caruso, L. (2006). Assessment of cognitive changes. In N. LaRocca & R. Kalb (Eds.), *Multiple sclerosis: Understanding the cognitive challenges* (pp. 42–45). New York: Demos Medical Publishing.

Lazarus, R.S. (1993). From psychological stress to the emotions: A history of changing outlooks. *Annual Review of Psychology, 44*, 1.

Lyros, E., Messinis, L., Papageorgiou, S.G., & Papathanasopoulos, P. (2010). Cognitive dysfunction in multiple sclerosis: The effect of pharmacological interventions. *International Review of Psychiatry, 22*, 35–42.

Migliore, L., & Coppede, F. (2009). Genetics, environmental factors and the emerging role of epigenetics in neurodegenerative diseases. *Mutation Research, 667*, 82–97.

Miller, A., Bourdette, D., Ritvo, P., & Stuart, W. (1994). The neurologist's perspective: What do we know and where do we go? *Journal of Neurologic Rehabilitation*. Special Focus Issue: *Comprehensive Care in Multiple Sclerosis, 8*, 105–111.

Mitchell, J.D., & Borasio, G.D. (2007). Amyotrophic lateral sclerosis. *Lancet, 369*, 2031–2041.

Mitsonis, C.I., Potagas, C., Zervas, I., & Sfagos, K. (2009). The effects of stressful life events on the course of multiple sclerosis: A review. *International Journal of Neuroscience, 119*, 315–335.

Mohr, D.C., Boudewyn, A.C., Goodkin, D.E., Bostrom, A., & Epstein, L. (2001). Comparative outcomes for individual cognitive-behavior therapy, supportive-expressive group psychotherapy, and sertraline for the treatment of depression in multiple sclerosis. *Journal of Consulting and Clinical Psychology, 69*, 942–949.

Mohr, D.C., Boudewyn, A.C., Likosky, W., Levine, E., & Goodkin, D.E. (2001). Injectable medication for the treatment of multiple sclerosis: The influence of self-efficacy expectations and injection anxiety on adherence and ability to self-inject. *Annals of Behavioral Medicine, 23*, 125–132.

Mohr, D.C., & Cox, D. (2001). Multiple sclerosis: Empirical literature for the clinical health psychologist. *Journal of Clinical Psychology, 57*, 479–499.

Mohr, D.C., & Goodkin, D.E. (1999). Treatment of depression in multiple sclerosis: Review and meta-analysis. *Clinical Psychology: Science and Practice, 6*, 1–9.

Mohr, D.C., Hart, S.L., Julian, L., Catledge, C., Honos-Webb, L., Vella, L., & Tasch, E.T. (2005). Telephone-administered psychotherapy for depression. *Archives of General Psychiatry, 62*, 1007–1014.

Multiple Sclerosis Council for Clinical Practice Guidelines. (1998). *Fatigue and multiple sclerosis: Evidence-based management strategies for fatigue in multiple sclerosis*. Washington: Paralyzed Veterans of America.

Multiple Sclerosis (MS) Society of Canada (2012). Multiple sclerosis information. Retrieved from www.mssociety.ca/en/information/default.htm

O'Connor, A.B., Schwid, S.R., Herrmann, D.N., Markman, J.D., & Dworkin, R.H. (2008). Pain associated with multiple sclerosis: Systematic review and proposed classification. *Pain, 137*, 96–111.

Peyser, C.E., & Folstein, S.E. (1990). Huntington's disease as a model for mood disorders: Clues from neuropathology and neurochemistry. *Molecular and Chemical Neuropathology, 12*, 99–119.

Pugliatti, M., Sotgiu, S., & Rosati, G. (2002). The worldwide prevalence of multiple sclerosis. *Clinical Neurology and Neurosurgery, 104*, 182–191.

Qiu, J. (2010). Venous abnormalities and multiple sclerosis: Another breakthrough claim? *Lancet Neurology, 9*, 464–465.

Rabkin, J.G., Albert, S.M., Del Bene, M., O'Sullivan, R., Tider, T., Rowland, L.P., & Mitsumoto, H. (2005). Prevalence of depressive disorders and change over time in late-stage ALS. *Neurology, 65*, 62–67.

Radloff, L.S. (1977). The CES-D scale: A self-report depression scale for research in the general population. *Applied Psychological Measurement, 1*, 385–401.

Ranen, N.C. (2002). Psychiatric management of Huntington's disease. *Psychiatric Annals, 32*, 105–110.

Rosati, G. (2001). The prevalence of multiple sclerosis in the world: An update. *Neurological Sciences, 22*, 117–139.

Sanders, A.S., Foley, F.W., LaRocca, N.G., & Zemon, V. (2000). The Multiple Sclerosis Intimacy and Sexuality Questionnaire-19 (MSISQ-19). *Sexuality and Disability, 18*, 3–26.

Shah, A. (2009). Fatigue in multiple sclerosis. *Physical Medicine and Rehabilitation Clinics of North America, 20*, 363–372.

Spielberger, C.D. (1985). Assessment of state and trait anxiety: Conceptual and methodological issues. *Southern Psychologist, 2*, 6–16.

Stroud, N.M., & Minahan, C.L. (2009). The impact of regular physical activity on fatigue, depression and quality of life in persons with multiple sclerosis. *Health and Quality of Life Outcomes, 7*, 68.

Thompson, A.J., Toosy, A.T., & Ciccarelli, O. (2010). Pharmacological management of symptoms in multiple sclerosis: Current approaches and future directions. *Lancet Neurology, 9*, 1182–1199.

van Vugt, J.P.P., & Roos, R.A.C. (1999). Huntington's disease: Options for controlling symptoms. *CNS Drugs, 11*(2), 105–123.

Vattakatuchery, J.J., Rickards, H., & Cavanna, A.E. (2011). Pathogenic mechanisms of depression in multiple sclerosis. *Journal of Neuropsychiatry and Clinical Neurosciences, 23*, 261–276.

Walker, F.O. (2007). Huntington's disease. *Lancet, 369*, 218–228.

World Health Organization (WHO). (2008). *Atlas multiple sclerosis resources in the world*. Geneva: World Health Organization Press.

Zamboni, P., Galeotti, R., Menegatti, E., Malagoni, A.M., Tacconi, G., Dall'Ara, S., ... Salvi, F. (2009). Chronic cerebrospinal venous insufficiency in patients with multiple sclerosis. *Journal of Neurology, Neurosurgery, and Psychiatry, 80*, 392–399.

Zigmond, A.S., & Snaith, R.P. (1983). The Hospital Anxiety and Depression Rating Scale. *Acta Psychiatrica Scandinavica, 67*, 361–370.

Zivadinov, R., Zorzon, M., Bosco, A., Bragadin, L.M., Moretti, R., Bonfigli, L., ... Cazzato, G. (1999). Sexual dysfunction in multiple sclerosis: II. correlation analysis. *Multiple Sclerosis, 5*, 428–431.

Zorzon, M., Zivadinov, R., Bosco, A., Bragadin, L. M., Moretti, R., Bonfigli, L., ... Cazzato, G. (1999). Sexual dysfunction in multiple sclerosis: A case-control study. I. frequency and comparison of groups. *Multiple Sclerosis, 5*, 418–427.

Chapter 13

Abramowitz, J.S., Meltzer-Brody, S., Leserman, J., Killenberg, S., Rinaldi, K., Mahaffey, B.L., & Pedersen, C. (2010). Obsessional thoughts and compulsive behaviors in a sample of women with postpartum mood symptoms. *Archives of Women's Mental Health, 13*, 523–530.

Alhusen, J.L., Gross, D., Hayat, M.J., Woods, A.B., & Sharps, P.W. (2012). The influence of maternal–fetal attachment and health practices on neonatal outcomes in low-income, urban women. *Research in Nursing & Health, 35*, 112–120.

American Diabetes Association. (2012). What is gestational diabetes? Retrieved from www.diabetes.org/diabetes-basics/gestational/what-is-gestational-diabetes.html

Andersen, A.M.N., Wohlfahrt, J., Christens, P., Olsen, J., & Melbye, M. (2000). Maternal age and fetal loss: Population-based register linkage study. *British Medical Journal, 320*, 1708–1712.

Aranda, M.P., & Knight, B.G. (1997). The influence of ethnicity and culture on the caregiver stress and coping process: A sociocultural review and analysis. *The Gerontologist, 37*, 342–354.

Armstrong, D., & Hutti, M. (1998). Pregnancy after perinatal loss: The relationship between anxiety and prenatal attachment. *Journal of Obstetric, Gynecologic, & Neonatal Nursing, 27*, 183–189.

Attard, C.L., Kohli, M.A., Coleman, S., Bradley, C., Hux, M., Atanackovic, G., & Torrance, G.W. (2002). The burden of illness of severe nausea and vomiting of pregnancy in the United States. *American Journal of Obstetrics and Gynecology, 186*, S220–S227.

Austin, M.P.V., Hadzi-Pavlovic, D., Priest, S.R., Reilly, N., Wilhelm, K., Saint, K., & Parker, G. (2010). Depressive and anxiety disorders in the postpartum period: How prevalent are they and can we improve their detection? *Archives of Women's Mental Health, 13*, 395–401.

Avis, N.E., Stellato, R., Crawford, S., Bromberger, J., Ganz, P., Cain, V., & Kagawa-Singer, M. (2001). Is there a menopausal syndrome? Menopausal status and symptoms across racial/ethnic groups. *Social Science & Medicine, 52*(3), 345–356.

Ayers, B., Forshaw, M., & Hunter, M. (2010). The impact of attitudes towards the menopause on women's symptom experience: A systematic review. *Maturitas, 65*, 28–36.

Beck, C.T., & Gable, R.K. (2000). Postpartum Depression Screening Scale: Development and psychometric testing. *Nursing Research, 49*, 272–282.

Berg, J.A. (2011). The stress of caregiving in midlife women. *The Female Patient, 36*, 33–36.

Berle, J., Mykletun, A., Daltveit, A.K., Rasmussen, S., Holsten, F., & Dahl, A.A. (2005). Neonatal outcomes in offspring of women with anxiety and depression during pregnancy. *Archives of Women's Mental Health, 8*, 181–189.

Blalock, J.A., Fouladi, R.T., Wetter, D.W., & Cinciripini, P.M. (2005). Depression in pregnant women seeking smoking cessation treatment. *Addictive behaviors, 30*, 1195–1208.

Boivin, J., Takefman, J., & Braverman, A. (2011). The fertility quality of life (FertiQoL) tool: Development and general psychometric properties. *Fertility and Sterility, 96*, 409–415.

Borg, S., & Lasker, J. (1981). *When pregnancy fails: Families coping with miscarriage, stillbirth, and infant death.* Boston: Beacon Press.

Boyd, R.C., Le, H.N., & Somberg, R. (2005). Review of screening instruments for postpartum depression. *Archives of Women's Mental Health, 8*, 141–153.

Buist, A., Gotman, N., & Yonkers, K.A. (2011). Generalized anxiety disorder: Course and risk factors in pregnancy. *Journal of Affective Disorders, 131*, 277–283.

Burns, L.H. (2007). Psychiatric aspects of infertility and infertility treatments. *Psychiatric Clinics of North America, 30*, 689–716.

Bushnik, T., Cook, J.L., Yuzpe, A.A., Tough, S., & Collins, J. (2012). Estimating the prevalence of infertility in Canada. *Human Reproduction, 27*, 738–746.

Canadian Diabetes Association. (2012). Gestational diabetes: Preventing complications in pregnancy. Retrieved from www.diabetes.ca/diabetes-and-you/what/gestational/

Centers for Disease Control and Prevention (CDC). (2012). Health effects of cigarette smoking. Retrieved from www.cdc.gov/tobacco/data_statistics/fact_sheets/health_effects/effects_cig_smoking/

Chandra, A., Martinez, G.M., Mosher, W.D., Abma, J.C., & Jones, J. (2005). *Fertility, family planning, and reproductive health of US women: Data from the 2002 National Survey of Family Growth.* Vital and Health Statistics, Series 23, no. 25. Hyattsville, Md: US Department of Health and Human Services, National Center for Health Statistics.

Chen, T.-H., Shang, S.-P., Tsai, C.-F., & Juang, K.-D. (2004). Prevalence of depressive and anxiety disorders in an assisted reproductive technique clinic. *Human Reproduction, 19*, 2313–2318.

Cohen, L.S., Altshuler, L.L., Harlow, B.L., Nonacs, R., Newport, D.J., Viguera, A.C., … Reminick, A.M. (2006). Relapse of major depression during pregnancy in women who maintain or discontinue antidepressant treatment. *Journal of the American Medical Association, 295*, 499–507.

Cox, J.L., Holden, J.M., & Sagovsky, R. (1987). Detection of postnatal depression: Development of the 10-item Edinburgh Postnatal Depression Scale. *British Journal of Psychiatry, 150*, 782–786.

Curbow, B., Khoury, A.J., & Weisman, C.S. (1998). Provision of mental health services in women's health centers. *Women's Health: Research on Gender, Behavior, and Policy, 4*, 71–91.

Curry, S.J., McBride, C., Grothaus, L., Lando, H., & Pirie, P. (2001). Motivation for smoking cessation among pregnant women. *Psychology of Addictive Behaviors, 15*, 126.

Derry, P.S., & Dillaway, H.E. (2013). Rethinking menopause. In M.V. Spiers, P.A. Geller, & J.D. Kloss (Eds.), *Women's Health Psychology* (pp. 440–463). Hoboken, NJ: John Wiley & Sons.

DiClemente, C.C., Dolan-Mullen, P., & Windsor, R.A. (2000). The process of pregnancy smoking cessation: Implications for interventions. *Tobacco control, 9*(Suppl. 3), iii16–iii21.

Dobie, D.J., Kivlahan, D.R., Maynard, C., Bush, K.R., Davis, T.M., & Bradley, K.A. (2004). Posttraumatic stress disorder in female veterans: Association with self-reported health problems and functional impairment. *Archives of Internal Medicine, 164*, 394.

Engelhard, I.M., van den Hout, M.A., & Arntz, A. (2001). Posttraumatic stress disorder after pregnancy loss. *General Hospital Psychiatry, 23*, 62–66.

Evans, M.I., Ayoub, M.A., Shalhoub, A.G., Feldman, B., & Yaron, Y. (2002). Spontaneous abortions in couples declining multifetal pregnancy reduction. *Fetal Diagnosis and Therapy, 17*, 343–346.

Farr, S.L., Bitsko, R.H., Hayes, D.K., & Dietz, P.M. (2010). Mental health and access to services among US women of reproductive age. *American Journal of Obstetrics and Gynecology, 203*, 542.e1–9.

Field, T., Hernandez-Reif, M., & Feijo, L. (2002). Breastfeeding in depressed mother–infant dyads. *Early Child Development and Care, 172*, 539–545.

Flynn, H.A., Davis, M., Marcus, S.M., Cunningham, R., & Blow, F.C. (2004). Rates of maternal depression in pediatric emergency department and relationship to child service utilization. *General Hospital Psychiatry, 26*, 316–322.

Gaynes, B.N., Gavin, N., Meltzer-Brody, S., Lohr, K.N., Swinson, T., Gartlehner, G., … Miller, W.C. (2005). Perinatal depression: prevalence, screening accuracy, and screening outcomes. *Evidence Report/Technology Assessment (Summary), 119*, 1–8.

Geller, P.A. (2004). Pregnancy as a stressful life event. *CNS Spectrums, 9*, 188–197.

Geller, P.A. (2012). The role of emerging technology in women's response to pregnancy loss. *Expert Review of Obstetrics & Gynecology, 7*, 19–23.

Geller, P.A., Klier, C.M., & Neugebauer, R. (2001). Anxiety disorders following miscarriage. *Journal of Clinical Psychiatry, 62*, 432–438.

Geller, P.A., Nelson, A.R., Kornfield, S.L., & Silverman, D.G. (2014). Women's health: Obstetrics & gynecology. In C.M. Hunter, C.L. Hunter, & R. Kessler (Eds.), *Handbook of clinical psychology in medical settings: Evidence-based assessment and intervention*. New York: Springer.

Geller, P.A., Psaros, C., & Kerns, D. (2006). Web-based resources for health care providers and women following pregnancy loss. *Journal of Obstetric, Gynecologic, & Neonatal Nursing, 35*, 523–532.

Geller, P.A., Psaros, C., & Kornfield, S.L. (2010). Satisfaction with pregnancy loss aftercare: Are women getting what they want? *Archives of Women's Mental health, 13*, 111–124.

Glover, V. (2011). Prenatal stress and the origins of psychopathology: An evolutionary perspective. *Journal of Child Psychology and Psychiatry, 52*, 356–367.

Gold, K.J., Boggs, M.E., Mugisha, E., & Palladino, C.L. (2011). Internet message boards for pregnancy loss: Who's online and why? *Women's Health Issues, 22*, 67–72.

Gossier, S.M. (2010). Use of complementary and alternative therapies during pregnancy, postpartum, and lactation. *Journal of Psychosocial Nursing and Mental Health Services, 48*, 30–36.

Grimes, D.A. (2006). Estimation of pregnancy-related mortality risk by pregnancy outcome, United States, 1991 to 1999. *American Journal of Obstetrics & Gynecology,194*, 92–94.

Health Canada. (2002). Women and smoking in Canada. Canadian Tobacco Use Monitoring Survey. Retrieved from www.hc-sc.gc.ca/hc-ps/tobac-tabac/research-recherche/stat/_ctums-esutc_fs-if/2002_women-eng.php

Henshaw, C. (2003). Mood disturbance in the early puerperium: A review. *Archives of Women's Mental Health, 6*, 33–42.

Hughes, M.J., & Jones, L. (2000). *Women, domestic violence and posttraumatic stress disorder (PTSD)*. A report for the California State University Faculty Research Fellows Program Office for the California Governor's Office of Planning and Research.

Hughes, P., Turton, P., Hopper, E., McGauley, G.A., & Fonagy, P. (2001). Disorganised attachment behaviour among infants born subsequent to stillbirth. *Journal of Child Psychology and Psychiatry, 42*, 791–801.

Issokson, D. (2004). Effects of childhood abuse on childbearing and perinatal health. In K.A. Kendall-Tacket (Ed.), *Health consequences of abuse in the family: A clinical guide for evidence-based practice*. Washington: American Psychological Association.

Jaffe, J., & Diamond, M. (2011). *Reproductive trauma: Psychotherapy with infertility and pregnancy loss clients*. Washington: American Psychological Association.

Janssen, H.J.E.M., Cuisinier, M.C.J., Hoogduin, K.A.L., & de Graauw, K.P.H.M. (1996). Controlled prospective study of the mental health of women following pregnancy loss. *American Journal of Psychiatry, 153*, 226–230.

Jennings, K.D., Ross, S., Popper, S., & Elmore, M. (1999). Thoughts of harming infants in depressed and nondepressed mothers. *Journal of Affective Disorders, 5*(1–2), 21–28.

Jones, I., & Cantwell, R. (2010). The classification of perinatal mood disorders—Suggestions for DSMV and ICD11. *Archives of Women's Mental Health, 13*, 33–36.

Jones, I., & Craddock, N. (2001). Familiality of the puerperal trigger in bipolar disorder: Results of a family study. *American Journal of Psychiatry, 158*, 913–917.

Kendell, R.E., Chalmers, J.C., & Platz, C. (1987). Epidemiology of puerperal psychoses. *British Journal of Psychiatry, 150*, 662–673.

Kessler, R.C., McGonagle, K.A., Swartz, M., Blazer, D.G., & Nelson, C.B. (1993). Sex and depression in the National Comorbidity Survey I: Lifetime prevalence, chronicity and recurrence. *Journal of Affective Disorders, 29*, 85–96.

Klier, C.M., Geller, P.A., & Ritsher, J.B. (2002). Affective disorders in the aftermath of miscarriage: A comprehensive review. *Archives of Women's Mental Health, 5*, 129–149.

Koleva, H., Stuart, S., O'Hara, M.W., & Bowman-Reif, J. (2011). Risk factors for depressive symptoms during pregnancy. *Archives of Women's Mental Health, 14*, 99–105.

Kuehn, B.M. (2010). Depression guideline highlights choices, care for hard-to-treat or pregnant patients. *Journal of the American Medical Association, 304*, 2465–2466.

Kumar, R. (1994). Postnatal mental illness: A transcultural perspective. *Social Psychiatry and Psychiatric Epidemiology, 29*, 250–264.

Lee, C. (1998). *Women's health: Psychological and social perspectives*. London: Sage.

Lee, C., & Slade, P. (1996). Miscarriage as a traumatic event: A review of the literature and new implications for intervention. *Journal of Psychosomatic Research, 40*, 235–244.

Llewellyn, A.M., Stowe, Z.N., & Nemeroff, C.B. (1997). Depression during pregnancy and the puerperium. *Journal of Clinical Psychiatry, 58*, 26–32.

Lumley, J., Chamberlain, C., Dowswell, T., Oliver, S., Oakley, L., & Watson, L. (2009). Interventions for promoting smoking cessation during pregnancy. *Cochrane Database of Systematic Reviews, 3*.

Lydon, K., Dunne, F., Owens, L., Avalos, G., Sarma, K., O'Connor, C., … McGuire, B. (2012). Psychological stress associated with diabetes during pregnancy: A pilot study. *Irish Medical Journal, 105*(Suppl. 5), 26.

MacDorman, M.F., Menacker, F., & Declercq, E. (2008). Cesarean birth in the United States: Epidemiology, trends, and outcomes. *Clinics in Perinatology, 35*, 293–307.

Mann, J.R., McKeown, R.E., Bacon, J., Vesselinov, R., & Bush, F. (2008). Predicting depressive symptoms and grief after pregnancy loss. *Journal of Psychosomatic Obstetrics & Gynecology, 29*, 274–279.

Marchand, W.R., & Thatcher, J.W. (2008). Psychopharmacologic management of depression in pregnant women and breastfeeding mothers. *Hospital Physician*, 8–16.

Martin, J.A., Hamilton, B.E., Sutton, P.D., Ventura, S.J., Menacker, F., Kirmeyer, S., & Munson, M.L. (2007). Births: Final data for 2005. *National Vital Statistics Reports, 56*(6), 1–103.

Mauri, M., Oppo, A., Montagnani, M.S., Borri, C., Banti, S., Camilleri, V., … Cassano, G.B. (2010). Beyond "postpartum depressions": Specific anxiety diagnoses during pregnancy predict different outcomes: Results from PND-ReScU. *Journal of Affective Disorders, 127*, 177–184.

Mechanic, M.B., Weaver, T.L., & Resick, P.A. (2008). Mental health consequences of intimate partner abuse: A multidimensional assessment of four different forms of abuse. *Violence Against Women, 14*, 634–654.

Neugebauer, R., Kline, J., Shrout, P., Skodol, A., O'Connor, P., Geller, P.A., … Susser, M. (1997). Major depressive disorder in the 6 months after miscarriage. *Journal of the American Medical Association, 277*, 383–388.

Newton, C.R., Sherrard, W., & Glavac, I. (1999). The Fertility Problem Inventory: Measuring perceived infertility-related stress. *Fertility and Sterility, 72*, 54–62.

Novick, D., & Flynn, H.A. (2013). Psychiatric symptoms and pregnancy. In M.V. Spiers, P.A. Geller, & J.D. Kloss (Eds.), *Women's health psychology*. New York: John Wiley and Sons.

O'Connor, T.G., Heron, J., Golding, J., Beveridge, M., & Glover, V. (2002). Maternal antenatal anxiety and children's behavioural/emotional problems at 4 years. *British Journal of Psychiatry, 180*, 502–508.

Office on Women's Health (2009). Infertility fact sheet. Retrieved from womenshealth.gov/publications/our-publications/fact-sheet/infertility.pdf

O'Hara, M.W., Schlechte, J.A., Lewis, D.A., & Varner, M.W. (1991). Controlled prospective study of postpartum mood disorders: Psychological, environmental, and hormonal variables. *Journal of Abnormal Psychology, 100*, 63.

O'Hara, M.W., Stuart, S., Gorman, L.L., & Wenzel, A. (2000). Efficacy of interpersonal psychotherapy for postpartum depression. *Archives of General Psychiatry, 57*(11), 1039.

O'Hara, M.W., & Swain, A.M. (1996). Rates and risk of postpartum depression—A meta-analysis. *International Review of Psychiatry, 8*, 37–54.

Pavalko, E.K., & Woodbury, S. (2000). Social roles as process: Caregiving careers and women's health. *Journal of Health and Social Behavior, 41*, 91–105.

Prince, L.B., & Domar, A.D. (2013). The stress of infertility. In M.V. Spiers, P.A. Geller, & J.D. Kloss (Eds.), *Women's health psychology*. New York: John Wiley and Sons.

Remennick, L.I. (2001). "All my life is one big nursing home": Russian immigrant women in Israel speak about double caregiver stress. *Women's Studies International Forum, 24*, 685–700.

Righetti-Veltema, M., Conne-Perréard, E., Bousquet, A., & Manzano, J. (2002). Postpartum depression and mother–infant relationship at 3 months old. *Journal of Affective Disorders, 70*, 291–306.

Robertson, E., Grace, S., Wallington, T., & Stewart, D.E. (2004). Antenatal risk factors for postpartum depression: A synthesis of recent literature. *General Hospital Psychiatry, 26*, 289–295.

Robinson, K. (1988). Older women who are caregivers. *Health Care for Women International, 9*, 239–249.

Ross, L.E., & McLean, L.M. (2006). Anxiety disorders during pregnancy and the postpartum period: A systematic review. *Journal of Clinical Psychiatry, 67*, 1285–1298.

Saisto, T., Salmela-Aro, K., Nurmi, J.E., Könönen, T., & Halmesmäki, E. (2001). A randomized controlled trial of intervention in fear of childbirth. *Obstetrics & Gynecology, 98*(5, Part 1), 820.

Saraiya, M., Green, C.A., Berg, C.J., Hopkins, F.W., Koonin, L.M., & Atrash, H.K. (1999). Spontaneous abortion-related deaths among women in the United States—1981–1991. *Obstetrics & Gynecology, 9*, 172–176.

Schiller, J.S., Lucas, J.W., Ward, B.W., & Peregoy, J.A. (2012). *Summary health statistics for US adults: National Health Interview Survey, 2010*. Vital and Health Statistics, Series 10, no. 252. Hyattsville, Md: US Department of Health and Human Services, National Center for Health Statistics.

Sinha, M. (2012). Violence against intimate partners. Received from www.statcan.gc.ca/pub/85-002-x/2012001/article/11643/11643-2-eng.htm

Sjögren, B., & Thomassen, P. (1997). Obstetric outcome in 100 women with severe anxiety over childbirth. *Actaobstetricia et gynecologica Scandinavica, 76*, 948–952.

Sockol, L.E., Epperson, C.N., & Barber, J.P. (2011). A meta-analysis of treatments for perinatal depression. *Clinical Psychology Review, 31*, 839–849.

Striepe, M.I., & Coons, H.L. (2002). Women's health in primary care: Interdisciplinary interventions. *Families, Systems, & Health, 20*, 237.

Swanson, L.M., Flynn, H.A., Wilburn, K., Marcus, S., & Armitage, R. (2010). Maternal mood and sleep in children of women at risk for perinatal depression. *Archives of Women's Mental Health, 13*, 531–534.

Thapar, A.K., & Thapar, A. (1992). Psychological sequelae of miscarriage: A controlled study using the general health questionnaire and the hospital anxiety and depression scale. *British Journal of General Practice, 42*, 94.

Theut, S.K., Pedersen, F.A., Zaslow, M.J., & Rabinovich, B.A. (1988). Pregnancy subsequent to perinatal loss: Parental anxiety and depression. *Journal of the American Academy of Child & Adolescent Psychiatry, 27*, 289–292.

Tjaden, P., & Thoennes, N. (1998).*Stalking in America: Findings from the National Violence against Women Survey*. Washington: US Department of Justice, Office of Justice Programs, National Institute of Justice.

Tjaden, P., & Thoennes, N. (2000). *Extent, nature, and consequences of intimate partner violence: Findings from the National Violence against Women Survey*. Washington: US Department of Justice, Office of Justice Programs, National Institute of Justice.

Toedter, L.J., Lasker, J.N., & Janssen, H.J.E.M. (2001). International comparison of studies using the Perinatal Grief Scale: A decade of research on pregnancy loss. *Death Studies, 25*, 205–228.

Turner, C., Boyle, F., & O'Rourke, P. (2003). Mothers' health post-partum and their patterns of seeking vaccination for their infants. *International Journal of Nursing Practice, 9,* 120–126.

Verhaak, C.M., Smeenk, J.M.J., van Minnen, A., Kremer, J.A.M., & Kraaimaat, F.W. (2005). A longitudinal, prospective study on emotional adjustment before, during and after consecutive fertility treatment cycles. *Human Reproduction, 20,* 2253–2260.

Vesga-Lopez, O., Blanco, C., Keyes, K., Olfson, M., Grant, B.F., & Hasin, D.S. (2008). Psychiatric disorders in pregnant and postpartum women in the United States. *Archives of General Psychiatry, 65,* 805.

Viguera, A.C., Tondo, L., Koukopoulos, A.E., Reginaldi, D., Lepri, B., & Baldessarini, R.J. (2011). Episodes of mood disorders in 2,252 pregnancies and postpartum periods. *American Journal of Psychiatry, 168,* 1179–1185.

Vogel, L. (2011). Tailored treatment for postpartum depression. *Canadian Medical Association Journal, 183,* 1163–1164.

Watkins, S., Meltzer-Brody, S., Zolnoun, D., & Stuebe, A. (2011). Early breastfeeding experiences and postpartum depression. *Obstetrics & Gynecology, 118*(2, Part 1), 214–221.

West, A.E., & Newman, D.L. (2003). Worried and blue: Mild parental anxiety and depression in relation to the development of young children's temperament and behavior problems. *Parenting: Science and Practice, 3,* 133–154.

Willinger, M., Ko, C.W., & Reddy, U.M. (2009). Racial disparities in stillbirth risk across gestation in the United States. *American Journal of Obstetrics and Gynecology, 201*(5), 469. e1–8.

Wisner, K.L., Parry, B.L., & Piontek, C.M. (2002). Postpartum depression. *New England Journal of Medicine, 347,* 194–199.

Wisner, K.L., Peindl, K.S., Gigliotti, T., & Hanusa, B.H. (1999). Obsessions and compulsions in women with postpartum depression. *Journal of Clinical Psychiatry, 60,* 176.

World Health Organization (WHO). (1999). Definition, diagnosis and classification of diabetes mellitus and its complications. Retrieved from www.staff.ncl.ac.uk/philip.home/who_dmc.htm#DiagGDM

Yonkers, K.A., Vigod, S., & Ross, L.E. (2011). Diagnosis, pathophysiology, and management of mood disorders in pregnant and postpartum women. *Obstetrics & Gynecology, 117,* 961–977.

Chapter 14

Aalto, A.M., Harkapaa, K., Aro, A.R., & Rissanen, P. (2002). Ways of coping with asthma in everyday life: Validation of the Asthma Specific Coping Scale. *Journal of Psychosomatic Research, 53,* 1061–1069.

Alexander, F. (1950). *Psychosomatic medicine: Its principles and applications.* New York: Norton.

Anthonisen, N.R., Connett, J.E., Murray, R.P., for the Lung Health Study Research Group (2002). Smoking and lung function of lung health study participants after 11 Years. *American Journal of Respiratory and Critical Care Medicine, 166,* 675–679.

Apfelbacher, C.J., Hankins, M., Stenner, P., Frew, A.J., & Smith, H.E. (2011). Measuring asthma-specific quality of life: Structured review. *Allergy, 66,* 439–457.

Bailey, E.J., Cates, C.J., Kruske, S.G., Morris, P.S., Brown, N., & Chang, A.B. (2009). Culture-specific programs for children and adults from minority groups who have asthma. *Cochrane Database of Systematic Reviews, 2,* CD006580.

Banzett, R.B., Dempsey, J.A., O'Donnell, D.E., & Wamboldt, M.Z. (2000). Symptom perception and respiratory sensation in asthma. *American Journal of Respiratory and Critical Care Medicine, 162,* 1178–1182.

Baraniak, A., & Sheffield, D. (2010). The efficacy of psychologically based interventions to improve anxiety, depression and quality of life in COPD: A systematic review and meta-analysis. *Patient Education and Counseling, 83,* 29–36.

Bender, B.G., Milgrom, H., & Apter, A. (2003). Adherence intervention research: What have we learned and what do we do next? *Journal of Allergy and Clinical Immunology, 112,* 489–494.

Bobb, C., Ritz, T., Rowlands, G., & Griffiths, C. (2010). Effects of allergen and trigger avoidance advice in primary care on asthma control—A randomized controlled trial. *Clinical and Experimental Allergy, 40,* 143–152.

Bogaerts, K., Notebaert, K., Van Diest, I., Devriese, S., De Peuter, S., & Van den Bergh, O. (2005). Accuracy of respiratory symptom perception in different affective contexts. *Journal of Psychosomatic Research, 58,* 537–543.

Bourbeau, J., & Bartlett, S. J. (2008). Patient adherence in COPD. *Thorax, 63,* 831–838.

Bourbeau, J., & van der Palen, J. (2009). Promoting effective self-management programmes to improve COPD. *European Respiratory Journal, 33,* 461–463.

Braman, S.S. (2006). The global burden of asthma. *Chest, 130,* 4S–12S.

Brenes, G.A. (2003). Anxiety and chronic obstructive pulmonary disease: Prevalence, impact, and treatment. *Psychosomatic Medicine, 65,* 963–970.

Broadbent, E., Petrie, K.J., Main, J., & Weinman, J. (2006). The Brief Illness Perception Questionnaire. *Journal of Psychosomatic Research, 60,* 631–637.

Bruton, A., & Thomas, M. (2011). The role of breathing training in asthma management. *Current Opinion in Allergy and Clinical Immunology, 11,* 53–57.

Bruzzese, J.M., Sheares, B.J., Vincent, E.J., Du, Y., Sadeghi, H., Levison, M.J., ... Evans, D. (2011). Effects of a school-based intervention for urban adolescents with asthma: A controlled trial. *American Journal of Respiratory and Critical Care Medicine, 183,* 998–1006.

Buist, A.S., McBurnie, M.A., Vollmer, W.M., Gillespie, S., Burney, P., Mannino, D.M., ... Nizankowska-Mogilnicka, E. (2007). International variation in the prevalence of COPD (The BOLD Study): A population-based prevalence study. *Lancet, 370*(9589), 741–750.

Burgess, A., Kunik, M.E., & Stanley, M.A. (2005). Chronic obstructive pulmonary disease: Assessing and treating psychological issues in patients with COPD. *Geriatrics, 60*(12), 18–21.

Bush, A. (2007). Diagnosis of asthma in children under five. *Primary Care Respiratory Journal, 16*(1), 7–15.

Carrieri-Kohlman, V., Gormley, J.M., Eiser, S., Demir-Deviren, S., Nguyen, H., Paul, S.M., & Stulbarg, M.S. (2001). Dyspnea and the affective response during exercise training in obstructive pulmonary disease. *Nursing Research, 50,* 136–146.

Carson, K.V., Chandratilleke, M.G., Picot, J., Brinn, M.P., Esterman, A.J., & Smith, B.J. (2013). Physical training for asthma. *Cochrane Database of Systematic Reviews* (9), CD001116.

Chen, E., Chim, L.S., Strunk, R.C., & Miller, G.E. (2007). The role of the social environment in children and adolescents with asthma. *American Journal of Respiratory Critical Care Medicine, 176*, 644–649.

Cookson, H., Granell, R., Joinson, C., Ben-Shlomo, Y., & Henderson, A.J. (2009). Mothers' anxiety during pregnancy is associated with asthma in their children. *Journal of Allergy and Clinical Immunology, 123*, 847–853.

Coventry, P.A. (2009). Does pulmonary rehabilitation reduce anxiety and depression in chronic obstructive pulmonary disease? *Current Opinion in Pulmonary Medicine, 15*, 143–149.

Coventry, P.A., & Gellatly, J.L. (2008). Improving outcomes for COPD patients with mild-to-moderate anxiety and depression: A systematic review of cognitive behavioural therapy. *British Journal of Health Psychology, 13*, 381–400.

Dahlén, I., & Janson, C. (2002). Anxiety and depression are related to the outcome of emergency treatment in patients with obstructive pulmonary disease. *Chest, 122*, 1633–1637.

de Godoy, D.V., & de Godoy, R.F. (2003). A randomized controlled trial of the effect of psychotherapy on anxiety and depression in chronic obstructive pulmonary disease. *Archives of Physical Medicine and Rehabilitation, 84*, 1154–1157.

De Peuter, S., Janssens, T., Van Diest, I., Stans, L., Troosters, T., Decramer, M., … Vlaeyen, J.W.S. (2011). Dyspnea-related anxiety: The Dutch version of the Breathlessness Beliefs Questionnaire. *Chronic Respiratory Disease, 8*, 11–19.

Donaldson, G.C., Seemungal, T.A.R., Bhowmik, A., & Wedzicha, J.A. (2002). Relationship between exacerbation frequency and lung function decline in chronic obstructive pulmonary disease. *Thorax, 57*, 847–852.

Dowson, C.A., Town, G.I., Frampton, C., & Mulder, R.T. (2004). Psychopathology and illness beliefs influence COPD self-management. *Journal of Psychosomatic Research, 56*(3), 333–340.

Effing, T., Monninkhof, E.M., van der Valk, P.D., van der Palen, J., van Herwaarden, C.L., Partidge, M.R., … Zielhuis, G.A. (2007). Self-management education for patients with chronic obstructive pulmonary disease. *Cochrane Database of Systematic Reviews, 4*, CD002990.

Eisner, M.D., Blanc, P.D., Yelin, E.H., Katz, P.P., Sanchez, G., Iribarren, C., & Omachi, T.A. (2010). Influence of anxiety on health outcomes in COPD. *Thorax, 65*, 229–234.

Emery, C.F., Schein, R.L., Hauck, E.R., & MacIntyre, N.R. (1998). Psychological and cognitive outcomes of a randomized trial of exercise among patients with chronic obstructive pulmonary disease. *Health Psychology, 17*, 232–240.

Eneli, I.U., Skybo, T., & Camargo, C.A. Jr. (2008). Weight loss and asthma: A systematic review. *Thorax, 63*, 671–676.

First, M.B., Gibbon, M., Spitzer, R.L., & Williams, J.B.W. (2002). *User's guide for the SCID-I: Structured Clinical Interview for DSM-IV-TR Axis I Disorders* (Research version). Biometrics Research Department, New York State Psychiatric Institute.

Fischer, M.J., Scharloo, M., Abbink, J.J., van't Hul, A.J., van Ranst, D., Rudolphus, A., … Kaptein, A.A. (2009).

Drop-out and attendance in pulmonary rehabilitation: The role of clinical and psychosocial variables. *Respiratory Medicine, 103*, 1564–1571.

George, J., Kong, D.C.M., Thoman, R., & Stewart, K. (2005). Factors associated with medication nonadherence in patients with COPD. *Chest, 128*, 3198–3204.

Gershon, A.S., Wang, C., Wilton, A.S., Raut, R., & To, T. (2010). Trends in chronic obstructive pulmonary disease prevalence, incidence, and mortality in Ontario, Canada, 1996 to 2007: A population-based study. *Archives of Internal Medicine, 170*, 560–565.

Giardino, N.D., Curtis, J.L., Abelson, J.L., King, A.P., Pamp, B., Liberzon, I., & Martinez, F. J. (2010a). The impact of panic disorder on interoception and dyspnea reports in chronic obstructive pulmonary disease. *Biological Psychology, 84*, 142–146.

Giardino, N.D., Curtis, J.L., Andrei, A.-C., Fan, V.S., Benditt, J.O., Lyubkin, M., … the NETT Research Group. (2010b). Anxiety is associated with diminished exercise performance and quality of life in severe emphysema: A cross-sectional study. *Respiratory Research, 11*, 29.

Glassman, A.H., Helzer, J.E., Covey, L.S., Cottler, L.B., Stetner, F., Tipp, J.E., & Johnson, J. (1990). Smoking, smoking cessation, and major depression. *Journal of the American Medical Association, 264*, 1546–1549.

Global Initiative for Asthma (GINA). (2010). *Global strategy for asthma management and prevention*. Retrieved from www.ginasthma.org/

Global Initiative for Chronic Obstructive Lung Disease (GOLD). (2011). *Global strategy for the diagnosis, management and prevention of COPD*. Retrieved from www.goldcopd.org/

Goodwin, R.D., Jacobi, F., & Thefeld, W. (2003). Mental disorders and asthma in the community. *Archives of General Psychiatry, 60*, 1125–1130.

Guyatt, G.H., Berman, L.B., Townsend, M., Pugsley, S.O., & Chambers, L.W. (1987). A measure of quality of life for clinical trials in chronic lung disease. *Thorax, 42*, 773–778.

Guyatt, G.H., Feeny, D.H., & Patrick, D.L. (1993). Measuring health-related quality of life. *Annals of Internal Medicine, 118*, 622–629.

Hackman, R.M., Stern, J.S., & Gershwin, M.E. (2000). Hypnosis and asthma: A critical review. *Journal of Asthma, 37*, 1–15.

Hajiro, T., Nishimura, K., Tsukino, M., Ikeda, A., Oga, T., & Izumi, T. (1999). A comparison of the level of dyspnea vs disease severity in indicating the health-related quality of life of patients with COPD. *Chest, 116*, 1632–1637.

Halm, E.A., Mora, P., & Leventhal, H. (2006). No symptoms, no asthma: The acute episodic disease belief is associated with poor self-management among inner-city adults with persistent asthma. *Chest, 129*, 573–580.

Halterman, J.S., Riekert, K., Bayer, A., Fagnano, M., Tremblay, P., Blaakman, S., & Borrelli, B. (2011). A pilot study to enhance preventive asthma care among urban adolescents with asthma. *Journal of Asthma, 48*, 523–530.

Hardie, G.E., Janson, S., Gold, W.M., Carrieri-Kohlman, V., & Boushey, H.A. (2000). Ethnic differences: Word descriptors used by African-American and White asthma patients during induced bronchoconstriction. *Chest, 117*, 935–943.

Hasler, G., Gergen, P.J., Kleinbaum, D.G., Ajdacic, V., Gamma, A., Eich, D., ... Angst, J. (2005). Asthma and panic in young adults: A 20-year prospective community study. *American Journal of Respiratory and Critical Care Medicine, 171*, 1224–1230.

Huntley, A., White, A.R., & Ernst, E. (2002). Relaxation therapies for asthma: A systematic review. *Thorax, 57*, 127–131.

Hyland, M.E., Kenyon, C.A., Taylor, M., & Morice, A.H. (1993). Steroid prescribing for asthmatics: Relationship with asthma symptom checklist and living with asthma questionnaire. *British Journal of Clinical Psychology, 32*, 505–511.

Isenberg, S.A., Lehrer, P.M., & Hochron, S. (1992). The effects of suggestion and emotional arousal on pulmonary function in asthma: A review and a hypothesis regarding vagal mediation. *Psychosomatic Medicine, 54*, 192–216.

Janssens, T., De Peuter, S., Stans, L., Verleden, G., Troosters, T., Decramer, M., & Van den Bergh, O. (2011). Dyspnea perception in COPD: Association between anxiety, dyspnea-related fear and dyspnea in a pulmonary rehabilitation. *Chest, 140*, 618–625.

Janssens, T., Verleden, G., De Peuter, S., Van Diest, I., & Van den Bergh, O. (2009). Inaccurate perception of asthma symptoms: A cognitive-affective framework and implications for asthma treatment. *Clinical Psychology Review, 29*, 317–327.

Jones, P.W., Harding, G., Berry, P., Wiklund, I., Chen, W.-H., & Kline Leidy, N. (2009). Development and first validation of the COPD Assessment Test. *European Respiratory Journal, 34*, 648–654.

Jones, P.W., Quirk, F.H., & Baveystock, C.M. (1991). The St George's Respiratory Questionnaire. *Respiratory Medicine, 85* (Suppl. 2), 25–31.

Joyce, D.P., Jackevicius, C., Chapman, K.R., McIvor, R.A., & Kesten, S. (2000). The placebo effect in asthma drug therapy trials: A meta-analysis. *Journal of Asthma, 37*, 303–318.

Juniper, E.F., Guyatt, G.H., Cox, F.M., Ferrie, P.J., & King, D.R. (1999a). Development and validation of the Mini Asthma Quality of Life Questionnaire. *European Respiratory Journal, 14*, 32–38.

Juniper, E.F., O'Byrne, P.M., Guyatt, G.H., Ferrie, P.J., & King, D.R. (1999b). Development and validation of a questionnaire to measure asthma control. *European Respiratory Journal, 14*, 902–907.

Kaptein, A.A., Klok, T., Moss-Morris, R., & Brand, P.L. (2010). Illness perceptions: Impact on self-management and control in asthma. *Current Opinion in Allergy and Clinical Immunology, 10*, 194–199.

Kaptein, A.A., Scharloo, M., Fischer, M.J., Snoei, L., Cameron, L.D., Sont, J.K., ... Weinman, J. (2008). Illness perceptions and COPD: An emerging field for COPD patient management. *Journal of Asthma, 45*, 625–629.

Katz, P.P., Yelin, E.H., Eisner, M.D., & Blanc, P.D. (2002). Perceived control of asthma and quality of life among adults with asthma. *Annals of Allergy Asthma and Immunology, 89*, 251–258.

Kinsman, R.A., Luparello, T., O'Banion, K., & Spector, S. (1973). Multidimensional analysis of the subjective symptomatology of asthma. *Psychosomatic Medicine, 35*, 250–267.

Klinnert, M.D., Nelson, H.S., Price, M.R., Adinoff, A.D., Leung, D.Y., & Mrazek, D.A. (2001). Onset and persistence of childhood asthma: Predictors from infancy. *Pediatrics, 108*, E69.

Koinis-Mitchell, D., McQuaid, E.L., Friedman, D., Colon, A., Soto, J., Rivera, D.V., ... Canino, G. (2008). Latino caregivers' beliefs about asthma: Causes, symptoms, and practices. *Journal of Asthma, 45*, 205–210.

Kolbe, J., Fergusson, W., Vamos, M., & Garrett, J. (2002). Case-control study of severe life threatening asthma (SLTA) in adults: Psychological factors. *Thorax, 57*, 317–322.

Kopp, M.S., Thege, B.K., Balog, P., Stauder, A., Salavecz, G., Rózsa, S., ... Ádám, S. (2010). Measures of stress in epidemiological research. *Journal of Psychosomatic Research, 69*, 211–225.

Laurin, C., Moullec, G.G., Bacon, S.L., & Lavoie, K.L. (2012). Impact of anxiety and depression on COPD exacerbation risk. *American Journal of Respiratory and Critical Care Medicine, 185*, 918–923.

Lavoie, K.L., Boudreau, M., Plourde, A., Campbell, T.S., & Bacon, S.L. (2011). Association between generalized anxiety disorder and asthma morbidity. *Psychosomatic Medicine, 73*, 504–513.

Lebowitz, K.R., Suh, S., Diaz, P.T., & Emery, C.F. (2011). Effects of humor and laughter on psychological functioning, quality of life, health status, and pulmonary functioning among patients with chronic obstructive pulmonary disease: A preliminary investigation. *Heart & Lung: The Journal of Acute and Critical Care, 40*, 310–319.

Lehrer, P.M., Isenberg, S., & Hochron, S.M. (1993). Asthma and emotion: A review. *Journal of Asthma, 30*, 5–21.

Lehrer, P.M., Karavidas, M.K., Lu, S.E., Feldman, J., Kranitz, L., Abraham, S., ... Reynolds, R. (2008). Psychological treatment of comorbid asthma and panic disorder: A pilot study. *Journal of Anxiety Disorders, 22*, 671–683.

Lehrer, P.M., Vaschillo, E., Vaschillo, B., Lu, S.E., Scardella, A., Siddique, M., & Habib, R.H. (2004). Biofeedback treatment for asthma. *Chest, 126*, 352–361.

Leong, A.B., Ramsey, C.D., & Celedón, J.C. (2012). The challenge of asthma in minority populations. *Clinical Reviews in Allergy and Immunology, 43*, 156–183.

Leventhal, H., Meyer, D., & Nerenz, D. (1980). The common sense representation of illness danger. *Contributions to Medical Psychology, 2*, 7–30.

Liangas, G., Morton, J.R., and Henry, R.L. (2003). Mirth-triggered asthma: is laughter really the best medicine? *Pediatric Pulmonology, 36*, 107-112.

Livermore, N., Sharpe, L., & McKenzie, D. (2010). Prevention of panic attacks and panic disorder in COPD. *European Respiratory Journal, 35*, 557–563.

Lord, V., Hume, V., Kelly, J., Cave, P., Silver, J., Waldman, M., ... Hopkinson, N. (2012). Singing classes for chronic obstructive pulmonary disease: A randomized controlled trial. *BMC Pulmonary Medicine, 12*, 69.

McLean, S., Chandler, D., Nurmatov, U., Liu, J., Pagliari, C., Car, J., & Sheikh, A. (2011). Telehealthcare for asthma: A Cochrane review. *Canadian Medical Association Journal, 183*, E733–E742.

Mallia, P., & Johnston, S.L. (2006). How viral infections cause exacerbation of airway diseases. *Chest, 130*, 1203–1210.

Marks, G.B., Dunn, S.M., & Woolcock, A.J. (1992). A scale for the measurement of quality of life in adults with asthma. *Journal of Clinical Epidemiology, 45*, 461–472.

Mathers, C. D., & Loncar, D. (2006). Projections of global mortality and burden of disease from 2002 to 2030. *PLoS Medicine, 3*, e442.

Maurer, J., Rebbapragada, V., Borson, S., Goldstein, R., Kunik, M.E., Yohannes, A. M., & Hanania, N.A. (2008). Anxiety and depression in COPD. *Chest, 134*, 43S–56S.

Meek, P.M., Banzett, R., Parshall, M.B., Gracely, R.H., Schwartzstein, R.M., & Lansing, R. (2012). Reliability and validity of the multidimensional Dyspnea profile (MDP). *Chest, 141*, 1546–1553.

Meuret, A.E., & Ritz, T. (2010). Hyperventilation in panic disorder and asthma: Empirical evidence and clinical strategies. *International Journal of Psychophysiology, 78*, 68–79.

Millard, M.W. (2003). Dispelling the myths of exercise and asthma. *Proceedings (Baylor University Medical Center), 16*, 388–391.

Miller, B.D., & Strunk, R.C. (1989). Circumstances surrounding the deaths of children due to asthma. A case-control study. *American Journal of Diseases of Children, 143*, 1294–1299.

Miller, G.E., Cohen, S., & Ritchey, A.K. (2002). Chronic psychological stress and the regulation of pro-inflammatory cytokines: A glucocorticoid-resistance model, *Health Psychology, 21*, 531–541.

Nathan, R.A., Sorkness, C.A., Kosinski, M., Schatz, M., Li, J.T., Marcus, P., … Pendergraft, T.B. (2004). Development of the asthma control test: A survey for assessing asthma control. *Journal of Allergy and Clinical Immunology, 113*, 59–65.

National Heart, Lung, and Blood Institute/National Asthma Education and Prevention Program (NHLBI/NAEPP). (2007). *Expert panel report: Guidelines for the diagnosis and management of asthma* (NIH Publication No. 07-4051). Bethesda, Md: National Institutes of Health.

Ng, S.M., Li, A.M., Lou, V.W., Tso, I.F., Wan, P.Y., & Chan, D.F. (2008). Incorporating family therapy into asthma group intervention: A randomized waitlist-controlled trial. *Family Process, 47*, 115–130.

Nurmatov, U., Devereux, G., & Sheikh, A. (2011). Nutrients and foods for the primary prevention of asthma and allergy: Systematic review and meta-analysis. *Journal of Allergy and Clinical Immunology, 127*, 724–733.

Papi, A., Bellettato, C.M., Braccioni, F., Romagnoli, M., Casolari, P., Caramori, G., … Johnston, S.L. (2006). Infections and airway inflammation in chronic obstructive pulmonary disease severe exacerbations. *American Journal of Respiratory and Critical Care Medicine, 173*, 1114–1121.

Pearce, N., Pekkanen, J., & Beasley, R. (1999). How much asthma is really attributable to atopy? *Thorax, 54*, 268–272.

Pedersen, M.S., Benros, M.E., Agerbo, E., Børglum, A.D., & Mortensen, P.B. (2012). Schizophrenia in patients with atopic disorders with particular emphasis on asthma: A Danish population-based study. *Schizophrenia Research, 138*, 58–62.

Peytremann-Bridevaux, I., Staeger, P., Bridevaux, P.-O., Ghali, W.A., & Burnand, B. (2008). Effectiveness of chronic obstructive pulmonary disease-management programs: Systematic review and meta-analysis. *American Journal of Medicine, 121*, 433–443.

Polednak, A. P. (2010). Trends in mortality from COPD in selected U.S. states differing in tobacco control efforts. *COPD: Journal of Chronic Obstructive Pulmonary Disease, 7*, 63–69.

Posadzki, P., & Ernst, E. (2011). Yoga for asthma? A systematic review of randomized clinical trials. *Journal of Asthma, 48*, 632–639.

Postma, J., Karr, C., & Kieckhefer, G. (2009). Community health workers and environmental interventions for children with asthma: A systematic review. *Journal of Asthma, 46*, 564–576.

Proust, M. (1956). *Marcel Proust: Letters to his mother*. London: Rider.

Ritz, T. (2004). Probing the psychophysiology of the airways: Physical activity, experienced emotion, and facially expressed emotion. *Psychophysiology, 41*, 809–821.

Ritz, T. (2012). Airway responsiveness to psychological processes in asthma and health. *Frontiers in Physiology, 3*, 343.

Ritz, T., Dahme, B., & Roth, W.T. (2004). Behavioral interventions in asthma: Biofeedback techniques. *Journal of Psychosomatic Research, 56*, 711–720.

Ritz, T., Steptoe, A., Bobb, C., Harris, A., & Edwards, M. (2006). The Asthma Trigger Inventory: Development and evaluation of a questionnaire measuring perceived triggers of asthma. *Psychosomatic Medicine, 68*, 956–965.

Sandberg, S., Jarvenpaa, S., Penttinen, A., Paton, J.Y., & McCann, D.C. (2004). Asthma exacerbations in children immediately following stressful life events: A Cox's hierarchical regression. *Thorax, 59*, 1046–1051.

Scharloo, M., Kaptein, A.A., Schlösser, M., Pouwels, H., Bel, E.H., Rabe, K.F., & Wouters, E.F.M. (2007). Illness perceptions and quality of life in patients with chronic obstructive pulmonary disease. *Journal of Asthma, 44*, 575–581.

Spitzer, R.L., Williams, J.B., Kroenke, K., Linzer, M., deGruy, F.V., Hahn, S.R., … Johnson, J.G. (1994). Utility of a new procedure for diagnosing mental disorders in primary care: The PRIME-MD 1000 study. *Journal of the American Medical Association, 272*, 1749–1756.

Statistics Canada. (2010). Asthma. Retrieved from www.statcan.gc.ca/pub/82-625-x/2011001/article/11458-eng.htm

Steen, N., Hutchinson, A., McColl, E., Eccles, M.P., Hewison, J., Meadows, K.A., … Fowler, P. (1994). Development of a symptom-based outcome measure for asthma. *British Medical Journal, 309*, 1065–1068.

Stehr, D.E., Klein, B.J., & Murata, G.H. (1991). Emergency department return visits in chronic obstructive pulmonary disease: The importance of psychosocial factors. *Annals of Emergency Medicine, 20*, 1113–1116.

Stout, C., Kotses, H., & Creer, T.L. (1997). Improving perception of air flow obstruction in asthma patients. *Psychosomatic Medicine, 59*, 201–206.

Thomson, N.C., & Chaudhuri, R. (2009). Asthma in smokers: Challenges and opportunities. *Current Opinion in Pulmonary Medicine, 15*, 39–45.

Tønnesen, P., Carrozzi, L., Fagerström, K.O., Gratziou, C., Jimenez-Ruiz, C., Nardini, S., … West, R. (2007). Smoking cessation in patients with respiratory diseases: A high priority, integral component of therapy. *European Respiratory Journal, 29*, 390–417.

Troosters, T., Casaburi, R., Gosselink, R., & Decramer, M. (2005). Pulmonary rehabilitation in chronic obstructive pulmonary disease. *American Journal of Respiratory and Critical Care Medicine, 172*, 19–38.

Troosters, T., Gosselink, R., Janssens, W., & Decramer, M. (2010). Exercise training and pulmonary rehabilitation: New insights and remaining challenges. *European Respiratory Review, 19*, 24–29.

Vercelli, D. (2010). Gene–environment interactions in asthma and allergy: The end of the beginning? *Current Opinion in Allergy and Clinical Immunology, 10*, 145–148.

von Leupoldt, A., Sommer, T., Kegat, S., Eippert, F., Baumann, H.J., Klose, H., … Büchel, C. (2009). Down-regulation of insular cortex responses to dyspnea and pain in asthma. *American Journal of Respiratory and Critical Care Medicine, 180*, 232–238.

von Leupoldt, A., Taube, K., Henkhus, M., Dahme, B., & Magnussen, H. (2010). The impact of affective states on the perception of dyspnea in patients with chronic obstructive pulmonary disease. *Biological Psychology, 84*, 129–134.

von Leupoldt, A., Taube, K., Lehmann, K., Fritzsche, A., & Magnussen, H. (2011). The impact of anxiety and depression on outcomes of pulmonary rehabilitation in patients with COPD. *Chest, 140*, 730–736.

Vos, R., De Vusser, K., Schaevers, V., Schoonis, A., Lemaigre, V., Dobbels, F., … Verleden, G.M. (2010). Smoking resumption after lung transplantation: A sobering truth. *European Respiratory Journal, 35*, 1411–1413.

Ware, J.E. Jr. (2000). Using generic measures of functional health and well-being to increase understanding of disease burden. *Spine, 25*, 1467.

Warner, L.J., Lumley, M.A., Casey, R.J., Pierantoni, W., Salazar, R., Zoratti, E.M., … Simon, M.R. (2006). Health effects of written emotional disclosure in adolescents with asthma: A randomized, controlled trial. *Journal of Pediatric Psychology, 31*, 557–568.

Watson, L., Vonk, J.M., Löfdahl, C.G., Pride, N.B., Pauwels, R.A., Laitinen, L.A., … Postma, D.S. (2006). Predictors of lung function and its decline in mild to moderate COPD in association with gender: Results from the Euroscop study. *Respiratory Medicine, 100*, 746–753.

Weiner, H. (1977). *Psychobiology and human disease*. New York: Elsevier.

Weinstein, A.G. (1984). Crying-induced bronchospasm in childhood asthma. *Journal of Asthma, 21*, 161–165.

Wigal, J.K., Stout, C., Brandon, M., Winder, J.A., McConnaughy, K., Creer, T.L., & Kotses, H. (1993). The Knowledge, Attitude, and Self-Efficacy Asthma Questionnaire. *Chest, 104*, 1144–1148.

Wilson, R.C., & Jones, P.W. (1989). A comparison of the visual analogue scale and modified Borg scale for the measurement of dyspnoea during exercise. *Clinical Science, 76*, 277–282.

Wood, B.L., Cheah, P.A., Lim, J.H., Ritz, T., Miller, B.D., Stern, T., & Ballow, M. (2007). Reliability and validity of the Asthma Trigger Inventory applied to a pediatric population. *Journal of Pediatric Psychology, 32*, 552–560.

Wright, R.J. (2010). Perinatal stress and early life programming of lung structure and function. *Biological Psychology, 84*, 46–56.

Xu, W., Collet, J.-P., Shapiro, S., Lin, Y., Yang, T., Platt, R.W., … Bourbeau, J. (2008). Independent effect of depression and anxiety on chronic obstructive pulmonary disease exacerbations and hospitalizations. *American Journal of Respiratory and Critical Care Medicine, 178*, 913–920.

Yorke, J., & Shuldham, C. (2005). Family therapy for chronic asthma in children. *Cochrane Database of Systematic Reviews, 18*, CD000089.

Zigmond, A.S., & Snaith, R.P. (1983). The hospital anxiety and depression scale. *Acta Psychiatrica Scandavica, 67*, 361–370.

Zimmerman, D.M., Sehnert, S.S., Epstein, D.H., Pickworth, W.B., Robinson, M.L., & Moolchan, E.T. (2004). Smoking topography and trajectory of asthmatic adolescents requesting cessation treatment. *Preventative Medicine, 39*, 940–942.

Chapter 15

American Psychiatric Association (2013). *Diagnostic and statistical manual of mental disorders* (5th ed.). Washington: Author.

Ashworth, L.A., Billett, A., Mitchell, P., Nuti, F., Siegel, C., & Bousvaros, A. (2012). Lymphoma risk in children and young adults with inflammatory bowel disease: Analysis of a large single-center cohort. *Inflammatory Bowel Disease, 18*, 838–843.

Baars, J.E., Siegel, C.A., van't Spijker, A., Markus, T., Kuipers, E.J., & van der Woude, C.J. (2010). Inflammatory bowel disease patients are insufficiently educated about the basic characteristics of their disease and the associated risk of colorectal cancer. *Digestive and Liver Disease, 42*, 777–784.

Baumgart, D.C., & Sandborn, W.J. (2012). Crohn's disease. *Lancet, 380*, 1590–1605.

Berman, S.M., Naliboff, B.D., Suyenobu, B., Labus, J.S., Stains, J., Ohning, G., … Mayer, E.A. (2008). Reduced brainstem inhibition during anticipated pelvic visceral pain correlates with enhanced brain response to the visceral stimulus in women with irritable bowel syndrome. *Journal of Neuroscience, 28*, 349–359.

Bernstein, C.N., Wajda, A., Svenson, L.W., MacKenzie, A., Koehoorn, M., Jackson, M., … Blanchard, J.F. (2006). The epidemiology of inflammatory bowel disease in Canada: A population-based study. *American Journal of Gastroenterology, 101*, 1559–1568.

Bitton, A., Peppercorn, M.A., Antonioli, D.A., Niles, J.L., Shah, S., Bousvaros, A., … Stevens, A.C. (2001). Clinical, biological, and histologic parameters as predictors of relapse in ulcerative colitis. *Gastroenterology, 120*, 13–20.

Blanchard, E.B., Lackner, J.M., Sanders, K., Krasner, S., Keefer, L., Payne, A., … Dulgar-Tulloch, L. (2007). A controlled evaluation of group cognitive therapy in the treatment of irritable bowel syndrome. *Behaviour Research and Therapy, 45*, 633–648.

Bousvaros, A., Morley-Fletcher, A., Pensabene, L., & Cucchiara, S. (2008). Research and clinical challenges in paediatric inflammatory bowel disease. *Digestive and Liver Disease, 40*, 32–38.

Braganza, J.M., Lee, S.H., McCloy, R.F., & McMahon, M.J. (2011). Chronic pancreatitis. *Lancet, 377*, 1184–1197.

Brandt, L.J., Chey, W.D., Foxx-Orenstein, A.E., Schiller, L.R., Schoenfeld, P.S., Spiegel, B.M., … Quigley, E.M. (2009a).

An evidence-based position statement on the management of irritable bowel syndrome. *American Journal of Gastroenterology, 104*, S1–35.

Carter, M.J., Lobo, A.J., & Travis, S.P. (2004). Guidelines for the management of inflammatory bowel disease in adults. *Gut, 53*(Suppl 5), V1–16.

Chang, L., Sundaresh, S., Elliott, J., Anton, P.A., Baldi, P., Licudine, A., ... Mayer, E.A. (2009). Dysregulation of the hypothalamic-pituitary-adrenal (HPA) axis in irritable bowel syndrome. *Neurogastroenterology and Motility, 21*, 149–159.

Chiarioni, G., Palsson, O.S., & Whitehead, W.E. (2008). Hypnosis and upper digestive function and disease. *World Journal of Gastroenterology, 14*, 6276–6284.

Cohen, H., Jotkowitz, A., Buskila, D., Pelles-Avraham, S., Kaplan, Z., Neumann, L., & Sperber, A.D. (2006). Post-traumatic stress disorder and other co-morbidities in a sample population of patients with irritable bowel syndrome. *European Journal of Internal Medicine, 17*, 567–571.

Collins, S.M. (2001). Stress and the gastrointestinal tract IV. Modulation of intestinal inflammation by stress: Basic mechanisms and clinical relevance. *American Journal of Physiology—Gastrointestinal and Liver Physiology, 280*, G315–318.

Cottone, M., Renna, S., Orlando, A., & Mocciaro, F. (2011). Medical management of Crohn's disease. *Expert Opinion on Pharmacotherapy, 12*, 2505–2525.

Deechakawan, W., Cain, K.C., Jarrett, M.E., Burr, R.L., & Heitkemper, M.M. (2011). Effect of self-management intervention on cortisol and daily stress levels in irritable bowel syndrome. *Biological Research for Nursing, 14*. Retrieved from brn.sagepub.com/content/early/2011/07/05/1099800411414047.full.pdf+html

Drossman, D.A., Camilleri, M., Mayer, E.A., & Whitehead, W.E. (2002). AGA technical review on irritable bowel syndrome. *Gastroenterology, 123*(6), 2108–2131.

Drossman, D.A., Toner, B.B., Whitehead, W.E., Diamant, N.E., Dalton, C.B., Duncan, S., ... Bangdiwala, S.I. (2003). Cognitive-behavioural therapy versus education and desipramine versus placebo for moderate to severe functional bowel disorders. *Gastroenterology, 125*, 19–31.

Engel, G.L. (1977). The need for a new medical model: A challenge for biomedicine. *Science, 196*, 129–136.

Ford, A.C., Talley, N.J., Schoenfeld, P.S., Quigley, E.M., & Moayyedi, P. (2009). Efficacy of antidepressants and psychological therapies in irritable bowel syndrome: Systematic review and meta-analysis. *Gut, 58*, 367–378.

Francis, C.Y., Duffy, J.N., Whorwell, P.J., & Morris, J. (1997). High prevalence of irritable bowel syndrome in patients attending urological outpatient departments. *Digestive Diseases and Sciences, 42*, 404–407.

Fukudo, S., Nomura, T., Muranaka, M., & Taguchi, F. (1993). Brain–gut response to stress and cholinergic stimulation in irritable bowel syndrome: A preliminary study. *Journal of Clinical Gastroenterology, 17*, 133–141.

Goodhand, J.R., Wahed, M., Mawdsley, J.E., Farmer, A.D., Aziz, Q., & Rampton, D.S. (2012). Mood disorders in inflammatory bowel disease: Relation to diagnosis, disease activity, perceived stress, and other factors. *Inflammatory Bowel Disorders, 18*, 2301–2309.

Gros, D.F., Antony, M.M., McCabe, R.E., & Swinson, R.P. (2009). Frequency and severity of the symptoms of irritable bowel syndrome across the anxiety disorders and depression. *Journal of Anxiety Disorders, 23*, 290–296.

Grover, M., & Drossman, D.A. (2011). Centrally acting therapies for irritable bowel syndrome. *Gastroenterology Clinics of North America, 40*, 183–206.

Guo, Y.J., Ho, C.H., Chen, S.C., Yang, S.S., Chiu, H.M., & Huang, K.H. (2010). Lower urinary tract symptoms in women with irritable bowel syndrome. *International Journal of Urology, 17*, 175–181.

Hahn, B.A., Kirchdoerfer, L.J., Fullerton, S., & Mayer, E. (1997). Patient-perceived severity of irritable bowel syndrome in relation to symptoms, health resource utilization and quality of life. *Alimentary Pharmacology & Therapeutics, 11*, 553–559.

Heitkemper, M., Jarrett, M., Burr, R., Cain, K.C., Landis, C., Lentz, M., & Poppe, A. (2005). Subjective and objective sleep indices in women with irritable bowel syndrome. *Neurogastroenterology and Motility, 17*, 523–530.

Heitkemper, M.M., Jarrett, M.E., Levy, R.L., Cain, K.C., Burr, R.L., Feld, A., ... Weisman, P. (2004). Self-management for women with irritable bowel syndrome. *Clinical Gastroenterology and Hepatology, 2*, 585–596.

Hommel, K.A., Hente, E.A., Odell, S., Herzer, M., Ingerski, L.M., Guilfoyle, S.M., & Denson, L.A. (2012). Evaluation of a group-based behavioural intervention to promote adherence in adolescents with inflammatory bowel disease. *European Journal of Gastroenterology and Hepatology, 24*, 64–69.

Hsueh, H.F., Jarrett, M.E., Cain, K.C., Burr, R.L., Deechakawan, W., & Heitkemper, M.M. (2011). Does a self-management program change dietary intake in adults with irritable bowel syndrome? *Gastroenterology Nursing, 34*, 108–116.

Hungin, A.P., Chang, L., Locke, G.R., Dennis, E.H., & Barghout, V. (2005). Irritable bowel syndrome in the United States: Prevalence, symptom patterns and impact. *Alimentary Pharmacology & Therapeutics, 21*, 1365–1375.

Jarrett, M.E., Cain, K.C., Burr, R.L., Hertig, V.L., Rosen, S.N., & Heitkemper, M.M. (2009). Comprehensive self-management for irritable bowel syndrome: Randomized trial of in-person vs. combined in-person and telephone sessions. *American Journal of Gastroenterology, 104*, 3004–3014.

Kane, S., & Shaya, F. (2008). Medication non-adherence is associated with increased medical health care costs. *Digestive Diseases and Sciences, 53*, 1020–1024.

Karban, A., & Eliakim, R. (2007). Effect of smoking on inflammatory bowel disease: Is it disease or organ specific? *World Journal of Gastroenterology, 13*, 2150–2152.

Keefer, L., Doerfler, B., & Artz, C. (2012). Optimizing management of Crohn's disease within a project management framework: Results of a pilot study. *Inflammatory Bowel Diseases, 18*, 254–260.

Keefer, L., & Keshavarzian, A. (2007). Feasibility and acceptability of gut-directed hypnosis on inflammatory bowel disease: A brief communication. *International Journal of Clinical and Experimental Hypnosis, 55*, 457–466.

Kiebles, J.L., Doerfler, B., & Keefer, L. (2010). Preliminary evidence supporting a framework of psychological adjustment to inflammatory bowel disease. *Inflammatory Bowel Diseases, 16*, 1685–1695.

Kiebles, J.L., Kwiatek, M.A., Pandolfino, J.E., Kahrilas, P.J., & Keefer, L. (2010). Do patients with globus sensation respond to hypnotically assisted relaxation therapy? A case series report. *Dis Esophagus, 23*, 545–553.

Koloski, N.A., Talley, N.J., & Boyce, P.M. (2000). The impact of functional gastrointestinal disorders on quality of life. *American Journal of Gastroenterology, 95*, 67–71.

Kovacs, Z., & Kovacs, F. (2007). [Depressive and anxiety symptoms, coping strategies in patients with irritable bowel syndrome and inflammatory bowel disease]. *Psychiatria Hungaria, 22*(3), 212–221.

Lackner, J.M., Gudleski, G.D., Keefer, L., Krasner, S.S., Powell, C., & Katz, L.A. (2010). Rapid response to cognitive behavior therapy predicts treatment outcome in patients with irritable bowel syndrome. *Clinical Gastroenterology and Hepatology, 8*, 426–432.

Lackner, J.M., Jaccard, J., Krasner, S.S., Katz, L.A., Gudleski, G.D., & Holroyd, K. (2008). Self-administered cognitive behavior therapy for moderate to severe irritable bowel syndrome: Clinical efficacy, tolerability, feasibility. *Clinical Gastroenterology and Hepatology, 6*, 899–906.

Lackner, J.M., Lou Coad, M., Mertz, H.R., Wack, D.S., Katz, L.A., Krasner, S.S., ... Lockwood, A.H. (2006). Cognitive therapy for irritable bowel syndrome is associated with re-duced limbic activity, GI symptoms, and anxiety. *Behaviour Research and Therapy, 44*(5), 621–638.

Lakatos, P.L. (2006). Recent trends in the epidemiology of inflammatory bowel diseases: Up or down? *World Journal of Gastroenterology, 12*(38), 6102–6108.

Lee, S., Wu, J., Ma, Y.L., Tsang, A., Guo, W.J., & Sung, J. (2009). Irritable bowel syndrome is strongly associated with generalized anxiety disorder: A community study. *Alimentary Pharmacology and Therapeutics, 30*, 643–651.

Lesbros-Pantoflickova, D., Michetti, P., Fried, M., Beglinger, C., & Blum, A.L. (2004a). Meta-analysis: The treatment of irritable bowel syndrome. *Alimentary Pharmacology and Therapeutics, 20*, 1253–1269.

Leserman, J. (2007). Association of sexual and physical abuse with functional gastrointestinal and pelvic pain. *Primary Psychiatry, 14*, 58–63.

Leserman, J., & Drossman, D.A. (2007). Relationship of abuse history to functional gastrointestinal disorders and symptoms: Some possible mediating mechanisms. *Trauma Violence Abuse, 8*, 331–343.

Levenstein, S. (2002). Psychosocial factors in peptic ulcer and inflammatory bowel disease. *Journal of Consulting and Clinical Psychology, 70*, 739–750.

Lindfors, P., Unge, P., Arvidsson, P., Nyhlin, H., Bjornsson, E., Abrahamsson, H., & Simren, M. (2012). Effects of gut-di-rected hypnotherapy on IBS in different clinical settings—Results from two randomized, controlled trials. *American Journal of Gastroenterology, 107*, 276–285.

Longstreth, G.F., Thompson, W.G., Chey, W.D., Houghton, L.A., Mearin, F., & Spiller, R.C. (2006). Functional bowel disorders. *Gastroenterology, 130*, 1480–1491.

Lydiard, R.B. (2005). Increased prevalence of functional gastro-intestinal disorders in panic disorder: Clinical and theoretical implications. *CNS Spectrums, 10*, 899–908.

Mahid, S.S., Minor, K.S., Soto, R.E., Hornung, C.A., & Galandiuk, S. (2006). Smoking and inflammatory bowel disease: A meta-analysis. *Mayo Clinic Proceedings, 81*, 1462–1471.

Mardini, H.E., Kip, K.E., & Wilson, J.W. (2004). Crohn's dis-ease: A two-year prospective study of the association between psychological distress and disease activity. *Digestive Diseases and Sciences, 49*, 492–497.

Mawdsley, J.E., Jenkins, D.G., Macey, M.G., Langmead, L., & Rampton, D.S. (2008). The effect of hypnosis on systemic and rectal mucosal measures of inflammation in ulcerative colitis. *American Journal of Gastroenterology, 103*, 1460–1469.

Mertz, H., Morgan, V., Tanner, G., Pickens, D., Price, R., Shyr, Y., & Kessler, R. (2000). Regional cerebral activation in irri-table bowel syndrome and control subjects with painful and nonpainful rectal distention. *Gastroenterology, 118*, 842–848.

Mikocka-Walus, A.A., Turnbull, D.A., Moulding, N.T., Wilson, I.G., Holtmann, G.J., & Andrews, J.M. (2008). Does psy-chological status influence clinical outcomes in patients with inflammatory bowel disease (IBD) and other chronic gastro-enterological diseases: An observational cohort prospective study. *BioPsychoSocial Medicine, 2*, 11.

Miller, V., Hopkins, L., & Whorwell, P.J. (2004). Suicidal ideation in patients with irritable bowel syndrome. *Clinical Gastroenterology and Hepatology, 2*, 1064–1068.

Misiewicz, J., Lennard-Jones, J.E., Connell, A., Baron, J.H., & Avery Jones, F. (1965). Controlled trial of sulphasalazine in maintenance therapy for ulcerative colitis. *Lancet, 1*, 185–188.

Mittermaier, C., Dejaco, C., Waldhoer, T., Oefferlbauer-Ernst, A., Michsler, W., Beier, M., ... Moser, G. (2004). Impact of depressive mood on relapse in patients with inflammatory bowel disease: A prospective 18-month follow-up study. *Psychosomatic Medicine, 66*, 79–84.

Moser, G., Tillinger, W., Sachs, G., Genser, D., Maier-Dobersberger, T., Spiess, K., ... Gangl, A. (1995). Disease-related worries and concerns: A study on out-patients with inflammatory bowel disease. *European Journal of Gastroenterology and Hepatology, 7*, 853–858.

Murray, C.D., Flynn, J., Ratcliffe, L., Jacyna, M.R., Kamm, M.A., & Emmanuel, A.V. (2004). Effect of acute physical and psychological stress on gut autonomic innervation in irritable bowel syndrome. *Gastroenterology, 127*, 1695–1703.

Mykletun, A., Jacka, F., Williams, L., Pasco, J., Henry, M., Nicholson, G.C., ... Berk, M. (2010). Prevalence of mood and anxiety disorder in self-reported irritable bowel syn-drome (IBS): An epidemiological population-based study of women. *BMC Gastroenterology, 10*, 88.

Nahon, S., Lahmek, P., Durance, C., Olympie, A., Lesgourgues, B., Colombel, J.F., & Gendre, J.P. (2012). Risk factors of anxiety and depression in inflammatory bowel disease. *Inflammastory Bowel Diseases, 18*, 2086–2091.

Naliboff, B.D., Munakata, J., Fullerton, S., Gracely, R.H., Kodner, A., Harraf, F., & Mayer, E.A. (1997). Evidence for two distinct perceptual alterations in irritable bowel syndrome. *Gut, 41*, 505–512.

Ordás, I., Eckmann, L., Talamini, M., Baumgart, D.C., & Sandborn, W.J. (2012). Ulcerative colitis. *Lancet, 380*, 1606–1619.

Osterberg, E., Blomquist, L., Krakau, I., Weinryb, R.M., Asberg, M., & Hultcrantz, R. (2000). A population study on irritable bowel syndrome and mental health. *Scandinavian Journal of Gastroenterology, 35*, 264–268.

Palsson, O.S. (2010). Hypnosis treatment for gut problems. *European Gastroenterology and Hepatology Review, 6*, 42–46.

Palsson, O.S., Turner, M.J., Johnson, D.A., Burnett, C.K., & Whitehead, W.E. (2002). Hypnosis treatment for severe irritable bowel syndrome: Investigation of mechanism and effects on symptoms. *Digestive Diseases and Sciences, 47*, 2605–2614.

Palsson, O.S., & Whitehead, W.E. (2006). Hypnosis for non-cardiac chest pain. *Gut, 55*, 1381–1384.

Remes-Troche, J., Bernal-Reyes, R., Valladares-Lepine, M., Alonso-Larraga, O., Gomez-Escudero, O., & Melendez-Mena, D. (2009). Gastroenterology diagnosis and treatment guidelines of irritable bowel syndrome: Clinical features and diagnostic criteria. *Revista de Gastroenterología de México, 74*, 58–62.

Riedl, A., Schmidtmann, M., Stengel, A., Goebel, M., Wisser, A.S., Klapp, B.F., & Monnikes, H. (2008). Somatic comorbidities of irritable bowel syndrome: A systematic analysis. *Journal of Psychosomatic Research, 64*, 573–582.

Rifai, M.A., Gleason, O.C., & Sabouni, D. (2010). Psychiatric care of the patient with hepatitis C: A review of the literature. *Primary Care Companion to the Journal of Clinical Psychiatry, 12*.

Ringstrom, G., Storsrud, S., & Simren, M. (2012). A comparison of a short nurse-based and a long multidisciplinary version of structured patient education in irritable bowel syndrome. *European Journal of Gastroenterology and Hepatology, 24*, 950–957.

Schmulson, M., Chang, L., Naliboff, B., Lee, O.Y., & Mayer, E.A. (2000). Correlation of symptom criteria with perception thresholds during rectosigmoid distension in irritable bowel syndrome patients. *American Journal of Gastroenterology, 95*, 152–156.

Sewitch, M., Abrahamowicz, M., Barkun, A., Bitton, A., Wild, G.E., Cohen, A., & Dobkin, P.L. (2003). Patient non-adherence to medication in inflammatory bowel disease. *American Journal of Gastroenterology, 98*, 1535–1544.

Sewitch, M., Leffondre, K., & Dobkin, P.L. (2004). Clustering patients according to health perceptions: Relationships to psychosocial characteristics and medication non-adherence. *Journal of Psychosomatic Research, 56*, 323–332.

Silberbogen, A.K., Ulloa, E.W., Janke, E.A., & Mori, D.L. (2009). Psychosocial issues and mental health treatment recommendations for patients with hepatitis C. *Psychosomatics, 50*, 114–122.

Smith, M.D., Russell, A., & Hodges, P.W. (2008). How common is back pain in women with gastrointestinal problems? *Clinical Journal of Pain, 24*, 199–203.

Sperber, A.D., Atzmon, Y., Neumann, L., Weisberg, I., Shalit, Y., Abu-Shakrah, M., ... Buskila, D. (1999). Fibromyalgia in the irritable bowel syndrome: Studies of prevalence and clinical implications. *American Journal of Gastroenterology, 94*, 3541–3546.

Stout, C., & Snyder, R.L. (1969). Ulcerative colitis-like lesion in Siamang gibbons. *Gastroenterology, 57*, 256–261.

Sykes, M.A., Blanchard, E.B., Lackner, J., Keefer, L., & Krasner, S. (2003). Psychopathology in irritable bowel syndrome: Support for a psychophysiological model. *Journal of Behavioral Medicine, 26*, 361–372.

Taft, T.H., Ballou, S., & Keefer, L. (2012). Preliminary evaluation of maternal caregiver stress in pediatric eosinophilic gastrointestinal disorders. *Journal of Pediatric Psychology, 37*, 523–532.

Taft, T.H., Keefer, L., Leonhard, C., & Nealon-Woods, M. (2009). Impact of perceived stigma on inflammatory bowel disease patient outcomes. *Inflammatory Bowel Diseases, 15*, 1224–1232.

Taft, T.H., Kern, E., Keefer, L., Burstein, D., & Hirano, I. (2011). Qualitative assessment of patient-reported outcomes in adults with eosinophilic esophagitis. *Journal of Clinical Gastroenterology, 45*, 769–774.

Thompson, W.G., Irvine, E.J., Pare, P., Ferrazzi, S., & Rance, L. (2002). Functional gastrointestinal disorders in Canada: First population-based survey using Rome II criteria with suggestions for improving the questionnaire. *Digestive Diseases and Sciences, 47*, 225–235.

Tillisch, K., & Chang, L. (2005). Diagnosis and treatment of irritable bowel syndrome: State of the art. *Current Gastroenterology Reports, 7*, 249–256.

Verne, G.N., Robinson, M.E., & Price, D.D. (2001). Hypersensitivity to visceral and cutaneous pain in the irritable bowel syndrome. *Pain, 93*(1), 7–14.

White, D.L., Savas, L.S., Daci, K., Elserag, R., Graham, D.P., Fitzgerald, S.J., ... El-Serag, H.B. (2010). Trauma history and risk of the irritable bowel syndrome in women veterans. *Alimentary Pharmacology & Therapeutics, 32*, 551–561.

Whitehead, W.E. (2002). Fecal incontinence: A neglected area of gastroenterology. *Gastroenterology, 122*, 5.

Whitehead, W.E., Borrud, L., Goode, P.S., Meikle, S., Mueller, E.R., Tuteja, A., ... Ye, W. (2009). Fecal incontinence in US adults: Epidemiology and risk factors. *Gastroenterology, 137*, 512–517.e2.

Whorwell, P.J. (2008). Hypnotherapy for irritable bowel syndrome: The response of colonic and noncolonic symptoms. *Journal of Psychosomatic Research, 64*, 621–623.

Wood, J.D., Peck, O.C., Tefend, K.S., Stonerook, M.J., Caniano, D.A., Mutabagani, K.H., ... Sharma, H.M. (2000). Evidence that colitis is initiated by environmental stress and sustained by fecal factors in the cotton-top tamarin (Saguinus oedipus). *Digestive Diseases and Sciences, 45*, 385–393.

World Health Organization (WHO). (2008). *ICD-10: International statistical classification of diseases and related health problems* (10th rev. ed.). New York: Author.

Wright, J., O'Keefe, E.A., Cuming, L., Jaskiewicz, K. (1993). Olsalazine in maintenance of clinical remission in patients with ulcerative colitis. *Digestive Diseases and Sciences, 38*, 1837–1842.

Chapter 16

Bandura A. (1997). *Self-efficacy: The exercise of control.* New York: W.H. Freeman.

Barlow, J., Wright, C., Sheasby, J., Turner, A., & Hainsworth, J. (2002). Self-management approaches for people with chronic conditions: A review. *Patient Education and Counseling, 48,* 177–187.

Basile, C. (2008). The long-term prognosis of acute kidney injury: Acute renal failure as a cause of chronic kidney disease. *Journal of Nephrology, 21,* 657–662.

Boateng, E.A., & East, L. (2011). The impact of dialysis modality on quality of life: A systematic review. *Journal of Renal Care, 37,* 190–200.

Boulware, L.E., Liu, Y., Fink, N.E., Coresh, J., Ford, D.E., Klag, M.J., & Powe, N.R. (2006). Temporal relation among depression symptoms, cardiovascular disease events, and mortality in end-stage renal disease: Contribution of reverse causality. *Clinical Journal of the American Society of Nephrology, 1,* 496–504.

Brown, C.T., Yap, T., Cromwell, D.A., Rixon, L., Steed, L., Mulligan, K., … Emberton, M. (2007). Self management for men with lower urinary tract symptoms: Randomised controlled trial. *British Medical Journal, 334,* 25.

Brown, E.S., Woolston, J.D., Frol, A., Bobadilla, L., Khan, D.A., Hanczyc, M., … Cullum, C.M. (2004). Hippocampal volume, spectroscopy, cognition, and mood in patients receiving corticosteroid therapy. *Biological Psychiatry, 55,* 538–545.

Browne, T., & Merighi, J.R. (2010). Barriers to adult hemodialysis patients' self-management of oral medications. *American Journal of Kidney Diseases, 56,* 547–557.

Butler, J.A., Roderick, P., Mullee, M., Mason, J.C., & Peveler, R.C. (2004). Frequency and impact of nonadherence to immunosuppressants after renal transplantation: A systematic review. *Transplantation, 77,* 769.

Cameron, J.I., Whiteside, C., Katz, J., & Devins, G.M. (2000). Differences in quality of life across renal replacement therapies: A meta-analytic comparison. *American Journal of Kidney Diseases, 35,* 629–637.

Canadian Institute for Health Information (CIHI). (2011a, January 20). Number of Canadians living with kidney failure triples over 20 years: Renal transplantation saving millions in dialysis costs. Retrieved from www.cihi.ca/CIHI-ext-portal/internet/en/Document/types+of+care/specialized+services/organ+replacements/RELEASE_20JAN11

Canadian Institute for Health Information (CIHI). (2011b). *The Canadian organ replacement register: Annual report 2000–2009.* Retrieved from publications.gc.ca/pub?id=390122&sl=0

Chan, R., Brooks, R., Steel, Z., Heung, T., Erlich, J., Chow, J., & Suranyi, M. (2012). The psychosocial correlates of quality of life in the dialysis population: A systematic review and meta-regression analysis. *Quality of Life Research, 21,* 563–580.

Chen, S.H., Tsai, Y.F., Sun, C.Y., Wu, I.W., Lee, C.C., & Wu, M.S. (2011). The impact of self-management support on the progression of chronic kidney disease—A prospective randomized controlled trial. *Nephrology Dialysis Transplantation, 26,* 3560–3566.

Chilcot, J., Wellsted, D., & Farrington, K. (2010). Depression in end-stage renal disease: Current advances and research. *Seminars in Dialysis, 23,* 74–82.

Chilcot, J., Wellsted, D., & Farrington, K. (2011). Illness perceptions predict survival in haemodialysis patients. *American Journal of Nephrology, 33,* 358–363.

Christensen, A.J., Turner, C.W., Smith, T.W., Holman, J.M., & Gregory, M.C. (1991). Health locus of control and depression in end-stage renal disease. *Journal of Consulting and Clinical Psychology, 59,* 419–424.

Clemens, K.K., Thiessen-Philbrook, H., Parikh, C.R., Yang, R.C., Karley, M.L., Boudville, N., … Garg, A.X. (2006). Psychosocial health of living kidney donors: A systematic review. *American Journal of Transplantation, 6,* 2965–2977.

Cohen, S.D., Sharma, T., Acquaviva, K., Peterson, R.A., Patel, S.S., & Kimmel, P.L. (2007). Social support and chronic kidney disease: An update. *Advances in Chronic Kidney Disease, 14,* 335–344.

Collins, A.J., Chen, S.C., Gilbertson, D.T., & Foley, R.N. (2009). CKD surveillance using administrative data: Impact on the health care system. *American Journal of Kidney Diseases, 53,* S27–S36.

Coresh, J., Selvin, E., Stevens, L.A., Manzi, J., Kusek, J.W., Eggers, P., … Levey, A.S. (2007). Prevalence of chronic kidney disease in the United States. *Journal of the American Medical Association, 298,* 2038–2047.

Couser, W.G., Remuzzi, G., Mendis, S., & Tonelli, M. (2011). The contribution of chronic kidney disease to the global burden of major noncommunicable diseases. *Kidney International, 80,* 1258–1270.

Cukor, D., Cohen, S.D., Peterson, R.A., & Kimmel, P.L. (2007). Psychosocial aspects of chronic disease: ESRD as a paradigmatic illness. *Journal of the American Society of Nephrology, 18,* 3042–3055.

Cukor, D., Rosenthal, D.S., & Kimmel, P.L. (2010). Depression and neurocognitive function in chronic kidney disease. In J. Himmelfarb & M.H. Sayegh (Eds.), *Chronic kidney disease, dialysis, and transplantation.* (3rd ed., pp. 218–230). New York: Elsevier.

Danquah, F.V.N., Wasserman, J., Meininger, J., & Bergstrom, N. (2010). Quality of life measures for patients on hemodialysis: A review of psychometric properties. *Nephrology Nursing Journal, 37,* 255–270.

Davison, S.N. (2010). End-of-life care preferences and needs: Perceptions of patients with chronic kidney disease. *Clinical Journal of the American Society of Nephrology, 5,* 195–204.

Denhaerynck, K., Dobbels, F., Cleemput, I., Desmyttere, A., Schäfer-Keller, P., Schaub, S., & De Geest, S. (2005). Prevalence, consequences, and determinants of nonadherence in adult renal transplant patients: A literature review. *Transplant International, 18,* 1121–1133.

Denhaerynck, K., Manhaeve, D., Dobbels, F., Garzoni, D., Nolte, C., & De Geest, S. (2007). Prevalence and consequences of nonadherence to hemodialysis regimens. *American Journal of Critical Care, 16,* 222–235.

Dew, M.A., DiMartini, A.F., De Vito Dabbs, A., Myaskovsky, L., Steel, J., Unruh, M., … Greenhouse, J.B. (2007). Rates and risk factors for nonadherence to the medical regimen after adult solid organ transplantation. *Transplantation, 83,* 858–873.

Diseth, T., Tangeraas, T., Reinfjell, T., & Bjerre, A. (2011). Kidney transplantation in childhood: Mental health and quality of life of children and caregivers. *Pediatric Nephrology, 26*, 1881–1892.

Duarte, P.S., Miyazaki, M.C., Blay, S.L., & Sesso, R. (2009). Cognitive-behavioral group therapy is an effective treatment for major depression in hemodialysis patients. *Kidney International, 76*, 414–421.

Eitel, P., Hatchett, L., Friend, R., Griffin, K.W., & Wadhwa, N.K. (1995). Burden of self-care in seriously ill patients: Impact on adjustment. *Health Psychology, 14*, 457–463.

ERA-EDTA Registry. (2012). *ERA-EDTA registry annual report 2010*. Amsterdam: Academic Medical Center, Department of Medical Informatics.

Finkelstein, F.O., Wuerth, D., & Finkelstein, S.H. (2009). Health-related quality of life and the CKD patient: Challenges for the nephrology community. *Kidney International, 76*, 946–952.

Foley, R.N., Parfrey, P.S., & Sarnak, M.J. (1998) Clinical epidemiology of cardiovascular disease in chronic renal failure. *American Journal of Kidney Diseases, 32*, S112–119.

Franklin, P.M., & Crombie, A.K. (2003). Live related renal transplantation: Psychological, social, and cultural issues. *Transplantation, 76*, 1247.

Gelb, S., Shapiro, R.J., Hill, A., & Thornton, W.L. (2008). Cognitive outcome following kidney transplantation. *Nephrology Dialysis Transplantation, 23*, 1032–1038.

Goodkin, D.A., Bragg-Gresham, J.L., Koenig, K.G., Wolfe, R.A., Akiba, T., Andreucci, V.E., … Young, E.W. (2003). Association of comorbid conditions and mortality in hemodialysis patients in Europe, Japan, and the United States: The dialysis outcomes and practice patterns study (DOPPS). *Journal of the American Society of Nephrology, 14*, 3270–3277.

Griva, K., Davenport, A., Harrison, M., & Newman, S.P. (2010). An evaluation of illness, treatment perceptions, and depression in hospital- vs. home-based dialysis modalities. *Journal of Psychosomatic Research, 69*, 363–370.

Griva, K., Davenport, A., Harrison, M., & Newman, S.P. (2012). The impact of treatment transitions between dialysis and transplantation on illness cognitions and quality of life—A prospective study. *British Journal of Health Psychology, 17*, 812–827.

Griva, K., Jayasena, D., Davenport, A., Harrison, M., & Newman, S.P. (2009). Illness and treatment cognitions and health related quality of life in end stage renal disease. *British Journal of Health Psychology, 14*, 17–34.

Griva, K., Lai, A.Y., Lim, H., Yu, Z., Foo, M.W.Y., & Newman, S.P. (2014). Non-adherence in patients on peritoneal dialysis: A systematic review. *PloS ONE* (in press).

Griva, K., Newman, S.P., Harrison, M.J., Hankins, M., Davenport, A., Hansraj, S., & Thompson, D. (2003). Acute neuropsychological changes in hemodialysis and peritoneal dialysis patients. *Health Psychology, 22*, 570–578.

Griva, K., Stygall, J., Hankins, M., Davenport, A., Harrison, M., & Newman, S.P. (2010). Cognitive impairment and 7-year mortality in dialysis patients. *American Journal of Kidney Diseases, 56*, 693–703.

Griva, K., Ziegelmann, J.P., Thompson, D., Jayasena, D., Davenport, A., Harrison, M., & Newman, S.P. (2002). Quality of life and emotional responses in cadaver and living related renal transplant recipients. *Nephrology Dialysis Transplantation, 17*, 2204–2211.

Groothoff, J.W., Grootenhuis, M.A., Offringa, M., Stronks, K., Hutten, G.J., & Heymans, H.S.A. (2005). Social consequences in adult life of end-stage renal disease in childhood. *Journal of Pediatrics, 146*, 512–517.

Hallan, S.I., Coresh, J., Astor, B.C., Åsberg, A., Powe, N.R., Romundstad, S., … Holmen, J. (2006). International comparison of the relationship of chronic kidney disease prevalence and ESRD risk. *Journal of the American Society of Nephrology, 17*, 2275–2284.

Hays, R.D., Kallich, J.D., Mapes, D.L., Coons, S.J., & Carter, W.B. (1994). Development of the kidney disease quality of life (KDQOL TM) instrument. *Quality of Life Research, 3*, 329–338.

Hedayati, S.S., & Finkelstein, F.O. (2009). Epidemiology, diagnosis, and management of depression in patients with CKD. *American Journal of Kidney Diseases, 54*, 741–752.

Heijnsdijk, E.A.M., Wever, E.M., Auvinen, A., Hugosson, J., Ciatto, S., Nelen, V., … de Koning, H.J. (2012). Quality-of-life effects of prostate-specific antigen screening. *New England Journal of Medicine, 367*, 595–605.

House, J.S., Landis, K.R., & Umberson, D. (1988). Social relationships and health. *Science 241*, 540–545.

Johansen, K.L. (2008). Exercise and dialysis. *Hemodialysis International, 12*, 290–300.

Joshi, S., Gaynor, J., & Ciancio, G. (2012). Review of ethnic disparities in access to renal transplantation. *Clinical Transplantation, 26*, 337–343.

Kalender, B., Ozdemir, A.C., Dervisoglu, E., & Ozdemir, O. (2007). Quality of life in chronic kidney disease: Effects of treatment modality, depression, malnutrition and inflammation. *International Journal of Clinical Practice, 61*, 569–576.

Karamanidou, C., Clatworthy, J., Weinman, J., & Horne, R. (2008). A systematic review of the prevalence and determinants of nonadherence to phosphate binding medication in patients with end-stage renal disease. *BMC Nephrology, 9*, 2.

Kimmel, P.L., Cukor, D., Cohen, S.D., & Peterson, R.A. (2007). Depression in end-stage renal disease patients: A critical review. *Advances in Chronic Kidney Disease, 14*, 328–334.

Koushik, N., McArthur, S., & Baird, A. (2010). Adult chronic kidney disease: Neurocognition in chronic renal failure. *Neuropsychology Review, 20*, 33–51.

Kurella, M., Chertow, G.M., Luan, J., & Yaffe, K. (2004). Cognitive impairment in chronic kidney disease. *Journal of the American Geriatrics Society, 52*, 1863–1869.

Lacson, E., Li, N.C., Guerra-Dean, S., Lazarus, M., Hakim, R., & Finkelstein, F.O. (2012). Depressive symptoms associate with high mortality risk and dialysis withdrawal in incident hemodialysis patients. *Nephrology Dialysis Transplantation, 27*, 2921–2928.

Leggat, J.E., Bloembergen, W.E., Levine, G., Hulbert-Shearon, T.E., & Port, F.K. (1997). An analysis of risk factors for withdrawal from dialysis before death. *Journal of the American Society of Nephrology, 8*, 1755–1763.

Leventhal, H., Brissette, I., & Leventhal, E.A. (2003). The common-sense model of self-regulation of health and illness. In L.D. Cameron & H. Leventhal (Eds.), *The self-regulation of health and illness behaviour* (pp. 42–65). New York: Routledge.

Lopes, A.A., Bragg, J., Young, E., Goodkin, D., Mapes, D., Combe, C., ... Port, F.K. (2002). Depression as a predictor of mortality and hospitalization among hemodialysis patients in the United States and Europe. *Kidney International, 62*, 199–207.

McDonald, S.P., & Craig, J.C. (2004). Long-term survival of children with end-stage renal disease. *New England Journal of Medicine, 350*, 2654–2662.

Madero, M., Gul, A., & Sarnak, M.J. (2008). Review: Cognitive function in chronic kidney disease. *Seminars in Dialysis, 21*, 29–37.

Mason, J., Khunti, K., Stone, M., Farooqi, A., & Carr, S. (2008). Educational interventions in kidney disease care: A systematic review of randomized trials. *American Journal of Kidney Diseases, 51*, 933–951.

Matteson, M.L., & Russell, C. (2010). Interventions to improve hemodialysis adherence: A systematic review of randomized-controlled trials. *Hemodialysis International, 14*, 370–382.

Mehrotra, R., Chiu, Y.W., Kalantar-Zadeh, K., Bargman, J., & Vonesh, E. (2011). Similar outcomes with hemodialysis and peritoneal dialysis in patients with end-stage renal disease. *Archives of Internal Medicine, 171*, 110.

Mendelssohn, D.C., Mujais, S.K., Soroka, S.D., Brouillette, J., Takano, T., Barre, P.E., ... Finkelstein, F.O. (2009). A prospective evaluation of renal replacement therapy modality eligibility. *Nephrology Dialysis Transplantation, 24*, 555–561.

Moist, L.M., Bragg-Gresham, J.L., Pisoni, R.L., Saran, R., Akiba, T., Jacobson, R.H., ... Port, F.K. (2008). Travel time to dialysis as a predictor of health-related quality of life, adherence, and mortality: The Dialysis Outcomes and Practice Patterns Study (DOPPS). *American Journal of Kidney Diseases, 51*, 641–650.

Morton, R.L., Tong, A., Howard, K., Snelling, P., & Webster, A. (2010). The views of patients and carers in treatment decision making for chronic kidney disease: Systematic review and thematic synthesis of qualitative studies. *British Medical Journal, 340*(c112).

Morton, R.L., Turner, R.M., Howard, K., Snelling, P., & Webster, A.C. (2012). Patients who plan for conservative care rather than dialysis: A national observational study in Australia. *American Journal of Kidney Diseases, 59*, 419–427.

Muntner, P., He, J., Hamm, L., Loria, C., & Whelton, P.K. (2002). Renal insufficiency and subsequent death resulting from cardiovascular disease in the United States. *Journal of the American Society of Nephrology, 13*, 745–753.

Murray, A.M., Pederson, S.L., Tupper, D.E., Hochhalter, A.K., Miller, W.A., Li, Q., ... Foley, R.N. (2007). Acute variation in cognitive function in hemodialysis patients: A cohort study with repeated measures. *American Journal of Kidney Diseases, 50*, 270–278.

Murray, M.A., Brunier, G., Chung, J.O., Craig, L.A., Mills, C., Thomas, A., & Dawn, S. (2009). A systematic review of factors influencing decision making in adults living with chronic kidney disease. *Patient Education and Counseling, 76*, 149–58.

Murtagh, F.E.M., Marsh, J.E., Donohoe, P., Ekbal, N.J., Sheerin, N.S., & Harris, F.E. (2007). Dialysis or not? A comparative survival study of patients over 75 years with chronic kidney disease stage 5. *Nephrology Dialysis Transplantation, 22*, 1955–1962.

National Kidney Foundation. (2002). Kidney disease outcomes quality initiative (KDOQI) clinical practice guidelines for chronic kidney disease: Evaluation, classfication, and stratification. Retrieved from www.kidney.org/professionals/kdoqi/guidelines_ckd/p4_class_g1.htm

O'Connor, S.M., Jardine, A.G., & Millar, K. (2008). The prediction of self-care behaviours in end-stage renal disease patients using Leventhal's self-regulatory model. *Journal of Psychosomatic Research, 65*, 191–200.

Orr, A., Willis, S., Holmes, M., Britton, P., & Orr, D. (2007). Living with a kidney transplant: A qualitative investigation of quality of life. *Journal of Health Psychology, 12*, 653–662.

Penedo, F.J., & Dahn, J.R. (2004). Prostate cancer and QOL: Impact of treatment, disease burden and psychosocial interventions. *Expert Review of Pharmacoeconomics & Outcomes Research, 4*, 525–535.

Penedo, F.J., Molton, I., Dahn, J.R., Shen, B.J., Kinsinger, D., Traeger, L., & Antoni, M. (2006). A randomized clinical trial of group-based cognitive-behavioral stress management in localized prostate cancer: Development of stress management skills improves quality of life and benefit finding. *Annals of Behavioral Medicine, 31*, 261–270.

Plantinga, L.C., Fink, N.E., Sadler, J.H., Levey, A.S., Levin, N.W., Rubin, H.R., ... Powe, N.R. (2004). Frequency of patient–physician contact and patient outcomes in hemodialysis care. *Journal of the American Society of Nephrology, 15*, 210–218.

Saran, R., Bragg-Gresham, J.L., Rayner, H.C., Goodkin, D.A., Keen, M.L., Van Dijk, P.C., ... Port, F.K. (2003). Nonadherence in hemodialysis: associations with mortality, hospitalization, and practice patterns in the DOPPS. *Kidney International, 64*, 254–262.

Sayin, A., Mutluay, R., & Sindel, S. (2007). Quality of life in hemodialysis, peritoneal dialysis, and transplantation patients. *Transplantation Proceedings, 39*, 3047–3053.

Sharp, J., Wild, M.R., & Gumley, A.I. (2005). A systematic review of psychological interventions for the treatment of nonadherence to fluid-intake restrictions in people receiving hemodialysis. *American Journal of Kidney Diseases, 45*, 15–27.

Smith, C., Da Silva-Gane, M., Chandna, S., Warwicker, P., Greenwood, R., & Farrington, K. (2003). Choosing not to dialyse: Evaluation of planned non-dialytic management in a cohort of patients with end-stage renal failure. *Nephron Clinical Practice, 95*, c40–c46.

Tong, A., Chapman, J.R., Wong, G., Kanellis, J., McCarthy, G., & Craig, J.C. (2012). The motivations and experiences of living kidney donors: A thematic synthesis. *American Journal of Kidney Diseases, 60*, 15–26.

Tong, A., Lowe, A., Sainsbury, P., & Craig, J.C. (2008). Experiences of parents who have children with chronic kidney disease: A systematic review of qualitative studies. *Pediatrics, 121*, 349–360.

United Nations. (2011). *Political declaration of the High-level Meeting of the General Assembly on the Prevention and Control of Non-communicable Diseases.* Retrieved from www.un.org/en/ga/ncdmeeting2011/

United States Renal Data System (USRDS). (2011). *USRDS 2011 Annual data report: Atlas of chronic kidney disease and end-stage renal disease in the United States.* Bethesda, Md: National Institutes of Health, National Institute of Diabetes and Digestive and Kidney Diseases. Retrieved from www.usrds.org/adr.aspx

Untas, A., Thumma, J., Rascle, N., Rayner, H., Mapes, D., Lopes, A.A., … Combe, C. (2011). The associations of social support and other psychosocial factors with mortality and quality of life in the dialysis outcomes and practice patterns study. *Clinical Journal of American Society of Nephrology, 6,*142–152.

Watnick, S., Wang, P.L., Demadura, T., & Ganzini, L. (2005). Validation of 2 depression screening tools in dialysis patients. *American Journal of Kidney Diseases, 46,* 919–924.

Wolfe, R.A., Ashby, V.B., Milford, E.L., Ojo, A.O., Ettenger, R.E., Agodoa, L.Y.C., … Port, F.K. (1999). Comparison of mortality in all patients on dialysis, patients on dialysis awaiting transplantation, and recipients of a first cadaveric transplant. *New England Journal of Medicine, 341,* 1725–1730.

Wu, A.W., Fink, N.E., Cagney, K.A., Bass, E.B., Rubin, H.R., Meyer, K.B., … Powe, N.R. (2001). Developing a health-related quality-of-life measure for end-stage renal disease: The CHOICE health experience questionnaire. *American Journal of Kidney Diseases, 37,* 11–21.

Wu, A.W., Fink, N.E., Marsh-Manzi, J.V.R., Meyer, K.B., Finkelstein, F.O., Chapman, M.M., & Powe, N.R. (2004). Changes in quality of life during hemodialysis and peritoneal dialysis treatment: Generic and disease specific measures. *Journal of the American Society of Nephrology, 15,* 743–753.

Wuerth, D.B., Finkelstein, S.H., Schwetz, O., Carey, H., Kliger, A.S., & Finkelstein, F.O. (2002). Patients' descriptions of specific factors leading to modality selection of chronic peritoneal dialysis or hemodialysis. *Peritoneal Dialysis International, 22,* 184–190.

Yeh, S.C.J., & Chou, H.C. (2007). Coping strategies and stressors in patients with hemodialysis. *Psychosomatic Medicine, 69,* 182–190.

Ziegelmann, J.P., Griva, K., Hankins, M., Harrison, M., Davenport, A., Thompson, D., & Newman, S.P. (2002). The transplant effects questionnaire (TxEQ): The development of a questionnaire for assessing the multidimensional outcome of organ transplantation—Example of end stage renal disease (ESRD). *British Journal of Health Psychology, 7,* 393–408.

Chapter 17

Barlow, J.H., & Ellard, D.R. (2004). Psycho-educational interventions for children with chronic disease, parents and siblings: An overview of the research evidence base. *Child: Care, Health & Development, 30,* 637–645.

Beale, I.L. (2006). Scholarly literature review: Efficacy of psychological interventions for pediatric chronic illnesses. *Journal of Pediatric Psychology, 31,* 437–451.

Beck, M.H., Cataldo, M., Slifer, K.J., Pulbrook, V., & Ghuman, J.K. (2005). Teaching children with attention deficit hyperactivity disorder (ADHD) and autistic disorder (AD) how to swallow pills. *Clinical Pediatrics, 44,* 515–526.

Bergstraesser, E. (2012). Pediatric palliative care—When quality of life becomes the main focus of treatment. *European Journal of Pediatrics.* doi: 10.1007/s00431-012-1710-z

Bethell, C.D., Kogan, M.D., Strickland, B.B., Schor, E.L., Robertson, J., & Newacheck, P.W. (2011). A national and state profile of leading health problems and health care quality for US children: Key insurance disparities and across-state variations. *Academic Pediatrics, 11,* S22–33.

Birch, L.L., & Fisher, J.A. (1995). Appetite and eating behavior in children. *Pediatric Nutrition, 42,* 931–953.

Birch, L.L., & Fisher, J.A. (1998). Development of eating behaviors among children and adolescents. *Pediatrics, 101,* 539–549.

Birnie, K.A., Boerner, K.E., & Chambers, C.T. (2013). Families and pain. In P.J. McGrath, B. Stevens, S. Walker, & W. Zempsky (Eds.), *Oxford text of paediatric pain* (pp. 111–118). Oxford: Oxford University Press.

Birnie, K.A., Uman, L.S., & Chambers, C.T. (2013). Impact of familial factors on children's chronic pain. In R.F. Schmidt & G.F. Gebhart (Eds.), *Encyclopedia of pain* (2nd ed., pp. 1577–1584). New York: Springer-Verlag.

Blount, R.L., Cohen, L.L., Frank, N.C., Bachanas, P.J., Smith, A.J., Manimala, M.R., & Pate, J.T. (1997). The child–adult medical procedure interaction scale-revised: An assessment of validity. *Journal of Pediatric Psychology, 22,* 73–88.

Blount, R.L., Corbin, S.M., Sturges, J.W., Wolfe, V.V., Prater, J.M., & James, L.D. (1989). The relationship between adult's behavior and child coping and distress during BMA LP procedures: A sequential analysis. *Behavior Therapy, 20,* 585–601.

Blount, R.L., Dahlquist, L.M., Baer, R.A., & Wuori, D. (1984). A brief effective method for teaching children to swallow pills. *Behavior Therapy, 15,* 381–387.

Blount, R.L., Simons, L.E., Devine, K.A., Jaaniste, T., Cohen, L.L., Chambers, C.T., & Hayutin, L.G. (2008). Evidence-based assessment of coping and stress in pediatric psychology. *Journal of Pediatric Psychology, 33,* 1021–1045.

Broome, M.E., Bates, T.A., Lillis, P.P., & McGahee, T.W. (1990). Children's medical fears, coping behaviors, and pain perceptions during a lumbar puncture. *Oncology Nursing Society, 17,* 361–367.

Brown, M.L., Pope, A.W., & Brown, E.J. (2010). Treatment of primary noctural enuresis in children: A review. *Child: Care, Health and Development, 37,* 153–160.

Brummelte, S., Grunau, R.E., Chau, V., Poskitt, K.J., Brant, R., Vinall, J., … Miller, S.P. (2012). Procedural pain and brain development in premature newborns. *Annals of Neurology, 71,* 385–396.

Canadian Institute of Child Health. (2001). *The health of canada's children: A CICH profile* (3rd ed.). Ottawa.

Chambers, C.T. (2003). The role of family factors in pediatric pain. In P.J. McGrath & G.A. Finley (Eds.), *Pediatric pain: Biological and social context* (pp. 99–130). Seattle: IASP Press.

Chambers, C.T. (2012). Pill swallowing and children. *Progress Notes: Newsletter of the Society for Pediatric Psychology, 36*(2), 4–5.

Chambers, C.T., & Craig, K.D. (1998). An intrusive impact of anchors in children's faces pain scales. *Pain, 78*, 27–37.

Chambers, C.T., Craig, K.D., & Bennett, S.M. (2002). The impact of maternal behavior on children's pain experiences: An experimental analysis. *Journal of Pediatric Psychology, 27*, 293–301.

Chambers, C.T., Giesbrecht, K., Craig, K.D., Bennett, S.M., & Huntsman, E. (1999). A comparison of faces scales for the measurement of pediatric pain: Children's and parents' ratings. *Pain, 83*, 25–35.

Chambers, C.T., Hardial, J., Craig, K.D., Court, C., & Montgomery, C. (2005). Faces scales for the measurement of postoperative pain intensity in children following minor surgery. *Clinical Journal of Pain, 21*, 277–285.

Chambers, C.T., Reid, G.J., Craig, K.D., McGrath, P.J., & Finley, G.A. (1998). Agreement between child and parent reports of pain. *Clinical Journal of Pain, 14*, 336–342.

Chambers, C.T., Taddio, A., Uman, L.S., & McMurtry, C.M. (2009). Psychological interventions for reducing pain and distress during routine childhood immunizations: A systematic review. *Clinical Therapeutics, 31*(Suppl. B), S77–S103.

Christopherson, E. (2010). *Elimination disorders in children and adolescents*. New York: Hogrefe & Huber.

Cohen, L.L., & MacLaren, J.E. (2007). Breaking down the barriers to pediatric procedural preparation. *Clinical Psychology: Science and Practice, 14*, 144.

Compas, B.E., Jaser, S.S., Dunn, M.J., & Rodriguez, E.M. (2012). Coping with chronic illness in childhood and adolescence. *Annual Review of Clinical Psychology, 8*, 455–480.

Coulombe, J.A., Reid, G.J., Boyle, M.H., & Racine, Y. (2010). Concurrent associations among sleep problems, indicators of inadequate sleep, psychopathology, and shared risk factors in a population-based sample of healthy Ontario children. *Journal of Pediatric Psychology, 35*, 790–799.

Craig, K.D., Lilley, C.M., & Gilbert, C.A. (1996). Social barriers to optimal pain management in infants and children. *Clinical Journal of Pain, 12*, 232–242.

Craig, K.D., Whitfield, M.F., Grunau, R.V.E., Linton, J., & Hadjistavropoulos, H.D. (1993). Pain in the preterm neonate: Behavioral and physiological indices. *Pain, 52*, 287–299.

Crist, W., & Napier-Phillips, A. (2001). Mealtime behaviors of young children: A comparison of normative and clinical data. *Journal of Developmental and Behavioral Pediatrics, 22*, 279–286.

Cruz-Arrieta, E. (2008). Pill-swallowing training: A brief pediatric oncology report. *Primary Psychiatry, 15*, 49–53.

Culbert, T.P., & Banez, G.A. (2007). Integrative approaches to childhood constipation and encopresis. *Pediatric Clinics of North America, 54*, 927–947.

Curran, E. (2007) *Guided imagery for healing children and teens*. New York: Atria Books.

Dean, A.J., Walters, J., & Hall, A. (2010). A systematic review of interventions to enhance medication adherence in children and adolescents with chronic illness. *Archives of Disease in Childhood, 95*, 717–723.

Drotar, D., & Bonner, M.S. (2009). Influences on adherence to pediatric asthma treatment: A review of correlates and predictors. *Journal of Developmental and Behavioral Pediatrics, 30*, 574–582.

Eccleston, C., Malleson, P.N., Clinch, J., Connell, H., & Sourbut, C. (2003). Chronic pain in adolescents: Evaluation of a programme of interdisciplinary cognitive behaviour therapy. *Archives of Disease in Childhood, 88*, 881-885.

Eccleston, C., Palermo, T.M., Fisher, E., & Law, E. (2012). Psychological interventions for parents of children and adolescents with chronic illness. *Cochrane Database of Systematic Reviews (Online), 8*, CD009660.

Eccleston, C., Palermo, T.M., Williams, A.C., Lewandowski, A., Morley, S., Fisher, E., & Law, E. (2012). Psychological therapies for the management of chronic and recurrent pain in children and adolescents (review). *Cochrane Database of Systematic Reviews (Online), 12*, CD003968.

Feeney, J.A., (2000). Implications of attachment style for patterns of health and illness. *Child: Care, Health and Development, 26*, 277–288.

Funk, M.J., Mullins, L.L., & Olson, R.A. (1984). Teaching children to swallow pills: A case study. *Children's Health Care, 3*, 20–23.

Garvie, P.A., Lensing, S., & Rai, S.N. (2007). Efficacy of a pill-swallowing training intervention to improve antiretroviral medication adherence in pediatric patients with HIV/AIDS. *Pediatrics, 119*, e893–e899.

Ghuman, J.K., Cataldo, M.D., Beck, M.H., & Slifer, K.J. (2004). Behavioral training for pill-swallowing difficulties in young children with autistic disorder. *Journal of Child and Adolescent Psychopharmacology, 14*, 601–611.

Grunau, R.V.E., Whitfield, M.F., Petrie, J.H., & Fryer, E.L. (1994). Early pain experience, child and family factors, as precursors of somatization: A prospective study of extremely premature and fullterm children. *Pain, 56*, 353–359.

Hadjistavropoulos, T., Craig, K.D., Duck, S., Cano, A., Goubert, L., Jackson, P.L., … Fitzgerald, T.D. (2011). A biopsychosocial formulation of pain communication. *Psychological Bulletin, 137*, 910–939.

Henderson, E.M., Rosser, B.A., Keogh, E., & Eccleston, C. (2012). Internet sites offering adolescents help with headache, abdominal pain, and dysmenorrhoea: A description of content, quality, and peer interactions. *Journal of Pediatric Psychology, 37*, 262–271.

Hicks, C.L., von Baeyer, C.L., Spafford, P.A., van Korlaar, I., & Goodenough, B. (2001). The faces pain scale—revised: Toward a common metric in pediatric pain measurement. *Pain, 93*, 173–183.

Huguet, A., & Miro, J. (2008). The severity of chronic pediatric pain: An epidemiological study. *Journal of Pain, 9*, 226–236.

Jaaniste, T., Hayes, B., & von Baeyer, C.L. (2007). Providing children with information about forthcoming medical procedures: A review and synthesis. *Clinical Psychology: Science and Practice, 14*, 124–143.

Jannoun, L., & Chessels, J.M. (1987). Long-term psychological effects of childhood leukemia and its treatment. *Pediatric Hematology & Oncology, 4*, 293–308.

Kahana, S., Drotar, D., & Frazier, T. (2008). Meta-analysis of psychological interventions to promote adherence to treatment in pediatric chronic health conditions. *Journal of Pediatric Psychology, 33*, 590–611.

Kerwin, M.E. (1999). Empirically supported treatments in pediatric psychology: Severe feeding problems. *Journal of Pediatric Psychology, 24*, 193–214.

King, S., Chambers, C.T., Huguet, A., MacNevin, R.C., McGrath, P.J., Parker, L., & MacDonald, A.J. (2011). The epidemiology of chronic pain in children and adolescents revisited: A systematic review. *Pain, 152*, 2729–2738.

La Greca, A.M., & Race Mackey, E. (2009). Adherence to pediatric treatment regimens. In M.C. Roberts & R.G. Steele (Eds.), *Handbook of pediatric psychology* (4th ed., pp. 130–152). New York: Guilford Press.

Lewandowski, A.S., Ward, T.M., & Palermo, T.M. (2011). Sleep problems in children and adolescents with common medical conditions. *Pediatric Clinics of North America, 58*, 699–713.

Logan, D.E., Engle, L., Feinstein, A.B., Sieberg, C.B., Sparling, P., Cohen, L.L., … Masuda, A. (2012). Ecological system influences in the treatment of pediatric chronic pain. *Pain Research & Management, 17*, 407–411.

Luersen, K., Davis, S.A., Kaplan, S.G., Abel, T.D., Winchester, W.W., & Feldman, S.R. (2012). Sticker charts: A method for improving adherence to treatment of chronic diseases in children. *Pediatric Dermatology, 29*, 403–408.

McCulloch, R., Comac, M., & Craig, F. (2008). Paediatric palliative care: Coming of age in oncology? *European Journal of Cancer, 44*, 1139–1145.

McGrath, P.J., Walco, G.A., Turk, D.C., Dworkin, R.H., Brown, M.T., Davidson, K., … Zeltzer, L. (2008). Core outcome domains and measures for pediatric acute and chronic/recurrent pain clinical trials: PedIMMPACT recommendations. *Journal of Pain, 9*, 771–783.

McMurtry, C.M., Chambers, C.T., McGrath, P.J., & Asp, E. (2010). When "don't worry" communicates fear: Children's perceptions of parental reassurance and distraction during a painful medical procedure. *Pain, 150*, 52–58.

McMurtry, C.M., McGrath, P.J., Asp, E., & Chambers, C.T. (2007). Parental reassurance and pediatric procedural pain: A linguistic description. *Journal of Pain, 8*, 95–101.

McMurtry, C.M., McGrath, P.J., & Chambers, C.T. (2006). Reassurance can hurt: Parental behavior and painful medical procedures. *Journal of Pediatrics, 148*, 560–561.

Meltzer, L.J., Johnson, C., Crosette, J., Ramos, M., & Mindell, J.A. (2010). Prevalence of diagnosed sleep disorders in pediatric primary care practices. *Pediatrics, 125*, e1410–e1418.

Meltzer, L.J., & Mindell, J.A. (2009). Pediatric sleep. In M.C. Roberts & R.G. Steele (Eds.), *Handbook of pediatric psychology* (4th ed., pp. 491–507). New York: Guilford Press.

Meltzer, L.J., & Montgomery-Downs, H.E. (2011). Sleep in the family. *Pediatric Clinics of North America, 58*, 765–774.

Meltzer, E.O., Welch, M.J., & Ostrom, N.K. (2006). Pill swallowing ability and training in children 6 to 11 years of age. *Clinical Pediatrics, 45*, 725–733.

Mindell, J.A., Kuhn, B., Lewin, D.S., Meltzer, L.J., Sadeh, A., & American Academy of Sleep Medicine. (2006). Behavioral treatment of bedtime problems and night wakings in infants and young children. *Sleep, 29*, 1263–1276.

Modi, A.C., Pai, A.L., Hommel, K.A., Hood, K.K., Cortina, S., Hilliard, M.E., … Drotar, D. (2012). Pediatric self-management: A framework for research, practice, and policy. *Pediatrics, 129*, e473–e485.

Moody, K., Siegel, L., Scharbach, K., Cunningham, L., & Cantor, R.M. (2011). Pediatric palliative care. *Primary Care: Clinics in Office Practice, 38*, 327–361.

Moon, E.C., Chambers, C.T., & McGrath, P.J. (2011). "He says, she says": A comparison of fathers' and mothers' verbal behavior during child cold pressor pain. *Journal of Pain, 12*, 1174–1181.

Noel, M., Petter, M., Parker, J.A., & Chambers, C.T. (2012). Cognitive behavioural therapy for pediatric chronic pain: The problem, research, and practice. *Journal of Cognitive Psychotherapy, 26*, 143–156.

O'Brien, I., Duffy, A., & Nicholl, H. (2009). Impact of childhood chronic illnesses on siblings: A literature review. *British Journal of Nursing, 18*, 1358, 1360–1365.

Olson, A.L., Johansen, S.G., Powers, L.E., Pope, J.B., & Klein, R.B. (1993). Cognitive coping strategies of children with chronic illness. *Journal of Developmental and Behavioral Pediatrics, 14*, 217–223.

Palermo, T.M. (2000). Impact of recurrent and chronic pain on child and family daily functioning: A critical review of the literature. *Journal of Developmental & Behavioral Pediatrics, 21*, 58–69.

Pless, I.B., Power, C., & Peckham, C.S. (1993). Long-term psychosocial sequelae of chronic physical disorders in childhood. *Pediatrics, 91*, 1131–1136.

Porter, F.L., Grunau, R.E., & Anand, K.J.S. (1999). Long-term effects of pain in infants. *Journal of Developmental and Behavioral Pediatrics, 20*, 253–261.

Powers, K.S., & Rubenstein, J.S. (1999). Family presence during invasive procedures in the pediatric intensive care unit. *Archives of Pediatric and Adolescent Medicine, 153*, 955–958.

Prchal, A., & Landolt, M.A. (2009). Psychological interventions with siblings of pediatric cancer patients: A systematic review. *Psycho-Oncology, 18*, 1241–1251.

Pui, C.H., Mullighan, C.G., Evans, W.E., & Relling, M.V. (2012). Pediatric acute lymphoblastic leukemia: Where are we going and how do we get there? *Blood, 120*, 1165–1174.

Reid, G.J., Gilbert, C.A., & McGrath, P.J. (1998). The pain coping questionnaire: Preliminary validation. *Pain, 76*, 83–96.

Reid, G.J., Hong, R.Y., & Wade, T.J. (2009). The relation between common sleep problems and emotional and behavioral problems among 2- and 3-year-olds in the context of known risk factors for psychopathology. *Journal of Sleep Research, 18*, 49–59.

Reitman, D., & Passeri, C. (2008). Use of stimulus fading and functional assessment to treat pill refusal with an 8-year-old boy diagnosed with ADHD. *Clinical Case Studies, 7*, 224–237.

Repetti, R.L., Taylor, S.E., Seeman, T.E. (2002). Risky families: Family social environments and the mental and physical health of offspring. *Psychological Bulletin, 128*, 330–336.

Rodriguez, E.M., Dunn, M.J., Zuckerman, T., Vannatta, K., Gerhardt, C.A., & Compas, B.E. (2012). Cancer-related sources of stress for children with cancer and their parents. *Journal of Pediatric Psychology, 37*, 185–197.

Rubenstein, C.L., Varni, J.W., & Katz, E.R. (1990). Cognitive functioning in long-term survivors of childhood leukemia: A prospective analysis. *Journal of Developmental and Behavioral Pediatrics, 11*, 301–305.

Rudolph, K.D., Dennig, M.D., & Weisz, J.R. (1995). Determinants and consequences of children's coping in the medical setting: Conceptualization, review and critique. *Psychological Bulletin, 118,* 328–357.

Schmidt, S., Peterson, C., & Bullinger, M. (2003). Coping with chronic disease from the perspective of children and adolescents: A conceptual framework and its implications for participation. *Child: Care, Health and Development, 29,* 63–75.

Schwartz, L.A., Tuchman, L.K., Hobbie, W.L., & Ginsberg, J.P. (2011). A social-ecological model of readiness for transition to adult-oriented care for adolescents and young adults with chronic health conditions. *Child: Care, Health & Development, 37,* 883–895.

Shah, V., Taddio, A., & Rieder, M.J. (2009). Effectiveness and tolerability of pharmacologic and combined interventions for reducing injection pain during routine childhood immunizations: Systematic review and meta-analyses. *Clinical Therapeutics, 31*(Suppl. B), S104–S151.

Spirito, A., Brown, R.T., D'Angelo, E., Delamater, A., Rodrigue, J., & Siegel, L. (2003). Society of Pediatric Psychology Task Force Report: Recommendations for the training of pediatric psychologists. *Journal of Pediatric Psychology, 28,* 85–98.

Spirito, A., Stark, L.J., & Williams, C. (1988). Development of a brief coping checklist for use with pediatric populations. *Journal of Pediatric Psychology, 13,* 555–574.

Stanford, E.A., Chambers, C.T., Biesanz, J.C., & Chen, E. (2007). The frequency, trajectories and predictors of adolescent recurrent pain: A population-based approach. *Pain, 138,* 11–21.

Stevens, B., Johnston, C., Petryshen, P., & Taddio, A. (1996). Premature infant pain profile: Development and initial validation. *Clinical Journal of Pain, 12,* 13–22.

Stevens, B.J., Abbott, L.K., Yamada, J., Harrison, D., Stinson, J., Taddio, A., … Finley, G.A. (2011). Epidemiology and management of painful procedures in children in Canadian hospitals. *Canadian Medical Association Journal, 183,* E403–E410.

Stinson, J.N. (2009). Improving the assessment of pediatric chronic pain: Harnessing the potential of electronic diaries. *Pain Research & Management: Journal of the Canadian Pain Society, 14,* 59–64.

Stinson, J., Wilson, R., Gill, N., Yamada, J., & Holt, J. (2009). A systematic review of Internet-based self-management interventions for youth with health conditions. *Journal of Pediatric Psychology, 34,* 495–510.

Taddio, A., Appleton, M., Bortolussi, R., Chambers, C., Dubey, V., Halperin, S., … Shah, V. (2010). Reducing the pain of childhood vaccination: An evidence-based clinical practice guideline. *Canadian Medical Association Journal, 182,* E843–E855.

Taddio, A., Chambers, C.T., Halperin, S.A., Ipp, M., Lockett, D., Rieder, M.J., & Shah, V. (2009). Inadequate pain management during routine childhood immunizations: The nerve of it. *Clinical Therapeutic, 31*(Suppl. B), S152–S167.

Taddio, A., Goldbach, M., Ipp, M., Stevens, B., & Koren, G. (1995). Effect of neonatal circumcision on pain responses during vaccinations in boys. *Lancet, 345,* 291–292.

Taddio, A., Ilersich, A.L., Ipp, M., Kikuta, A., & Shah, V. (2009). Physical interventions and injection techniques for reducing injection pain during routine childhood immunizations: Systematic review of randomized controlled trials and quasi-randomized controlled trials. *Clinical Therapeutics, 31*(Suppl. B), S48–S76.

Taddio, A., Katz, J., Ilersich, A.L., & Koren, G. (1997). Effect of neonatal circumcision on pain response during subsequent routine vaccination. *Lancet, 349,* 599–603.

Thompson, R.J., & Gustafson, K.E. (1996). *Adaptation to chronic childhood illness.* Washington: APA.

Thompson Jr, R.J., Gustafson, K.E., Hamlett, K.W., & Spock, A. (1992). Stress, coping, and family functioning in the psychological adjustment of mothers of children and adolescents with cystic fibrosis. *Journal of Pediatric Psychology, 17,* 573–585.

Uman, L.S., Chambers, C.T., McGrath, P.J., & Kisely, S. (2006). Psychological interventions for needle-related procedural pain and distress in children and adolescents. *Cochrane Database of Systematic Reviews, 4,* 1–72.

Uman, L.S., Chambers, C.T., McGrath, P.J., & Kisely, S. (2008). A systematic review of randomized controlled trials examining psychological interventions for needle-related procedural pain and distress in children and adolescents: An abbreviated Cochrane review. *Journal of Pediatric Psychology, 33,* 842–854.

US Department of Health and Human Services, Health Resources and Services Administration. (2009). *The health and well-being of children: A portrait of states and the nation 2007.* Retrieved from mchb.hrsa.gov/nsch/07main/moreinfo/pdf/nsch07.pdf

Van Allen, J., Davis, A.M., & Lassen, S. (2011). The use of telemedicine in pediatric psychology: Research review and current applications. *Child and Adolescent Psychiatric Clinics of North America, 20,* 55–66.

von Gontard, A. (2003). Elimination disorders in childhood. How to make children dry and clean. [Ausscheidungsstorungen differenziert behandeln. Wie Sie Kinder trocken und sauber bekommen] *MMW Fortschritte Der Medizin, 145,* 26–30.

von Gontard, A., Baeyens, D., Van Hoecke, E., Warzak, W.J., & Bachmann, C. (2011). Psychological and psychiatric issues in urinary and fecal incontinence. *Journal of Urology, 185,* 1432–1436.

Walco, G.A. (1986). A behavioral treatment for difficulty in swallowing pills. *Journal of Behavior Therapy and Experimental Psychiatry, 17,* 127–128.

Walker, L.S., Sherman, A.L., Bruehl, S., Garber, J., & Smith, C.A. (2012). Functional abdominal pain patient subtypes in childhood predict functional gastrointestinal disorders with chronic pain and psychiatric comorbidities in adolescence and adulthood. *Pain, 153,* 1798–1806.

Wallander, J.L., & Varni, J.W. (1992). Adjustment in children with chronic physical disorders: Programmatic research on a disability-stress-coping model. In A.M. LaGreca, L. Siegal, J.L. Wallander, & C.E. Walker (Eds.), *Stress and coping in child health* (pp. 279–298). New York: Guilford Press.

Wright, L. (1967). The pediatric psychologist: A role model. *American Psychologist, 22*(4), 323–325.

Zhou, H., Roberts, P., & Horgan, L. (2008). Association between self-report pain ratings of child and parent, child and nurse and parent and nurse dyads: Meta-analysis. *Journal of Advanced Nursing, 63*, 334–342.

Chapter 18

Abrahamson, K., Clark, D., Perkins, A., & Arling, G. (2012). Does cognitive impairment influence quality of life among nursing home residents? *Gerontologist, 52*, 632–640.

Aguirre, E., Spector, A., Hoe, J., Russell, I.T., Knapp, M., Woods, R.T., & Orrell, M. (2010). Maintenance Cognitive Stimulation Therapy (CST) for dementia: A single-blind, multi-centre, randomized controlled trial of maintenance CST versus CST for dementia. *Trials, 11*, 1–10.

Allen, R.S. (2009). The Legacy Project intervention to enhance meaningful family interactions: Case examples. *Clinical Gerontologist, 32*, 164–176.

Allen, R.S., Harris, G.M., Burgio, L.D., Azuero, C.B., Miller, L.A., Shin, H., … Parmelee, P. (2014). Can senior volunteers deliver reminiscence and creative activity interventions? Results of the Legacy Intervention Family Enactment (LIFE) randomized controlled trial. *Journal of Pain and Symptom Management.* doi:10.1016/j.jpainsymman.2013.11.012.

Allen, R.S., Hilgeman, M.M., Ege, M.A., Shuster, J.L., Jr, & Burgio, L.D. (2008). Legacy activities as interventions approaching the end of life. *Journal of Palliative Medicine, 11*, 1029–1038.

Alm, N., Dye, R., Gowans, G., Campbell, J., Astell, A., & Ellis, M. (2007). A communication support system for older people with dementia. *Computer, 35*–41.

Aneshensel, C.S., Pearlin, L.I., Mullan, J.T., Zarit, S.H., & Whitlatch, C.J. (1995). *Profiles in caregiving: The unexpected career.* San Diego: Academic Press.

Balfour, J.E., & O'Rourke, N. (2003). Older adults with Alzheimer disease, comorbid arthritis and prescription of psychotropic medications. *Pain Research and Management, 8*, 198–204.

Ballard, C., Hanney, M.L., Theodoulou, M., Douglas, S., McShane, R., Kossakowski, K., … Jacoby, R. (2009). The dementia antipsychotic withdrawal trial (DART-AD): Long-term follow-up of a randomised placebo-controlled trial. *Lancet Neurology, 8*, 151–157.

Beck, A.M., & Katcher, A.H. (2003). Future directions in human–animal bond research. *American Behavioral Scientist, 47*, 79–93.

Bohlmeijer, E., Smit, F. & Cuijpers, P. (2003). Effects of reminiscence and life review on late-life depression. *International Journal of Geriatric Psychiatry, 18*, 1088–1094.

Bourgeois, M.S., Dijkstra, K., Burgio, L., & Allen-Burge, R. (2001). Memory aids as an augmentative and alternative communication strategy for nursing home residents with dementia. *Augmentative and Alternative Communication, 17*, 196–210.

Boyd, C.M., Darer, J., Boult, C., Fried, L.P., Boult, L., & Wu, A.W. (2005). Clinical practice guidelines and quality of care for older patients with multiple comorbid diseases: Implications for pay for performance. *Journal of the American Medical Association, 294*, 716–724.

Boyle, P.A., Yu, L., Wilson, R.S., Gamble, K., Buchman, A.S., & Bennett, D.A. (2012). Poor decision making is a consequence of cognitive decline among older persons without Alzheimer's disease or mild cognitive impairment. *PLoS ONE 7*(8), e43647.

Brummel-Smith, K. (1989). Falls in the aged. *Primary Care, 16*(2), 377–393.

Burgio, L.D., Allen-Burge, R., Roth, D.L., Bourgeois, M.S., Dijkstra, K., Gerstle, J., … Bankester, L. (2001). Come talk with me: Improving communication between nursing assistants and nursing home residents during care routines. *Gerontologist, 41*, 449–460.

Butler, A.C., Chapman, J.E., Forman, E.M., & Beck, A.T. (2006). The empirical status of cognitive-behavioural therapy: A review of meta-analyses. *Clinical Psychology Review, 26*, 17–31.

Camp, C.J., Cohen-Mansfield, J., & Capezuti, E.A. (2002). Use of nonpharmacologic interventions among nursing home residents with dementia. *Psychiatric Services, 53*, 1397–1401.

Canadian Study of Health and Aging Working Group. (1994). Canadian study of health and aging: Study methods and prevalence of dementia. *Canadian Medical Association Journal, 150*, 899–913.

Candy, B., Jones, L., Drake, R., Leurent, B., & King, M. (2011). Interventions for supporting informal caregivers of patients in the terminal phase of a disease. *Cochrane Database of Systematic Reviews, 7*, 1–77.

Centers for Disease Control (2012). Health disparities. Retrieved from www.cdc.gov/healthyyouth/disparities/index.html

Chan, S., Hadjistavropoulos, T., Williams, J., & Lints-Martindale, A. (in press). Evidence-based development and initial validation of the Pain Assessment Checklist for Seniors with Limited Ability to Communicate-II (PACSLAC-II). *Clinical Journal of Pain.*

Charlton, J.E. (2005). *Core curriculum for professional education in pain* (3rd ed.). Seattle: IASP Press.

Chochinov, H.M. (2012). *Dignity therapy: Final words for final days.* New York: Oxford University Press.

Chochinov, H.M., Kristjanson, L.J., Breitbart, W., McClement, S., Hack, T.F., Hassard, T., & Harlos, M. (2011). Effect of dignity therapy on distress and end-of-life experience in terminally ill patients: A randomised controlled trial. *Lancet Oncology, 12*(8): 753–62.

Clare, L., & Woods, B. (2003). Cognitive rehabilitation and cognitive training for early-stage Alzheimer's disease and vascular dementia. *Cochrane Database of Systematic Reviews, 4.*

Cohen-Mansfield, J. (2001). Nonpharmacologic interventions for inappropriate behaviours in dementia: A review, summary, and critique. *American Journal of Geriatric Psychiatry, 9*, 361–381.

Cohen-Mansfield, J., Golander, H., & Arnheim, G. (2000). Self-identity in older persons suffering from dementia: Preliminary results. *Social Science & Medicine, 51*, 381–394.

Cohen-Mansfield, J., Parpura-Gill, A., & Golander, H. (2006) Utilization of self-identity roles for designing interventions for persons with dementia. *Journals of Gerontology, Series B: Psychological Sciences and Social Sciences, 61*, 202–212.

Colombo, G., Dello Buono, M., Smania, K., Raviola, R., & De Leo, D. (2006). Pet therapy and institutionalized elderly: A study on 144 cognitively unimpaired subjects. *Archives of Gerontology and Geriatrics, 42,* 207–216.

Delbaere, K., Sturnieks, D.L., Crombez, G., & Lord, S.R. (2009). Concern about falls elicits changes in gait parameters in conditions of postural threat in older people. *Journals of Gerontology, Series A: Biological Sciences and Medical Sciences, 64,* 237–242.

Family Caregiver Alliance. (2006). *Caregiver assessment: Voices and views from the field.* Report form a National Consensus Development Conference (Vol. II). San Francisco: Family Caregiver Alliance.

Feltner, M.E., MacRae, P.G., & McNitt-Gray, J.L. (1994). Quantitative gait assessment as a predictor of prospective and retrospective falls in community-dwelling older women. *Archives of Physical Medicine and Rehabilitation, 75,* 447–453.

Fields, J.A., Kramer, J.A., & Lubin, W. (1993). Challenges and opportunities in the provision of long-term care. *Benefits Quarterly, 9,* 6–11.

Fisher, J.E., Drossel, C., Ferguson, K., Cherup, S., & Sylvester, M. (2008). Treating persons with dementia in context. In D. Gallagher-Thompson, A.M. Steffen, & L.W. Thompson (Eds.), *Handbook of behavioral and cognitive therapies with older adults* (pp. 200–218). New York: Springer Science + Business Media, LLC.

Fuchs-Lacelle, S., Hadjistavropoulos, T., & Lix, L. (2008). Pain assessment as intervention: A study of older adults with severe dementia. *Clinical Journal of Pain, 24,* 697–707.

Gauthier, L.R., & Gagliese, L. (2010). Assessment of pain in older persons. In D.C. Turk & R. Melzack (Eds.), *Handbook of pain assessment* (3rd ed., pp. 242–259). New York: Guilford Press.

Glass, T.A., de Leon, C.F., Bassuk, S.S., & Berkman, L.F. (2006). Social engagement and depressive symptoms in late life: Longitudinal findings. *Journal of Aging and Health, 18,* 604–628.

Green, S.M., Hadjistavropoulos, T., Hadjistavropoulos, H., Martin, R., & Sharpe, D. (2009). A controlled investigation of a cognitive behavioural pain management program for older adults. *Behavioural and Cognitive Psychotherapy, 37,* 221–226.

Haber, D. (2006). Life review: Implementation, theory, research, and therapy. *International Journal on Aging and Human Development, 63,* 153–171.

Hadjistavropoulos, T. (2012). Self-management of pain in older persons: Helping people help themselves. *Pain Medicine, 13,* S67–S71.

Hadjistavropoulos, T., Carleton, R.N., Delbaere, K., Barden, J., Zwakhalen, S., Fitzgerald, B., ... Hadjistavropoulos, H. (2012). The relationship of fear of falling and balance confidence with balance and dual tasking performance. *Psychology and Aging, 27,* 1–13.

Hadjistavropoulos, T., Craig, K.D., Duck, S., Cano, A., Goubert, L., Jackson, P., ... Fitzgerald, T.D. (2011). A biopsychosocial formulation of pain communication. *Psychological Bulletin, 137,* 910–939.

Hadjistavropoulos, T., Fitzgerald, T.D., & Marchildon, G. (2010). Practice guidelines for assessing pain in older persons who reside in long-term care facilities. *Physiotherapy Canada, 62,* 104–113.

Hadjistavropoulos, T., & Hadjistavropoulos, H.D. (Eds.). (2008). *Pain management for older adults: A self help guide.* Seattle: IASP Press.

Hadjistavropoulos, T., Herr, K., Turk, D.C., Fine, P.G., Dworkin, R.H., Helme, R., ... Williams, J. (2007). An interdisciplinary expert consensus statement on assessment of pain in older persons. *Clinical Journal of Pain, 23,* S1–S43.

Hadjistavropoulos, T., Marchildon, G., Fine, P., Herr, K., Palley, H., Kaasalainen, S., & Beland, F. (2009). Transforming long-term care pain management in North America: The policy clinical interface. *Pain Medicine, 10,* 506–520.

Hadjistavropoulos, T., Martin, R., Sharpe, D., Lints-Martindale, A.C., McCreary, D., & Asmundson, G.J.G. (2007). A longitudinal investigation of fear of falling, fear of pain, and activity avoidance in community dwelling older adults. *Journal of Aging and Health, 19,* 965–984.

Haight, B., Michel, Y., & Hendrix, S. (2000). The extended effects of the life review in nursing home residents. *International Journal on Aging and Human Development, 50,* 151–168.

Haight, B., & Webster, J.D. (1995). *The art and science of reminiscing: Theory, research, methods and applications.* Washington: Taylor and Francis.

Hawk, C., Hyland, J.K., Rupert, R., Colonvega, M., & Hall, S. (2006). Assessment of balance and risk for falls in a sample of community-dwelling adults aged 65 and older. *Chiropractic & Osteopathy, 14.* Retrieved from www.chiroandosteo.com/content/14/1/3

Health Canada (2003). *Arthritis in Canada—An ongoing challenge.* Ottawa: Health Canada. Retrieved from www.phac-aspc.gc.ca/publicat/ac/pdf/ac_e.pdf

Herr, K. (2010). Pain in the older adult: An imperative across all health care settings. *Pain Management Nursing, 11,* S1–S10.

Horgas, A.L., Nichols, A.L., Schapson, C.A., & Vietes, K. (2007). Assessing pain in persons with dementia: Relationships among the non-communicative patient's pain assessment instrument, self-report, and behavioral observations. *Pain Management Nursing, 8,* 77–85.

Ivzeku, D., Matarese, M., & Pedone, C. (2011). Predictive validity of the Hendrich fall risk model II in an acute geriatric unit. *International Journal of Nursing Studies, 48*(4), 468–474.

Karel, M., Emery, E., & Molinari, V. (2010). Development of a tool to evaluate geropsychology knowledge and skill competencies. *International Psychogeriatrics, 22,* 886–895.

Kazdin, A.E., & Blase, S.L. (2011). Rebooting psychotherapy research and practice to reduce the burden of mental illness. *Perspectives on Psychological Science, 6,* 21–37.

Kitwood, T. (1997). *Dementia reconsidered: The person comes first.* Buckingham, UK: Open University Press.

Knight, B.G., Karel, M.J., Hinrichsen, G.A., Qualls, S.H., & Duffy, M. (2009). Pikes Peak model for training in professional gerospsychology. *American Psychologist, 64,* 205–214.

Kurz, A., Thone-Otto, A., Cramer, B., Egert, S., Frolich, L., Gertz, H., ... Werheid, K. (2012). CORDIAL: Cognitive rehabilitation and Cognitive-behavioral Treatment for Early Dementia in Alzheimer Disease: A multicenter, randomized, controlled trial. *Alzheimer Disease & Associated Disorders, 26,* 246–253.

Lawton, M.P. (1997). Positive and negative affective states among older people in long-term care. In R.L. Rubenstein & M.P. Lawton (Eds.), *Depression in long term and residential care: Advances in research and treatment* (pp. 29–54). New York: Springer.

Lejuez, C.W., Hopko, D.R., & Hopko, S.D. (2001). A brief behavioral activation treatment for depression: Treatment manual. *Behavior Modification, 25*, 255–286.

Lezak, M.D., Howieson, D.B., & Loring, D.W. (2004). *Neuropsychological assessment*. Oxford: Oxford University Press.

Lints-Martindale, A.C., Hadjistavropoulos, T., Lix, L.M., & Thorpe, L. (2012). A comparative investigation of observational pain assessment tools for older adults with dementia. *Clinical Journal of Pain, 28*, 226–237.

Lunde, L., Nordhus, I.H., & Pallesen, S. (2009). The effectiveness of cognitive and behavioural treatment of chronic pain in the elderly: A quantitative review. *Journal of Clinical Psychology in Medical Settings, 16*, 254–262.

McDougall, G.J., Buxen, C.E., & Suen, L.J. (1997). The process and outcome of life review psychotherapy with depressed homebound older adults. *Nursing Research, 46*, 277–283.

McMillan, S.C. (2005). Interventions to facilitate family caregiving at the end of life. *Journal of Palliative Medicine, 8*(S1), S132–S139.

McMillan, S.C., Small, B.J., Weitzer, M., Schonwetter, R., Tittle, M., Moody, L., & Haley, W. (2006). Impact of a coping skills intervention with family caregivers of hospice patients with cancer: A randomized clinical trial. *Cancer, 106*, 214–222.

Martin, R., Williams, J., Hadjistavropoulos, T., Hadjistavropoulos, H.D., & MacLean, M. (2005). A qualitative investigation of seniors' and caregivers' views on pain assessment and management. *Canadian Journal of Nursing Research, 37*, 142–164.

Meeks, S., & Depp, C.A. (2002). Pleasant events-based behavioral intervention for depression in nursing home residents: A conceptual and empirical foundation. *Clinical Gerontologist, 25*, 125–148.

Meeks, S., Looney, S.W., Van Haitsma, K., & Teri, L. (2008). BE-ACTIV: A staff-assisted behavioral intervention for depression in nursing homes. *Gerontologist, 48*, 105–114.

Meeks, S., Young, C.M., & Looney, S.W. (2007). Activity participation and affect among nursing home residents: Support for a behavioural model of depression. *Aging and Mental Health, 11*, 751–760.

Monin, J.K., & Schulz, R. (2009). Interpersonal effects of suffering in older adult caregiving relationships. *Psychology and Aging, 24*, 681–695.

Moos, I., & Björn, A. (2006). Use of the life story in the institutional care of people with dementia: A review of intervention studies. *Ageing and Society, 26*, 431–454.

Morrison, R.S., & Siu, A.L. (2000). A comparison of pain and its treatment in advanced dementia and cognitively impaired patients with hip fracture. *Journal of Pain and Symptom Management, 19*, 240–248.

Opie, J., Doyle, C., & O'Connor, D.W. (2002). Challenging behaviours in nursing home residents with dementia: A randomised controlled trial of multi-disciplinary interventions. *International Journal of Geriatric Psychiatry, 17*, 6–13.

Parekh, A.K., & Barton, M.B. (2010). The challenge of multiple comorbidity for the US healthcare system. *Journal of the American Medical Association, 202*, 1303–1304.

Parmelee, P.A., Katz, I.R., & Lawton, M.P. (1992). Incidence of depression in long-term care settings. *Journals of Gerontology: Series A, Biological and Medical Sciences, 47*, M189–M196.

Pearson, W.S., Bhat-Schelbert, K., & Probst, J.C. (2012). Multiple chronic conditions and the aging of America. *Journal of Primary Care & Community Health, 3*, 51–56.

Plassman, B.L., Williams, J.W., Burke, J.R., Holsinger, T., & Benjamin, S. (2009). NIH conference and systematic review: Factors associated with risk for and possible prevention of cognitive decline in later life. *Annals of Internal Medicine, 153*, 182–193.

Public Health Agency of Canada (PHAC). (2009a). *Tracking heart disease and stroke in Canada*. Retrieved from www.phac-aspc.gc.ca/publicat/2009/cvd-avc/pdf/cvd-avs-2009-eng.pdf

Public Health Agency of Canada (PHAC). (2009b). *Obesity in Canada—snapshot*. Retrieved from www.phac-aspc.gc.ca/publicat/2009/oc/pdf/oc-eng.pdf

Public Health Agency of Canada (PHAC). (2011). *Diabetes in Canada: Facts and figures from a public health perspective*. Retrieved from www.phac-aspc.gc.ca/cd-mc/publications/diabetes-diabete/facts-figures-faits-chiffres-2011/pdf/facts-figures-faits-chiffres-eng.pdf

Public Health Agency of Canada (PHAC). (2012). *Asthma facts and figures*. Retrieved from www.phac-aspc.gc.ca/cd-mc/crd-mrc/asthma_figures-asthme_figures-eng.php

Radvansky, G.A. (2011). *Human memory* (2nd ed.). New York: Pearson.

Robinson, C.L. (2007). Relieving pain in the elderly. *Health Progress, 88*, 48–53, 70.

Rosland, A.M., Heisler, M., & Piette, J.D. (2012). The impact of family behaviors and communication patterns on chronic illness outcomes: A systematic review. *Journal of Behavioral Medicine, 35*, 221–239.

Rossen, E.K. (2007). Assessing older persons' readiness to move to independent congregate living. *Clinical nurse specialist, 21*, 292–296. Retrieved from www.ncbi.nlm.nih.gov/pubmed/18000442

Rubenstein, L.Z. (2006). Falls in older people: Epidemiology, risk factors and strategies for prevention. *Age and Ageing, 35*, 37–41.

Scherrer, J.F., Bucholz, K.K., Eisen, S.A., Lyons, M.J., Goldberg, J., Tsuang, M., & True, W.R. (2003). A twin study of depression symptoms, hypertension, and heart disease in middle-aged men. *Psychosomatic Medicine, 65*, 548–557.

Scogin, F., Hanson, A., & Welsh, D. (2003). Self-administered treatment in stepped-care models of depression treatment. *Journal of Clinical Psychology, 59*, 341–349.

Scogin, F., & Shah, A. (2006). Screening older adults for depression in primary care settings. *Health Psychology, 25*, 675–677.

Scogin, F., Welsh, D., Hanson, A., Stump, J., & Coates, A. (2005). Evidence-based psychotherapies for depression in older adults. *Clinical Psychology: Science and Practice, 12*, 222–237.

Snarski, M., Scogin, F., DiNapoli, E., Presnell, A., McAlpine, J., & Marcinak, J. (2011). The effects of behavioral activation therapy with inpatient geriatric psychiatry patients. *Behavior Therapy, 42*, 100–108.

Solano, J.P., Gomes, B., & Higginson, I.J. (2006). A comparison of symptom prevalence in far advanced cancer, AIDS, heart disease, chronic obstructive pulmonary disease and renal disease. *Journal of Pain and Symptom Management, 31*, 58–69.

Sperling, R.A., Aisen, P.S., Beckett, L.A., Bennett, D.A., Craft, S., Fagan, A.M., … Phelps, C.H. (2011). Toward defining the preclinical stages of Alzheimer's disease: Recommendations from the National Institute on Aging-Alzheimer's Association workgroups on diagnostic guidelines for Alzheimer's disease. *Alzheimer's Dementia 7*, 280–292.

Statistics Canada. (2013). National seniors day … by the numbers. Retrieved from www42.statcan.gc.ca/smr08/2013/smr08_178_2013-eng.htm

Stevens, J.A., Mack, K.A., Paulozzi, L.J., & Ballesteros, M.F. (2008). Self-reported falls and fall-related injuries among persons aged greater than or equal to 65 years—United States, 2006. *Journal of Safety Research, 39*, 345–349.

Stone, R.I., & Reinhard, S.C. (2007). The place of assisted living in long-term care and related service systems. *Gerontologist, 47*, 23–32. Retrieved from www.ncbi.nlm.nih.gov/pubmed/18162566

Teresi, J., Abrams, R., Holmes, D., Ramirez, M., & Eimicke, J. (2001). Prevalence of depression and depression recognition in nursing homes. *Social Psychiatry and Psychiatric Epidemiology, 36*, 613–620.

Thielke, S., Vannoy, S., & Unützer, J. (2007). Integrating mental health and primary care. *Primary Care: Clinics in Office Practice, 34*(3), 571–592.

Volker, D.L. (2005). Control and end-of-life care: Does ethnicity matter? *American Journal of Hospice and Palliative Medicine, 22*, 442–446.

Werner, C. (2011). *The older population: 2010*. Washington: US Census Bureau. Retrieved from www.census.gov/prod/cen2010/briefs/c2010br-09.pdf

Willis, S.L., Tennstedt, S.L., Marsiske, M., Ball, K., Elias, J., Koepke, J.M., … Wright, E. (2006). Long-term effects of cognitive training on everyday functional outcomes in older adults. *Journal of the American Medical Association, 296*, 2805–2814.

Wilson, B.A. (1997). Cognitive rehabilitation: How it is and how it might be. *Journal of the International Neuropsychological Society, 3*, 487–496.

Yamaguchi, H., Maki, Y., & Yamagami, T. (2010). Overview of non-pharmacological intervention for dementia and principles of brain-activating rehabilitation. *Psychogeratrics: Official Journal of the Japanese Psychogeriatric Society, 10*, 206–213.

Zijlstra, G.A.R., Van Haastregt, J.C.M., Ambergen, T., Van Rossum, E., Van Eijk, J.T.M., Tennstedt, S.L., & Kempen, G. (2009). Effects of a multicomponent cognitive behavioral group intervention on fear of falling and activity avoidance in community-dwelling older adults: Results of a randomized controlled trial. *Journal of the American Geriatrics Society, 57*, 2020–2028.

Zijlstra, G.A.R., Van Haastregt, J.C.M., Van Rossum, E., Van Eijk, J.T.M., Yardley, L., & Kempen, G. (2007). Interventions to reduce fear of falling in community-living older people: A systematic review. *Journal of the American Geriatrics Society, 55*, 603–615.

Chapter 19

Abraham, C., Sheeran, P., & Johnston, M. (1998). From health beliefs to self-regulation: Theoretical advances in the psychology of action control. *Psychology and Health, 13*, 569–591.

Adelson, N. (2005). The embodiment of inequality: Health disparities in Aboriginal Canada. *Canadian Journal of Public Health, 96*, S45–S61.

Adler, N.E., & Ostrove, J.M. (1999). Socioeconomic status and health: What we know and what we don't. *Annals of the New York Academy of Sciences, 896*, 3–15.

Airhihenbuwa, C.O., & Liburd, L. (2006). Eliminating health disparities in the African American population: The interface of culture, gender, and power. *Health Education & Behavior, 33*, 488–501.

Alarcon, R.D., Westermeyer, J., Foulks, E.F., & Ruiz, P. (1999). Clinical relevance of contemporary cultural psychiatry. *Journal of Nervous and Mental Disease, 187*, 465–471.

American Diabetes Association. (2012). Living with diabetes: Native American complications. Retrieved from www.diabetes.org/living-with-diabetes/complications/native-americans.html

American Psychiatric Association. (2000). *Diagnostic and statistical manual of mental disorders*, (4th ed. text revision.). Washington: American Psychiatric Association.

American Psychological Association (APA). (2002). *Guidelines on multicultural education, training, research, practice, and organizational change for psychologists*. Retrieved from www.apa.org/pi/oema/resources/policy/multicultural-guideline.pdf

American Psychological Association (APA). (2007). *Report of the APA task force on socioeconomic status*. Retrieved from www.apa.org/pi/ses/resources/publications/task-force-2006.pdf

American Psychological Association (APA). (2012). *Public description of clinical health psychology*. Retrieved from www.apa.org/ed/graduate/specialize/health.aspx

American Psychological Association Presidential Task Force on Evidence-Based Practice. (2006). Evidence-based practice in psychology. *American Psychologist, 61*, 271–285.

Anderson, N.B., Bulatao, R.A., & Cohen, B. (Eds.). (2004). *Critical perspectives on racial and ethnic differences in health and late life*. Washington: National Academies Press.

Anderson, R.J., Freedland, K.E., Clouse, R.E., & Lustman, P.J. (2001). The prevalence of comorbid depression in adults with diabetes: A meta-analysis. *Diabetes Care, 24*, 1069–1078.

Andrews, M.M., & Boyle, J.S. (1995). *Transcultural concepts in nursing care* (5th ed.). Philadelphia: Lippincott Williams & Wilkins.

Attewell, P., Kasinitz, P., & Dunn. K. (2010). Black Canadians and Black Americans: Racial income inequality in comparative perspective. *Ethnic and Racial Studies, 33*, 473–495.

Bartlett, J.G. (2003). Involuntary cultural change, stress phenomenon and aboriginal health status. *Canadian Journal of Public Health, 94*, 165–167.

Battiste, M., & Henderson, J. (2000). *Protecting indigenous knowledge and heritage: A global challenge.* Saskatoon: Purich Publishing.

Bernal, G., & Scharrón-Del-Río, M. (2001). Are empirically supported treatments valid for ethnic minorities? Toward an alternative approach for treatment research. *Journal of Cultural Diversity and Ethnic Minority Psychology, 7,* 328–342.

Berry, J.W. (1990). Acculturation and adaptation: Healthy consequences of culture contact among circumpolar peoples. *Arctic Medical Research, 49,* 142–150.

Berry, J.W. (1997). Immigration, acculturation, and adaptation. *Applied Psychology, 46,* 5–34.

Bhugra, D., & Jones, P. (2001). *Advances in Psychiatric Treatment, 7,* 216–222.

Blumentritt, T.L., Angle, R.L., & Brown, J.M. (2004). MACI personality patterns and DSM-IV symptomology in a sample of troubled Mexican-American adolescents. *Journal of Child & Family Studies, 13,* 163–178.

Brawley, O.W. (2007). Health-care disparities, civil rights, and human rights. *Oncology, 21,* 499–503.

Brisline, R. (1990). *Applied cross-cultural psychology.* Newbury Park, Calif.: Sage.

Browne, A.J., Smye, V.L., & Varcoe, C. (2005). The relevance of postcolonial theoretical perspectives to research in Aboriginal health. *Canadian Journal of Nursing Research, 37,* 16–37.

Cajete, G. (1999). *Native science: Natural laws of interdependence.* Sante Fe, NM: Clear Light Publishers.

Campinha-Bacote, J. (1999). A model and instrument for addressing cultural competence in health care. *Journal of Nursing Education, 38,* 203–207.

Carter-Pokras, O., & Baquet, C. (2002). What is a "health disparity"? *Public Health Reports, 117,* 426–434.

Centers for Disease Control and Prevention (CDC), US Department of Health and Human Services. (2011). *CDC health disparities and inequalities report—United States 2011* (Morbidity and Mortality Weekly Report, No. 60). Retrieved from www.cdc.gov/mmwr/pdf/other/su6001.pdf

Chandler, M.J., Lalonde, C.E., Sokol, B.W., & Hallet, D. (2003). Personal persistence, identity, development, and suicide: A study of Native and non-Native North American adolescents. *Monographs for the Society for Research in Child Development, 68*(2), 1–130.

Chang, D.F., & Yoon, P. (2011). Ethnic minority clients' perceptions of the significance of race in cross-racial therapy relationships. *PsychotherapyResearch, 21,* 567–582.

Cohen, K. (2003). Honoring the medicine: The essential guide to Native American healing. *Alternative Therapies in Health and Medicine, 9,* 68–73.

Constantine, M.G., & Ladany, N. (2000). Self-report multicultural counseling competence scales: Their relation to social desirability attitudes and multicultural case conceptualization ability. *Journal of Counseling Psychology, 47,* 155–164.

Corbie-Smith, G., Thomas, S.B., & St George, D.M.M. (2002). Distrust, race, and research. *Archives of Internal Medicine, 162,* 2458–2463.

Corbie-Smith, G., Thomas, S.B., Williams, M.V., & Moody-Ayers, S. (1999). Attitudes and beliefs of African Americans toward participation in medical research. *Journal of General Internal Medicine, 14,* 537–546.

Cramer, H., Lauche, R., Langhorst, J., & Dobos, G. (2013). Yoga for rheumatic diseases: A systematic review. *Rheumatology.* doi: 0.1093/rheumatology/ket264

Culler, J. (1997). *Literary theory: A very short introduction.* New York: Oxford.

Cutler, D.M., Lleras-Muney, A., & Vogl, T. (2008). *Socioeconomic status and health: Dimensions and mechanisms.* NBER Working Paper No. 1433.

Dana, R.H. (2002). Mental health services for African Americans: A cultural/racial perspective. *Cultural Diversity and Ethnic Minority Psychology, 8,* 3–18.

Danish, S.J., Forneris, T., & Wilder Schaaf, K. (2007). Counseling psychology and culturally competent health care: Limitations and challenges. *Counseling Psychologist, 35,* 716–725.

Ermine, W., Nilson, R., Sauchyn, D., Sauve, E., & Smith, R.Y. (2005). Isi Askiwan—The state of the land: Summary of the Prince Albert grand council Elders' forum on climate change. *Journal of Aboriginal Health, 2,* 62–72.

Fernandez, D.R., Carlson, D.S., Stepina, L.P., & Nicholson, J.D. (1997). Hofstede's country classification 25 years later. *Journal of Social Psychology, 137,* 43–54.

Fisher, J.A., & Kalbaugh, C.A. (2011). Challenging assumptions about minority participation in US clinical research. *American Journal of Public Health, 101*(12), 2217.

Flaskerud, J.H. (1990). Matching client and therapist ethnicity, language, and gender: A review of research. *Issues in Mental Health Nursing, 11,* 321–336.

Ford, M.E., & Kelly, P.A. (2005). Conceptualizing and categorizing race and ethnicity in health services research. *Health Research and Educational Trust, 40,* 1659–1675.

Frideres, J.S. (2011). *First nations in the twenty-first century.* Toronto: Oxford University Press.

Frohlich, K.L., Ross, N., & Richmond, C. (2006). Health disparities in Canada today: Some evidence and a theoretical framework. *Health Policy, 79,* 132–143.

Fuertes, J.N., & Brobst, K. (2002). Clients' ratings of counselor multicultural competency. *Cultural Diversity and Ethnic Minority Psychology, 8,* 214–223.

Fuertes, J.N., Costa, C.I., Mueller, L.N., & Hersh, M. (2005). Psychotherapy process and outcome from a racial-ethnic perspective. In R.T. Carter (Ed.), *Handbook of racial-cultural psychology and counseling, Volume One, Theory and Research* (pp. 256–277). Hoboken, NJ: Wiley.

Gamble, V.N. (1997). Under the shadow of Tuskegee: African Americans and health care. *American Journal of Public Health, 87,* 1773–1778.

Gamst, G., Dana, R.H., Der-Karaberian, A., & Kramer, T. (2000). Ethnic match and client ethnicity effects on global assessment and visitation. *Journal of Community Psychology, 28,* 547–564.

Gideon, V., Gray, J., Nicholas, W., & Ha, P. (2008). First Nations youth health: Recognizing the challenges, recognizing the potential. *Horizons: Policy Research Initiative, 10,* 83–87.

Government of Canada. (2011). TCPS 2—2nd edition of Tri-Council Policy Statement: Ethical conduct for research involving humans. Panel on Research Ethics. Retrieved from www.pre.ethics.gc.ca/eng/policy-politique/initiatives/tcps2-eptc2/Default/

Gracey, M., & King, M. (2009). Indigenous health part 1: Determinants and disease patterns. *Lancet, 374*, 65–75.

Guimond, E., & Cooke, M.J. (2008). The current well-being of registered Indian youth: Concerns for the future? *Horizons: Policy Research Initiative, 10*, 26–30.

Gurung, R.A.R. (2011). Cultural influences on health. In K.D. Keith (Ed.), *Cross-cultural psychology: Contemporary themes and perspectives* (pp. 259–273). West Sussex, UK: Wiley-Blackwell.

Hall, G.C.N. (2001). Psychotherapy research with ethnic minorities: Empirical, ethical, and conceptual issues. *Journal of Consulting and Clinical Psychology, 69*, 502–510.

Hayward, M.D., Miles, T.P., Crimmins, E.M., & Yang, Y. (2000). The significance of socioeconomic status in explaining the racial gap in chronic health conditions. *American Sociological Review, 65*, 910–930.

Hazuda, H.P., Haffner, S.M., Stern, M.P., & Eifler, C.W. (1988). Effects of acculturation and socioeconomic status on obesity and diabetes in Mexican Americans. *American Journal of Epidemiology, 128*, 1289–1301.

Health Canada. (2008). *A statistical profile on the health of First Nations in Canada: Self-rated health and selected conditions, 2002 to 2005* (Government of Canada Publication, No. 3556). Retrieved from www.hc-sc.gc.ca/fniah-spnia/pubs/aborig-autoch/index-eng.php

Health Canada. (2011). *Diabetes in Canada: Facts and figures from a public health perspective*. Ottawa. Retrieved from www.phac-aspc.gc.ca/cd-mc/diabetes-diabete/index-eng.php

HealthyPeople.gov. (2012). *Healthy People 2020: Improving the health of Americans*. Washington: US Department of Health and Human Services. Retrieved from www.healthypeople.gov/2020/default.aspx

Helms, J.E., & Talleyrand, R.M. (1997). Race is not ethnicity. *American Psychologist, 52*, 1246–1247.

Henao-Martinez, A.F., & Castillo-Mancilla, J.R. (2013). The Hispanic HIV epidemic. *Current Infectious Disease Reports, 15*, 46–51.

Hofstede, G. (2001). *Culture's consequences: Comparing values, behaviors, institutions, and organizations across nations* (2nd ed.). Thousand Oaks, Calif.: Sage.

Hofstede, G., & Bond, M.H. (1988). The Confucius connection: From cultural roots to economic growth. *OrganizationalDynamics, 16*, 5–21.

Jacob, K.S., & Kuruvilla, A. (2012). Psychotherapy across cultures: The form-content dichotomy. *Clinical Psychology and Psychotherapy, 19*, 91–95.

Jones, M.L. (2007). Hofstede – Culturally questionable? (Published for Research Online [University of Wollongong]). Retrieved from ro.uow.edu.au/cgi/viewcontent.cgi?article=1389&context=commpapers

Kao, H.F.S., Hsu, M.T., & Clark, L. (2004). Conceptualizing and critiquing culture in health research. *Journal of Transcultural Nursing, 15*, 269–277.

Kaplan, J.B., & Bennett, T. (2003). Use of race and ethnicity in biomedical publication. *Journal of the American Medical Association, 289*, 2709–2716.

Kazarian, S.S., & Evans, D.R. (Eds.). (2001). *Handbook of cultural health psychology*. San Diego: Academic Press.

Keefe, F.J., & Blumenthal, J.A. (2004). Health psychology: What will the future bring? *Health Psychology, 23*, 156–157.

Keenan, M.L., & Shaw, K.M. (2011). Coronary heart disease and stroke deaths—United States, 2006. In Centers for Disease Control and Prevention, US Department of Health and Human Services, *CDC health disparities and inequalities report—United States 2011* (pp. 62–66) (Morbidity and Mortality Weekly Report, No. 60). Retrieved from www.cdc.gov/mmwr/pdf/other/su6001.pdf

Kim, K.I., Li, D., Kiang, Z., Cui, X., Lin, L., Kang, J.J., … Kim, C.L. (1993). Schizophrenic delusions among Koreans, Korean-Chinese and Chinese: A transcultural study. *International Journal of Social Psychiatry, 39*, 190–199.

Kirmayer, L.J. (1994). Suicide among Canadian Aboriginal people. *Transcultural Psychiatric Research Review, 31*, 3–58.

Kirmayer, L.J. (2001). Cultural variations in the presentation of depression and anxiety: Implications for diagnosis and treatment. *Journal of Clinical Psychiatry, 63*(suppl. 13), 22–28.

Kirmayer, L.J., Gill, K., Fletcher, C., Ternar, Y., Boothroyd, L., Quesney, C., … Hayton, B. (1993). *Emerging trends in research on mental health among Canadian Aboriginal people*. Montreal: Sir Mortimer B. Davis—Jewish General Hospital and Department of Psychiatry, McGill University.

Kirmayer, L.J., & Sartorius, N. (2007). Cultural models and somatic syndromes. *Psychosomatic Medicine, 69*, 832–840.

Kitaoka, S.K. (2005). Multicultural counseling competencies: Lessons from assessment. *Journal of Multicultural Counseling and Development, 33*, 37–47.

Kottak, C.P. (2011). *Cultural anthropology: Appreciating cultural diversity*. New York: McGraw-Hill.

Kressin, N.R., Raymond, K.L., & Manze, M. (2008). Perceptions of race/ethnicity-based discrimination: A review of measures of evaluation of their usefulness for the health care setting. *Journal of Health Care for the Poor and Underserved, 19*, 697–730.

Lara, M., Gamboa, C., Kahramanian, M.I., Morales, L.S., & Hayes Bautista, D.E. (2005). Acculturation and Latino health in the United States: A review of the literature and its socio-political context. *Annual Review of Public Health, 26*, 367–397.

Lewis-Fernandez, R., Hinton, D.E., Laria, A.J., Patterson, E.H., Hofmann, S.G., Craske, M., … Liao, B. (2009). Culture and the anxiety disorders: Recommendations for DSM-V. *Depression and Anxiety, 27*, 212–229.

Lopez-Class, M., Castro, F.G., & Ramirez, A.G. (2011). Conceptions of acculturation: A review and statement of critical issues. *Social Science & Medicine, 72*, 1555–1562.

Luginaah, I., Smith, K., & Lockridge, A. (2010). Surrounded by chemical valley and "living in a bubble": Health impacts and coping strategies of the Aamjiwnaang First Nation, Ontario. *Journal of Environmental Planning and Management, 53*, 353–370.

MacDorman, M.F., & Mathews, T.J. (2011). Infant Deaths—United States, 2000–2007. In Centers for Disease Control and Prevention, US Department of Health and Human Services, *CDC health disparities and inequalities report—United States 2011* (pp. 59–61) (Morbidity and Mortality Weekly Report, No. 60). Retrieved from www.cdc.gov/mmwr/pdf/other/su6001.pdf

McSweeney, B. (2002). Hofstede's model of national cultural differences and their consequences: A triumph of faith—a failure of analysis. *Human Relations, 55*, 89–118.

Majumdar, B., Browne, G., Roberts, J., & Carpio, B. (2004). Effects of cultural sensitivity training on health care provider attitudes and patient outcomes. *Journal of Nursing Scholarship, 36*, 161–166.

Maramba, C.G., & Hall, G.C.N. (2002). Meta-analyses of ethnic match as a predictor of dropout, utilization, and level of functioning. *Cultural Diversity and Ethnic Minority Psychology, 8*, 290–297.

Marshall, C.A., Larkey, L.K., Curran, M.A., Weihs, K.L., Badger, T.A., Armin, J., & Garcia, F. (2011). Considerations of culture and social class for families facing cancer: The need for a new model for health promotion and psychosocial intervention. *Families, Systems, & Health, 29*, 81–94.

Mensah, G.A., Mokdad, A.H., Ford, E.S., Greenlund, K.J., & Croft, J.B. (2005). State of disparities in cardiovascular health in the United States. *Epidemiology, 111*, 1233–1241.

Möller-Leimkühler, A.M. (2007). Gender differences in cardiovascular disease and comorbid depression. *Dialogues in Clinical Neuroscience, 9*, 71–83.

Morales, E., & Norcross, J.C. (2010). Evidence-based practices with ethnic minorities: Strange bedfellows no more. *Journal of Clinical Psychology, 66*, 821–829.

Morales, L.S., Lara, M., Kington, R.S., & Valdez, R.O. (2002). Socioeconomic, cultural, behavioral factors affecting Hispanic health outcomes. *Journal of Health Care for the Poor and Underserved, 13*, 477–503.

Moulettes, A. (2007). The absence of women's voices in Hofstede's *Cultural consequences:* A postcolonial reading. *Women in Management Review, 22*, 443–455.

Mountain, J.L., & Risch, N. (2004). Assessing genetic contributions to phenotypic differences among "racial" and "ethnic" groups. *Natural Genetics, 36*, S48–S53.

Mulatu, M.S., & Berry, J.W. (2001). Health care practice in a multicultural context: Western and non-western assumptions. In S.S. Kazarian & J.W. Berry (Eds.), *Handbook of cultural health psychology* (pp. 46–63). New York: Academic Press.

Muris, P., Schmidt, H., Engelbrecht, P., & Perold, M. (2002). DSM-IV-defined anxiety disorder symptoms in South African children. *Journal of the American Academy of Child & Adolescent Psychiatry, 41*, 1360–1368.

National Center for Complementary and Alternative Medicine (NCCAM). (2013). Complementary, alternative, or integrative health: What's in a name. Retrieved from nccam.nih.gov/health/whatiscam

National Institutes of Health. (2012). National Institute on minority health and health disparities. Retrieved from www.nih.gov/about/almanac/organization/NIMHD.htm

Oates, M.R., Cox, J.L., Neema, S., Asten, P., Glangeaud-Freudenthal, N., Figueiredo, B., … Yoshida, K. (2004). Postnatal depression across countries and cultures: A qualitative study. *British Journal of Psychiatry, 184*, s10–s16.

Ortega, A.N., Feldman, J.M., Canino, G., Steinman, K., & Alegria, M. (2006). Co-occurrence of mental and physical illness in U.S. Latinos. *Social Psychiatry and Psychiatric Epidemiology, 41*, 927–934.

Osborn, C.Y., de Groot, M., & Wagner, J.A. (2013). Racial and ethnic disparities in diabetes complications in the northeastern United States: The role of socioeconomic status. *Journal of the National Medical Association, 105*, 51–58.

Parlee, B., Berkes, F., Gwich'in, T. (2005). Health of the land, health of the people: A case study on Gwich'in berry harvesting in northern Canada. *Ecohealth, 2*, 127–137.

Purnell, L. (2002). The Purnell Model for cultural competence. *Journal of Transcultural Nursing, 13*, 193–196.

Rabia, M., Knauper, B., & Miquelon, P. (2006). The eternal quest for optimal balance between maximizing pleasure and minimizing harm: The compensatory health beliefs model. *British Journal of Health Psychology, 11*, 139–153.

Ram, R. (2006). Further examination of the cross-country association between income inequality and population health. *Social Science & Medicine, 62*, 779–791.

Reading, C.L., & Wien, F. (2009). *Health inequalities and social determinants of Aboriginal peoples' health.* Retrieved from www.nccah.ca/docs/social%20determinates/NCCAH-Loppie-Wien_Report.pdf

Richmond, C.A.M. (2007). Social support, material circumstance and health: Understanding the links in Canada's Aboriginal population. Doctoral dissertation, McGill University.

Richmond, C., Elliott, S.J., Mathews, R., and Elliott, B. (2005). The political ecology of health: Perceptions of environment, economy, health and well-being among "Namgis First Nation." *Health & Place, 11*, 349–365.

Richmond, C.A.M., & Ross, N.A. (2008). Social support, material circumstance and health behaviour: Influences on health in First Nation and Inuit communities in Canada. *Social Science & Medicine, 67*, 1423–1433.

Richmond, C.A.M., & Ross, N.A. (2009). The determinants of First Nation and Inuit health: A critical population health approach. *Health and Place, 15*, 403–411.

Rosenstock, I. (1974). Historical origins of the health belief model. *Health Education Monographs, 2*(4).

Rosenstock, I.M., Strecher, V.J., & Becker, M.H. (1988). Social learning theory and the Health Belief Model. *Health Education & Behavior, 15*, 175–183.

Royal Commission on Aboriginal Peoples. (1995). *Choosing life: Special report on suicide among Aboriginal people.* Ottawa: Supply and Services.

Rudell, K., & Deifenbach, M.A. (2008). Current issues and new directions in psychology and health: Culture and health psychology. Why health psychologists should care about culture. *Psychology and Health, 23*, 387–390.

Saha, S., Arbelaez, J.J., & Cooper, L.A. (2003). Patient–physician relationships and racial disparities in the quality of health care. *American Journal of Public Health, 93*, 1713–1719.

Scott, K.M., Kokaua, J., & Baxter, J. (2011). Does having a chronic physical condition affect the likelihood of treatment seeking for a mental health problem and does this vary by ethnicity? *International Journal of Psychiatry in Medicine, 42*, 421–436.

Scott, K., McGee, M.A., Schaaf, D., & Baxter, J. (2008). Mental–physical comorbidity in an ethnically diverse population. *Social Science & Medicine, 66*, 1165–1173.

Sheikh, S., & Furnham, A. (2000). A cross-cultural study of mental health beliefs and attitudes towards seeking profession help. *Social Psychiatry and Psychiatric Epidemiology, 35*, 326–334.

Shin, S.M., Chow, C., Camacho-Gonsalves, T., Levy, R., Allen, I.E., & Leff, H.S. (2005). A meta-analytic review of racial-ethnic matching for African American and Caucasian American clients and clinicians. *Journal of Counseling Psychology, 52*, 45–56.

Skrentny, J.D. (2008). Culture and race/ethnicity: Bolder, deeper, and broader. *Annals of the American Academy of Political and Social Science, 619*, 59–77.

Smedley, B.D., Stith, A.Y., & Nelson, A.R. (2002). *Unequal treatment: Confronting racial and ethnic disparities in health care.* Institute of Medicine Report. Washington: National Academy Press.

Smith, M.L., & Glass, G.V. (1977). Meta-analysis of psychotherapy outcome studies. *American Psychologist, 32*, 752–760.

Smylie, J., Fell, D., & Ohlsson, A. (2010). A review of Aboriginal infant mortality rates in Canada: Striking and persistent Aboriginal/non-Aboriginal inequities. *Canadian Journal of Public Health, 101*, 143–148.

Statistics Canada, Ministry of Finance. (2003). Census 2001 highlights.

Statistics Canada. (2005). *Projections of the Aboriginal populations, Canada, provinces and territories 2001 to 2017.* Ottawa.

Statistics Canada. (2008). *Canada's ethnocultural mosaic, 2006 census.* Ottawa: Minister of Industry. Retrieved from www12.statcan.ca/census-recensement/2006/as-sa/97-562/pdf/97-562-XIE2006001.pdf

Stephens, C. (2011). Narrative analysis in health psychology research: Personal, dialogical and social stories of health. *Health Psychology Review, 5*, 62–78.

Strecher, V.J., & Rosenstock, I.M. (1997). The health belief model. In A. Baum, S. Newman, J. Weinman, R. West, & C. McManus (Eds.), *Cambridge handbook of psychology, health, and medicine* (pp. 113–116). Cambridge: Cambridge University Press.

Sue, D.W. (2001). Multidimensional facets of cultural competence. *Counseling Psychologist, 29*, 790–821.

Sue, D.W., Ivey, A.I., & Pederson, P.B. (1996). *A theory of multicultural counseling and therapy.* Pacific Grove, Calif.: Brooks/Cole.

Sue, S. (1998). In search of cultural competence in psychotherapy and counseling. *American Psychologist, 53*, 440–448.

Sue, S., Fujino, D., Hu, L.T., Takeuchi, D.T., & Zane, N.W. (1991). Community mental health services for ethnic minority groups: A test of the cultural responsiveness hypothesis. *Journal of Consulting and Clinical Psychology, 59*, 533–540.

Sue, S., Zane, N., Nagayama Hall, G.C., & Berger, L.K. (2009). The case for cultural competency in psychotherapeutic interventions. *Annual Review of Psychology, 60*, 525–548.

Suls, J., & Rothman, A. (2004). Evolution of the biopsychosocial model: Prospects and challenges for health psychology. *Health Psychology, 23*, 119–125.

Suzuki, K., Takei, N., Kawai, M., Minabe, Y., & Mori, N. (2003). Is Taijin Kyofusho a culture-bound syndrome? *American Journal of Psychiatry, 160*, 1358–1358.

Taras, V., & Kirkman, B.L. (2010). Examining the impact of *Culture's consequences:* A three-decade, multilevel, meta-analytic review of Hofstede's cultural value dimensions. *Journal of Applied Psychology, 95*, 405–439.

Teferra, S., & Shibre, T. (2012). Perceived causes of severe mental disturbance and preferred interventions by the Borana semi-nomadic population in southern Ethiopia: A qualitative study. *BMC Psychiatry, 12*, 1–9.

Tenkorang, E.Y., Gyimah, S.O., Maticka-Tyndale, E., & Adiei, J. (2011). Superstition, witchcraft and HIV prevention in sub-Saharan Africa: The case of Ghana. *Culture, Health, and Sexuality, 13*, 1001–1014.

Thakker, J., & Ward, T. (1998). Culture and classification: An international follow-up study. *Clinical Psychology Review, 18*, 501–529.

Tucker, C.M., Marsiske, M., Rice, K.G., Jones, J.D., & Herman, K.C. (2011). Patient-centered culturally sensitive health care: Model testing and refinement. *Health Psychology, 30*, 342–350.

US Census Bureau. (2001, January 13). *Projections of the total resident population by 5-year age groups, race, and Hispanic origin with special age categories: Middle series, 2050 to 2070.* Retrieved from www.census.gov/population/projections/nation/summary/np-t4-g.txt

US Census Bureau. (2011, March). *Overview of race and Hispanic origin: 2010.* 2010 Census Briefs. Retrieved from www.census.gov/prod/cen2010/briefs/c2010br-02.pdf

Vaughn, L.M., Jacquez, F., & Baker, R.C. (2009). Cultural health attributions, beliefs, and practices: Effects on healthcare and medical education. *Open Medical Education Journal, 2*, 64–74.

Vega, W.A., Rodriguez, M.A., & Gruskin, E. (2009). Health disparities in the Latino population. *Epidemiological Review, 31*, 99–112.

Ward, L., Stebbings, S., Cherkin, D., & Baxter, G.D. (2013). Yoga for functional ability, pain and psychosocial outcomes in musculoskeletal conditions: A systematic review and meta-analysis. *Musculoskeletal Care.* doi: 10.1002/msc.1042

Watt, S., & Norton, D. (2004). Culture, ethnicity, race: What's the difference? *Paediatric Nursing, 16*, 37–42.

Weisz, J.R., Suwanlert, S., Chaiyasit, W., Weiss, B., Achenback, T.M., & Eastman, K.L. (1993). Behavioral and emotional problems among Thai and American adolescents: Parent reports for ages 12–16. *Journal of Abnormal Psychology, 102*, 395–403.

Wendler, D., Kington, R., Madans, J., Wye, G.V., Christ-Schmidt, H., Pratt, L.A., ... Emanuel, E. (2005). Are racial and ethnic minorities less willing to participate in health research? *PLoS Medicine, 3*, 201–210.

Whaley, A.L., & Davis, K.E. (2007). Cultural competence and evidence-based practice in mental health services: A complementary perspective. *American Psychologist, 62*, 563–574.

Wilson, D., & Macdonald, D. (2010, April). *The income gap between Aboriginal peoples and the rest of Canada.* Retrieved from v4.policyalternatives.ca/sites/default/files/uploads/publications/reports/docs/Aboriginal%20Income%20Gap.pdf

Wilson, K. (2003). Therapeutic landscapes and First Nations peoples: An exploration of culture, health and place. *Health & Place, 9*, 83–93.

Wilson, K., & Rosenberg, M.W. (2002). Exploring the determinants of health for First Nations peoples in Canada: Can existing frameworks accommodate traditional activities? *Social Science & Medicine, 55*, 2017–2031.

World Health Organization (WHO). (1998). *Health promotion glossary*. Geneva. Retrieved from www.who.int/healthpromotion/about/HPR%20Glossary%201998.pdf

Xanthos, C., Treadwell, H.M., & Braithwaite Holden, K. (2010). Social determinants of health among African-American men. *Journal of Men's Health, 7*, 11–19.

Yali, A.M., & Revenson, T.A. (2004). How changes in population demographics will impact health psychology: Incorporating a broader notion of cultural competence into the field. *Health Psychology, 23*, 147–155.

Yancey, A.K., Ortega, A.N., & Kumanyika, S.K. (2006). Effective recruitment and retention of minority research participants. *Annual Review of Public Health, 27*, 1–28.

Yang, J.M. (1997). *The essence of Taiji Qigong: The internal foundation of Taijiquan*. Boston: YMAA Publication Center.

Yeh, R.S. (1988). On Hofstede's treatment of Chinese and Japanese values. *Asia Pacific Journal of Management, 6*, 149–160.

Zheng, H. (2009). Rising U.S. income inequality, gender and individual self-rated health, 1972–2004. *Social Science & Medicine, 69*, 1333–1342.

Name Index

Subject Index